HANDGUNS

A BUYER'S AND SHOOTER'S GUIDE

by

Steve Markwith

Part of the *Survival Guns* series of books
published by:

Your Survival Library

PrepperPress.com/SurvivalGuns

Handguns: A Buyer's and Shooter's Guide

ISBN 13: 978-1-939473-93-6

Copyright © 2019 by Steve Markwith

All rights reserved.

Printed in the United States of America.

Prepper Press Trade Paperback Edition: July 2019

Prepper Press is a division of Kennebec Publishing, LLC

No part of this book may be reproduced or utilized in any form or by any means, electronic or mechanical, including photocopying, recording, or by any information storage or retrieval system, without permission in writing from Kennebec Publishing, LLC.

Photos and illustrations used throughout the book are privately owned, public domain, or licensed under the Creative Commons Attributions-Share Alike or GNU Free Documentation License, except where credits are otherwise noted.

Disclaimer. This book is intended to offer general guidance relating to firearms. It is sold with the understanding that every effort was made to provide accurate information; however, errors are still possible. The author and publisher make no warrantees or claims as to the truth or validity of the information. The author and publisher shall have neither liability nor responsibility to any person or entity over any loss or damage caused, or alleged to have been caused, directly or indirectly, by the information contained within this book.

ABOUT THE AUTHOR

Steve has a lifelong interest in just about all things that shoot: rifles, shotguns, revolvers, pistols, air guns, and black powder guns, as well as vertical or horizontal bows. He began formal firearms training at eleven during NRA-sanctioned smallbore target rifle events, and was an active hunter by twelve. He began reloading shotgun shells at fourteen, using a handheld Lee Loader to feed his addiction. After joining the U.S. Army, he served two combat tours in Vietnam, gaining experience with numerous military firearms during Air Cavalry helicopter operations and ground-based reconnaissance missions.

Upon returning to civilian life, Steve resumed shooting, participating in NRA bullseye, combat pistol, and trap events. These activities expanded his reloading experience to metallic ammunition and bullet casting. Steve eventually became an NRA-certified pistol, rifle & shotgun instructor, as well as a certifying official for state firearms permit applicants. He also worked for a well-known gunsmith and PO Ackley disciple, until an untimely death forced a career change.

Joining a major state correctional agency, Steve was soon appointed as a firearms instructor, eventually assuming control of all state correctional firearms operations. He held a master instructor rating, plus numerous other federal, state, and industry certifications. He has over 25 years of full-time firearms training experience, and numerous industry connections. Although now mostly retired, he still consults and participates as needed. Whether officially or not, he can often be found on a range shooting everything from handgun silhouettes to long-range targets or clay pigeons.

Steve also has extensive hunting experience in the Northeast, and at other locations throughout the United States. He holds an archery deer record, and actively remains afield on a year-round basis, whether chasing turkeys, waterfowl and upland birds, winter coyotes with night-vision, or other varmints.

He also actively writes, and has had numerous articles published about firearms and the great outdoors. Five books pertaining to survival guns, shotguns, rimfire rifles, airguns, and centerfire rifles; all based upon hands-on experience and geared toward practical choices.

Special thanks to Sgt. Domenick Leonard (retired) for his comments regarding Sig pistols, and other photos within this edition. Thanks also to Mike Garan, who juggles the duties my former position with his Mid-Maine Firearms business; the source of more photos. Ryan Dearborn, another of our able cadre members, graciously extended the use of several fine single-action revolvers for pictures.

PREFACE

BANG! Among our firing line of ten trainees, Shooter #3 looked befuddled. His pistol was part way out of battery, with a small curl of smoke seeping from a place where none should appear. As we soon discovered, that's because the gun unraveled; a supposedly serviceable specimen no less, of many within our inventory, from a big-name manufacturer. Turned out, the right side of the barrel's thick chamber section bore a half-inch long split, and an adjacent section of the slide was bowed dramatically outward. This, with factory-fresh ammo also of a well-known brand.

Our first concern was the shooter, who was shaken but uninjured. The obvious concern was cause. One immediate suspect was a bore obstruction; an event we'd seen before. But in this case, none was apparent, leading to the possibility of an overloaded cartridge. We segregate our ammunition inventories by receiving dates and lot numbers, so the program went on hold long enough for a switch to a different batch. Although phone calls were in progress, the show went on with reasonable confidence that no further issues would occur. And there weren't any either – at least not for the next five days. At that point, a second pistol failed with identical results. Again, no injuries, in part due to mandatory hearing and eye protection. But the confidence of our troops was rattled and we were in a pickle.

By total coincidence, a leading gun magazine arrived at my residence the next day with a story on this very subject. The author deemed such situations rare, having never seen one firsthand, but that didn't alter the fact that we'd witnessed two "ka-booms" in one week.

Meanwhile, back to the problem at hand, further firing was suspended to determine the cause. Complicating a timely resolution, the gun and ammo manufacturers each assigned blame to the other. And, of course, everyone had a theory. So, digging deeper, as experienced hand-loaders, we began our own investigative process by recording velocities and examining disassembled components. Long story short, although some initial head-butting occurred, both companies soon stepped up to the plate. When the dust settled, we had dozens of brand new pistols and 100,000+ rounds of replacement ammo for no real out-of-pocket cost; no small feat given shortages at that time. Factors that saved us were first and foremost the reputability of both manufacturers. Also, we had anal records that documented proper maintenance protocols for each gun, along with ammo consumption details, and other systematic processes.

Would we buy from either manufacturer again? Absolutely! We still do. Good thing both were well-established firms with reputations to uphold. Using mainstream sources also ensured greater odds of locating replacement products without untimely delays.

If nothing else, this example should justify cautious shopping. The following excerpt from *Centerfire Rifles: A Buyer's and Shooter's Guide* will shed more light on the subject.

While shiny new toys are nice, a few of us had been here before with things like supposedly high-end firearms that wound up going full-auto. There was the massive large-caliber bolt-gun that gutted its scope on the third shot. Another military-type rifle fired out of battery when the bolt went home, spraying brass shrapnel in all directions. We've also had a few pistols blow up for no apparent reason. These episodes illustrate why we do "testing and evaluation" prior to embracing the latest marvel. For that matter, T&E never really stops. A few decades behind a firing line present further opportunities to see what works – as well as what doesn't. "Works" by the way, means more than reliable function. Ergonomics, control, and ease of operation also count, as does requisite training. The last factor is often overlooked, and accounts for a recurring KISS theme throughout the entire Survival Guns series. In keeping with the other editions, I've tried to stick with firearms, ammunition, and equipment with which we've had the most experience. The "we" refers to not only me, but also a well-seasoned group of firearms cadre, and other trusted contacts from the fascinating world of shooting.

The downside. Of course, when using this approach, it's impossible to examine everything. Some readers will be distressed to note an absence of their favorite handgun, whether it be H&K, Ruger, Walther, or another good manufacturer. Fair point, but coverage of every good handgun would result in one humongous edition - and cursory coverage at best. You can bet each design has its share of attributes *and* quirks, too. Since these are best revealed through several specimens, judgement will be deferred to those possessing the requisite experience.

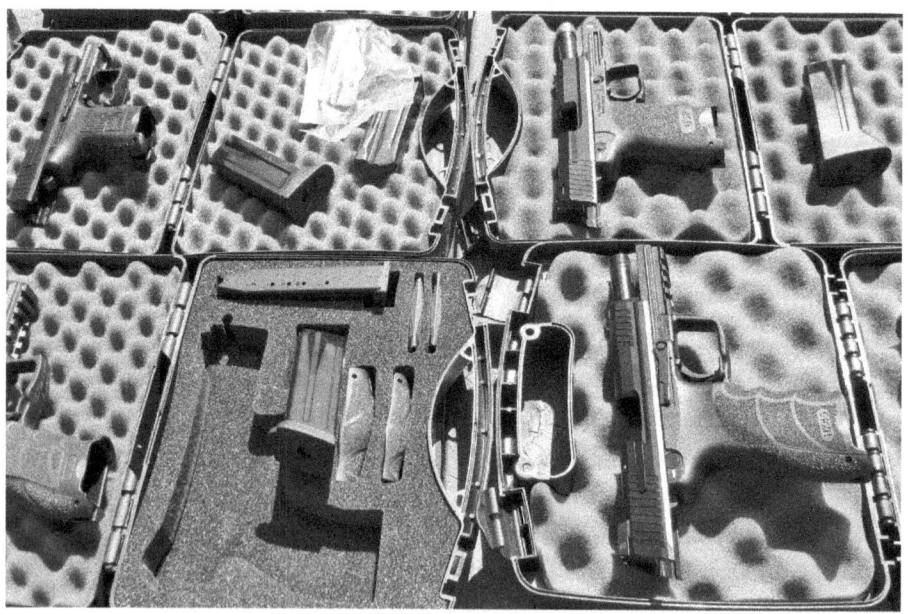

Extensive first-hand experience being the benchmark, a number of strong contenders will miss out. Too bad, because we really liked this sampling of H&Ks, abused during a one-day range session.

What about those two pistols? Truthfully, I'm not sure anyone is 100% certain of the cause. The final deal was to not assign any specific blame, but to resolve the situation in a fair and timely manner. That's what happened. Based on circumstantial evidence, it's possible that a handful of pistols built on one date could've had a run of bad barrels. That's the prevailing theory, but several months later I dipped into one surviving partial box of the exchanged ammunition – and promptly blew the barrel bushing out of my 1911.

THE SURVIVAL GUNS FIREARMS SERIES

This book is the sixth of several *Survival Guns* firearm publications. The first lays out some basic principles, while the others deal with specific firearm systems. It should be noted that a "system" consists not only of a gun, but also its ammunition and related equipment. A thorough understanding of each type can fully exploit capabilities without undue expense. A planned procurement strategy is of further benefit, since firearms with similar function can improve overall proficiency. The upcoming *selection guidelines* govern the whole process, and the series runs as follows:

SURVIVAL GUNS: A BEGINNER'S GUIDE

In the first publication, we laid out some groundwork for a practical collection of firearms. Each was geared toward "prepper" use, and chosen from key requirements: widespread use; dependability; ease of operation; and availability of parts, accessories, and ammunition. Also covered was a hard look at firearms safety and responsible firearms ownership. Part of that process involved secure storage methods. We procured a gun safe and then framed up a small but practical inventory of firearms based on these requirements, adding a shotgun, rimfire rifle, centerfire rifle, and a handgun. The idea was to choose, when possible, types with similar function. Use of each would thus promote skills with another to improve overall proficiency. Toward that goal, our initial selections were based on the K.I.S.S. principle (Keep It Simple, Stupid). We had to start *somewhere,* and most of us don't have deep enough pockets to rush headlong into the nearest Guns –R-Us for an arm load of shootin' irons. We needed something to cover the basics while developing resources to fund other items. That's where the second book began…

SHOTGUNS: A COMPREHENSIVE GUIDE

The second edition served as a specific firearm starting point, and examined this versatile but often misunderstood firearm. You'll sometimes hear it called a "scattergun" in reference to its multiple-projectile payload. However, pellet distribution is based on factors ranging from gauges to chokes. A carefully selected shotgun can also utilize single projectiles to extend its range or tackle the largest North American game animals. From birds to defense, a shotgun offers many useful options, making it a good first choice for our safe. The right shotgun also makes a great foundation for future acquisitions, which leads us to the next edition…

RIMFIRE RIFLES: A BUYER'S AND SHOOTER'S GUIDE

Several different calibers are classified as rimfires, beginning with the well-known .22 Long Rifle. The venerable "twenty-two" hosts a wide array of interesting loads, including some ultra-quiet choices and fairly nasty high-speed rounds. Even hotter rimfire calibers include the .22 Winchester Magnum Rimfire; plus three small-bore derivatives, the .17 Mach II, .17 Hornady Rimfire Magnum, and Winchester's high velocity .17 Super Magnum. Careful shopping can provide a useful rimfire (or maybe even two to quietly harvest small game or eliminate pests. An economical .22 LR firearm can also serve as a great rifle trainer if similar function is considered beforehand. A rimfire can't do *everything,* but it can do a lot once fully understood.

AIR RIFLES: A BUYER'S AND SHOOTER'S GUIDE

Air-powered guns offer several useful advantages. For starters, they are unregulated by the Bureau of Alcohol, Tobacco, Firearms and Explosives, meaning they have non-firearm status. Some state and local restrictions exist but, in most municipalities, you can order one by mail. Many airguns are also very quiet - a useful advantage if low-impact hunting is necessary. Uninformed people will lump them all together as simple BB guns, but the field has greatly evolved. The general lack of knowledge does provide an additional benefit. An airgun tends to be more acceptable in areas that would raise firearm concerns. Not everyone will need or want an air-powered system, choosing low-powered .22 loads instead. Confusion can play a role in this decision due to the various power-plants and types. Performance and pricing varies widely. Some of are even available in head-turning calibers like 9mm, .45, or .50! The airgun is an interesting specialty tool for clandestine subsistence, quiet practice, and all around fun.

CENTERFIRE RIFLES: A BUYER'S AND SHOOTER'S GUIDE

A properly equipped shotgun can stand in as a surrogate rifle of sorts using powerful slugs which function as large, heavy bullets. Since most are designed to be fired through smoothbore barrels, stability is reduced, resulting in mediocre accuracy which, combined with the poor ballistic qualities of the projectiles, limits range to around 100 yards. For the most part, the same is true of much smaller rimfire and air-powered rifles; still perfectly fine for use on small game. However, acquiring both power and range calls for some sort of centerfire rifle. Long-range shooting now involves distances beyond 1000 yards, made possible due to recent technological developments. But even lacking pricey equipment, a wide variety pedestrian but popular rifles can cover most bases out to a quarter-mile or more. This edition expands the system-based approach through compatible choices broken into general sporting-type rifles, and a separate AR-15 section. Once duly armed, the harvesting of larger animals will be possible while maintaining solid defensive footing. However, one thing still missing the means for a hands-free defensive capability, and that of course, is best served through a handgun…

THIS EDITION: HANDGUNS

Before jumping into the world of handguns, let's examine several key considerations referenced in the previous editions. These factors can steer us to practical choices that won't leave us high and dry regarding spare parts, ammo, and accessories. With apologies to readers who labored through them in other editions, the criteria laid out here just might save future headaches.

Whatever we're looking at must be in widespread use. An established design is reassuring. It takes time for a system to gain recognition and grow in numbers. Well-established firearms have plenty of history behind them, and will hold few surprises. In that regard, the immortal Government Model Pistol is a classic example. At this point, so is the Glock. S&W has been churning out revolvers since the 1800s so they also fit the bill. Widespread use is an indicator of numerous desirable traits.

Whatever we choose should be something with a solid reputation for dependability. Confidence in a chosen tool is always comforting. As explained in *Survival Guns*, there are teething pains with many new products and firearms are no exception. It's not uncommon to run into issues ranging from function to ergonomics. Anecdotal experience based on one or two examples can give you a false read and often seems to be the basis for unswerving opinions. A well-established track record is the better bet. For the most part, the handguns that follow will be ones involving extensive first-hand experience involving numerous specimens.

Glock pretty much nails the whole list. Its lineage has been preserved throughout the entire family tree. This G-17 is a 4th Generation.

It must be easy to operate. Disparate function is never a good thing during stressful circumstances, and operational proficiency is commensurate with training. The more complicated something is, the more training will be necessary. If time and range access are issues, simple is better. A basic revolver fits this description although polymer pistols are now in high demand. Also, simpler designs normally offer less opportunity for breakage. But, even the simplest systems can quit working at some point, so…

More specimens provide more data. These M&Ps are just part of a much larger inventory, used heavily for a decade. Consider them "tested".

Although less trendy, revolvers are simple and reliable. The bases are well-covered by this S&W Model 625. Its moon clips provide extremely fast reloads, using the same combat-proven .45 ACP rounds as the 1911 pistol.

The legendary .45 ACP 1911 Government Model (named for its year of adoption) certainly qualifies as "well established". Production continues unabated and spare parts abound. Negatives? Perhaps, more complex operation.

Parts must be readily available. In *Shotguns: A Comprehensive Guide,* we held up the Remington Model 870 as an example of ten million-plus firearms that have been in continuous production since 1950. In other words, plenty of spare parts abound. The same is true of heavily produced military systems like the U.S. M-16/AR-15 rifle, now more than fifty years old. But S&W's revolvers and the .45 ACP 1911 pistol have crossed the century mark with unceasing vitality. The Glock is younger, but it still qualifies thanks to huge distribution. Using a proven system, you can predict which parts are likely to fail and stock up on spares.

Ammunition must be widely available. You can't go wrong with an established military caliber like the 5.56mm (.223 Remington) or 9mm NATO (9mm Luger). Just about any hardware store with an FFL will have .30/06 cartridges on hand. The .45 ACP is another time-tested favorite. By comparison, the .40 S&W is a newbie, but it caught on in a big enough way to qualify here. When you're buying, mainstream choices will just about always be cheaper and if you're scrounging, the odds will tip in your favor. You can also benefit from a much wider selection of loads to match individual requirements.

It must be easy to maintain. In a survival situation, function is crucial. At some point, even the best-designed firearm will quit without cleaning. Simple disassembly facilitates the process while prolonging the life of your investment. Polished bluing may be esthetically pleasing, but stainless steel is better in rough weather. Captive parts and easy disassembly also help when on the go. A spring-loaded guide-rod that launches to parts unknown is bad enough in daylight let alone around a campfire in snow.

It should accommodate practical accessories. By sticking with the most popular handguns, availability of accessories is assured. Aftermarket parts abound for the 1911 Government Model Pistol, and Glock is hot on its heels. But, beyond nifty custom upgrades, lights and lasers are now in vogue, calling for practical ways to mount them. One expedient solution is an accessory rail; now more common, but by no means universal.

Mainstream calibers translate to more handgun choices. When factoring in defense, the "big three" pistol choices are (L-R): 9mm Luger, .40 S&W, and .45 ACP.

It must represent good value. The well-known rule of thumb is to buy the best equipment you can afford. However, when it comes to firearms, "equipment" means more than just a gun. Looking at a handgun, basic extras will include a holster, magazine or loader pouch, ammo, and a few spare magazines or speed-loaders. Adding up the essentials (with extra room for training), constitutes the bottom line. We call this our "system cost," which will mushroom without educated planning.

THE NEXT STEPS

These guidelines can steer us toward a practical firearm, but the possibilities still seem nearly endless! Furthermore, what's best for me may not be for you. Recoil, weight, complexity, and operation can pose problems

With raw power as a priority (L-R) the .357 Magnum, .41 Magnum, and .44 Magnum dominate revolver sales. But, with defense thrown in, the latter two could be excessive. However, a .357 will also fire manageable .38 Special loads.

related to experience or physique. Education is essential, starting with the various handgun types and how they work. From there we can narrow down some practical choices with proven track records.

TABLE OF CONTENTS

SECTION ONE: THE BASICS 1

Chapter 1: INTRODUCTION 5

Chapter 2: HANDGUN BASICS 9

Chapter 3: AMMUNTION BASICS 23

Chapter 4: GUIDELINES AND USEFUL FEATURES 39

Chapter 5: THE PERSONAL INTERFACE 55

Chapter 6: SIGHTS, LASERS, AND LIGHTS 73

Chapter 7: THOUGHTS ON ACCURACY AND RANGE 97

Chapter 8: CUSTODY AND CARRY BASICS 105

SECTION TWO: THE REVOLVER - 19th CENTURY TECHNOLOGY THAT REFUSES TO DIE **117**

Chapter 9: REVOLVER BASICS 119

Chapter 10: USEFUL REVOLVER CARTRIDGES 123

Chapter 11: SINGLE-ACTION REVOLVERS 143

Chapter 12: DOUBLE-ACTION REVOLVERS 149

Chapter 13: MORE DOUBLE-ACTIONS: S&W'S LINE 155

Chapter 14: GOOD REVOLVER PICKS: S&W – AND OTHERS 173

Chapter 15: HANDY REVOLVER ACCESSORIES 181

Chapter 16: KEEP YOUR WHEELGUN RUNNING 189

SECTION III: THE SEMIAUTOMATIC PISTOL WAVE **203**

Chapter 17: SEMIAUTOMATIC PISTOL BASICS 205

Chapter 18: USEFUL PISTOL CARTRIDGES 217

Chapter 19: SINGLE-ACTION PISTOLS 231

Chapter 20: DOUBLE-ACTION PISTOLS 259

Chapter 21: STRIKER-FIRED PISTOLS 273

Chapter 22: HANDY PISTOL ACCESSORIES 295

Chapter 23: KEEP YOUR PISTOL RUNNING 299

SECTION IV: ALA CARTE HANDGUNS, CARRY SYSTEMS, GADGETS, AND OTHER CONCERNS **307**

Chapter 24: CONVENTIONAL RIMFIRE HANDGUNS 309

Chapter 25: SINGLE-SHOT AND DERRINGER-TYPE HANDGUNS 323

Chapter 26: AN AR-15 PISTOL? 331

Chapter 27: INTO THE CARRY WEEDS; HOLSTERS, ETC. 345

Chapter 28: MORE ACCESSORIES: ESSENTIAL AND USEFUL ITEMS...... 361

Chapter 29: MORE ON AMMUNITION AND RELIABILITY 371

Chapter 30: DON'T FORGET TRANING! 381

CLOSING THOUGHTS 393

GLOSSARY... 395

SECTION ONE
THE BASICS

Chapter 1: INTRODUCTION 5

Chapter 2: HANDGUN BASICS 9

Chapter 3: AMMUNTION BASICS 23

Chapter 4: GUIDELINES AND USEFUL FEATURES 39

Chapter 5: THE PERSONAL INTERFACE 55

Chapter 6: SIGHTS, LASERS, AND LIGHTS 73

Chapter 7: THOUGHTS ON ACCURACY AND RANGE 97

Chapter 8: CUSTODY AND CARRY BASICS 105

CHAPTER 1
INTRODUCTION

Within the previous five books, the focus has been on arms capable of fulfilling two survival-based requirements: defense and hunting. Gun owners will typically work off an existing collection, but others could be starting from scratch. For the latter group, prioritized procurement makes sense, and the previous editions mirrored this approach. If at any time you are finding words abbreviations that are unfamiliar to you, I would advise consulting the Glossary at the end.

TIME TO ADD A HANDGUN

Until now in this series of books, the handgun has been conspicuously absent. Remember, the overall premise involved multi-use guns when reasonably possible, the shotgun being a prime example. Again, this assumes *both* hunting and defense are envisioned. But, if critters are not on your list, a handgun can move higher up the ladder. In that case, it might even become the first or second pick.

As for hunting with handguns, many people lack the skills necessary for reliable hits on small game; or for that matter, even deer-sized game taken at further distances. This statement is based on the observation of thousands of people during formalized training programs. Some are even paramilitary types with handgun backgrounds. And this is without the physiological effects of a defensive engagement factored in. Adrenaline will quickly degrade fine motor skills and, defensively, you should expect plenty of it! Furthermore, a handgun small enough to comfortably carry will be more difficult to shoot, even at closer ranges. I'm not talking about the smallest deep-cover pocket-rockets, either. This generalized statement applies to standard-sized pistols or revolvers against man-sized targets as close as 12-15 yards. Yes, a hit might appear *somewhere* on the target, but it might not be a good one. So-called "stopping power" is always a concern with handgun projectiles, which lack centerfire rifle punch. We *could* step up to more serious calibers, but a useful handgun requires a practical balance of portability AND control during recoil. Mass can help tame recoil but, when concealment is factored in, bigger isn't necessarily better! And, for most of us, concealment will be of interest.

RATIONALE

First off, if things look ugly, get a shotgun or rifle. As we say, only a fool would bring a handgun to a gun fight. During tough times, you probably won't be hunting purely for sport, where most dedicated handguns are more like "hand-rifles" set up with longer barrels and optical sights. They're fun to shoot and they present an alternative challenge for experienced sportsmen but, during a national calamity, the greater challenge may involve just staying alive. So, if you can, bring something with a shoulder-stock attached. The odds of ending the day secure with a full belly will greatly increase.

Of course, a shoulder-fired firearm can pose defensive challenges related to maneuverability as well as concealment. A shorter-barreled shotgun or centerfire carbine helps in tight places, but a carefully chosen handgun is often the more practical close-quarter choice – in the hands of a competent user. Again, this capability is best supported by a handgun with sufficient power to inspire defensive confidence. And, through careful shopping, we still might gain a modicum of hunting capability. To that end, the more useful pick will be a general-purpose compromise. Of course, the assumption here is that efforts will be made to become a highly skilled shot.

Right off the bat though, a question is what type of handgun? Should it be a revolver or a pistol? In fact, what's the difference? And, what caliber is best? The latter can produce lots of confusion by itself. But for now, let's start with basic gun types.

A general-purpose revolver? Those considering hunting will be better served by slightly larger handguns (or possibly a second gun). After all, power comes with a price beyond dollars, which is recoil. A bigger gun just soaks up more of it, so big-boomers like the .44 Magnum are sized accordingly, and are seen most often in the bush. Sometimes, the longer-barreled types that provide greater velocities are carried in cross-chest holsters to support their extra weight. As such, they don't really qualify as "general purpose."

On the other hand, a .357 Magnum double-action revolver with a four-inch barrel was the standard law enforcement preference for decades. A medium-sized version offers good portability with plenty of power for defense, as well as hunting. The .357 can take whitetail deer-sized quarry out to around 50 yards, and a switch to less powerful, non-expanding, .38 Special rounds will transform the same revolver into a small game tool. The beauty of a .357 Magnum is that it can digest either caliber, although point-of-impact (POI) will vary. The simple fix is a gun with adjustable sights. This flexibility also allows use of hotter .38 Special +Ps, which offer a compromise of recoil and power sufficient for self-defense. In other words, thanks to its great versatility, one well-chosen .357 Magnum revolver can cover many bases.

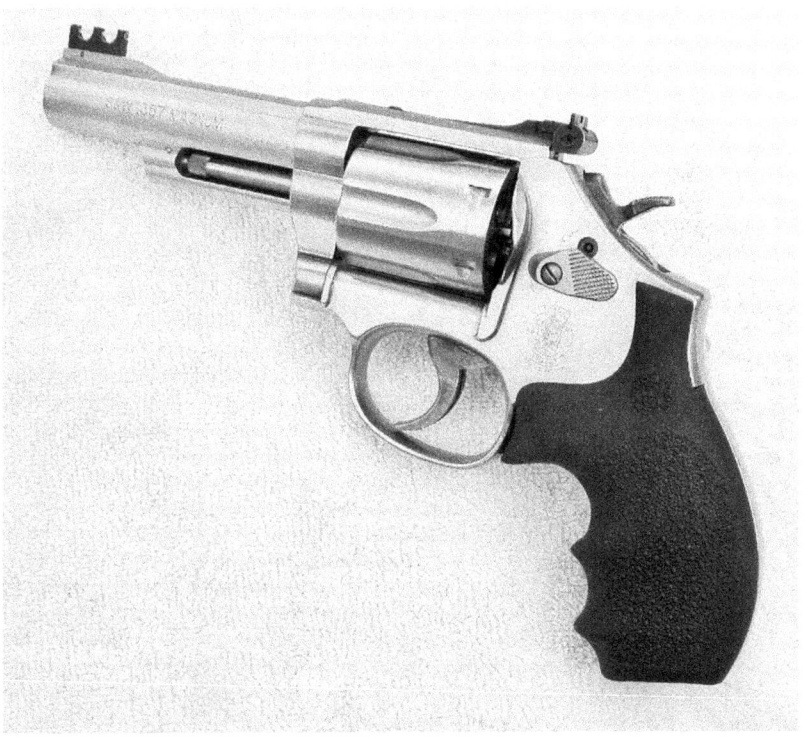

S&W's Model 66 .357 Magnum fits the description of a general-purpose revolver.

Plenty of smaller guns are also sold for concealed-carry use, often with short "snub-nose" barrels, frequently loaded with milder .38 Special cartridges. They'll carry and hide well, but their size and power constraints take hunting off the table - as well as anything other than close-range practice. As such, they're not good general-purpose picks, like most of the .380 pistols touched upon below.

General-purpose pistols? Interests will likely shift to guns no larger than medium-sized, high-capacity semi-automatics if hunting is off the table. But, one caliber with adequate power to take larger game is the 10mm Automatic. Like the .357 Magnum, it's a potent cartridge with similar if not greater power. In fact, the "Ten" gets close to a .41 Magnum (a notch below the .44 Mag.), but with an overall cartridge length only slightly greater than a 9mm or .40 S&W round. Actually, a .45 ACP size frame will often accommodate the 10mm. A classic example is the 1911 Government Model Pistol, which will work with either (using different magazines), accounting for the growing list of 10mms. Many of these 1911s are six-inch "long-slide" models geared toward feral hogs. Capitalizing on such interest, other 10 mm pistol types have appeared, branded by Glock, Sig, etc. But for defensive purposes, none are small pistols. Recoil and muzzle-flash are also quite pronounced, although a few milder 10 mm loads are offered. These will be more on the order of a .40 S&W, but will cost more with limited availability. Too bad the .40 can't be fired in a 10mm, but rimless pistol cartridges preclude this possibility (possible in a revolver though).

For more than a century, the 1911 Government Model Pistol has been "the choice" among die-hards. Smaller versions now abound, but simpler polymer alternatives have made serious inroads.

Entering general-purpose territory, a 1911 pistol is manageable for many in .45 ACP, and some diehards will settle for nothing else. The slide and/or frame may be shortened for carry purposes, and the 9mm has made recent Government Model inroads thanks largely to better bullets. In fact, odds are strong *any* new semiauto will debut in 9mm Luger, with a decreasing but still likely possibility of a .40 S&W choice. Such pistols can be smaller and both calibers will fit most medium-sized pistol frames. However, the improved 9mm performance has slowed .40 sales. Capacity is greater, recoil is less, and so is ammunition cost; due at least in part to abundance of 9mm ammunition, which can be found pretty much anywhere. While you *could* enlist these cartridges for hunting duties, they are really geared toward defense.

Small pistols have become popular for deep concealment carry, or for use as a second "back-up gun." The smallest are usually chambered for the less powerful .380 ACP, although some now appear as 9mms. They fill the similar roles of small-frame revolvers and while they're all extremely handy, none are ideal general-purpose picks.

We'll examine some good picks in the upcoming chapters but, before we delve into specifics, let's think about how you'll fit in…

PERSONAL CONSIDERATIONS

Your "right" handgun might not be mine. Sorta like vehicles, a good choice should be based on personalized factors. Since we're talking guns, fit, controllability (recoil), complexity, and cost should be considered. Concerning the latter, essential gear will increase the final tab; things like a holster, loader devices or magazines, ammunition, and a secure storage container. And, ammo is related to proficiency, which won't come with just a few boxes. In fact, since shooting is a perishable skill, more will be needed later, along with some provision for regular range time. The travel aspect alone may create additional burdens, both monetarily and time-wise, and these concerns should be factored into a total "system cost."

Thoughts on proficiency. Some readers may have a bit of history with a BB gun or .22 rifle. It counts as useful experience, but a handgun is harder to shoot than a shoulder-fired gun due to less stability and a shorter sight radius. The basics are still pretty much the same though, although competency doesn't stop with marksmanship. Several skill-sets apply from operation through tactics, grounded in a firm grasp of safety. If the process is rooted in Murphy's Law, so much the better: anything which can go wrong *will go wrong* – at the worst possible moment! Think about reloading minus the use of your dominant hand to get a handle on this principle. It's doable with proper training and practice, but it's *not* a safe starting point!

Our Firearms Training Unit is tasked with "qualifying" staff for armed duties. From management's view, it's as if some magic wand exists to anoint personnel. Presto, they're good to go! But of course, there's more to it than that. A week on the range and 800+ rounds are just the *minimum* process. For those showing promise, it could be the first phase of later tactical programs. Ideally, we'd extend such training to everyone. Ideally, we'd all vacation on a Mediterranean coast in our yachts, too. Unfortunately, constraints imposed by time, budget, and ability count. Management seeks economy and cadre wants a Ninja. Somewhere in the middle is reality.

So, what constitutes "qualified"? Everyone has their own take here. Some states have concealed-carry permit requirements, including proficiency standards, but they're typically minimal. A nebulous but acceptably higher degree of proficiency is a personal question based upon the aforementioned constraints. While anticipated circumstances and commitment play significant roles, it's better to be over-prepared than under-prepared. Plugging in Murphy's Law, a fully "qualified" individual should be able to effectively employ their firearm with either hand, from any position, in any light. That's a tall order since, besides the necessary resources, serious commitment is required. Realities will probably dictate a lower standard, hopefully still above the basic. Some folks will be starting from scratch and, if so, here's a reassuring thought: We often find that the person finishing first within our Basic Pistol Program is the one with no firearms experience at all. Why? No bad habits!

Gender-based myths. The number of female shooters has grown by leaps and bounds, so manufacturers have responded accordingly, with many good semiautomatics. A pistol is, perhaps, a tad more complex than a revolver, but it's certainly no more difficult to operate than a vehicle. The notion that a revolver is best for a woman due to its simplicity is a gender-based myth.

But, one size doesn't fit all. It may come as a major disappointment to some readers looking for a simple fix but, bottom line: there really isn't one best handgun OR training regimen. Although it sounds like a cop-out, we say "best choices" should really be tailored ones. When it comes to handguns, some users could have strength issues or be less mechanically inclined. In that case, coupled with only limited opportunities for practice, the KISS principle will gain more importance. Again, think about the handgun's anticipated role and your degree of commitment.

No matter what type of handgun is chosen, *its function must be clearly understood.* And, since safety is another crucial aspect, a baseline level of training is critical. So is a more advanced firearms school. Each source tends to operate off its own unique culture, grounded on a few common tenets. It's the depth of training that that could govern the choice. We all have practical limits based on budget, time, travel, fitness, and desire. Some schools fall into the "one size fits all" mindset while missing the bigger picture. As often as not there are *several* good ways to accomplish a task, indicating the value of ongoing training – preferably from different sources.

CHAPTER 2
HANDGUN BASICS

The FBI is headed back into a 9mm pistol and the U.S. Army is about to join suit with their own new high-capacity, polymer-frame wonder. In western military parlance, the cartridge itself is known as the *9mm NATO* (or 9x19mm). Globally, the same load is often listed as *9mm Parabellum*. A box of American-made cartridges will probably be labeled *9mm Luger*. Georg Luger's 9mm 1902 technology appears to be more than a fad.

A BIT OF EARLY HISTORY

All of today's handguns are intertwined with a fascinating period of 19th century evolution. During the 1830s, smokeless powder and self-contained metallic cartridges were far over the horizon. For centuries, attempts had been made to produce a reliable repeating firearm, but none were entirely satisfactory. Part of the problem was the heavy, corrosive residue resulting from combustion of the black powder propellant, but the flintlock ignition system then in use posed even greater challenges. So, the conventional handgun (like other circa 1800 firearms), was loaded through its muzzle with loose powder, followed by a lead round ball. The projectile was seated with a ramrod and small pan was then primed with a separate charge of fine powder. Ignition occurred when a hammer containing a piece of flint was triggered to strike a steel arm (a frizzen), directing a shower of sparks into the pan. From there, a small orifice (touch-hole) allowed the burning priming charge to reach the main powder load. The hoped-for result was a shower of sparks and heavy noxious smoke, accompanied by the exit of the ball. Obviously, reloading was a tedious event, so a brace of pistols was sometimes employed, often in conjunction with a shoulder-fired musket.

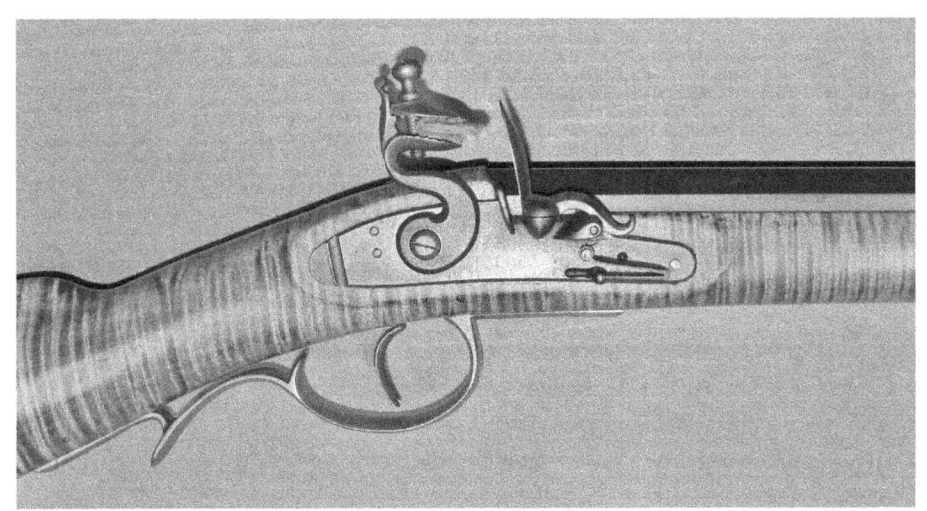

This flintlock is cocked and ready to fire. Upon pulling the trigger, a flint within the hammer will strike the "frizzen", exposing its primed "pan" to a shower of sparks.

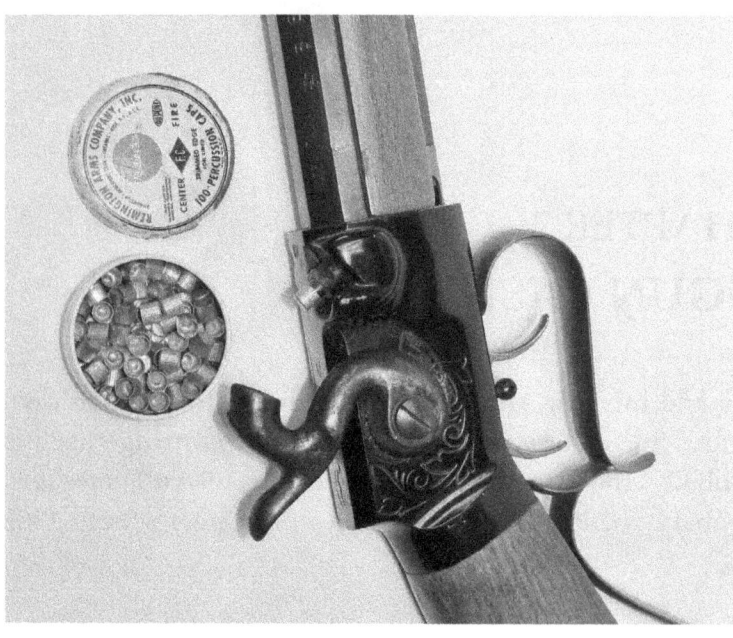

The invention of the percussion cap was a major breakthrough, but metallic cartridges were yet to come.

Many defensive/military arms had smoothbore barrels for easier loading with fouled bores, resulting in lackluster accuracy. Elegant Pennsylvania (or Kentucky) long rifles offered useful accuracy in the hands of skilled frontiersmen, but their primary use was for hunting. A cloth patch surrounded the projectile during seating for optimum engagement of the barrel's "lands and grooves," so reloads were even slower. But, these spiral cuts provided gyroscopic stability much like a properly thrown football, resulting in vastly improved accuracy. Rifled barrels are alive and well today, but seating a projectile in a muzzle-loading barrel often required a short ball-starting rod and a mallet. Fortunately, this situation was about to change for the better…

Birth of the revolver. Sam Colt revolutionized handgun design through an innovative concept. His revolving cylinder represented a quantum leap, made possible by a new percussion cap. The cap itself was just a small copper cup that contained a small explosive compound. After pre-loading five chambers within the cylinder, each could be aligned with the rear of a stationary .28-caliber barrel through a hammer-connected linkage. Loose powder was dispensed into each chamber, the rear of which contained a

Nineteenth century muzzle-loading systems evolved from a flint and fine black powder priming charge (L), to a percussion cap. Patched round balls gave way to soft lead bullets, but loading remained tedious.

steel nipple. The projectile was a lead ball, seated on top of the powder charge. The mouth of each chamber was then sealed with grease to prevent "chain firing" (an exciting event caused by sparks igniting adjacent loads). The nipples were finally "capped" for ignition by a hammer blow, presenting five quick shots. This "Patterson Colt" was primitive by today's standards, requiring partial disassembly to load its cylinder. Still, it was a big advancement beyond existing muzzle-loading firearms that offered one hopeful shot. By 1839, refinements included a built-in arm to ram the ball home. A rifled barrel thus became practical, resulting in good accuracy, and as word got out, Colt incorporated larger calibers.

Colt's Model 1851 percussion revolver was a hugely successful design.

The Patterson venture failed during the 1840s, but the design was too good to die. By 1847, Connecticut-built Colts were rolling off a new factory floor thanks to government contracts. The line was well-established by the Civil War and cavalry units from both sides often carried a brace of cap & ball revolvers during fast-paced skirmishes. Calibers were .31, .36, or .44, built in sizes commensurate with their projectiles. Colt not only defined the revolver, but also died as one of America's wealthiest men, a testament to the value of a reliable repeating firearm.

Who cares? Well, some readers might, since guns of this type are not federally regulated. If you get on the websites of sporting suppliers like Cabelas or Midway USA, you'll see a large assortment of surprisingly affordable replica cap & ball revolvers. These guns don't require any ATF paperwork so they can be purchased by mail in many locales (depending on their restrictions). As such, they could have appeal for some readers, although their use will be much more complicated. For safety's sake, the propellant must be loose black powder *or an approved substitute!* Byproducts include lots of noxious white smoke and heavy, corrosive fouling which will quickly cause rust unless cleaned promptly using hot soapy water (followed by oil). Smokeless powders will blow the gun to hell so that option is clearly out. Of course, reloading will also be a tedious event, which is why many gunfighters carried two guns. Others sometimes packed an extra loaded cylinder, although dropping one posed risks. That said, extra cylinders are still sold today.

EVOLUTION

Back to the second half of the 19th century, it wasn't long before purpose-built metallic cartridge revolvers began to appear. This process began with self-contained "pinfire" cartridges, each of which had small individual firing pins. But, S&W's anemic self-contained .22 Short rimfire revolver really sparked a revolution after combining a bored-through cylinder with a truly practical self-contained cartridge that fired an elongated bullet. Appearing in 1857, its patents ensured success during a period of further refinements. After they expired in 1869, growth was exponential, coinciding with further cartridge development. Conical bullets offered improved performance through the stabilizing effects of rifling, and some serious defensive loads appeared.

Two ground-breaking self-contained metallic cartridges were the anemic rimfire .22 Short, and potent centerfire .44 WCF (.44-40).

Single-action refinement. During 1873, a now legendary Peacemaker stole the show as the Colt Frontier Six-Shooter. Like its percussion predecessors, the new Colt was of single-action design, requiring manual cocking of a hammer to fire each shot. However, it was strong enough to handle a new and potent .44 Winchester Centerfire cartridge (.44 WCF), which gained further widespread favor in Winchester Model 1873 rifles. Otherwise known as the .44/40, this dual-use cartridge had huge appeal, and this concept still survives as a practical option that simplifies ammo procurement. Other calibers followed including the perennial .45 Colt, which quickly gained favor as reliable man-stopper upon adoption by U.S. Army as the Model 1873.

Double-action evolution. D/A revolvers got an early start, but stayed in the background until the 1870s. A D/A revolver could be fired two ways. The first using the conventional manual hammer-cocking method of that period. The second option required a long, deliberate trigger pull which rotated the cylinder while activating the hammer. The gun was timed so the hammer fell of its own accord upon a properly indexed chamber. Some, like the first double-action Colts, were like the Peacemakers. Others, including the early S&Ws, were top-break designs that ejected spent cases when their hinged frames were opened to expose their cylinders. However, it's safe to say that Colt's 1889 swing-out cylinders was a breakthrough. Because of its solid frame, the gun was much stronger, and its easily accessible cylinder was much faster to reload than the single-action models. S&W jumped on this design with their .32-caliber "Hand Ejector" in 1896. It was followed by their Model 1899 with a new .38 Special cartridge. We know this gun today as S&W's immortal Model 10; still in production!

Ammunition evolution and repeaters. The advent of smokeless powder was a parallel breakthrough that eliminated excessive fouling. Without it, reliable semi-automatic function would have been difficult to achieve. Interestingly, although smokeless propellants were non-corrosive, the mercuric priming compounds in use at that time could still raise havoc with steel. It's not uncommon to see older barrels with finely pitted bores which resulted from lack of immediate attention. Beginning around World War II, especially in the USA, non-corrosive priming came into play, effectively solving this problem.

Self-loading concepts. An early pistol cartridge was the .30 Borchardt, developed in 1893 for the first successful semi-automatic pistol. It was a radical design, but it was also impractically large. Georg Luger improved upon the concept in 1900, launching the famous Luger Pistol with greatly improved ergonomics. By 1902, a new cartridge appeared for this pistol, which is still referred to as the 9mm Luger. Its projectile and ballistics are not all that different from the circa 1899 .38 Special (the forerunner of .357 Magnum), but the cartridge case differs. The 9mm Luger uses a shorter rimless case, achieving good velocities through lighter bullets, loaded to higher pressure. Eight stacked rounds could be loaded into a detachable magazine, housed within its grip. The shorter cartridges resulted in a more manageable package, and offered extra shots with rapid reloads.

During the early 1900s, longer, bottleneck cartridges like the .30 Borchardt were shortened to afford better grip-frame ergonomics. The later 9mm Luger (R) looks stubby by comparison.

Semiauto pistol refinement. Meanwhile, the U.S. Army was shopping for a better handgun. Unsatisfactory combat results with late 19th century smaller-caliber revolvers indicated the need for extra punch. John Browning's brilliant .45 ACP "Government Model" offered the stopping power of a storied .45 Colt Single Action Army revolver in a modern 8-shot pistol. Adopted in 1911, it's still going strong today. Not only that, the .45 Automatic Colt Pistol Cartridge remains a benchmark of terminal semi-automatic pistol performance. The Model 1911 concept also established the nearly universal blueprint for future pistol designs. The toggle-action P-08 Luger served Germany through two global conflicts, but it was on the way out before World War II ended. The recoil-operated, locked breech, tilt-

The iconic Luger Pistol is often associated with its 9mm namesake but a .30-caliber version came first, for use by the Swiss. The Germans demanded a bigger bullet.

John Browning's 1911 Government Model soldiers on. Today's examples incorporate more bells and whistles than this early .45 ACP, but the basic platform remains.

ing-barrel 1911 is still seeing combat, and many other modern pistols like the Glock employ its tilting-barrel principle.

The seismic semiauto shift. The Brits stayed with revolvers throughout this period, as did U.S. law enforcement agencies. While military pistol interest was strong before World War I, civilian transition didn't blossom until the late 1980s. Before then, the revolver of choice was a .357 Magnum made by S&W or Colt, with a smattering of Rugers thrown in. By the mid-90s the law enforcement situation had completely reversed course and the handgun of choice became some sort of semiautomatic pistol, more than likely chambered for 9mm, or a new .40-caliber upstart. However, to this day the renowned .357 Magnum remains another standard used to quantify so-called stopping power. Regardless, civilian handgun preference rapidly changed during the late 20th century, reflecting military and law enforcement trends. Revolver sales declined and were relegated to smaller concealed-carry types. Connected to the latter, other manufacturing innovations spawned some interest in long-range handgun shooting.

Long-range handguns. The stage was really set during the 1960s when Thompson/Center came out with their *Contender*, a unique single-shot break-action pistol with easily interchangeable barrels. This innovative gun had dual firing pins and a hammer-selector, which provided rimfire and centerfire possibilities starting with .22 LR or .22 Hornet. The list of calibers grew and rifle scopes were catching on during this period so, inevitably, pistol scopes appeared. Before long, serious sportsmen were stretching out handgun distances to unheard of ranges, using all sorts of hot-rock calibers. The sport of Metallic Silhouette followed with 200-yard events. Other specialty hunting handguns arrived and performance increased again. Some, like Remington's XP-100, were bolt-actions, chambered for centerfire rifle calibers. For the most part though, these handguns occupy a specialized sporting niche.

TODAY'S HANDGUNS

Technically, it would be correct to refer to any handheld firearm as a pistol and, in fact, Samuel Colt sold his revolvers this way. Of course, the field has grown considerably since then. Today's general handgun types reflect several evolutionary species.

Modern revolver types. As touched upon previously, the beauty of a revolver is its relative simplicity. Being a self-contained system, it doesn't rely on detachable magazines and will fire any cartridge of the correct caliber, regardless of its power level. Within the generalized classification of revolvers two sub-categories exist which have not only survived, but continue to prosper.

Single-action revolvers are alive and well. The hammer of this example is on "half-cock", and must be fully cocked (by hand) to fire. Note the loading gate.

Single-action (S/A) revolvers. Although these guns represent the first practical repeaters, production continues today. Development of self-contained metallic ammunition greatly sped up the reloading process, but individual handling of each cartridge is still necessary. Thumb-cocking the external hammer will ready the gun to fire, and this step also advances the cylinder for each successive shot. The cylinder revolves around a central axle (or pin), which remains captured within the frame. A small hinged loading gate can be swung open to expose an individual chamber for loading, and manual rotation of the cylinder will index each one. Unloading occurs similarly, using a barrel-mounted ejector rod to punch out fired cases. Later during cleaning, the pin can be withdrawn, permitting the cylinder to be removed. Again, think "Peacemaker" to visualize this sort of gun, which has appeared in dozens of Hollywood Westerns. The S/A revolver design endures as a true American classic, offering a taste of nostalgia with some additional sportsman's attributes, including strength and reliability.

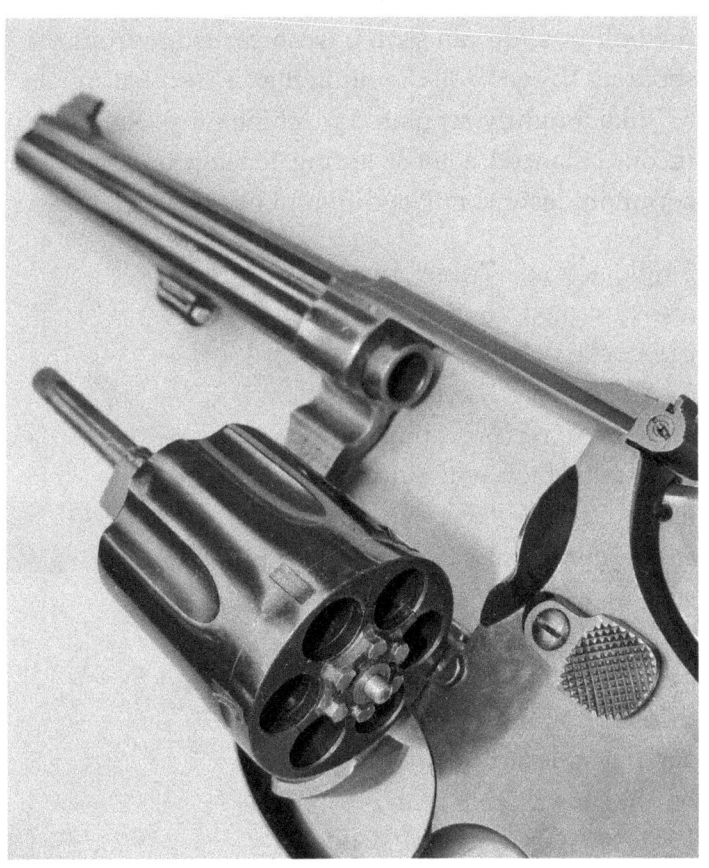

The double-action revolver with its swing-out cylinder evolved as the handgun of choice for decades. In fact, it's still a viable choice.

Double-action (D/A) revolvers. This evolution adds an alternate trigger-cocking capability to the single-action system. In

Handgun Basics | 15

"double-action" mode, a long and deliberate trigger pull will draw back the hammer while cycling the cylinder for rapid, successive shots. A swing-out cylinder permits simultaneous ejection of fired cases and use of speed-loading devices. The cylinder still revolves around a central axis but the rod is relocated to a hinged, swing-out arm (or crane). Pushing a frame-mounted release tab will unlock this assembly, allowing the cylinder to swing left. The spring-loaded rod is then exposed for use as an ejector. Since it penetrates the cylinder, the breech end can be connected to one central ejector "star" for clearance of empties. The rear face of the cylinder is also fully exposed for fast access of the chambers for reloading. D/A revolvers can be safely carried with their hammers at rest, but an instantaneous response is just a trigger-stroke away. Back to Hollywood, think 1940 gangster movies. The same guns also gained rapid favor among law enforcement agencies, serving well into the 1980s. Some will still be found in ankle holsters and of late, the D/A revolver has reemerged as a viable civilian defensive and sporting choice.

Semiautomatic pistols. More often today, the term "pistol" refers to a self-loading handgun with a detachable magazine. Upon discharge, a reciprocating mechanism with some sort of bolt or slide is driven rearward, extracting and ejecting a spent cartridge case while re-cocking its action. After full travel, a heavily compressed recoil spring then drives the mechanism forward. Along the way, the bolt or slide can strip a fresh cartridge from the magazine and chamber it. Each shot requires a separate trigger pull denoting it as a "semiautomatic" design (a gun that continues to fire is 'full-auto" like a tightly regulated machine gun). Reliable function is dependent on cartridge pressure and recoil, balanced against spring tension and gun mass. Within the semiauto pistol category, three common designs reflect different operational approaches.

Single-action. These pistols are designed to fire from a pre-cocked hammer, like a S/A revolver. The big difference is a reciprocating bolt or slide, which will automatically re-cock the hammer for subsequent shots. Some sort of external safety lever is usually employed so the pistol can be rendered "safe" during carry. In fact, most such pistols are designed to be holstered this way, the 1911 .45 Government Model being a classic example. Its frame-mounted safety lever prevents the pistol from

Single-actions aren't all 1911, although this .22 Browning Buckmark's controls will be recognizable. However, it fires from an internal hammer (Photo by Domenick Leonard).

firing when engaged, and a grip-safety provides additional insurance. Like a cocked revolver, an S/A pistol's trigger pull is typically light and consistent with a short travel. Although the 1911 and many other S/A pistols have an external hammer, some employ an internal design. A series of smaller-caliber Browning-designed pistols employed this system for non-snagging pocket carry. Many .22 LR target pistols work the same way. The pre-cocked hammer provides ignition but it's tucked securely out of sight, inside the frame.

Walther's double-action PP-series is a classic DA/SA design. Of reasonably compact size and chambered for smaller calibers (like this .22 LR), they remain in production today (Photo by Domenick Leonard).

Double-action. A typical double-action/single-action (DA/SA) incorporates the uncocked mode of a D/A revolver with a cocked S/A pistol, within one semiautomatic system. A double-action pistol is carried with its hammer at rest. A long, deliberate trigger stroke will cock and fire the gun, whereupon, like a S/A pistol, its hammer will be automatically re-cocked during slide cycling. Unless uncocked, all subsequent shots will occur via the shorter and lighter S/A pull. The U.S. Military Beretta M-9 and James Bond's Walther PPK are two representative DA/SA examples. These pistols (and many others) employ some sort of de-cocking lever to safely drop the hammer before re-holstering the gun. Most DA/SA designs will also permit manual cocking of the hammer for a lighter first-shot trigger pull.

Another variant is the double-action-only (DAO), in which the hammer always returns to rest between shots. The design relies upon a long and heavy trigger pull to initiate each shot, and its hammer-down carry solves the need for any de-cocking levers. Some have external safeties. Most of today's DAO pistols are smaller

Most of today's DAOs are smaller deep-cover designs. This S&W .380 Bodyguard fires from a shrouded hammer through a long, deliberate trigger stroke. Although harder to master, practical accuracy is attainable.

Handgun Basics | 17

deep-cover designs that can be safely secreted in pockets or purses. When at rest, the hammer may be shrouded within the rear of the slide for a more streamlined "no-snag" profile. Manual cocking of the hammer is generally precluded, but is of no real concern for this type of pistol.

Striker-fired pistols. A Glock embodies this system. Instead of a hammer-fired mechanism, a partially cocked spring-loaded striker is used. Pulling the trigger draws the striker further rearward until it finally disengages, lunging forward to strike the primer. This design requires a somewhat heavier trigger than a fully pre-cocked S/A, but less than required for a D/A release. Furthermore, each trigger pull remains the same. Because the striker is not fully cocked, an external safety is often omitted, which further simplifies operation. Since the appearance of the Glock, striker-fired pistols have gained *huge* popularity. Like a Glock, you can bet that its many rivals will have polymer frames.

Three common pistol types (L-R): Single-action, double-action, and striker-fired.

Other pistols. This category includes derringers, single-shots, bolt-actions, and AR-type handguns. The contrast between these guns is huge, with demure derringers serving for concealed carry. The others are large specialty tools designed primarily for hunting, long-range shooting, or defensive purposes.

Derringers. Today's big player is *Bond Arms*. This company has aggressively marketed a modern series of smaller two-barreled handguns based loosely on the old 19th century Remington break-action Derringers. What Bond has done is offer a switch-barrel capability with lots of interesting calibers, offered in several lengths. No doubt many of these guns are carried by joggers or hikers in outdoor settings, but their downside is just two shots. Bond is not the only manufacturer, and there are even some multi-barrel four-shot versions. Based more on size than anything, some folks also lump very tiny revolvers into the Derringer classification.

Single-shots. The modern single-shot handguns present intriguing possibilities, especially the switch-barrel Encores and G-2 Contenders from Thompson/Center (T/C). Whereas the derringer appeared as a vest pocket gun, the T/C was presented as a large break-barrel sporting tool designed for long-range shooting and handgun hunting. The T/C can even transform into a shoulder-fired system (the trick is to maintain compliance with NFA regulations during this process). At the other end of the spectrum is the very small Heizer Defense PS-1 Pocket Shotgun. A few other companies sell interesting examples, but one thing they have in common is being limited to one shot.

Bolt-actions. These handguns are more like rifles than pistols. Remington's XP-100 single-shot had a space gun appearance with its racy synthetic stock and long barrel. It eventually morphed into a similar bolt-action repeater that fed centerfire rifle cartridges. Long-range Metallic Silhouette competition and hunting were the primary markets, but such "handguns" have faded a bit, perhaps because a shorter-barreled carbine is just a better general-purpose choice.

AR-types. The so-called AR-type "pistols" are essentially short-barreled AR-15 carbines that lack conventional butt-stocks. The ensuing package is more compact, but by no means small, so normal holster carry is out. It will also be loud in a rifle caliber like the 5.56 NATO (.223 Rem), and it will be more difficult to shoot than a carbine. I could see some use for one, possibly if stashed in a trunk, but I'd much rather have a telescoping stock. Trouble is, at that point, like any other shoulder-fired rifle with a barrel less than 16-inches long, you'll have a federally regulated "short-barreled rifle" (SBR). Without the legally required $200 NFA stamp and paperwork, you'll need a good lawyer to avoid an extended stay at Club Fed.

For our intents, these "other" pistols are really niche items. Our first order of business should be some practical means for defense. A sport-shooting aspect, although useful, should be secondary. To cover both, we'll be better served by a general-purpose sidearm which will need to be a repeater of some sort.

WHERE DO WE GO FROM HERE?

Each handgun type will get full attention in the upcoming chapters. Meanwhile, since an established track record is reassuring, an older design is not necessarily a bad one. Many of today's shooters have grown up in The Polymer Age, and have no other frame of reference. A steel-framed handgun – especially one with a revolving cylinder - is viewed as little more than an arcane relic. However, the polymer pistol crowd has also experienced its share of accidental discharges (ADs). Granted, an "accidental discharge" is certainly possible with *any* type of firearm, but it's less likely with a gun that doesn't require pulling its trigger for disassembly. That's Step #1 for many striker-fired designs. A universal requirement for any handgun choice is plain old common sense and with that, from the perspective of safety, design becomes less of a concern. However, practice opportunities and complexity can affect proficient operation.

Tiers of complexity. Many serious "gun people" will consider – if not own – a 1911 pistol. This time-tested gun will be carried "cocked and locked" with its hammer back and a safety-lever engaged. A virtue of this design is a light and consistent trigger pull. The drawback is some additional complexity and the need for unrelenting attention. Those who shoot less often may be better served by simpler designs since KISS is good, especially under stress.

To a large extent, the latest genre of striker-fired, polymer pistols addresses the KISS principle nicely, but the devil is in the details. Most rely upon a somewhat heavier trigger sans a separate safety. In theory, such pistols won't fire until the shooter's finger depresses some sort of trigger-actuated blocking system. With training, this system *should* be safe. Heck, all we need to do is follow the widely taught *Four Rules of Firearms Safety*, right?

A similar rimfire is a worthy addition. These S&Ws, in .22 LR and .357 Magnum, will cover just about everything. Speed-strips are but one of many loading options.

Rule #1: Treat all guns as though loaded – always!

Rule #2: Don't point the gun at something you don't intend to shoot!

Rule #3: Keep you finger off the trigger until the sights are on the target!

Rule #4: Be sure of your target, and what is beyond it!

Sounds simple enough, but more than one pistol has fired from nether regions due to unanticipated pressure on its trigger. The cause could be a wad of bunched up loose clothing but an errant lipstick or lighter can cause similar havoc from inside a fanny-pack or purse. Carry is a significant concern which should not be underestimated and, to some extent, the handgun can dictate the means.

Rumors to the contrary, a revolver is far from obsolete. The double-action type is the primary defensive choice because of its long and heavy trigger pull. Many smaller models reside in ankle-holsters, pockets, or purses. Since operation is simple and easily understood, these attributes go a long way toward preventing unintentional discharges. Shooters with limited strength may also appreciate the lack of heavily spring-loaded parts common to some semiautomatic pistols.

A DAO pistol shares much common ground, although like snub-nose revolvers, most run smaller, making them somewhat harder to shoot accurately. Many DA/SA pistols solve the size issue, but extra complexity can result from two different trigger pulls, and the need for de-cocking. Master these skills and you'll gain a reassuringly safe companion piece.

Education is the best way to narrow down a good personal choice. While we're at it, let's throw another consideration into the mix. A rimfire .22 can be a darned handy addition. One with functional similarity can support economical practice while providing lots of fun and, possibly, even some meat for the pot. It's something to bear in mind when shopping, since not every center-fire type can be matched to a rimfire twin.

Handgun designs aside, some readers may be uncertain about the various calibers, not to mention bullet types, etc. So, let's take a quick time out to nail down some ammunition basics…

CHAPTER 3
AMMUNITION BASICS

A little bit of knowledge can indeed be a dangerous thing. The purchase of a box of .45 pistol cartridges seems simple enough, right? Well, my son appeared with a new box of .45 GAP, which was sold to him by a supposedly knowledgeable salesman at a big sporting emporium. Trouble was, he needed .45 ACP. Neither of them knew the difference and luckily, this problem only involved one box of ammo. Although the .45 Glock Automatic Pistol seemed like a good idea several years ago, it's already semi-obsolete. Furthermore, the cartridge is not interchangeable with common .45 Automatic Colt Pistol (.45 ACP) ammo.

Now picture a complete listing of *all* pistol and revolver cartridges. The domestic list alone is imposing enough but, fortunately for us, it won't be necessary. If we stick with our theme of widespread availability, life gets a bit simpler – and safer!

TERMINOLOGY

One problem for many newer shooters is the jargon. Some of the information you'll find below is condensed from the first *Survival Guns* edition, which contains further details about cartridge terminology and anatomy. There you can see the difference between rimfire and centerfire cartridges. Since not everyone will have a copy on hand, let's begin with some basics.

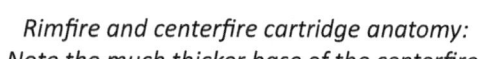

METALLIC AMMUNITION COMPONENTS

RIMFIRE — CENTERFIRE

Rimfire and centerfire cartridge anatomy: Note the much thicker base of the centerfire.

Examples of rimfire and centerfire ignition systems, both fired and unfired. The centerfire's headstamp indicates a .223 Remington, manufactured by the Federal Cartridge Company.

Rimfire and centerfire differences. The original rimfire .22 Short eventually evolved into a series of somewhat more powerful cartridges but, owing to their design, none were particularly strong. The priming compound was spun within a thin annular brass rim, and ignition occurred from a firing pin blow sufficient to pinch the brass case, causing detonation. The .22 Long Rifle is a classic example of today's thinly populated and non-reloadable rimfire cartridge alternatives. This ignition system works very well, but more potent cartridges need robust cartridge cases to safely contain their increased pressure. The centerfire system permits use of a much thicker base that houses a small centrally located (and often replaceable) primer.

Caliber (Cal.). A caliber equals one one-hundredth (0.01") of an inch. A .22-caliber bullet is therefore roughly twenty-two one hundredths (0.22") in diameter. I use the term "roughly" because great license has been used by firearms manufacturers when labeling new cartridges. The true diameter may vary from its label. For example:

The most popular rimfire load is the .22 Long Rifle (.22 LR). Its true diameter is 0.0223.

The hotter .22 Winchester Rimfire Magnum measures 0.0224, and uses a longer, straight-walled case of greater diameter. These rounds are similar in design, but not interchangeable (although a few revolvers are sold with both cylinders). Firing a .22 LR in a larger-diameter .22 Magnum (WMR) chamber is unsafe.

The centerfire .38 Special isn't really a .38-caliber at all. The name no doubt stuck because the cartridge case evolved from an even older .38 Long Colt load, which fired a "heeled bullet." The .22 LR survives as an example of such designs where both the bullet and cartridge case share the same external diameter. In other words, the true .380" diameter of the old .38 LC applied to the whole cartridge. When the longer .38 Special evolved, a non-heeled bullet was developed to fit snugly inside its case. The inside diameter was .357, so this dimension also applied to the bullet and the .38 Special's barrel was rifled accordingly. The longer, hotter, and more accurately described ".357 Magnum" uses bullets of the same diameter, and both cartridges fire bullets closer to .36-caliber (averaging 0.357 to 0.358). The external .380 case diameter of both goes back beyond the .38 Long Colt, to a .38 Short Colt, which itself evolved from a bored-through conversion of a cap & ball cylinder. Say what? But, wait, there's more…

Here's another mind-bender: the .38 S&W. This old and milder cartridge dates to 1877, and is entirely different from the .38 Special. It fires a larger .361 diameter bullet and uses a different case. Ruger built some .38 S&Ws for overseas sales, and the Brits built a bunch of Webley MK-1 revolvers in this caliber. There are plenty of old domestic .38 S&Ws languishing in drawers. Colt's old .38 New Police is essentially the same cartridge. Don't shoot these loads in a .38 Special or .357 Magnum gun.

The .32 Rimfire cartridge is long gone, but various .32 centerfires survive. The former (L) employed an outside-lubricated "heeled" bullet of the same diameter as its case. Typical of most centerfire cartridges, the old .32 S&W Long uses a smaller-diameter inside-lubricated bullet.

The .38 Super is an entirely different cartridge, itself a hotter version of an older semi-rimmed .38 Automatic cartridge designed for semiauto pistols. The Super is too hot for older pistols and neither should be fired in a .38 Special or .357 Magnum chamber.

A .44 Special can be fired in a .44 Magnum but neither is a true .44-caliber since they fire bullets measuring 0.429". The older .44/40 (.44 WCF) is not interchangeable and uses a 0.427" projectile.

The whole thing can be very confusing and, since many loads are not interchangeable, you can get in serious trouble by firing an incorrect round. If in doubt, first check with a trustworthy source! A full-line gun shop is a safer bet than the big-box retailers, but life becomes even simpler when mainstream chamberings are chosen.

This lineup includes (L-R) .22 LR, .22 WMR, .223, 30/06, .308, 38 Special, and .357 Magnum cartridges. The power of the bottleneck rifle cartridges is in a whole different league than the others.

Ammunition Basics | 25

Millimeter (mm). The metric cartridge system is much more logical, although still imperfect. One millimeter (mm) equals roughly four calibers, so a 9mm is approximately .36-caliber (.355). The question is which 9mm? There are several common types to choose from, plus a bunch of more obscure versions.

The very popular 9mm Luger is a 9x19mm, and the second number refers to the length of its cartridge case. It's different than the shorter 9x17mm, otherwise known as a .380 ACP (or 9mm Kurz). Then, there is the 9mm Makarov (or 9x18mm), along with several other 9mms. These rounds are not interchangeable, so you need to be sure what you're firing.

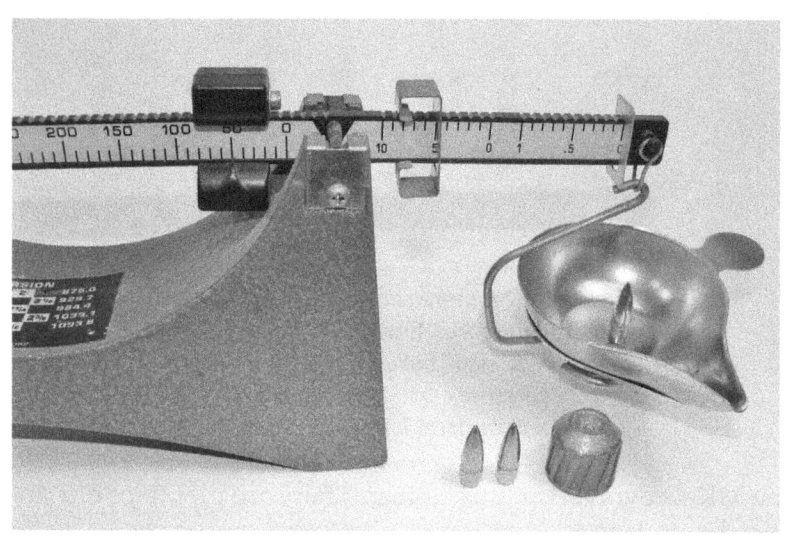

The 12 Gauge slug in the foreground weighs 437.5 grains (one ounce). The military .223/5.56mm bullet on the scale weighs 55 grains.

Grains. We can use this unit of measurement to quantify the weight of a bullet. It's also used by reloaders to determine a powder charge weight, and should not be confused with individual grains of powder. As a unit of weight, there are 7,000 grains in a pound and 437.5 grains in an ounce. A standard .22 LR bullet weighs only 40 grains. A common 9mm bullet weighs 115-grains, whereas a .45 ACP is twice that. Cartridges like the .30/06 Springfield often use bullets weighing 150 grains. More mass may mean more terminal punch, but velocity is also important. Rest assured, the terminal effects of a 165 grain 30/06 will be a quantum leap above any conventional 165 grain handgun round, regardless of its caliber. The velocity of the rifle round will be roughly three times greater, placing it in another realm.

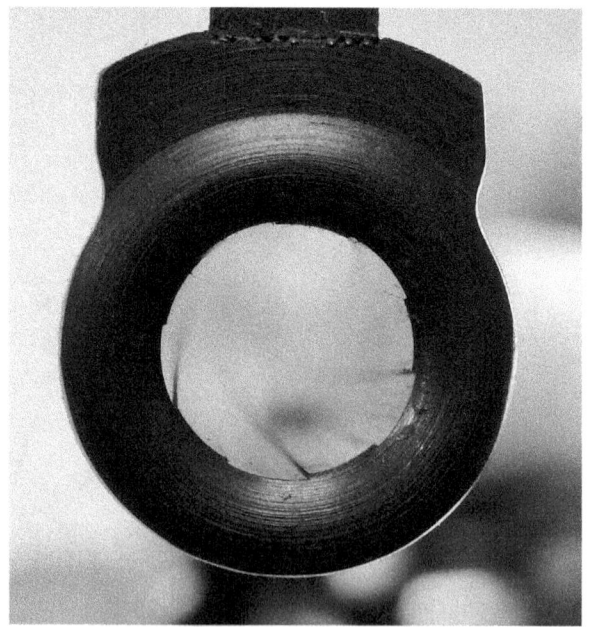

Rifling is visible in the muzzle of this S&W .38 Special, showing five lands and grooves.

Rifling. Without a way to stabilize conical bullets, their flight paths would become erratic, and tumbling would occur. So, by cutting spiral grooves within a barrel, the resulting "lands" between them can bite into a bullet, imparting the necessary spin for nose-forward flight, much like a properly thrown football. The actual rate-of-twist will vary based on several factors including projectile length, weight, and velocity. But less recognized is the effect of rifling upon a bullet after impact due to centrifugal force. Today's manufacturers take this into account when developing projectiles to meet defensive penetration and expansion standards, most commonly associated with F.B.I. Protocols (more on this shortly). Firearm manufacturers have also jumped on board through more uniform twist rates to assist in this process. For example, a common 9mm twist for years has been 1x10, meaning a bullet achieved one complete 360-degree revolution with ten inches of bore travel. I personally preferred S&W's slower 1x15 rate (based on better accuracy results), but they too have recently changed to a faster 1x10 barrel. Such consistency can prove helpful for those seeking quantifiable bullet performance, per the above protocols.

MORE ON BULLETS

For years, bullets were made from lead. This substance still works well in revolvers if velocities are kept low, but "leading" can accumulate within rifling grooves, affecting accuracy and pressures. This condition is exacerbated through increased velocities, and the original .357 Magnum load was notorious in that regard. One fix was a gas check, which is just a short copper cup swaged on to the base of a lead bullet. Better yet was a jacketed bullet, which encased all or part of the lead core in a copper sheathing. This design became essential for reliable semiauto feeding and such "cup & core bullets" remain in widespread use today. They may leave some lead exposed at their tips to initiate expansion. The latest "monolithic" bullets are made entirely from solid copper or bronze. When fired at their intended velocities, they expand nicely and shed little mass. "Bonded" bullets have lead cores soldered to copper jackets, another way to improve bullet integrity while promoting "controlled expansion." They will often be referred to as "premium bullets" with costs reflecting this category.

Varmint hunters will seek fragile, high-velocity projectiles designed for "pink mist." Small game hunters may be looking for just the opposite, non-destructive bullets to help minimize meat damage. Target shooters usually just need to punch a clean hole in paper. The military employs non-expanding bullets to meet international treaties, but most intended for LE or civilian defense (and big game hunting) are designed to expand. Upon impact, the front portion upsets, growing larger in diameter. The bugaboo for manufacturers has been a satisfactory combination of expansion, weight-reten-

Results of a controlled test, showing classic expansion. The bullet is a 9mm Speer 124 grain Gold Dot Hollow-Point (GDHP), recovered from ballistic gelatin.

tion, and penetration. Ideally, a nicely-expanded jacketed bullet will display "banana-peeled" petals ahead of an unexpanded shank, closely resembling a mushroom. The hope is that its weight will also remain close to that of its unfired mass. Reality may prove otherwise since impact with foreign objects or bone can cause core and jacket separation, or even disintegration (as noted above, rifling can also skive results). Such damage can greatly limit penetration for reduced terminal results.

In the end, we wind up with a huge assortment of projectiles to choose from. When buying reputable commercial ammunition, the box will display the caliber, bullet-weight, and type. The latter may be identified by an abbreviation, or actually spelled out.

These recovered cup & core bullets include two non-deformed FMJs and a properly expanded JHP. Rifling marks are clearly visible.

Useful information is often printed on the box – assuming you understand the vernacular.

FMJ stands for "full-metal jacket" bullet. Typically, the bullet will be lead, encased in a thin copper jacket for reliable feeding in semi-automatic firearms. Expansion is usually non-existent, but penetration may be deep. The Hague Convention limits signatories to FMJs, which are supposedly less destructive, explaining their widespread military use.

JHP stands for "jacketed hollow-point." The design is similar to an FMJ, but the bullet will have a cavity in its nose. It is usually designed to expand or "mushroom" in tissue, creating a larger wound-cavity for more rapid incapacitation, perhaps with less penetration. A JHP (or HP) is a popular choice for civilian self-defense or hunting.

JSP stands for "jacketed soft-point," again with construction similar to an FMJ. However, a small portion of the nose may be exposed lead. Some of the latest polymer-tipped bullets are a hybrid JHP/SP with a plastic nose-cap insert, designed to initiate expansion upon contact with tissue. Hornady's *Critical Defense* loads employ this construction.

RN means a "round-nose" profile. The bullet may be plain lead (RNL) like a .22 LR, or jacketed like a 9mm FMJ. Such bullets chamber easily, but cause minimal tissue damage. The old .38 Special RNL was a classic example of a widespread choice that was easy to chamber, but a poor defensive stopper.

TC is for "truncated cone." Picture a RN with a flat tip and you'll have a truncated cone. You'll see them often in .40 S&W or some lighter .45 ACP loads.

SWC is for "semi-wadcutter." Like the above TC, a semi-wadcutter bullet has a cylindrical body with a tapered forward section, ending in a flat nose. It became a popular centerfire revolver successor to the older RN loads, and is usually composed entirely of lead. A SWCHP has a hole in its nose to promote expansion and still works well for defensive revolver purposes.

WC: A "wadcutter" is like a SWC, but without its tapered nose section. In other words, a WC is essentially a lead cylinder. It was a preferred choice in the era of revolver target shooting because it cut nice round holes in paper. Although its terminal effects are theoretically better than a RN or SWC, loading full-wadcutters in revolver chambers is more difficult under pressure. Feeding is even more problematic in pistols.

Homogenous bullets, otherwise known as monolithic solids, are machined from one solid piece of brass or copper alloy. They're expensive but tough. Barnes led the way with their expanding X-Bullets and TSX rifle bullets, but the line now includes loaded TAC-XPD and VOR-TX handgun cartridges. Concerns about jacket and core separation are eliminated and, since their weight retention is very good, penetration also tends to be deep.

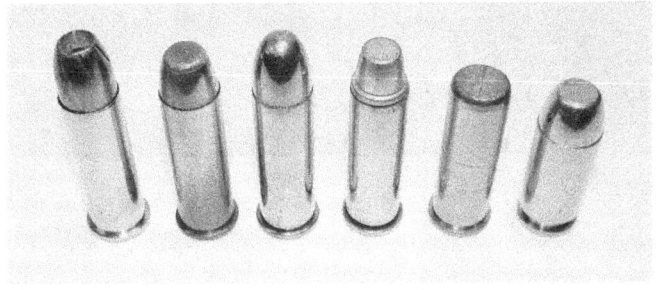

Common handgun bullets (L-R) include: JHP, JSP, FMJ (RN), SWC, WC, and TC (FMJ).

Frangible bullets are designed to disintegrate upon contact with hard surfaces, such as indoor range backstops or reactive steel targets. In that regard they work well, if the surfaces are smooth. Since concrete isn't, don't assume complete disintegration will occur. The core is often a sintered copper/polymer mix with some type of coating. Many are electro-plated but polymers have recently been used, and a few now have unusual deep fluted noses to disrupt tissue. Owing to their lighter weights, velocities tend to be higher, which *may* result in different POIs (sometimes lower).

Lead-free loads should be self-explanatory.

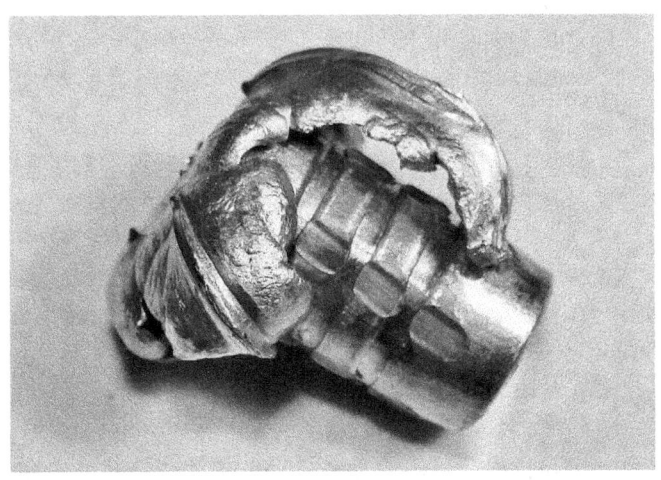

Typical expansion from a solid-copper Barnes TSX. This .338 example penetrated a big buck lengthwise, retaining nearly all of its weight.

Ammunition Basics | 29

Lead toxicity is a major concern, especially for indoor ranges. Besides projectile impacts, airborne lead can be produced from barrel heat or friction, and conventional lead styphnate primers. The latest lead-free loads use non-lead priming compounds and frangible (or sometimes, monolithic)

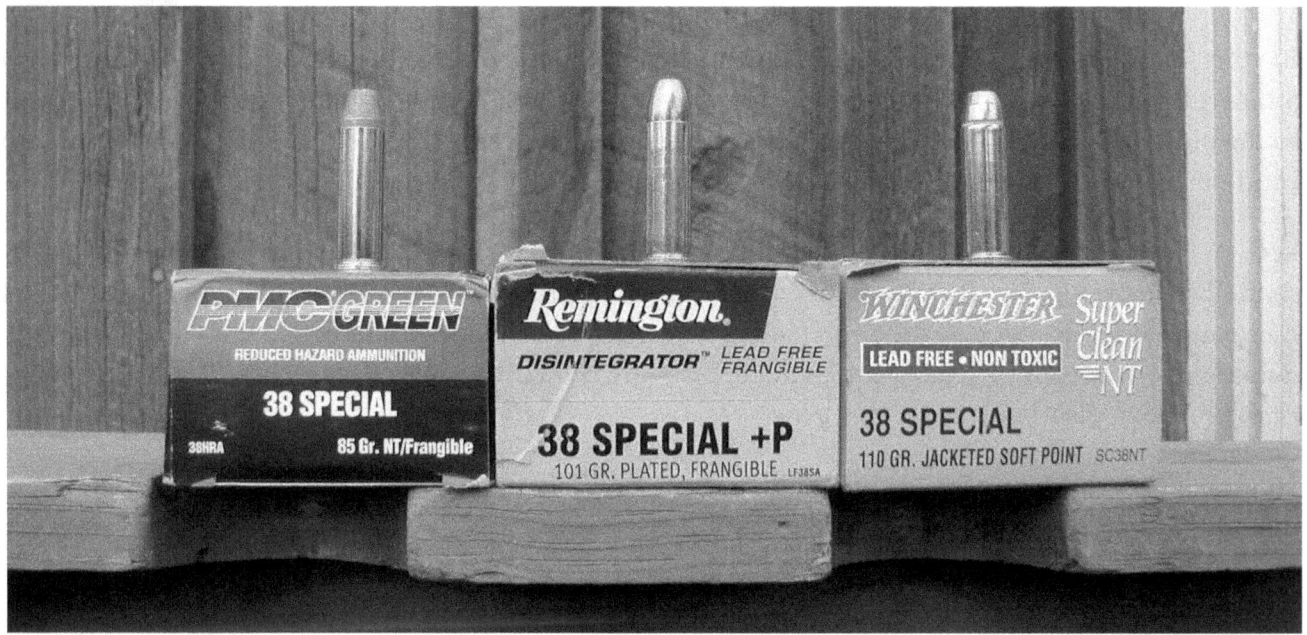

An assortment of .38 Special "lead-free" loads. "NT" stands for non-toxic. BUT, only the first two are listed as frangible!

bullets. Even outdoors, we shoot lead-free frangible loads on steel plate stages to cut down on ricochet hazards while at the same time minimizing our lead exposure. Ammo costs are higher but the benefits are a fair trade. We have noted a slight increase in pistol stoppages, no doubt due to cycling dynamics related to light-for-caliber bullets. Since this ammo is used for training, we treat any malfunctions as good stoppage-clearance practice.

CARTRIDGES AND PRESSURES

A cartridge must closely fit its chamber to safely contain the high pressures generated upon discharge. A ductile cartridge case can thus expand to seal the rear (or breech) end of the barrel without rupturing. Once the bullet exits, pressure will quickly subside and a properly alloyed case will shrink a bit to ease extraction. Brass is the metal of choice due to its elastic properties, with thickness dependent upon pressure. A .22 LR case is made from very thin brass and, due to its rimfire priming design, becomes disposable. Center-fire cases are thicker, and may even be salvageable for reloading depending on the priming system. Many of us chase fired brass cases for cost savings after purchasing new components. Another option is commercial ammunition made with aluminum or mild steel cartridge casings which are more affordable but also less ductile, and therefore non-reloadable. We keep a large magnetic stick on the range which is great for policing fired steel cases. They'll hop on as well as hungry fleas on a sleeping cat.

Ammo ID tip: To help segregate any practice ammo from serious defensive loads, buy the latter with nickel-plated cases. The difference will be obvious and useful in pistols with chamber-checking ports.

SAAMI cartridges and chambers. Here in the U.S., dimensional cartridge and chamber standards are maintained through voluntary manufacturer compliance with Sporting Arms and Ammunition Institute (SAAMI) specifications. The mainstream firearms and ammunition makers rely on SAAMI drawings, and barrels are stamped to indicate their caliber, millimeter, or gauge. Any cartridges adopted by SAAMI will also have specified pressure parameters. For example, the "Maximum Average Pressure" (MAP) of a .40 S&W is 35,000 PSI. That's a whole lot of pressure to be holding in our hands so we better hope things go right! There's a good chance they will since the .40 S&W is a recent U.S. brainchild, less likely to have relatives of

A conventional .45 ACP 230-grain FMJ is shown beside two equivalent CCI "Blasers". The aluminum cases reduce cost, but can't be reloaded.

questionable origins. On the other hand, the popular 9mm Luger is a global citizen. There are stories involving hotter imported rounds that have damaged pistols. We haven't had any such episodes, simply because we buy from established domestic manufacturers. A good, strong firearm also helps, especially when heavy shooting is anticipated.

Hotter +P loads. The recent .40 S&W is already warm, but several older cartridges have been souped up for use in stronger, modern handguns. The .38 Special operates at 17,000 MAP. The hotter .38 Special +P MAP is 20,000 PSI. A .357 Magnum can develop 35,000 PSI so, a +P .38 has plenty of leeway in its chambers. However, old or small-frame lightweight .38 Special revolvers will take a pounding through use of +Ps. A few other common pistol calibers have also been loaded to +P pressures (or even +P+ levels). Today's SAAMI-spec +P 9mm Luger or .45 ACP loads develop about 10% more pressure to provide a small boost in velocity. They should only be fired in firearms rated for these rounds. We choose to skip them entirely, benefiting from longer gun life. Ultra-hot +P+ loads exceed SAAMI pressures, putting you in uncharted waters.

Muzzle velocity (MV). The speed with which a projectile exits a barrel is most often expressed in feet per second (fps). This data is usually recorded a few feet off the muzzle with a chronograph, a special instrument which can "see" and precisely calculate the speed of a projectile. The ammo makers conform to SAAMI specs through pressure and velocity (P&V) testing. The broad gamut of modern cartridges has quite a spread, from below 1,000 fps up to 4,000 fps or more. A .22 LR will start out somewhere around 1,000 fps, depending on the load. Most center-fire handgun MVs run a bit above or below that speed, depending on the load. Rifle calibers like a .30/06 will start near 3,000 fps, but for every action there is a reaction. Recoil aside, conventional handgun barrels lack sufficient volume in which to consume slower burning rifle-type powders. A fast, standard-weight .357 Magnum load will clock less than 1500 fps, but this velocity is more than adequate to ensure reliable expansion with properly designed bullets. Low-velocity bullets can fail to expand at all, a problem .380 ammo makers have been dealing with for years - fortunately with recent success. In the past, many advertised velocities were "optimistic," but like other electronic devices, chronograph prices have fallen, affording consumers with the means to glean accurate data. Nowadays, manufacturer-published velocities are more likely to mirror real-life expectations, but note any test-barrel information. Look for length and whether the barrel was vented. The latter is a concern for revolver shooters, since it can more accurately simulate the pressure loss associated with barrel/cylinder gaps.

POA & POI. *Point-of-aim* is the spot we're aiming at. We hope the bullet will strike this mark, but *point-of-impact* could be different. In fact, both coincide at two points, reflecting the bullet's parabolic trajectory as it intersects a straight line-of-sight (LOS).

Sight-in (or zero). If we "sight in" a handgun for 25 yards, bullet impacts at that range should coincide with the sights. To achieve this, a small amount of barrel and sight divergence is factored in. Remember, the bore is under the sights. For this reason, if we aim at a bug from just a few steps, the bullet should strike a tad low. When POA and POI converge at 25 yards, out at 50 yards POI will be low again due to gravitational effects upon the bullet. With adjustable sights, we could alter their relationship to the barrel, raising the rear sight enough to achieve a true 50-yard "zero." However, due to the parabolic trajectory of the bullet, POI would then shift a bit high at 25 yards. This same effect could be noted on that irritating little close-range bug. For handgunning purposes, individual grip tension, recoil, and velocity can further affect POI.

Chronographs have become affordable. The velocity is displayed in feet-per-second (fps). Bullets pass above two sensor windows on the unit's upper surface.

Most handgun manufacturers attempt to address these variables by offering sights regulated to generic 15-25 yard zeros with more common loads.

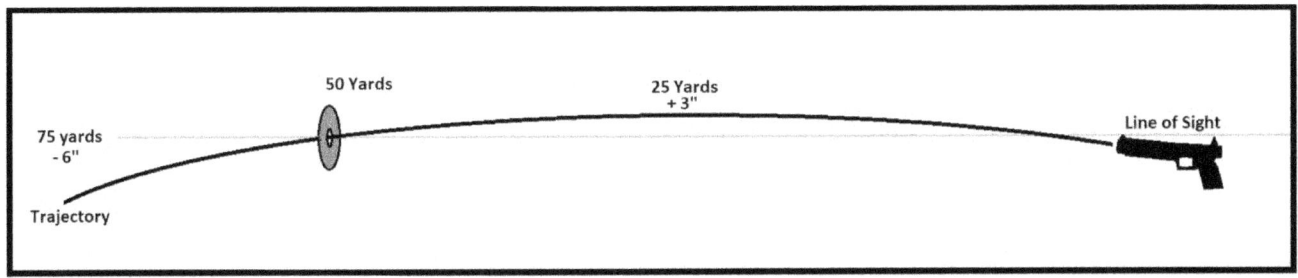

An exaggerated illustration of POA and POI. In this example, the 50-yard zero results in a +3" mid-range trajectory.

HG-3 Sight Picture & Trajectory: Stopping power. Defining so-called "stopping power" is a difficult task due to numerous influences. Besides caliber and velocity, mass and bullet design are important factors, along with the actual physiology of a target. There are several formulas to quantify terminal force, but foot-pounds (ft-lbs) of energy is most often listed. The figure is a product of projectile mass and velocity, expressed as "muzzle energy."

Muzzle energy. ME by itself can be deceiving. Some state wildlife agencies mandate minimums for big game hunting calibers. You may see a requirement for an expanding bullet of at least .24-caliber, with a 1,000 ft-lbs minimum. This is one approach to help ensure humane harvest of deer or other larger-sized animals, but an easy thing to overlook is the effect of an expanding bullet, which will cause more tissue damage than a non-expanding type. Some states prohibit the use of FMJs for exactly this reason so, bottom line, foot-pounds alone won't provide a complete picture. We need to consider bullet construction as well. Furthermore, although the foot-pound spread is large, running from 100 ft-lbs for a .22 LR, to center-fire rifle figures exceeding 3,000 ft-lbs, these numbers don't directly translate to actual force delivered on-target. We often see 300 ft-lb pistol hits that leave knock-down steel "pepper-popper" targets standing. It's educational for trainees since we can walk up afterward and push them over with just one finger!

So-called knockdown power. People have been trying to quantify "knockdown power" for eons. The 1904 Thompson-LeGarde studies involved use of live cattle and human cadavers which were shot with representative handgun calibers of that time. None of the results were particularly inspiring although a general conclusion was that big .45-caliber bullets were the better choice. It's no coincidence that the .45 ACP appeared shortly thereafter with the 1911 Government Model Pistol. Of course, this was a century before the refinement of today's expanding bullets, many of which have been engineered to meet specific terminal criteria. During 1975, The National Institute of Justice funded comprehensive testing of expanding bullets in ballistic gelatin designed to replicate flesh. Wound cavities were transposed to computer simulations of human anatomy to scientifically quantify stopping power. Based on the aftermath of the famous 1986 FBI Miami Shootout, it became clear that people were not made from Jell-O.

Meanwhile, the highly-regarded team of Marshall and Sanow assembled an impressive list of actual LE shootings and sifted through the results by caliber and bullet type to rate their effectiveness. Some questioned the criteria they used to define a "one shot stop," but their data is revealing nonetheless. Hits to the central nervous system were not factored in since very large animals can be killed by a .22 LR through the brain. No handgun cartridge earned a 100% rating, not even the .44 Magnum. Actually, .357 Magnum 125 gr. JHPs were among the most effective, producing one-shot stops of around 90%. Good, 230-gr. 45 ACP JHPs were also right up there, and the lighter .40 S&W JHPs also got good marks. Even the 9x19mm fared well with a couple lighter loads.

Testing in progress, per FBI standards. A bare gel-block is visible to the left of the others.

An outcome of the Miami Shootout was a more precise set of standards. Based on numerous resources, the FBI developed concise protocols involving calibrated ballistic gelatin and real-world influences on expansion and penetration such as clothing, wallboard, plywood, sheet-metal, and glass barriers. As it turned out, some supposedly "good" expanding bullets failed to expand at all when their noses became plugged by fabric, sheet-rock, or wood. Others flattened upon impacting sheet metal, or unraveled during passage through glass. One thing that shook out was a need for sufficient penetration on the order of 12-inches. Having participated in several tests, it's always interesting to pluck bullets from the blocks with a set of surgical forceps. Penetration, weight, and expansion are three quantifiable measurements which can vary

The path of each bullet is measured for penetration. Once recovered, expansion and remaining weight will be recorded for comparison.

34 | *Handguns: A Buyer's And Shooter's Guide*

depending on the barriers. Glass and sheet metal are part of the testing because of law enforcement (LE) incidents involving vehicles.

Bullets and shot placement. Today, the FBI protocols are often used for bullet design purposes and many LE ammo manufacturers post specific performance results. We shoot CCI Speer Gold Dot 9mm and .40 loads, but some of the test-phases are not necessarily pertinent to civilian users due to over-penetration concerns. Hornady is one firm that addresses both markets through two distinct product lines involving use of their "flex-tip" bullet technology. Their Critical Defense rounds are a bit more fragile so they'll expand in shorter barrels, while the Critical Duty loads are built to meet FBI requirements in full-size handguns. Both employ soft synthetic red inserts, originally developed to help streamline blunt-tipped rifle bullets necessary in tubular magazines (to prevent primer detonations). The small, flexible plastic nose sections provided cushioning while improving aerodynamics, but the idea has since been applied to defensive handgun rounds to prevent clogging of JHPs while promoting good expansion. The Critical Defense line may be of interest to civilians..

Examples of bullet expansion - or lack thereof. Except for its rifling marks, the FMJ (L) remained intact. Among the center HPs, wood clogged one while the other expanded nicely. The bullet on the right was stopped by body armor.

Nowadays, all the major ammo players offer LE and civilian defensive ammo choices, which are generally formulated for reduced muzzle flash, an important factor in the dark. Stiff competition has resulted in better bullets, to the point where the formerly suspect 9mm is beginning to shine. Ironically, the FBI adopted the 10mm after 9mm bullet failures. The hot 10mm gave birth to the somewhat more controllable .40 S&W. Now the FBI is headed back to where it all started, simply because of vastly improved 9mm bullets.

The age-old 9mm versus .45 ACP argument is far from dead but given military rounds, I'd take 230 grain .45 hard-ball every time over 115 grain 9mm FMJs. Back in my recon days I carried a trusted 1911 full of 230 grain FMJs. Today, I'd rather pack my trusty single-stack S&W Model 3913 9mm – *if it was loaded with a good expanding bullet!* The latest data shows its terminal effects would be better than .45 hardball *and* I could carry more ammo, important on the move. When possible, scratch FMJ (or lead round-nose) for defense. And remember, bullet design is everything.

Where mobility is less of a concern one could make a case for the biggest, reliable expanding bullets able to be fired in a controlled manner. However, the Newtonian Laws are incontrovertible. Every action will cause an opposite reaction. Don't believe the images portrayed by Hollywood, with bad guys blown skyward from torso hits. If you fired a weapon capable of delivering that much force, what do you suppose it would do to you? I have no personal desire to find out! We need a practical balance of performance and manageable recoil. Terminal effects will be largely governed by a bullet's design, but we'll still need to put it in the right spot.

REVOLVER AND PISTOL CARTRIDGE CHARACTERISTICS

Traditional revolver cartridges have rims which are well suited for cylinders. The rims support solid firing pin contact, while maintaining consistent breech-face clearance known as "headspace." Rimmed designs offer some interesting options, too. Sharing the same diameter cartridge case, a shorter .38 Special will headspace in a longer .357 Magnum chamber. On the other hand, a .357 Magnum will (hopefully) not fully seat within a .38 Special-only chamber. Assuming the .38 is reamed to SAAMI specifications, the mouth of a longer .357 case should contact the forward chamber edge, preventing full insertion and closure of the cylinder. The same is true for the .44 Magnum/.44 Special. A few exceptions are the handful of rimless rounds designed for reliable function in pistols, adapted to work in revolvers.

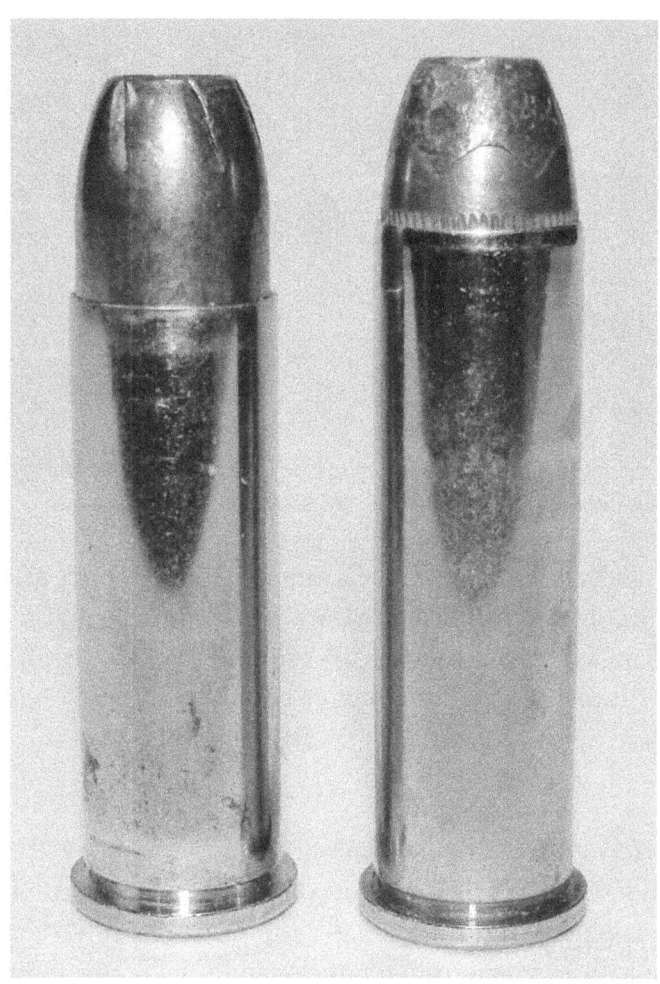

A .38 Special can be fired in the longer chamber of a .357 Magnum thanks to the identical headspace of their rims.

Rimless pistol cartridges in revolvers. Pistol cartridges like the 9mm Luger and .45 ACP establish headspace off their case mouths by abutting the front edge of their chambers. Normally, a slide-mounted extractor will engage the cartridge's head for positive extraction force, but a double-action revolver poses challenges with rimless pistol cartridges, simply because there is nothing for its extractor to engage. A clever WW 1 moon clip adaptation solved this problem while permitting simultaneous unloading and reloading. Each rimless round is snapped into a thin steel plate with corresponding cartridge cuts, and the "clip" spans the extractor-star. A single-action revolver makes life a bit simpler, and Ruger sells one with a pair of interchangeable .45 Colt (rimmed), and .45 ACP cylinders. The latter will work in *carefully* cut chambers thanks to the barrel-mounted ejector rod. Theoretically, a rimless pistol round should fire in any chamber, extraction issues aside, however, a couple .45 ACP S&W N-frames I've used needed moon clips for reliable ignition. Some clever engineering has resulted in the occasional alternate extractor design, as sold by Charter Arms. On top of that, an obscure .45 ACP Auto Rim cartridge appeared during the 1920s for use in surplus M-1917 .45 ACP revolvers. It was a good idea in principle but today moon clips rule the roost for D/A revolver use.

Rimmed revolver cartridges in pistols. Rimmed cartridges can pose feeding issues when stacked on top of each other in magazines. Their greater length can also negatively affect ergonomics. The anemic .25 ACP is a circa 1905 Browning designed, semi-rimmed alternative to a .22 rimfire. The Colt 1908 vest Pocket Pistol among others offered claims of increased reliability in a short-gripped, ultra-small, semiauto. Today, successful magazine-fed .22 LR pistols abound. The small rimmed cartridges are short enough to fit within an average-sized frame and most will feed them reliably.

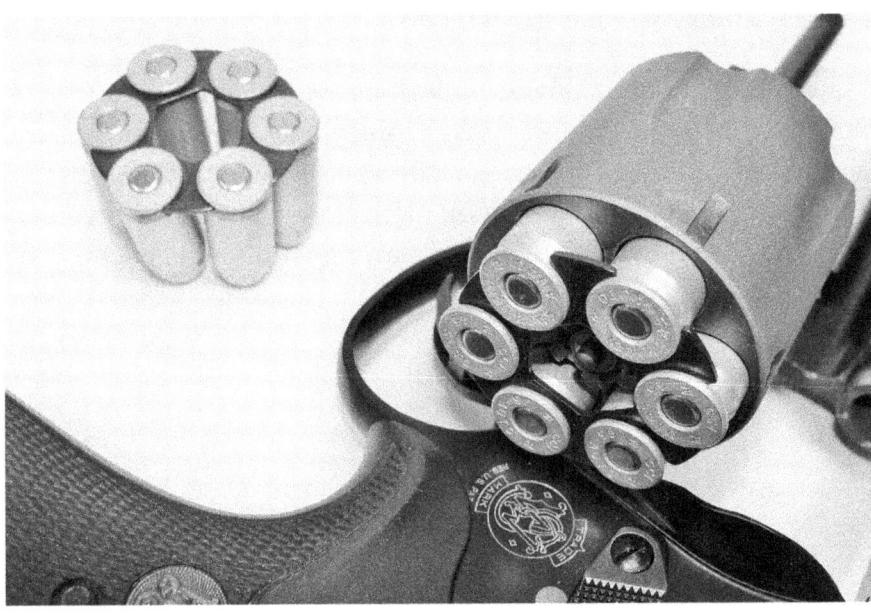

Rimless pistol cartridges pose challenges for revolvers, but these .45 ACPs will reliably fire from moon-clips, which also speed loading and unloading.

As we get into larger, conventional revolver cartridges, things begin to get challenging. Case in point: Coonan's .357 Magnum hybrid 1911 pistol, and the behemoth Desert Eagle. The Coonan works thanks to careful engineering, but the grip frame is unusually deep to accommodate long .357 cartridges. Reliable function with milder .38 specials introduces other unique challenges (which Coonan has overcome using +P loads). At different times, I've owned 1911 and S&W Model 52 pistols chambered for .38 Special, but these semiautos were strictly bullseye target guns with low-capacity magazines. They could only accept flush-seated wadcutter bullets, the price paid to use standard-sized frames. The Desert Eagle dispenses with any concerns about size. Its gas-operated action more closely resembles a rifle. The first one I fired was a .357 Magnum, which had almost no recoil. The .41 Magnum and .44 Magnum versions are manageable but all are just plain big.

NO MAGIC BULLET?

Early on, semiautomatic pistol designers developed shorter, rimless cartridges, which were loaded to higher pressures than their rimmed revolver counterparts. Similar velocities could thus be achieved through rounds like the 9mm Luger and .45 ACP. The 9mm Luger roughly approximates the power of a .38 Special +P, despite its shorter cartridge case. Bullet diameters are similar but the 9mm runs at much higher pressure. The .45 ACP was developed to preserve the virtues of the .45 Colt, clobbering targets with big fat heavy bullets launched at more moderate pressures. These approaches made sense a century ago and they still do today. Good bullets have made things even better.

However, there is no "magic bullet," per se. Whether fired from a revolver or pistol, most practical defensive handgun rounds travel somewhere north or south of 1000 fps in order to be manageable. Considerable effort has gone into perfecting bullet designs among the flagship calibers but shot placement still counts. We'll look more closely at specific revolver and pistol cartridge options later. For now, let's return to handguns, starting with some generalized guidelines.

CHAPTER 4
GUIDELINES AND USEFUL FEATURES

This chapter covers some generalized concerns worth mulling over before committing to a handgun purchase. There are so many available choices that it's tough to pick a winner. You could buy a highly-rated model but it still might not be the best choice for you so, before delving into details, think about why you're considering a handgun. Will it serve primarily for concealed-carry? Or, will it cover multiple uses like home defense, target shooting, and outdoor chores?

If a multi-use role is in the cards, a general-purpose handgun may serve well – more so if even a peripheral subsistence capability is anticipated. Bigger handguns, within reason, are easier to shoot well and they also afford better recoil control. We'll lump them in the "full-size" category, more on the order of LE duty-type side arms.

To the other extreme, deep concealment requires a very small gun, relegating it to close-range defense. Smaller handguns are the most difficult to master, and they tend to generate more recoil. It's a safe bet that most are carried much more often than they are shot. There's also a very good chance you'll never suspect the person wearing one is armed.

If competitive target events or handgun hunting comes off the table, an in-between choice may meet your needs quite well. Perhaps the most rapidly growing handgun segment consists of compact pistols designed for defensive carry by civilians. These guns carry well in belt holsters while affording enough accuracy for meaningful range practice.

Those unsure may wish to hedge their bets with that general-purpose choice. Otherwise known as "full-size," it need not be gargantuan, but it should be large enough to promote accurate shooting. Solid marksmanship skills only come with practice, and a shootable choice solves part of the battle. Marksmanship really boils down to sight picture (aiming) and trigger control. The longer sight radius afforded by a larger handgun tends to minimize subtle alignment errors, and weight promotes steadiness. Also, the trick is to release the trigger in such a manner that the sights are not disturbed. A yank won't cut the mustard, and an excessively heavy or hard-to-reach trigger will only make matters worse.

This brings us to suitability. Operational complexity should be balanced against personal experience (along with other factors like recoil), but stature and strength may also come into play. Some semi-

Handguns designed for LE use often have general-purpose value. S&W's M&P semiauto represents the current genre, and their Model 65 revolver is a time-tested alternative. Both offer simplicity in effective, reasonably-sized packages.

automatic pistols have stiff springs that can impede manual operation. Access of controls could pose further challenges, particularly for those with smaller hands. The comparative simplicity of a revolver might seem like an expedient solution, but its trigger reach and pull-weight could cause other issues.

Fortunately, small, medium, large, or extra-large applies to more than shirts. Revolvers come in different sizes and their grips are often replaceable. Most metal-framed semiauto pistols permit similar grip options, and some polymer versions permit personalized fitting via inserts. In fact, complete reconfiguration is even possible with a pistol like Sig's P320. It usually takes some hands-on shopping to sort through potential challenges.

Lastly, don't forget about adaptability. Integral rail sections are the latest rage, permitting easy mounting of lights or lasers. Electronic dot sights are also catching on, and the list of conventional aiming systems is expanding. It's reassuring to know you can always upgrade later, so adaptability is a good thing. The challenge is to understand these finer points *prior* to making a purchase.

FULL-SIZE, ITTY-BITY, AND COMPACT PLATFORMS

We're in the zenith of handgun production, which is good for consumers. Trouble is, those starting from scratch have an overwhelming assortment of types from which to choose.

When it comes to revolvers, a double-action type is the preferred defensive choice. The good news is that all the D/A revolvers function in a similar manner. They offer reliability and simplicity in platforms of several sizes, from small to extremely large. The most popular caliber by far is the .357 Magnum, which can also digest milder .38 Special ammunition. It's nice to have both options but, since hot loads in small revolvers are hard on both a shooter and the gun, the latter caliber is a popular choice. Yes, there are others, but this combination rules the roost.

Pistols can be tougher to sort through because, aside from the numerous brands, they fall into different functional categories. On top of that, the caliber choices are much more diverse, which a further relationship to size. Although there's no hard and fast rule. the fat .45 ACP most often seen in full-size pistols, .40 S&W and 9mms tend to occupy middle ground, with the smallest being demure .380 ACPs.

Worth noting is the relationship of LE qualification courses to gun size. Most are geared toward full-size handguns with stages that go out to around 25 yards. Some agencies adjust these standards for compact guns simply because they can be harder to shoot, with a max range of 15 yards.

Full-size, compact, and itty-bitty pistols: S&W's 9mm M&P, 9mm Shield, and small .380 Bodyguard. All share similar function.

Nowadays, the two preeminent handgun systems are a single-action 1911 Government variant, or some sort of striker-fired polymer pistol. Either offers a consistent trigger pull, and the latter has surged in part due to a minimum of controls – a concept reaching back to the same KISS principles shared by revolvers.

The venerable steel-framed 1911 was designed around its large .45 ACP cartridge. It's still king but the 9mm Luger has gained recent ground. With either caliber, the front-to-rear grip size remains consistent among standard 1911 frames which employ "single-stack" magazines holding 7-9 shots, depending upon their calibers. Internal modifications to the magazines regulate the feeding process.

More modern "high-cap" striker-fired polymer designs (like the Glock) were scaled to the smaller 9mm Luger cartridge from their inception. The fore-to-aft grip dimension is thus reduced, while still permitting use of "double-stack" magazines, some of which hold 17 rounds, or more. Beyond 9mm Luger, the .40 S&W is also popular because it will fit in the same frame. A larger frame is used for the .45 ACP, and most will also accommodate increasingly popular 10mm Automatic versions. But, the 9mm and .40 chamberings dominate the hi-capacity field due to their manageable ergonomics.

Most full-size guns including the S&W Model 10 revolver, 1911 Government Model, and Glock M-17 were developed for military or law enforcement use, where concealment was less of a concern. Such a handgun with its four to five-inch barrel can provide useful accuracy and reasonable comfort when carried in a duty-type holster. Fully loaded, most are heavy, but a well-designed carry system helps spread the load (which also includes extra magazines).

The rules change when concealed-carry is part of the game. Some, enamored by full-sized models, will be happy with range results, but less so with comfort after several days of carry. Especially in warmer climes, concealment poses further challenges so, as time goes by, full-size handguns can wind up staying behind. Of course, the scale of a handgun to its user plays a role. Let's face it, a big handgun is not going to play well with most petite users regardless of their best intentions. However, those who can manage a full-size gun will be suitably armed for just about any circumstance. Ample room will also exist for rails, permitting use of lights or lasers. In fact, some of the latest holsters use these increasingly popular rails to retain the gun. Being less dependent on exact fitting, they have evolved to generic types with cost saving benefits for some multiple-gun owners.

One indicator of a handgun's usefulness is a law enforcement qualification course, which will typically involve humanoid silhouette targets and timed stages of fire. Most are geared toward duty-type handguns, reflecting real-life distances, fired at 3, 7, 10, and 15 yards. A 25-yard stage is often included because it corresponds with the accuracy limits of most trained shooters – *when firing under stress*. Adrenaline does funny things and, even with more shootable handguns, loss of fine motor skills take their toll. A small gun may be handier to carry, but results downrange will be even less inspiring. Bottom line: a full-size handgun does provide an edge!

Itty-bitty (or micro) pocket rockets. Shifting gears, a little gun is a whole lot better than *no* gun, but where do we draw the line? Of late, a series of *really* tiny pistols have appeared. Barrels can run well under three inches, and frames are often chopped, which limits capacity – and grip. Two popular pistol calibers are 9mm or .380 ACP. The .32 ACP was popular but faded as manufacturers perfected small .380 designs. Even dimunitive .25 ACP models have given way to miniaturized .380 offerings, some of which are scaled-down "micro" versions of larger models.

The recent expansion of CCW permits accounts for these small guns and, while they just beg to be carried, their inherent shootability suffers. Sometimes it's hard enough just figuring where extra fingers will go when trying to establish a grip. Quick follow-up shots can be tough for not only this reason, but also due to increased recoil. Lights and lasers are *sometimes* possible through innovative designs, but for the most part, there just isn't much room to work with.

We call firearms of this genre "back-up guns" for good reason. Many are purchased by experienced shooters for use as last-ditch spares. Beyond more conventional carry modes, they are frequently hidden in ankle holsters, pockets, or other discreet locations. Being strictly close-range defensive tools, although practice is essential, true target shooting is out. In fact, most published accuracy testing is limited to seven yards. For real world use, a truly skilled shooter might double that distance, but most will struggle beyond conversation distance, even on silhouette targets. That said, I wouldn't rule one completely out. If just one gun is in the cards something a tad larger would be better. As a second gun, though, a micro-sized handgun could still fill a niche.

The compact pistol option. The latest vogue is a series small (but not miniature) pistols, often of single-stack design, chambered in 9mm. To a lesser extent, .40 S&W and .45 ACP variants are popular alternatives. Barrel lengths often run around 3 ½ inches, and capacity may be 7-10 rounds (although a few double-stack types can hold more). These guns offer reasonable carry comfort while still feeling good in the hand. An accessory rail may not be present due to size constraints. Although many such pistols are polymer, some smaller, aluminum-frame 1911-type pistols are part of this mix.

Handguns in this size are generally small enough to hide and large enough to shoot reasonably well. Their practical accuracy will cover nearly all defensive situations. Target scores will be hampered by a shorter sight radius, but decent results are still attainable on standard LE silhouette Q-courses. Many trained shooters can squeak through a 25-yard stage, while most can perform acceptably well out to 15 yards. For this reason, some agencies run separate, shorter-range courses for their concealed-carry officers. The closer-range stages still exist, but 15 yards is the furthest.

Revolver comparisons. For the most part, "wheel guns" can be lumped into the above pistol categories. Size-wise, a double-action .357 S&W Model 66 revolver has much in common with many popular 9mm or .40 semiautos. This makes some sense since they were all created to address similar requirements.

Full-sized, four-inch, double-action .38 Special and .357 Magnums ruled for decades, but they gradually lost ground to smaller hide-out guns. However, this doesn't mean they're kaput. The old FBI Q-course had some interesting service revolver stages including one at 50 yards, shot two-handed, as a righty *and*

A blast from the past: Revolver qualification using S&W M-65. Two decades later, the guns have changed but the targets and general format remain.

lefty. The guns were obviously up to the job although timed reloading kept everyone busy. During the late 1980s, auto-pistols began sweeping law enforcement circles, accounting for the revolver decline. The wheel gun is far from dead though, being simple and ammo tolerant. Full-size types still make great general-purpose handguns, or dedicated sporting-type firearms. For the latter use, barrel lengths of six inches or more are not uncommon, particularly in more potent calibers. The .357 Magnum is still a great choice and will work on deer with careful shooting. The .44 Magnum remains the more popular dedicated big game hunting caliber - at the expense of much greater recoil. It used to be king, but some *really* potent calibers now reign supreme. Of course, the Newtonian laws cannot be ignored, meaning the .44 Magnum is pushing the recoil envelope for most handgun shooters.

With today's CCW in full swing, smaller revolvers are not only popular, but gaining new momentum. It's possible to get into absolutely tiny-mode, too! The miniature single-action, five-shot .22 LR and .22 Magnum North American Arms revolvers certainly qualify as "itty bitty" since they can fit in an eyeglass pouch. I'd view one as a last-ditch defensive choice where *any gun* is better than no gun.

In the "compact" category, S&W's small 5-shot .38 (or more recently, .357) J-frames have always been popular for concealed carry. The Chief's Special became an even bigger hit with the appearance of a stainless steel version. Colt's similar Detective Special offered an extra shot. It disappeared but, after years of absence, Colt just jumped back in with a similar, small 6-shot D/A revolver – and the fact that they did so is telling. Ruger has also expanded their small-frame revolver line with some polymer-framed versions to help shed extra weight. But even the smallest S&W short-barreled, alumi-

A trio of S&W revolvers: The .44 Magnum N-frame Model 629 (L) is NOT for beginners, but the .357 Magnum K-frame Model 66 can also fire milder .38 Special loads. The smallest J-frame .22 LR Model 63 is available in .357/.38 versions.

num-framed revolvers are *really* light and although less steady in the hand, hide extremely well. In fact, if necessary, you can shoot a small D/A revolver from inside a pocket. Some even have shrouded hammers so, lacking reciprocating parts, they'll reliably fire multiple shots. Stubby 1 7/8" barrels are often the norm, making them close-range propositions. For what it's worth, I've found that I can shoot a slightly larger 3-inch J-frame with much more confidence – enough to approach full-size accuracy results.

When it comes to a general-purpose revolver, a 4-inch K-frame .357 S&W works as well now as it did in the early 80s. When hotter loads are in the cards, a slightly heftier L-frame is even better. A revolver can still do the job and, like pistols, two in different sizes may be better!

MATERIALS AND FINISHES

Glock wasn't the first company to pitch a polymer-framed pistol, but they certainly deserve credit for popularizing this design. Up until the 1980s, handguns were built entirely of metal with steel being the preeminent choice. The finish was most often blued. Stainless steel arrived in the mid 1960s, and being difficult to blue, was usually left bright. Aluminum-framed handguns were a radical departure that actually preceded stainless steel, offered as a weight-saving feature in smaller guns. It was sometimes accompanied by concerns about long-term durability, so the introduction of polymer caused grave consternation among experienced pistoleros. I remember wondering who in their right mind would buy one. This was in reference to the appearance of the Glock around 1982. A few years later I was shooting my own. The anti-gunners went nuts over its ability to slip through metal detectors but, of course, this was false since the slides and barrels are still made of steel. The frame is the major plastic component, and it typically contains reinforced steel inserts for the slide to ride on. You can also run into lower-cost handguns constructed largely out of painted pot-metal, except for a few key components like cylinders, barrels, or action parts.

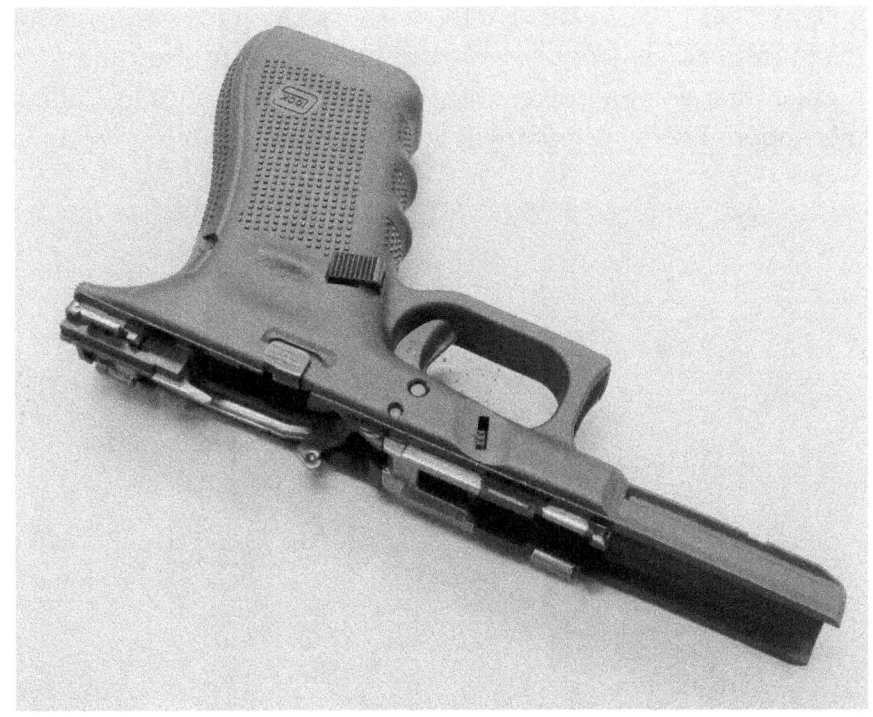

Proof positive polymer works: Glock's sound design endures through their 4th generation frame - still with steel rail inserts. And, now there's even a Gen-5!

Materials. At this point, it's safe to say that these materials are well-proven. Steel is timeless. Aluminum-framed handguns have been around for more than sixty years, and production of polymer framed pistols is approaching its fourth decade. S&W has more recently introduced a series of very lightweight handguns with scandium frames and titanium cylinders. The slides of most centerfire pistols are steel since they operate off locked-breech principles, requiring durable barrel/slide interfaces. However, some blow-back pistols – particularly .22 rimfires – function better with less reciprocating mass, accounting for the use of lighter materials. A magnet can provide answers about construction. It will literally hop right on to carbon steel. You'll detect some attraction with stainless. Aluminum will cause no reaction, and the same applies for scandium, titanium, or non-ferrous castings.

<u>Steel-framed handguns.</u> Nearly all firearms were made from steel until the late 20th century. Carbon steel was standard, finished with blued surfaces or, to a lesser extent, nickel (or chrome) plating. After some initial manufacturing challenges, stainless steel became increasingly popular for its greater resistance to rust. With either alloy, manufacturing may commence from a rough forging, a casting, or solid bar-stock. The strength of these materials is greatly enhanced through special heat-treating processes, making today's handguns much more resistant to high pressures. Production efficiency has also improved thanks to CNC machining, although MIM (metal-injected molding) is often used for smaller parts like triggers or hammers. Regardless, steel remains a strong and dependable choice. Let's face it, nobody advertises something as "stronger than plastic." Cost is generally higher, and weight tends to be greater, but there is something reassuring about a solid-steel 1911 pistol or brawny magnum revolver. Highly polished, blued steel is also candy for the eyes, although it will require regular attention for prevention of rust. When it comes to maintenance, stainless is the more forgiving option. Either material will accept metal-checkering for a nice custom option on a 1911's front strap.

Classic blued steel: S&W's K-38 was a purpose-built 6" target revolver.

<u>Aluminum and other weight-saving alloys.</u> Shortly after its split from the Army, the U.S. Air Force fielded a small quantity of aluminum .38 Special revolvers. Durability was poor, which gave such guns a bad rap. However, Colt succeeded in lightening up a shortened 1911 pistol, and launched their new .45 ACP Lightweight Commander. You'll have no trouble tracking down

a current-production example, which certainly legitimizes this concept. While attending an S&W Academy range session during the mid-80s, I was handed an aluminum-framed 9mm Model 39 school pistol. After enquiring about its round-count, the instructor asked me to give it a close examination. It seemed plenty tight to me, with no excessive wear. Turned out the pistol I was holding had consumed around 25,000 rounds!

My 3rd-Gen Model 3913 is a compact successor, which I bought during the late 1980s. It saw a huge amount shooting during daily range duties, and it's still going strong. We procured around 100 more during the mid-90s for plain-clothes issuance. Each officer fired around 750 rounds during initial training, followed by several hundred more annually. Some of these pistols had higher mileage caused by turn-over and re-issuance but, during a decade of use, we had no major problems (like cracked frames). Besides good engineering, part of the success was no doubt due to a scheduled maintenance regimen that involved periodic recoil spring replacement. Also, ammunition was limited to standard 9mm loads (as opposed to +P). During the same era, we were shopping for a full-size duty pistol, and procured some larger T&E, 3rd Gen .40 S&Ws. Some of our troops found recoil to be stout with the aluminum-framed versions. We went with stainless M-4006s, despite their considerable extra weight, but durability was also factored in to this decision. The .40 is fairly hot and high-volume shooting was in the cards. I'd be less eager to embrace aluminum for feisty pistol calibers like the 10mm if regular shooting was likely. For similar reasons, S&W's small aluminum-framed revolvers should be limited to standard .38 Special loads. Of course, these little J-frames aren't target guns by any stretch of the imagination, so they seldom see much shooting.

S&W's 9mm Model 39 set the stage for a number of double-action successors. Its aluminum frame has an anodized finish.

Some rimfire pistols employ blow-back steel breech-bolts (similar to slides) that cycle on aluminum frames. However, others reverse this metallurgy. At the moment, a Kimber .22 LR aluminum 1911 conversion kit is attached to the stainless frame of my Kimber .45 ACP. It works remarkably well; the only kicker being that the slide won't lock open on the last shot. You can latch it open manually like any other 1911, but Kimber's rimfire magazines intentionally prevent this function. The softness of aluminum can otherwise result in gradual deformation of the slide-stop notch.

The now-defunct Lorcin was one of several inexpensive zinc-alloy blow-backs, chambered for smaller calibers. Such handguns have been referred to as "Saturday Night Specials".

Some other blow-back designs employ non-ferrous (pot metal) castings to hold the line on cost. A few use jumbo-sized parts to resist the forces of centerfire pistol cartridges. Most probably see minimal use which may be for the best. I'd question their long-term durability.

More recently, S&W began offering scandium-framed handguns. This alloy is aluminum-based with some scandium mixed in. The resulting alloy is strong but extremely light, creating a surprisingly portable package - even in a large N-frame revolver. My .45 ACP Model 325 has a four-inch barrel and a titanium cylinder. A small steel insert in its top-strap, above the barrel/cylinder gap, serves as a blast shield. This area is subject to erosion, even with steel-framed guns, so the insert is a revealing but prudent touch. However, on the hip, a 4" Scandium N-frame weighs almost nothing, making it a handy north woods kit gun. The price beyond extra cost is an increase in recoil. I can tolerate a couple boxes of 230 grain G.I. hardball in one session, but I'm ready for a break after that. A Scandium .357 Magnum should get anyone's attention, and I can't imagine their .44 Magnum version! On the other hand, my Son's .22 Magnum M-351 PD is as light as a feather, with only negligible recoil. Supposedly, it needs an extra-power hammer spring just to overcome lack of inertial resistance! S&W also sells a scandium 1911 in a Commander-sized platform.

For most users, the reduced weight of these alloys offers real advantages during concealed-carry. The same qualities extend to other possible uses, such as a bug-out kit.

The .45 ACP isn't just for pistols. Although S&W's Scandium Model 325 is built on their large N-frame, this snub-nose version weighs next to nothing. Loading is also a snap thanks to moon-clips.

Polymer pistols. Logic dictates that a plastic pistol should unravel in short order but, since Glock has been in the game from the get-go, they've had ample opportunity to dispel this notion. There are examples out there with absurdly high counts of *well* over 50,000 rounds. Tactical Tupperware is here to stay for other good reasons, including light weight without the penalty of excessive recoil. Turns out the flex associated with polymer frames can soak up some of the kick, which can be further reduced through good ergonomics. It's just easier to manufacture a molded frame without sharp corners or other irritations. The necessary steel slide rails are usually just small inserts that don't take up much room, and the racy frame can nestle lower in the hand to minimize recoil leverage.

The new look is polymer. Glock wrote the book regarding construction as well as function.

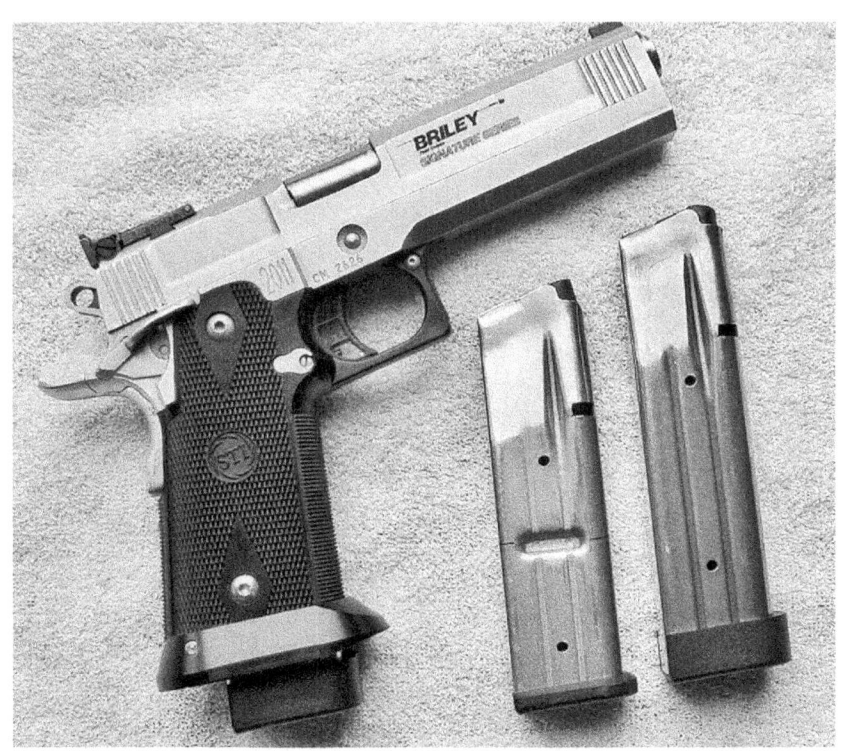

Modernized high-capacity 1911s gained rapid favor among serious combat competitors. Some, like this .40 STI, are referred to as "2011s". They combine double-stack magazines with synthetic sub-frames to preserve ergonomics.

At this point, most handgun manufacturers are producing some sort of polymer handgun. Many look and function suspiciously like a Glock, although a few polymer-framed revolvers have recently appeared. Somehow, the concept seems more tenable in a semiauto and even the timeless 1911 isn't immune from the onslaught of plastic. Some of the recent introductions represent an interesting merge of old and new technologies, although firms like STI were on this material earlier in the game. You'll see their pistols often during combat-type competitions due to cavernous molded sub-frames, capable of accepting special hi-cap magazines with little increase in girth. My custom

.40 S&W shot as well as any steel-framed 1911 could, in part because of its ample steel chassis, which not only interfaced with the slide, but also housed the fire-control parts. The polymer lower grip and trigger guard constituted a separate and replaceable unit, which bolted to the serial numbered steel frame section.

Lately, other manufacturers have gone this route, Sig being one of them. Different-sized polymer grip assemblies can be interchanged, along with slides of various lengths. More, like S&W, use easily interchangeable grip inserts to personalize fit. Such a feature is worth shopping for – especially if more than one user is planned. Many metal-framed handguns have separate grip panels with the means to add after-market grips of various sizes, whereas polymer pistols without such features leave few options other than rubber slip-on "hand-alls" that will only increase size. A cottage industry has sprung up around polymer grip-frame reduction services, with Glocks constituting much of the demand. I mailed out the polymer sub-frame of my STI for thinning and stippling after removing a few screws. It felt good before, but even better afterwards!

Many polymer pistol frames employ imbedded steel rail sections. Some are permanently molded in while others can be removed. Our 1st Gen S&W M&Ps employ steel insert sections which were secured by roll pins. The pistols have worked well, but you'll see elsewhere that a couple rail surfaces chipped off our .40s. They were back in business within minutes, thanks to easy installation of spares (S&W's latest 2.0 M&Ps use longer rails).

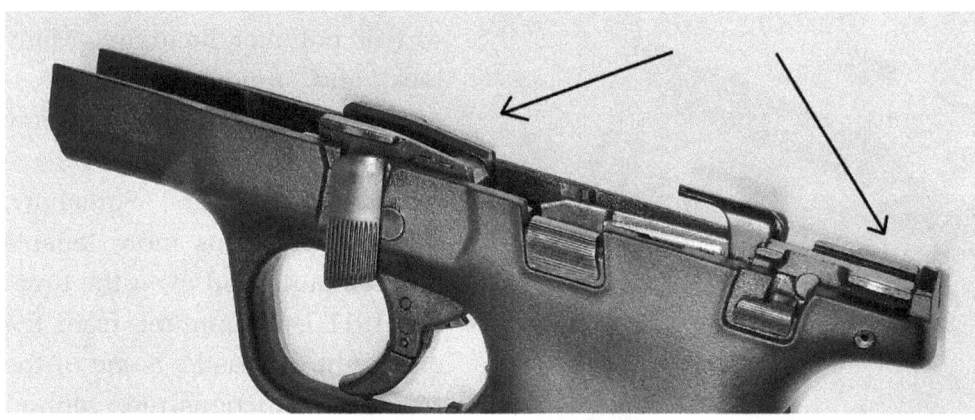

Two steel rail sections (arrows) are pinned within the polymer frame of this compact S&W Shield.

As mentioned above, the generous steel insert on an STI provides enough support for match-grade accuracy. Most other polymer pistols are built for service-type markets and priced accordingly, with less slide interface. The resulting extra flex may degrade accuracy to some extent, but how much is really necessary? Most of these guns will equal their pedestrian metal-framed rivals, placing 5 shots within three inches at 25 yards. Perhaps the manufacturers have learned how to build more accurate polymer pistols. Much as it pains me, for general combat-course shooting, my pretty steel 1911s often remain in the safe, in favor of racy, hi-cap polymer alternatives. Polymer may not embody the classic esthetics of steel, but it certainly does eliminate concerns about rust.

Finishes. Today, there are plenty of options to choose from. Some are recent developments, while others have been used for centuries. Blued steel is one obvious example, although some anodized aluminum surfaces can present a similar appearance (a magnet will tell the story). Some people confuse nickel-plating with stainless steel and sometimes it can be hard to tell the difference. I've seen a few stainless guns that received a custom polish, shining as brightly as nickel. More recently, a spate of tough industrial treatments has arrived, along with spiffy colored coatings.

Bluing. Blued steel is the traditional surface treatment for carbon steel firearms and, although it does provide some corrosion protection, bluing itself is actually a form of controlled rust. There are several different bluing techniques, but most steel firearms are "hot-blued" by immersion in heated tanks containing special salt solutions. Metal preparation is a key part of the process which has developed as a fine art. Major manufacturers like Colt or Smith & Wesson employed skilled polishers, and experienced staff claimed they could tell who had done the work just by looking at a gun. The smoothly polished and deeply blued steel surfaces of a pristine pre-war revolver are a joy to behold, especially when accented by the rainbow colors of its case-hardened hammer and trigger. The latter treatment is also seen on other old firearms like Winchester lever-action rifles. This special heat-treating imparts a thin but hard surface to steel, and can decrease wear. Case hardened colors tend to fade over time, and very old bluing will eventually display a brown patina. Except for nostalgic recreations, new induction-hardening techniques have replaced case-hardening. Blued steel firearms are still common, more often with less detailed polishing. That's not always a bad thing since matte or brushed-type surfaces will minimize reflections while holding oil. Matte finishes are often the result of bead-blasted metal prep, which requires less time and lowers cost. Sometimes a steel surface will be left "bright," meaning it has no treatment at all. In handguns, this most often applies to smaller moving parts.

The biggest enemy of bluing is rust, which can develop in almost no time at all. The sweat and natural salts from our bodies are prime offenders, and some people seem more caustic than others in ways beyond demeanor. Protection of blued steel surfaces in normal conditions is as simple as wiping down metal surfaces with a lightly oiled rag, *each and every time the gun is handled!* Blood will quickly cause rust, but a blued firearm stored in a drawer or other area containing clothing may also become a casualty. Rust can develop with surprising rapidity through moisture absorbed by fibers. Long-term storage in a holster may cause similar problems. It'll start as a fine reddish sheen which, if caught early enough, can sometimes be removed with four-ought steel wool and WD-40. A neglected surface will gradually fester to the point where it develops irreversible pitting.

Well-maintained handguns that have seen much use will typically display holster wear, evidenced by thin bluing near the muzzle. Sometimes, such bare spots, dings, or light scratches can be touched up with a commercial "cold blue" solution after thoroughly degreasing the steel. A gun in need of total rebluing will require gunsmith servicing, with complete disassembly, metal prep, and another dunk in a hot-blue tank. A re-blued firearm will often be revealed by softer lettering or slightly rounded edges. Bluing is pretty, but it's also high-maintenance.

Platings and coatings. Nickel appeared during the late 1800s as a popular alternative to bluing. While it improved resistance to rust, older examples often have blotches where the plating flaked off. The great attention to polishing at Colt and S&W resulted in a series of spectacular nickel-plated revolvers which were further enhanced by accompanying display cases. I've never been a fan of nickel, in part because the front sight is often plated, making it harder to see. Also, it will invariably be scratched during use with no expedient fix, and anything other than brief exposure to solvents can attack plated surfaces. Although nickel is still in use, newer and more durable alternatives like chrome or *Armaloy* have appeared. These finishes often closely resemble stainless steel, and most are extremely resistant to wear and corrosion.

Some of the latest colored finishes like FDE or Desert Tan (among many others) are done with a ceramic-type coating such as *Cerakote*. Others employ the exotic high-tech deposits used on industrial cutting tool surfaces. Some gun owners go it alone with home finish alternatives like DuraCoat, which can be applied from a kit. In nearly all cases, steel surfaces will be more resistant to corrosion, but that doesn't mean they should be ignored. A brief wipe-down after handling will still go a long way toward protecting your investment.

Peruse a gun shop and you may see a few older .22 rifles or shotguns with scratched up trigger guards. Good bet they were cast from pot-metal or aluminum and finished using black paint. Some inexpensive handguns receive the same treatment, although the Cold War era Communist Block CZ-75s were initially painted. More recently, the lines have blurred on painted firearms, since some are fairly tough, epoxy-based solutions. Proprietary coatings have also appeared and some require curing with heat. A few, like DuraCoat, will work with or without it. Another big coating is film-dipping, used to create camouflage finishes. You'll see it more often on waterfowl shotguns, which eventually display nicks and dings from hard use in boats and blinds. Film-dipped handguns seem more common as rimfire models.

Anodizing. Aluminum-framed handguns are finished differently, using an electrochemical process. Anodizing is especially well-suited for this material, providing a durable surface with an attractive finish. S&W's scandium handguns also receive this treatment. Besides the classic darker tones, many color alternatives are available from clear-coat to electric-blue. Aluminum won't rust but it is soft, so any dings or scratches can penetrate the finish, leaving a shiny mark. It can also flake off in small spots after heavy use. Cold blue won't cure the problem, but an easy fix is Brownell's Aluma-hyde II, available in different colors. For small touch-ups, I sometimes just apply a blob of Magic Marker. My old S&W Model 3913 pistol has been through the wringer, but you'd never know that because of its clear-anodized frame. The few minor bright dings are badges of honor. Of course, I still treat the whole pistol as a blued-steel gun, wiping it down after handling.

Stainless steel. A local gun dealer calls me "Stainless Steve." Guilty as charged. I'll take stainless whenever it's offered over any other choice. As an agency, we used an inventory of stainless S&W Model 65 revolvers for years. They took a licking but kept on… shooting. They received nothing more than routine (but not obsessive) maintenance. Eventually, they were replaced by stainless 3rd Gen S&W pistols (some being the previously mentioned aluminum-framed 3913s). These pistols held up extremely well and like our older revolvers, any surface defects were strictly minor cosmetic dings.

Our present S&W M&P pistols have Polymer frames, but their slides are Melonite-treated stainless steel. No, the finish isn't made of melons. It's actually applied through an industrial salt-bath nitriding process, which provides an extremely hard and durable finish resembling matte-bluing (Glock uses a similar, tough Tenifer finish). The nitride finishes are thicker than bluing and harder than nails, so metal-wear is greatly reduced. Although some minor cosmetic thinning can occur, these treatments hold up well with a modicum of care. Note that they result from a special salt bath. Sure enough, stainless steel is by no means immune from rust. It does, however, afford extra resistance using chromium alloys.

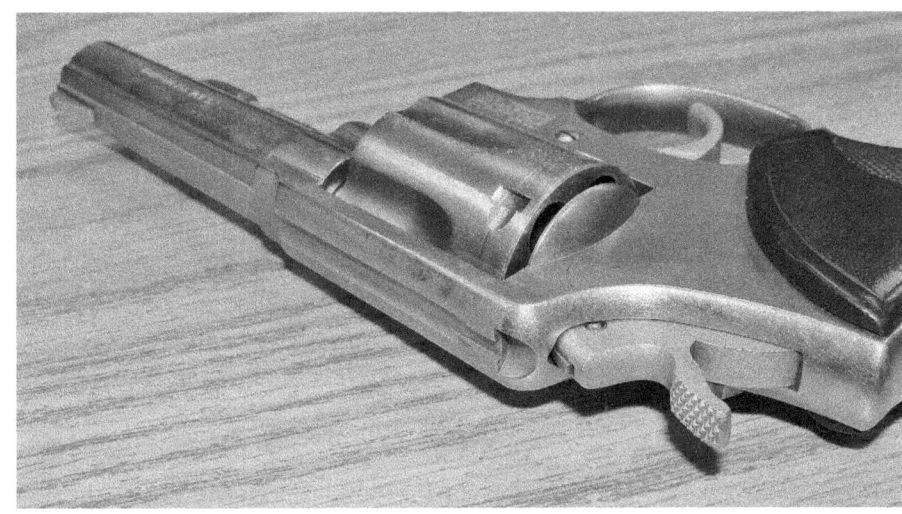

Although this circa 1989 S&W Model 65 saw years of service, the stainless finish displays little of its interesting history.

Although stainless steel was occasionally used for gun parts, S&W broke new ground in 1965 when they introduced a little .38 Special Model 60. This J-frame version of their Chief's Special was made almost entirely from stainless steel. Since hide-out guns are prone to corrosion from close body contact, sales soared. The same gun is available today along with many other models, and five decades of engineering has refined stainless production throughout the industry. Manufacturers encountered initial difficulties during machining, and galling

Although this S&W M&P has seen a decade of regular use, its treated stainless slide has held up well. The frame is polymer so its color is "baked in".

Guidelines And Useful Features | 53

issues arose with some early slides and frames. Fortunately, thanks to metallurgical refinements, today's firearms will run reliably. Proper lubrication is as important as it always has been, regardless of the materials.

Again, the stainless alloys used for firearms manufacturing can in fact rust. It'll happen more gradually, and one common spot is underneath any grip panels. A bag full of Doritos, followed by a long-range session on a hot day, might offer future surprises without prompt attention. For this reason, I stick with my standard regimen of a simple post-use wipe down. Occasionally, I'll also remove the set of grips on *any* steel-framed handguns. The occasional ding in a stainless surface can often be buffed out by hand with fine emery cloth, lapping compound, or steel wool. After using steel wool, fine particles can imbed in the surface causing rust, but you can carefully brush the spot with a stainless toothbrush and some WD-40 to "pacify" it.

This leads to another main reason why I prefer stainless. Unlike some other finishes, there's nothing to chip or flake off. The finish is simply built-in. Some serious gun people don't like it for cosmetic reasons, while others worry about shiny guns for defense. Well, matte-finished stainless steel solves some of these concerns. The new dark nitride alternatives are another easy fix, but bare, bead-blasted stainless is quite subdued. However, like completely nickel-finished guns, I don't care for stainless front sights. They're just harder to see in many light conditions. Most of my revolvers are stainless S&Ws, but each has a removable front sight, whether pinned or dovetailed in place. As such, customized aiming improvements are possible – just one example of a personalized approach to purchasing.

PERSONALIZED FACTORS

For use in tough conditions, weatherproof options provide huge advantages. Non-ferrous materials take rust off the table but, whether carbon or stainless, at least *some* steel remains within them all so maintenance still matters. And, of course, the type of materials used can also affect a handgun's weight, which has a further effect upon portability, steadiness, and recoil. These and other factors can make or break a purchase, so that's where we're headed next…

CHAPTER 5
THE PERSONAL INTERFACE

With a few basics behind us, let's weave in a few personal factors. The first one is glitz. It's tempting to fixate on the latest, greatest firearm and the gun press has hyped more than one new trinket which then faded into obscurity. At that point, anyone who jumped onboard was left holding the bag as far as spare parts or servicing went.

But, even a well-built firearm with a lengthy track record won't necessarily qualify as a top choice. And, since not everyone is a died-in-the-wool gun person, what actually constitutes the "right gun"? Muddying the waters even more, some couples can wind up sharing a handgun for household defense. In our stereotyped world, the Alpha Male typically determines the selection, meaning the "Other Half" will be stuck with the choice regardless of its suitability. Experience, complexity, and fit all come into play here. Without careful shopping, proficiency may come more slowly, or could never be fully realized. A large, complex gun as loud and heavy as Thor's hammer just ain't gonna cut it for everyone, including some "experienced" folks.

We've noticed the ladies have a penchant for smaller guns. Part of the allure may be appearance, but other attractions include less weight. Macho guys on the other hand, get excited over a truck axle-size handgun like a Desert Eagle; particularly one chambered for the behemoth .50 Action Express. In either case, like many other things in life including prune juice, moderation is often beneficial. Shorter-barreled handguns are often described as "cute." Maybe, but they also tend to amplify firing effects. Besides being louder, they tend to generate more flash and muzzle-blast – all of which are disconcerting to novice shooters (because they have a shorter sight radius, small handguns can also be harder to shoot accurately). We regularly issue double hearing protection to female shooters, who seem more noise- sensitive than men. Most of the guys are deafer than stumps by their mid-forties, probably from loud music, machinery, and guns. We Neanderthals just take extra noise for granted, but the concussive effects of muzzle-blast are very real concerns. Younger shooters are in the same boat and many will jump through their skin upon a shot.

Recoil can cause further worries. Beyond discomfort, loss of control is possible, and this can pose serious safety concerns. The muzzle of a handgun can wind up pointed in the wrong direction within an instant. Moving parts can cause further difficulties. Watch new shooters firing autoloaders and you'll see many closing their eyes while jerking their heads rearward. This reaction is a reflexive effort to avoid a reciprocating slide as it travels toward the face. Without a proper introduction, aiming and follow-through will be inconsistent at best. Remember: the sights are on the slide. A competent shot will see the sights before, during, and after each shot – something that can never happen with closed eyes!

Here's where our gun choice can play a role. A revolver's sights remain stationary, which makes them easier to focus on *throughout* each firing sequence. Because of its simplicity, a revolver also makes a good starter gun. That said, since we're all individuals, other factors also come into play - beginning with fit.

GUN FIT

A universal truism is, it's darned hard to shoot *any* handgun well without lots of practice. Competent shooters have one thing in common: they have mastered the basics and learned how to employ them *consistently*. One key fundamental is a proper grip. A well-chosen gun will nestle in the hand, permitting comfortable access to the trigger and any other controls such as magazine releases, slide releases, or de-cocking levers. A handgun that provides a comfortable grip angle will also support natural target indexing but, like shoes or gloves, one size won't fit all.

Trigger reach. To some extent, natural hand placement simplifies the complex repertoire of marksmanship details. An important dimension is the distance from the web of the hand to the trigger finger's distal joint. With a handgun nestled into the web, the trigger should fall somewhere around the outermost crease if the finger is extended in line with the forearm. Depending to some extent upon the type of gun, most folks will shoot well with the pad of the index finger located on the trigger's face. This is just a general rule of thumb since a few experienced D/A revolver shooters use their crease to gain extra leverage. Some pistol shooters use the outer finger tip but, as a general principle, the crease makes a good point of reference when evaluating fit. I normally use the pad of my trigger finger, which works with many types of handguns, but I recently struggled with a very small D/A-only pistol. A simple switch to the tip of my finger was all it took to fix my problem (although it may not work for those with weaker hands).

Grip geometry plays a major role regarding target indexing. Ideally, the handgun should align as an extension of the shooter's forearm. However, we've watched some petite users struggle to properly acquire the trigger, resulting in a major gun shift while trying to shorten the distance. It's a losing proposition that will degrade marksmanship while magnifying recoil. To the other extreme, we've encountered ham-sized hands that blocked access to controls, or even obstructed complete trigger travel. When factoring in trigger-reach, remember that double-action designs present two different strokes. The first D/A pull will involve a longer stroke, followed by shorter S/A resets. Standby for more comments pertinent to pull-weights in this chapter.

Trigger guard comments and cautions. Some semiautos are sold with hooked forward faces while others may have metal-checkered front section. This feature is included to accommodate those who shoot with their support-hand's trigger finger hooked forward to contact that area. Today though, it's mostly passé, which is all for the best since it can develop an unsafe revolver style. Extending that finger below the barrel/cylinder gap of a powerful revolver presents an opportunity for injury from escaping high-pressure gas. So, the safer bet is to skip this technique, thus rendering the feature moot.

Grip. Comfort can often be improved through use of different grips. Most revolvers offer plenty of options on both sides of the size spectrum from small to extra-large. Many metal-framed pistols also accept replaceable grip panels. Often, they are attached by just one or two screws. Polymer pistols typically provide a streamlined monolithic grip frame that offers plenty of ammo capacity but less versatility concerning grips. Shooters with larger hands sometimes slip on elastic "hand-all" adapters to increase girth but more recently, interchangeable grip sections have caught on in a big way.

Pachmayer grips are a simple fix for skimpy revolver panels. Elastic "hand-alls" are an easy pistol solution – but not for those with grip safeties! Fortunately, 1911 panels can be easily exchanged with a screw driver. Swapping that one-piece S&W 3rd-Gen grip is trickier.

While finger grooves have appeal, they need to match a shooter's hand. Since commercial designs are generic, this is easier said than done. As a general principle, the gun should sit low in the hand when grasped. With double-action revolvers, the sloping rear of the frame should flow into the web, or just above it. Pistols typically have a tang or overhanging rear, designed to firmly contact this point. Extra space between the gun and web will locate the axis of the bore higher, generating extra recoil leverage. Recovery time between shots will suffer as a result. If finger grooves support proper fit, then so much the better. Trouble is, there's a good chance they won't. For better or worse, the grip initially established will be the one you'll be stuck with during fast-paced multiple shots.

A proper tang can also prevent semiauto hammer bite. While striker-fired designs are immune from this problem, the slide still reciprocates. A fleshy hand may be nipped and odds are higher with some designs. The older Walther PPKs and Browning Hi Powers will bite some shooters mercilessly, along with a host of smaller pocket rockets. This hazard can often be identified at a gun counter after assuming a solid grip.

Soft rubber grips can soak up recoil and are often seen on the hard-kicking magnum revolvers, but

I've encountered some single-action types with seemingly innocuous checkering that quickly rubbed my shooting hand raw during recoil (one simple fix was a glove). A large and somewhat tacky surface can have another negative effect, somewhat analogous to finger grooves. Namely, where your hand initially winds up during the draw is where it'll want to stay. When speed is of the essence, the grip problems identified above can appear. On the other hand, a very slick grip can degrade control during recoil. Once again, moderation helps. A bit of checkering on a set of grip panels isn't a bad thing. Most of the Polymer-framed pistols now sport molded-in stippling and that helps. Some of us die-hards have even done it on our own with a soldering iron on *replaceable* synthetic grips.

More on indexing. When the gun comes up to eye level it should index near the target. If the sights consistently point up or downhill, quick shooting will be compromised, and accuracy may further suffer in low light. Rumors to the contrary, some supposedly excellent guns don't fit all users. A pistol with a reputation for good ergonomics is John Browning's 1911. Its 13-degree grip angle remains in use on several modern designs. The angle of the hugely popular Glock is similar to a P-08 Luger, at around 22 degrees which, unfortunately for me, causes these pistols to point uphill. Many shooters extol the handling qualities of another Browning inspired design, the Hi Power. It was my strong favorite until I finally got my hands on an S&W M&P pistol with its 18-degree rake. After installing the smallest of three included rear grip inserts, the feel was near nirvana. Legions of Glock fans will hotly debate this observation while less experienced shooters may never note a difference. Still, grip angle is at least worth considering.

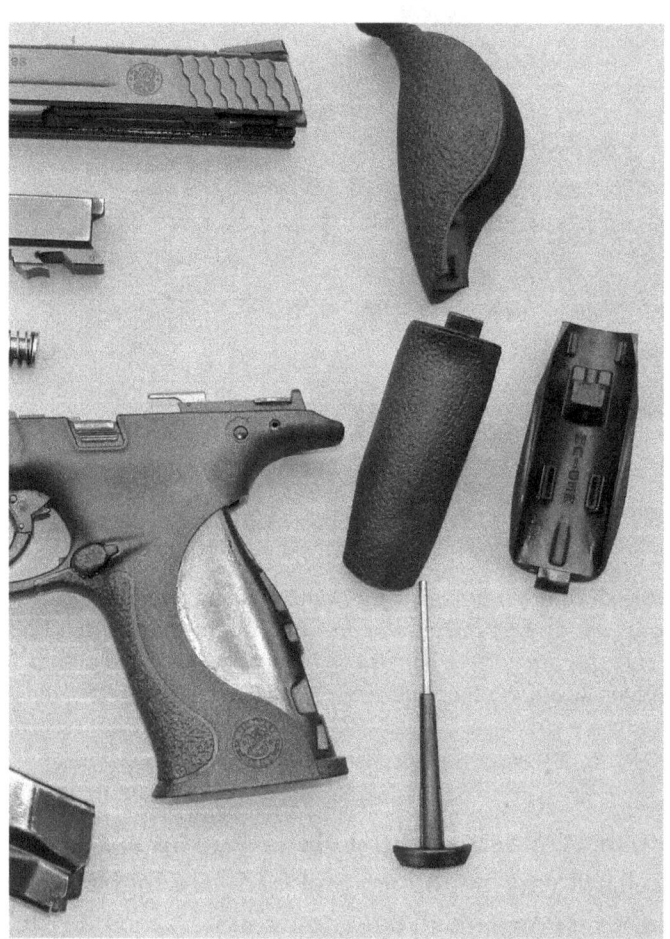

Some polymer pistols offer grip options. Earlier M&P came with three interchangeable inserts, but the latest version adds a fourth. Exchange them by withdrawing the retaining pin after a quarter-twist.

Tip: A gun shop with a large assortment of different makes and models is a good place to sort through the various issues noted above. More food for thought: I've found it's generally easier to shoot a handgun that's a bit too small than one that is oversized.

OPERATION

People with extensive firearms experience can usually adapt to operational idiosyncrasies after some hands-on practice. Furthermore, hard corps handgunners tend to have good hand strength thanks to regular manipulation of slides and controls. Filling hi-cap magazines is also a great way to toughen up fingers! Operation is often taken for granted, but even the basics can pose real challenges for some individuals.

Occasional design quirks can also cause stumbling blocks for well-seasoned folks. One thing that bugs me is the magazine-release button on some small pistols. My thumb just doesn't want to cooperate without unnatural hand contortions and, since the issue is size-driven, there is no easy fix beyond lots of extra practice. But why hamstring yourself if better options exist? To that end, revolvers have minimal controls. The primary double-action control is a thumb-piece (or button) that unlatches the cylinder.

As for semiautomatic pistols, two common controls will be a slide-stop (which often serves as a dual-use slide release), and a magazine release. Some designs may also include a safety-lever. Besides trigger reach, the effort required to activate these devices should be considered. The slide itself is a large spring-loaded component which often requires substantial effort to manually retract. Those who struggle with basic operation will be ineffective at best, and much more likely to be unsafe. It's easy to let a muzzle wander while battling controls, so potential difficulties are best discovered *prior* to a purchase.

Semiautomatic operation. Most defensive handgun shooting involves both hands which are often referred to by firearms instructors as the "dominant" and "support" hands. The dominant - or strong hand - does the shooting, but both control the gun (in a pinch it's reassuring to know how either can be used on its own). Ideally, semiauto pistol controls will accommodate dominant hand-only operation. This speeds up the reloading process (although there are other reasons), and most service-type semiautos are laid out accordingly. Back to that dual-use slide-stop/slide release lever: when functioning as a slide-stop, an arm on the lever will be engaged by an empty magazine to lock the slide rearward; a great cue to reload! To expedite this process, a magazine release button is typically located on the left side of the pistol's frame behind the trigger guard (some are now reversible or ambidextrous). This is a preferred American design, ideal for activation by the thumb of a right-handed

Although many of today's semiautomatics offer simplified operation, proper clearance requires practice. On the other hand, a D/A revolver's cylinder can be opened by pushing a button. A shove of the rod will clear its chambers.

shooter. Depressing the button will permit a magazine to drop while, at the same time, the support hand can retrieve and present a fresh magazine for reloading. Once seated, the slide release can be used to allow the slide to run home and chamber a fresh round (or the slide can be retracted a bit to permit disengagement).

Typical of polymer pistols, S&W's M&P has few active controls. The take-down lever is strictly for disassembly.

Sounds good in principle and it is – assuming the gun fits properly to begin with. I sometimes need to shift a pistol in my hand to activate a magazine release. This is usually no big deal with practice, using a slight flip inboard. With proper technique, the reloading procedure can happen at dazzling speed, but well-positioned controls help, even for non-Ninjas. Those who can walk while chewing gum should be able to perfect the technique – assuming they've picked the right pistol. But, don't ignore magazines since some can be a bear to load, especially when nearly full. Taped fingers are a common sight during multi-day schools with some types of pistols. There are special loading tools to help ease the effort but, sometimes, seating a fully loaded magazine can be a battle of its own. This problem won't become evident until the slide is in battery, at which point magazines without clearance for a bit of cartridge compression may require a stiff bump. Omission of this step could cause a malfunction or, possibly, the loss of the magazine. A pistol with a magazine disconnect feature will also be rendered inert unless the magazine is fully seated. Regardless of the gun, it's worth

Some European designs like this smaller .380 Sig P232 use a heel-type magazine release. Operation requires two hands, possibly no big backup gun issue - assuming the value of familiar function is weighed.

tugging on the magazine just to make sure it has fully engaged because, sooner or later, you'll find one that hasn't.

As we can see, a design that doesn't require a wrestling match can save lots of irritations. A few annoyances may not become fully evident until the gun has seen some range time, but a batch of dummy cartridges may reveal some in advance. To that end, smaller gun shops are more likely to be helpful. Hit one at a quieter time and you may be able to avoid later problems on the range.

Revolver operation. Things become simpler with a double-action wheel-gun. Most of the above concerns will disappear, although ammo capacity will probably decrease. As far as loading goes, a D/A revolver will have a simple release-button, permitting the cylinder to swing open for easy access of its chambers. Next, pushing a spring-loaded rod will simultaneously eject any fired cases or live rounds. Gravity factors in, and fired cases will eject more reliably if the muzzle is elevated before punching the rod. Fresh rounds will chamber more efficiently if the muzzle is first depressed. Although a proper technique requires some extra two-handed juggling, the whole process can be deftly accomplished with practice (there are also single-hand reloading techniques that will work during an emergency). A swing-out revolver affords both simplicity and safety. Its load status can be verified at a glance and the two active controls (latch and rod) are easily mastered by everyone. The hardest part for some may be the heavier D/A trigger stroke. It serves as good insurance against an unintentional discharge but can create a struggle for those without much hand-strength. Thumb-cocking to S/A mode may solve this problem, but the resulting lighter trigger pull can be risky under stress.

Accessing the chambers of a single-action revolver is typically accomplished through a hinged loading gate. After exposing a chamber (normally at 2:00), a long, barrel-mounted rod is pushed to knock out each individual empty case. Manual rotation of the non-swing-out cylinder aligns each chamber with the gate and rod, so the system is a bit more "fiddly." Its chambers are also harder to inspect. Manual cocking of the hammer is necessary for each shot, but the result is a light trigger pull. Of course, that will introduce the same concerns as those of a D/A revolver cocked to its S/A mode.

One thing many people forget is the un-cocking process. It's a non-issue with most striker-fired pistols, but should be considered a vital part of any hammer-gun's operation, whether revolver or pistol. The right techniques are necessary to prevent an AD (although a shrouded-hammer, D/A-only revolver eliminates this concern). Before dry-firing or cocking a gun in a store, ask the person behind the counter for permission. It's not only proper etiquette, but a good chance to receive some guidance. Regardless of where you are, remember to manage the muzzle at all times!

Complexity. It boils down to this: *a shooter should be able to operate his or her handgun on demand, smoothly and with confidence!* This is impossible without a clear understanding of a gun's function.

We employ check-off criteria to assess the operational skills of our staff. Using a semiauto pistol as an example, there are basic steps related to *proper* administrative loading, administrative unloading, and clearance. The administrative process is used when not in harm's way, such as while beginning

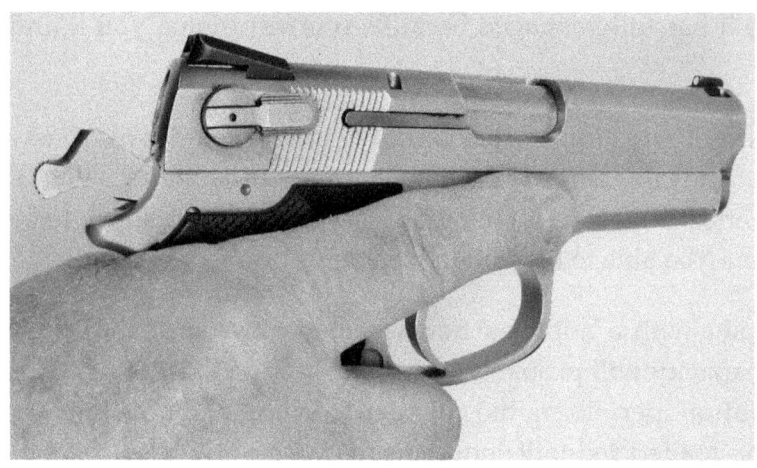

This D/A pistol is cocked to its single-action mode. The slide-mounted lever can safely lower it, but trigger finger discipline is essential. Hence, the need for proper training!

or ending armed duties. The safety of everyone is a major concern anytime a gun is handled, so there are designated areas for this purpose. Anyone struggling during scheduled check-off sessions is flagged for remedial training. Competent gun handlers will sail right through, but not everyone is in this boat.

Personal experience also counts. A complex system can be overwhelming for those starting from scratch and, while proper training can develop competency, shooting – including safe gun handling – is a perishable skill. We need to be honest about our commitment, resources, and abilities. While decked-out tactical firearms may be cool, the KISS approach has merits.

Disassembly and maintenance. Part of "operation on demand" includes field stripping the handgun for routine cleaning. A design that supports this process will go a long way toward ensuring reliability. Two very popular John Browning designed pistols are the 1911 Government Model and the Hi Power. As a big fan of both, I find the P-35 Hi-power evolution much easier to maintain. For disassembly purposes, there are several 1911 variations and, to my mind, none of them are completely simple. The original system is downright "fiddly," with the added possibility of launching a recoil-plug to places unknown. The standard reassembly routine for all 1911s involves holding your mouth just right, while attempting to insert the slide-stop axle through both the frame and a pivoting barrel link. By comparison, the later P-35 is a breeze to field-strip for cleaning. For this reason, I'd often reach for a 9mm Hi Power when it came to punching paper. Fortunately, this simplicity now extends to several modern pistol designs, and some make the Hi-Power look arcane.

Many LEOs shoot only when paid to do so, meaning they're not really "gun people." Some civilian gun owners are in a similar league with the added burden of ammo expense. We used to issue S&W Model 3913s to plain-clothes staff and, although they were easier to disassemble than a 1911, some still made funny faces during reassembly. It was easy to see who had a firm handle on the process during post live-fire maintenance. We *made* them do it. Disinterested private owners might avoid the process until any marginal ability fades to none.

Malfunctions were uncommon with our little single-stack 9mms, and the few encountered were attributable to neglect. Considering their lives were literally on the line, one might expect more dedication, but that's not how human nature works. Eventually, we switched to our present M&Ps, which follow other polymer, striker-fired designs. Thanks to their greatly simplified field-stripping process, cleanliness immediately improved. An easy-to-maintain handgun can provide similar benefits to informed consumers and there are plenty of good choices, although some have quirks.

Unlike some other modern makes, you also don't need to dry-fire an M&P prior to disassembly. We consider this a plus although others will argue it's no big deal, so long as common sense is exercised. Sounds simple: clear the pistol *before* pulling the trigger. In theory, there's no excuse for a "negligent" (or accidental) discharge. If we extend the same logic to driving, accidents should be extremely rare, but there's a good chance some proponents of this AD theory have initiated a crash. The one AD on our range happened during a Glock disassembly. Fortunately, the bonehead who caused it exercised muzzle control. We're quite sure he'll be more careful next time. We also suspect he needed new underwear.

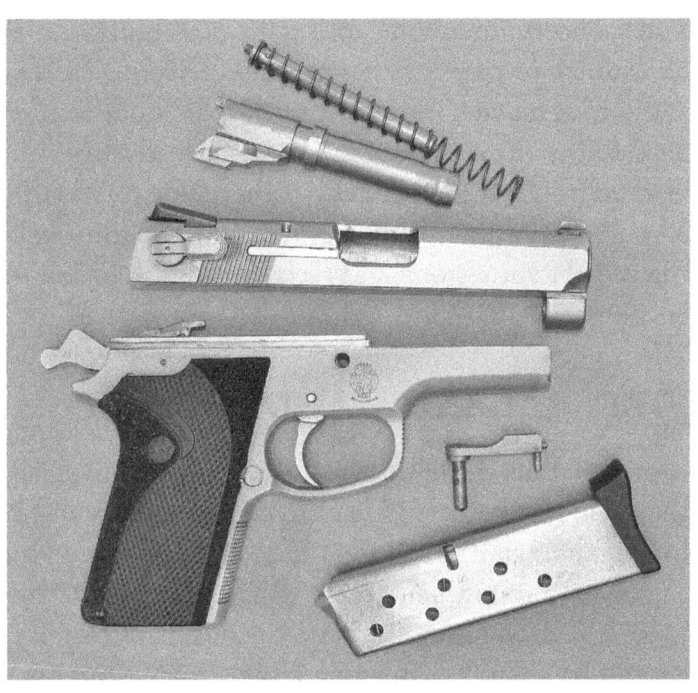

S&W's Model 3913 (still a good gun) was a compact evolution of their M-39. Field-stripping loosely mirrored a 1911 pistol with the possibility of lost parts.

Revolvers solve just about all disassembly concerns. The fouling from a normal post-range session can be scrubbed off without dismantling the gun. S/A designs facilitate easy cylinder removal, presenting no real extra work. After *lots* of shooting, a D/A cylinder should also be removed, and removal of one screw is all it takes with an S&W. Delving into the lock-work will be attempted by some, while others will be better off with gunsmith services. More on this later…

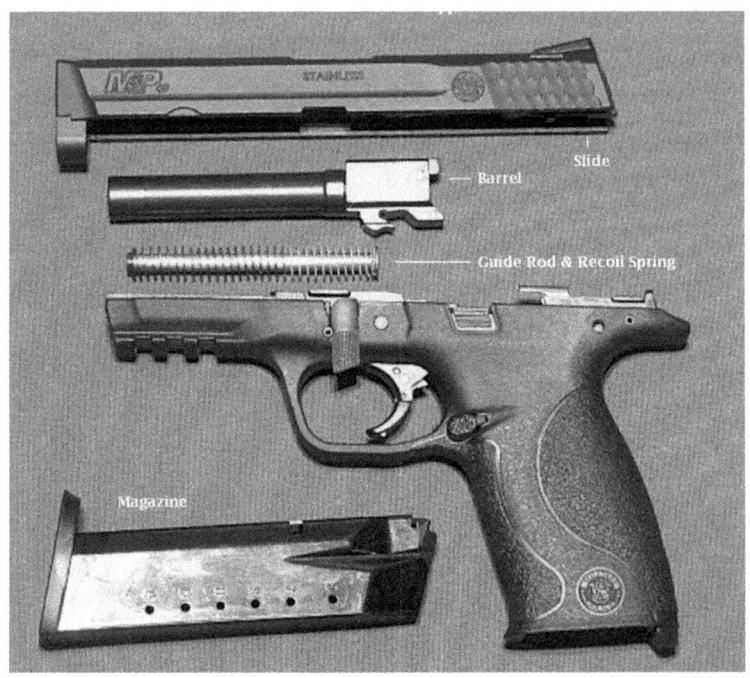

Like many newer striker-fired designs, M&P disassembly simple. A rotating a take-down lever is the key and, unlike some others, dry-firing isn't necessary.

The big takeaway is to select a handgun appropriate for its user. Two concerns are ease of operation *and* maintenance. A third concern for anyone facing the possibility of maintenance on the fly is captive parts. Things that can launch to parts unknown are worrisome. Picture this happening in the woods. Then, add some snow to achieve a new level of despair - not to mention darkness. During less dire circumstances, availability of replacement parts is also reassuring. One common feature many of the latest striker-fired polymer pistols share is easy slide dismounting without removal of their slide-stops. There's a good chance their recoil springs will be captured on their guide-rods, too. Makes me wonder how many 1911 slide-stops and recoil spring plugs lay undiscovered in far-flung locales throughout the South Pacific and Europe!

SIZE, BALANCE, AND WEIGHT

A gun that fits the hand will go a long way toward delivering a well-centered shot, but what if more than one is necessary? Defensively, the ability to control and quickly recover from recoil is what it may take to stay in the fight long enough to stop a threat. In that case, a manageable compromise of power and gun-mass can soak up some recoil. Here's how it works: a heavier gun will offer more inertial resistance and soak up the effects of recoil. By going with a smaller caliber, perceived recoil should be even less. Burning less powder also cuts down on muzzle-blast, especially with a longer barrel. A design that locates the bore lower in the hand will exert less leverage during recoil. Less kick and muzzle-blast reduce the involuntary tendency to flinch, resulting in better marksmanship.

Size matters. Of course, besides the handgun itself, a shooter's physique, experience, and attitude count. Even marginal defensive calibers can be feisty in a small enough gun. For an experienced shooter, the magnified recoil may be little more than a minor annoyance, whereas a small-statured beginner could be totally intimidated by a tiny .380 pistol, or an ultra-lightweight .38 Special revolver – especially for those lacking any previous frame of reference. A standard-size .22 rimfire makes a nice starting point for this reason.

Little handguns are generally harder to shoot since, besides increased recoil, less gun mass translates to more wobble while aiming. The distance between the front and rear sights on a smaller gun will also be shorter, which can magnify seemingly minor alignment errors. Target guns have longer barrels to minimize this effect. A practical all-around handgun choice will probably fall somewhere in the middle. Often, a useful threshold will be met at somewhere around four inches of barrel length, explaining why most LE handguns fall into this size-range.

Barrel length introduces other considerations. A longer-barreled handgun can be harder to conceal, and an extreme example can be difficult to carry in a traditional manner. On a positive note, the resulting extra sight radius can do more than improve accuracy. Increased velocity is a dividend of a longer barrel. The additional bore volume provides more space for powder consumption, which can further reduce muzzle flash. In low light, the latter is a serious concern since the dazzling effects of some heavy-hitters can immediately disrupt a shooter's vision. I've occasionally touched off a .44 Magnum during a night-fire program and it's pretty much a one-shot event. A .357 from a short barrel isn't a whole lot better. The concussive effects of either are another big concern. Imagine these effects indoors at night without hearing protection!

Balance. Many moons ago, when D/A revolvers were king, my agency decided to run a three-day competition for its ten top-scoring shooters. I was among them and, since personal facsimiles of our duty handguns were permitted, I chose a four-inch S&W Model 67. This adjustable-sight K-frame closely matched our old issued, fixed-sight, .38 Special Model 64s, but had a lighter, tapered barrel. After three days of fast and furious shooting, I managed to take first-place. Immediately afterward, I sold the M-67 to the second-place shooter who'd been hot on my heels throughout. When I noted some unexpected difficulty posting good scores with this gun, he wasn't buying in. So, he bought the gun and shortly thereafter, arrived at the same conclusion. It's light, tapered barrel was great in a holster, but less mass up front compromised steadiness. He sold it too, and in short order, we were both happily shooting new Model 686 four-inch L-frames with much heavier barrels (I was glad he didn't use one during that competition).

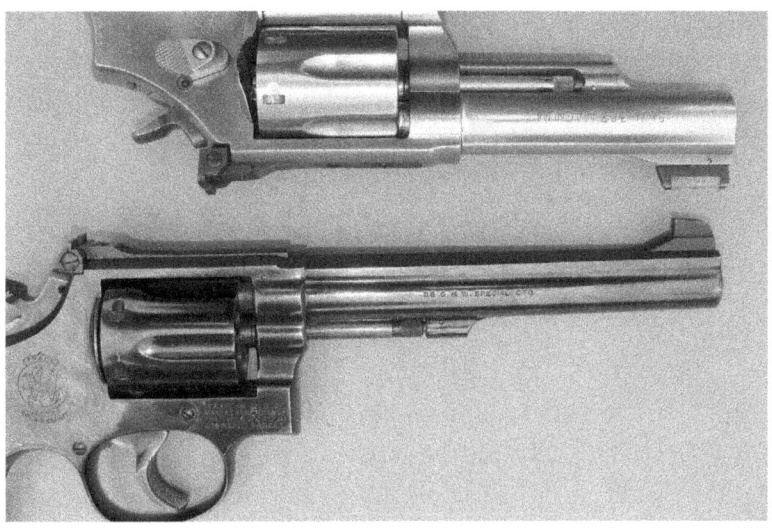

The six-inch K-38 target revolver has a longer sight radius to minimize aiming errors, but the handier four-inch .357 will still be usefully accurate. It'll also be concussive and bright with magnum loads.

Nowadays, semiauto pistols rule the course and many are six-inch "long-slide" versions, which increase sight radius while improving steadiness. The handguns of either genre handle great, and while their downrange effectiveness is obvious, most never see real street time. They're just too big for daily carry.

Liveliness also counts. Having tried several longer-barreled types, the evolution of standard-length handguns make lots of sense. Among the latest fast-paced combat-oriented competitions like IPSC and IDPA, five-inch pistols remain popular simply because they offer an ideal balance of speed and accuracy. Some long-slides may be part of the mix but they'll probably have weight-saving sections milled out to impart better balance. You won't see the shorter compact iterations in anything other than concealed-carry courses, which are usually run as separate matches.

Balance is one of the intangibles that often won't become apparent until rounds have been expended so, for those unsure, the safest one-gun bet is probably a middle-of-the-road selection.

Weight. Although gun mass can soften perceived recoil, too much weight can create problems. An obvious one is carry comfort. Less obvious is a shooter's ability to support the gun in a firing stance, or during a prolonged "ready" position. The latter issue is perhaps less of a concern for civilians, but it's still worth considering. Picture holding someone at bay until help arrives. After several minutes, a seemingly "light" handgun will start gaining weight faster than Bubba at a Super Bowl party.

As to what constitutes a practical general-purpose gun, a couple popular LE choices might shed some light. Remember, the folks behind a badge wear a sidearm every day. These two mainstay sidearms encompass more than half-a-century of use, legitimizing each as a "practical" example.

Type	Make	Model	Caliber	Bbl	Unloaded	Loaded
Revolver	S&W	66	.357 Mag	4 ¼"	36.09 oz.	39.50 oz.
Pistol	Glock	17	9mm Luger	4 ½"	25.06 oz.	32.12 oz.

The Glock looks like a gimmee, being lighter fully loaded than the revolver is empty. *But don't forget about reloads!* The typical basic load for LE revolver was 18 rounds, counting 6 in the gun, plus 12 spares. Heck, a 17 +1 Glock covers that without any extra magazines! Add the standard two reloads and you'll be lugging more than a 50-round box of ammo. Of course, you may not need two extra mags, but I'd want at least one spare. Heavier bullets and larger calibers will pile on even more weight. Also, note that recoil will increase as ammunition is expended, which further affects the gun's handling. The perceived difference could be negligible with a 6-shot steel-frame revolver, but an 18-shot polymer pistol is a different animal.

The Glock Model 17 embodies another general-purpose handgun choice, wrapping a reasonably-sized semiauto platform around a controllable cartridge. Given today's cartridge options, the concept of variable power and recoil can be extended to the 9mm through standard or +P loads. The right-sized pistol can allow us to strike a useful balance of portability and control. Fortunately, there is no shortage of great choices in all sorts of sizes and calibers.

Whatever strikes your fancy, Newton's Law should be considered before jumping into the purchase. As a frame of reference, the weights of some popular handguns in their most common chamberings are shown below.

HANDGUN WEIGHT COMPARISON   *Unloaded

Type	Make	Model	Frame	Caliber	Bbl	Weight *
Pistol	S&W	Bodyguard	Polymer	.380 ACP	2 ¾"	12 oz.
Pistol	Glock	17	Polymer	9mm	4 ½"	25 oz.
Pistol	Colt 1911	Commander	Aluminum	.45 ACP	4 ¼"	29.4 oz.
Pistol	Colt 1911	Standard Gvt	Steel	.45 ACP	5"	37.5 oz.

D/A Rev	S&W J-frame	M-642	Aluminum	.38 Special	1 7/8"	14.6 oz.
D/A Rev	S&W K-frame	M-66	Stain Steel	.357 Mag	4 ¼"	37 oz.
D/A Rev	S&W N-frame	M-29	Steel	.44 Mag	4"	43.8 oz.
S/A Rev	Ruger	Blackhawk	Steel	.357 Mag	4 5/8"	42 oz.

Note the light weights of the small .380 pistol and .38 Special revolver. Although either will carry well, both will be harder to master and, even though neither is a powerhouse, recoil will be snappy. While the latter will be a non-issue for experienced shooters, many won't be in that league.

CALIBER CONCERNS

Without adequate experience or proper guidance, an appropriate caliber choice can be a daunting proposition. Safe to assume, most people with a strong firearm background already have clear caliber preferences. We'd like to think that no one from this group would start a novice shooter on a hard-kicking magnum, but we also know it happens.

Experience versus recoil. The effects of a full-strength .357 Magnum on a novice shooter would be bad enough. A .44 Magnum would be devastating and potentially unsafe. A longer-term result for either would be a nearly incurable flinch. Most magnum revolvers are built on larger frames for durability and shooter comfort. Their extra mass helps dampen recoil, *but many of them can be a handful for even able-bodied individuals.* Muzzle-blast also tends to be severe. The combined effects can be quite debilitating, so it's wiser to start with something smaller. Same story for pistols. What follows is just a short list of the more popular options.

A few useful examples. Again, one dual-caliber revolver chambering has much to offer. The .357 Magnum is versatile, but a full-power load can be unpleasant. The simple fix is a switch to milder but interchangeable .38 Special loads, which provide a *much* more sensible starting-point. Later, a switch

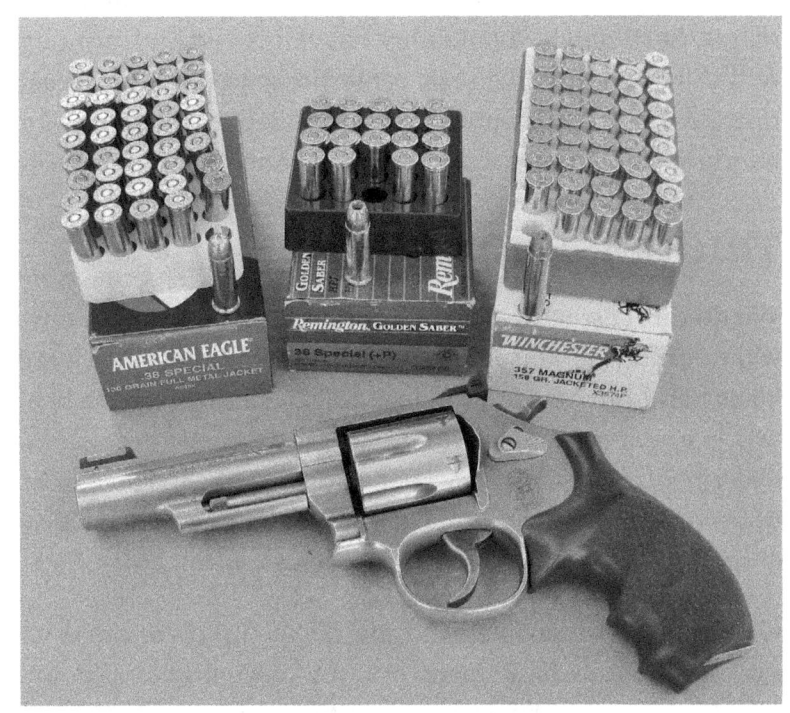

S&W's medium-frame Model 66 offers a practical compromise of size and versatility. Each class of ammunition represents a progressive level of power.

to .38 Special +Ps can provide a practical power upgrade without the penalties of full-strength Magnums. As noted, gun size must be considered since a standard .38 Special can be snappy in a small, lightweight revolver.

The 9mm Luger (sometimes listed as 9mm Parabellum) remains an ever-popular choice, producing noticeably milder recoil than its two biggest rivals: the .40 S&W and .45 ACP. On top of that, 9mm cartridges are smaller, so more will fit within a reasonably sized pistol. Ammo is also cheaper and somewhat easier to find. Ballistically, the 9mm is similar to a .38 Special, making it a good choice for many shooters.

Yes, the .380 is even milder in a similarly-sized pistol. The reason is simple: it has less power. This cartridge is often considered the minimum threshold for defensive purposes, and is most commonly seen in small backup pistols. In fact, it's easier to find a tiny .380 than any normal-sized version. The few larger examples tend to be compact, so some can be difficult to shoot. A few recent exceptions are .380 knock-offs of 1911s built to a smaller scale, and S&W's new .380 Shield EZ. As for the smallest .380s, recoil can be stout because of minimal mass. Experienced shooters will manage without undue difficulties, but beginners could be better off with a larger example like the above S&W.

In fact, a newer shooter would be well-served by starting even smaller in caliber. An understudy .22 rimfire makes a great addition, whether as a pistol or a revolver. By matching up similar rimfire and centerfire models, you can gain a winning combination. Until recently, .22 LR ammunition was scarce. Fortunately, availability has improved and, although prices have risen somewhat, .22 rimfire will still be cheaper than any centerfire load (and much easier to shoot). Thanks to minimal recoil and muzzle-blast, full attention can be applied to marksmanship fundamentals. Skills with larger-caliber handguns will improve as a result; a concept worth a dedicated rimfire handgun chapter.

TRIGGERS AND SIGHTS

We do our best to deliver relevant firearms training programs and, since each has a defensive slant, it only stands to reason that the shooters will need to learn how to function under stress. Using our basic handgun course as an example, we'll turn up the heat once mastery of the shooting fundamentals is apparent. In fact, after several days, some stages will advance to what might charitably be described as "fast-paced." That's how we like to run a final qualification course, which often leads to questions from participants about how to most effectively complete a good run. The answer will be short and sweet: *sight picture and trigger control!*

One ongoing defensive handgun debate involves point-shooting versus aimed fire. In our opinion, both techniques have merit but, for most shooters, point-shooting should be limited to last-ditch efforts *at very close range*. Beyond a few steps, employment of sights will greatly increase our hit probability. Any defensive reaction will occur with great urgency, so sights that can be quickly acquired offer real advantages. But, all bets are off if we ignore that trigger. Cranking on it won't work so proper control is essential. This leads to the question of what constitutes "a good trigger."

Trigger pull. Good bullseye-type accuracy is difficult to achieve without a light and predictable trigger release. The idea is to align the sights and release the trigger in a manner that won't disrupt the process. So, true target guns usually offer a nice, crisp single-action release of 2-3 pounds (or less). While that may be fine on a controlled range environment, it's just asking for trouble during rougher circumstances, particularly those involving stress! One of the initial casualties of adrenaline is fine-motor skills, at which point a "hair trigger" will be a liability. Since even justifiable use of deadly force will likely result in a trip through the legal system, a "reasonable pull" is advised.

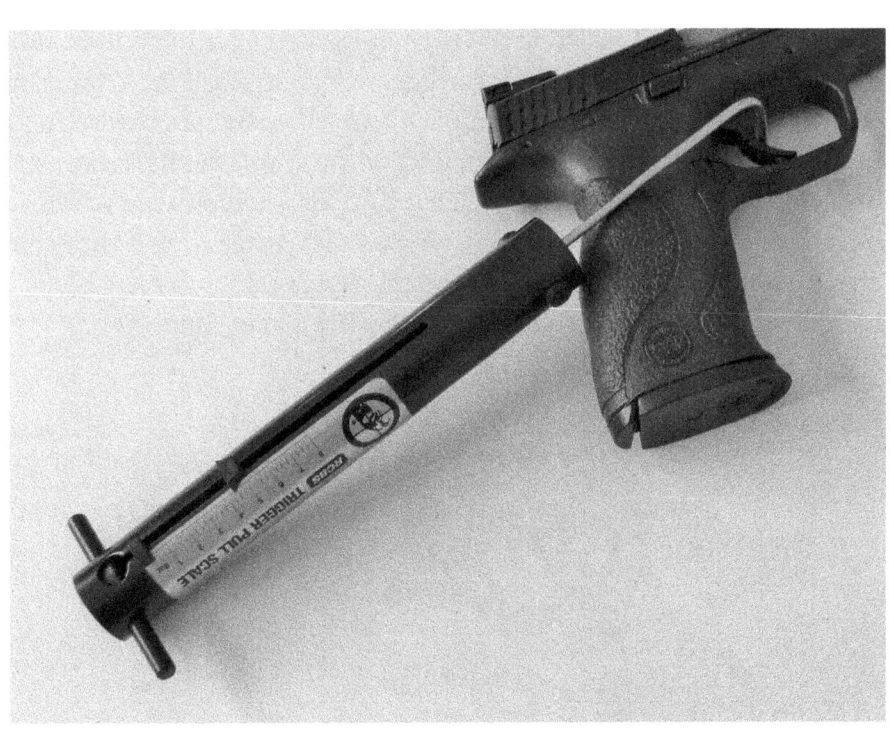

Pull weight is measured by a trigger scale, but other factors count, including smoothness, travel - and safety!

Revolvers. Regardless of the type, single-action pulls tend to be light, running 2 ½ -5 pounds. A double-action type will offer a heavier, longer, and more deliberate trigger-cocking mode which can exceed 10 pounds but, defensively, this will work fine if the action is smooth. A medium-frame S&W is an example of such a gun, geared toward defensive double-action shooting. The perennial .38 Special Model 10 (still in production today) was a hugely popular law enforcement choice for good reason. Like S&W's larger frame revolvers, its hammer is powered by a long leaf spring which compresses during double-action in a smooth and consistent manner. The hammers of S&W's smallest J-frames are powered by coil springs due to space constraints and, although ignition is reliable, their D/A pull tends to "stack" as the coils are compressed. The result is a stiffer trigger pull toward the end of the cycle; still manageable, but lacking the silkiness of the larger frames. Today, coil springs are quite common among other manufacturers, but recent geometric refinements have overcome some of the stacking issues.

Pistols. Single-actions like the 1911 can be tuned to run with short, crisp triggers of less than 3 lbs., but that's too light for general-purpose use where a 4 ½ - 5 ½ lb. pull is the safer bet. Most double-action pistols run a bit heavier in S/A mode (maybe 5-6 lbs.), with stout D/A pulls that can exceed revolver standards. Striker-fired types like a Glock, S&W M&P, etc., tend to run around 5 ½ - 6 ½ lbs. with a slightly mushier pull that remains consistent. That is, until people start adding after-market parts that can reduce the release to around 3 lbs. I'd never consider holstering a 1911 of any type with its safety "off," but that's essentially where you're at with some striker-fired trigger mods - in most cases with no provision for an active safety lever. After-market custom work involving tuned or lightened triggers can be asking for trouble during any post-shooting proceedings so the safer bet is a gun with a factory trigger. Fortunately, most of today's handguns are sold with manageable triggers if for no other reason than to survive in a crowded market.

Many people who obsess over lighter triggers could benefit more from proper training and practice. The idea is to avoid mashing the trigger, instead exerting good tactile control. In practice, after breaking a shot, the idea is to hold the trigger fully rearward for a nanosecond and then ease it forward just to the point where sear engagement occurs; somewhere before full forward trigger travel. This takes practice and reset won't be mastered without full tactile awareness, but the reward will be greatly improved control and accuracy. That said, defensively, the whole idea is probably overblown for all but a handful of highly trained professionals. Adrenaline wreaks havoc on fine motor skills and most engagements are up close and personal anyway. Plus, a reset is absent on any double-action systems, including revolvers that have withstood the test of time.

Refinements to the 1911 Government Model typically begin with precise fitting, good sights, and tuned triggers. The result will be a shootable pistol like this S&W, chambered for .45 ACP.

Sights. Most factory-issue aiming systems are just variations of an age-old principle employing front and rear sights. In theory, when both are properly aligned on a target, a hit should result. This assumes they are properly regulated to the gun, and can also be seen by the shooter. Lighting, background, and visual acuity can affect the latter, more so with older eyes. Fortunately, several clever new sight designs have appeared to counter these concerns. Other recent aiming technologies include optical sights such as scopes, dot-sights, and lasers.

THE HANDGUN RUB

A poorly chosen gun is a hindrance at best, but even the best pick will offer challenges simply because a handgun is so darned hard to master. Proficiency won't come without practice and, as distances increase (or targets shrink), well-aimed shots will become increasingly necessary. Centered hits also count during practice, simply because they inspire confidence. But, since there is more to aiming systems than first meets the eye (sorry), a dedicated chapter follows.

CHAPTER 6
SIGHTS, LASERS, AND LIGHTS

Have you noticed that many older handguns have minimal sights? Some seem more like afterthoughts. The original U.S. 1911 Government .45 comes to mind with its tiny front blade. But for starters, pistol craft was different then, and shooters had eyes that weren't fried by artificial lighting, TVs, monitors, or other electronics. I used such a pistol with good effect as a young soldier but those days are over. Many modern pocket-type pistols are still produced with small sights, the rationale being distances will be close and they'll be less likely to snag on clothing. It's a logical justification, but I'll take a set of sights I can *see*.

By the time most of us hit our mid-forties, Presbyopia has begun to set in. Printed text becomes fuzzy, and those afflicted will suddenly need longer arms, brighter light, or glasses to resolve small details. There's a good chance one of these details will be that front sight! For me, the choices are a set of store-bought reading glasses, bigger and brighter sights, or both. Since, like most folks, I don't normally wander around with reading glasses, my compromise solution is a bold set of sights - often of an aftermarket design. A fiber-optic design can help quite a bit, especially when those store-bought reading glasses are elsewhere. More drastic measures could include an electronic dot-sight. Dot-sights are becoming more mainstream thanks to miniaturized designs, but they introduce the foibles of electronics, not to mention extra expense. Lasers *have* become main stream, but should be considered auxiliary system due to battery life and background light. Positive identification of friend or foe justifies the need for an effective light. Some manufacturers now incorporate both features within one weapon-mounted unit but, despite these technological gains, a good set of sights remains worthwhile.

SIGHT FUNDAMENTALS

As noted, we believe a case can be made for un-aimed fire, otherwise known as "point-shooting." In fact, many supposedly "trained" shooters resort to it - despite intentions to the contrary. The basic tenets of marksmanship are abandoned during moments of sheer panic. Results speak for themselves, with surprisingly low hit statistics, running below 20% among uniformed personnel during close range encounters. Although we incorporate point-shooting techniques within our handgun programs, we keep the ranges *very* short, running from contact distance out to three yards, maximum. Beyond that, out to maybe nine yards, we go with "combat sighting," which is essentially a rough sight-picture with the front sight located on the threat. As distances increase, more aiming refinement is necessary. Assuming proper alignment of both sights has been established, clear focus on the front sight is the key to handgun accuracy. A fully established sight picture offers the best odds of putting rounds on target at any range. To that end, a set of sights that can be quickly acquired helps!

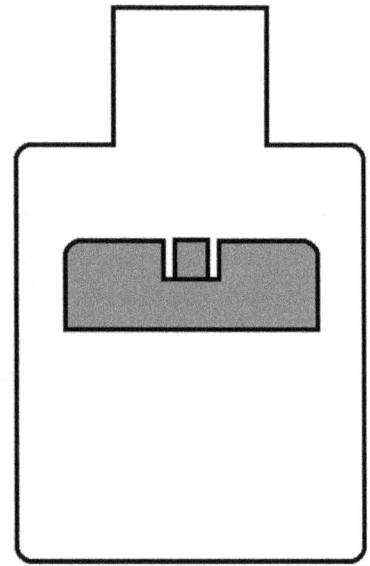

When the front and rear sights are aligned on a target (in this case a combat silhouette), a "sight picture" results. Focus should be on the front sight!

Old eyes introduce challenges, but so does lighting. A fiber-optic element won't work in total darkness, but will stand out as daylight fades.

Different-colored elements can eliminate alignment confusion. No-snag contours provide a defensive edge, and dovetailed slides permit changes. A set-screw affords extra insurance against movement.

Mounting. Many sights are mounted in dovetail cuts, but some front sights are staked or pinned in place. A few are even made from plastic, while others are forged as an integral part of the handgun for maximum durability. Although a one-piece design is strong, I often look for a handgun featuring replaceable sights. With a fixed-sighted handgun, it may then be possible to install a front sight of a different height for elevation corrections. Windage – left or right – can be adjusted through minor lateral movements of a rear sight in its dovetail. A gun with adjustable sights makes life simpler, since elevation and windage can be tweaked through rear sight movements. Still, it's always nice to be able to install a different front sight, suited to personal needs.

A few other design details. A no-snag design is helpful on a handgun slated for concealed carry. Sharp-edged sights can tear up holsters or clothing while interfering with a draw. Sleek-bodied sights are an obvious solution, and one of the more popular rear-sight designs is the streamlined Novak with its forward-sloping contour. Many manufacturers offer it as a non-adjustable version with a pair of white dots and more recently, an adjustable version has appeared. Some also now offer a small ledge just above the slide. A forward 90-degree surface on a rear sight body can prove invaluable if single-handed operation is ever necessary. Hooking a rear sight against a belt edge can cycle a slide through a downward shove. Granted, this is more of an advanced skill, but it's still one worth understanding.

FIXED AND ADJUSTABLE SIGHTS

Fixed sights are "built-in," affording little or no means to regulate bullet impacts. However, most are inherently strong and less prone to disturbance. Adjustable sights contain extra parts, but provide latitude to compensate for various impact points caused by different shooting styles or ammunition types.

Fixed sights. Semiautomatic pistols operate most reliably within narrow pressure parameters, so they can often be built with regulated fixed sights. The typical design employs a reciprocating slide to which both the rear and front sights are securely attached. One or both may be mounted in dovetail cuts that permit some horizontal adjustment. Look closely and a small set-screw may be visible in the rear sight. Its job is to help prevent drift within the dovetail. Regardless of whether this feature is present, most stay put thanks to a very tight press-fit. They can often be budged, but the right tools and knowledge will be necessary, along with some caution. It's possible to damage the gun or a night sight element with indiscriminate pounding. Elevation is factory-set, although front sights of varying heights are sometimes available. A taller front-sight will lower point-of-impact (POI), but a different load can sometimes accomplish the same thing with velocity and recoil differences. When trying a new fixed-sighted handgun, a standard load makes a good starting point. Odds are better of achieving closer POI than more exotic ultra-fast or heavier, slow alternatives.

A proper fixture can move dovetailed sights without inflicting damage.

Lacking a sight fixture, damage is possible. This night-sight lost its Tritium element.

Revolvers aren't functionally dependent on recoil forces and can digest a broader array of ammunition. A .357 Magnum revolver can also digest lower-velocity .38 Specials so, considering the various bullet weights in each caliber, varying POI should be expected. Those considering both loads may appreciate adjustable sights and, although they'll be a bit less rugged, the trade-off could be worthwhile. Many smaller revolvers are equipped with short barrels and snag-free fixed sights for optimum concealed carry. The rear sight will typically be a simple groove, milled into the top of the frame. The front sight is often an integral blade so the whole sighting arrangement is quite literally "fixed." Our old S&W Model 65s were surprisingly well regulated for our duty loads. I never hesitated to randomly grab one for a live-fire demonstration, and even an occasional fly was vaporized from seven paces on a friendly bet. However, at long distances, or for hunting, I'll take adjustable sights.

Adjustable sights. I find there's nothing quite as aggravating as a firearm that won't shoot to its sights. This is a bigger deal with rifles, which offer more precision, but it can still pose problems at shorter handgun ranges. Granted, you can employ "Kentucky Windage," holding lower, higher, left, or right, to compensate for impact discrepancies; but it's just one more loose end that'll invariably bite you in the butt. A few fast-paced 10-yard runs through six falling 8" steel plates will illustrate the foibles of this technique. From a combat perspective, a handgun that will place its chosen load right on top of the front sight at around 15 yards will serve admirably. Adjustable sights can provide this capability, probably with latitude for other distances and loads. In fact, with an accurate handgun up to the task, I may establish a final zero out at 50 yards.

The fixed sights on this S&W Model 65 are rugged, and also well-regulated for most common loads.

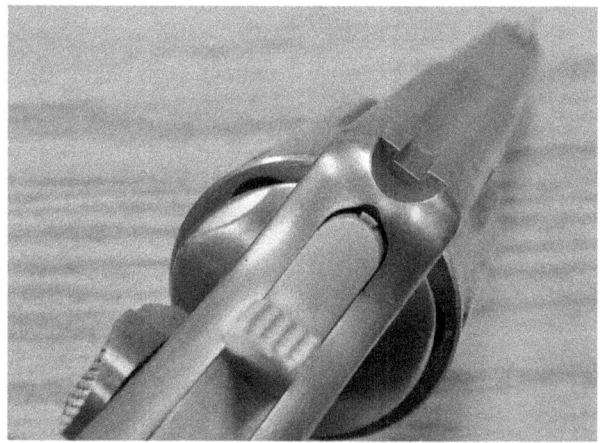

Like other tried and true revolvers, the Model 65's fixed rear sight is entirely "built in".

Most commonly, the rear sight is used to adjust point of impact (POI). For example, moving the rear sight upwards will cause bullets to strike higher. Finite adjustments are often accomplished using screws with click-stops. Sometimes, little directional arrows provide cues for elevation (up & down), or windage (left & right). Small witness lines are occasionally engraved to reference miniscule movements, and it usually won't take much to change POI. Lacking this feature, you can scribe a temporary pencil mark to serve as a guide. Clicks are also helpful because you can count them. Ideally, the final adjustment will locate the rear sight somewhere around the middle of its range, providing sufficient latitude for other loads. Some metallic silhouette aficionados even use feeler gauges to determine and record various rear sight settings. Others just note the requisite number of clicks.

The windage and elevation screws on this S&W adjustable rear will accommodate various loads. They have tactile clicks for precise, repeatable movements.

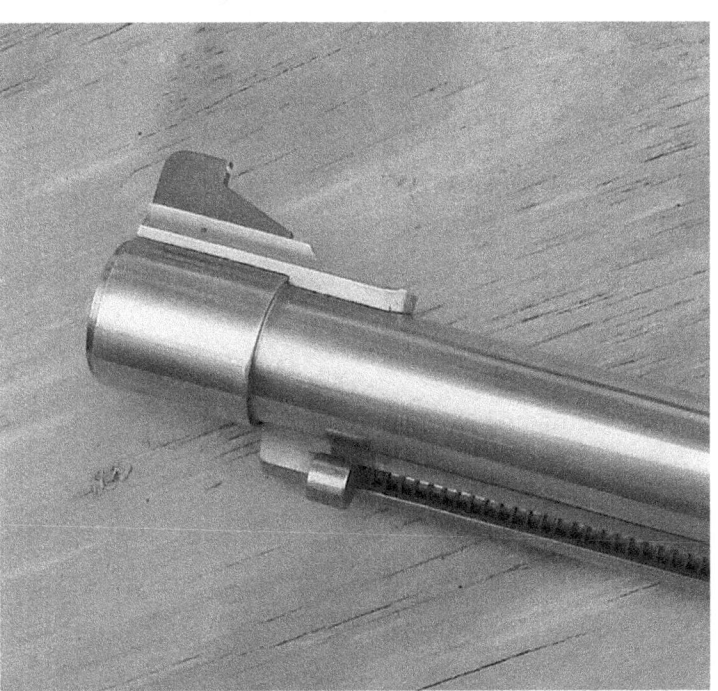

Once sight alignment is understood an elevation bar makes sense. The extra line offers a precise point of reference for long-range holdover.

Always move the rear sight in the same direction you want your bullets to go. For example, moving the rear sight toward the left will cause a corresponding leftward POI shift. You're really changing the relationship of the sighting plane to the bore. Picture an imaginary rear sight of some ridiculous height, like six inches. Then extend a line from its upper surface through the top edge of the front sight, to a target around ten paces away. At that point, the barrel will be pointed grossly uphill, resulting in an extremely high shot. Lowering the rear sight should eventually cause everything to coincide. Got it? Good, because everything happens in reverse with the front sight!

It should be noted that POI differences are possible between shooters. Sometimes these discrepancies are minor, but larger variations can exist. No two individuals will see a sight picture in the exact same manner, and physiological differences can contribute to this phenomenon. Why? Because the bullet is traveling through the barrel as the handgun climbs in recoil. A strong shooter with a solid grip will experience less upward gun movement, which can result in somewhat lower POI. For what it's worth, the installation of a different set of grips can also affect point-of-impact. A soft rubber grip can improve hand purchase, limiting recoil-induced rotation, resulting in lower POI.

Occasionally, we'll run into a shooter with an extreme shot-group deviation. Sometimes we'll be asked to try the handgun, just to see how things pan out. After many moons of shooting I know I'm fairly neutral when it comes to sight regulation. Often, the problem lies with the shooter rather than the gun, but sometimes things really can be out of whack. A loose rear sight may explain a windage issue, but so can non-centered sights - including the front one. A misaligned sight becomes obvious after eyeballing the gun, and even factory installations aren't immune from this problem. Factory sights of the wrong height can be encountered, more commonly with fixed types.

Here's where some type of replaceable front-sight design can save the day. Assuming POI is too high, a taller front sight could fix the problem. If the situation was reversed, filing down the front-sight might be easier than installing a shorter version. Changes to the height of a rear sight can accomplish the same thing, but recessed dots or inserts in either could give you grief. This is the beauty of a properly calibrated adjustable rear sight.

Fixed versus adjustable? For close-quarter defense and concealed carry use, fixed sights are good. There's little to go wrong and, despite the problems noted above, a handgun from a major manufacturer will likely have usefully regulated sights. When adding sporting use to the mix (hunting, plinking, etc.), adjustable sights have value. Sights that can be seen in other than ideal conditions are equally important! For defensive carry, so is a no-snag design. Look for rounded corners on the edges of an adjustable rear sight, and locate a well-fitted screwdriver for its windage and elevation screws.

SIGHT DESIGNS

Even with 20/20 vision, environmental factors can create difficulties. Target shooters often like flat-black sights for 6:00 holds on bullseyes, but as light fades and/or against darker targets, resolving them can become difficult. Fiber-optic designs are an eye-grabbing option for daylight use while remaining visible at dawn or dusk. In total darkness, forget it. Night sights solve this problem through small radioactive sight inserts which glow in the dark (and they also provide useful contrast against many daytime targets). Three-dot sights are another common but more basic type, often seen on pistols.

Fiber-optic sights. I like these sights because they grab my tired old eyes in almost any light except true darkness. This increasingly popular design employs small plastic rods imbedded within the sights, their ends glowing brightly from nothing more than ambient light. The rear notch may have a pair of elements - one per side, with a single insert up front. Others use a F/O front sight alone. Since I have trouble seeing red, I shop for those with green front elements. The little plastic rods can sometimes be switched using built-in retainers, or replaced using a nail clipper and butane lighter. The material is sold through the more serious shooting emporiums and it's worth having a few replacement rods on hand.

The earlier F/O designs were fragile but things have improved. Still, these sights are best for sporting or range use. Maximum durability counts for defensive use and, although they are protected by the sight bodies themselves, some of the plastic inserts are tiny. This concern hasn't deterred combat match shooters from adopting F/O sights in a big way though. The green front sight on my five-inch S&W M&P Pro Model is highly effective on combat-type courses. The rear sight is just flat-black, for a non-cluttered image that's quick to resolve.

Several of my S&W revolvers are similarly equipped for sporting use. Although they won't replace true night sights, the fiber-optic elements remain visible in light that would render conventional iron sights useless. I love them in the woods, particularly during early morning or late afternoon. If a F/O aiming system is considered for a general-purpose handgun, consider one with enough surrounding metal to work without its element. That way you'll still have a small hole, which could still act like an element of sorts.

Night sights. Tritium sights are a great defensive choice because they are always "on." Like fiber-optic types, small glowing elements are installed within the sights. The difference is that the night sight elements are small transparent vials, charged with radioactive Tritium gas. At some point they'll fade out, but their life is ten years or more. I just checked the set on my .45 Kimber Eclipse and they're dimmer, but still going after 15 years. The oldest night sights on our S&W M&P duty pistols are only half that age and plenty bright. During night-fire ranges, a pair of glowing dots is visible in each shooter's holster from behind the firing line. These are the two elements imbedded in the rear sight. They are a potential giveaway during exposed nocturnal carry, but most civilian users will use a concealed system. Once on target, acquiring a useful low-light sight picture is a piece of cake. In fact, we often see marksmanship improve somewhat, probably for no other reason than complete attention to the sight picture.

The green fiber-optic front sight of this big-bore S&W is highly visible in the woods. It's a factory installation, secured by a traverse pin.

The factory night sights on our large inventory of older S&W Model 4006s held up well throughout the service life of the guns, and our newer M&Ps may be a bit more durable. One prime suspect in the few failures we've seen is caustic cleaning agents. Some of them can attack the sealant that bonds the vials, causing loss of gas. Also, even though the vials are well protected within metal sight bodies, a sharp blow can kill an element. For this reason, those considering aftermarket units will be better served through a professional installation involving a special vise-type fixture.

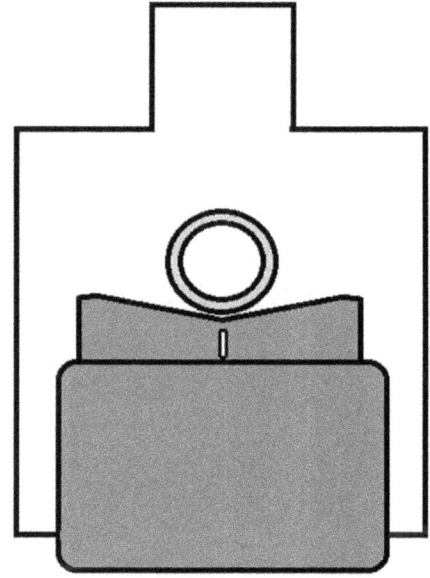

XS "Big Dot" sights support fast close-quarter shooting. The front has a highly visible Tritium night-sight element.

Alignment of XS "Big Dot" sights: Float the front dot in the shallow express rear V and superimpose it on the target.

The XS Big Dot front sight, which seems only slightly smaller than a bowling ball, is floated above a shallow express-type V rear blade. This aiming system gained favor among African professional hunters for fast, close shooting on dangerous game. Although the similar XS arrangement may seem imprecise, it affords fast combat-grade accuracy in all lighting conditions. An identical set on a slightly larger S&W 9mm Shield has proven surprisingly effective during dynamic shooting drills, being fast to acquire and easy to see when shooting on the move. The XS line changed during early 2018, with some new names for existing products, plus a very interesting version incorporating a bold, deep rear sight notch that should meld speed with precision.

An accurate five-inch 1911 pistol would benefit from a more refined sight picture, and more precise designs are available from a number of manufacturers. A downside to Tritium-powered sights is their cost. Anyone considering a set will probably be better off by purchasing a night sight equipped handgun right from the start.

Dual fiber-optic/night sight designs. Sounds like the best of both worlds! They're a recent design which you can see the concept on the Truglo website. Look for their *Brite-Sites*, which are also listed by various distributors. They're also now offered as a factory option on several well-known pistols. Again, consider a proper means of installation prior to an aftermarket purchase.

Three-dot sights. This lower-cost option often comes standard on defensive pistols. Instead of imbedded elements, shallow circular depressions are filled with white paint to improve combat-type sight acquisition. Lately, some luminescent versions have appeared which require exposure to light for activation.

Some shooters hate these sights, preferring the simplicity of plain black types. During proper sight alignment, the front blade is centered in the rear notch, with the tops of both on the same plane. Trouble is, the dots don't always coincide with a level front and rear alignment. This can really discombobulate some shooters for understandable reasons. Worst case, it's easy enough to cover the dots with blobs of permanent marker (Shooter's choice solvent will dissolve it later if desired). We've also seen plenty of front sight indents filled with orange or yellow paint. The tip of a toothpick makes a good applicator for this.

I just tune out the dots when they don't coincide with the sight tops. The three-dot sights work for me against targets of varying colors including B-27 black combat silhouettes. They're also cheaper to produce than F/O or Tritium types.

MORE DETAILS

If some sort of element-enhanced aiming system is chosen, consider front and rear patterns that are different. This visual cue can prevent misalignment errors during low light or fast-paced situations. Some shooters will pick up three identical dots during night-fire events, thinking the middle dot is the front sight. In actuality, the front dot might be the one on the far left or right. The result will be a shot far off the mark, even at relatively close range.

Three-dot sights are common and many are fixed types.

As we know, some sights can be integral to a handgun. This is often the case with small pocket pistols and revolvers, the rationale being they'll be used for last-ditch defense at card table distances. Since presentation may occur from a pocket, no-snag sights are preferred. In fact, a few small handguns have been sold without any sights at all. The idea is to point-shoot as fast as possible. In our experience, this technique can work, but you'd better be darned close! Personally, I'll take a *visible* set of sights every time. Some of the hardest to pick up are stainless (or nickel) front sights, typically of integral designs bearing the same finish as a barrel or slide.

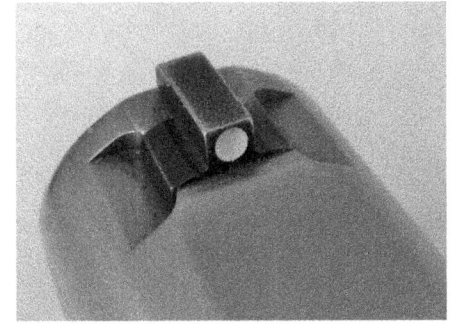

The small indent containing a dot can be filled with a dab of visible paint - or, if dovetailed, exchanged for a different sight.

Baughman front ramp. Our old duty-sized S&W M-65 revolvers come to mind with their sloping front sight blades, designed to clear holsters. A series of fine serrations was applied to the face which helped reduce reflections, but the shiny stainless finish was still bright enough to cause problems. Since the blade was an integral part of the barrel, an expedient fix involved swiping the surface with a black felt-tipped marker.

The Model 65's integral Baughman ramp can be hard to see in sunlight, but it's nearly indestructible.

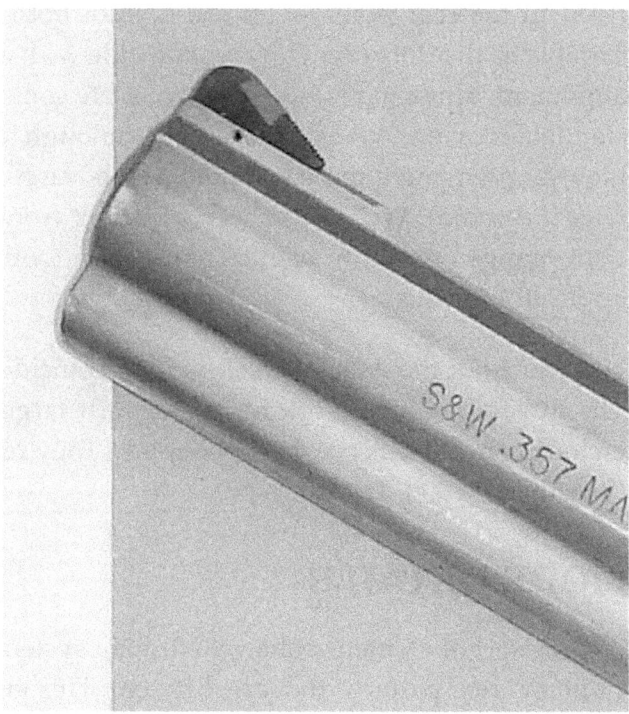

S&W has been offering revolvers with "red ramp" front sights for years, often with a white-outline rear.

Front colored inserts (non-F/O). These differ from fiber-optic inserts. S&W has sold plenty of revolvers with small red plastic inserts, dovetailed into their front ramps through the sides. The resulting image presents a colored face section, and a small white outline surrounding an adjustable rear sight notch often accompanies this option. The red-ramp feature works for many shooters but is of little use for me. For starters, I have trouble seeing red, but low light can raise problems for everyone. I sometimes just give them the same black Magic Marker treatment.

Front "Patridge" blade. Some experienced shooters prefer flat-black sights, and often the front blade will be a "Patridge." Its vertical rear surface presents a sharp 90-degree edge for precise alignment with a rear sight and the target. The front sight's forward corner is often rounded for easier re-holstering, but the sharp edge can snag during a draw. I own a few handguns with Patridge front sights and, while they do present nice sharp sight pictures, they serve mostly as range guns.

Picture a small shiny brass ball, inserted into the rear of a Patridge front sight blade. It's a good enough eye-grabber that the sharp upper edge can be softened a bit to reduce snagging. Before the advent of F/O front sights, the Mc Givern was among my favorites. It still works well and offers better durability than many of today's plastic inserts.

Interchangeable front sights. Examine a newer S&W revolver and you may spot a small cross-pin, located just below the front sight blade. If so, the blade, which is seated within a longitudinal barrel slot, can be swapped for a custom version. However, a replacement blade will not have the corresponding pin hole

A "Patridge" front sight is popular among target shooters who normally shoot in well-lit conditions. The F/O unit is less precise but better in the field. Worse case, its cross-pin permits a change.

so it must be located and then drilled (with caution). A few S&W DX models employ a clever retaining system with a forward-facing, spring-loaded plunger. Ruger used a similar design with their Red Hawks but it has since been replaced by a front dovetail cut. This same system seems to be catching on with pistols, presenting opportunities for after-market sights. A key concern for all is a replacement of the correct height, needed to avoid elevation errors.

Bo-Mar rear sights. The refinement of the 1911 as a target pistol involved more than better fitting. A precise aiming system was necessary and Bo-Mar had the solution. Many of today's higher-end 1911 pistols incorporate a version of this fully adjustable rear sight, which is "melted" into the slide. Careful machining of a special "Bo-Mar Cut," allows the entire rear sight to be inset for a low-profile system (there are two versions of the cut). Positive click-stops permit precise windage and elevation adjustments, and rear blades may be a flat-black or insert types. Some also have rounded corners,

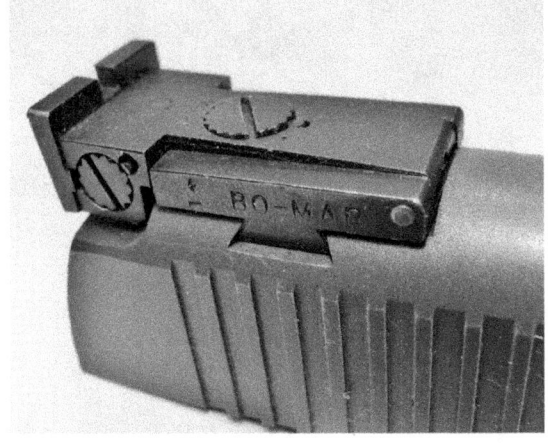

The precise Bo-Mar rear is a classic target sight. The 1911's slide has been machined for its low-profile installation.

Adjustable sights can also fight. Tritium vials and rounded corners cover most bases.

which make more sense in holsters. Still, a Bo-Mar sight, by nature of its design, is more susceptible to damage during hard use. For this reason, one rugged rear sight design became a popular defensive alternative...

No one will deny the ruggedness of a Novak. The design is rock-solid and it employs a sloping profile to minimize snagging. The front edge is flush (or nearly so) with the slide, while the higher rear end is machined to provide a clean aiming notch. A slide with a "Novak Cut" is one machined to accommodate this type of rear sight. Both fixed and adjustable versions are sold with three-dot, Tritium, or F/O inserts. The design is popular enough to be standard-issue for many manufacturers, most being fixed three-dot types. Some include a small set-screw for extra insurance against lateral movement, but most are pressed in with impressive force – possibly by The Incredible Hulk.

Slide-racking note: the only gripe I have with a Novak design involves single-handed slide-racking, where the sight is hooked against a belt. The sloping profile kills this technique, but some modified versions now have a corner to solve this concern. It's anal perhaps but, defensively, the devil is in the details. I must not be the only one thinking this way since a forward ledge of some sort is now more common among factory-issued sights.

Other sights. Dawson Precision offers a great assortment of excellent handgun sights, along with installation services. When I shopped for an adjustable replacement rear sight for my 5-inch S&W 9mm M&P Pro, Dawson was the first stop. Their streamlined proprietary unit easily replaced the factory

A basic but streamlined Novak rear sight with a set-screw for extra insurance.

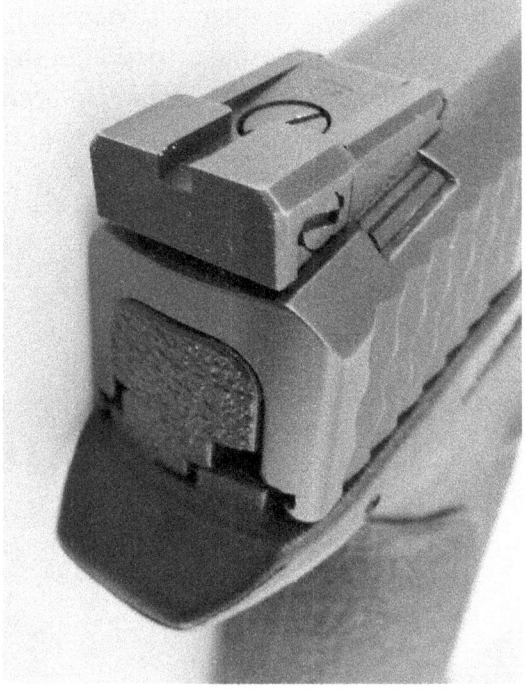

Dawson's adjustable rear is a refinement of the basic Novak. Its rounded corners and forward shelf are practical improvements.

fixed sight, permitting plenty of adjustment for a variety of loads. Dawson also sells other great choices from firms like LPA, Heinie, Warren Tactical, etc. Several of my 1911s sport Dawson Fiber-Optic front sights, backed up by a collection of spare green rods. Brownells is another good source with a large variety of front and rear sights from Truglo, Hiviz, Meprolight, Trijicon, Ed Brown, and others.

Fitting and tools. Whenever dovetails are involved, expect a tight fit! Without one, the reciprocating slide would quickly cause loosening or loss of a sight. A hobby gunsmith can be in for a real challenge just removing an original sight, let alone installing a replacement. While it *can* be done with a brass or aluminum drift-punch and a hammer, the specter of damage is real. Aftermarket purchasing also requires sights with matching dovetails, built to proper heights. Front sight width will also need to be visually compatible with a rear sight's notch, whether for target or combat shooting use. The specialty sight-pushing fixtures are expensive enough to justify a gunsmith's services. And again, all things considered, Tritium night sights are probably a better overall deal when purchased as a factory option.

PRACTICALITY VERSUS PRECISION

One custom 1911 in my safe is a real tack-driver. The gunsmith's test target reveals much potential and my own results back it up. However, this pistol is set up for defensive use with fairly bold and de-horned adjustable night sights. Its wide front sight is easy to pick up and the sloping outer edges of the rear sight's blade are snag-free. The gun is also "Commander" size with a shorter, four-inch barrel. It performs exactly as intended, but I can shoot a couple less accurate, factory-built, five-inch 1911s better – depending on conditions. The less costly rivals have adjustable target-type rea sights with square-shouldered blades. The front sights are taller, narrow, front posts with F/O inserts. They align precisely, affording an excellent sight picture on just about any target – assuming enough light exists to see them…

Bold versus fine sights. For combat-type shooting, my custom 1911 is hard to beat. Its bold sight picture can be acquired on the move, in any light, from various positions and, if I do my part, bullets will strike darned close to the front sight. However, as range increases, the somewhat less accurate production guns begin to shine. The difference becomes apparent somewhere around 25 - 30 yards, and at 50 yards it's obvious. When aiming at large, humanoid-type silhouettes from fifty paces, the custom gun's sights blot out much of the target. The finer sights on the production-class pistols permit more precise aiming, which inspires confidence. As such, it's possible to back out further, switching to 75-yard neck holds for trajectory compensation. Lobbing bullets into a 100-yard steel IPSC target is doable by holding on its "head." At that range, just about the entire target will disappear behind the coarser sights on my custom gun, but for real-world use, who cares? Odds are any defensive use will be up close and dirty, probably in low light, where a set of highly visible sights will be a whole lot more useful. Try shooting on the move at a fast-paced walking speed to a get an idea of what's involved.

If the wheels fall completely off our current social order, well, then anything goes. In that case, some extra longer-range capability *could* be reassuring. Meanwhile, a 50-100-yard civilian engagement seems iffy at best from any legal point of view. Justifiable use of deadly force is predicated upon a reasonable belief that such force is *necessary*, meaning there is no other *reasonable* alternative. Extreme distance throws both tenets into doubt, and even a 25-yard shot could be questionable.

The large XS Big Dots on my small S&W Shield might cover up a Buick at longer distances, but again, so what? I fired this 9mm extensively with its factory sights and was impressed by its accuracy (it also shot right to the sights at 15 yards). After installing the giant XS Sights, POI remained unchanged, group sizes still looked useful, and Ninja-type CQB maneuvers yielded highly effective hits on Q-targets. Back around 25-yards, groups opened somewhat compared to previous results, but the trade-off was more than acceptable.

This entirely useful group was fired offhand from 15 yards, using a 9mm S&W Shield, fitted with XS Big Dots.

OPTICAL SIGHTS

Here, we're talking about sighting systems with lenses of some sort. The big three are handgun scopes, so-called "dot-sights," and lasers.

Scopes. Thompson Center Arms and Remington probably did more to promote handgun scopes than anyone. The arrival of accurate Contender and XP-100 single-shot handguns created a need for maximum aiming precision to fully exploit their rifle cartridge capabilities. A few major optics manufacturers responded with dedicated handgun scopes and a new era of long-range handgunning commenced. I enjoyed great results with these "hand-rifles" on varmint hunts, using cartridges like .22 Hornet, .223 Remington, etc. With careful shooting, rifle-like groups were possible, so woodchucks inside 200 yards were in mortal danger using improvised rests. I eschewed a holster in favor of a sling, which could also be used as a neck-tensioned brace. One of our cadre has a 4X Leupold mounted to an S&W .41 Magnum revolver for use on deer. He carries this rig in a chest-mounted holster which helps support its extra mass.

Adding a scope to an accurate handgun will often result in dramatic improvements on bullseyes, especially from a rest. However, unsupported shooting takes some getting used to, since every tremor or wobble is magnified. Extra practice will also be needed to efficiently locate targets through a scope held at arm's length. True handgun scopes are built with much longer eye-relief to accommodate this position, but due to the involved optical physics, field-of-view can become relatively small. Higher magnification will result in an even smaller FOV (the area visible through the scope), while perceived tremors will also increase. Less magnification is the more practical solution, but the whole scope-mounted handgun package will still be large.

A specialized hunting revolver from muzzle to grips: This customized Ruger single-action sports a Leupold 2.5-8 handgun scope. The three mounting rings help resist the recoil of its potent, flat-shooting, .300 GNR chambering. Odds of finding spare ammo are close to zero.

Strictly as a sport-shooting proposition, a scoped handgun is fine. Defensively, I'll pass.

Dot-sights. This aiming system should not be confused with a laser-sight. The latter projects a narrow beam used for aiming, while the former has more in common with a scope. One dot-sight difference though is lack of any magnification. This solves eye-relief issues and wobbles are much less pronounced. Field-of-view is not optically reduced, so an image viewed through the sight becomes an extension of the surrounding area.

Dot-sight types. The initial versions were similar to scopes, with tubular bodies that housed an electronically powered, non-magnified red element in lieu of crosshairs. Placement of a bright dot upon the target eliminated the need for front/rear sight alignment and the dot arrangement turned out to be both intuitive and fast – assuming the dot popped immediately into view. Some disciplined competition handgun shooters embraced the technology with good results, developed after *lots* of practice. However, the sights themselves had large-diameter bodies of 30mm or more, requiring complex mounting systems and special holsters. Although some tube-type dots are still in use, a new generation of miniature red-dot sights has gained favor. Resembling tiny circa 1985 TV sets or computer monitors, they mount directly to handguns, adding only minimal bulk. On a shoulder-fired firearm either system works well, permitting almost instantaneous target acquisition. But, a handgun extended to arm's length presents a much less stabile image. Throw in the smaller housing of an MRDS and a dot hunt can result. I have several handguns so equipped, and I still struggle a bit with each one – from a speed point of view. On the other hand, for sporting purposes, the improvement over iron sights is dramatic.

Sights, Lasers, And Lights

A collection of dot sights: The Aimpoint (top) is battlefield tough with a price reflecting its quality. The tube-sights are affordable, while the Burris MRDS (bottom) falls in between.

Tube-type dot sights are getting tougher and smaller. This electronic Sig Romeo is designed for AR use, and backed up by folding irons.

Accuracy with a dot. My aging eyes have trouble resolving the clear front sight necessary for accurate shooting, whereas a dot handily solves this problem. True, it's aiming-point affords a bit less precision than a finer set of crosshairs, but results speak for themselves. If the dot is wandering around within the target, a decent hit is likely through proper trigger control. And, strangely, the shot-group is often much smaller than any perceived wobbles. Here's another phenomenon: groups are often smaller without any aiming point at all. I have recorded several excellent groups from fifty or even one hundred yards, using nothing more than white IPSC cardboard humanoid silhouettes. The dot is simply placed on the target's "chest" area, which seems counterintuitive until you try it. The good news is that this same technique relates to real-world shooting scenarios. Ever the consummate tinkerer, I managed to rig a long nylon sling to my S&W Model 629 revolver. It attaches to the QD studs seen on sporting rifles, and serves as a handy brace when the sling is looped cross-body. At full arm extension, everything tightens up for accurate offhand delivery of large .44 Magnum bullets.

More MRDS. Many of these miniaturized red-dot sights use a disk-type CR-1632 (or CR2032) battery to energize a small diode, located in the bottom of the sight. The light is reflected upward to a lens, for use as an aiming point. Dot sizes vary but many average 2-8 MOA. Since a "minute of angle" equals roughly one inch at 100 yards, at that distance, a 2 MOA dot will subtend roughly two inches. I like smaller dots, which afford a bit more precision (without obstructing smaller targets), but some speed-shooters go with larger dots for use on close-range combat silhouettes. We ran an inventory of AR-15 carbines with non-electronic Trijicon Reflex Sights for years. Their Tritium-powered lamps had 6.5 MOA dots, but we still made effective steel silhouette hits out to 300 yards or beyond. We have since switched to electronic Aimpoint Pro tube-type sights with 2 MOA dots. Battery life is measured in years, which is not the case with most MRDS types. In my experience, it's darned easy to find one with a dead battery that has somehow been stored "on." Better to discover this at the ranch with some hope of a spare, at which point a sight with an accessible battery compartment will

Dot sights can yield outstanding results. This 75-yard cluster of .44 Magnums was fired from an S&W Model 629. Note the absence of a precise aiming point.

The "dot" viewed from a shooter's perspective. Directions: Place dot on target and press trigger.

be greatly appreciated. Some units require dismounting for a battery swap from underneath. There's a good chance zero will be lost afterward, so a top-loading model makes more sense. A few also have motion-sensing cut-offs to help conserve power.

Miniaturized dots can be a nuisance in bad weather simply because of their shape. Unlike a tube-sight, lens caps are problematic. Most of them do have a removable plastic cover and some will power-down with it on. I use mine strictly for storage and go with the switch. I'll also admit to a fundamental mistrust of their long-term dependability, checking them often during use. However, the Burris Fast-Fire III on my 12 Gauge Beretta autoloading shotgun has so far survived two spring/fall turkey seasons with its original battery. Since three-inch Magnum turkey shells are energetic to say the least, I'll have to assume the sight is fairly durable. The latest FF-III generation also has a top-loading battery and is supposedly waterproof. Fast-fire

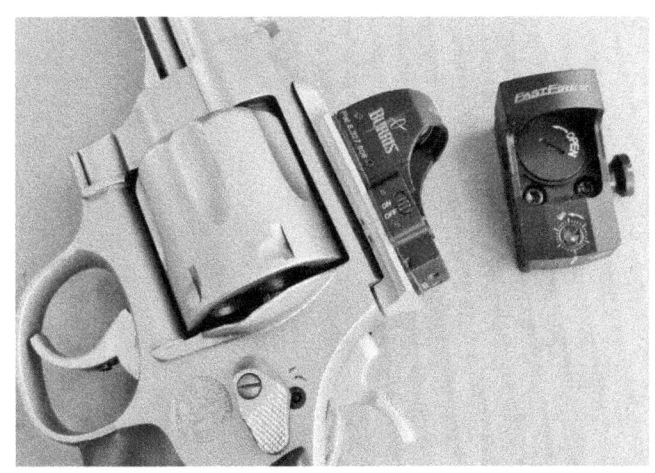

The latest Burris FFIII offers easy battery swaps thanks to its top-mounted compartment. But, the earlier FFII version will need to be removed from its base, resulting in loss of zero.

Sights, Lasers, And Lights | 89

IIs use a sliding on-off switch instead of an adjustable-intensity push-button, and dismounting is necessary for battery changes. Both types are still sold and I have one of each mounted on S&W .357 and .44 Magnum revolvers. So far, so good using small Alchin Bases, which replace the factory rear sights of newer S&W 3-hole drilled & tapped frames. Weaver's rugged base works just as well and Warne sells a rail with back-up iron sights installed.

The small Burris Fast-Fire sights could be described as "mid-priced," running around $235. I could see spending less on a .22 plinking pistol, but the extra cost of the higher-end models could easily be justified for any defensive purposes. Trijicon, C-More, Docter, Eotech, JP, Leupold, Vortex, and several other manufacturers offer MRDS products. Their mounting systems, although similar, have proprietary differences. The sight bodies are typically secured to separate base-plates using non-slip locating posts. The lower bases are machined to fit various firearms, and many ship with a Picatinny-type base.

<u>Optic-ready pistols.</u> The latest rage is the series of modified pistols from major manufacturers like S&W, Glock, SIG, FN, etc. Their slides are machined to accept MRDS optics, reflecting more widespread acceptance. I find the concept hard to resist – at least for range or outdoor use. Since the hole and stud patterns differ somewhat between dot-sight brands, the pistol manufacturers try to accommodate the more popular types. In some cases, the slides themselves become an integral base section for low-profile mounting. When not in use, an accessory cover-plate fills the relieved mounting section. Conventional sights are also furnished, and some are taller for use through the optic, providing back-up capability. One might question the survivability of an optical sight on a reciprocating pistol slide but apparently, it works. Based on my own experience with various Magnum 12 Gauge loads, I'm a believer. One neat thing about some "optic-ready" pistols is that they can be used with or without the MRDS installed. Just remember that the holster needs to fit!

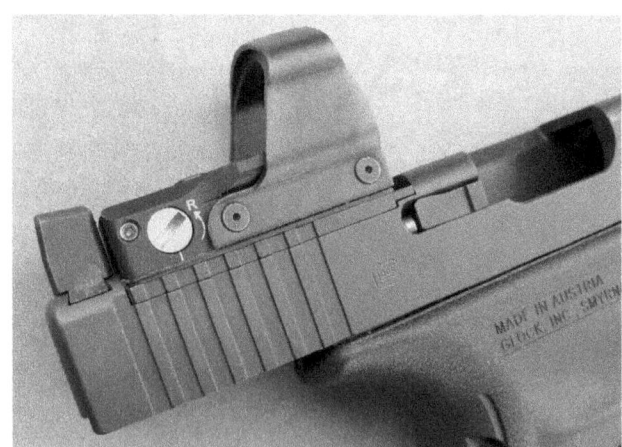

The slide of this Glock is machined for a mounting plate. The MRDS mounts to the plate. Unlike some others, its rear sight is independent of the plate.

Another tack: A complete, sight-equipped insert has been substituted for the optics mount. Either unit will screw to the machined slide of this customized Glock.

Limitations. A highly regarded long-time LEO connection recently corresponded about the use of dot-sights on defensive handguns. Turns out we independently arrived at the same conclusion: we'll pass – for now. A big problem is trying to find the dot at all with a hand-held system. Durability is another concern. The industry gaining ground, but we might not be there yet for tough defensive use. The sights also need to be powered up in advance, and although battery life is improving, it's not infinite. This raises real concerns about NO dot when one is needed. A possible back-up solution is an instant-on laser, since odds of both failing simultaneously should be less.

We really liked this system! Acquisition of the dot within Leupold's Delta-point Pro was extremely fast and intuitive. The shielded lens, although rugged, was backed up by decent iron sights. It's a game-changer!

Rear view of Leupold's Delta. Once zeroed, a hit should result - even if the dot isn't centered within the sight!

Stop the press. MRDS have finally gone mainstream for serious defensive use. The inevitable breakthrough resulted from recent efforts to improve battery life and construction. Looks like mission accomplished, based on SOCOM's adoption of Trijicon's Type 2 RMR! Aimpoint followed in 2019 with a new contender, their ACRO P-1. Others are in the works, designed to withstand the rigors of daily use, aboard reciprocating pistol slides (no small feat). With the bugs now largely worked out, law enforcement agencies are embracing the technology, which greatly simplify training. Low mounting and good pistol ergonomics also make dot acquisition much easier - in nearly any type of light. So, expect exponential growth and more good products.

LASERS AND LIGHTS

Light and laser systems have blossomed during recent years, with all sorts of high-tech possibilities. Numerous weapon-mounted laser systems now exist, so the concept has clearly advanced from a fringe novelty status to the norm. The same is true regarding the huge assortment of so-called tactical lights, as evidenced by a growing list of pistols with integral accessory rails; now often referred to as "rail guns." Revolvers so equipped are scarcer commodities but even rail-less semiautos won't be left completely in the dark. Where there's a need, some clever entrepreneur is almost guaranteed to fill it, with alternate laser mounting systems being one example.

Lasers. The laser concept involves projecting a concentrated red or green beam on to a target for use as an aiming point. In theory, if the firearm and laser are properly "sighted in," effective hits should be possible. Urban legend would also have us believe that the appearance of a laser on the chest of a threat could act as a strong deterrent; a theory which could have some merit – assuming the beam is even noticed. One issue involves locating the small spot during dynamic scenarios; especially in bright light, which poses additional challenges by itself. Throw in a busy background and the laser dot may be hard to pick up. When these conditions converge, recoil can bounce the laser off-target, increasing the time needed for reacquisition. Depending on the design, further drawback may be extra motions needed for activation the laser. The units themselves have come a long way, but they all require batteries. Some of the newer polymer pistols also pose mounting challenges, resulting in some semi-Rube Goldberg solutions.

We consider a laser an *extremely* useful accessory, rather than a complete substitute for sights. When viewed in this context, a laser can provide a few unique capabilities, including the ability to fire from cover with minimal exposure. Also, many smaller handguns have minimal sights which are hard enough to use in ideal light, let alone low-light conditions. Here is where a laser can really "shine" – assuming it can quickly be activated. Some designs require an awkward grip shift (or even the use of the support hand) to get them into action. A great solution is the grip-activated system developed by Crimson Trace, and a handgun with replaceable grips is the perfect host for this technology. One CT panel contains a battery and the other has an integral laser diode that projects from its upper surface. The diode is located high enough to clear a shooter's hand, and a small squeeze-pad activates the la-

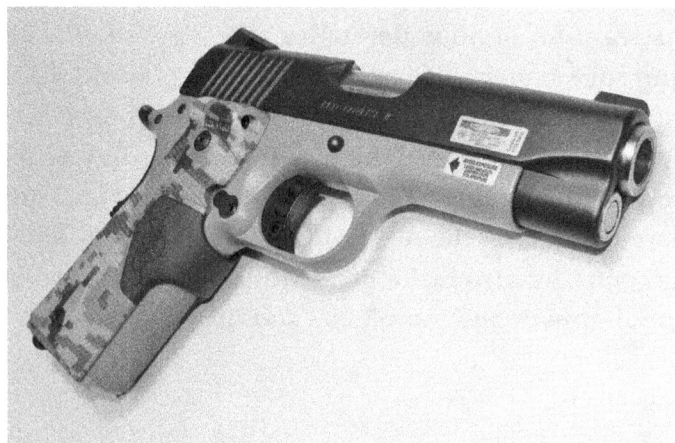

Squeeze-activated Crimson Trace Laser-Grips, installed on a 1911 pistol. The actual laser is visible in the upper corner of the grip.

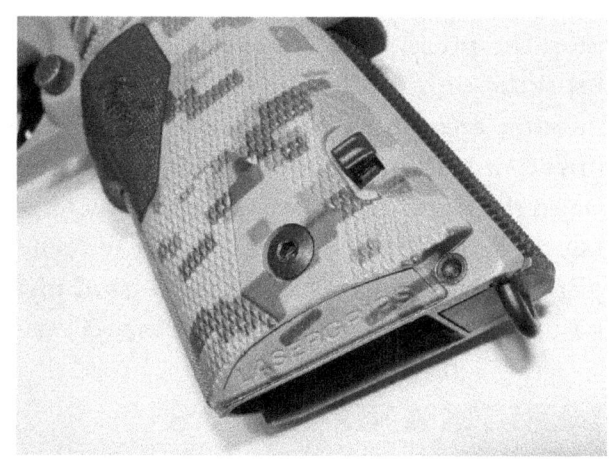

If desired, the Crimson Trace laser can be deactivated by a simple on/off switch.

ser. A separate on/off switch will also power the unit at the user's discretion. Small set-screws permit fine adjustments for final laser sight-in and, if the handgun's sights are on the money, laser zero is as simple as adjusting the beam to coincide while both systems are aimed at a target. A couple strong contenders for laser grips are D/A revolvers and 1911 pistols with easily replaceable grips. Of course, there are plenty of other designs with innovative approaches, including rail-mounted systems, and even guide-rod replacement types. Green lasers are also making inroads on the classic red types, with claims of improved visibility.

Extra insurance. A small D/A revolver is a strong laser-grip candidate. Its sights will probably be rudimentary and engagements will likely be close-range affairs, with a good chance of poor lighting to boot. As mentioned, a laser could provide extra insurance for use with red dot sights. I nearly went with the factory laser option for my small S&W .380 Bodyguard pistol, but the on-off button was a bit too awkward for my taste. However, thanks to today's competitive laser market, I can always add one later – something worth considering *prior* to a handgun purchase.

HG-6 Sight Laser Integral: <u>Carry.</u> Holster fit is another concern. The laser-grip versions will be less of an issue, but most forward-mounted designs can cause problems. Lately, some useful weapon-mounted combination laser and light units have appeared, as covered below. This technology nicely solves potential low-light issues from threat identification to aiming. The latest trend, all for the good, is a polymer-frame pistol with a molded-in laser, located ahead of the trigger guard. This design offers a streamlined profile which may or may not fit an existing holster. If not, the holster makers generally follow suit to accommodate the more popular pistols.

Small handguns are prime laser candidates. This S&W .380 Bodyguard has an integral system, activated by the forward button.

Laser bonus. Back to marksmanship, a laser does provide an often-overlooked opportunity to improve trigger skills. Although dry-firing is great practice by itself, from several yards, a sudden laser-beam bounce will quickly reveal any trigger-control shortcomings. To that end, there are some interesting laser-related training items, covered further in the *Accessories Chapter*.

Lights. Any type of emergency preparedness strategy will require some means for illumination and, while a basic flashlight is a whole lot better than nothing, a strong case can be made for some type of "tactical" light, whether hand-held or weapon-mounted. The latter use will require an accessory rail, but all is not lost without one. Either way, the extra investment for a light will provide some practical advantages, among them the ability to navigate, identify friendlies, and disorient or engage threats. The latest lights are downright amazing and seem almost bright enough to weld with! Output is typically expressed in Lumens with more being brighter. The smaller hand-held types might generate

Like many of today's handguns, this Glock will accommodate a rail-mounted light.

50-60 Lumens, more than adequate for mundane uses such as navigating a parking lot or locating a door lock. The higher-end tactical models are sometimes rated as 300 Lumens or more.

Combo light/laser units. Some of the higher-end rail-mounted units incorporate both features. The user has the option of running the light and laser simultaneously through use of tail-cap controls. Such a dual-use design tends to be somewhat larger to accommodate the parts and batteries, making them dedicated weapon systems. Other tactical-grade lights may have a strobe feature which can be extremely debilitating for an opponent. A bright but steady beam directed at a face can produce somewhat similar effects in low light.

Weapon-mounted systems. One concern with any weapon-mounted light involves muzzle discipline. Your light beam (or laser) will follow your muzzle, which can be good - or very bad. Attachment of a light to a handgun is typically accomplished with a purpose-built light that clamps to short rail section on the gun, either with screws or some type of QD arrangement. The latter will require lots of practice with an unloaded gun, given the light's proximity to the muzzle. And again, a semi-permanent type will probably require a special holster.

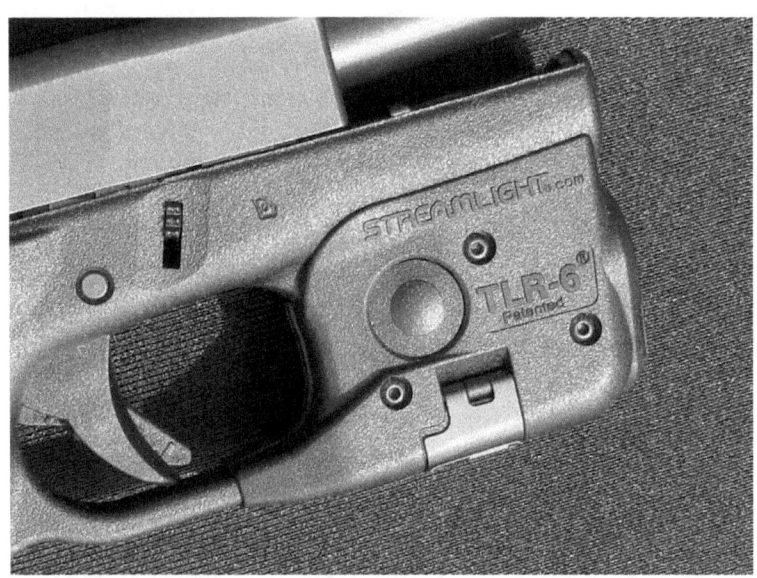

Streamlight's ultra-compact TLR-6 light & laser unit works on small rail-less pistols. Clamped to the trigger guard by three screws, battery exchanges won't require disassembly.

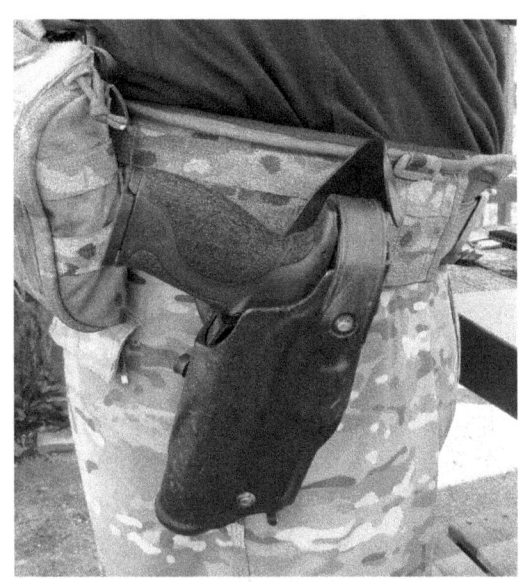

A closer look at this tactical holster reveals space for a weapon-mounted light.

Hand-held lights. There are also plenty of excellent compact lights which can be carried on a belt or in a pocket for independent use; a feature which will be appreciated during normal routines. Plus, the same light can be effectively deployed via hand-held techniques in concert with a handgun; good news for revolver owners. But regardless of the firearm, in the interest of safety, formal training is strongly advised! Once understood, handheld gun and light strategies can be employed using coordinated or independent techniques.

More information about lights is contained in the *Accessories Chapter*.

CLOSING THOUGHTS

It's worth at least considering any future upgrades when shopping for a handgun. Dovetails or pinned front sights will more readily accommodate replacements. Same story for drilled and tapped revolver frames (like the latest S&Ws). If a laser or light is in the cards, a practical mounting system will be needed. A handgun with an accessory rail could solve these issues without adding any appreciable size or cost. The newest wave of small dot-sights offers further intriguing possibilities, which will no doubt lead to even better products. Meanwhile, since most of the latest "optics-ready" pistols will work with their factory iron sights, it won't hurt to have an MRDS option.

CHAPTER 7
THOUGHTS ON ACCURACY AND RANGE

The major manufacturers produce reasonably accurate handguns for their intended purposes. Feeding them a diet of mainstream ammunition improves the odds of determining both accuracy *and* reliability, although nothing is guaranteed. An agency showed up on our range with a bunch of brand new .40 pistols from a major manufacturer. During the initial test-fire, function was fine but we experienced wash-tub sized groups at 15-yards. At 25 yards, five shots wouldn't stay inside an FBI Q-target! Just as panic set in, I dragged out a factory load of the same bullet weight from another manufacturer. Viola, 25-yard groups ran around 2 ½ inches! Crisis over, except for one remaining problem: the agency was stuck with cases of unusable ammo. Since their problem load shot well in other pistol makes, this was a classic example of incompatibility. The lesson here is to experiment before buying in bulk.

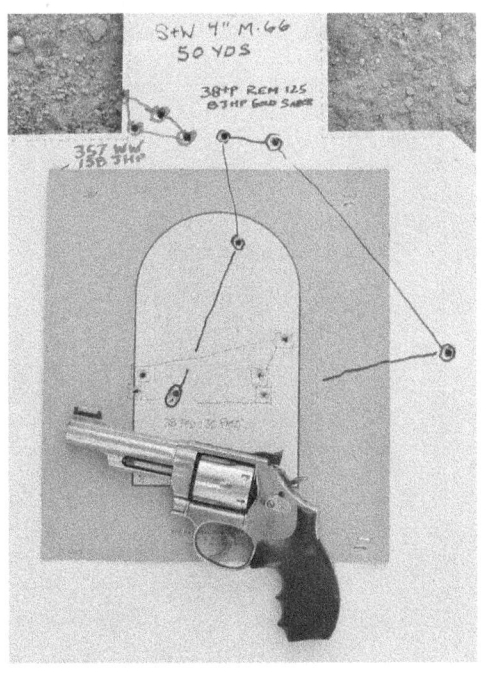

Testing has value. This 4" S&W M-66 produced great 50-yard sandbag accuracy with .38 Special FMJs, or .357 JHPs! But, .38 +P results were abysmal (confirmed through further shooting). Note the varying POIs.

The Ransom Rest eliminates human errors. The spare inserts fit S&W's K-frame, round-butts. The board will be clamped to a sturdy bench.

Accuracy testing protocols. Centerfire rifle accuracy is normally assessed at 100 yards. Every effort is made to eliminate the human factor, so bench-rest techniques are employed. A rifle capable of placing 3-5 shots within one inch at that distance is generally deemed "accurate." Handgun testing, on the other hand, is much more haphazard. A common protocol involves the use of sandbag rests for five-shot groups, fired from 25 yards. Some testers (usually gun writers) may even employ a Ransom Rest; a mechanical fixture similar to a vise designed to eliminate human wobbles and vision issues. The handgun is sandwiched between a pair of fitted pliable inserts, which firmly clamp around the grip-frame on a pivoting steel arm. The trigger is tripped remotely and the arm then climbs in recoil, requiring a manual but repeatable reset.

Given the expense of a Ransom Rest and different inserts, most shooters will be stuck with less precise assessment methods. In fact, even much published gun-rag data is based on sand-bag results. Lately, a few gun writers have begun counting only the best three out of five shots. The well-known writer, Massad Ayoob, popularized this protocol after discovering his closest three shots approximated the results of all five from a Ransom Rest; the two wider sand-bag rounds being attributable to human error. Lately, his sandbag tests list both three *and* five-shot measurements, which seem like a better approach. I've shot sandbag and Ransom Rest groups for comparison, using a highly accurate .22 target pistol. I could rival mechanical results, but only for about 30 rounds. After that, the sandbag groups began to gradually degrade, which I blame on fading concentration and eye strain. Of course,

Careful testing in progress over sandbags. The handgun is a dot sight-equipped .22LR target pistol, S&W's Model 41.

This phenomenal 100-yard group was a product of careful sandbag testing (three previous groups on steel were similar). No distinct bullseye either! The "X" was applied afterward to indicate POA. The load is Federal's .22 LR Gold Medal Target.

the Ransom Rest suffers none of these maladies, so it just keeps cranking out consistent results.

Other writers may be less meticulous, and some even cut loose from off-hand without any support at all. I suppose that's better than nothing – but not by much. It's also not uncommon to see published results from oddball distances like 7, 10, 15, or 20 yards. A few gun writers have even declared the whole exercise pointless. Truth be known, some of the so-called professional testers may not shoot all that well, explaining their looser standards. Others are limited to indoor ranges, where conditions can limit results.

So, what constitutes "good" handgun accuracy? Although the answer may seem like a cop-out, I think it depends. I have a few larger revolvers and pistols that have been wrung out to the nth degree from 25 yards with all sorts of ammunition. A few finalist loads have even been tested at 50, and sometimes, 100 yards. In stark contrast, I own a few small carry guns that have never been through any serious accuracy testing at all – function testing yes, but nothing for accuracy other than some deliberate offhand shooting at close range. For the most part, POI is the greater concern.

ACCURACY EXPECTATIONS

First, there is no general accuracy standard per se, although an agency may post requirements, and some manufacturers have in-house limits. All sorts of factors come into play from ammunition quality, rifling rate-of-twist, subtle dimensional variables, and fitting, etc. Of course, the biggest wildcard is the shooter behind the gun! To help quantify accuracy expectations, here are some *general* guidelines based on personal experience:

Match-gun performance. Handguns in this category will probably be custom or semi-custom builds fitted to tighter tolerances with match-grade barrels, priced accordingly. Barrel-length may run around 5 inches, and sights will often be adjustable. Longer length translates to greater sight radius for more precise alignment, although the barrel by itself may not be more accurate. Fitting is important. Once in a while, the accuracy gods will smile and deliver similar results from a production gun, thanks to a happy coincidence of tighter tolerances.

A handgun capable of placing five rounds within three inches at 50 yards is a real ringer. If it's a semi-auto there's a good chance it'll be a custom 1911, carefully fitted, at extra expense. In fact, some of these guns will shoot even better. These higher-end masterpieces are sometimes sold with accuracy guarantees and test targets to back up expectations. The gorgeous 1911s from firms Les Baer, Wilson, Nighthawk, Ed Brown, etc. are built exceptionally tight thanks to careful hand-fitting. You can easily shell out $3,000 or more for such a pistol, reflecting the efforts of skilled craftsmen.

You *may* see fifty-yard accuracy on the order of three inches from a well-built factory revolver simply because its barrel is stationary. Yes, the individual chambers must properly align, so the "well-built" caveat applies. I'd have high hopes of an S&W .357 Magnum Model 686 achieving such accuracy – for less than $800.

Service (or duty-type) handguns: These production-grade guns often have barrels running around four inches in length. Although optimum accuracy is desirable, reliability is paramount, so such semiauto firearms are built with slightly looser tolerances to function in harsh conditions. Less fitting also helps keep a lid on cost.

Great 50 yard results from a well-fitted 1911 with iron sights. The magic combination? An STI long-slide 9mm Trojan, and plain-Jane Federal 124-grain American Eagle FMJ! Again, no specific aiming point.

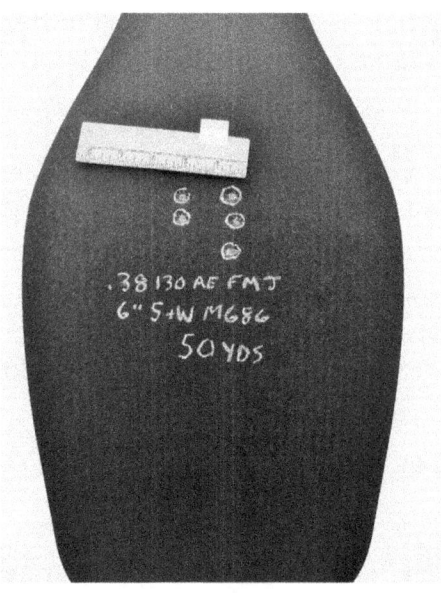

Another 50-yard group, fired from an S&W Model 686 .357 Magnum revolver with its factory sights. Affordable .38 Special 130-grain American Eagle FMJs produced excellent accuracy despite the long chambers.

A semiautomatic pistol that will reliably put five shots inside two inches at 25 yards should be considered an accurate specimen. For the reasons noted, there's a better chance that a good four-inch barrel revolver will achieve this goal.

Most service-type pistols (Glock, S&W, etc.) will probably cut three-inch, 25-yard groups -still perfectly adequate for defensive purposes. Plenty of other such pistols will shoot more on the order of four inches – an often considered acceptable 25-yard spread. Supposedly, the arsenal standard for a WW II 1911 pistol was four inches or less at 15 yards!

Overall, accuracy is improving, probably due to CNC machining and the polymer-pistol learning curve. The good news is that the pistols are affordable with many selling for less than $600.

Small concealed-carry types. We can lump the smaller .380 semiautos and snub-nose revolvers into this category. Often, published accuracy results are based on 7-yard groups. The rationale is that these guns are intended for close-range use, but little guns are also just harder to shoot well. Five-shot

Match-grade accuracy from a factory-built 1911, thanks to modern manufacturing. Same shooter and 15-yard distance as the .380 test. But, this .40 STI put five rounds through almost the same hole!

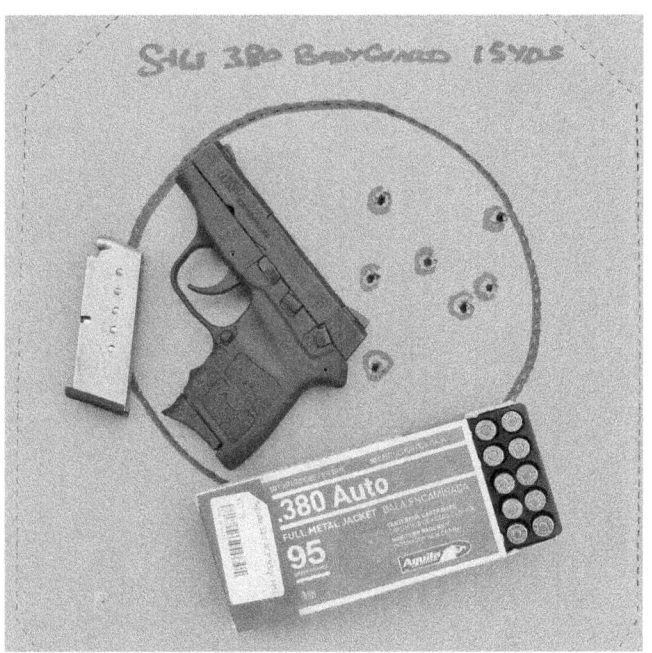

This 15-yard group was fired offhand with a small S&W Bodyguard .380 and FMJ practice ammo. Although accuracy isn't match-grade, it's certainly more than adequate.

groups running around 2 ½ - 3" are the norm, although the guns themselves can sometimes do better. You could expect similar accuracy at perhaps, 15 yards, although many will do better in the hands of good shooters.

Rimfire notes. Most centerfire semiautos employ reciprocating slides that unlock through tilting barrels. On the other hand, .22 pistols are usually blow-back designs using stationary barrels. Thanks to this feature rimfire pistols can be inherently more accurate. Five-shot 25-yard groups of 1 ½ inches or less are not uncommon, and some rimfires can do *much* better. Instead of the several thousand dollars it might take to achieve such centerfire performance, this degree of rimfire accuracy can often be had for $400 or less.

Rimfire revolver accuracy expectations may flip a bit because of minor chamber misalignments. Still, like a centerfire version, a good .22 revolver should shoot into two inches or less. A rimfire S&W Model 617 is built a lot like its centerfire M-686 brother and is thus priced similarly. However, there are plenty of other good D/A and S/A revolvers on the market for less.

Since all rimfires seem to have individual ammo preferences, some testing may be needed to find a winning combination - great practice! The accuracy of a quality .22 makes it a great tool for developing marksmanship skills.

PRACTICAL PERFORMANCE

A handgun is hard enough to shoot without impediments like mediocre accuracy, poor ergonomics, an excessively heavy trigger, or hard-to-see sights. And, of course, a further irritation is a fixed-sighted gun that doesn't shoot to the sights. Some people compensate for errors by aiming off-target an appropriate amount (Kentucky Windage). We wish you well in that endeavor, especially if things become hectic. For combat use I'd prefer a reliable service-grade handgun that shot spot-on over a match-grade gun that didn't.

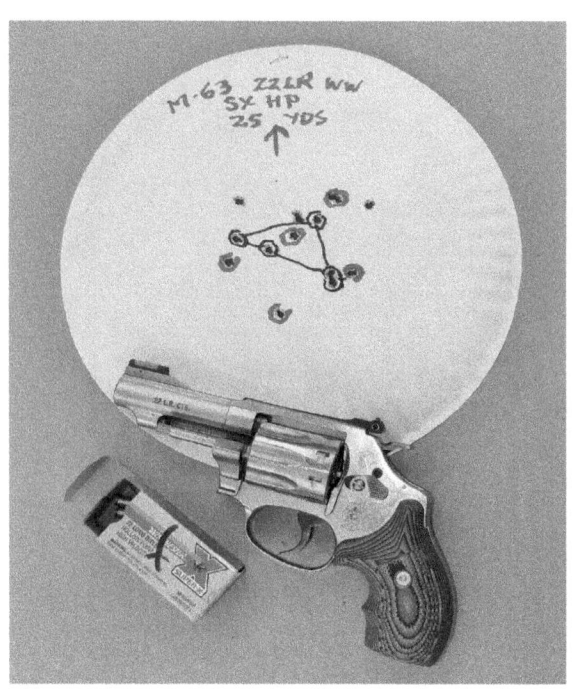

This S&W M-63 kit-gun produced useful .22 LR accuracy at 25 yards. The three 5-shot groups are smaller than its 3" barrel.

Inherent versus practical accuracy. I've owned a few handguns capable of stellar accuracy, but difficult to shoot to their full potential. A few were high-capacity 1911 variants with thicker grip-frames than a standard Government Model. I experimented with grip reductions and other modifications, but eventually returned to thinner single-stack 1911s. Since many top shooters employ the high-cap versions with great results, the problem was obviously me.

At one point I also owned a couple switch-barrel, single-shot, Thompson/Center Contender pistols, well known for their exceptional accuracy. Despite years of searching, I never did find a truly comfortable set of grips, so I decided to conduct a multi-session range experiment. First, I installed a 10-inch .22 LR T/C barrel which shot about as well as any rimfire handgun could. Next, I dug out my old 7 3/8-inch barrel, S&W .22 LR Model 41 target pistol. Both handguns were equipped with optical sights to wring out their full potential. Shooting them offhand at 25 yards illustrated the difference between mechanical and practical accuracy. Despite similar mechanical accuracy, the M-41 was a whole lot more shootable from real-world positions. Next, I swapped out the T/C's rimfire barrel for a 10-inch .44 Magnum. Out came another .44 Magnum; this time a 6-inch S&W Model 629. Again, both guns wore optical sights. From previous bench-rest testing at 50 yards, I knew the Contender barrel was more accurate. However, from field positions, the S&W revolver held a clear advantage despite its stiffer recoil. This is by no means a knock on T/C's excellent and unique handguns. The point is that personal comfort (ergonomics) shouldn't be overlooked.

The snob factor can also be counterproductive and expensive. Yes, custom guns are pretty, but a few higher-end 1911s on hand here see less recent use. Although my S&W 9mm Pro is less accurate, it has become my go-to pistol for combat-type courses. Its svelte lines and utter simplicity translate to better results when speed is a part of scoring. If pure accuracy is the primary requirement though, I'll still reach for a match-grade 1911. An edge-on playing card is a darned small target, even at seven paces. If betting (or ego) is involved, a precisely placed .45 bullet has the better chance of cutting it in half; and shooting from 50 yards can be another eye-opener. But again, while match-grade accuracy is great, it isn't everything. Take all that you can get, but temper your expectations by broader concerns like ergonomics, useful sights, and utter reliability.

Effective range. This one is a pet peeve. The military seems especially fond of empirical pronouncements. Let's say for argument's sake, a .45 ACP Government Model is listed as having an effective range of 50 meters. I guess, at 51 meters, the bullets either evaporate or fall straight down to earth. We say effective range depends more upon a shooter, most of whom will fall a whole lot shorter than the potential of their handguns. In fact, just about all calibers retain lethality out to their maximum carrying distances, in excess of a mile. The two limiting factors are marksmanship ability and trajectory, with the former generally trumping the latter.

However, many practical handguns impose further limits. Small handguns can restrict accurate shot placement to ranges well inside ballistic capabilities; a reason why many LE Q-courses go with shorter distances for back-up guns. Partly for this reason, many defensive academies consider anything but close-quarter shooting superfluous. Much of it occurs at 3 -7 yards, with a dash of further distances (10-15 yards) thrown in. We generally train the same way but, since our statewide LE qualification course has a 25-yard stage, this distance gets some attention. Personally, I'm all for it. That's where we see people throwing most their shots. Sight alignment and trigger control are important, and a 25-yard stage will reveal any sloppiness. In fact, some 50-yard shooting can be educational. We often run drills from that distance, combining use of cover with prone techniques.

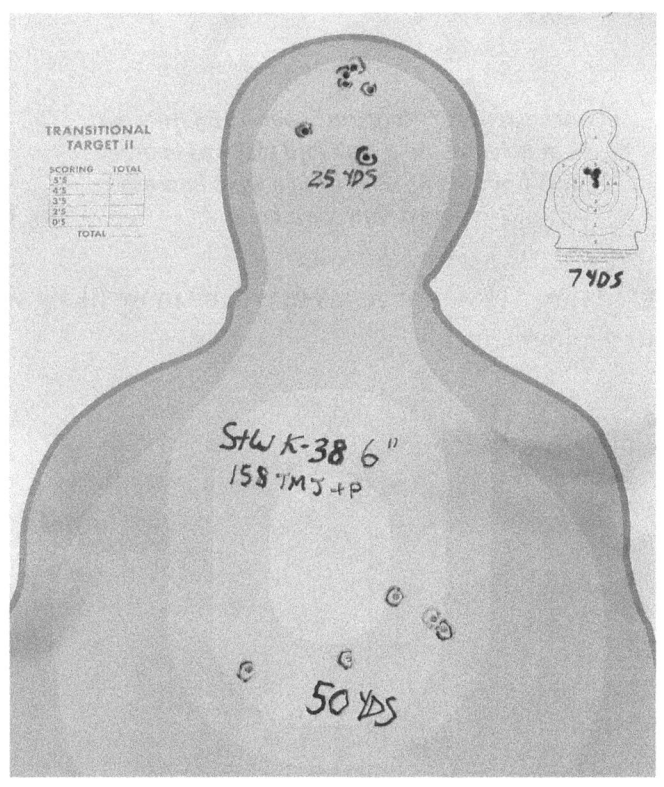

The average fight occurs inside 7 yards and most are even closer. But, averages are also based on extremes. I had the fortune to survive a long-range engagement, armed solely with a .45 ACP 1911.The distance was so far that it'll lack any credibility, so I'll just skip the estimated yardage and go with *"really far!"* Conventional aiming was out so, as we say in the military, I had to "adapt and overcome." It didn't hurt a bit that I had done lots of previous shooting with this pistol at 100 yards and further. At extreme

Offhand results from a 6" S&W K-38 revolver and CCI .38 +P TMJ, zeroed at 25 yards. The warmer +P load flattens trajectory somewhat, reducing hold-over at longer range.

Thoughts On Accuracy And Range | 103

distances, the big, slow .45 bullets lobbed in like rocks. A hard-to-come-by stash of tracers revealed just how loopy the trajectory really was. This research later saved my bacon - along with seven extra magazines.

Winchester .357 Magnum Super-X 158 JHPs did well at 50 yards, so a 100-yard test was in order. Results from the 6" S&W M-686 were impressive using a high chest hold!

Lighter, faster 9mm or .357 rounds drop less, making them more doable on 100-yard steel combat silhouettes. You'll probably need a head-hold (or more) with a conventional zero, but assuming your marksmanship skills are improving, why not give it a go? Partner up with somebody who can shoot and place a bet on the lunch tab because motivation helps! But, the 50-yard line is a better starting point when coupled with a gun of reasonable accuracy.

REALITY CHECK

Longer-range shooting can be educational assuming the gun is up to the task. I'd want one capable of reliably producing three-inch groups at 25 yards (although 2" would be better). Mechanically, this translates to fifty-yard results of 6 inches, and a foot at 100 yards. Of course, the human element can only make things worse, accounting for the comment about "improving skills." Worst case, adjust the distance inward until reliable hits result.

Odds are a close-range event will be more likely with the need for a rapid response, so let's move on to deployment.

CHAPTER 8
CUSTODY AND CARRY: THE BASICS

Although shoulder-fired weapons are more effective, a handgun is a whole lot better than no gun; and on a day-to-day basis, there's a darn better chance of having a sidearm with you - especially if it's easy to carry! Experienced gun people get there through trial and error meaning, sooner or later, they'll wind up with a practical handgun and holster. Others may view the gun as little more than a survival tool to be stuffed in a bug-out bag or pack along with other emergency supplies, but, both groups could face similar concerns regarding home-storage issues. This could be the sole purpose of firearm ownership for a third group of people more interested in bedside security.

Static defense often translates to home defense, involving not only responsible custody, but also some means of rapid access. Solutions can vary greatly, from hidden guns to hi-tech biometric containers. The thing to remember is that, sooner or later, the firearm will be unattended. The expedient solution will likely be driven by one's living situation, with children being a huge concern.

Mobile defense introduces variables related to lifestyle, physique, and climate. An appropriate gun and holster combination can provide concealment and hands-free carry comfort, but once again, rapid access should be considered. Good chance you won't be sleeping with a sidearm strapped to your waist though, so let's kick things off at the hacienda.

STATIC DEFENSE

Although the stereotypical static strategy centers on the home, the same gun could be staged at alternate locations. Trips between the residence and place of employment are but one example that introduces mobility, not always in a conventional sense. State laws can vary so, in some instances, the firearm may need to be isolated and secured during transportation. Movement to a bug-out destination would impose similar concerns, although a status quo lifestyle could quickly evaporate.

Legalities. Since transportation or use of a firearm outside the

A full-blown gun safe affords the greatest level of security. Many are fire-resistant but, since none are portable, additional measures may be necessary.

home may introduce sticky issues, your first responsibility should be a clear understanding of all pertinent statutes, ordinances, and employer policies. Next up (and often required) are appropriate security measures, which could conflict with ready access. These concerns are usually a balancing act with no perfect solution. For example, some regulations require a handgun to be transported unloaded in a locked container, isolated from a driver's compartment. Other CCW laws make life simpler by allowing loaded weapons; although some require direct control – meaning the gun must be worn. A few locales are much laxer concerning personal carry or storage of a loaded gun inside a vehicle. However, one obligation for everyone is reasonable control of the firearm.

Storage. Back on the home-front, kids and guns don't mix. Even if your own children are versed on firearm safety, there's no guarantee their playmates are, so a handgun hidden on a shelf or in a drawer is just a recipe for disaster. In fact, *any* unattended firearm incurs serious liabilities, including haphazard storage in a vehicle. Fortunately, some of the latest gun vaults and other creative storage options provide practical solutions to this age-old quandary.

Secure containers. One big question is whether to maintain a loaded firearm or not. No easy answers here, although the type of handgun can affect the decision. We issue a large quantity of pistols to civilian-dressed officers who don't work out of centralized locations. Since most operate directly from their homes, each is provided with a GunVault MV-500 Micro-vault. Essentially, it's a reinforced, portable steel lock-box with a hinged lid that opens from a coded push-button sequence. The unit is powered by a long-lasting 9-volt battery, but it also has a key override feature. Each user can program a personalized button sequence, which will deny access upon several incorrect entries. The buttons are large enough to work well in the dark, although this isn't the main reason for their issu-

GunVault's battery-powered MV-500 can be accessed by a programmable push-button sequence, backed up by a key.

The MV-500's supplied cable can be looped around hard-points. This S&W M&P has the dreaded magazine-disconnect feature. Some may find it useful with this system.

ance. We were more worried about safe storage, and here's where the type of firearm can play a part. As we delve into semiauto pistols, you'll see a discussion about magazine disconnect systems. Many well-qualified professionals consider them an abomination since a pistol so equipped won't fire if its magazine is removed. Factoring in Murphy's Law, it's a legitimate concern, but in this case, there is one advantage. By removing the magazine prior to secure storage, safer gun handling ensues. Yes, a live round will remain in the chamber, but the gun won't fire until its magazine is reinserted. Both removal and reinsertion can be done while the pistol remains holstered using the right selections of gear. This procedure is safer than daily clearance and loading, which is also hard on ammunition (more on this later). Plus, the disconnect serves as another safety layer of sorts during storage.

Others might opt for a completely unloaded gun, which solves any magazine-disconnect concerns. Of course, so will a fully loaded handgun; in which case an active safety could have merit. After all, gun handling could occur under stress, in the dark, possibly while half-asleep. This is also not the best time to be fumbling through a button sequence, so one alternative is a nighttime ritual involving an opened container, secured during daytime hours. Of course, the big concern is remembering to close the box whenever it is unattended. For some extra security, the special hardened cable provided with most such units can be looped around something like a bed frame. A simple shove will then slide it out of sight when the unit is unattended.

The same box can be discretely shunted between a residence and vehicle inside a bag or brief case. Its cable system is designed to loop around hard-points, so it will also attach to trunk hinges, seat frames, etc. Of course, while security is important, a box won't help much if the vehicle is stolen. Having seen both situations we're not big fans of any such long-term storage.

Still, a gun box remains a good option, best viewed as a theft deterrent; and while a full-size gun safe will be a whole lot harder to lug off, no system is perfect. Many shooters use both, securing their main collection in a fire-resistant safe, while staging an emergency firearm in a more accessible location. Besides biometric locks as sold by Liberty Safe, new RFID technologies exist, permitting wireless access through remote controls, special decals, and wrist bracelets; Hornady's Rapid Safes being an example. Some of these products are large enough to hold a long-gun, while others are designed for vehicles or permanent structural installations. One benefit of a handgun assigned solely to storage is its ability to be fully decked out with the latest light and lasers without concerns for holster fit or excess weight. If something goes bump in the night, their value will be appreciated.

<u>Hidden guns.</u> These are another possibility, and all sorts of innovative products have appeared for this purpose including strong magnets, hollowed-out books, clocks, and even furniture. *Tactical Walls* sells a fascinating line of the latter which can locate a firearm in a well-trafficked space, completely out of sight, while affording rapid access. Some gun owners will use this approach as a fast-response layer in their static-defense plan

<u>Unsecured guns.</u> As for loaded guns, plenty of people go this route and some no doubt live alone – which doesn't eliminate the possibility of guests. Some conscious effort for access is recommended

since more than one visitor or family member has been unintentionally shot by someone not fully awake. An unsecured, loaded gun is a risky proposition - *maybe* in all but a few special circumstances.

As for unsecured, empty guns, some types like SA revolvers can be difficult to load in hurry, even during daylight hours; but others can be loaded with little effort, including D/A revolvers that use full-moon clips. With this design the cylinder's full content can be swiftly loaded en masse (you'll see more about this system in the upcoming revolver sections). It also doesn't take long to shove a loaded magazine into a pistol and rack its slide. Of course, this assumes the ammunition source can be located in a hurry. An alternate method is to store a pistol with a loaded magazine inserted under an empty chamber. One quick slide-rack will put the gun in action and many designs employ stout enough springs to make this difficult for untrained or very young people. An active safety can serve as a further security barrier, but the whole approach is far from secure.

<u>Other options.</u> These include trigger and cable-locks, the latter using a hardened coated wire which can be looped through an action, cylinder, or barrel. A padlock will work on the opened frames of most D/A revolvers, so will a set of handcuffs. A disassembled pistol offers similar possibilities at the expense of emergency access. Some handgun manufacturers now incorporate integral locking systems designed to render an action inoperable when engaged. These usually work even if loaded, requiring the use of a small proprietary key. The trick is to not only have the key on hand, but also to be able to use it in a pinch. Better turn out the lights for some educational practice first. I'd be leery of using these designs as a stand-alone measure.

Whatever measures you employ, responsible custody should remain the priority. This concern only increases whenever the firearm is not under our direct control. Mobility can solve this concern, which leads us to personalized carry alternatives.

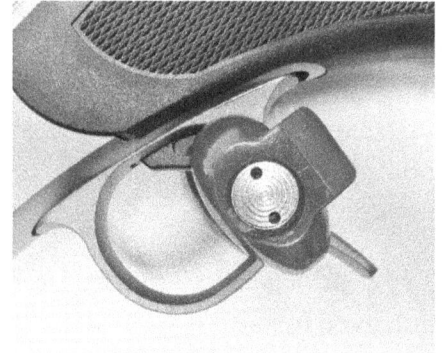

Nowadays, a safety device of some sort is included with most new firearms. Trigger locks are one type. Many can be defeated with a simple screwdriver.

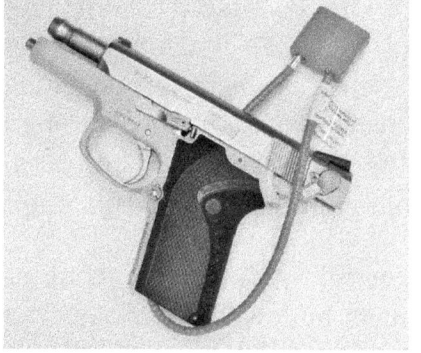

Safety cables are another option. When passed through a mag-well or revolver frame, the loops can be secured to a hard-point.

Another old revolver trick is a set of handcuffs. A padlock can also work.

MOBILITY

Gun size and weather resistance are less of a concern on the home front. Firearms of all types from shotguns to pocket-pistols languish in closets or night stands, unaffected by their size. Mobility is the big game-changer, requiring practical solutions that provide comfort, concealment, and ready access; and although concealment might not always be a primary concern, it does afford a layer of extra security for the user, meaning it shouldn't be discounted. The environment is of further concern through direct or indirect exposure. Inclement weather can result in rust, but so can perspiration. These concerns more often relate to on-person carry, but some preppers may have a different take.

Although a holster is by far the most common carry method, the handgun could be just part of a larger pre-packed kit constituting part of a larger load. Either way, extra mass counts, including the weight of spare ammo. Access should also be considered.

Carry modes. The mere fact that a handgun is under consideration implies a need for ready access. A gun tucked inside a bug-out kit or backpack could be reassuring, but an emergency response will be better served by a decent holster. On top of that, any range practice will be a whole lot safer. Besides freeing up both hands, it will serve as an effective muzzle-control device for the shooter and any bystanders. So, toward that end, let's consider some options…

First off, a survival situation is beyond any sport hunting, so for subsistence purposes, go with a rifle or shotgun whenever possible (either will be a better defensive choice, too). The most effective hunting handguns are typically large for extra sight radius and velocity. Although they may carry well in specialized holster systems, some create muzzle-control issues for both users and bystanders. A cross-chest rig can support a heavy handgun with relative comfort, but it will typically orient the muzzle in a horizontal slant. The supporting harness straps bear weight effectively, but the overall size of the resulting system is best managed through exposed carry, meaning garment changes can be a hassle. Still, this arrangement has merit for those fishing Alaskan streams where bears are a real concern.

Back in the Lower 48, cross-draw and shoulder holsters can drive range officers nuts. Good chance the muzzle will sweep adjacent shooters at some point, and horizontal shoulder rigs guarantee this result (stand behind someone wearing one and note where the muzzle is pointed). Vertical shoulder holsters can create similar risks for their users during both a draw and recovery process. Concealed carry comes to mind as a principle use for such a system, especially when a jacket and tie are involved. However, a shoulder rig can be useful during extreme weather when a heavy winter parka becomes a necessity. Access is a whole lot easier than fishing around under a thigh-length coat. Most handgunners will probably never face such outdoor extremes, so for many a belt-holster will serve admirably - assuming the handgun is of reasonable size.

Size versus concealment. Using a standard-size gun as a frame of reference, it's often harder to hide a handgun with a larger grip than one with a longer barrel. Compact handguns eliminate most such concerns, but some rubber grips (or those with sharp checkering) can hang up on clothing to "print" a gun. So, in other words, size alone is not always the deciding factor. A simple way to determine if a handgun prints is to holster it in normal attire. You might encounter some initial difficulties that can be overcome though minor wardrobe changes. As previously discussed, the micro-sized handguns that eliminate all such concerns can seem like the expedient solution, but will likely compromise general utility, meaning they're a better back-up choice.

CARRY LANGUAGE

The recent expansion of concealed carry laws has given rise to legions of armed citizens, many of whom are toting compact handguns. Carry methods have expanded to follow this trend, resulting in some new descriptive terms. The gun publications often assume everyone is familiar with them, but that's not always the case…

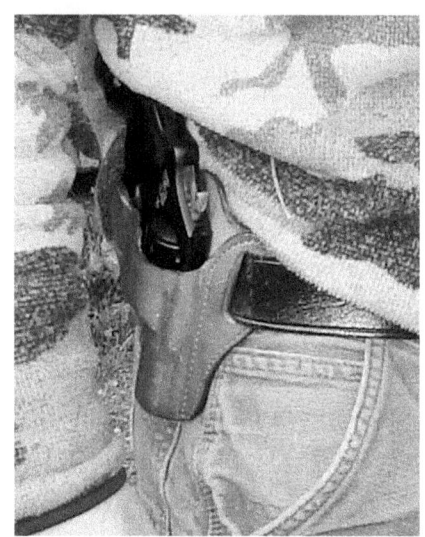

A holster like this 3:00 OWB (see below) can free up both hands while improving muzzle control. The gun is a small-frame revolver, well-suited for OC or CCW purposes.

OC. Open carry refers to a firearm carried in an exposed manner, such as a handgun in a belt holster. This method is legal in some states for residents without permits, giving rise to a similar "Constitutional Carry" reference. Just because something is legal doesn't necessarily make it the best choice. Furthermore, open carry can introduce retention concerns, while advertising exactly who is armed. From a sporting perspective, open carry can be entirely practical. Size becomes much less of a concern, even with six-inch barreled handguns. In the North Woods of my state, or other wilderness areas, a gun on a belt is a common sight, and it's often a large revolver.

CCW. Thankfully, most states now recognize our 2nd Amendment rights, meaning Concealed-Carry Weapons have blossomed. Many require some sort of "CCW Permit," although permit-less carry has become increasingly legal. My home state recently joined this movement, at least partially thanks to our largely rural population. While running previously required CCW permit classes, I discovered many of the applicants were actually sportsmen bent on avoiding inadvertent concealment infractions resulting from coats. Nationally though, CCW use is no doubt geared toward self-defense.

EDC. Stands for every day carry, reflecting a user's chosen method of handgun carry. There is a good chance that most EDC (sometimes just EC) handguns will be compact. If not, it probably won't be long before the gun stays behind. An EDC carry method will probably have two other things in common beyond size: simplicity and comfort. Two extremely popular EDC choices involve IWB and OWB holsters.

OWB. Outside-the-waistband refers to a holster secured to a belt, often on the user's strong side, between 2:00 to 4:00. To a lesser extent, cross-draw holsters are worn at a 10:00 position for easier vehicular access. These methods most often pertain to CCW. As noted, open carry is much less of a size issue, so some gun and holster combinations can run large. In fact, a 7 ½" single-action revolver is often carried this way. If we want to make a gun disappear inside a jacket, a barrel length of around four inches or less makes more sense.

IWB. Inside-the-waistband holsters locate a gun similarly, but tucked inside the pants. Holsters in this category are increasingly popular for EDC purposes, and many will even work with tucked-in shirts. A smaller gun provides more comfort, so a compact model is often the largest practical choice – sometimes with trousers running one size larger.

IWB-A (sometimes reversed to AIWB). Like above, the gun is in the appendix area, at around 2:00. Gun size will become more critical, with shorter barrel-lengths providing better comfort. Plenty of compact handguns are carried this way, and IWB-A carry methods no doubt account for the recent explosion of micro-sized .380 and 9mm pistols; and speaking of "explosions," it's worth considering the proximity of valued anatomical features to the muzzle of your handgun.

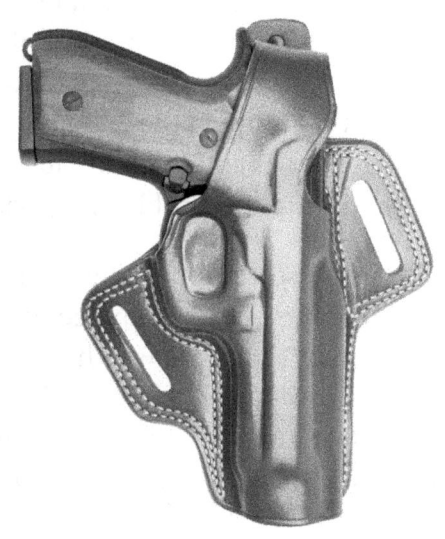

Classic OWB holster with molded-leather and a thumb-break, raked for 4:00 carry.

The list of carry options goes on, but these will do for now. Once the ins and outs of handguns have been fully explored, we'll return to more specific carry details (holster designs, etc.). But first, let's connect our operating environment to some additional firearm concerns.

ENVIRONMENTAL ISSUES

Since where we live affects the way we dress, clothing can introduce challenges. Spring in Northern New England is winter across much of the United States. Coats are standard dress for all but twelve weeks, some of which are still jacket weather. As this is written in mid- March, it's 10 degrees and the wind is howling. I could hide a pistol-grip shotgun without much difficulty right now. Meanwhile, my retired LEO buddy in Florida is suffering through eighty-degree weather (a pox upon him). For concealment purposes, he not only needs a small handgun, but a comfortable means of concealment. Inevitably, his gun will be in close body contact raising sweat-induced corrosion concerns.

Occasionally, in the Bad Old Days, I'd stuff a full-size G.I. 45 Government Model underneath my jungle shirt for rare R&R excursions. It disappeared fairly well, but this holsterless "Mexican Carry" technique soon caused a red pistol silhouette on each of my precious OD undershirts. Retention issues aside, it was hard on the gun, although even the most sensible tropical carry methods required zealous maintenance. We'll come back to holsters later. For now, think about a firearm appropriate for your weather.

All firearms need regular maintenance regardless of their finish. Dirt, dust, or fabric tufts will accumulate in small nooks and crannies as products of regular carry. Lubricants can help ward off rust, and they can also affect reliability – for better or worse. Too much will attract the junk described above. Too little and the gun may quit working. The tables can sometimes turn in cold weather where some lubes can stiffen up to cause malfunctions. Revolvers will usually run fine, but some pistols are susceptible to this problem, especially when periodic spring replacement regimens are haphazard.

We've also seen supposedly unbreakable polymer duty-gear snap during frigid weather. Some were polymer buckles that snapped after storage in cold vehicle trunks, while others were plastic holsters that couldn't hack the weather. Ironically, we've also seen some heat induced problems, and among the worst was a pistol hopelessly lodged in its hi-tech holster. We finally narrowed down the cause to vehicular storage in direct sunlight on a hot summer day. The synthetic holster softened just enough to change shape, remaining unnoticeable until the pistol snapped in – and stayed there.

CARRY AND USE-DRIVEN EXAMPLES

We've examined some static and mobile factors somewhat loosely tied to use. Now, how about more specific mission requirements? They can vary, and what works for me may not work for you. In any case, I'll share some considerations that governed two recent handgun purchases. Their intended missions set the stage for a list of specifications from which it was easier to narrow down a list of finalists. The first gun reflects a general-purpose choice, intended for OWB carry. Of course, holster availability was equally important.

General-purpose missions. I was looking for a dependable sidearm, suitable for woods use, self-defense, combat courses, and informal shooting. A strong contender was a .357 Magnum double-action revolver with dual-use .38 Special capabilities. There are several good revolver brands, but for me, the choice was easy enough; it had to be an S&W. Why? Experience, and an existing collection of accessories like grips, loader-devices, etc.

Size & weight. The gun needed to bridge the gap between the smallest J-frames and the larger N-frame models - small enough for comfortable carry, but big enough for accurate shooting. Manageable recoil was another consideration. Based on experience, a revolver weighing a bit above two pounds seemed about right.

Barrel. Something in the three to four-inch range would promote easier OWB carry. Going shorter would sacrifice some accuracy and velocity. An odd-ball five-inch barrel would add size while limiting holster choices. The six-inch length, although common, was deemed excessively long for this revolver's intended uses.

Finish. Since bad weather was in the cards, stainless steel was a given.

Grips. I wanted a round-butt frame to help maintain a compact package. Fortunately, this was easy.

There are many older square-butts in circulation and S&W offered both types, but they've since standardized on the round-butt (those preferring the larger square-butt design can replicate that effect by adding similarly profiled grips). One thing was certain: buying an S&W, grip choices would be almost limitless.

Sights. Fixed sights won't snag, but adjustable sights permit spot-on groups with a variety of loads. A pinned front-sight was a must. So was S&W's latest adjustable rear sight, mounted to a drilled & tapped frame. These features will accommodate aftermarket sights, including the latest optical designs.

Holsters and accessories. Popular handguns ensure the largest selection of holsters, speed-loaders, parts, and accessories. I planned on slicking up the action, with the possibility of installing custom springs (best skipped for pure defense), so…

Final choice. When all was said and done the logical choice became a 4" S&W K-frame Model 66. These guns (and their blued Model 19 counterparts) have been around for years. Although some of the older S&Ws are exceptionally nice, only the latest M-66 addressed my specifications. Due to limited availability, I wound up buying a new one and, after carefully going through the gun, I shot it for accuracy. Later, I added a small synthetic Hogue Bantam Grip, a green Hi-Viz fiber-optic front sight, and eventually, a Bowen Rough Country adjustable rear (not necessary but cool). Subsequent tuning resulted in a slick but reliable action. Holsters and loader devices were no worry thanks to a large existing collection.

Carry methods. The smallish grip keeps a lid on size, and at around 36 ounces, this M-66 carries quite well. It will snug up close enough to the body for decent CCW purposes in a leather Bianchi 7/7L Pancake holster. Two belt slots in its forward edge permit height and angle adjustment. Result: the gun rides tight and high enough to disappear inside an un-tucked shirt, and a thumb-break strap affords security beyond its molded fit. A couple 6-shot rubber speed-strips inside a right rear right pocket provide a low-profile source of spare ammo in the woods, equaling 18 total rounds.

A second synthetic Bladetech holster affords more belt-drop for range use, or for sporting purposes when worn with a coat. This holster has no active retention device per se, relying instead on its flexible, form-fitting shell. However, tension can be regulated by two Allen-head screws that pass-through rubber spacers, sandwiched between a gap along the rear of its shell. An adjustable belt-slide feature also provides plenty of latitude for solid mounting, contributing to an efficient draw. With concealment, less of a concern, one or two speed-loaders can be carried on a belt, directly ahead of the holster. Those and an extra speed-strip will boost the basic load to 24 rounds.

The pre-planning was worthwhile. I'm more than happy with the outcome and there's little this system can't handle, including most two or four-legged varmints. Still, a very small handgun can prove useful at times…

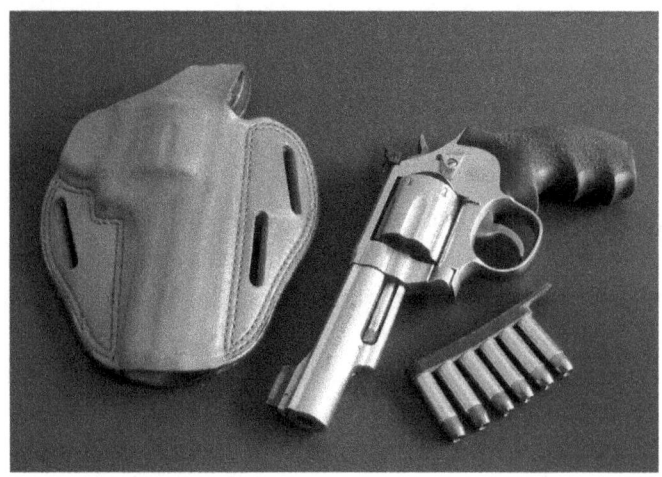
The finished Model 66, with its Bianchi "pancake" holster and a speed-strip. A thumb-break provides some retention as the gun rides high and tight.

A second, Bladetech holster provides easier access with a heavy coat. Its synthetic shell provides molded-in tension, further regulated by screws.

Deep-cover CCW mission. Although I own a few compact handguns, I was looking for a more discreet alternative that could be grabbed on the fly, mostly for local errands. In other words, it would serve strictly for self-defense. Some of the so-called derringers are in this league, but they suffer from limited capacity. The smallest 5-shot revolvers will go in a pocket, but pistols are generally flatter. A logical choice became a 5-7 shot .380 ACP. Brand allegiance was less of a concern than several key features, one being familiar operation.

Size and weight. Some .380s are not much smaller than the latest crop of miniaturized 9mms. I was after something a full notch below them, and although size was important, the gun still had to handle reasonably well. As for weight, one pound was deemed excessive. Again, there are 9mms that come close, but something weighing less than 13 ounces was more appealing.

General function. Some small pistols have bottom-mounted magazine catches instead of push-button releases. A few employ the latter feature but require a downward shove. Other micro-sized pistols won't lock back upon the last shot. Granted, they are not true fighting guns, but why not strive for similar operation? A full-function slide-stop is a darned good reload indicator that also allows a pistol to be manually locked open for safe handling and inspection. A heavy trigger seemed prudent for a pistol carried near nether regions, and a safety lever wasn't ruled out.

Finish. Once again, the choice was stainless, whether treated or bare.

Replaceable sights. Fixed sights are pretty much a given on concealable guns. However, many of the smallest guns employ rudimentary sights, integral with their slides. Although they are viewed as last-ditch, close-range tools, a visible no-snag aiming system can't hurt. In this case, I already had XS Big Dots in mind. They're streamlined, fast, and highly visible in all lighting conditions. Tritium night sight technology is part of their design, so a pistol that could accommodate them became a priority. This narrowed the choices to just a few popular pistols with replaceable sights.

Laser feature. I wrestled with this one. There's no denying the value of a laser but it does add another layer of complexity, not to mention cost. The activation of some designs also can be fiddly. Since this applied to a couple finalists, a laser went in the "maybe" section.

Holsters and accessories. Pocket pistols are a whole lot safer when their triggers are shielded by *something*. Thin, tacky-surfaced pocket holsters are sold just for this reason, but I had other carry modes in mind as well. Magazine floor-plate extensions and thin adhesive grip panels were possible extras, intended to improve recoil control. Other more exotic enhancements (trick triggers, etc.) were a lower priority, in part because of post-shooting liability concerns. Vulnerability generally increases as extra goodies are installed.

Maintenance & repairs. Since several brands were in the running, ease of disassembly for routine maintenance, spare parts, repairs and factory turn-around times were considered.

Final choice. Three pistols made the final cut. I held out on declaring a winner, pending a hands-on examination of each. In the end, I went with an S&W .380 Bodyguard; the simpler non-laser version with a manual safety. Besides addressing all the above requirements, it had a certain familiarity born by M&P Pistol experience. Two notable dissimilarities are the Bodyguard's D/A-only hammer (instead of a striker) and a somewhat different disassembly procedure. However, it handled better than expected, given its very small size. A mixed bag of ammo was digested without incident so it was time for a few extra touches. First on the list was a set of XS Big Dot Sights. A third magazine was next (the pistol comes with two). My pinky was looking for a home so I sprung for two Garrison extended magazine floor-plates.

S&W's small .380 Bodyguard with XS Big Dot Sights, a Techna Clip, and Garrison magazine extenders. Its shrouded hammer is a common DAO feature.

Carry. I picked up a basic OWB clip-on holster at a local gun show, but it didn't float my boat. After all, the idea was to make this small pistol totally disappear with a minimum amount of effort. Plan B became a metal Techna Clip, which bolts right to the gun for holsterless, IWB carry (it looks like a money-clip). You can install it right at a kitchen table with a minimum of tools and afterward, the gun will still fit inside some holsters. Although I picked up another IWB holster, the clip thingy is simple and it works.

Custody And Carry: The Basics | 115

During winter's heavy coat season (darned near year-round here), I can just drop the gun in a pocket, but the safety will go on first. That's about the only time I use it though. A more conventional presentation will be similar to that of our agency's safety-less M&Ps. Pocket-carry is not the best method by itself, and in this case, I've introduced another variable (the safety) that negates the KISS approach. The safety-lever introduces an extra step, assuming I even remember it's engaged. Clearly, more discipline is called for. Meanwhile, I'll settle for this slothful compromise-strategy with no real excuse for ignorance.

Stay tuned for more about the Bodyguard in the pistol chapter. Meanwhile, for better or worse, mission accomplished!

SUMMARY

Shopping for a firearm is always fun for us gun nuts. If nothing else, it's a good excuse to hit a few gun shops and ogle the toys. The same process can be daunting for beginners, but so some basic information helps. The big thing to remember is, when all is said and done, we'll really be shopping for a "system." The gun is only part of it. Holsters, accessories, ammunition, training, and security devices represent the real bottom line, and since the type of handgun will play a pivotal role in a personalized security plan, the most practical options come next.

SECTION II
THE REVOLVER - 19th CENTURY TECHNOLOGY THAT REFUSES TO DIE

Chapter 9: REVOLVER BASICS 119

Chapter 10: USEFUL REVOLVER CARTRIDGES 123

Chapter 11: SINGLE-ACTION REVOLVERS 143

Chapter 12: DOUBLE-ACTION REVOLVERS 149

Chapter 13: MORE DOUBLE-ACTIONS: S&W'S LINE 155

Chapter 14: GOOD REVOLVER PICKS: S&W – AND OTHERS 173

Chapter 15: HANDY REVOLVER ACCESSORIES 181

Chapter 16: KEEP YOUR WHEELGUN RUNNING 189

CHAPTER 9
REVOLVER BASICS

With the luxury of a decent range, our Firearms Training Unit periodically hosts staff development courses. During 2013, we hosted a preeminent field school, filling the firing line with certified firearms instructors from various state LE agencies. A couple of us "experienced" types (as in older) were anxiously awaiting a session pertaining to revolvers. When that time arrived, one of our younger cadre exclaimed, "Oh, it's time for the antiques!" As it turned out, several shooters from other state agencies had zero revolver experience. Two managed to cobble together makeshift revolver packages after viewing the itinerary, but others were completely stumped. Fortunately, we'd stashed an inventory of well-used 4-inch S&W double-action Model 65s from our revolver era. The M-65 is an evolution of the Model 10, and both were a mainstay LE choice for years. Besides some revolvers, we'd also hung on to a collection of holsters, speed-loaders and ammo. As we doled out the goodies, a twinkle in our guest instructor's eyes was evident. A retired LEO himself, he'd served during the transitional period from revolvers to semi-autos. Like many others from that era, he considered a wheel-gun an old but still-reliable friend.

It was time to load up. The M-65 is a .357 Magnum, but it will also fire milder .38 Special cartridges. When the dust finally settled, we'd burned through a bunch of 130-grain .38 Special full-metal-jacket round-nose loads (FMJ RN). Any disparaging comments about the viability of a good D/A revolver had also disappeared. We'd made a point of locating Mr. Antique amidst the most experienced revolver shooters and it's fair to say he got one heck of an education. It probably didn't hurt that the guy to his right just happened to be an International Defensive Pistol Association (IDPA) "Stock Service Revolver" champion with first-place wins from several states. It's doubtful he could've kept up, even with his polymer wonder-nine.

One of the actual S&W M-65s described above, still going strong after thousands of rounds.

IT'S THE NUT BEHIND THE WHEELGUN

While this may sound like a stretch, we have a basis for comparison. We have occasionally run multi-agency programs involving a mix of pistol and revolver shooters. Our agency stayed with revolvers longer than most, so we took great pains to offer the best training possible. Beyond pure accuracy, much emphasis was directed toward reloading skills, and this paid off. I'll never forget a joint qualification course with a mixed group of officers. Our revolver shooters absolutely hammered the pistol crew, much to their dismay. Adding insult to injury, the first shots after a timed reloading stage were fired from a revolver. Chalk up another education, compliments of well-versed wheelgun shooters.

Everyone gets fixated on equipment at the expense of operator skills, but they're *both* important. I'll take a group of well-trained shooters with mediocre equipment over another crew with top-flight gear and mediocre skills every time. Here's a chilling hypothetical question: how would one of today's wonder-nine shooters fare against old Wild Bill Hickock? My money is on Mr. Hickock and his brace of well-maintained percussion-fired, black powder Navy Colts. He'd no doubt lose on reloading stages, but that's why he carried a second gun. A pair of modern S&W .357s would certainly be no less of a threat, although one alone would likely cover most bases. So rest assured, a place still exists for a solidly built revolver.

Besides IDPA, another skillful revolver group participates in the sport of "cowboy action shooting," which is governed by the Single-Action Shooting Society (SASS). Although the D/A revolver was developed for rapidity of shots, there are plenty of SASS members who can thumb-cock through a cylinder full of lead with blazing speed. In deference to slower S/A reloads, two guns are often still the norm, and the revolver of choice remains a facsimile of Colt's Model 1873. We'll look closer at some S/A and D/A choices after a few generalized revolver comments.

REVOLVER PLUSSES AND MINUSES

Here's a question: why does the revolver show up first here? Beyond the chronological progression, it's a dependable choice. Rumors to the contrary, it's certainly not foolproof. We've witnessed many live-fire debacles, most attributable to operator error. Yes, a revolver is simple, but it's still possible to get in a heap of trouble with one, making a case for proper training!

Advantages. For starters, a revolver is simple. Particularly with the double-action, swing-out cylinder types in common use today, load-status can be verified at a glance. A revolver is also self-contained, not requiring separate magazines. Furthermore, because the action is manually cycled, a revolver is much more ammo tolerant.

Ammo advantages. You'll know right away if a cartridge will properly chamber, so the entire cylinder full is "pre-checked" during the loading process. Also, unlike a semiauto pistol, repeat chamberings won't ding up your ammo. Just handle the same rounds with respect and they should work fine.

Semi-autos function through a careful orchestration of ammo-generated pressure and recoil. Gun mass, spring-tension, and the shooter's physique are parts of this equation. Not so with a revolver. Given enough strength to pull the trigger, and a cartridge that will fit, the gun will probably go bang. If it doesn't, another shot is only a trigger-pull away. Great versatility is also possible through dual-caliber options like .38 Special/.357 Magnum, etc.

Operation. During dire circumstances, many revolvers will fire from the confines of a pocket or purse. The same is true during a hard-contact struggle which can shove a pistol slightly out of battery (at that point its disconnector will disengage the firing mechanism, preventing the gun from firing). Thanks to a minimum of controls, revolver basics can also be easily understood, and operation may be less physically challenging than those semiauto pistols with stiffer spring-powered slides (which must be manipulated for loading or clearance). Access to a cylinder requires nothing more than finger pressure, and loading or unloading is assisted by gravity.

Marksmanship development. Because the barrel and sights are rigidly mounted to the frame, a revolver tends to be accurate, and stationary sights play a further role regarding marksmanship. Accomplished shooters "call their shots," meaning they know exactly where their sights are in relationship to the target when the gun discharges. It's a harder skill to master with centerfire pistols because the sights are normally located on a reciprocating slide. The first reaction is to blink when an object is headed towards our eyes – something we often see with newer pistol shooters, some of whom even jerk their heads rearward. Obviously, this reaction is not conducive to shot-calling!

Practice makes perfect and dry-firing is a great off-range exercise for marksmanship improvement. After verifying the gun as empty, the shooter acquires sight alignment on some makeshift target with a safe backstop (just in case things go wrong). Proper trigger control can then be practiced, along with follow-through. It's easy with a revolver since the fire-control mechanism isn't dependent on a reciprocating slide, and unlike some pistols, a revolver's trigger pulls will remain consistent.

On a range, the revolver is also great for "ball & dummy" exercises. Spent cases can be randomly mixed in with live rounds, causing occasional "duds." Flinching is a major handgun curse resulting from an involuntary reaction to noise and recoil, evident through convulsive downward hand movements. If attention remains focused on the sights, these involuntary movements will be apparent when a dummy round is encountered. The ball & dummy route is the best cure for flinching by far, and it's *much* easier to set up with a revolver.

Personalized grips. Most revolvers incorporate separate grip panels which are easy to replace, and the more popular models ensure a wide variety of after-market options. Personalized fit can improve results on-target, and although not necessary, ornamental designs are a further possibility.

Durability. To a large extent, the life a gun is dependent on maintenance and the type of ammo fired, so quantifiable service can be hard to predict. but remember that 2013 S&W Field School? The Model 65s we handed out had been purchased in 1991. They had certainly digested 50,000+ rounds, and the actual number might've been closer to 75,000. They ran fine.

Disadvantages. Two big revolver drawbacks are limited capacity (at least, compared to the current crop of high-cap nines), and generally slower reloading times. By the nature of its design, a revolver also has a small but necessary gap between the cylinder face and barrel. As noted, especially with potent calibers, considerable blast can be emitted through this juncture, posing a hazard for any adjacent digits. Pacing the support hand's index finger on the forward surface of a trigger guard is therefore an ill-advised revolver habit, and one we universally discourage! Finally, lacking an active safety mechanism, a revolver is a snatch-and-shoot weapon (also true of many so-called "safe-action" pistols).

Barrel/cylinder gap damage from the blast of just five .357 Magnums!

Capacity. General-purpose revolvers typically provide six shots. The smallest versions hold five and a few large specimens afford eight. Although some of the rimfire models accept ten rounds, their defensive capability will be seriously hamstrung by marginal power, but all of these numbers pale in comparison to 17-round magazines typical of 9mm pistols. In theory, we might be able to offset revolver limitations through expedited reloads, but one large magazine is just a whole lot easier to manage. Revolver loading-devices attempt to remedy the problem by consolidating loose rounds into speed-loaders, moon clips, or speed-strips, all of which we'll examine. With the right techniques, some are pretty darned fast, but given two equally accomplished shooters, expect the pistol to be back in action first. That said, it's still possible to reload a revolver in short order.

Snatch & shoot. If we examine a typical D/A revolver, its lack of controls will be evident. With the cylinder closed, the most conspicuous gizmo will be a frame-mounted tab which some may mistake for a safety button. In actuality, it's a "thumb-piece," that unlocks the cylinder. There isn't any active safety per-se. Instead, the odds of inadvertent firing are minimized by a long and heavy D/A trigger pull. So, if the revolver was ever lost during a struggle, someone with zero firearms experience could shoot you with it by simply pulling its trigger. On the other hand, many semi-auto pistols (including a military-issued D/A Beretta M-9, or S/A 1911 Government Model) have some type of active safety lever. But here's where it gets interesting: the latest genre of striker-fired pistols (Glock, M&P, Sig, etc.) are devoid of active safety levers. Instead, they rely on heavier trigger pulls and/or built-in interrupters to resist rearward travel. Glock's "safe-action trigger" is a prime example. It'll prevent the pistol from firing if dropped, because a thin blade within the trigger-face must be depressed to allow rearward movement. In a gun-snatch situation, these designs are no more reassuring than a revolver - with the added threat of extra shots. One fix with any handgun type is this: don't give up the gun! Proper mindset, effective clothing, and the right holster are important considerations.

IDIOSYNCRACIES

To some extent, a single-action revolver is a different animal. For starters, the many iterations of the Peacemaker won't fire unless the hammer is first manually cocked. With revolver knowledge waning, this *could* be a lifesaver during a struggle. Then again, a traditional S/A revolver design may fire even when un-cocked through an inadvertent blow to its hammer! A modern hammer-block design (like a current Ruger) can be safely loaded to full capacity. The traditional S/As should be carried one round shy, with an empty chamber resting under the hammer, for insurance against the consequences of an impact. Cocking the hammer will simultaneously index a live round and ready the gun to fire, but this extra step - and lack of a swing-out cylinder - account for the popularity of D/A revolvers for defense.

Cylinder rotation. This should be another concern for revolver owners: to locate an empty chamber underneath a single-action's hammer, we'll need to know which way it turns. No big deal here; we can just eyeball the alignment (safely please), but things get more interesting during any partial loads. Let's say you want to load just two rounds in a D/A revolver. Easy enough; just swing open the cylinder and toss them in, right? Trouble is, when the cylinder is closed, where will they wind up? Without an understanding of cylinder rotation, you might be in for a version of Russian roulette. As a believer in Murphy's Law, I for one have no interest in owning any guns with opposite rotations.

Fool proof? It IS possible to jam a revolver! The cause is operator error related to swing-out cylinder designs. One common stoppage is a fired case, lodged underneath the extractor. Game over until it's removed, which can be a challenge for some so-called operators, even in broad daylight. Insurance against this nasty stoppage is the correct, muzzle-up, unloading technique, followed by a good smack to the extractor (more on this later).

A fired case lodged under an extractor can be tough to clear. More often, the cause is operator error combined with shorter .38 Specials in .357 Magnum cylinders. (Rotation tip: The small scallops adjacent to the cylinder notches serve as arrows.)

Trigger-control issues. Some double-action revolvers actually aren't at all, because their S/A modes have been omitted. Most are defensive, small-frame types designed for deep-concealment, and many have shrouded or internal hammers to prevent snagging within pockets. Although most large D/A revolvers offer two firing modes, defensive responses are typically initiated through long, deliberate double-action trigger pulls. During deep trouble, whatever is happening will probably require a quick reaction. A D/A response is plenty fast and less prone to unintended discharges, but here's the rub: some people have a heck of a time mastering proper D/A trigger technique. It should be more of a stroke than a squeeze, as opposed to a "crank & yank." Once you figure out the right technique, everything feels smooth, and at some point, the hammer will fall during the long and continuous stroke, promoting good follow-through, without flinching. Trouble is, in our experience, some people – maybe 20% - never fully get it, resorting to a staple gun technique. Since the trigger is traveling a relatively long distance during the yank, the violently applied force permits extra muzzle movement. Hits will usually be biased toward the right for a right-handed shooter. The problem is curable with remedial work and frequent practice, but then again, the road to Hell is also paved with good intentions. Many of these folks show marked improvements after transitioning to striker-fired pistols with shorter and somewhat lighter trigger pulls. This switch also eliminates first-shot difficulties with double-action pistols, which typically employ revolver-like trigger strokes.

Another class of shooters just might not have enough strength to cycle a D/A trigger at all. A good indicator is the inclination to employ *both* trigger fingers. That won't work any better than two people attempting to steer a car. In that case, strength issues will require a different gun, hand exercises, or both steps. The trigger-pull problem is eliminated with a single-action revolver, but loading will be slow. I'd hate to wake up to breaking glass with an empty S/A. While the spate of new fast-access gun storage containers could provide enough security to justify a loaded gun, reloads would be problematic.

Unique training concerns. We always recommend professional training, especially when self-defense is considered. Nowadays though, finding a fully-qualified revolver source can be a challenge, especially if younger instructors are involved. I just watched an interesting online review of a new S&W revolver from a well-respected source, but while watching his loading and unloading techniques, the lack of in-depth experience was obvious. This makes perfect sense considering his high-speed military background, a phenomenon we've observed among others with similar sandbox experience. Keep that in mind before investing in a revolver, and maybe, look for an Old Fart (like me).

MOVING ON

Professional defensive training will center on a double-action type revolver, but not everyone will be thinking in terms of two-legged threats, as evidenced by the common use of large singe-actions in bear country. These guns are typically chambered for some serious calibers with enough power to pose real control issues during more typical uses that center around self-defense. This leads to questions about what constitutes a good revolver cartridge.

CHAPTER 10
USEFUL REVOLVER CARTRIDGES

What follows is by no means a complete list of revolver cartridges. Instead, the focus is on those calibers more likely to be found on retail shelves. Some readers might be surprised to see the ever-popular 9mm Luger pistol cartridge listed among revolver choices, but this option does in fact exist. It may be of some interest to prospective revolver owners who already have semiautomatic pistols and, for that matter, 9mm Luger ammo might now be more common than classic .38 Special/.357 Magnum rounds.

Not shown is the popular .40 S&W, only because so few revolvers have been built in this caliber. S&W sold some neat 10mm/.40 moon clip revolvers but they've disappeared. However, this situation may reverse to some extent, driven largely by the revival of 10mm handguns. Ruger just launched a dual-cylinder 10mm/.40 S/A Blackhawk, and a 10mm Super Redhawk which will also fire .40 rounds thanks to moon clips. Charter Arms also lists a small-framed 5-shot *Pitbull* .40 S&W snubby. You can read more about these cartridges in the Pistol Cartridge Section.

COMMON CALIBERS

The cartridges listed below have a loose dimensional relationship with revolver size, but of course, there are exceptions to every rule, as evidenced by Charter Arms' small 5-shot revolvers that can fire large .44 Special bullets. For the most part, the smaller calibers often appear in smaller guns, simply because they make the best fit. Some of the largest calibers could possibly be engineered to fit in smaller-framed revolvers, but capacity would suffer and recoil would become excessive, with dramatic reduction in gun life. So, let's start small and work our way up…

Small calibers. First up, two rimfire choices: the hugely popular .22 Long Rifle (.22 LR), and the somewhat popular .22 Winchester Magnum Rimfire (.22 WMR). These chamberings are sold in both small and medium-frame revolvers, but the smaller types remain more popular, serving as so-called "kit-guns."

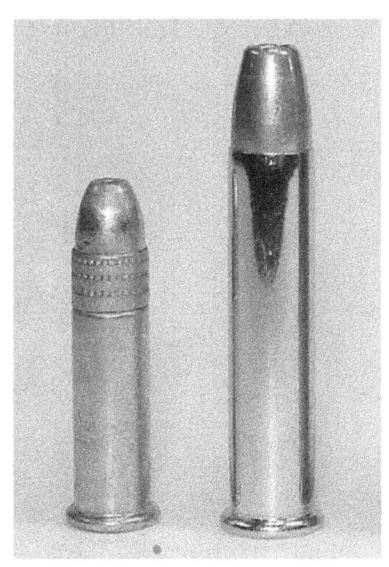

Caution: .22 LR and .22 WMR cartridges are not interchangeable! Beyond extra pressure and length, the .22 Magnum (R) also has a fatter case.

The old centerfire .32 Long (L) evolved to the .32 H&R Magnum, which later spawned the .327 Federal. The latter can fire all three.

The high-pressure .357 Magnum (L) achieves its velocity through use of a lengthened .38 Special case stoked with extra powder. The .38 +P (C) shares standard .38 Special dimensions (R), but is loaded to higher pressure.

A relative newcomer is the centerfire .327 Federal, which will also fire .32 H&R Magnum ammo, plus .32 Long cartridges. It often appears as a small-framed revolver chambering because six cartridges will fit and the recoil associated with larger calibers will be noticeably lessened.

Mid calibers. The preeminent choice is the indomitable .357 Magnum, which will also fire standard-velocity .38 Special and hotter +P versions. The .357 is more often see in 6-shot medium-framed revolvers, but large 7 or 8-shot, and small 5-shot guns are also available. Since recoil can be severe in the smallest lightweight revolvers, many are sold as five-shot .38 Specials.

A .38 Special +P (L) looks more potent, but its performance isn't all that different from the higher-pressure 9mm.

A more obscure revolver chambering accommodates one of most widespread handgun calibers, the rimless 9mm Luger. Power is roughly the equivalent of .38 +P loads. This chambering is growing new legs in small-frame revolvers, which are scaled for a perfect fit. The rimless cartridges require some reengineering for headspace and ejection, but manufacturers have successfully risen to this challenge.

Large calibers. The .41 Magnum falls roughly midway between the .357 and .44 Magnums, where it languishes as a useful niche caliber, employed by experienced shooters, most often in larger-frame revolvers.

Although the .44 Magnum of Dirty Harry fame is no longer the most powerful load, it's certainly stout. In fact, for all but the most experience shooters, the .44 Magnum is probably pushing the envelope to point of excess. However, it can also fire .44 Special cartridges which are fairly manageable in a full-size revolver. The smaller Charter Arms, 5-shot, .44 Special-only revolvers are in interesting spin-off, although they generate a fair amount of recoil.

A non-conventional revolver chambering is the very popular .45 ACP. Although widely associated with the 1911 Pistol, this cartridge has been successfully adapted thanks to WW 1 technology for use in large-frame revolvers.

Among revolver calibers qualifying as "large", (L-R) the .41 Magnum, .44 Magnum, and .45 Colt are more common.

We know that the older *.45 Colt* (also known as the .45 Long Colt or .45 LC) was a revolver caliber from its inception. Both .45 loads hit with authority, but in modern guns, the .45 LC can be loaded hotter than a .45 ACP due to its greater case capacity. In strong Ruger SAs, hand-loaders push the .45 Colt to near .44 Magnum levels. Factory loads are still fine in Colt-type single-action six-shooters or large S&W D/A revolvers.

The dual-purpose .45 LC/.410 is an unorthodox possibility in a revolver large enough to accommodate 2 ½-inch (or, sometimes, 3-inch) .410 shells, as well as .45 Colt cartridges. Taurus and S&W sell stretched-frame D/A revolvers just for this purpose.

Most of the above offerings are sold as larger, steel-frame revolvers, scaled to accommodate six shots. However, use of lighter alloys can help reduce weight, which is fine to a point. The lighter we go, the more recoil we'll encounter; especially in a .44 Magnum!

Big boomers. The *.454 Casull* is a magnumized (stretched-out) .45 Colt loaded to higher pressure. Its performance and recoil climb to entirely new levels, but the older .45 LC cartridge can also be fired. Not to be outdone, Smith & Wesson more recently came out with large X-frame D/A revolvers in .460 S&W, and .500 S&W. The newer and even hotter .460 will digest .454 Casull *and* .45 LC, presenting some interesting possibilities. Eventually, Magnum Research jumped on board with BFR single-action revolvers. Taurus came out with a double-action .454 Casull in their Raging Series. Recoil-wise, the big .500 S&W is in a league of its own. Many of these big-boomers reappear in gun shops as "barely used," due to exciting effects encountered upon their discharge. The group of owners most likely to remain owners are Alaskan bush people, for whom bears are a threat. Ruger's *.480* is somewhat less fierce but a notch above the .44 Magnum. You can buy one as a Super Redhawk in either caliber, as well as in .454 Casull. However, recoil issues aside, consider the odds of finding any ammo.

A .357 Magnum, shown for comparison beside (L-R): A .41 Magnum, .44 Magnum, .45 Colt, and .500 S&W big-boomer.

Not available in your local hardware store! The previously mentioned .300 GNR is a custom "wildcat" cartridge formed from shortened .30/30 brass. Velocity (2100 fps with 110 JHPs) exceeds an M-1 .30 Carbine, from a standard S/A Ruger cylinder!

Other oddities. Magnum Research has broken the mold with their single-action BFR Revolver. Supposedly, this stands for "big frame revolver," but you get the idea. Besides some of the above big revolver calibers, its extra-long cylinder can handle rifle rounds like the .30/30, .45/70, and .450 Marlin. Because of its size, recoil from the .30/30 is surprisingly mild, whereas I found the others to be quite invigorating!

Sometimes, what's old is new again. The rimless .30 Carbine (L) performed similarly to an older high-velocity .32-20 load (C). Ballistically, both have much in common with the latest .327 Federal.

The .30 Carbine deserves mention because of Ruger's single-action, 7 ½," .30 Carbine Blackhawk. As a stand-alone handgun, I can think of better choices, but some people still own useful M-1 Carbines. Given today's better ammo, a shoulder-fired .30 Carbine is not a bad defensive choice (as mentioned in *Centerfire Rifles: A Buyer's Guide*). The 18-inch barrel will spit out a 110 grain .308-diameter bullet at nearly 2000 fps. Barrel length is a major factor, but a .30 Carbine 7 ½-inch Blackhawk should still be good for around 1500 fps. One thing's for certain - it'll be loud!

AN ALL-AROUND REVOLVER CHOICE

A winning pick becomes simpler when we think "general purpose," which leads directly to the well-proven and versatile .357 Magnum. It's time for an in-depth look at the various .357 Magnum and .38 Special options.

.357 Magnum. Although it dates to 1935, "The Three-Fifty-Seven" remains a benchmark for defensive "stopping power." The magnum cartridge-case is based on a slightly lengthened .38 Special (+0.125"), loaded to higher pressure. Recoil is stiff with lots of muzzle-blast to boot, but many serious handgunners can manage this cartridge. Other aspiring shooters could work up to full-strength .357 Magnums after plenty of .38 Special practice. Casual shooters could hold the line with .38 Special +P loads, and beginners should always start with mild .38 Specials.

.38 Special +P. These loads are just warmer versions of a standard .38 Special. You can feel a noticeable difference, but recoil isn't extreme. The cartridge case is a regular .38 Special and bullet weights are similar. Velocity will be higher for better terminal results; however, many older revolvers should not be fired with +P ammunition. The same is true for some of the smallest S&W J-Frames. You won't blow one up, but a steady diet may loosen the gun. In a modern .357 medium-size K-Frame, .38 Special +P may be the optimum choice for many. Power will fall between standard .38 Special loads and full-house .357 Magnums, recoil will remain manageable, and muzzle-flash won't be excessive. And, of course, the full-power Magnum option is still available if needed.

.38 Special. This circa 1899 load is mild in all but the very lightest little J-Frames. As such, the venerable .38 provides plenty of control for follow-up shots. The original 158-grain lead round-nose bullets were pretty anemic, but bullet technology has come a long way. Many people shoot milder .38 Specials during practice and switch to hotter +Ps or .357s for serious work. It's not a bad concept, saving money as well as wear and tear.

Putting all three loads to work. A well-built, medium-frame revolver (like an S&W K-frame) should live up to all reasonable accuracy expectations, and with most loads it will probably shoot two-inch or better groups at 25 yards. In theory, a .38 Special might be a bit less accurate in a longer .357 Magnum chamber due to bullet jump. Maybe, but in my experience any degradation is minimal.

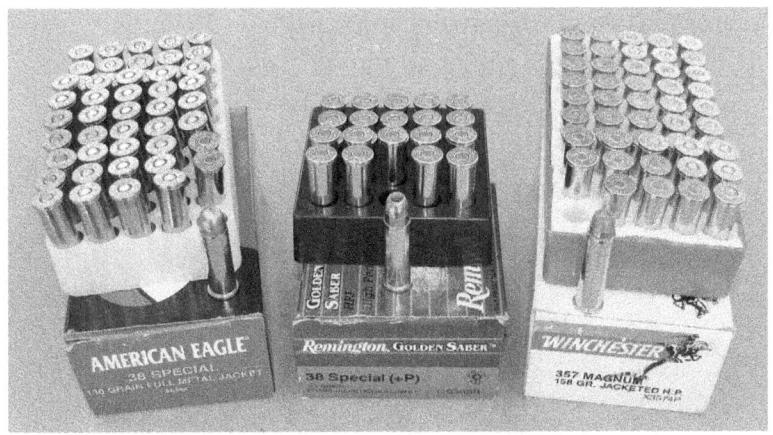

The .357 Magnum is a versatile choice. Shop carefully and you'll gain three distinct power-levels that can cover most bases. These are just a few of many competing offerings.

<u>Point of impact.</u> The three different loads have varying velocities, which will almost certainly affect POI. Believe it or not, at closer range, the faster loads may shoot lower due to less bore-time during recoil. Somewhat strangely, at greater distances POI could reverse due to trajectory. Again, this is a good reason to consider adjustable sights. Many have repeatable click-stops for both windage and elevation. You can either count clicks when switching loads, or use a feeler gauge. During our agency's

Useful Revolver Cartridges | 129

revolver days, we shot .38 Special across the board, using 130-grain .38 Special FMJ for practice; and warmer 125 grain +P JHP for carry. Both loads shot darn close to point of aim and recoil wasn't an issue with either. The +Ps were a bit brighter at night, but nothing like full-house magnums. You could probably cover at least 90% of your needs using a similar strategy.

Target practice and small game hunting. The same .38 Special Federal American Eagle 130-grain FMJ we used for range-ammo should work just fine here. Most major manufacturers offer a similar and affordable "Q-load" (qualification load). Besides Federal AE, we've shots tons (literally) of *Winchester USA 130s*. A paper target won't care what it's drilled by, and rabbits won't be blown to smithereens. I've shot larger snowshoe hares with round-nose FMJs and some ran a short distance, illustrating why we shouldn't choose such a bullet for defense. A 158-grain lead semi-wadcutter (LSWC) works more effectively without wrecking much meat, but it can produce some barrel leading. The same type of bullet with a hole in its nose is a LSWCHP. There's a good chance of at least some expansion from a 4-inch or longer barrel, making it a more effective multi-purpose "stopper," something the FBI figured out years ago.

Up through the 1970s, full wad-cutter .38 Special target loads were as common as warts. The cylindrical lead bullets weighed 148 grains and, lacking any sort of nose, they were seated flush or nearly so within the cartridge cases. The virtue of a LWC was clean holes in paper. Accuracy was extremely good but fast reloads were quite a challenge. The commercial types were (are) swaged from fairly soft lead with hollow bases. They flew like badminton birdies so they were stable and accurate. Some people even hand-loaded them backwards for use as jumbo hollow-points. I haven't shot one in years or, for that matter, any sort of lead .357 - .358 bullet (lead types often measure .358"). Plated bullets from outfits like Berry's and Rainier have become popular alternatives for hand-loaders, mainly because they are much less likely to cause leading.

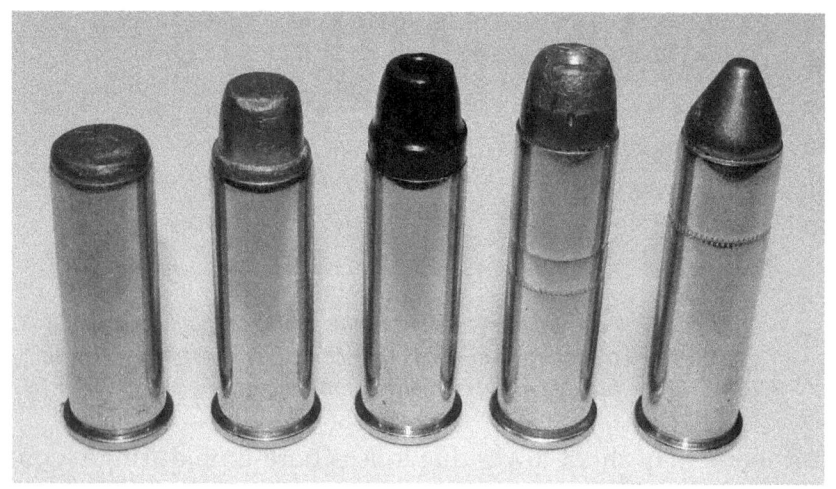

A sampling of .38/.357 loads (L-R): .38 Special LWC, LSWC, LSWCHP; .357 Magnum JHP, and even an old pointed "metal-case" for use against vehicles!

Today's revolvers and factory-loaded ammunition will seldom cause problems regardless of a bullet's composition, but caution is advised with older guns of varying barrel/cylinder gaps, or chamber and bore diameters. If looser tolerances bleed off too much pressure, milder loads, particularly jacket types, can wind up stuck in a barrel. Softer lead bullets can be the safer bet and most commercially loaded types do use such types. But, one problem with lead bullets – especially those driven to higher velocities – is leading. An accumulation can rapidly develop in the chambers, forcing cone, and barrel. If left unchecked, it can degrade accuracy while increasing pressures to unsafe levels. Hobby bullet casters often create harder lead alloys through the addition of tin (or even old linotype), but many commercial bullets are swaged from softer mixes. Such alloys are more prone to leading, but they all can cause problems. A "gas-check" is a small copper cup that helps shield the bullet's base, and while it helps with warmer loads, sooner or later, every barrel will need attention. The Lewis Lead Remover is one fix. An alternate trick involves following up lead bullets with a few jacketed rounds, the theory being accumulated lead will solder itself to the hot copper jackets. This practice can be unsafe, depending upon the amount of residual lead. I've gone both routes, reserving the jacketed-bullet trick for low volume range work in modern revolvers.

Load choices really boil down to personal preference although you might want to consider similar bullet-weights so impact variations will be minimized. Winchester has capitalized on this concept with their Train & Defend line of handgun cartridges. For example, they offer a pair of 130 grain .38 Special loads in FMJ and JHP which offer identical POI.

Defense. One of the all-time best fight-stoppers is a .357 Magnum 125-grain, jacketed hollow-point – period. You'll pay a price for such performance extending beyond cost, since recoil and muzzle flash will be significant. If you can handle these effects, then great, use the Magnums. But shoot a few in low-light, where the effects could be dramatic! The latest defense loads are formulated for less flash, but a full-house magnum still burns a lot of powder.

If you are searching for something less dramatic, we tested a few different .38 +P loads using the FBI Protocols. We went with Remington .38 Special, 125 grain +P, Golden Saber, brass-jacketed hollow-points (BJHPs). Out of a 3-inch Model 65, expansion and weight-retention were very good. Wondering about the upper limits of this bullet's velocity integrity, I managed to shoot a 135-pound whitetail buck (dressed weight) broadside. I used a Marlin .357 lever-action rifle, and the range was around 30 yards. This .38 +P load really cranks on some horsepower from a longer rifle barrel. The Marlin's 24-inch tube clocked 1,400 fps through our chronograph! I wish the bullet had

Remington's .38 Special +P "Golden Saber" BJHPs: The expanded bullet was fired from a 3" revolver. Typical of many HPs, wood clogged the other one (but it will still leave a mark).

been recovered, but it passed completely through the ribcage, leaving a thumb-sized exit. The deer ran *maybe* 50 yards and piled up. Since then, I've used .38 +P GS to shoot a few other critters, leading me to conclude that it's a reasonably rugged bullet. I wouldn't doubt that Speer's Gold Dot would be an equally good choice and, for that matter, the big-name manufacturers all offer darned good loads, driven in part by those FBI protocols.

The above mentioned 158 grain LSWCHPs were, at one point, a popular expanding .38 +P choice. Expansion was reliable, but again, all-lead bullets are fading in deference to the many excellent jacketed types. Speer's 135 grain +P JHP is worth a look, especially for use in shorter barreled revolvers. Velocity is high enough to initiate expansion and the lighter bullet is less subject to inertial creep. Very light 110-grain .38 Special JHP loads have become popular for similar reasons, with the bonus of less recoil.

Hunting larger game. A dedicated hunting revolver could benefit from a bigger caliber like the .41 or .44 Magnum, but if we're trying to cover all bases with just one gun, the .357 will do. So, consider a combination of power, expansion and penetration. A 140-grain bullet would be a good starting point, but if black bears are in the mix, Federal's 180 grain Power-Shok would be a better choice. Shoot carefully and plan on a sight adjustment first. Barnes also catalogs a 140-grain VOR-TX, which employs a solid-copper bullet. If it works as well as their rifle bullets, all three requirements should be easily met. I'd still expect a sight adjustment, but it might be less extreme. The .357 standard has been a 158-grain bullet whether soft-point or hollow-point. I shoot the latter as Winchester Super-X, and so far, accuracy has been excellent from several guns. The additional mass ensures decent penetration, making it a good all-around choice for defense and hunting.

Barnes solid-copper .357 Magnums are worthy of consideration for deer-size game. Expansion, weight retention, and penetration are typically excellent.

Accuracy of shorter .38 Special loads in .357 Magnum chambers. Some shooters worry about a decline in accuracy resulting from chamber jump. This concern seems plausible so I set up a simple test involving loads of proven accuracy. Two batches of Hornady swaged LWC hollow-base 148-grain handloads were carefully assembled using new .38 Special *and* .357 Magnum cases. Both loads were then fired through the same .357 Magnum S&W 6-inch Model 686 from 25 yards. The difference in accuracy was negligible, so shooting progressed to 50 yards. No clear winner was apparent despite the extra 0.125" of chamber jump required of the .38 Specials. Five-shot groups averaged just above three inches with either.

Later, I fired some jacketed factory .38 Special and .357 Magnum loads through a spare ten-inch .357 Maximum barrel mounted to a T/C Contender frame. The plan was to discover the effects of substantial chamber jump on accuracy, since a .357 Maximum case is a full 0.300" longer than a .357 Magnum - and a whopping 0.425" more than a .38 Special! In theory, bullets – especially the .38s - should develop a bit of wobble as they jumped this extra chamber space. One might then expect off-center engagement of the rifling and poorer accuracy. At 50 yards, POI was lower, but accuracy was more than acceptable, with group sizes being only minimally larger.

Conclusion. Nowadays, I worry more about the effects of individual loads on .38/.357 accuracy. The .357 Magnum has always been a great caliber and recent bullet improvements only make it better. The capability to fire additional standard-velocity and +P .38 Special loads makes the .357 an excellent all-around choice - particularly for someone looking to streamline their firearm inventory.

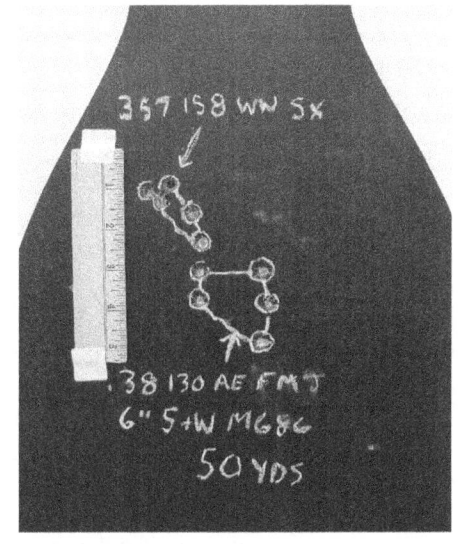

Accuracy of shorter .38 Specials won't always suffer in .357 magnum chambers. At 50 yards, both groups were tight from an S&W M-686. Its heavy 6" barrel may account for the surprisingly close POIs.

OTHER POTENTIAL REVOLVER CANDIDATES

We could end it right here with the .357 Magnum, but there are other points to ponder. An under-study rimfire is always handy for practice, plinking, or potting small game; and if recoil is an issue, a lighter-kicking alternative could also be considered. Others may just wish to simplify logistics through use of an on-hand horde. Finally, there are certain circumstances where raw power is a must.

.22 Long Rifle (.22 LR). The "Twenty-two," or .22 Long Rifle, is too light for self-defense, but perfect for small game and practice. For anyone considering a second revolver, a .22 makes sense as a great trainer, plinker, and camp-meat provider. You can also stuff in

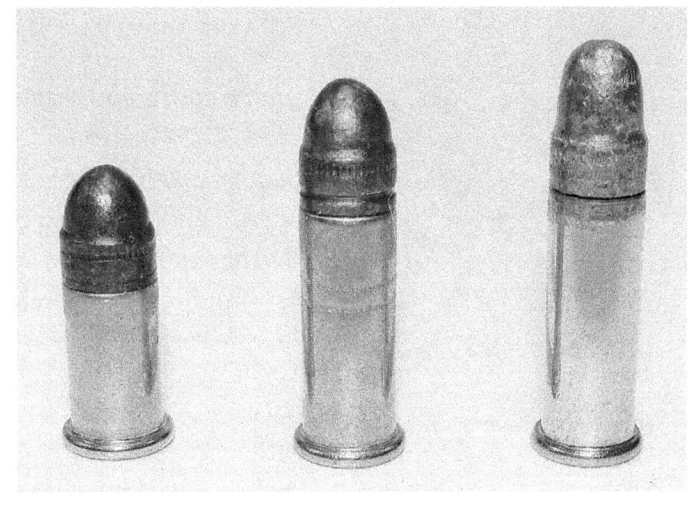

A .22 LR revolver will digest several shorter options. The .22 Long (C) is now semi-obsolete, but .22 Shorts (R) remain popular.

Useful Revolver Cartridges | 133

some intriguing loads like .22 Shorts, CB Caps or shot-shells. The latter are strictly a close-range option, best reserved for use against snakes, since their effectiveness is measured in feet instead of yards. CB Caps behave like even milder .22 Short loads, and both are much quieter than standard .22 LR cartridges. Feeding is also a non-issue in a manually cycled revolver. CCI's "Quiet" .22 LR is another short-range possibility for small game or beverage cans within 20 yards or thereabout.

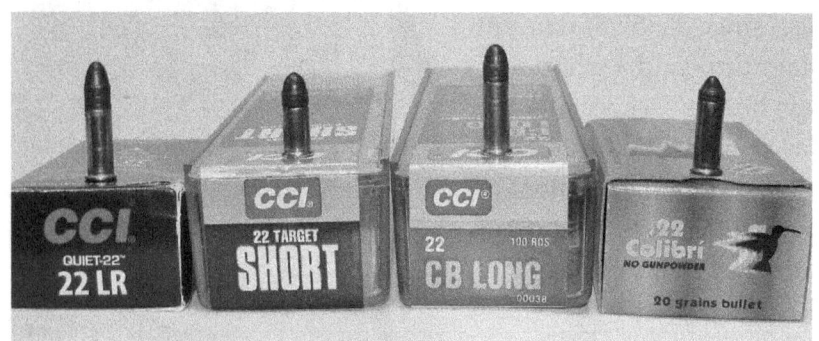

Further options include quiet, lower-velocity loads, shown (L-R) in descending levels of power.

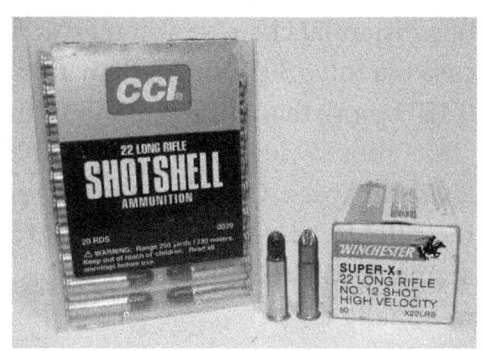

Rimfire shot-loads are strictly short-range propositions due to their miniscule payloads. BUT, they will function in revolvers.

.22 LR cartridges of any type were scarce until recently, but the situation has greatly improved. Rimfires can be picky eaters so the greater variety of choices is beneficial for accuracy testing, which also provides extra practice. With just a bit of luck you'll find an economical load with which to perforate cans or other inanimate targets, regardless of whether the bullet is a hollow-point or solid-nose design. Depending on your quarry though, an HP is often the better small game choice.

Some confusion exists concerning the interchangeability .22 Long Rifle and .22 Winchester Magnum Rimfire cartridges. The big question is, can you safely fire .22 LR cartridges in a .22 WMR chamber? The answer is *no!* Because the longer .22 Magnum cartridge develops much higher pressure, its diameter is increased a bit to prevent chambering in standard .22 LR chambers. A .22 LR *will* drop into a .22 WMR chamber, but firing one will result in a ruptured case and lots of escaping high-pressure gas – don't even try it!

The .22 Magnum (.22 WMR) enjoys some popularity in revolvers, and this Speer load is marketed for short-barreled versions. Again, firing a standard .22 cartridge in one is unsafe!

Interchangeable cylinders: you can buy dual cylinder .22 LR/.22 WMR revolvers; mostly single-action types (Ruger, Heritage), with easy cylinder removal. Taurus sells a nice-looking M-992 dual cylinder double-action with a 6 ½-inch barrel to help boost velocity. A concern for all such designs is optimum accuracy with the .22 LR cylinder installed. A .22 WMR requires a .224" barrel; just a hair bigger than the standard .223 diameter of a .22 LR. That extra one-thousandth of an inch might not seem like much and probably won't matter for mundane work – but may degrade .22 LR accuracy a bit.

.22 Winchester Magnum Rimfire (.22 WMR). In a handgun, the .22 Magnum gives up much of its velocity. You'll still gain a bit over a .22 Long Rifle, but it won't be dramatic in a practical gun. Expect .22 WMR revolver muzzle velocity (MV) to approximate that of .22 LR from a rifle. For plinking purposes, I'd just buy a .22 Long Rifle handgun. Same story for *most* small game, although the extra .22 WMR punch could prove useful against raccoons, etc. It might also be a consideration for anyone unable to handle a .38 Special. Smith & Wesson sells a 6-shot .22 Magnum K-Frame (Model 48) and some petit J-Frames. My son has a little Model 351 PD, which stands for "personal defense." It's a 7-shot, 11-ounce aluminum gun with fixed sights and a 1 7/8" barrel. The bright fiber-optic front sight is easy to see, although bullets strike slightly high and right. The difference wouldn't matter in a defensive situation, but could cost you a squirrel dinner. Since the sights are fixed, it's necessary to use "Kentucky windage," meaning some degree of hold-off. We shot the new .22 WMR Speer 40-grain Gold Dot Short Barrel load through our chronograph, and it averaged 1050 fps – a far cry from the 1900 fps possible with a rifle. Defensively, I'd feel a whole lot more comfortable with a plain old .38 Special.

327 Federal. Neat idea! I view it as a modern day .32/20 of sorts, with the added flexibility to fire shorter .32 H&R Magnum, or even shorter .32 S&W Long cartridges. The concept is like shooting .22 Short or .22 Long rounds through a .22 Long Rifle chamber. The .327 Federal appeared in 2007 as a low-recoil "magnum," offering a bonus 6th round in a small-framed revolver. It's an even more

S&W's .22 WMR Model 351 PD gives up much velocity, but carries like a feather, and still hits as hard as a standard .22 rifle.

Result of a close encounter with a hare. A well-placed GDHP from the S&W M-351 PD has "procured dinner".

"magnumized" rendition of the circa 1984 .32 H&R Magnum, itself a lengthened rendition of the old .32 S&W Long. All three cartridges (and the .32/20) use .312-caliber bullets weighing around 100 grains. From a four-inch barrel, the .327 Federal can crank out around 1400 fps; enough to permanently ruin anyone's day. I don't have experience with this load, but I'm familiar with the others. They're all neat cartridges, but to my mind, even the .327 Magnum would be too light for deer - other than as a last resort. I'd love one in a 4" *Ruger SP101*, which would make a dandy outdoorsman's kit gun. Some handgunners who struggle with .357 Magnum recoil could no doubt manage the .327 Federal, gaining a quantum defensive handgun jump beyond the .22 WMR. Of course, lighter .38 Special loads are another practical option, with much greater odds of locating ammo.

9mm Luger in revolvers. Many gun owners have some kind of 9mm on-hand, so perhaps a small D/A revolver could make sense for some. Ballistic performance is the equivalent of a lighter-bullet .38 Special +P loads, and relatively inexpensive 9mm Q-loads can support range sessions or incidental smaller critter collecting. If you match up an FMJ with a good defensive 9mm bullet of equivalent weight (115 or 124 grains), POI should remain similar. Charter Arms 9mm revolvers (and their .380s) work without moon clips thanks to an innovative extractor system. S&W's present 9mm revolver line is built on larger 7-8 shot L and N-frame guns that load from moon clips, the latter being geared for competition. Taurus announced a line of switch-cylinder .357/9mm mid-frame D/A revolvers for 2018. These 9mm versions also use moon clips; not necessarily a bad thing given the ease and speed of reloads. Ruger's little D/A-only 5-shot LCR works the same way. The thin metal moon clips have slots between each recess, greatly reducing the force needed to strip or refill the clips. A downside is the 9mm Luger offers less versatility than a .38/.357 Magnum revolver, so scratch hunting off the list for quarry larger than small pig-like javelina, coyotes, etc.

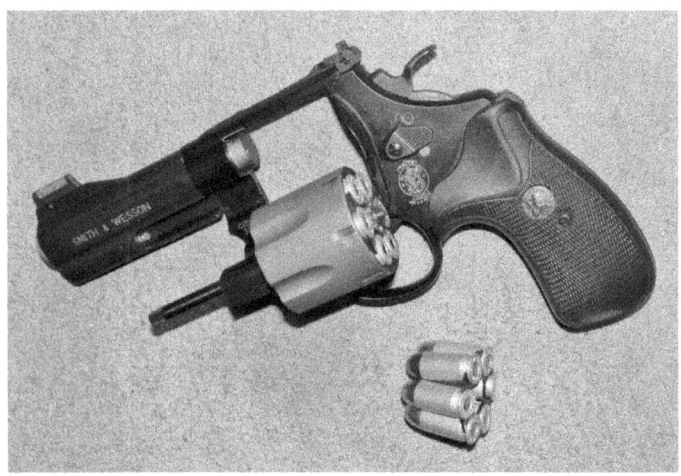

Moon clips permit extraction of rimless pistol cartridges in revolvers. Full-moon types like those shown with this lightweight .45 ACP M-325 support fast reloads.

.45 ACP revolver option. Ballistics will be similar to the .44 Special, but ammo should be easier to find. It makes the most sense for pistol owners with a stash of .45 ACP on hand and an itch for a revolver. If so, unlike 1911s, much less time will be spent chasing fired brass. The empties will still be attached to those moon clips making them especially attractive for hand-loaders. Of course, fiddling with moon clips is a minor bother, but once set up, you'll gain an ammo tolerant .45-caliber thumper. My 4-inch N-Frame S&W Model 325 has a scandium frame, and although surprisingly light, is well within the realm of control. With round-nose 230 grain bullets, you can just throw a full-moon clip in the cylinder's general direction for a reload. Unloading is equally easy. S&W now catalogs the 4-inch "Model

325 Thunder Ranch," which weighs 31 ounces. I wouldn't want a much lighter gun either since, after two boxes of G.I. 230 grain FMJ, I'm ready for a break with my similar M-325. Recoil is well below a .44 magnum, but you'll still know you've been shooting an authoritative gun. The effectiveness of the .45 ACP for defense is undisputed – assuming the right bullets are chosen and, rumors to the contrary, G.I. round-nose FMJs are *not* your best choice (don't ask me how I know this). Expanding bullets change the game completely though. When so armed, I'd also be willing to try a .45 ACP revolver on larger game within reasonable ranges of 25-50 yards. Owing to its extremely loopy trajectory, these distances would most likely reflect the practical envelope, anyway.

.45 Auto Rim note: this cartridge was introduced after World War 1 for use in surplus Model 1917 revolvers. As its name implies the Auto Rim is a rimmed adaptation of the .45 ACP which eliminates the need for moon clips. Although obscure, loaded ammo is still available from a few smaller manufacturers, although cost is relatively high.

.44 Magnum and .44 Special. Buy a .44 Magnum and you'll be able to use either cartridge. However, a true .44 Special will limit you to just that caliber (discounting obscure .44 Russian rounds), so factoring in availability of ammo, the .44 Magnum is usually the better choice. The Magnum version will also handle just about any animate target, but recoil will be stiff. Like the other magnum handguns, so will muzzle flash. As for the .44 Special, power-wise, it's not that dissimilar from the .45 ACP and once again, bullet choices matter! The old 246-grain lead round-nose .44 Special load was not quite as "special" as this cartridge's name implied, but modern loads have changed things for the better. A surprising amount of excellent defensive loads are now sold with lighter 180-200 grain expanding bullets in this caliber and the beauty of a revolver is that it will digest anything within reason. With the incidental need for more power, a 5-shot S&W .44 Magnum Model 96 L-frame could be close to perfect. The larger Scandium N-frame guns will also carry well while offering a 6th shot. Although tolerable with .44 Special loads, its durability could be a concern with .44 Magnums – for both the gun and its shooter! The small 5-shot Charter Arms .44 Special snubbies are intriguing, and I'm a fan of their 4" Target Bulldog, which is in essence a big-bore kit-gun.

.44 Special ammunition (L) can be fired in a .44 Magnum. The pointed bullet is a cast-lead handload, guaranteed to penetrate.

.45 Colt. This grand old cartridge remains a popular choice among single-action shooters. On the other hand, double-action .45 Colt revolvers are limited. One that stands out as a solid contender for those who can manage its weight is Ruger's rugged 44-ounce stainless D/A *Redhawk* - a brilliant idea which will fire either .45 Colt or .45 ACP from the same cylinder. The .45 Colt has enough oomph to clobber just about anything in the lower 48, while the shorter .45 ACP rounds head-

The old .45 Colt 255-grain LSWC had plenty of clout. Hornady's Flex-Tip gives it a modern spin but, either way, it remains a serious cartridge. Beside it are 2 ½ and 3" .410 shotgun shells.

space off moon clips, affording a useful dual-caliber gun that could offset ammo scarcity. The beauty of this Redhawk is that it's sold as a round-butt version, making it more amenable to regular carry. S&W's big, blued M-25 .45 Colt N-frame is a very pretty gun, but not nearly as versatile.

Dual-use .45 Colt/.410 shot-shell handguns. As it turns out, a .45 Colt and .410-bore shotgun shell have some dimensional similarities. Hence the development of the large Taurus Judge.45 Colt/.410, followed by S&W's similar Governor, and a few other intriguing handguns that warrant a further look.

.410 HANDGUNS?

A smoothbore handgun would require additional BATF permitting so instead, a few manufacturers sell rifled guns with .45 Colt chambers that have been lengthened to accept .410 shells. Unfortunately, as the shot charge is spun, centrifugal force rapidly dissipates the pellets, causing sparse shot patterns beyond several yards. To work around this issue, some manufacturers have developed unusual .410 loads. Hornady sells a Triple Defense, which uses two .35-caliber lead balls topped by a .41-caliber FTX expanding bullet, sized to be spun by rifling. This ensures it'll strike nose-forward so the flexible plastic tip can work its magic. Other ammo makers have come up with equally unconventional solutions, all designed to increase the lethality of a .410 revolver.

Taurus Judge and S&W Governor revolvers. As for conventional shot loads, the age-old standard 2 ½" .410 shell holds only ½-ounce of shot. A 3" Magnum boosts the payload to 11/16 oz. – still much less than a 12-gauge 1 1/8-ounce shell. The patterns we fired with 2 ½" Federal #4s from a Judge were impressive at close range, but by fifteen feet they had opened up to around a foot and a half. Loads containing smaller pellets (#6 or # 7 ½) might improve pattern density enough to squeak out a few extra yards, but their use would only be advised for small game. Wing-shooting would be pretty much a fantasy, even with 3" shells. Still, there are plenty of areas with cottontail rabbits that tend to sit tight. If you can see one before it bolts, there's a good chance of potting supper. The .410 shot loads would also be highly effective against snakes. Defensively, these guns might have potential in confined areas like apartment complexes, where over-penetration is a concern. Recoil may be excessive for some users, although Taurus uses soft, ribbed grips which help. Unlike Hollywood's portrayals of massive area destruction, aiming is still necessary. The shot loads are more forgiving but they are not wire-guided. Anyone interested in their performance can view YouTube clips. You'll see more information about these innovative revolvers in the upcoming S&W chapters.

Magnum Research BFR Revolver. I have no experience with the .45/.410 Magnum Research BFR, which appears to bring .410 performance to a whole new level. The BFR is clearly a dedicated hand-shotgun. Beside an extra-long cylinder, it has a shotgun-like ventilated-rib with no rear sight and a simple bead up front. The 7 ½" barrel is equipped with a removable choke-tube and the cylinder can handle longer 3" .410 shells. It also weighs 4 ½ pounds! The Magnum Research site has a video showing this gun in action against launched clay pigeons that break with regularity. I believe this is an honest depiction based on my experience with a T/C Contender.

The Taurus Judge has an extended cylinder that can fire .45 Colt or .410 shotshells.

Single-shot .45 Colt/.410 pistols. The extra length of even the shortest 2 ½" shells requires a *much* longer revolver cylinder, but a break-action single-shot design solves this problem, and some even feature interchangeable barrels. These guns will receive more attention during the '"*Other Handguns* section.

Conventional-caliber shot loads. At this point, some readers may be wondering about conventional shot-shell alternatives. Commercial variations have been produced for years in various calibers, from .22 LR upwards. They are available for the more popular revolver and pistol calibers so we'll look at them more thoroughly later.

LOGISTICAL CONCERNS

For the purposes of the chart, the most common revolver cartridges drive the list. For this reason, the biggest magnums and other oddities are absent. Unless you already have a very large stash of some other ammo, why not stay with the most popular choices? Also, for what it's worth, "standard loads" have blurred during recent years, the .44 Special being one example. At this point, the old 246-grain RNL offering has no doubt been supplanted by a series of great expanding bullets, many of which weigh 200 grains. Same story for jacketed .45 ACP alternatives, while moving in the opposite direction, 124-grain 9mm loads could now be as popular as the old classic 115s. And, of course, bullet construction has a huge bearing on the effectiveness of a give load.

A comparative sampling of popular revolver calibers from 4" barrels:

Caliber	Weights	Standard load &	MV FS	Use
.22 LR	29-40 grains	40 grains	1000	Targets, plinking & small game
.22 WMR	30-40	40	1300	Defense* & small game
.327 Federal	85-100	100	1500	Defense; game up to coyote-size
9mm Luger	90-147	115	1150	Defense; game up to coyote-size
.38 Special	110-158	158	750	Defense; game up to coyote-size
.38 Special +P	110-158	158	900	Defense; game up to coyote-size
.357 Magnum	110-180	158	1200	Defense; deer out to 75 yards
.41 Magnum	170-210	210	1300	Deer, hogs, black bear to 75 yards: defense
.44 Special	180-246	246	760	Defense; close-range hogs & deer
.44 Magnum	180-300	240	1350	Big game out to 100 yards
.45 ACP	185-230	230	830	Defense; Close-range hogs, deer, black bear
.45 Colt	185-255	255	860	Defense; Hogs, deer, black bear to 50 yards

Only for recoil sensitive shooters; not recommended

Another big consideration is cumulative weight. A GI ammo can full of any type of ammunition will be *really* heavy. If you need to bug out, assuming you can grab it, you'll have lots more rounds with smaller cartridges. The .22 LR certainly has the advantage here, but for general-purpose use it's insufficient. Weight-wise, the 9mm ranks as a "maybe" if subsistence hunting is involved, so once again, the immortal .357 Magnum strikes a fair balance of portability and power.

And here's a related logistical thought: what if you had a shoulder-fired weapon that could share the same round?

The companion carbine concept. Reviewing the birth of the .44 WCF (.44/40), it debuted in Winchester's Model 1873 lever-action rifle, and it wasn't long before Colt had a matching revolver. Of course, other firearm manufacturers quickly followed suit with a host of dual-purpose cartridges. A handgun and rifle that could share the same ammunition made sense on the edges of civilization back then, and it still does. Compared to conventional rifle cartridges like the .308 Winchester, you give up some power, but today's good handgun bullets can help close the gap.

More than a century later, lever-guns and revolvers continue to dominate the companion-firearm field. In fact, you can still buy a Winchester Model 1873 reproduction and a real Colt Single-Action Army. However, I'd prefer a double-action revolver and a somewhat more modern lever-action rifle capable of accommodating an optical sight. Winchester's Model 92 was a successor to the '73 but both eject through the top. On the other hand, Marlin's Model 1894 and Henry's Big-Bores employ solid-top receivers which come drilled and tapped for scope mounts. Caliber choices won't be an issue so long as the all-stars are picked. Today's "big three" are the .357 Magnum, .44 Magnum, and .45 Colt.

Useful revolver/carbine choices include the .22 LR, .327 Federal, .357 Magnum, .44 Magnum, and .45 Colt. Most, being offspring of shorter versions, provide even greater versatility.

The 9mm Luger might seem like another viable alternative, especially considering 9mm AR-15 carbine popularity. Trouble is, the 9mm doesn't gain much steam in these longer barrels. The .45 ACP is in the same boat. Their relatively small powder charges are consumed within the first few inches of bore travel, and a .45 ACP bullet can actually *slow down* through friction in a carbine-length barrel! However, for those less interested in hunting larger game, a 9mm AR-15 does have much to offer, extending useful defensive range to around 100 yards. To that end, several neat, dedicated 9mm AR carbines have appeared that accept popular pistol magazines, with Glock-types being the most common.

However, my two-gun choice would be a .357 Magnum, which picks up considerable velocity in a rifle-length barrel. We're talking about hundreds of feet per second! The .44 Magnum burns plenty of propellant, making it another great two-gun candidate. The same is true of the .41 Magnum, although rifle choices are limited. I'm betting the .327 Federal would also crank on velocity.

One issue is reliable feeding with non-magnum .38 Special or .44 Special alternate loads in some lever-guns. Bullet profiles play a part here but so does overall cartridge length. Some combinations are touchy so research is advised. The

These evolutions includes the .32 Long/.327 Federal, .38 Special/ .357 Magnum, and .44 Special/.44 Magnum. Revolvers will eat 'em up, although some rifles might be pickier feeders.

Useful Revolver Cartridges | 141

shape of a bullet's nose can also pose hazards in tubular magazines because they bear against successive primers. Round-nose types are usually not recommended, but fortunately, there are flat-points to choose from, including most JHPS or SPs types. Hornady's "flex-tip" loads are another great option since their pointed soft plastic noses provide the necessary cushioning.

Ruger's M-77 based bolt-action .357 and .44 Magnums solve this problem through detachable, rotary magazines. Unfortunately, these neat rifles no longer appear in the 2017 listings, although some are no doubt languishing within the supply chain. My own companion carbine is just a simple Rossi break-action single-shot .357 Magnum with a 21" barrel that eats everything. I feed it from speedstrips and it easily disassembles for storage, but since it offers only one shot, we could do better for defensive purposes.

Repeaters aside, single-shot rifle can still be handy. This low-budget .357 Rossi shoots surprisingly well and digests everything. Thanks to its 21" barrel, some .38 +Ps clock 1400 fps!

Based on current listings, my companion-gun choice would boil down to a couple weather-proof lever-actions. The Henry Big Boy All Weather .357 Magnum/.38 Special is set up for tough conditions with industrial hard-chrome plated metal and a poly urethane-coated stock. Its 20" barrel should maximize .357 Magnum velocities while maintaining a handy, fully ambidextrous package. Milder .38 specials would work well for practice and FMJ types would limit small game meat damage. Supposedly, they'll feed either load. Meanwhile, Marlin has just introduced a stainless version of their timeless Model 1894, the overall concept being like the Henry. Such a rifle, when paired with a sturdy mid-sized .357 Magnum revolver, would constitute a darned useful, if not tactical-looking, combination absent regulatory concerns associated with "black guns."

ONWARD TO GUNS

If a common-caliber carbine/revolver system is considered, the shorter list of available shoulder-fired chamberings will impose some limits on handgun options; but using the .357 Magnum as an example, lots of good revolver choices still exist as single or double-action types. So, that's where we're headed next, starting with some rugged single-actions.

CHAPTER 11
SINGLE-ACTION REVOLVERS

Like earlier percussion revolvers, the single-action Colt Peacemaker was fired by thumb-cocking its hammer for each shot. Most S/A revolvers in use today are Model 1873 clones and some are even genuine Colts which have come and gone at various times. Colt's Single Action Army .45 is legendary, but it has also been produced in many other calibers and barrel lengths, with fixed or 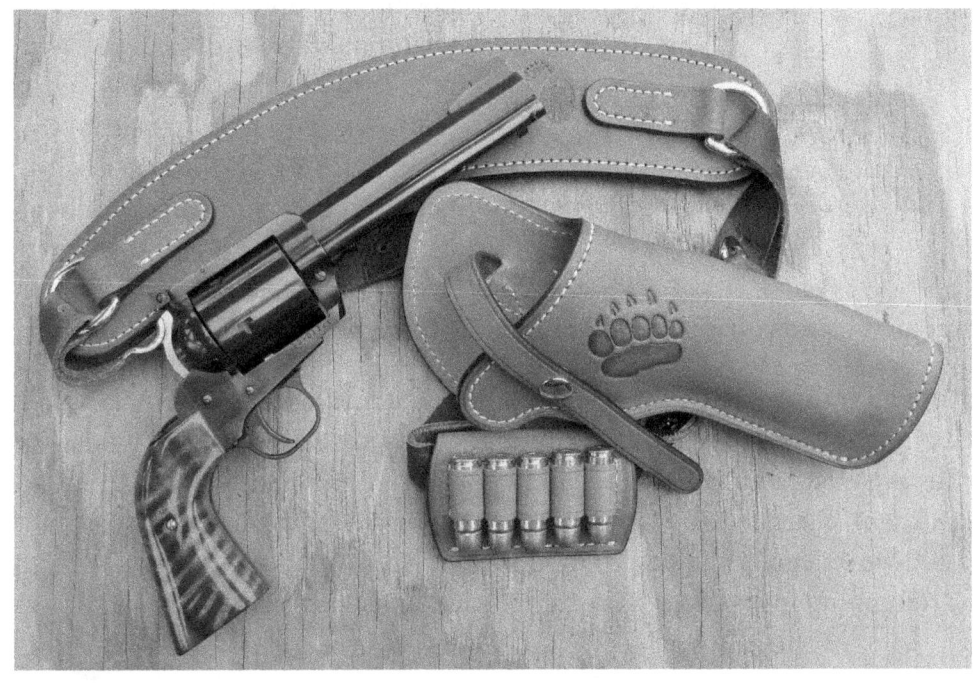 adjustable sights. Original chamberings included .32/20 (32. WCF), .38/40 (.38 WCF), and .44/40 (.44 WCF). Many older Winchester Model 73 and 92 lever-action rifles used the same calibers, permitting true versatility; and performance-wise, the old .38/40 was not too different from the modern .40 S&W pistol round. Although the so-called .45 Colt was not an original chambering, the Army stipulated that caliber. It was an effective choice which later became a ballistic benchmark when the .45 ACP Government Model Pistol was developed. Today, when we mention an 1873 Colt Revolver, the .45 Colt chambering goes hand-in-hand. To separate it from other .45-caliber cartridges, it will often be referred to by the unofficial title of .45 Long Colt (or .45 LC).

OPERATIONAL CONCERNS

To load the typical S/A revolver, each cartridge must be inserted individually. When using a gun built to the classic design, its hammer is first pulled back to half-cock, which permits free cylin-

Early SA cartridges: The .32/20, .38/40, and .44/40. Previously semi-obsolete, this "Winchester Centerfire" series (WCF) has regained popularity with Cowboy Action shooters.

der rotation. Next, a small hinged gate on the right side of the frame is swung open. At that point, the cylinder can be manually indexed to expose each chamber for loading. The same process will also align it with a barrel-mounted housing that contains a spring-loaded ejector rod. A tab on the rod extends through a slot in the housing, and shoving the tab rearward will cause the ejector to knock out a fired case. Sounds simple, and it is, but for eons, experienced S/A users have only loaded five rounds. The empty sixth chamber was positioned underneath the un-cocked hammer to prevent an unintentional discharge. With the hammer fully down on a loaded chamber, the firing pin will rest on a primer. A half-cock setting will position the hammer rearward a bit. If it slips during cocking the half-cock notch *should* arrest the hammer, but here's the problem: a hard blow can shear off its notch. At that point, the firing pin can impact a primer to fire the revolver. This phenomenon is more common than imagined, and has resulted in numerous tragedies resulting from dropped guns or other impacts.

Ruger's transfer-bar solution. The advent of television spawned a series of new western programs during the 1950s and, since Sturm Ruger always has a handle on what shooters want, they jumped on the single-action bandwagon. First up was a .22 rimfire, followed by a two-cylinder .22 LR/.22 WMR package. A larger .357 Magnum appeared next, leading to the robust .44 Magnum Super Blackhawk. The Rugers can be viewed as modernized Colts, with excellent metallurgy and modern coil springs. A remaining loose end was the single-action hazard associated with loading six rounds. Ruger came

Ruger probably did more to preserve the SA legacy than any other manufacturer, blending traditional lines with rugged construction and modern features, all for a fair price.

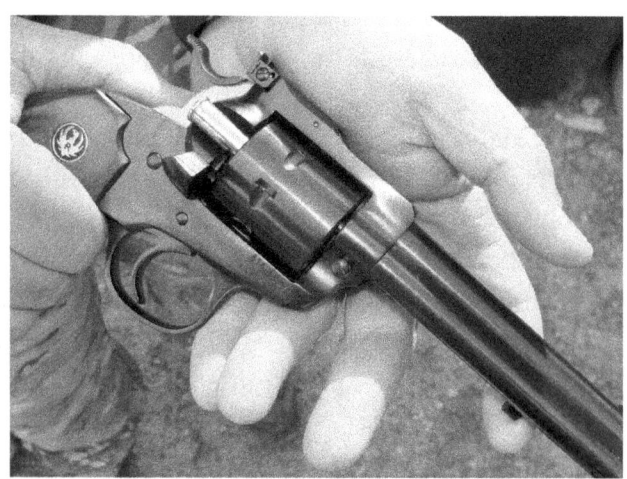

Despite some grumbling from traditionalists, Ruger's new models do provide a safer system. Note the hammer-forward position during loading.

up with a fix during the 1970s, when their traditional hammer-mounted firing pin was relocated to the frame. The redesign also added a steel "transfer-bar," which bridged the hammer and firing pin gap only when the trigger was pulled fully rearward. Loading and unloading was done with the hammer fully forward instead of at half-cock. This system proved reliable and it continues today. Despite some grumbling from purists, this new design is safer. Ruger still offers a free retrofit for those with older guns and a revolver so equipped can be safely carried with all six rounds.

Traditional precautions. Several other single-action clones have appeared, and the sport of Cowboy Action Shooting accounts for the recent spike in choices. Since some are of traditional designs, the load-five rule may still apply. If so, the procedure is easier and safer if we first place the hammer on half-cock and swing open the loading gate. We can then load one round, skip the next chamber, and load four more. Then the loading gate is shut, the hammer is cocked, and it is carefully lowered. With the right technique, an empty chamber should be underneath it. This is a much better plan than peering into the business end of the chambers. If still in doubt, the muzzle can be carefully pointed in a safe direction while peering sideways through the cylinder/frame gap. Along this vein, one way to discern a questionable design is to unload the revolver. Then fully lower the hammer and, with the revolver held sideways, carefully peer into the rear gap between the cylinder and frame. With good light behind it, the firing pin tip should be visible in an original Peacemaker design. This condition won't occur with a transfer-bar type unless the trigger is held to the rear while simultaneously lowering its hammer. With either version, it's worth giving the hammer spur an extra forward nudge while watching for any firing pin protrusion. Do this without contacting the trigger.

Cocking the hammer will rotate the cylinder to align a chamber with the barrel, and rotation is often clockwise as viewed from behind the gun. If rounds are not fully expended, the hammer will remain above the last fired case so long as it remains forward. However, once it is re-cocked, the potential live round-under-hammer hazard can reappear. Either take the shot or re-index the cylinder. Half-cock is strictly for loading and unloading. By no means is it a safety device!

Here's another original S/A quirk: You can sometimes tie up an action by attempting to fully lower a hammer from half-cock. The hammer should first be fully cocked and then carefully let down. Of course, un-cocking requires a good deal of attention. If the hammer slips near full-cock it will immediately snap forward. With a traditional design the half-cock notch *may* catch it – or not. When un-cocking a transfer-bar design, a rearward trigger is needed to "complete the circuit." By releasing pressure from the trigger as soon as the hammer disengages, this connection can be interrupted. The same process works with a D/A revolver in its single-action mode.

While single-action loading can be slow, firing can be pretty darned quick *with practice*. You'll see some cowboy shooters who can really make a peacemaker sing, and they won't be "fanning" the hammer. Instead, each shot will be preceded by a thumb-cocked hammer, probably using the support-hand. A few stages may even involve a pair of guns, employing single-hand cocking and firing, but while fire-power is doubled, two-gun shooting is tricky business. For most of us, single-action "reloads" will be a tedious one-gun affair. Visual verification of "cleared" cylinder status will also be more involved than the swing-out cylinders typical of D/A designs.

SINGLE-ACTIONS TODAY

The sport of Cowboy Action Shooting, as governed by SASS (Single Action Shooting Society), has no doubt done more to spark new life into single-action revolver sales than any other activity. In order to remain faithful to 19th century designs, the firearms must be SASS approved, and since the participants are traditionalists, much emphasis is heaped on Colt SA Army revolvers or copies, produced by offshore firms like Uberti. These guns invariably have fixed sights and are chambered for popular period cartridges like .45 Colt and .44/40, although lots of low-recoil .38 Specials are fired through reproductions chambered for this cartridge or .357 Magnum. Good chance the shooters will own a pair carried in fancy two-holster rigs!

Even prior to this interest, single-action army types always had a following, a trend which continues today. Recent popularity may be attributable to manufacturing improvements that greatly strengthened Colt's design. This has not escaped the attention of some serious outdoors folks who require raw power. While double-action revolvers probably make more sense against two-legged varmints, there are still wild places where serious four-legged threats exist. A modern S/A revolver can be strong enough to handle not only .44 Magnum varieties, but also fiercer handgun calibers like the .454 Casull.

Freedom Arms sells some beautiful single-action big-bores, and the .454 is popular among those who tread in bear country. This cartridge is a lengthened and "magnum-ized" .45 Colt with significant extra thump, and the chambers will accept either load. Those with deep pockets won't go wrong with any type of Freedom Arms single-action. Their attention to details is beyond dispute, and numerous models are offered including useful .44 Magnums, .357s, and even .22 LR versions.

Freedom Arms builds premium single-actions. This .44 Special, with its 5-shot cylinder, makes a handy carry piece.

Ruger is no doubt the largest single-action manufacturer with lots of great choices that strike a fair balance of features versus cost. I've owned a few of their .44 Magnum Super Blackhawks (among other models), including two with 10 ½" barrels. At times, I'd join a friend for some informal sandpit shooting. Targets were often claybirds lined up on a bank at 50 – 75 yards. The long-Tom Ruger was so effective from offhand that it became known as my "hand-rifle." After much shooting, I replaced the smooth wooden grip panels with a checkered rubber set. Recoil then seemed less violent but major skin abrasion developed. A thin glove solved that problem, but reloading became more difficult. Undaunted, I persevered and finally, during one extended session, I blew the crystal out of a watch. This was with a stout 300-grain .44 Magnum load.

For greater excitement, try a giant Magnum Research BFR single-action in a caliber like .45/70. There will be no mistaking its appearance due to use of an extra-long cylinder needed to chamber this grand old rifle cartridge. You'll certainly know when it goes off!

Colt (among several other Italian clones) still catalogs several SA Army models built along traditional lines with fixed sights, no doubt to satisfy the lust of SASS members and others looking for *the* classic six-shooter. The current Colt choices boil down to the time-honored .45 Colt, or .357 Magnum, the latter no doubt for Cowboy Action shooters firing .38 Specials. The larger magnum calibers are absent although even the original .45 Colt is no slouch.

Unlike the humped grip common to most D/A revolvers, a single-action plow-handle grip will rotate through the firing hand in recoil, making it more tolerable with powerful cartridges. Maintenance is also easy, which is helpful in the field. Disengagement of a small detent will typically free the axle that captures the cylinder and, at that point, it can be removed from the frame for easy cleaning. You'll see big S/A revolvers on the hips of many Alaskans and Rocky Mountain outdoor folks for exactly these reasons.

More Rugers. These rugged guns can be purchased in blued or stainless steel. Several frame sizes are available to accommodate various cartridge classes. Our theme of widespread ammunition availability is a non-issue because popular chamberings abound.

<u>Smaller choices.</u> Especially neat for camp-gun use is the demure .22 Bearcat, which has returned from a lengthy absence. It fits the "kit gun" description nicely, making a handy backpack or tackle box addition.

A niche exists for custom single-actions. This Ruger Blackhawk is a 5-shot .45 Colt, with a Bisley-type grip and hammer. Like other SAs, it offers easy maintenance.

The somewhat larger Single Six is the gun that got Ruger's single-actions rolling. It makes a great general-purpose rimfire choice, and can still be purchased as a two-cylinder .22 LR/.22 WMR package. Both will be covered again in the rimfire chapter.

The new .327 Federal Single Nine is a severe temptation. It offers greater power than a rimfire without .357 Magnum recoil. It'll also shoot .32 S&W Long and .32 H&R Magnum loads, although none of these cartridges are as common as .357 Magnum options. The .327 has the most steam of all three .32s, but it's still a marginal choice for deer-size quarry.

Blackhawks. Various barrel lengths and calibers are sold. Among them, a time-proven .357 Magnum Blackhawk is a manageable choice thanks to its weight and grip design. Adjustable sights also permit the use of affordable and readily available .38 Special loads for practice and small game. The 4 5/8" version weighs 40 ounces. The same frame will also accommodate a .41 Magnum while shaving off 2 ounces. Other intriguing Blackhawks include a dual-cylinder .357/9mm for true versatility. A similar option is sold with both .45 Long Colt and .45 ACP cylinders. Some M-1 Carbine owners will no doubt be interested in Ruger's extremely loud .30 Carbine Blackhawk.

Super Blackhawks. The well-established .44 Magnum is available in everything from a 10 ½" cannon to a compact 3.75" Super Bisley. The latter option uses a straighter, downturned grip that Colt developed for target shooting back in 1894. Some folks love 'em and some don't. It's really a matter of personal preference and either style can be purchased. A good all-around choice is a stainless 5 ½" Super Blackhawk with a weight-saving fluted cylinder. The rear of the trigger guard is rounded to spare adjacent fingers from the full effects of recoil. At 46 ounces, it's still no flyweight, which is not necessarily a bad thing given the caliber. The smaller Super Bisley has a non-fluted cylinder, but its shorter barrel trims two ounces.

More eye-candy: A customized Ruger Super Blackhawk in .44 Magnum with Bisley features and an octagonal barrel.

The Bisley Series extends beyond the Super Blackhawk. Those immune to recoil will be enthralled by .454 Casull and .480 Ruger Super Blackhawks. These calibers are just too much for an average shooter, but a softer-shooting .44 Special "Flattop" is built on a mid-sized Blackhawk frame. In fact, for gun nuts, the various Ruger choices constitute a real crisis!

CLOSING SINGLE-ACTION COMMENTS

I still have a soft spot for a well-made single-action; or better yet, several! But, as much as it pains me to say this, if defensive use is factored in, a D/A revolver is just a better choice. Faster reloads are possible, and its load status can be verified by simply unlocking the cylinder. So, from this point forward, the revolver focus will be on double-action types.

CHAPTER 12
DOUBLE-ACTION REVOLVERS

Quick review: a well-built D/A revolver remains a dependable choice, its principle attributes being simplicity and reliability. The swing-out cylinder permits easy loading and simultaneous ejection of empty cases. It doesn't have a safety-switch, nor does it really need one. The gun can be safely carried with its hammer forward and all six chambers loaded. Consider this example: my agency SOP calls for rubber mats inside our armories. They provide extra insurance if a firearm is ever dropped, but they only address a small portion of a much larger operational environment. During a three-year period, I encountered two S&W Model 65s with snapped off hammer spurs. It turned out each had been dropped on a hard surface *raising further concerns about muzzle orientation*! The fact that neither discharged was at least reassuring.

THE DOUBLE-ACTION CONCEPT

Defensive doctrine calls for an immediate double-action response via a long and deliberate trigger stroke. Using this technique, some precision is sacrificed for a gain in speed, but since manual dexterity is often impaired by the effects of stress anyway, the odds of an unintentional discharge are reduced. If the hammer is manually cocked before firing (like a single-action revolver), a much shorter and lighter trigger pull will result, so better accuracy should be possible. If I faced the challenge of shooting a small target from twenty paces, I'd use the single-action mode. Odds would be better of winning a bet or dining on roasted rabbit. One could argue the same for a longer-range defensive situation. Well, maybe, but we have run experimental drills on fairly large combat silhouette targets at greater distances. To add a small degree of realism, we turned up the heat with sharp verbal commands. Shooting was preceded by a 25-yard sprint beginning at 75 yards. From 50 yards, most of our shooters were stunned to see better D/A results. Why? Because a properly executed double-action shot involves a long, smooth stroke. The hammer will fall at *some point* while the shooter "steers" the gun using its sights. The exact instant at which the hammer drops is more of a surprise, which helps eliminate flinching. On the other hand, a short and predictable single-action break is easily anticipated, inviting negative reactions. In fairness, many of those from the above test were older hands with years of D/A revolver qualifications, meaning they had mastered the long continuous stroke necessary for accurate shooting.

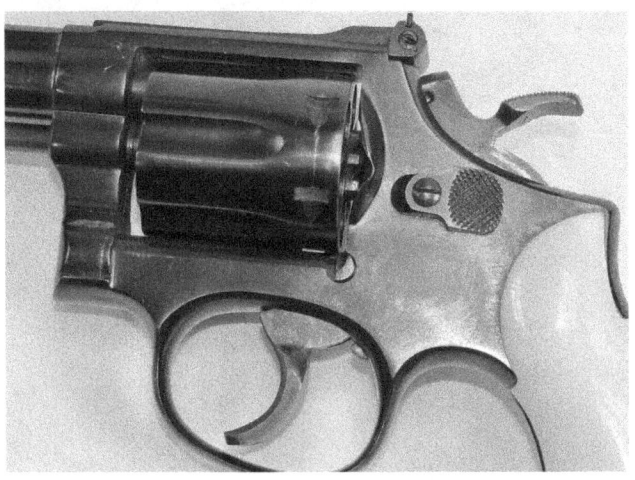

From double-action, a long deliberate trigger-stroke causes the cylinder to rotate and index a cartridge, simultaneously drawing the hammer rearward until it drops.

The other option is a single-action shot. Manually cocking the hammer also indexes a cartridge. The gun can then be fired by a shorter and lighter trigger pull.

D/A trigger nuances. Early in my instructor days, I encountered a new trainee who was struggling with the whole D/A concept. Being a military-trained shooter, a revolver of any kind was a foreign object. In frustration, he blurted out that he could shoot a G.I. issued .45 automatic with *much* better accuracy. I wasn't buying it, but by complete luck, I had a 1911 in my range bag. I handed him the pistol so he could put his money where his mouth was and shazam! A decent shot group developed, which taught me a lesson. Thinking things over, the Government Model's single-action trigger was not only lighter, but also had much shorter travel. My trainee was consequently experiencing less gun movement while cranking on its trigger. Other prior military staff faced similar difficulties but all was not lost. The fix involved extensive dry-firing while maintaining a stabile sight picture. Proper D/A trigger control is somewhat like riding a bike; it takes time to master, but then it's ingrained. This skill may fade over time but the "wobbles" usually disappear after a short-range session. Not everybody will shine with a long D/A pull. For some, it's crank n' yank no matter what.

THE CASE FOR A 21st CENTURY REVOLVER

Those who can master a revolver's long D/A stroke (most shooters) will wind up with a safe and dependable handgun. The main negatives will then be limited capacity and slower reloading, BUT, they will still get six dependable shots - or thereabouts.; and with proper training, reloads won't be all that slow. The old police standard involving an HKS 6-second speed-loading device– 6 seconds! This is the difference between shots 6 and 7. We've seen plenty of slower times, but we've also clocked some reloads below 4 seconds. It all boils down to the right equipment, technique, *and practice*.

Today, the revolver is largely passé in law enforcement circles, but many officers still carry a small D/A type as a hidden, back-up gun. It will probably be a 5-shot model; and will more than likely contain .38 Specials. Plenty of civilians still carry small revolvers as well. Most will use .38s, but lots of .22 LR and .22 Magnums see regular use. The .32s had waned but newer Magnum iterations have changed that situation somewhat.

Before examining the smaller hideout revolvers, we'll look at general purpose choices. Although our focus is on defense, from a prepper point of view, we shouldn't rule out incidental hunting. In that case, we'll want a gun with controllable recoil but adequate power. Our geographic area could dictate the minimum caliber since, in some places animals could become not only targets of opportunity, but also threats. I'd have to be darned hungry to stalk a grizzly with a handgun, but the presence of a large gun would be reassuring. For decisive results, pure controllability would need to play second fiddle to raw power. The *minimum* threshold would be a .44 Magnum. One shot might work – or it might not. If it doesn't, well placed follow-up rounds will be necessary. The unfolding drama could occur quickly!

Most folks living in the lower 48 will be dealing with deer-sized quarry, in which case a carefully chosen defensive revolver chambering can work. The one jumping off the page is a .357 Magnum. When paired up with a medium-size revolver, a happy marriage of portability and control can be achieved.

Today's popular double-actions. Let's start with the original big-name revolver manufacturer and work our way through several others.

Colt. Colt still makes single-action revolvers, but their double-action line has all but vanished. The elegant .357 Python was a true example of the

If possible, leave quietly. You might need a bigger gun!

gunmaking art. Other "snake series" Colts (like the big-bore Anaconda or smaller Diamondback) now command premium prices, driven by Python envy. No Colt D/As survived for a while, but that sorry state of affairs has recently been remedied. New for 2017 was Colt's snub-nosed, 6-shot *Cobra*. Its 2" barrel is clearly intended for concealed carry, further validating the legitimacy of a good D/A revolver. Unlike a previous Cobra, this one is stainless steel. For 2018, a new night sight version joins the line, giving further credence to the defensive D/A revolver concept.

Smith & Wesson. Unlike Colt, S&W is synonymous with D/A revolvers. Their .38 Special Model 10 is a classic design that has seen the dawn of two centuries. In fact, S&W continues to crank them out, along with a broad selection of other models and calibers. Most their revolver production centers on four ascending frame sizes built from several specialized alloys, providing optimal weights and finishes for a variety of conditions. The S&W line is extensive enough to warrant its own detailed chapter.

Sturm Ruger. Although their initial foray into revolvers involved single-actions, Ruger is now well-established as a double-action manufacturer. Like S&W, they offer several sizes commensurate with popular calibers. I shot an older Security Six extensively, appreciating its simple disassembly. The GP-100 is it successor, with lots of interesting variants. In fact, Ruger's entire revolver line is diverse to say the least. Ascending in size and caliber offerings, we have their small and non-traditional LCR, a neat SP101, the general-purpose *GP-100*, a large Redhawk, and a jumbo Super Redhawk. All the Rugers are strongly built guns.

Dan Wesson. Wesson broke from the pack by offering interchangeable barrels in some interesting calibers. After on-again/off-again attempts, Dan Wesson is back as a CZ subsidiary, with a larger-framed D/A .357 Magnum revolver. The stainless steel Model 715 Pistol Pak ships with three barrels in 4, 6, and 8-inch lengths. These user-installed assemblies will interchange with older Model 15-2 (or later) guns.

Charter Arms. This company had a similar history, while specializing in small and affordable revolvers including their 5-shot .44 Special Bulldogs. I've owned a few of these little hand cannons and each one shot surprisingly well. Since feeding is a non-issue with a revolver, I used flat-nosed 200-grain wadcutter handloads. They resembled little lawnmower pistons which spoke with authority from both ends of the gun. The .38 Specials are probably the better bet for many shooters, and the shrouded-hammer Pink Lady is gender-biased in a good way. Of special interest to many pistol shooters will be the Pitbull Rimless Revolvers. How about a snubbie in 9mm, .40 S&W, or .45 ACP? These rimless pistol cartridges can be problematic with classic D/A ejector stars, but Charter Arms overcomes this through a patented spring-ejector system. Going back to basics, their .22 rimfire, 4.2" Pathfinders are handy adjustable-sight kit guns.

Taurus. These folks import an extensive line of South American-made double-actions, which strongly resemble S&W D/A revolvers. The gamut runs from snubbies through large D/A sporting revolvers, but the most unusual groundbreaking design has got to be the .410/.45 Colt Judge; an immediate hit that spawned the development of specialized .410 shot-shell loads. Taurus has established a small-frame market extending beyond .38 Special and .357 Magnums, to guns chambered for .380, 9mm, and .45 ACP pistol cartridges (fed from moon clips). A keyed TSS hammer locking system is standard and Taurus offers a lifetime warranty on each gun, regardless of its owner.

Kimber. Kimber is known for 1911-type pistols, but they just rocked the handgun industry with a well-made, small-frame, 6-shot, .357 Magnum, stainless steel revolver. An unusual departure is a cylinder with flats instead of flutes, designed to help minimize size. Replaceable low-profile fixed sights are another nice touch. The gun appears to be built like a tank and it's catching on, as evidenced by several new models.

Although better known for 1911 pistols, Kimber's expanding line of small D/A revolvers reflects a return to CCW-driven basics.

MORE DETAILS?

We'll take a closer look at some of the above revolvers later. Meanwhile, in keeping with the theme of well-established, Smith & Wesson's revolvers deserve closer scrutiny. For starters, they embody the classic double-action design.

CHAPTER 13
THE SMITH & WESSON LINE

Colt and Smith & Wesson have been key revolver players since the inception of metallic cartridges. Ruger jumped in comparatively late and Colt dropped out (save one recent D/A reintroduction), but S&W never wavered. They certainly satisfy our criteria of "well-established," having churned out an uninterrupted selection of good double-action guns for decades. In fact, S&W's revolver line alone is diverse enough to warrant its own chapter. As for personal experience, mine involves several hundred revolvers spread over four decades. So, without apologies, from here on, Smith & Wesson will become the primary focus.

S&W REVOLVER EVOLUTION

Blued and nickel-plated steel revolvers were the two early options, and since some shooters are still smitten by finely polished and deeply blued steel, S&W obliges. During the 1950s, a run of small aluminum-framed revolvers was developed to minimize weight. Then, during 1963, S&W achieved a real breakthrough with a diminutive .38 Chief's Special made from stainless steel. Although not truly rustproof, the stainless alloys offered much better resistance to corrosion. Stainless steel is harder to machine, but as the process evolved, the line expanded to larger revolvers, eventually replacing nickel-plating. Although stainless is extremely popular today, S&W has also delved into exotic alloys, resulting in some truly lightweight guns. Scandium frames and titanium cylinders are one such combination that can yield major weight savings. The further effect for consumers is a very diverse product line which can present challenges for those trying to narrow down a useful choice.

Models and such. At one point, S&W denoted their various offerings through descriptive titles such as "Combat Masterpiece," but nowadays, for the most part, numbers are employed instead. The first digit typically indicates the frame material. For example, the Model 29 is a large, carbon steel .44 Magnum. It will probably be blued, since nickel-plating has given way to stainless steel construction. The Model 629 is a stainless version, and the Model 329 has a scandium frame well-suited for exploration of personal recoil limits. All three of these guns are N-frames; the largest S&W offered until the recent introduction of the humongous X-frame. The ascending sizes as designated by S&W are J, K, L, N, a hybrid N/Z, and the X.

Beside the various materials, design can factor into the numerical soup. Let's back up to the stainless Chief's Special. Its blued steel predecessor is the Model 36. Since S&W's smallest revolvers are often carried concealed, some have shielded hammers to prevent hang-ups in clothing. The Model 442 is such an example. It couples a light aluminum frame with a carbon steel cylinder for non-snag carry. These guns are all J-frames. Throw in the others and choices become extensive to say the least. A comprehensive grasp of S&W's present revolver line will require exploration of their website.

The various models have also been tweaked over time. For example, my adjustable sight, stainless K-frame, .357 Magnum is a later-production Model 66-6. When it appeared around 1970 as a stainless version of the blued-steel Model 19, it was just a plain no-dash Model 66. As subsequent changes occurred, the M-66 progressed through the dashes (these iterations often reflect changes applied throughout revolver production). For example, earlier guns had "pinned barrels." The Model 66-2 eliminated a small frame-mounted indexing pin, in favor of a crush-fit barrel. Later evolutions reflected things like standardized rear sight frame holes, elimination of extractor alignment pins, etc. Eventually, the age-old hammer-mounted firing pin (hammer nose) was relocated to the frame. New metal-injected molded parts (MIM) appeared and a key-activated locking system arrived. The whole Model 66 then disappeared around 2005. Several years later it was back with other minor changes. Two significant ones are elimination of the hammer nose and the barrel mounting system. The original design had a floating pin that was secured to the hammer by a rivet. Breakage was rare, but it could happen. The barrel is now a separate liner housed within an exterior shroud, similar to Dan Wesson's design. Supposedly, its increased rigidity results in somewhat improved accuracy.

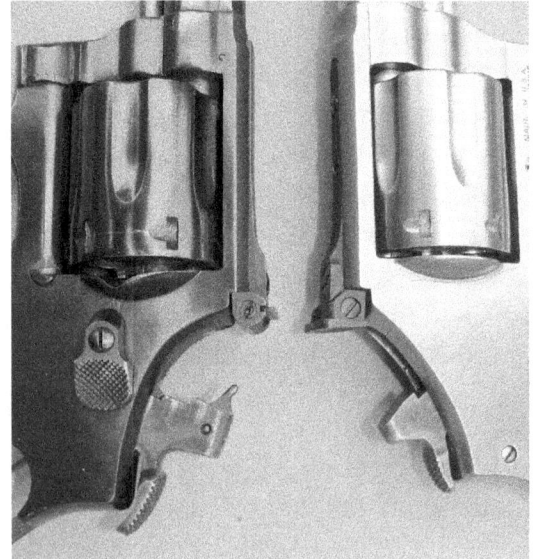

S&W K-frame evolutions: The older pinned barrel and hammer-nose (L) gave way to a crush-fit barrel and frame-mounted firing pin.

S&W's popular frame-sizes in descending order (L-R): N-frame M-629, L-frame M-686, K-frame M-66, and a J-frame M-63. Their common "6" indicates stainless construction.

S&W REVOLVER FRAMES

S&W's frames and cartridge offerings often share a dimensional relationship, so let's start with the smallest frame and work our way up.

J-Frame. It's the smallest size and most easily concealable, often sold as a short-barreled "snubbie" with a 1 7/8 – 3-inch barrel and fixed sights. Some have shrouded hammers for streamlined pocket carry, and one even uses moon clips (more on those later). Choices include carbon-steel, stainless, aluminum, and scandium. The latter alloys result in very lightweight guns, working well for deep-cover carry. Most of the J-frames are geared toward this market, but adjustable-sight versions are also offered. Calibers listed for 2018 include .22 LR, .22 Magnum (.22 WMR), .38 Special, and .357 Magnum.

The .22 LR M-63 is a stainless, 26-ounce, 3" J-frame with an 8-shot cylinder. The similar M-317 Kit Gun is an aluminum-framed version, weighing only 12.5 ounces. Both are nice sportsman's tools with adjustable sights. I opted for the heavier M-63 to promote steadiness, but it was a tough call.

.22 Magnum J-frames are sold as small hideout guns with 7-shot cylinders. The 10.8 ounce 351 PD (personal defense) has an exposed hammer, 1 7/8" barrel, and fixed sights. A similar 351-C has a concealed hammer. Much velocity is lost in such short barrels, but some recoil-sensitive folks tuck them into unobtrusive spots.

The .38 Specials and .357s employ 5-shot cylinders. Firing the latter caliber in a little J-Frame will certainly get your attention! The Scandium M-360 PD weighs a feathery 11.4 ounces, guaranteeing energetic recoil with even .38 +P ammo. On the flip side, a *3" M-60 Pro* is cataloged with adjustable sights and a semi-lugged barrel, boosting weight to 24.5 ounces. I shot one extensively without complaints using .38 +Ps. The venerable M-60 has a stumpy 2.125" barrel and fixed sights, shaving off a couple ounces. These small-frame revolvers are available in a wide assortment of materials, not all of which can withstand a .357 Magnum. The upper limit for aluminum-framed guns is .38 +P which, all things considered, is probably a relief. Shoot the warmer +Ps sparingly for the sake of the gun, and use standard .38 Specials for range work.

Hammer choices include a standard exposed type, a shrouded model, and an enclosed design. The fully enclosed version results in a very streamlined D/A-only action with no little nooks or crannies to accumulate pocket lint. Further options include factory supplied lasers – not a bad choice for a gun likely to see use in low light conditions.

The J-frame (unlike the larger S&Ws that employ long leaf-springs) uses a coiled hammer spring. This design generates sufficient force for positive primer indents from the smaller con-

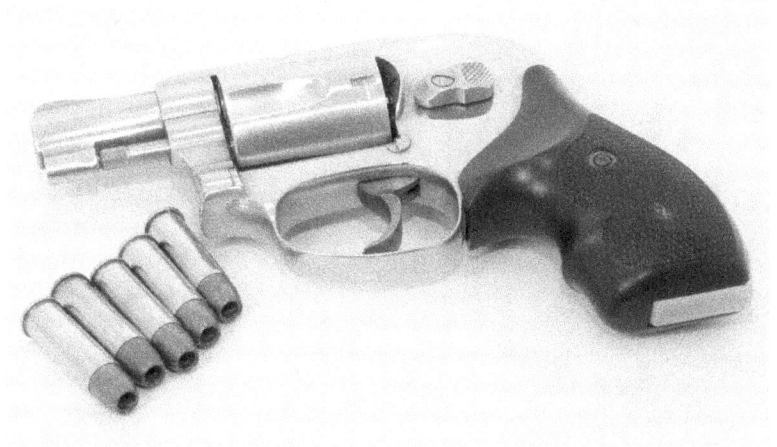

Shrouded or enclosed-hammer 5-shot S&W J-frames loaded with .38 Specials remain popular for good reasons, among them utter reliability and no-snag lines.

fines of the action. However, the trigger pull does tend to "stack" during compression in double-action mode. Of course, in single-action mode the hammer is pre-cocked, meaning a light trigger pull is possible.

S&W's J-frames employ a coiled hammer spring, shown here un-cocked in D/A mode. Note the grip locating-pins and lock above the thumb-piece.

Same J-frame cocked to S/A mode. A pin can be inserted through the hammer strut for removal of the assembly.

K-Frame. In one form or another, this medium-frame S&W has been around since 1899. The early .38 Special Military and Police Model 10 swiftly became the standard law enforcement sidearm, and S&W still catalogs it as part of their "Classic" line. The K-frame-sized platform soon evolved to numerous configurations from fixed-sight snub-noses to target guns with adjustable sights. Like the J-frame, newer alloys appeared, reflected by various model numbers. One difference between the smallest J-frame is the use of a long leaf-spring to power a K-frame's hammer. The K, L, and N-frames all share this older but entirely dependable design, which results in a very smooth and consistent double-action trigger throughout its travel. A small set-screw bears against the mainspring to regulate tension and its slotted head can be seen near the bottom of front-strap.

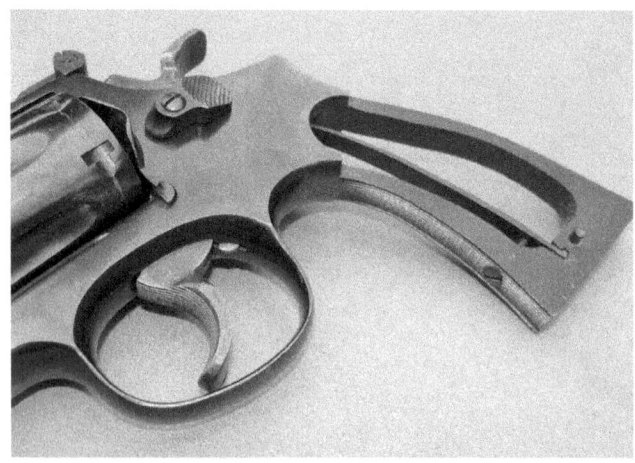

S&W's larger frames employ a long leaf-spring, tensioned by a screw. This K-frame also has a trigger-stop to limit overtravel – good for targets but bad for defense! Fortunately, it's removeable.

HG-13 S&W Stop & Mainspring: Current calibers include .22 LR, .22 Magnum, .38 Special, and .357 Magnum/.38 Special. The larger calibers have 6-shot cylinders, but the .22 LR can be purchased as a 10-shot version. When I first donned a badge, our agency carried well-worn .38 Special Model 64s, loaded with +P lead, 158 grain semi-wadcutters. These four-inch guns were essentially stainless Model 10s with fixed sights and heavy barrels. Later, we switched to nearly identical .357 Magnum Model 65s. Like many other agencies from that era, we still used .38 Special loads, although we did upgrade to +P jacketed hollow-points. The idea was to strike a balance of recoil control and so-called stopping power, while prolonging the service-life of our inventory. Most of our M-65s were square-butt 4" types, although we did field a smattering of 3" round-butt models for plainclothes carry (the same .357 in blued steel is a Model 13). Their fixed sights were foolproof and nearly indestructible. They were also regulated by the factory to our specified service load, and shot surprisingly close to the sights. The Model 19s and Model 66s are similar .357 Magnums in blued or stainless, sold with adjustable sights. Some models were dropped only to reappear, and beyond the Model 10, several blued examples are now back as "Classics." Among them is the elegant K-22, a rimfire version of S&W's prestigious K-38 target gun.

The K-frame was initially developed for .38 Special loads but improvements in metallurgy eventually permitted S&W to offer .357 Magnums. The 1950-era Model 19 "Combat Magnum" proved viable, providing a lighter revolver than the initial N-frame .357 chambering. The "magnumized" K-frame had a slightly longer cylinder than a .38, but existing holsters, grips, and loader devices still fit. Shortly thereafter, the predominant LE choice became some sort of 4," .357 Magnum K-frame. The fixed-sighted stainless M-65 was common, but the adjustable-sighted M-66 and its blued M-19 counterpart were also popular. Some agencies took advantage of the .357 chambering by carrying full-house loads. A common practice was to use cheaper, lower-powered .38 Specials on ranges, reserving magnums for service use. However, as liability-driven training evolved, it became prudent to qualify with what was carried on duty, resulting in steady magnum diets. The result was accelerated wear and a general loosening up of the guns. The hottest 125 grain .357 Magnum loads were supposedly the worst offenders. A flame-cut line would develop in the frame, just above the barrel's forcing cone, and the cone itself was subject to erosion and other problems. It protrudes into the frame window and has a small flat at 6:00 to provide necessary crane clearance (the swinging arm that holds the cylinder). Cracks sometimes developed at this thinnest section so S&W went to work on this issue, resulting in a new beefed up L-frame.

S&W's K-frame Model 65 is plenty tough - without a steady diet of .357 Magnums.

Those who stuck with .38 Special loads were in better shape. I'm not sure how long a Model 65 will last, but based on firsthand experience, it's a very long time. After assuming our Department's ordnance duties, I procured our M-65s. Because I managed our purchases and training, this provided an opportunity to track their ammo consumption. One batch of around 40 remained in service until 2005 and, although most of them had

The Smith & Wesson Line | 159

been procured around 1990, they had surprisingly few problems. Each one probably had digested at least 50,000 rounds of .38 Special; most being 130-grain FMJ, with a smattering of +P JHP thrown in. A few had slightly bulged bores attributable to lodged bullets. During fast-paced training a few underpowered "squibs" were likely perceived as misfires, whereupon following shots expelled the stuck bullets, causing barely visible rings. We had to look closely to see one, and each gun still functioned fine. The process is certainly not endorsed, but it is a testament to their durability. Put enough rounds down range and you'll see some weird stuff. The lodged bullets, by the way, were the product of an early batch lead-free ammo that gave us all sorts of fits.

We still have some M-65s in our inventory for old time's sake. A flame cut is visible in the usual problem area, but it's too minor to be of any consequence.

L-Frame. This slightly larger S&W appeared during 1980 as their Distinguished Combat Magnum. It's a reinforced K-frame with a larger-diameter cylinder, a thicker frame/barrel junction, and a full-lug barrel. The 6:00 flat on the forcing cone is gone, replaced by a round extension. These changes prolong gun life during sustained firing of .357 Magnums. In traditional alloys, the gun is heavier, but not by a huge extent. The newer super-light scandium models are a different story and, with full-house loads, they kick!

Blued and fixed-sight L-frame models have been offered, but the stainless Model 686 remains the most popular choice. S&W wisely retained the K-frame's grip dimensions for their new L-frame, so after-market choices remained extensive. However, the cylinder is larger in diameter, requiring the use of L-frame specific speed-loaders (which also work with Ruger GP-100s). The whole revolver is also somewhat bigger, which excludes the use of most K-frame holsters. These differences steered me toward M-65s as replacements for our agency's older K-frames, but it was a painful decision. On the other hand, personal logistics were minor so, in short order, I owned a four-inch Model-686. It may have racked up a higher round count than anything else I've owned. Our other FIs quickly followed suit, and one described the Model 686 as "elegant"; an observation no one disagreed with. Our four-inch guns handled superbly and were dead-nuts accurate, but I later added a six-inch version for use on steel plates, etc. Of course, it was a tack-driver, although less handy to carry. Various other barrels have appeared from 8 3/8" to snubbies. A 7-inch variant is another possibility although one kicker with oddball lengths can be holster fit. Many single-gun owners would probably be well served by an all-around 4" version.

Most L-frames are 6-shot .357s, but a 7-shooter is now available. In fact, S&W's Performance Center now offers a 9mm version as Model 986 Pro. Its titanium cylinder is cut for moon clips, and its reduced mass lessens the force required for double-action cycling, translating to a lighter trigger stroke. Weight is only 35 ounces but its 5-inch barrel will limit holster choices so, to me at least, this type of 9mm revolver is more of a range and competition piece. On the other hand, S&W's 2 ½" Performance Center M-986 is a much more portable 31.7-ounce gun, capable of roughly +P .38 ballistics and offers extremely quick reloads.

Possibly the most intriguing variant is the new 5-shot .44 Magnum, sold as the Model 69. Heretofore, this caliber was the province of S&W's larger N-frame, but elimination of one chamber permits an L-frame offering. Its 4.25" barrel is a nice match which keeps a lid on size while cutting weight to 37 ounces. By comparison, a large-frame 4" M-629 will provide a sixth chamber, but will add an extra quarter-pound. Since every extra ounce adds up when other gear is involved, the latest, 2.75" Model 69 Combat Magnum may have stronger appeal. In fact, this 34.4-ounce gun may be right at home with warmer .44 Special loads for general-purpose carry.

N-Frame. S&W's .44 Hand Ejector, 1st Model, New Century debuted around 1908 as a larger-framed revolver. The New Century is sometimes referred to as a "triple-lock" because of its extra cylinder-latching safeguard, and this since-simplified N-frame remained S&W's largest until the appearance of the mighty .500 S&W. Although the N-frame was designed as a heavy-duty platform for larger calibers like the .44 Special, during World War I a .45 ACP version was developed to supplant military handgun needs. However, since that cartridge was intended for the M-1911 Pistol, one hurdle was its rimless design. The fix was an ingenious "moon clip" solution designed for this U.S. Army Model 1917 revolver. Cartridges were coupled together in groups of three, using stamped moon clips. Today's stainless Model 625 .45 ACP is essentially the same N-frame with adjustable sights.

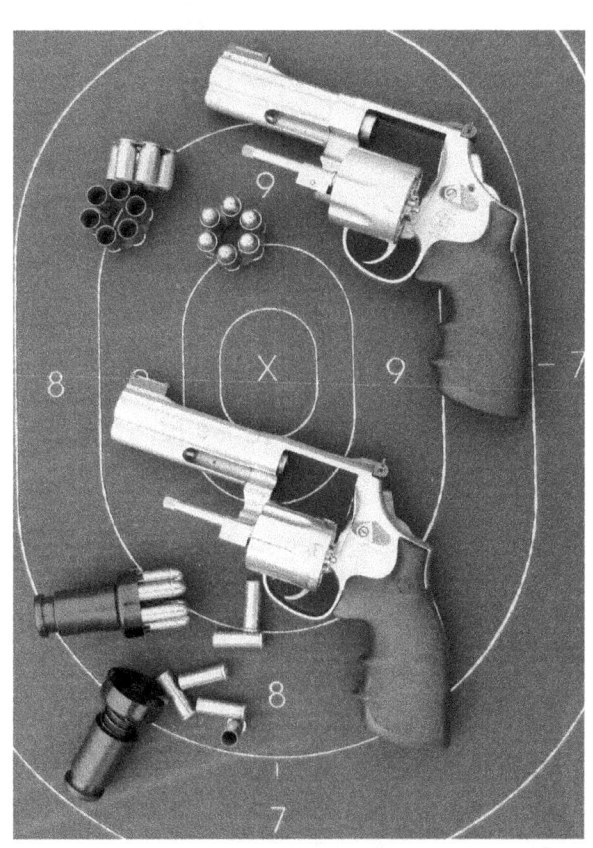

S&W's 4" N-frame Model 625 .45 ACP (top) accepts moon-clips. The .357 Model 686 L-frame can be fed from speed-loaders. Both have fired a huge amount of rounds during D/A competition. Note their bobbed hammers.

Hotter .38 Special loads resulted in the .38/44 Outdoorsman. Then, in 1935, a .357 Magnum version debuted as the .357/44. The first 5,500 were sold as prestigious Registered Magnums and were coveted prizes until production ceased for World War II efforts. During the 1950s, the same gun reappeared as the pretty Model 27, backed up by a more utilitarian M-28 Highway Patrolman. The .44 Magnum, Model 29 was a logical evolution of the .44 Special, appearing in 1955. A .41 Magnum, Model 57 followed as an in-between choice during 1963.

The current N-frame line includes .357 Magnum, .41 Magnum, .44 Magnum, .45 ACP, and .45 Colt calibers. Capacity is generally 6 shots, although 8-shot .357s are also offered. The latter uses full-moon clips similar in design to 6-shot .45 ACP. Now discontinued 10mm runs also employed moon clips, with an added advantage of .40 S&W capability. Full-moon clips, by the way, work like the lesser-capacity WW types, but offer en masse loading to full capacity (we'll take a closer look at moon clips shortly).

Today's N-frames are sold in various configurations, and as mentioned, some lightweight scandium models have appeared. I haven't fired one in .44 Magnum, and I'm in no rush to do so. My .45 ACP is snappy enough, thank you. And, regardless of its weight, an N-Frame revolver is still a big gun. I've owned a bunch in .44 Special, .44 Magnum, and .45 ACP. You could normally fire .44 Specials in any .44 Magnum, but S&W does rate a few of their Performance Center guns as .44 Magnum only. The reason no doubt has to do with barrel-porting. Mine has an over-bore section ahead of its true muzzle which redirects high-pressure gas upwards through slots (the ports). Lead can rapidly accumulate in such designs and, although most .44 Magnums use jacketed bullets, one common .44 Special load employs a 246-grain lead round-nose. The porting can exhaust lead fragments at high velocity, posing hazards to bystanders, which becomes a non-issue for revolvers with standard muzzles.

Z-frame Governor. Yes, it's a revolver *and* a shotgun! S&W's wild, quasi N-Frame spin-off was spurred by the Taurus Judge. The Z-frame S&W Governor has a stretched-out section to accommodate .45 ACP, .45 Long Colt, and 2 ½" .410 shotgun shells within its longer cylinder. The resulting package is large but a lightweight scandium frame cuts down on weight. A laser equipped model is available, and they all come with a Tritium front night sight. The Governor (and the Taurus Judge) will receive more attention momentarily.

X-Frame. If bigger is good, this new frame should be just the ticket! The X-frame is where S&W's biggest boomers dwell. The .500 S&W Magnum is an anti-beast cartridge for use against unhappy bears or resurrected dinosaurs. The faster and flatter-shooting .460 S&W Magnum is another big game revolver for handgun purists. Although it's hard to imagine, this cartridge takes the "shorter" .454 Casul to a whole new level. But, despite such thermonuclear performance, the long .460 can also digest .454 and .45 LC loads, providing the means for less violent shooting. When it comes to pure revolver cartridges though, the .500 S&W really has no equal. Any skeptics of this claim should be convinced within one cylinder's worth of energetic ammo. This probably explains why a disproportionate amount of used, low round-count X-frames are in circulation. S&W has a fairly broad selection of guns and, although most are oriented toward handgun hunters, a few fill a unique self-defense niche. The "smallest" .500 has a 3 ½"

This compensated N-frame Model 629 is a Performance Center .44 Magnum. The sling is a personal touch, along with the Burris dot-sight.

barrel, and weighs around 3 ½ pounds. That's a whole lot of gun to lug on a belt, but the weight will no doubt seem more tolerable when fishing Alaskan stream banks plastered with brown bear tracks. The longer-barreled X-frames sport recoil compensators for darned good reasons. They'll still get your attention, so this short-barreled canon should provide its share of thrills.

Performance Center options. S&W also offers some interesting semi-custom revolvers. Whereas a truly custom-built handgun can be an extremely costly proposition, the Performance Center models are more or less extensions of S&W's existing product lines. Costs are greater, but all things considered, not exorbitant. Shooters looking for special features may enjoy a visit to the PC site.

S&W REVOLVER FUNCTION

The overall simplicity of a revolver is legendary, but there is more going on under the hood than meets the eye. So, an understanding of basic function may prove useful for shoppers, or any existing Smith & Wesson revolver owners. In fact, some of this information could apply to other brands - at least in the loose sense of how a double-action revolver works.

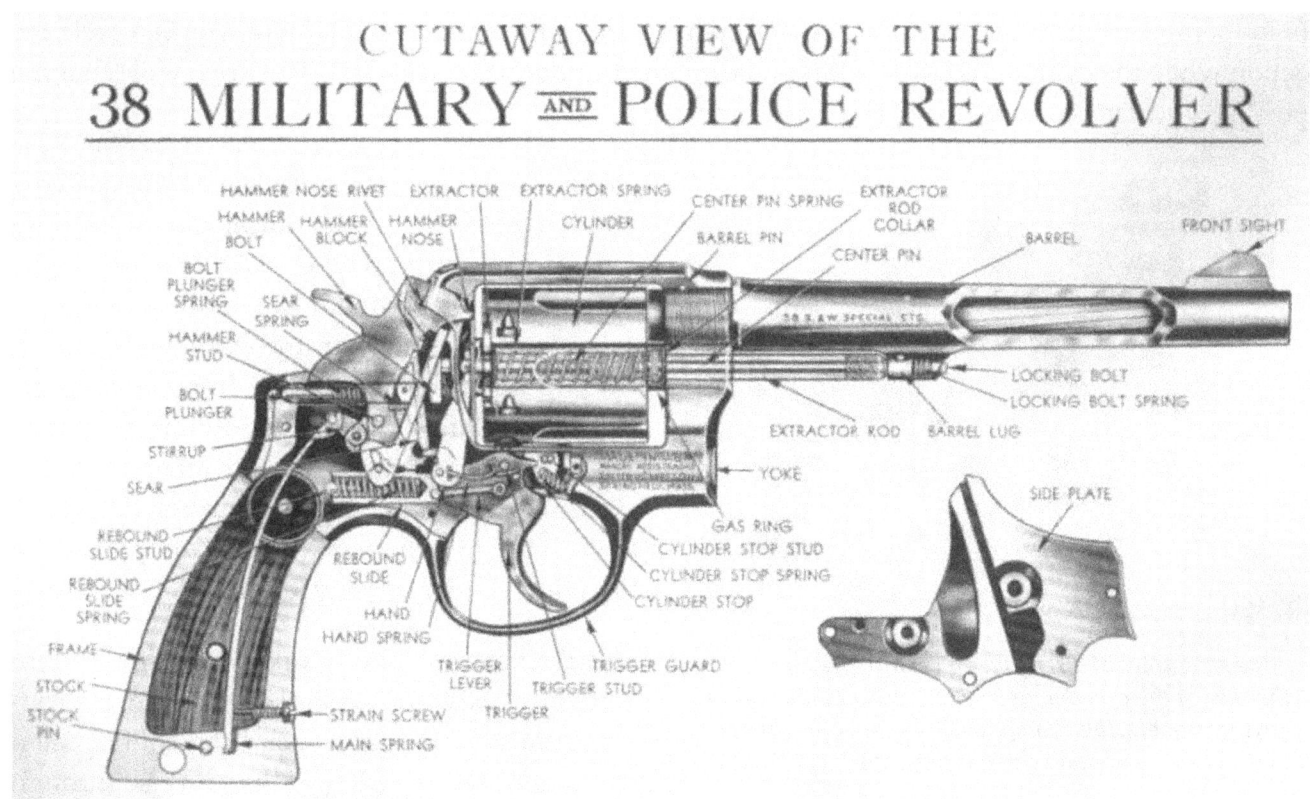

Lots going on under the hood of an S&W revolver! It's 19th century technology, too.

Disclaimer: I am not a factory-trained armorer. A couple other FTU cadre members performed complex servicing when they were available but there were occasional lapses in coverage so I sometimes filled in. Fortunately, problems were few. In fact, thanks to steady use, our Model 65s had actions slick enough to rival many custom-tuned revolvers. Regular maintenance kept them chugging along.

What follows is a brief tour of the workings of an average Smith & Wesson. If you can get your hands on an actual gun so much the better.

Thumb-piece. This button, located on the left side of the frame, is used to open the cylinder. As a right-handed shooter, sliding the button forward with that thumb will allow the cylinder to swing open upon a nudge at 3:00 (use your left finger tips). You'll see some high-speed competition shooters with oversized, trick thumb-pieces designed for instant access. They look cool but the factory-issue part will work just fine for most. In fact, S&W's latest tear-drop version is a close copy of a previous after-market unit. It's sleek and carries well without interfering with speed-loader devices. The various versions are all secured by a threaded fastener which can loosen and fall out, resulting in the loss of the thumb-piece. We just firmly cinch them up with a drop of blue thread-sealer, and the problem is solved.

The action will be immobilized when the thumb-piece is forward in normal open-cylinder mode, and in inoperable trigger is an indicator that the cylinder isn't fully shut. Knowing that, you can cycle the action while the cylinder is open by first holding the thumb-piece rearward. This trick will "fool the gun" so you can see how a few key parts function.

The thumb-piece disengages a central locking pin in the rear of the cylinder. Its ratchet teeth are part of the extractor-star. The chamfered chambers are custom, and don't extend to the star.

Action. To see how the thumb-piece unlocks the cylinder, note the small central pin protruding from its rear through a series of "ratchets" (the teeth that drive cylinder rotation). The pin is spring-loaded, and when the cylinder is shut, it will pop into a corresponding frame-hole to accomplish locking. Pushing the thumb-piece forward applies pressure from an internal "bolt," which depresses the cylinder pin for unlocking (as we'll see in a moment, this is only part of the story; the cylinder actually locks both fore and aft).

With the cylinder swung open, hold the thumb-piece fully rearward while *slowly* pulling the trigger. From double-action, you'll be able to see a frame-mounted "pawl" (or "hand") rise through a small window in the frame. Simultaneously, a small locking stud in the bottom of the frame will momentarily retract. The hand drives the ratchets when the cylinder is closed, and the stud arrests its rotation upon engagement with each notch. The shallow relieved "arrows" adjacent to each one initiate engagement and everything must be carefully timed for proper function. By the way, those little arrows also serve as excellent cylinder-rotation indicators.

The thumb-piece is forward, along with the central bolt. Above it is the firing pin and its bushing. The hand is visible in its window, as is the locking stud in the bottom of the frame.

The scallops adjacent to the locking slots serve as handy directionals. Some cylinders (like Colt's), rotate in an opposite, clockwise direction.

Again, with the cylinder open, cock the gun to single-action mode and note the fully extended hand. Then dry-fire it while holding the trigger rearward. The tip of the firing pin should be visible through the "recoil plate" (otherwise known as the breech face). As you let go of the trigger, the firing pin should retract. The same effect can be noted from double-action. If you press a fingertip against the firing pin hole, you'll feel a sharp strike when the hammer falls – a good indication of positive ignition. There's even more going on with trigger/hammer relationship, which we'll cover during problem-solving. Meanwhile, close the cylinder and draw the hammer back just far enough to drop the locking stud. The cylinder should "sing" (or spin freely) from a swipe to its side. If it doesn't there are problems which we'll cover in a bit.

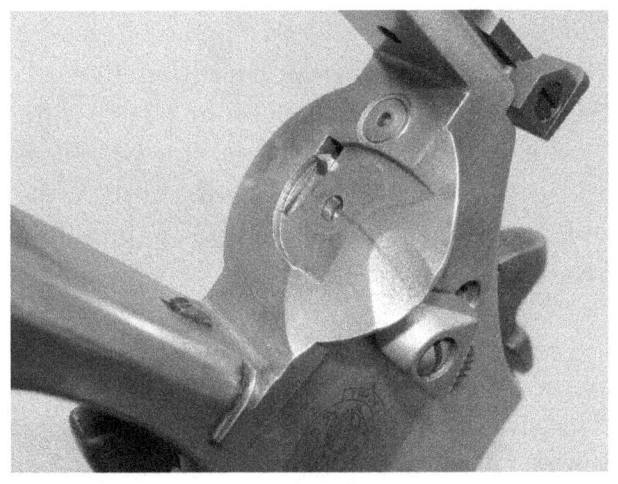

Cocked to S/A, the hand is elevated to its firing position. The frame's central bolt is retracted as it would be if the cylinder was closed.

Cylinder assembly. Swing the cylinder open and note its supporting arm, which pivots outward to the left from the lower forward corner of the frame. S&W calls this arm a "crane," which also incorporates a hollow axle upon which the cylinder rotates. You can spin the open cylinder to see how it works. While you're at it, take a close look at the front end of the ejector rod, and note a recess within its beveled end. This pocket engages another spring-loaded plunger (or stud) located underneath the barrel. In other words, the cylinder locks at both ends of its central axis. To understand the process, push firmly on the rear cylinder-pin while peering into the rod's front recess. You'll see it fill in as the rear pin is depressed. The ejector rod is really a hollow tube surrounding this long spring-loaded pin, its forward motion serving to disengage the front locking stud.

A second spring-loaded stud locks the front end of the ejector rod. Activating the thumb-piece drives a smaller, separate pin through the cylinder/rod assembly, providing disengagement.

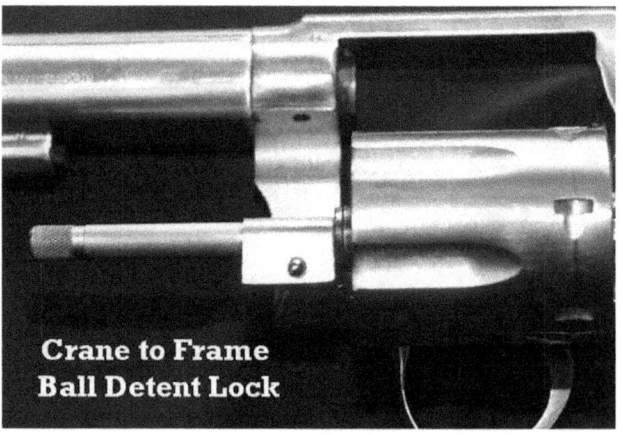

Beyond alternate factory ball-detents, others can be encountered as custom installations (photo by Domenick Leonard).

An exception is the occasional model with a small ball-detent captured within the front of the crane. The detent engages a corresponding recess to control side-play. My several-year-old .44 Magnum N-frame employs this system as does the recent L-frame M-69. The general concept goes way back to S&W's old "Triple Lock" N-frame, but a difference is that modern renditions dispense with forward ejector-rod locking altogether. One benefit may be improved accuracy since the effects of eccentric rod engagement are eliminated. As such, the cylinder can rotate truer on its axis. This feature has crept into other recent models including the current Model 66-8. Incidentally, although the ball and recess appear a bit off-center when engaged, this positioning is intentional.

As we can see, pushing the thumb-piece sets a fairly complicated mechanism in motion! Regardless of the locking design, the ejector rod passes through the crane which is also referred to as a "yoke." The crane's yoke supports the cylinder and smooth cycling is dependent on proper alignment of the various parts. Snapping the cylinder closed with a single-handed flip may look cool, but it's hard on the gun. Instead, just press the cylinder into battery as the crane pivots home. You don't want a bent ejector rod or excessive cylinder side-play.

Timing. Back to our old Model 65s, one thing that surprised me was how long they stayed "in time." Besides attention to maintenance, our ammo choices probably helped. The lion's share was standard velocity .38 Special, used for training and requalification, with a smaller percentage of +Ps thrown in the mix. Even though these revolvers were .357 Magnums, not much of it was fired. The timing of a few guns eventually became marginal, but it took a humongous amount of shooting.

Timing refers to how well a chamber is locked into alignment with the barrel. Theoretically, each one should lock tight as a drum without any wiggle at all. That would be fine so long as each chamber lined up precisely, but since tolerances and wear will introduce play, a bit of cylinder movement is acceptable. However, an excessive amount can shave bullets or cause misfires. The former condition can expel small bullet shavings with enough force to create bystander hazards. Offset primer dents are an indication of timing (or side-play) problems. In extreme examples, the entire primer may be missed; revealed by a small indent in an adjacent cartridge base.

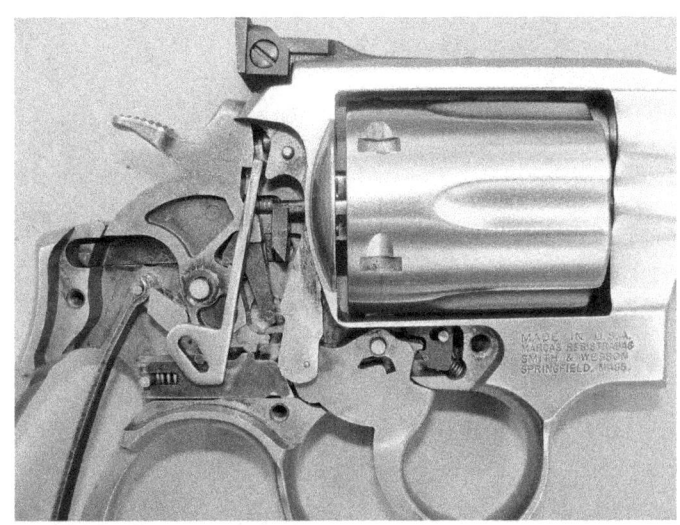

Removal of the side-plate reveals a complex design, along with the various parts that control timing.

Check timing from double-action because the hammer will fall earlier than when pre-cocked. Continue to hold the trigger rearward as the hammer falls to maintain maximum hand extension. This condition will replicate the moment when the gun fires for a truer indicator of cylinder locking. Again, a small amount of wiggle is okay. On the other hand, major movement is not. Be sure to check each chamber, and during this process, slowly manipulate the trigger so the upward pings of the stud can be heard. It should jump up, hit the cylinder, and pop into each notch *prior* to the hammer falling.

MORE ON MOON CLIPS

During World War I, the U.S. Model 1911 pistol was still in short supply so the Government turned to Colt and Smith & Wesson to increase handgun inventory. The result was the previously mentioned Model 1917 Revolver, adapted to rimless .45 ACP pistol rounds. Extraction was an immediate problem and the solution was a moon clip, which acted as a sort of surrogate rim that could capture multiple cartridges. These two-round, half, or full-moon clips are just thin steel stampings with cut-outs to accept the cartridges. You snap them in and throw the whole affair towards an open cylinder whereupon, with RN-type bullets, they'll be virtually inhaled. All the fired cases remain attached to the moon clip throughout the firing and ejection sequence. The biggest bother involves breaking the empties free afterward, and snapping fresh cartridges into the clips. Special tools are made for this purpose but the process still requires extra effort.

Even rimmed rounds like the .38/.357 have been adapted to moon clips. Besides an 8-shot Model 627 N-Frame, you can buy a J-Frame cut for 5-shot moon clips. Custom conversions are a further possibility. The cylinder's rear must be machined for adequate moon clip clearance, but TK Custom provides this service, as well as S&W. The conversion is done in such a way to accept individually loaded rounds or speed-loaders, as well as the clips. I had my Model 66 converted, but I like the big .45

Moon clips are associated with large-frame .45 ACP revolvers, but this .357 K-frame was converted by TK Custom. It'll also function normally without them.

ACP version more, even though it's moon clips or nothing. The smaller but longer .38/.357 cartridges are harder to align, and more difficult to snap in the clips. The moon clips themselves are also thinner, with tighter cartridge spacing necessary for K-frame indexing. The longer cartridges also tend to flop around a bit during loading, in part due to thinner clips. However, the .38/.357 moon clip system does work. Fortunately, since the gun loads conventionally too, I often go this route for casual shooting.

A *possible* concern could be degraded accuracy without use of the clips. The machining process leaves a small outboard section of each original chamber for a cartridge rim to bear against. The larger inboard area is relieved to the thickness of a moon clip for flush seating. This means without a moon clip, cartridge rims will receive only a portion of their normal support. Some shooters theorize that misalignment *could* result when primers are struck by the hammer, but I've shot some darn good 50-yard groups with individually loaded .38 Special and .357 Magnum rounds.

Of course, this concern disappears entirely with pistol cartridges like the 9mm and .45 ACP. Their rimless designs render individual loading moot so the entire rear of the cylinder is simply machined flat. Lately, moon clip 9mm revolvers have become increasingly popular, and their shorter length is more amenable to wiggle-free reloads. The downside to smaller cartridges is their tighter spacing which can make moon clip setup a bit fiddly.

I can usually snap cartridges into a moon clip by hand although the last round or two may be a battle; and in a pinch, it's possible to use a revolver's cylinder to strip out the first empty case. Removal of each one relieves progressively less tension so the job soon requires less effort. For higher volume purposes, both steps are *much* easier with the right tool. My favorite de-mooner is a simple piece of flat steel. Superficially, it resembles a blued "church key" with its end formed into a 180-degree curve. A small tab engages the edge of the moon clip, providing leverage while the curved section surrounds the fired case. You can then pry them out, one at a time. Another alternative is a tubular design resembling a jumbo magnetic screw-bit holder. The hollow shaft has a tab on its end which provides leverage to pop out fired cases, and it's long enough to accumulate a cylinder's worth. There are creative clip re-mooning devices too, some of which work like pliers or tongs. A neat gadget is pocket knife-size The Moonclip Tool that handles all related tasks. These specialized gadgets are real finger-savers during mass moon clip extravaganzas. Competitive shooters normally attend a match with lots of race-ready moon clips, worn in special belt-mounted holders. The expended clips are easily retrieved for refills at home.

Most revolver owners probably won't be entering matches, but a moon clip system can still be useful. Some locales prohibit loaded handguns in vehicles, ATVs, boats, etc. In such circumstances, a moon clip revolver is downright handy. Just dismount and toss in a full-moon clip. Unloading is just as easy. Fumble-free cartridge handling will also be appreciated in circumstances where individual rounds can disappear: deep snow, thick vegetation, low light, or any combination thereof.

MORE ON .45/.410 REVOLVERS

Although this chapter is about S&Ws, credit must go to Taurus for kicking off the whole .410 revolver concept. For years, I've heard stories of people stuffing .45 Long Colt cartridges into .410 shotguns. It's nothing I've ever cared to try, but Taurus seized upon the idea with a technical mindset, creating an unusual revolver large enough to safely handle either load.

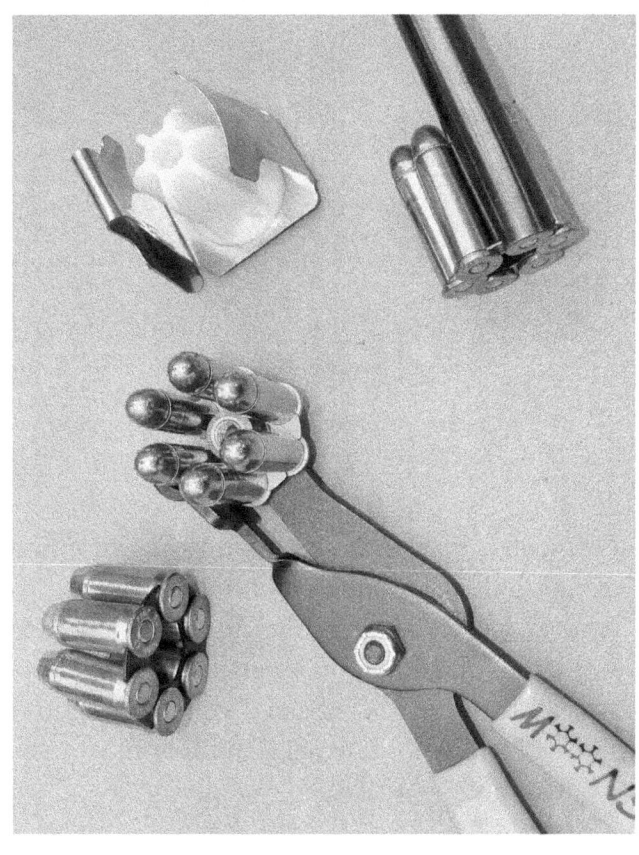

Although strong fingers work, the tubular tool is an easier way to de-moon fired cases. Tongs prevent sore fingers when snapping in new rounds. The holder is best reserved for ranges due to retention concerns.

Taurus Judge. After a decade of production, the Judge remains a strong seller. The original model was based on their Tracker, with a five-shot cylinder stretched to accommodate either .45 Colt cartridges, or 2 ½-inch .410 shotshells. The result was a somewhat odd looking and large revolver. Its bore was rifled for a couple reasons, one being to stabilize .45 bullets. The other was to avoid federal regulations pertaining to short-barreled, smoothbore shotguns. One wrinkle is that rifling can rapidly disperse shot, limiting its effectiveness to small-room ranges. Taurus supposedly worked on this problem, developing a barrel that improved patterns while maintaining useful bullet accuracy. Things got really interesting when Federal jumped on board with special 2 ½" shells containing either #4 shot, or four 000 buckshot pellets. Winchester followed with a 2 ½" combo-load containing three discs and twelve plated BBs. Nowadays, the Judge has grown to around a dozen offshoots, some of which will even accept 3-inch .410 shells. Barrels run from 6 ½-inches downward. The 2 ½" Public Defender Polymer is Taurus's most portable offering at 23 ounces.

S&W's Governor can fire 2 ½" .410 shells, plus .45 Colt, and .45 ACP cartridges (the latter using moon clips).

S&W Governor. During 2009, S&W introduced a similar gun. Besides the aforementioned loads, the Governor also offers the versatility of .45 ACP, thanks to moon clips. A scandium frame holds weight to a hair under 30 ounces. The 2.75" blackened stainless barrel limits size to some extent but it's still an N-frame. The cylinder is limited to 2 ½" shells, but offers a bonus sixth shot. Like the Taurus, the sights are fixed, although an S&W laser-equipped version is available.

.45/.410 revolver performance. Will these guns effectively fulfill both hunting and defense requirements? By most accounts, .45-caliber cartridge accuracy is decent. Assuming an appropriate load can be found that will shoot to the sights, big game *could* be harvested. The .45 Colt is no slouch and, for that matter, neither is the .45 ACP; and, using moon clips with a Governor, an easy switch to non-expanding .45 ACP FMJ bullets shouldn't demolish small game. Based on our limited experience, shot loads are probably out for anything other than small game at *very* close range. Combined with the negative effects of rifling, pellet count and shot density just aren't adequate for normal .410 shotgun distances. Of course, the several new unique defensive .410 options up the ante for self-defense.

ODDS AND ENDS

S&W has been making double-action revolvers for years, so many variations exist. Walk in a gun shop and there's no telling what you could run into between new or used guns. A new S&W comes with a lifetime warranty for the original owner - a reassuring feature! That said, there are plenty of good used S&Ws in circulation. Let's start with one unusual feature that has been in use for more than a century…

Bobbed, shrouded and internal hammers. Our lead FI raises general hell during IDPA matches, often finishing in first place against revolver *and* pistol competitors. His gun of choice is a slick S&W Model 686 with a bobbed hammer. He shoots it strictly in double-action so the superfluous spur has been ground off for a streamlined profile that affords somewhat faster lock-time. This modification was also popular during revolver PPC days, when Practical Police Course competitors shot highly customized .38 Special revolvers. On the opposite side of the spectrum, we'll find small revolvers with hammers designed for snag-free concealed carry. Choices include shrouded or internal hammer designs. The shrouded type has an extended frame that covers nearly the entire hammer, exposing only part of its spur for single-action access. An internal design completely encloses the hammer for snag and lint-free carry. As such, this design is D/A only. On any general-purpose revolver, I prefer a traditional hammer spur. In fact, I'd just as soon have one on a small J-frame. But that's just me. An internal-hammer design really does make lots of sense for a deep-cover revolver. Odds are any unpleasantness will be up close and personal, fired from double-action anyway.

Other D/A-only guns. You could also run into a larger-frame S&W that's strictly double-action. Some LE agencies stipulated this design so Smith & Wesson obliged with special DAO runs. Some eventually wound up in circulation on the used-gun market. If the hammer won't cock or its spur is missing, that could be what you've encountered.

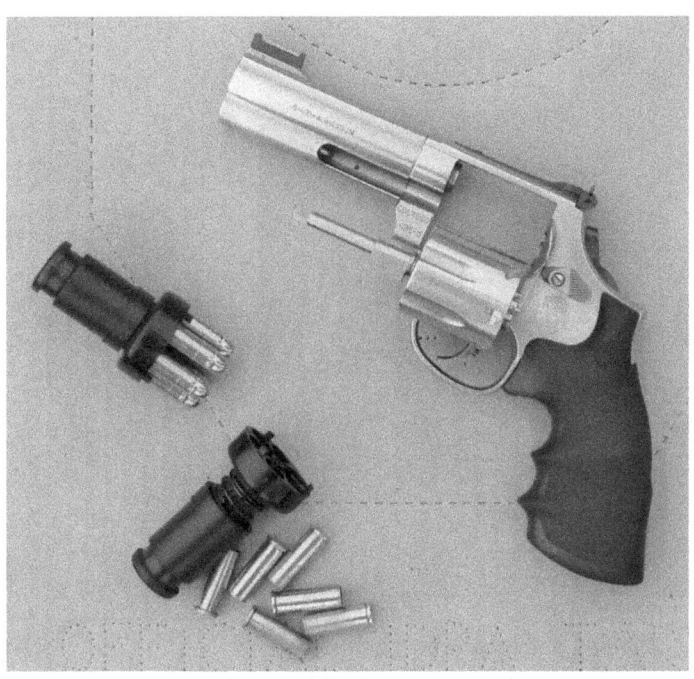

This bobbed-hammer S&W Model 686 has racked up numerous International Defensive Pistol Association (IDPA) wins, using Safariland's Comp III loaders.

Cut-away trigger guards. This non-factory modification is associated with some older, used revolvers. You'll know it when you see one because a chunk of the trigger guard will either be ground down or totally missing. The idea was to facilitate a faster D/A response. Maybe, but I'd pass in the interest of safety.

Key-lock. This feature was mentioned earlier. Look above the thumb-piece on a recent-production S&W revolver and you should see a small socket. The gun is sold with a key (of sorts), which can render the action inoperable. If you insert it and twist, a small metal tab should appear beside the hammer, indicating "locked." No doubt, this design has merit for some, but I'd rather lock the whole gun up and not worry about losing (or fiddling with) the key. Mine remain inside their factory boxes, speaking of which…

Boxes, serial, and model numbers. It's worth hanging onto a factory box. Some of them are basic plastic containers that could serve for trips to the range, while others are cardboard. Regardless, I just stash them in the attic, along with their paperwork and any extras – including the separate, obligatory cable locks. If nothing else, every relevant item is in one easy-to-find spot. In the event the gun needs factory service, the properly serial numbered box will be appreciated. Later, if you do decide to sell it, the box will be more attractive. LNIB means "like new in box," which should increase value somewhat. A factory box could also serve as a handy reference when some grip-types are installed. S&W stamps their serial numbers on the bottom of the grip-frame and some grips cover them up. The model number is usually stamped underneath the crane. Swinging it open should reveal something

The Smith & Wesson Line | 171

Thinned or cutaway trigger guards enjoyed some popularity when revolvers ruled the roost, and they're still in circulation.

S&W's key system is shown locked, as indicated by a small tab beside the hammer.

like 63-6, in this case indicating a .22 LR Model 63. My later-production S&Ws also have the serial number stamped in this location. An older gun might not, but if it ever disappears, the separately stored box could provide valuable information.

CHAPTER 14
GOOD PICKS: S&W – AND OTHERS

One more time: we need to strike a balance of something small enough to hide and big enough to shoot well, with a reasonable degree of power. That's hard to do with only one gun, which is why many folks have two. Since most of us are on a budget, let's start with one do-all gun.

With all due respect to the innovative Judge and Governor .45/.410 hand-canons, they're out as a single-gun choice (at least for most of us). Neither will provide the range of a true .410 shotgun, and although use of .45-caliber cartridges is possible, these guns are fairly large. However, those with a place to stash one will have a formidable close-range response. That spot *could* be purse, but a backpack or bug-out bag would be better, so would a readily accessible *but secure* indoor location. Of course, individual physique can play a further role in a final choice. A big strapping six-four shooter could probably manage an S&W N-frame as easily as a petite, J-frame toting woman. Since most of us fall in between, our gun choice should follow suit.

Revisited rationale. The previous editions focus on guns oriented toward survival use. Among them are a shotgun, rimfire rifle, air rifle, and centerfire rifle. The concept involves accumulating a modest but practical battery as time and resources permit, without going overboard on cost. As such, the focus has been on *one good gun* from each type. The hands-free carry option is, of course, a handgun. If the choice must boil down to just one, it might as well be the most versatile pick. Besides defense, subsistence hunting *could* be in the cards, but even if field use is discounted, the potential still exists for unpleasantness at longer ranges. A shootable choice could thus tip the odds toward a successful outcome – especially in the hands of a proficient user. Practice makes perfect, so a gun that supports this endeavor helps.

TOP PICK: S&W MODEL 66

Out of every revolver covered, I'd suggest a stainless 4-inch, K-frame .357 Magnum. It won't be the smallest or easiest to hide; it won't be the toughest or most powerful choice; but it will achieve a reasonable compromise, which is exactly why law enforcement personnel have carried a revolver of this size since 1900. Sure, the originals were .38 Specials, but the present .357s are fundamentally unchanged.

The most durable K-frame choice would be a fixed-sighted gun like a Model 65. As noted earlier, we had an armory full of 65s, which were shot non-stop for two decades. Although each one developed a shallow, flame-cut just above the barrel juncture, it didn't affect function in the least.

Model 66 rationale. Even though our trusty fixed-sighted M-65s were well-regulated, I'd go for a Model 66. *It's* essentially the same gun with adjustable sights. There's a very good chance that .38 special loads will be fired through this .357 Magnum, creating varying POIs. Granted, adjustable sights are less rugged than integral fixed sights, but that doesn't mean they are fragile. A good holster will also afford a bit of extra protection against bumps or even harder impacts. I added the Bowen Rough Country adjustable rear sight to my own Model 66. They appear to be aptly named, although windage is adjusted by opposing screws requiring trial and error. You can't make any minor corrections with graduated clicks like you could with a stock S&W rear sight, but most velocity corrections tend to be vertical. Truthfully though, the factory rear sight should work just fine for most of us.

Durability combines with grace through this battle-scarred, but still viable, S&W Model 65. The Magna-ported barrel is a recoil-reducing touch (photo by Domenick Leonard).

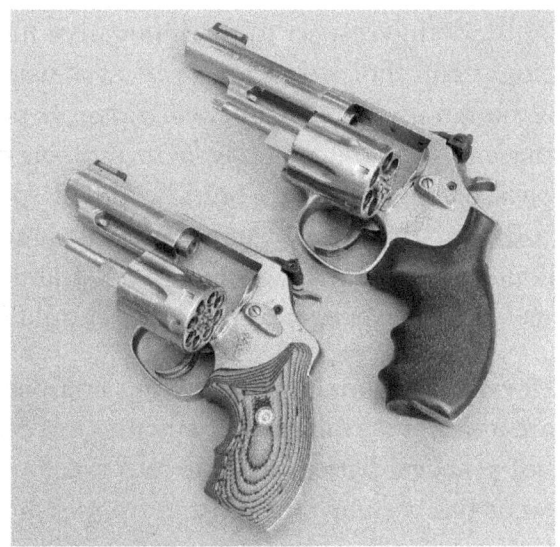

The .357/.38 Model 66 is a great solo choice, improved through a companion .22 LR.

Model 686 alternative. A steady diet of hotter .357s is the reason why the slightly larger L-Frame came into being. In other words, it's a stronger gun. Still, it's hard to beat the elegance of a stainless steel Model 686. Although S&W catalogs several versions of this revolver, a 4-inch gun seems "right." I can't see too many people burning through thousands of .357 rounds, but a M-686 does assure long-term durability. Weight will be a bit more but either frame will accept the same grips, and rear sight screw-hole spacing is identical.

THE TWO-GUN APPROACH

Some shoppers will have legitimate complaints about day-to-day carry with a K or L-frame revolver; particularly one with a barrel of four-inches or longer. If so, there's another option.

Model 60 or similar J-frame. Go for a smaller 5-shot choice and you'll gain a carry-friendly companion. There are plenty of versions to choose from between external and shrouded-hammer models. The barrels are typically less than 2-inches and some weigh less than a pound. The Bodyguard 340 CT is a D/A-only, shrouded-hammer, 13.5 ounce .357 Magnum pocket rocket. That's more excitement than I'd care to regularly experience, but this chambering does assure durability with 38 Special +P loads.

This two-gun .357/.38 approach includes an L-frame M-686 and a smaller J-frame M-60. The latter could serve as a stand-alone choice for some.

The "CT" stands for Crimson Trace, well-known for their excellent grip-activated lasers. A laser seems especially useful for small guns that are harder to aim, but the M-340 also has a 24/7 tritium front sight. Weight saving is accomplished by a scandium frame, and magnum strength results from its stainless steel cylinder and barrel. A somewhat similar Model 442 runs off .38 Special moon clips. The aluminum/ stainless Model 637s are lightweight double-action snubbies. These small revolvers could satisfy most CCW requirements but won't meet broader general-purpose needs, so let's jump up one more time…

Model 686 Pro Series SSR L-frame? A slightly larger general-purpose revolver makes the most sense when augmented by a small concealed-carry revolver. In that case a compromise gun becomes less of a concern, allowing a step up to gain some extra features. The Pros lack the full-underlug barrels of some other L-frame models, using a tapered rib instead. As such, the 6-shot Pro comes in just above 38 ounces. But, the 7-shot *Pro Series Plus* combines a 5-inch barrel with moon clip capability. Weight is nearly identical because of its extra chamber. Assuming you can find a holster that meets your needs, the *Plus* seems like one heck of a good revolver choice!

ADD A RIMFIRE?

Start saving pennies and down the road you might want to think about a .22 rimfire revolver. It would make a darned good addition to either menu for small game hunting, plinking, or relevant serious practice. S&W sells nicely scaled .22 LR alternatives which are based on J-frame and K-frame revolvers. A couple that come to mind are the smaller .22 LR Model 63 "Kit-Gun," and the medium-sized Model 617. Both will receive extra attention in the rimfire handgun chapter.

Incidentally, we are big advocates of dry-fire practice, especially for double-action proficiency. However, dry-firing rimfires can cause damage to chamber edges and firing pins so save dry-firing for your centerfire revolvers.

OTHER BRANDS: RUGERS

So far, it's been all S&W but, as we've seen, there are others. Two major double-action revolver competitors are Ruger and Taurus.

Ruger has been building solid double-action revolvers since 1972. Their Security Six laid the groundwork for future Ruger D/A models, including the larger Redhawk. Ruger made some changes during its 1980 introduction, rolling in a few clever features that eventually extended to other models. The original Security Six employed a forward extractor-rod locking design like S&W's, but that gave way to the Redhawk's crane-locking system (more like S&W's old Triple-lock). In 1985, the Security Six morphed into an updated GP100. Its traditional full-profile steel grip-frame was dropped for a smaller universal lug, which fit several GP100 grip options. Further D/A evolutions then blossomed, including an appropriately named Super Redhawk which is reminiscent of a bank vault. Ruger also addressed the opposite end of the spectrum with a handy SP101, followed by a very small LCR. The latter is the most unconventional, using everything from polymers through aluminum and, of course, steel.

Speaking of steel, Rugers are final-machined from investment castings. At the time of its inception, this construction raised the eyebrows of many within an entrenched forged-frame industry. However, several decades have proven this method to be both economical and sound. The D/A Rugers also share a push-button cylinder release instead of a sliding S&W-type thumb-piece, although cylinder rotation remains counter-clockwise. Coil springs are standard throughout the Ruger line, and disassembly is relatively simple. I wouldn't go so far as to call it tool-less, but it's pretty-darned close. A screwdriver will be needed to remove the grips. A small disassembly pin housed within can then be used to capture the hammer spring and strut-assembly for removal. At that point, plucking out a simple retainer will free the hammer. Unlike an S&W, there is no side-plate. Instead, a lower frame assembly can be popped free to reveal the entire fire-control system. When all is said and done, the cylinder will also disengage for maintenance (because of a few small parts this process is best done at home). The LCR is different animal which, for the most part, just survives on an occasional snort of oil.

LCR & LCR-X Series. These small revolvers present a non-traditional alternative to S&W J-frame line. Ruger has engineered their triggers for smooth non-stacking pulls. Weight runs from 13 ½ -17 ounces. The .38 +P rated 5-shot LCR has a stainless steel cylinder and barrel liner. The upper frame assembly is aluminum, and the lower frame is polymer. The marriage of these materials results in a corrosion-proof, lightweight revolver geared toward deep-cover carry. The .22 WMR and .22 LR options offer 6 or 8 shots, respectively. The hotter .357 Magnum, 9mm Luger, and .327 Federal versions use dark-finished stainless instead of aluminum. The LCRs are 1 7/8" "snubbies" with fixed-sights, DAO actions, and internal hammers, making them good concealed-carry choices. The LCR-X revolvers have exposed hammers. Two with great kit-gun potential are 3-inch adjustable-sight versions chambered for .22 LR or .38 +P. Their aluminum "monolithic frames" result in very handy D/A revolvers, weighing around one pound. One thing easy to overlook among the many unusual features is the well-thought out grips. The pinned front sights are another nice touch.

SP101. This line is a viable S&W J-frame competitor, constructed from stainless steel. The SP101s share many of the design features common to the GP100, but in a more compact package. Whereas the LCRs weigh close to a pound, the stainless SP101s run around 24 ounces; still quite comfortable when worn on a belt. However, there is nothing dainty about an SP101. One quick peek should alleviate concerns about its ability to handle .357 Magnum loads. You'll get five shots in this caliber, but the .327 Federal offers six, and a .22 LR version is good for eight. In its most basic form, the .357 Magnum SP101 has a 2 ¼-inch barrel and fixed sights. Other great-looking models have 4.2" barrels with F/O adjustable sights, extending their usefulness to general-purpose duties. Weight increases somewhat in the longer barreled SP101, but the heaviest .22 LR version is still only 30 ounces. Depending on the caliber, this compact revolver has either stand-alone or great second-gun potential.

HG-14 Revolver Ruger SP 101: GP100. Here's Ruger's answer to S&W's medium frame line. It's probably no coincidence that S&W L-frame speed-loaders also work with a GP100. Buyers on the prowl for one general-purpose (GP!) revolver could do a whole lot worse than this rugged, stainless steel revolver. The GP100 Standard is sold in several intriguing variations besides .357 Magnum. Two neat choices are a six-inch, 10-shot .22 LR, and a three-inch 5-shot .44 Special. Weights run from 36 – 42 ounces. The .44 Special will be especial-

The rugged construction of Ruger's SP101 is obvious.

ly appealing to diehard revolver fans, although a 4.2-inch .357 Magnum probably makes more sense. The standard version is fully up to all tasks, and the adjustable-sight, 4.2-inch Match Champion looks like a real winner. Its extras include a well-designed set of Hogue wood grips, polished internals, and F/O front sight.

Redhawk. This brawny gun is Ruger's answer to the S&W N-frame. The Redhawk is the domain of large-caliber cartridges like .41 Magnum, .44 Magnum, and .45 Colt; but two other interesting choices stand out. How about a fairly-compact 2 ¾," 8-shot .357 Magnum set up for moon clips? Adjustable sights permit great load flexibility and the round-butt frame is a good match which, to some extent, offsets its 44-ounce heft. Another *really interesting* and somewhat similar Redhawk is the 4.2-inch dual-caliber .45 LC /.45 ACP model. The latter cartridges can be fired by using moon clips and the whole gun just looks "right," although weight once again is 44 ounces.

The strength and simplicity of Ruger's Redhawk serves well with large calibers when the going gets tough.

If bigger is even better, the Super Redhawk fits the bill. The extra weight will be appreciated in its potent magnum chamberings.

Super Redhawk. Like S&W's X-frame, this beefed up Redhawk is *big*. Its massive frame extends forward to surround part of the barrel, providing plenty of strength for big cartridges like the .454 Casull and .480 Ruger - in addition to the other large magnums. The ample frame provides a good platform for use with optical sights and is machined to accept Ruger scope rings. The basic 7 ½-inch .44 Magnum Super Redhawk weighs 53 ounces – not something I'd care to wear on a belt. The 2 ½" Alaskan restores some order at 44 ounces, but it's certainly no conventional snubbie. Its name clearly denotes the most practical use for a gun in this size range, chambered for .44 Magnum, .454 Casull, and .480 Ruger. The latest Super Redhawk is a 10mm machined to accept full-moon clips, which means it'll also work with .40 S&W cartridges.

Decisions? A good one-gun choice would be a 4.2-inch GP-100, chambered for the versatile .357 Magnum. Budget would dictate the choice of a Standard Model or Match Champion, and either way you'll gain a rugged and maintenance-friendly revolver. Of course, the LCR-series would carry better concealed and while you *could* press a 3-inch LCR-X .38 Special into GP duties, I'd much prefer a rugged 4-inch, SP101 chambered in .357 Magnum. Mix and match as you choose, but don't forget about a useful .22 LR.

Disassembly and maintenance. All you'll need is a screwdriver and owner's manual to disassemble one of Ruger's steel-frame D/A revolvers. For that matter, lacking a manual, you can find directions on Ruger's web site. In fact, disassembly won't really be necessary during routine cleaning, which is pretty much the norm for any other D/A revolvers.

OTHER BRANDS: TAURUS REVOLVERS

At one point during the early 1970s, S&W was connected to this Brazilian firearm manufacturer. While that relationship no longer exists, the many double-action similarities are obvious. Taurus has put much recent effort into the quality of their product-line, resulting in a lifetime warranty that follows each gun. They are also big on the Taurus Security System, which employs a key to immobilize the hammer of their D/A revolvers. The firm has developed an extensive array of interesting choices based on both traditional and non-traditional materials, including an answer to Ruger's polymer LCR as well as S&W's titanium-cylinder creations. Rather than attempting to describe each model, we can lump them into size groupings.

Taurus small-frame guns. Based strictly on personal observation, I'm guessing these J-frame competitors are their strongest sellers. You can buy all sorts of variations with external or internal hammers, in different materials and calibers beyond the small-frame norm, including 9mm or even .380! The latter is admittedly an unorthodox revolver caliber, but then again, recoil should be minimal in such a 15-ounce gun, which no doubt is the point.

Medium-frames. Calibers and materials abound. As far as I'm concerned, some of the neatest revolvers in the whole Taurus line are the Tracker series. Check out their 7-shot, stainless steel .357 Magnum, which presents a nice balance of size and shootability. Its 4-inch barrel is ported to offset magnum recoil, and a set of soft ribbed grips is another helpful touch for this 28-ounce revolver. The front sight is pinned and the rear sight is adjustable. Shoppers seeking other calibers are also in luck. A 5-shot version is similarly equipped to help handle .44 Magnum recoil in a 34-ounce gun. I'd *probably* go with a good .44 Special defensive round for all but special circumstances, and I'd *certainly* go this route with their 28-ounce Taurus Ultralight Titanium version! Other options include 9-shot rimfires in .22 LR, .22 WMR, and even .17 HMR; the latter being more of a niche varmint choice. New for 2018 is a series of 7-shot Trackers sold with interchangeable .357 Magnum and 9mm Luger cylinders, which can be switched via a clever new release system.

Large frames. The Raging Series revolvers have been sold in some interesting calibers like .30 Carbine and .22 Hornet, along with large magnum-class cartridges. Today's smaller list includes .44 Magnum and .454 Casull guns. An odd but interesting addition is a snubbie .454 with a very long cylinder, designed to accept .410 shotgun shells (plus .45 Colt). A 6-inch variant is also listed but, at around 60 - 73 ounces, none of these stretch-cylinder choices are flyweights.

The Taurus M-692 Multi-caliber .357/9mm permits simple cylinder exchanges through a frame-mounted push-button.

SUMMARY

Of course, there are more guns to choose from than those covered above, including some recent off-shore brands which sell for less money than their domestic counterparts. A Turkish-built S&W clone is but one example. Whether such imports will survive on a long-term basis remains to be seen, raising concerns over parts and servicing. Meanwhile, back on the home front, Colt and Kimber have expanded their recent compact D/A revolver lines with a few new 2018 models. The Kimber revolvers seem especially well thought-out with fixed but replaceable front *and* rear sights, which being dovetailed into their frames, offer durability and a means to correct any POI discrepancies. Of course, when the product lines of well-known manufacturers expand, accessories soon follow, so that's where we're headed next.

CHAPTER 15
HANDY REVOLVER ACCESSORIES

For better or worse, those of us who are gun people love new gadgets and custom features. Heck, given the chance, we'd probably dab a touch of lipstick on the Mona Lisa. In other words, it's all too easy to get carried away. Any skeptics should purchase an AR-15 with rails and then ogle the vast assortment of irresistible bolt-on accessories. Better sit on your wallet, first. Fortunately, life is somewhat simpler in revolver land.

ESSENTIALS

For starters, you won't need extra pistol magazines. Of course, loading individual rounds is more difficult (particularly under stress), so a way to speed up this process is advised. You'll also want a holster if for no other reason than its safety benefits during practice sessions on uncontrolled ranges.

Holsters. Assuming you've chosen a general-purpose revolver, think about a strong-side design with a covered trigger guard that permits re-holstering with just the dominant hand. An exception might be a cross-chest rig for use in the bush with very large revolvers, especially during cold climates. Please refer to the holster chapters for more information.

Speed-loaders & pouch. Several types are available and most are fairly inexpensive. You could start with just a couple simple units like a pair of HKS #10s. It's the .38/.357 version that fits S&W K-frames like the Model 10 or Model 66. If you've gone with another gun, be sure to check the numbers for compatibility. For example, the diameter and hole-spacing of an HKS #586 is

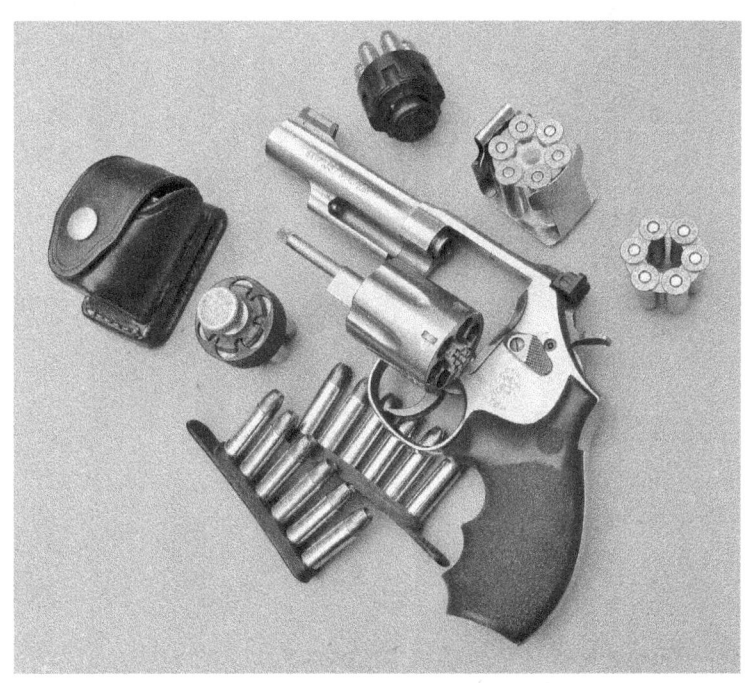

Speed-loaders are available to fit most D/A revolver models, whereas speed-strips are generic. Unless part of a factory offering, moon clips will require custom machining.

too big for a K-frame, being designed for a 6-shot L-frame or Ruger GP100. An HKS speed-loader is really just a plastic cylinder with holes that match your chambers. Cartridge rims are captured by a set of small metal teeth, and twisting an integral metal knob will release its contents. With the right technique and practice, once properly aligned, the rounds will drop right in your gun. A belt-mounted dual-loader pouch will work nicely when positioned ahead of your holster for dominant-hand access. As an alternate choice, check out the nice Safariland loaders, which are available in two types, the smaller push-button duty series being the better real-world choice. Others are available from 5-Star Firearms, Lyman, Maxfire, Speed Beez, etc. Once mastered, reloads can be surprisingly fast – assuming the device is present. Avoid any open-top pouches for general-purpose use. An optional accessory is a loading tray, designed to mesh with your loaders. The corresponding pockets can be pre-filled with cartridges for fast re-charging on the range. We used to maintain several ammo cans full of gang-loaded trays for fast-paced shooting sessions.

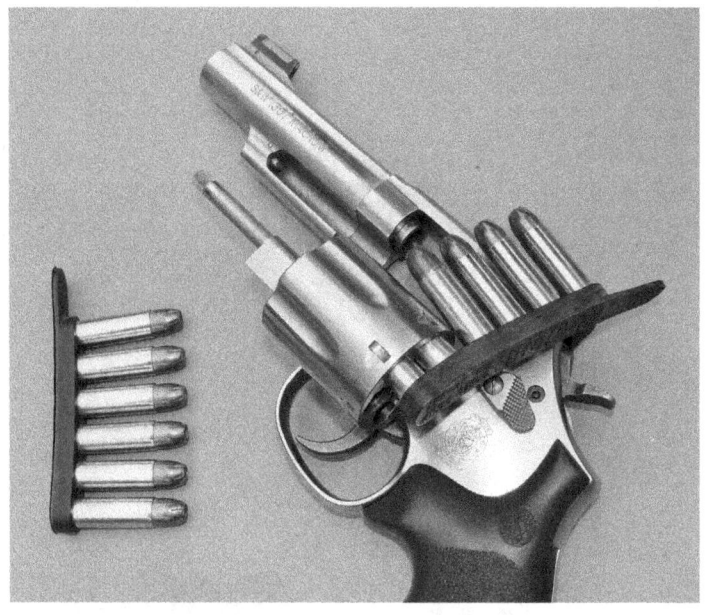

Although slower than speed-loaders, speed-strips are easy to carry, and handy for partial reloads.

Speed-strips. These affordable and handy little items are made from soft plastic or rubber. Just snap cartridge rims into their flexible recesses to gain a low-profile strip of spare ammo. A round will peel out with sideways pressure once it's been inserted in a chamber, and you can actually reload two chambers at once with practice. When cruising the woods, I'll often just slip a couple speed-strips in my back, right pocket, leaving the speed-loaders at home. At other times, I'll use both technologies, reserving a speed-strip for any partial loads. Some revolver owners may add a companion rifle, at which point a speed-strip will become an especially handy item! You can buy them in most popular calibers (including .410), with varying capacities, from makers like Bianchi, Safariland, and Tuff Products.

Moon clips and widgets for some. If you own a revolver that operates off this system, be sure to stock up on clips. However, don't go procure a large ammo supply until you check for proper fit, since minor differences in cartridge rim and clip dimensions can sometimes give you fits. Dillon Precision sells moon clips designed for optimum fit with specific cartridge brands, so does TK Custom, which also specializes in cylinder conversions. Brownells, Midway USA, and Wilson are further good sources for clips and related gear. Besides full-moons, partials are also available as half-moon, or 2-shot clips. Some shooters use the latter types as a solution for partial reloads since a "full" is all or nothing (although factoring in stress, especially with the lights turned out, a complete reload would be a whole lot simpler). With survival in the mix mobility should be considered, meaning elaborate moon clip tools are probably out. Still, you'll want at least something to help pop out spent cases. I use a small stamped-steel $3.00 Ranch Full-Moon Clip Case Extractor to pop out fired cases, with a speed-strip to top off any partially expended clips. A home-base re-mooning tool is worth having though for range preparations, and it can also minimize bent clip aggravations. Because the clips can become deformed during use, TK Custom's machined aluminum Moonclip Checkers are good insurance for proper fit. Your own cylinder will do the same thing but the gauge seems a whole lot safer when not on a range. TK Custom also sells purpose-built concealed-carry moon clip holders which are adjustable for improved retention. Most others are better for competition courses where maximum speed is the top concern, but after adding a simple foam filler to the bottom of a single-loader HKS pouch, I can access a full-moon N-frame clip without difficulty. It's possible to do custom conversions on many revolvers, including most S&Ws. Since TK Custom specializes in this service, anyone entertaining the idea should log into their website. Beyond possibilities and costs, you'll see cautions about maximum cartridge pressures, along with other useful snippets.

Cleaning kit. Since a handgun is more of an auxiliary weapon for use where a shotgun or rifle won't do, there's a good chance a cleaning kit of some type will already be on-hand. If not, a basic rifle kit should cover most handgun needs. The cleaning rod will probably be a sectioned type not ideal for match-grade rifle bores, but it'll be good enough to cover handguns. The kit will likely include a few bore brushes, a slotted tip, some cleaning patches, solvent, and oil; all the basics necessary for routine handgun maintenance. Because we operate on a larger scale, a few additional items are used (as covered in the maintenance chapters). Flexible kits are increasingly popular because they'll stow in small spaces, making them useful on the move. The "rod" is a coated pull-through wire with threaded ends to accept brushes

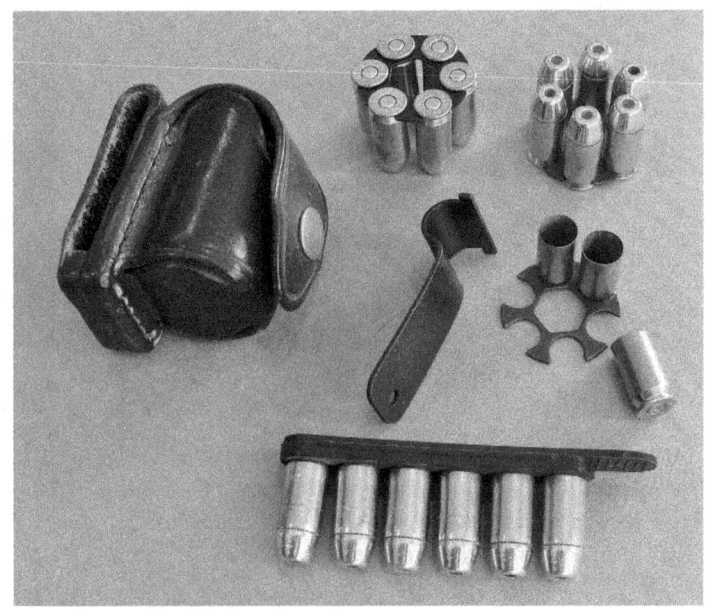

A speed-strip can also be useful for topping moon clips. Fired cases can be popped free with a simple Ranch Extractor.

or patch-jags, etc. Many rifle owners travel with one and, although they make a nice addition, threading one through each chamber of a revolver's cylinder wouldn't be much fun. On the home-front, I prefer one-piece rods with rotating handles that allow brushes and patches to turn as they engage the rifling. In addition to long rifle rods, a few shorter handgun-length versions always hang within arm's reach of the bench. Meanwhile, a simple take-down rod kit resides in my range bag.

USEFUL EXTRAS

Speed-loader trays. Although not essential, these simple units can be handy for fast refilling of speed-loaders. They're spaced to match popular K, L, or N-frame cylinders, so you can just drop an empty loader above its corresponding reload to lock it in place. The trays will fit in an ammo can for on-range mass production efforts that follow a whole lot of shooting. Casual shooters will survive just fine without them.

S&W Screwdriver. Our lead FI recently lost his vintage little factory supplied flat-tip all-metal screwdriver in the woods. He was almost as distraught as if his dog had died. I took pity on him and loaned him a spare from my precious hoard of obsolete S&W accessories. We were shocked to see them listed for $25 online; probably because of collectors, but possibly because they're also darned handy. Of course, any small screwdriver will do if it fits the sights, side-plate screws, etc.

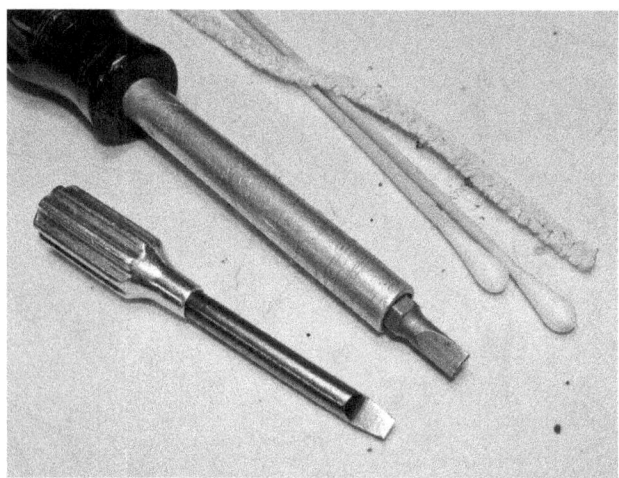

Although now scarce, S&W's screwdriver can be handy for minor tasks beyond rear-sight adjustments. However, a gunsmith screwdriver is the better choice for maintenance and disassembly.

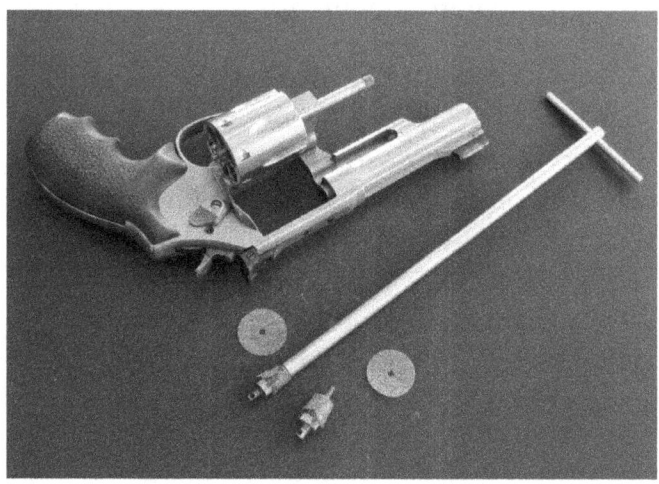

Available from Brownells, the Lewis Lead Remover lives up to its name. Lead deposits are dragged free by a tight-fitting copper screen and expandable rubber mandrel.

Lewis lead remover. I usually avoid plain lead bullets to avoid barrel-leading issues and related lead exposure. If you do wind up with heavy deposits of lead, cleaning can become a major chore, which is where this tool comes in handy. A tightly-fitting copper-mesh patch that surrounds an adjustable rubber mandrel is pulled through the barrel from breech to muzzle, using a stout rod furnished with the kit. The rod is first passed through the muzzle until its female end is exposed in the open action, and the mandrel is then threaded on. Once properly adjusted, the fine copper screen will do a pretty good job of dragging accumulated lead from the rifling. I don't use it often, but it's still worth keeping on hand.

Dummy cartridges. You may or may not want some, simply to use for handy off-range speed-loader practice. If so, avoid lighter plastic snap-cap types and go with the heavier A-Zooms.

CUSTOM TOUCHES

A little knowledge is a dangerous thing, especially when the wrong tools *and* firearms coincide. Adventuresome S&W owners would be well-served by a copy of *The S&W Revolver: A Shop Manual 5th Edition*," by Jerry Khunhausen. Another useful resource is TK Custom's website, where you can find videos pertaining to disassembly or reassembly of S&W and Ruger D/A revolvers, as well as the previously mentioned information about moon clip conversions, etc.

An "action job" has always been a prized custom revolver upgrade, whether needed or not. Back in the glory days of D/A revolvers, it was sort of a status symbol, one goal being to impress others by your silky-smooth and ultra-light double-action pull. A knowledgeable gunsmith could even get one to work properly! Many other "tuned" revolvers were unreliable or unsafe, being products of kitchen-table tinkering. With an S&W, this began through removal of the carefully-fitted side-plate. Beyond some possible initial damage, the next butchery involved snipping or replacement of springs to reduce their tensions. As often as not, an unrecognized result was an unsafe revolver; hence, the recommendation to seek educated first.

After-market springs. Spring kits are still available for the various S&W frames, and many are geared toward combat competition. These fast-paced events are fired almost exclusively from double-action, so some tricked-out revolvers even lack hammer spurs. The kits are intended to lighten D/A pull for improved trigger control, and they typically include a lighter rebound spring (or several), plus a different hammer spring (mainspring). Installing the lesser-tensioned springs can dramatically reduce trigger pull but, beyond safety issues, reliability can suffer. The competitors shoot through large piles of ammo between matches and practice, so many of them hand load to reduce cost. They also know what primers to avoid. Their lighter mainsprings can cause erratic ignition with the harder types designed for high-pressure loads. Misfires can tank a winning score but life will probably continue. The same cannot be said about an armed encounter, so I prefer a mainspring that will fire any type of cartridge reliably. It will also provide a bit of extra insurance during cold weather. The same holds true for the rebound spring, where a mushy return is just an invitation for trouble. You'll see more about the relationship of these internals during the upcoming chapter. Meanwhile, the factory-issue springs will probably get you by just fine. In fact, the whole gun will probably smooth up with more use. If you must have a tuned revolver, S&W can provide this service. They'll also be aware of less understood nuances like the inertial relationships of ultra-lightweight guns, springs, and consistent ignition. A factory-serviced firearm will also be a safer bet during any force-related litigation.

Chamfered chambers. Some serious revolver shooters speed up their reloads by slightly rounding the sharp edges of each chamber (S&W calls them "charge holes"). This job should be done professionally to prevent going overboard. The cartridge rims still need adequate support for reliable ignition, as well as positive ejection, so the extractor itself is best left as is. S&W provides this service and others do as well, including TK Custom.

Handy Revolver Accessories

Trick thumb-pieces. I've used custom S&W types off and on over the years, and now most of them are off. They look cool, but unless you plan on competition, a factory-issue unit will work just fine. In fact, some of the custom units have sharp corners that can ding your thumb with stiff loads during recoil.

After-market sights. An adjustable S&W rear sight blade travels on a horizontal screw to provide windage. However, the windage screw is staked, permitting no easy way to replace the actual blade. It's just a whole lot simpler to switch an entire rear sight assembly, so that's what drives the custom market. Older S&Ws used non-standard screw holes for attachment of their adjustable rear sights, but this situation has been rectified with the latest three-hole revolver frames. Switching an adjustable rear sight is now easy and there are several good replacements to choose from – assuming one is even necessary. The newer pinned S&W front sights permit further options from fiber-optics to Tritium; but there is a minor hurdle; the replacement will need to be drilled. A small integral sight tab nests into the corresponding barrel cut and the pin locks them together. Enough hole-variation exists from one gun to the next that the tab is left blank. Result: it's a gunsmith installation for most. By comparison, Rugers are easier. Some front sights dovetailed while others offer a QD feature. Ruger's rear sight blades can also be swapped which lowers the cost for a replacement.

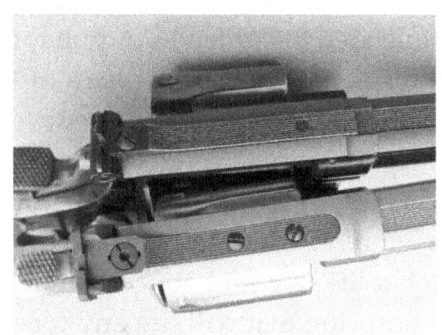

The upper S&W has a factory rear sight. The lower one has an aftermarket Bowen, secured to a newer 3-hole frame (one is covered by the sight).

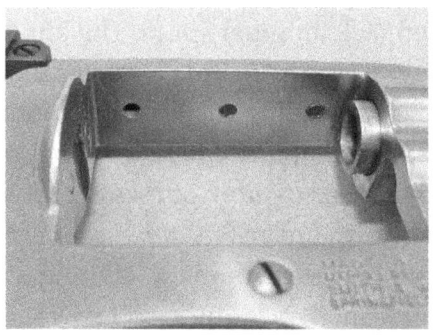

An underside view of the newer frame reveals all three drilled & tapped holes, spaced to a standard pattern. They provide extra holding-power with hard-kicking loads.

The extra shoulder on this S&W Weigand base engages the frame's rear sight cut. Combined with the screws, this low-mass system can withstand severe recoil.

Grips. Lately, S&W has been offering some of their revolvers with functional soft black-colored grips. Beauty is in the eye of the beholder and to me, they're (excuse the pun) butt-ugly. When it comes to most revolvers though, no custom touch is easier than a set of personalized grips, and there are plenty of great choices. Soft grips with finger grooves seem good in principle, but they can cause problems during fast, combat-type draws where a slightly fumbled grip can be harder to correct. We equipped our old square-butt Model 65s with Pachmayer Professional grips, which solved this problem for most staff thanks to hard-rubber construction. Actually, the smooth wooden "Roper" design without any finger-indents is by no means a bad thing. Some gun shops will have hands-on displays from makers like Hogue, along with Pachmayers, and others. The sky is the limit but factor in the use of any loader devices, which will require left-side grip clearance.

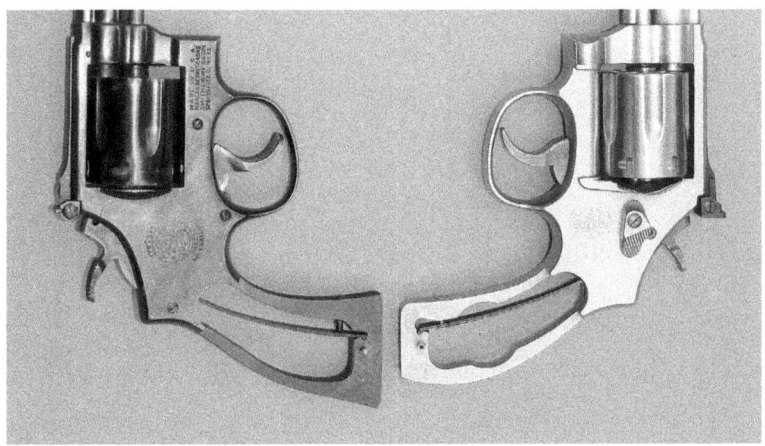

Two K-frames for comparison: S&W's square-butt (L) was the common service and target offering. Recently, a short-barrel, round-butt version (R) became the new standard. Check before ordering grips.

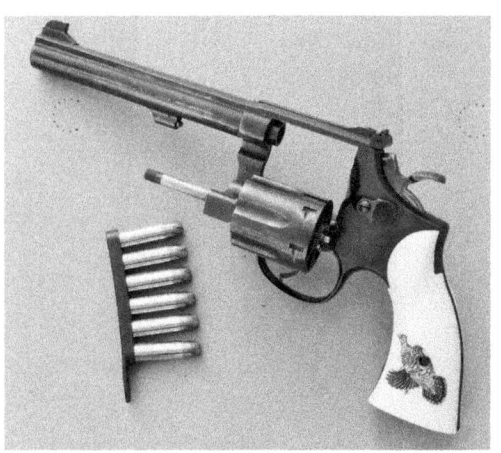

Custom grips from Altamont, mounted to a square-butt S&W K-38. They follow the profile of S&W's smaller service panels. Installation was simple with a screwdriver.

Customization and liability concerns. Pray that you never need to fire a shot in self-defense. One likely outcome will be a court date, even if your actions are completely justified. Beyond criminal liability, the prospect of civil litigation is real. At that point, a plaintiff's attorneys may try to depict a perfectly legal gun owner as a diabolical nut bent on homicide. With an uneducated jury, extra firearm touches could tip a verdict toward that direction, so minimal customization is prudent, meaning a stock gun is even better!

SIMPLICITY ISN'T BAD

A revolver doesn't require much in way of accessories to become field-ready. A holster, a couple loader devices, and a pouch will start the ball rolling quite nicely. Of course, since a simple cleaning kit is another essential, let's move on to basic maintenance.

CHAPTER 16
KEEP YOUR WHEEL-GUN RUNNING

Although much of what follows is S&W-based, for the most part, it'll also apply to other revolver types. The good news is that, barring unusual circumstances, detailed disassembly will seldom necessary for cleaning or routine maintenance. Same story for basic field-stripping other than the easy removal of a single-action's cylinder. Other than that, some basic cleaning gear and a bit of elbow grease should get the job done. The absence of loose or spring-loaded parts will be appreciated, especially during field conditions.

BASIC CRUD-CUTTING

Regardless of whether your revolver is a double or single-action type, it'll wind up with multiple dirty chambers, fouling on the cylinder face, and more around the adjacent frame and barrel. A simple examination will reveal three spots often overlooked; the recoil plate (or breech face), the cylinder's rear, and the underside of a D/A's extractor star. Proper cleaning of an S/A revolver will require removal of its cylinder, but that's usually as easy as depressing a small retainer that will allow its axle to be withdrawn. Consider the effects of "binding" to get a handle on cleaning priorities. Parts that rub are bad so thorough removal of fouling is good.

Brushes and solvents. A toothbrush and a jar of solvent can make short work of most fouled surfaces, and we use Shooter's Choice because it seems to dissolve just about anything. Besides plastic shotgun wad residue, an anti-reflective black marking pen swipe to a bright stainless front sight ramp can even be removed. Stainless guns can sometimes benefit from the added aggressiveness of a stainless toothbrush, but proceed with caution. Some surfaces are too delicate for this aggressive combination. A soft M-16 toothbrush is the better all-around choice for more delicate blued surfaces and smaller nooks and crannies; the underneath of an extractor being one prime example. Taurus cautions against excessive scrubbing of their titanium cylinder faces, which have a special coating. We routinely use a stainless toothbrush on the front face of stainless steel cylinders, as well as around the forcing cone, but I'd skip one entirely with any aluminum or scandium revolver.

A good solvent will cut most crud, but try to keep it out of the action. By cocking the hammer *after* opening the cylinder, the hand will rise to block its frame window. A bronze bore-brush with solvent will handle the chambers and bore, but don't reverse its direction inside the barrel. Also, proceed carefully toward the end of the stroke to avoid dinging a firing pin or bushing. Since you'll be cleaning through the muzzle, take care around that area while maintaining straight rod alignment. A handgun-specific brush is also the better choice simply because it's shorter than a rifle version. Thus, the entire brush should be able to emerge from the rear of a barrel before reversing its course. A shorter handgun-length rod provides much better control, and one with a rotating head will be easier on a rifled barrel. Don't twist a bore-brush through the rifling; just let rotate on its own.

These solvents and lubes should handle routine maintenance chores.

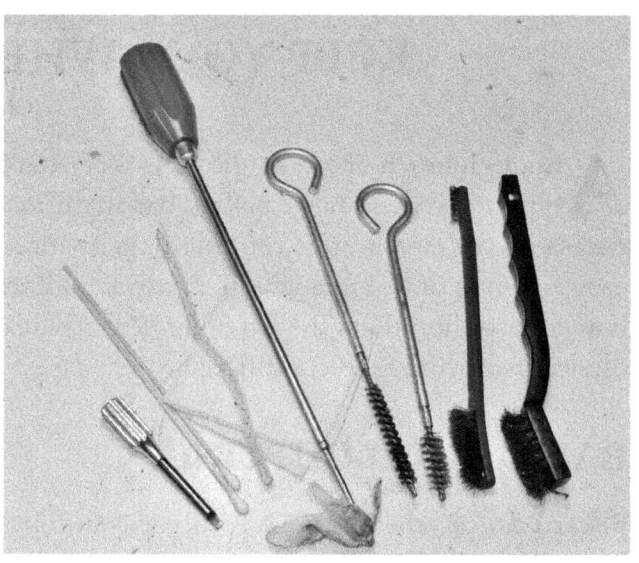

The longer rod is better than the one-piece types because its handle rotates. Brushes and patches will handle most cleanings, along with the solvents.

Back in our lead bullet days, we used a separate stainless chamber brush, which was a tad larger – and a whole lot more aggressive. But, a new bronze brush should do nearly as well, especially after use of jacketed or plated bullets. Of course, the chambers are a whole lot easier to inspect than a barrel. Actually, the cleanliness of a revolver barrel can be checked from both ends, *but first open the cylinder!* Next, you can orient a thumbnail behind the forcing cone to reflect light through the barrel. After swapping directions, point the muzzle toward a bright light source to view the forcing cone area of the bore. A few soft patches on a slotted tip should finish the job, but again, watch out for the firing pin hole. It's also worth checking for any potential problems as part of a cleaning regimen. Also, lead bullets could call for more serious efforts using a Lewis Lead Remover.

Inspection. We know that even stainless steel can rust, so an occasional peek underneath your grip panels is recommended. With most S&Ws and other types, removal of just one screw should free the panels for inspection of the frame. Most two-piece S&W types also engage a frame-mounted indexing-pin, but they'll come off with a bit of patience. After one side is freed, the other can be loosened by tapping its underside through the space within the frame. You might also run into a one-piece Hogue Grip secured by a bottom screw. If so, the grip can be worked off after wiggling it downward (the frame pin meshes with corresponding tracks inside the grip). The grip screw typically threads into a separate stirrup that surrounds the bottom of the frame, which could be captured by the same roll-pin used to index grips. On the other hand, Hogue's Bantams just snap on without any screw at all. Removal of these smaller-profiled "boot grips" is somewhat testy, but a provided plastic wedge will help spread the sides enough to clear the indexing pin. Once the frame is exposed, check for any rust spots. Often, they can be carefully scrubbed off with WD-40 and a stainless toothbrush.

Screws. Many grip designs surround the "strain screw" in the lower front of an S&W frame. The factory setting will seldom loosen up, but it's worth a check while the grips are removed. Remember, this screw controls mainspring tension for reliable ignition. A backed-out screw is a good indication of tinkering by *someone*, indicating a used gun. While the grips are off, check the exposed rear side-plate screw for tightness with a *properly* fitting screwdriver. It won't hurt to check the remaining two screws while you're at it. Same for the forward anchoring screw on an adjustable rear sight, which can loosen over time. Don't crank the rear one down though or you'll lower elevation! S&W used to include the previously mentioned nifty little flat-tip unit ground to fit their screws. To this day, another firearms instructor and I keep one in our pockets daily (the other FI also uses his to pry out stuck rubber ear-plugs). A small jeweler's screwdriver kit will work, and I sometimes use one in conjunction with a gunsmith set.

As for S/A revolvers, the retainer that secures the cylinder-pin (axle) is often tensioned by a small screw. The ejector-rod housing is typically secured to the barrel by a screw which can also loosen over time. Most of these guns also have separate upper and lower receiver sections, connected by multiple screws which should be periodically checked. Here, you'll appreciate a gunsmithing kit with removable, properly ground bits.

Light disassembly. Check your cylinder occasionally for free rotation. If it seems sluggish, fouling has probably accumulated within its axis; an easy fix with an S/A revolver. As for D/As, the forward S&W side-plate screw has a small spring-loaded plunger that captures an annular groove within the crane's pivoting extension. Removal of this screw will allow the cylinder and crane assembly to be withdrawn from the front of frame. Do this over-padding in case the cylinder slips off the yoke. Once separated, you may be surprised by the amount of gunk coating

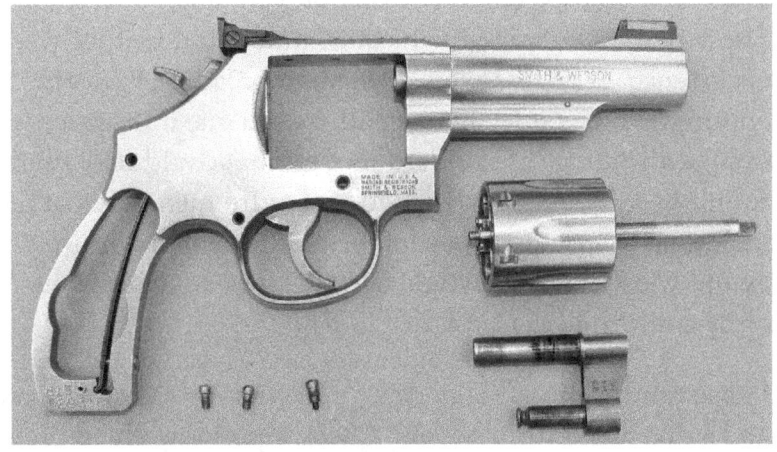

Removal of a cylinder will often reveal fouling. The side-plate screw secures an S&W cylinder assembly. It's different than the others (removed here for comparison).

the yoke. Never fear though, a bit of elbow grease, solvent, and oil should put you back in business. Older S&Ws used a fitted screw to capture the cylinder assembly instead of a plunger. Mixing it up with the other two side-plate screws will result in binding of the crane. Again, for single-action shooters, removal of the cylinder is SOP. The pin it travels around could be secured by a screw, or by a push-release.

That's about as far as you should go in the disassembly process. Over time, and after much shooting, the internals can accumulate glop. While you *could* remove the side-plate, most folks would be better off locating a qualified professional. S&W offers a lifetime warranty but they also stipulate approved servicing. In the past, the three options were either a factory return, use of factory-authorized service centers, or factory certified armorers. The latter were found at larger law enforcement agencies, most of whom now carry auto-pistols. S&W's web site doesn't show current domestic service centers, but their factory service gets consistently great reviews.

As far as maintenance goes for Taurus owners, think "Smith & Wesson." Things that could loosen on an S&W might also be worth watching with a Taurus. I say "might" based on my limited experience with these guns.

If you have a Ruger, accessing the innards is much easier. Just read the manual and then take it apart!

TROUBLE-SHOOTING

If nothing else, running daily revolver ranges does provide an opportunity to discover the most likely problems. We'll go down the list, but fortunately, only a few should bite an average owner. Here's what we saw with a pile of S&Ws…

Missing thumb-pieces were easily preventable, so were loosening ejector rods that could tie up a gun. These two issues were the most common, but neither was frequent. A broken firing pin was a rare occurrence, as well as a few even rarer maladies. Factoring in the huge amount of shooting our S&Ws endured, I'd be perfectly fine with a used one if the price was right. In fact, S&W has produced some unique variations of standard models that could really scratch an itch. I only missed out on a 3-inch round-butt Model 66 when a fellow cadre member beat me to the gun counter. I watched him give the gun a thorough inspection before he snapped it up. You'll see many of the issues he looked for below. Most, if not all, would need the services of a professional; either through a qualified gunsmith, or by a return to the factory.

Loose thumb-piece. Again, this problem is an easy fix for anyone with a properly fitting screw driver and some blue thread sealant. Check it periodically to prevent losing the parts.

Out-of- time. If the hammer falls at the same time the stud enters a notch, timing is marginal. Sometimes this condition will only occur with one or two chambers. By pulling the trigger *slowly* from double-action, you'll get a better read. Cranking it will induce more cylinder inertia; maybe enough to achieve false results. Pre-cocking the hammer to S/A will produce a similar effect through a bit more cylinder rotation. So, proceed slowly in double-action, cycling through each chamber. An out-of-time S&W is fixable by a qualified armorer or gunsmith and a high-mileage revolver is most likely to need such service. I remember an ancient inventory of WW II S&W Victory Models that resided in armory when I started. These old guns were as loose as a goose and many of them had several out-of-time chambers. Fortunately, there's a very good chance that an original S&W revolver owner will never need to worry about timing or other cylinder-related problems - like end-shake and side-play…

End-shake & side-play. I bought my trusty S&W M-686 CS sometime during the '80s, and shot the snot out of it for around 25 years. Eventually, it developed some end-shake. Grabbing the cylinder revealed a small amount of fore and aft movement which, if not corrected, could eventually lead to misfires or binding against the barrel's rear face. Stretching the yoke is the preferred gunsmith option, but a small end-shake bearing is another. The latter is less desirable for defensive purposes since the thin shim *could* deform, interfering with cylinder rotation. Still, that's the route I took to restore reliable function for another decade or so.

Side-play is excessive lateral movement of the cylinder when latched. As we've seen, the cylinder of most S&Ws locks both fore and aft. One good way to get side-play is to slam the cylinder home with reckless abandon. It looks cool but that's about it. Excessive side-play could lead to bullet shaving, or possibly even misfires. Correction of such problems is best done professionally.

Push-off. In single-action mode with its hammer cocked, a moderate shove on the spur should *not* cause it to fall. If it does the revolver is unsafe, probably due to a worn hammer notch or some kitchen table gunsmithing. Treat it as a professional repair!

Weak trigger return. The trigger should snap forward with enthusiasm if released from its rearward position. A sluggish return is unsafe, and although it *could* be due to neglect, it may be another sign of kitchen table gunsmithing. The interaction of the associated parts is complex enough to warrant further, detailed coverage so stay tuned for more.

Bent ejector rods. A bent rod is usually due to operator error. It will create eccentric cylinder rotation with front-locking S&Ws and, sometimes, the first clue is a harder or erratic D/A trigger pull caused by binding. As for operator error, an ejector rod can begin to unscrew (per below), preventing forward unlatching of the cylinder. Pounding the right side of the cylinder *may* force it open, but the rod can be bent in the process. From that point on, the cylinder won't rotate true to its axis, and it won't take much run-out for its face to bind against the rear of the barrel. The normal gap only measures around 0.006 – 0.008," just enough to provide a bit of clearance without bleeding off too much pressure.

Loose ejector rods. This problem relates to dual-end locking designs. If the cylinder won't swing open, there's a fair chance the ejector rod has loosened up, causing it to lengthen until it can't disengage from the forward stud. If so, at least one of the chambers could contain a live round. Any corrective actions will need to proceed with caution while maintaining full muzzle awareness!

One fix involves a matchbook cover or another thin shim. As we now know, the cylinder is locked into barrel alignment by a small spring-loaded stud that protrudes through the bottom of the frame. By carefully slipping the makeshift shim between the frame and cylinder, it can be used to depress the stud, which will then free the cylinder to rotate. At that point, a bit of pressure against the knurled end of the rod can immobilize it while the cylinder is manually rotated counter-clockwise. *This part is reverse-threaded.* Eventually, the rod should be drawn in enough to allow adequate clearance for unlocking.

Further tightening will require some disassembly. As previously explained, removal of the front side-plate screw will permit withdrawal of the crane and cylinder assembly. The cylinder can then be separated from the crane. Assuming the ejector rod has already loosened, you can just unscrew it (in reverse) with your fingers. The associated parts are fragile, and you can wreck your extractor "star" unless you slip a couple of fired cases in the cylinder to prevent twisting it out of alignment. Remember: the rod is reverse-threaded! Back in our agency's revolver days we used a special, split-collar wrench with a tightening screw. A well-padded vise can also do the job, but caution will be necessary to prevent bending the rod, so the much safer bet is a qualified gunsmith. There are other parts to deal with beyond the outer ejector rod, which is a hollow sleeve containing a spring and interior locking-rod. The extractor star and threaded ejector rod capture these parts, so the fix involves proper torque with a dab of thread-sealant.

Extractors (stars). Older extractor stars maintained chamber alignment by two small indexing pins, located 180 degrees apart. After hard use, we'd sometimes notice one was missing. A likely cause was aggressive scrubbing with a stainless steel toothbrush, but as long as one pin remained, the star would still align adequately for proper function. The latest design eliminates the pins altogether, in favor of a flat on the rod that mates with a corresponding cylinder-hole. That solves missing pins, but an accumulation of debris underneath any extractor can tie up the revolver. The usual culprits are accumulated fouling or unburned powder flakes. It won't take much to prevent the star from fully seating, causing it to bind against the frame's rear face. Some loads are more prone to this than others. I was forced to give up on a commercial .45 ACP brand that yielded great accuracy with moon clips in an S&W M-625. The components were probably formulated for use in semiauto pistols, but within less than two dozen shots, numerous powder granules accumulated, tying up this N-frame. One fix was as simple as brushing out the related extractor surfaces, but the better plan was just to switch loads. The offending cartridges were then reserved for use in

Older S&W extractors maintain their alignment though two small pins. The newer types align through corresponding flats on the cylinder and rod. No pin loss with this system.

1911 pistols, where no further issues were encountered.

Frame and forcing cone erosion. Supposedly, one load that's hard on a revolver is a full-power 125 grain .357 Magnum. As we've seen, the beefier L-frame evolved to counter steady Magnum effects. I suspect if our K-frame Model 65s had consumed a steady diet of such loads, they would've been reduced to smoking rubble within a relatively short period. As a general rule, besides general loosening up, the rear of a barrel and its adjacent area will experience erosion caused by hot gasses, powder particles, and violent bullet/barrel contact. Exactly how much depends upon the load, but regardless, an eroded strip can develop in the top-strap, directly above the forcing cone. The cone itself is a short-funneled section within the rear of the barrel, designed to swallow bullets. Given enough shooting of any kind, it will gradually erode, as evidenced by fine pitting. Hotter loads will exacerbate this process and, in extreme cases, the barrel might even develop a crack. The longevity of our nearly immortal K-frames was attributable to a mild .38 Special diet. They did develop some erosion over time, but it was never enough to be of any real concern.

Firing pins. Once in a blue moon a firing pin will break and if it happens, you're SOL. Every failure we've seen involved an extremely high round-count revolver. Although they had been dry-fired extensively during numerous week-long basic revolver schools, somewhat interestingly, each failed during a live-fire event. These were S&Ws with original "hammer-nose" firing pins, attached by a large rivet. The small tip would snap off and, sometimes, it would lodge in the frame's corresponding hole. However, the total number of instances was amazingly minimal. Although we always kept a few spare parts for in-house repairs, a professional fix is recommended. We don't have the same degree of ex-

S&W's scandium-frame revolvers incorporate a separate insert that guards against flame-cutting of their top-straps.

perience with frame-mounted firing pins, but we haven't heard any horror stories either. A recent breakage involved my lead instructor's Model 686 three days prior to his departure for an out-of-state IDPA championship. The gun was also an older hammer-mounted type with nearly 100,000 rounds through it. He had a spare gun, but still managed to affect a repair, and then traveled 1200 miles to win the match. In fact, by the time he arrived, he had four new pins to pick from, all expressed-mailed by acquaintances. The value of a firearm with widespread use cannot be underestimated!

Adjustable S&W rear sights. The forward screw secures the sight body to the frame. It can loosen up after some shooting, but it's an easy fix with a *properly fitting,* small flat-tip screwdriver. A small dab of blue thread-sealer will help keep it in place. The notched blade is captured by a staked, threaded screw that provides windage adjustments. Occasionally, you can run into one with a bit of blade wiggle caused by blade/slot tolerances. In the past, I've removed minor slop by carefully punching a small dimple into the steel sight body, just ahead of the blade slot (this trick can result in tighter groups). Overall, S&W does a good job regulating their sights for popular loads. The larger rear screw provides elevation adjustment, and you may stumble on a gun and load combination that requires plenty of upward clicks. An excessive amount can decrease tension, which could degrade accuracy or result in lost parts. To regain a mid-adjustment point, you could switch to a lower front sight. Lacking a replaceable design, a different load might be an alternative. Slower, heavier bullets often shoot higher simply because they spend more time within the bore during the upward arc caused by recoil. If the rear sight is bottomed out, everything is reversed. Fortunately, a loose mounting screw is usually the biggest concern.

OTHER REVOLVER QUIRKS

Your revolver is not the space shuttle. Function and operation are fairly basic, but nowadays, there are plenty of handgun shooters with little-to-no wheel-gun experience. For them, the system may seem disdainfully simple - until an unanticipated problem crops up. Some are attributable to nothing more than operator error.

High primers. If a primer isn't fully seated it can drag against the recoil plate (rear breech-face). This situation can bind up the cylinder and cause a heavy D/A trigger-pull. The safer way to check primer protrusion is to stand cartridges upright on a hard, smooth surface like a pane of glass. An alternate range method involves spinning the loaded cylinder with the hammer cocked just far enough to disengage the cylinder stop. A high primer can cause a misfire by absorbing some firing pin impact. Confounding the diagnosis, the primer may finish seating during impact, displaying no problem beyond a shallow indent. The round may go off with a second try – or not. Rather than randomly reloading it, index the cylinder so it will be the first one up, or better yet, discard it. By the way, don't be in a hurry to open the gun if a dud occurs since a hang-fire could be cooking.

Bullet creep. Hard-kicking cartridges can tie up a cylinder when bullets slip forward in their cases. They may creep enough to protrude from the cylinder, interfering with its rotation. Stiff revolver loads benefit from a firm crimp, so jacketed revolver bullets typically have corresponding annular knurled recesses (known as cannelures), which help hold them in place. These steps will help resist the effects of inertia – usually. Still, bullet creep is worth checking. You can mark the base of a cartridge and index it as the sixth shot. Then shoot the first five, unload, and compare its overall length to others in the box. A revolver like a .44 Magnum develops plenty of recoil, but the weight of a bullet *and* gun mass can also introduce creep. If a bullet moves far enough forward, it can protrude from the face of a cylinder to completely block rotation. Lesser movement isn't good either since pressures will vary, affecting velocity and accuracy. The .45 ACP is a useful revolver cartridge with power not unlike a .44 Special; however, since it normally head-spaces on its case mouth (in pistol chambers for which it was designed), a roll crimp is seldom applied. For this reason, .45 ACP bullets can sometimes creep forward in revolvers. Even .38 Specials are not immune from creep in flyweight revolvers. At its worst extreme this situation could prevent unlatching of a cylinder.

Revolver squib loads. A "squib" is an underpowered load, often caused by an incomplete powder charge. But, since the detonation of the primer does create some pressure, even without any powder, a small amount of bullet travel could be possible. With a revolver, the bullet often lodges part way inside the forcing cone, bridging the cylinder and barrel. At that point, Houston, we have a problem. Good chance other loaded rounds are somewhere in the cylinder, raising grave concerns about a safe remedy. We keep a "range rod" handy, which is just a short sub-caliber brass rod used to drive out lodged bullets. First, we flood the obstruction with oil from both ends of the barrel, while respecting the direction of its muzzle. Sometime later we can often bump the bullet far enough rearward to open the cylinder. The same trick *may* work when a bullet is lodged completely within the bore, but there's no guarantee. Much discretion is advised since pounding one can deform it, jamming it firmly in place. This situation is at least safer though, since the cylinder can be opened. In any case, be sure to flag and secure a gun with a plugged barrel.

Barrel/cylinder gap caution. A supposedly "helpful "pistol coach may not recognize the unpleasant side effects of an improper revolver grip. The small barrel gap necessary for cylinder rotation can expel some serious pressure. You can see this for yourself by draping a folded paper tent over a revolver in such a way that each side covers the gap. Fire a shot and watch what happens. The energetic reaction will include flying bits of paper followed by two large scorched tears. For this reason, we discourage the general practice of locating the support-hand's trigger finger on *any* trigger guard. Some semi-autos are sold with curved, checkered faces to support this shooting style, but we endorse an alternate and universal two-handed grip. A finger near the gap of a Magnum revolver could result in a serious burn, and the big boomers in calibers like .454 Casul could literally blast away chunks of flesh.

Fired cases under the extractor. So much for revolver reliability! This problem is more common than one might expect with D/A-type extractors, and when it happens, blame the operator. A contributing factor can also be the use of shorter .38 Special cases in a .357 Magnum-length extractor system. If a case does become wedged underneath the star, odds are it will be the inboard one, oriented closest to the frame. Removal during a fight would be no fun at all, and reloads wouldn't be possible until it was cleared. Shooters with stumpy fingers are in for one heck of a time, even without adrenaline flowing. I've had lots of practice clearing stuck cases

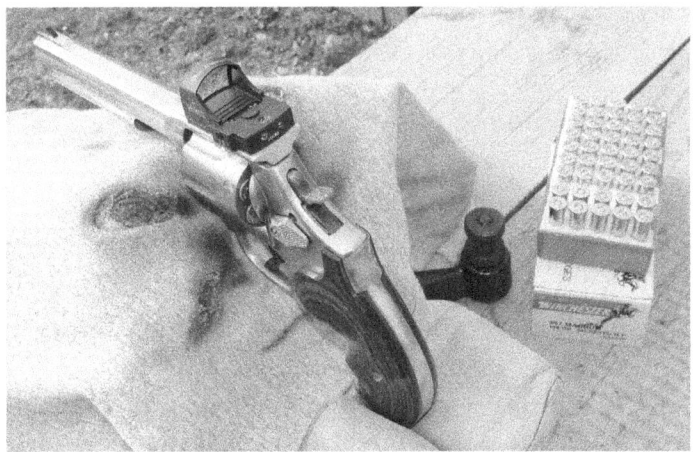

Five .357 Magnum rounds scorched the cloth adjacent to the barrel/cylinder gap. The sandbag shield was repositioned between each series so it wouldn't be blown to smithereens.

during on-range demonstrations, which start by rotating the cylinder until the offending case is outboard. At that point, I can pry it out with my trigger finger after holding my mouth just right. Those we had no mercy for – a few repeat offenders - were left to their own devices which often involved a pencil. Simple cure: elevate the muzzle *before* activating the ejector rod. Better yet, transfer the gun to the support hand and give it a good stiff smack with the palm of the dominant hand. This technique is the recommended defensive doctrine and it's quicker than you'd think. Remember: gravity is your friend with a revolver.

Short-stroking. Now and then we'll see a D/A revolver shooter get so wound up that, for lack of a better term, they'll "double-clutch" the trigger. The result is a live round/chamber that's entirely skipped, and one baffled-looking operator. Opening the gun in such instances will usually reveal a pristine primer. At that point, the next check is the firing pin. Assuming it's present, the fix is easy: calm down and smooth out.

S&W side-plates. The first thing I look for on a used S&W is its side-plate screws. If the slots are buggered up, someone with marginal skills has probably removed it for access to the action. In that case, further mischief is possible. The side-plate itself is tightly fitted so, during removal, it usually needs coercion. Prying is bad. Correct removal involves some judicious inertia, applied in concert with the edge of a wooden bench or block. At that point, all sorts of neat little parts will be exposed, some of which may separate. In the glory days of revolvers, custom tuning was big. Common modifications involved internal polishing and lighter springs, all intended to lighten double-action triggers. Plenty of kitchen table gunsmiths went to work and the fruits of their labor were sometimes unsafe. As a result, any revolvers sent to S&W for service would be returned with factory springs. A further understanding of fire-control function will account for this precaution.

Spring tension and safety. Like most other D/A revolvers, a *properly functioning* S&W can be safely carried with its hammer forward, above a loaded chamber. *But, it'll take an unloaded specimen* to safely explore the finer points of this design.

With the hammer at rest, push on its spur and you'll see the firing pin never protrudes through the recoil plate (in fact, there shouldn't be any forward movement at all). Next, dry-fire from either S/A or D/A mode, *while continuing to hold the trigger fully rearward*. The tip of the firing pin should now be visible, with enough protrusion to indent a primer. If you quickly let go of the trigger, it *should* snap forward with authority while the firing pin simultaneously retracts. At that point, forward hammer motion should be blocked. You can also try this is from double-action. Dry-fire a shot and continue to hold the trigger rearward. Then, *slowly* release the trigger while watching the hammer. As the trigger creeps forward the hammer should back out, again to the point where any forward travel is impossible. How can this be? The answer is the rebound block, a spring-powered steel part located underneath the hammer. When at rest, a step on the top of this block mates with a foot on the bottom of the hammer; their alignment preventing any forward hammer movement. The rebound-block's step will only clear the hammer-foot when the trigger is pulled to the rear. A rod connects the re-

 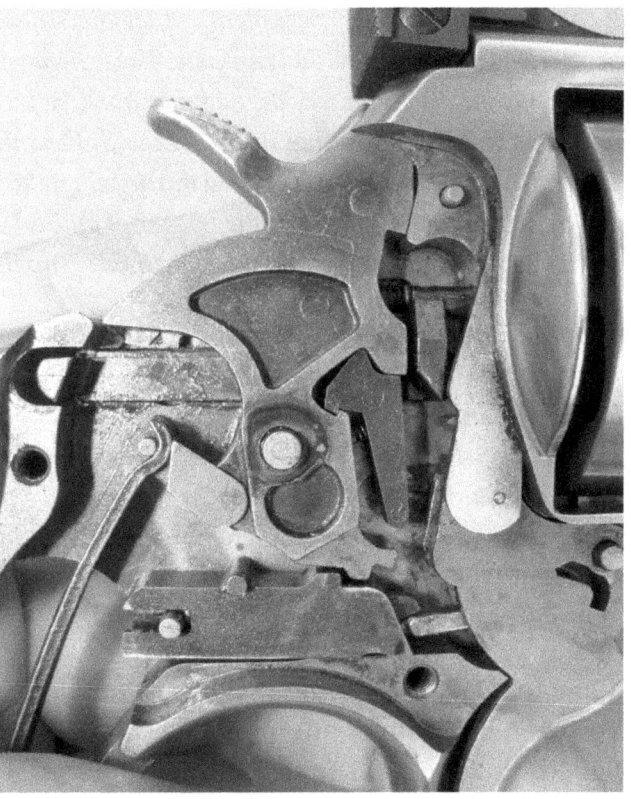

When the trigger is forward, a step on the spring-powered rebound block coincides with a foot on the hammer. Firing pin contact is thus prevented. Not shown is an extra hammer-blocking arm, removed to show the gap.	When the trigger travels rearward the rebound-block follows. The resulting clearance allows the hammer to strike the firing pin and detonate a primer.

bound-block to the trigger, and a stout coiled "rebound spring" within the block powers the return of both parts. Ingenious!

But wait, there's more! A separate reciprocating "hammer block" arm extends upward from the rebound-block, offering additional protection from hammer impacts. These features explain why the loaded M-65s we discovered with snapped-off hammer spurs never discharged. In fact, with factory springs installed, I doubt they would've fired even when cocked! In all probability, if the hammer was dislodged, the trigger and rebound-block would've snapped forward quickly enough to arrest its fall.

So, now we know why S&W took the precaution of reinstalling factory springs during servicing. Too many tinkerers were either snipping off rebound spring coils, or replacing them altogether with lesser-tensioned springs. The resulting lighter D/A trigger pulls came at the expense of some real hazards since, lacking sufficient return energy, a rebound-block might not arrive in time to intercept a hammer. This should be a concern for any prospective tuners, so here's a better idea: S&W will perform this service through their Performance Center.

Keep Your Wheel-Gun Running

Related safe uncocking trick: plenty of shooters have experience with hammer-fired guns like Winchester lever-actions, break-action shotguns, etc. These firearms are thumb-cocked immediately prior to firing. If for some reason no shot is presented, the hammer must be returned to its at-rest position. Most sportsmen will accomplish this task by controlling its descent with their thumb, while simultaneously holding the trigger rearward. This same technique is often applied during single-action revolver use; however, as we now know, the firing pin can only strike a primer when the trigger of an S&W is held rearward. Guess what happens if the thumb slips off the hammer with the good 'ol boy method? Yup, bang!

There's a safer way to un-cock an S&W, and it works with many other hammer-fired guns. We'll still need to control the hammer during its initial release, but we can then add two extra layers of safety. Trigger and hammer manipulation can still occur with the dominant hand, BUT the support-hand's index finger can be simultaneously inserted between the hammer and frame to block its initial descent. At that point, all trigger contact should cease, allowing the trigger to move forward on its own. If the hammer does somehow slip, the rebound-block in a properly functioning S&W should intercept it. Other firearms are often advertised as having a rebounding hammer, which works in a similar manner. This un-cocking technique is perhaps less stylish, but it sure is a whole lot safer!

Time to relax. We just ran down a list of things that *could* happen, but, there's a darned good chance you won't encounter any problems at all. Even with high-volume ammo consumption, our issues boiled down to a few missing thumb-pieces, loose ejector rods, or (rarely) broken firing pins. The first two are easily preventable with simple maintenance and thread-sealant. The several firing pins that snapped did so only after a bazillion rounds. So, once equipped with a bit of basic knowledge, expect your revolver to serve admirably as a simple and dependable companion. With proper care it will run almost forever. Those with more slothful habits will find a revolver to be a more forgiving choice than any semiauto pistol.

CLOSING REVOLVER COMMENTS

A revolver remains a darned good pick despite hyperbolae to the contrary. Simplicity, safety, and ease of operation can be rolled into one dependable handgun that offers power, accuracy, and versatility. Unlike a semi-automatic, you won't need to worry about load thresholds, lost/damaged magazines, or periodic replacement of recoil springs. In fact, none of the springs within a revolver undergo anything more than minimal compression throughout carry and storage. Truth be known, many firearm owners commit little-to-no time for anything other than very cursory maintenance – if even that. This can cause big problems with semiautos, more dependent on regular cleaning. Skip this process and pistol disassembly skills will soon perish. From that point forward, essential servicing is often ignored, resulting in inevitable malfunctions. For this reason, many casual shooters will be *much* better off with a revolver. People in this league will probably shoot less than 250 rounds annually, in which case no disassembly will be required – at least, not for a decade or so. Just about every gun owner should be able to swing open a D/A cylinder for cleaning; if not, consider something even simpler like a baseball bat.

A revolver will also fire sideways or upside-down, with no regard for grip tension. It will cycle inside a pocket or purse, or with solid muzzle contact. In the event of a dud, the much-vaunted double-strike pistol capability will advance a fresh cartridge. There is little to go wrong with a double-action revolver and much to like. As mentioned early-on though, professional training is highly recommended.

Apology in order. The heavy emphasis on Smith & Wesson revolvers is perhaps unfair, but this line represents the lion's share of our experience. One could easily make a stronger Ruger argument, for no other reason than its ease of disassembly; and the Taurus warranty is great. Truth be known, all three of these manufacturers (as well as others within the gun industry) will stand behind their products. In the end, choice boils down to personal preference.

SECTION III
THE SEMIAUTOMATIC PISTOL WAVE

Chapter 17: SEMIAUTOMATIC PISTOL BASICS 205

Chapter 18: USEFUL PISTOL CARTRIDGES 217

Chapter 19: SINGLE-ACTION PISTOLS 231

Chapter 20: DOUBLE-ACTION PISTOLS 259

Chapter 21: STRIKER-FIRED PISTOLS 273

Chapter 22: HANDY PISTOL ACCESSORIES 295

Chapter 23: KEEP YOUR PISTOL RUNNING 299

CHAPTER 17
SEMIAUTOMATIC PISTOL BASICS

When revolvers reigned supreme, the selection of a general-purpose sidearm was a relatively simple; at least, for those wearing badges. Choices boiled down to a Smith & Wesson or Colt, although in later years, it could've been a Ruger. The same mindset extended to the civilian market, with a smattering of other brands tossed in. I remember attending a Smith & Wesson Academy Firearm Instructor school in 1985. The use of a revolver was a given then, although a day of auto-pistol was included as harbinger of things to come. Shortly thereafter, a large-scale national transition to self-loading pistols kicked into high gear, driven largely by law enforcement. Although some agencies had used them earlier, official pistol use in the United States was more of a military thing. With U.S. forces adopting the Government Model .45 ACP in 1911, one wonders what the eighty-year delay was all about. Part of the reason is no doubt related to weapon complexity. Litigation drives training in law enforcement circles and that era was less litigious. Firearms training has always been budget-driven and less squeaky wheels receive less oil. Not that most PDs were Barney Fife class, but a D/A revolver was a whole lot easier to field. Perhaps, to a lesser extent, civilian use mirrored this trend, but by the 1990s, the entire situation had almost completely reversed. The service-type revolver became a dinosaur. The U.S. Military pistol had a foreign name and tactical Tupperware was surging. The process has continued unabated, complicating the selection process to the point where listing every choice would be nearly impossible. Truthfully, so many good pistols exist that picking one for you would be analogous to someone else choosing your vehicle. On the other hand, good cartridge choices are easier. We can narrow the pistol field to some extent after matching a few suitable candidates to one of several proven calibers. But first, let's look at pistol-function, which is largely governed by cartridge pressures.

PISTOL FUNCTION

Starting with the guns themselves, semiautomatic pistols share several common features. They feed ammunition from a detachable magazine housed within a grip-frame. Upon firing, recoil energy is harnessed to drive a slide rearward on a stationary frame. As the slide reciprocates, it ejects spent cases, strips new rounds from the magazine, and shoves them into the chamber. These are "self-loading" designs, but each shot requires a separate trigger pull, unlike a full-automatic gun. The latter will continue to cycle and fire if the trigger is held rearward. In the case of a handgun, we'd have a highly regulated "machine-pistol," which might, with lots of practice, spew its magazine contents in the loosely intended direction. By affixing a shoulder-fired stock and increasing its size somewhat, we could field a "sub-machinegun" (SMG), gaining improved control with pistol-caliber ammunition. Legalities aside, an easily carried semiauto sidearm makes more sense on all fronts, from procurement to ammo consumption.

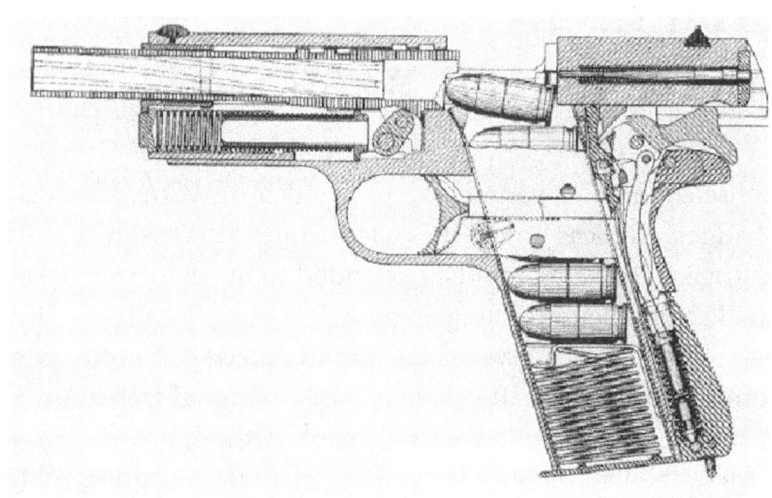

Semiautomatic function in progress, illustrated by a Model 1911. As its slide begins to close the breech-face strips a fresh .45 ACP cartridge from the magazine .

Because a semiautomatic pistol works through a careful balance of momentum and springs, to some extent, a shooter can affect its function. For example, a very weak grip could absorb some of the recoil energy required to fully cycle a slide. Mechanical timing is even more important since the considerable pressure generated to expel a bullet must be properly contained until it subsides. Premature slide and barrel separation could redirect high-pressure gas through the action, endangering the shooter. So, the solution is some sort of momentary delay, sufficient in duration to permit the exit of a bullet. Depending on the intensity of the cartridge, two prevalent systems are employed.

Blow-back pistols. Milder cartridges like the .22 LR, .25 ACP, .32 ACP, or .380 develop less thrust than rounds like the 9mm Luger, .40 S&W, .45 ACP, etc. So, concerning the milder calibers, unlocking can be delayed by a balance of slide mass and recoil spring tension. Nearly all .22 LR pistols are blow-back designs, and a good many .32 ACP or .380 ACP guns share this function. A classic example is the Walther PPK series which has been built in all three calibers. Its barrel remains affixed to the frame, serving double-duty as a guide for a stiff recoil spring. Upon discharge, the spring exerts enough forward pressure upon the slide to delay opening until the bullet clears the barrel. Other blow-back variations locate the recoil spring below the barrel, or employ a spring-loaded bolt. An example of the latter is Ruger's famous Mark-series .22 LR pistols. The Mark-1 appeared in 1949, morphed through three more iterations, and is still going strong as the Mark-IV. S&W's recent .22 LR Victory works the same way. Like most other blow-back designs, cost is reasonable thanks to less complicated construction. In fact, some blow-back pistols will even spit out fired cases with a missing extractor. However, the .22 Magnum is hot enough to require additional mechanical resistance, accounting for a scarcity of competitively priced pistols. The recent miniaturization of .380 pistols also poses blow-back challenges resulting from reduced slide mass. A stiffer recoil spring will help to some extent, but slide manipulation becomes more difficult, so a more practical solution is the same sort of locked-breech design employed with hotter calibers. This stronger mechanical lockup permits use of a lighter recoil spring, easing small-gun operation.

Short-recoil/locked-breech pistols. Mainstay cartridges like the 9mm luger, .40 S&W, or .45 ACP provide plenty of rearward thrust and lots of chamber-pressure, so as noted, unless the resistant force is extremely large, an action could open prematurely. However, some SMGs like the 9mm Sten or .45 Grease Gun are blow-back designs, which work through use of massive bolts. A smaller, holster-carried system needs a more practical way to delay unlocking, and several innovative approached have been tried.

Small-caliber locked-breech pistols are catching on for CCW use despite their greater costs. The simpler blow-back .380 (L) requires greater slide mass, resulting in a larger gun.

An early pistol concept was the toggle-action Luger, which had a two-piece bolt assembly. The toggle acted as a knee between both sections, and was knocked upward when it struck an inclined receiver surface. The effect was like a surprise bump of your knee from the rear, but with a Luger, recoil drove the assembly rearward to accomplish this function. John Browning went a different route with his Model 1911 Government Model. The Luger is long gone, but more than a century after its birth, factories continue to pump out droves of 1911 pistols.

In the Browning, design a heavy slide remains connected to the barrel through a series of interfacing lugs (located ahead of the breech), while both travel rearward during the short duration required for bullet-exit. At that point, the breech-end of the barrel is drawn downward by the camming action of a link, which pivots around the slide-stop axle within the frame. The barrel's upper set of lugs can then disengage from the corresponding set within the roof of the slide, allowing both parts to separate. Rearward barrel motion is quickly arrested by the link, but the slide continues for extraction,

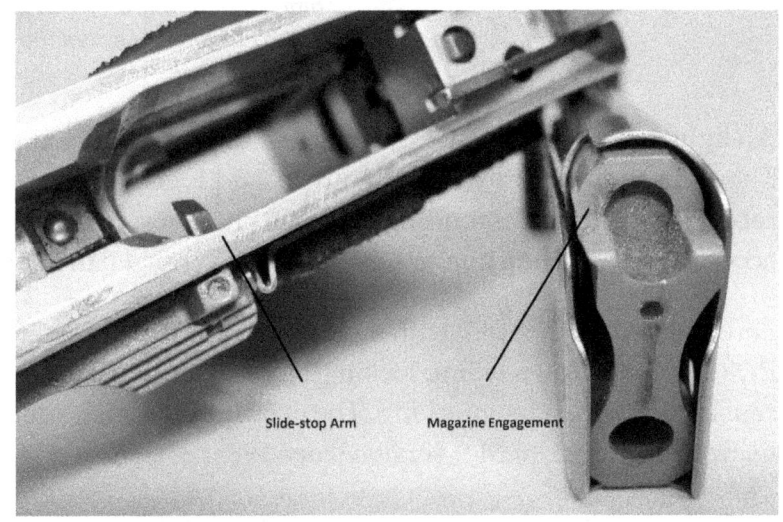

The slide-stop's arm is elevated through contact with the magazine's spring-powered follower. A lug on the stop then blocks the slide's return.

Semiautomatic Pistol Basics | 207

ejection, and hammer re-cocking. A heavy recoil-spring finally reverses this process, driving the slide forward to strip a round from the magazine, into the chamber. Once back in battery, the cycle can be repeated by firing another shot. The slide-stop also has a leg which penetrates the frame to engage an empty magazine's follower. The slide-stop will thus be elevated when the magazine runs dry, locking the slide rearward. Pushing a magazine release button will permit the magazine to drop free for rapid reloads. Hence the term "lock-back" reloads. Once a fresh magazine is inserted, depressing a tab on the slide-stop will cause it to serve as a "slide-release," allowing return to battery.

It's an ingenious system, and it works. Today, most major-caliber semiauto pistols are just variations of Browning's tilting-breech design. Instead of lugs, a square breech section may engage an opening in the slide, and the swinging link may be replaced by a kidney-shaped camming surface that conforms with the slide-stop axle. In the end, they all function similarly.

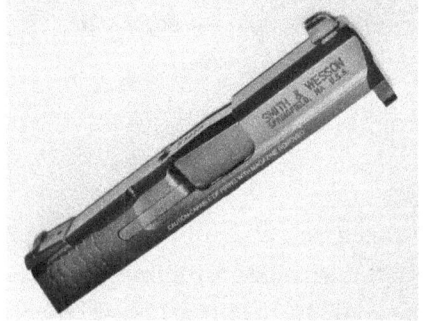

In battery, the square barrel-breech section locks into the slide's ejection port, forming a solid connection.

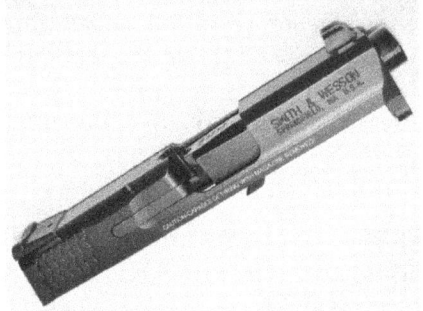

Unlocking begins as recoil drives the slide rearward. The diagonal lug beneath the barrel-breech contacts a corresponding frame incline, tilting it downward. At this point the bullet has already exited the muzzle, permitting pressure-free separation.

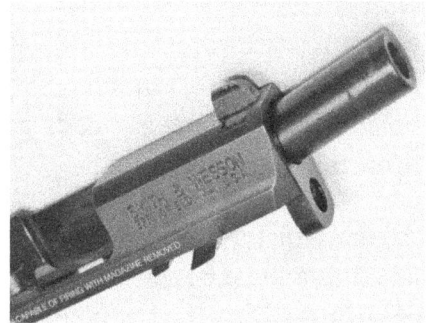

Now fully out of battery, the barrel's tilt is obvious. The inclined surfaces of its lower lug will cam it back up into battery as the slide cycles forward.

A slight twist (pun intended) is the rotating barrel used on a few pistols like Beretta'PX-4 Storm. The slide and barrel are still initially locked together, but recoil separates them when a series of barrel-lugs engage corresponding diagonal channels. In theory, this system may produce slightly better accuracy and feeding due to a consistently vertical barrel plane.

Beretta took another tack with their previous, well-known M-92 FS, itself a spin off Walther's pre-war P-38. Both employ a falling locking-block assembly cammed out of engagement during slide travel, causing barrel/slide unlocking. The concept obviously works since U.S. Military forces having been using the equivalent M-9 version since 1985.

These locked-breech variations are strong, durable, and reasonably affordable. Smaller pistols of this design typically need stout recoil springs to counter higher slide velocities. Nowadays, compact guns are where it's at, so recent efforts have resulted in clever recoil spring systems that facilitate easier manual slide retraction. Better 9mm bullets have shifted much interest back to this caliber, further reducing the necessary effort compared to rounds like a .40 S&W.

Other systems. We've examined actions that cycle off recoil impulses, but a stronger design is needed with the hotter calibers that push the limits of practical semiauto use. The solution is a "gas-operated" system, which employs propellant pressure to unlock a more complex mechanism. The Desert Eagle is a classic example. It's big, too! For starters, it must be if for no other reason than the cartridges it fires. The starting point is a .357 Magnum, followed by larger cartridges up through the .50 Action Express. Pressure and thrust are severe (not to mention recoil), so a strong, rotating-bolt locking system is employed, like a gas-operated M-16 rifle. The result is an imposing pistol that will pull your trousers down in conventional carry modes.

Lately, AR-15 "pistols" have become more popular as an end-around solution to NFA regulated SBRs. Function is classic AR; again, not much different from a Desert Eagle, meaning either way, you wind up with a big "handgun." In fact, hand-rifle is a better description. Personally, I'd rather tote a carbine equipped with a sling, but enough interest exists to further explore this alternative.

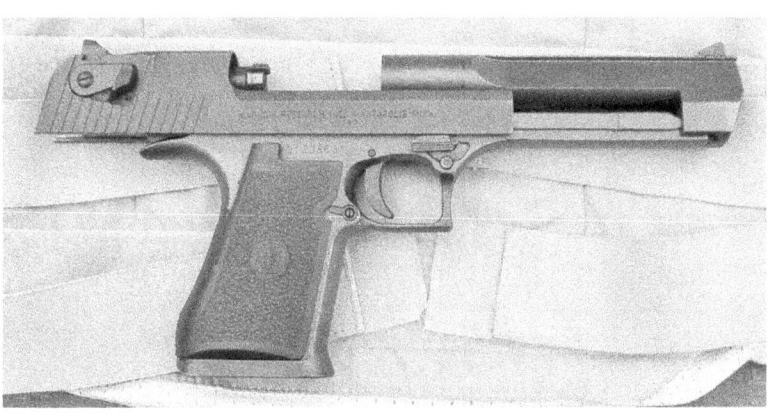

The gas-operated Desert Eagle is large by virtue of its design. Scratch concealed carry and, maybe, consider suspenders. The rotary bolt is visible in the ejection port.

HK came out with their compact P-7 squeeze-cocker during the 80s. It too was a gas design of sorts, but in this case, a small amount was siphoned from the barrel to activate a reverse piston, used to delay slide movement. It worked, and while the P-7 has been relegated to collector status, the piston-delay still appears from time to time. Walther now sells a compact SOFT-COIL CCP 9mm marketed for concealed-carry use. It's a gas-delayed blow-back design which can function with a lighter recoil spring for easier manual slide-cycling.

COMMON PISTOL TYPES

Semiautomatic pistols have evolved into several distinct types. Let's start at the beginning of this genesis and work our way forward.

Single-actions. Until well into the 20th century, most firearms had hammers, so the earliest single-action pistols were natural evolutions. These handguns were designed to be carried cocked with a manual safety engaged, and although the hammer was a distinct feature, some "hammerless" designs (like the old .380 Colt Model 1908) actually employed an enclosed hammer. Yes, such a pistol

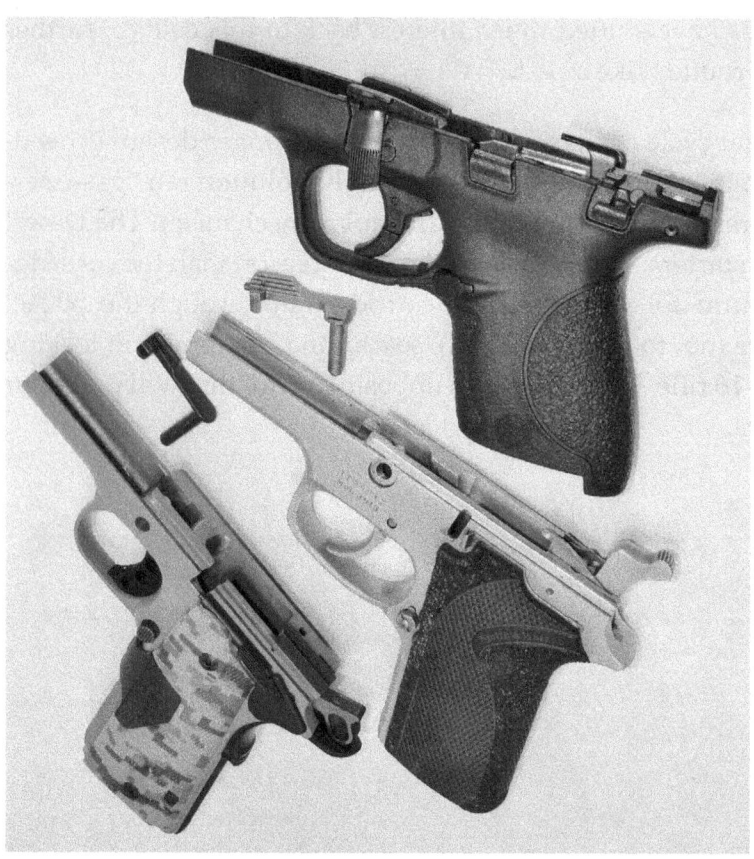

These smaller-frame evolutions include the classic single-action 1911, an S&W DA/SA type, and a striker-fired design. The latter has a captive takedown lever.

is still carried cocked, but you can't see the hammer. The same holds true more than a century later with S&W's modern polymer-framed .22 LR M&P. It is a close knockoff of their striker-fired centerfire M&P line (more on that system shortly), but since the rimfire has a hammer, a sear-blocking external safety is incorporated. The aforementioned Ruger Mark-series rimfires, which debuted in 1949, work the same way. In fact, S&W still builds the mid-50s era Model 41 .22 LR target pistol, known for a consistently great S/A trigger resulting from carefully honed sear and hammer surfaces. These blow-back designs employ a reciprocating slide or bolt which re-cocks the internal hammer during cycling.

Many centerfire versions function similarly, using an external hammer. In fact, the locked-breech Model 1911 .45 ACP Government Model Pistol embodies the single-action design. Like most others, its advantage is a consistent trigger pull with only minimal travel. Match guns, many of which are 1911-based, will have lightweight triggers tuned to three pounds or less. A less refined battle-worthy military version works the same way, although the pull will be intentionally heavier for safe handling during rough environments.

Double-actions. Think "double-action revolver." A classic DA/SA pistol can be safely carried with its hammer down on a loaded chamber. The first shot requires a long and deliberate trigger stroke. Upon discharge, the slide reciprocates and re-cocks the hammer, whereupon subsequent shots can be fired from a lighter single-action pull. Assuming a few shots have been fired, the hammer will remain cocked to S/A mode, presenting an unsafe condition for re-holstering. While the hammer *could* be manually uncocked, most D/A pistols have a de-cocking lever, designed to safely lower it without the risk of a discharge. The big concern involves remembering to do so *before* recovering the pistol to its holster. This step requires conscious thought, meaning it could be omitted during a stressful event. Furthermore, two distinctly different trigger-pulls will require mastery between the initial long stroke, and subsequent shorter S/A presses. Clearly, training is an important aspect of proper DA/SA pistol use. However, as a user of all the common systems, I feel the safest carrying a D/A pistol simply because it can be carried uncocked.

<u>Double-action-only variants.</u> These pistols dispense with a cocked single-action capability, firing only from their hammer-forward mode. Such a simplified variant eliminates any concerns over disparate trigger-pulls and de-cocking. The concept gained some traction during the heyday of D/A pistol uses within LE circles, and the transition from a revolver was also smoother due to familiar triggers. Lately, DAO pistols are back in force as small .380s from S&W, Ruger, Kahr, SCCY, etc. Many have a much-vaunted second-strike capability, meaning in the event of a dud, you could mindlessly try extra trigger-pulls - or maybe even throw the gun! This isn't true of most striker-fired pistols, which become partially cocked during slide cycling. (A few DAO designs work in a similar manner, the difference being the hammer is arrested prior to full forward travel.) Regardless of any second-strike capability, I'd rather execute an immediate malfunction-clearance procedure if experiencing a failure to fire.

Although not a preferred method of a carry, I'd resort to a DAO pistol in a pocket in a pinch – something I'd never consider with a S/A or striker-fired design. Some extra insurance is afforded by the heavy and deliberate DAO pull, with less chance of a foreign object-induced discharge. Some models even incorporate an external safety, and many are carried like small, shrouded-hammer revolvers.

Striker-fired pistols. The revolutionary, polymer-frame Glock is the most widely-recognized example of this design. You won't find a hammer of any sort. Instead, a deliberate trigger pull is used to retract an internal, spring-loaded "striker". Typically, each firing sequence begins with the striker partially cocked. Pulling the trigger draws it further rearward to the point where it eventually disengages, with sufficient tension to fire the gun. The pre-cocked condition excludes second-strike capability, but does result in a manageable trigger pull; heavier than a 1911, but lighter than a D/A stroke. Since each trigger pull is the same, it's also easier to learn. There is no de-cocking lever simply because it's unnecessary. Some striker-fired pistols now come with an external safety option, but the only visible safety on most is an extra vertical blade located within the trigger's face, which serves to block any movement. Unless full trigger contact is acquired, the pistol won't fire, and Glock calls theirs a "safe-action" trigger. In theory, it is – if nothing contacts the trigger assembly. Unanticipated things that *could* do that include an undisciplined trigger finger, a loose piece of clothing, or a wayward object in a purse, etc. Disassembly can be a further concern since some pistols require pulling the trigger first. But, of course, these issues can be mitigated through good 'ol common sense.

Glock's "safe-action trigger" has spread to other striker-fired pistols. The central tab must be depressed to activate the trigger.

From a marksmanship point of view, I'd rate a generic striker-fired pistol as the easiest route for developing basic skills. Based on the proliferation of such pistols within LE circles, others must share the same opinion - BUT, those agencies who were sloppy on trigger-finger discipline quickly re-visited Rule #3: keep the damn digit off the trigger until you're ready to fire! After some early misadventures, Glock developed a "New York Trigger" with a heavier, revolver-like pull. Over time, everyone paid more attention to holsters, and training tightened up. Today, we're mostly through the learning curve, but extra attention to firearms safety is equally important. I wouldn't want to stuff a striker-fired pistol in a purse, drawer, or baggy clothing. Pay attention to the details and you'll be good-to-go. But, one remaining hurdle is the mind-numbing assortment of "me too" striker-fired polymer pistols to wade through. Seems like a new one shows up every month, and even the biggest-name manufacturers have jumped in. These guns for the most part bear a suspicious resemblance to a Glock.

WHAT'S THE RIGHT CHOICE FOR YOU?

It depends. What is your level of firearm experience? Are you the only user? What about mechanical aptitude, physical limitations, or left-handed operation? Also, don't forget about commitment to training, time constraints, and related budgetary limitations. Personal living situations can also factor in, particularly when it comes to kids and safe storage, and carry modes are a further part of the equation.

Experience. Many serious gun people could make do with any of the systems we've examined, but one long-standing choice has been a single-action pistol; more than likely some type of 1911. It will probably be carried "cocked and locked," requiring some extra attention to details. Not too many law enforcement agencies went this route in part because a cocked hammer makes administrators nervous, but also because of simpler systems requiring less intensive training. The same concerns should serve as a cue for newer shooters.

Some LEOs or military folks may gravitate to DA/SA guns for no other reason than previous experience with issued S&Ws, SIGs, or Berettas. The hammer-down carry is reassuring, accounting for use within those circles. A caveat is users will need thorough de-cocking programming and lots of practice with two different trigger pulls. For these reasons, DA/SA pistols are, perhaps, no longer the optimum newbie choice. They might have been in 1985, but now we have simpler DAO and striker-fired designs that dominate both fields.

DAO pistols can wind up in the hands of nearly anyone simply because many small .380s work that way. They do solve most complexity issues since de-cocking and disparate trigger pulls are off the table. Of course, their longer trigger stroke is harder to master, and some pose additional marksmanship challenges related to small size.

Striker-fired pistols are likely to show up in the hands of just about anyone from high-speed tactical operators to beginners. KISS is good and a pistol like a Glock certainly meets this description, with only minimal active controls. De-cocking concerns become moot since there is no hammer at all. The consistent trigger pull is easy to learn, and many such pistols have no extra safety levers. Of course, pressure on the trigger will fire the gun – whether you want it to or not.

FEATURES AND CONTROLS

Glock stood pistol design on its ear through innovative concepts ranging from polymer construction through simplified operation. Of course, other manufacturers plagiarized this design as the concept caught fire, one outcome being that many of today's shooters have no other real frame of reference. When we were batting around the idea of a replacement pistol for our aging D/A S&W 3rd Gen pistols, I presented the idea of an active safety-lever. Most of the other cadre members sitting around our table were shocked by the very thought of one. For me at least, it was a revelation of how far the general pistol trend has moved since my prehistoric 1911 days.

Active safety lever? The theory is that a manual safety will just act as an impediment during a stressful situation. However, I've noticed the same serious gun people who pitch this doctrine won't think twice about the safety-lever on their AR-15s. In fact, watching them closely during live-fire drills, you'll see instantaneous manipulations, both before and after each volley. What's up with that? Good training methinks! Also, an AR is an AR; they all work pretty much the same way. With pistols, not so much - and therein lies the rub; but, if your handguns all work the same way, is an external safety a curse? Maybe not if you factor this into any multi-gun purchasing for commonality of function. Such owners can develop subconscious operation through training and repetition. Doubters should watch proficient 1911 shooters operate a safety and note their first-shot times on targets.

On the other hand, casual or multi-system shooters are probably better off without an active safety. Nowadays, I'm using more tactical Tupperware, and since most don't have active safety levers, the occasional conundrum is encountered. As an example, I holster my compact S&W Shield with its safety off; at which point function becomes identical to its larger M&P brethren (a non-safety Shield has since been introduced). Our lead instructor keeps a Shield in his truck, but he applies its safety for extra storage protection. Like the rest of our cadre he'll be messing with all sorts of different firearms, so hopefully, he'll remember that small lever thingy (I'm betting he will). I think the key to a safety lever is to *not* have a haphazard approach. Instead, treat it as an all-or-nothing feature, and assuming you're in, train on it religiously!

Ambidextrous features. Regarding access to controls and ease of operation, think about bilateral features. Many magazine release systems are now reversible, and dual-sided slide-releases have become more common. During the reign of D/A pistols (Beretta M-92, etc.), ambidextrous de-cocking levers were big for good reasons. Somewhere around 20% of the population is left-handed, and some could wind up as shared users of one pistol maintained for static defense. Beyond that, *everyone* should be versed in opposite-hand operation, simply because of Murphy's Law!

Magazine-disconnect safeties. With a pistol so designed, removal of the magazine will render it unfireable. Many so-called "professional" gun people consider this design abhorrent, and detractors argue they'll be rendered defenseless during reloads. Also, if the magazine somehow disengages, the pistol won't fire. We've even seen this occur while a pistol was still in its holster; often related to its selection process, and user contortions involving seat belts or armchairs. Of course, failure to fully seat a magazine can produce the same effect. We've seen some go airborne during draws, and for those without a high level of training, the immediate result is typically a blank look. Top-tier tactical operators train hard and often using firearms that can maximize their defensiveness, so odds are strong their pistols will fire with or without a magazine.

Nevertheless, a magazine-disconnect feature may have merit depending upon your personal situation. Such a pistol can be stored with a chambered round and its magazine removed. We factored this in to large group of armed caseworkers who were polar opposites of any tactical operators. Instead, they carried their handguns primarily for self-defense, in a manner like private CCW users. And likewise, most of them took their handguns home daily, arriving with a chambered round. So, each caseworker was issued an S&W M&P with a magazine-disconnect feature and a Gunvault MV500 pistol lock-box. They were trained to secure their weapons with loaded chambers, *after their magazines had been removed.* Wouldn't it be safer to unload the pistol first? Probably, but increased frequency can raise the risk of a very loud sound. Also, S&W will advise you to switch any round that's been chambered more than twice, since the process shoves the bullet into the feed-ramp with considerable force. The result can be a shortened round, and when a bullet is telescoped into the cartridge, chamber pressure can go through the roof. So, the magazine is simply removed *with the pistol remaining in its holster*, at which point it won't fire. Only then is the gun drawn for storage. The rearming procedures are simply reversed and the result is a safer environment for everyone in their proximity. Private citizens can use a similar approach with one of today's secure containers providing controlled but rapid access. Once the lid pops open it only takes a moment to reinsert a magazine.

Back to concerns about reloads during a fight: most shooters won't have true operator-grade training with strong emphasis on ammo management and tactical reloads. Many of today's pistols are fairly high-capacity, so assuming we have a 15-shot model, *and assuming we can accurately count rounds in a fight*, 14 shots have already gone somewhere – quite possibly with no effect.

For mag-disconnect skeptics, a drill worth running goes like this: take a group of formally-trained shooters and line them up at 7 yards. Each will have a pistol with a chambered round but no magazine. Beginning in a good defensive ready position, the goal is to fire 2 shots in 3 seconds. The pistols should all be capable of firing sans magazines. Results should also be worth capturing on video. For starters, when the gun goes bang it won't lock back. Instead, the slide will go forward on an empty chamber. Inserting a new magazine and pulling the trigger will only result in a disconcerting "click." Remember, the slide will need to be racked before shot #2 can occur! If you're thinking this over right now, that's the point. Some things are easier said than done. Those who can properly execute this drill from the start are truly proficient- and in the minority.

Defensively, we can minimize the magazine-disconnect hazard by presenting a fresh magazine to the pistol *before* removing the depleted one. With training, the switch only takes a second or two. As I said, it really depends on your personal situation. For anyone planning on competitive combat shooting, the magazine-disconnect feature can be a giant hassle. After most firing stages, you'll be required to unload and "show clear." Any pistol with a hammer will need to be un-cocked, which can't happen without the magazine. With a striker-fired pistol there isn't a hammer, so you may be all set. However, some ROs may ask you to pull the trigger on an empty pistol while it's pointed down-range.

That's one reason why S&W's "Pro" version of their M&P doesn't have a magazine disconnect. This trend has more recently extended to other M&Ps, perhaps in part to the large amount of negative press. But again, the concept could have merit, depending on your situation. As an EDC pistol, I wish my little Shield had the disconnect feature but it doesn't. S&W couldn't fit that sear housing into the narrow frame. I'm possibly the only one disappointed by this.

Loaded-chamber indicators. These are increasingly popular and the simplest is a small port or slot, cut into the rear of a barrel hood for visual identification of a chambered cartridge. A port is a worthwhile addition, but since darkness will throw you a curve, some sort of tactile indicator is better. Most incorporate a small tab in the top of a slide, which becomes elevated upon engagement with a chambered cartridge rim. Some extractors perform this job, too.

Magazine base-pads. Original G.I. Government Model magazines had non-removeable bottoms, but evolution led to improved types with easily removable base-pads. Today's versions are often made from soft materials for improved survivability during drops, and they also may be thicker to seat with magazine-well extensions. Other pistols now offer similar choices and yours could benefit through a bit of base-pad planning. For starters, life is much easier with a magazine base that can be easily removed for cleaning, as well as customization. Some of the smaller pistols come with two or more magazines, one of which may have a lower-profile bottom (capacity may also decrease by one round). Typically, the shorter mag is carried in the pistol to help minimize "printing," so before buying extra magazines, be sure to decide on your preference. Some after-market base-pads can also increase capacity a bit, while others just afford a better grip. Color options look cool but they can also help identify a magazine's contents or caliber. For what it's worth, a somewhat larger base-pad can help when trying to rip out a stuck magazine. Pearce Grips is just one of many good sources for these extensions.

Disassembly. Again, easy disassembly is worth shopping for (which also extends to magazines). The good news is that many of the latest pistols are a breeze to field-strip for routine maintenance. Some striker-fired types require pulling the trigger first, which is fine in principle, but less so in reality. Religiously follow the firearms safety rules and you'll be okay, but first, get rid of any live ammo and then double-check the pistol because of Murphy's Law!

Captive spring & guide-rod assemblies. I spent hours searching for a Beretta M-92s guide rod in my basement, and the planet must be strewn with errant 1911 recoil spring plugs that departed during field-stripping. They can launch with authority, too! After years of disassembling Government Models, one day a recoil plug launched without any time to react. It certainly would have caused an injury to my right eye if I wasn't wearing safety glasses.

ONE MORE LOOSE END

What about calibers? Before we delve into the various semiauto pistol choices, let's take a time-out for a more thorough look at some useful cartridges. Although several have already appeared as revolver listings, the full line of viable pistol options warrants examination.

CHAPTER 18
USEFUL PISTOL CARTRIDGES

Recent ammunition shortages provided a glimpse of what could happen during a national calamity. Some calibers were either scarce or unavailable; however, even during the midst of the crunch it was often possible to track down at least one box of 9mm Luger, .40 S&W, or .45 ACP. One centerfire commodity in short supply a few years back was .380 ACP, probably in part because of the spike in small pistol sales. Things are better today, but production is still directed toward higher volume products. The ubiquitous .22 LR is a prime example. Rimfire loads were extremely scarce, and although the availability of .22 LR has thankfully improved, .22 Shorts remained scarce until 2018.

COMMON CALIBERS

Small calibers. The .22 Long Rifle heads the list for the same good reasons noted within the revolver section. These pistols abound and many are quite affordable.

On the other hand, the .22 Winchester Magnum Rimfire (.22 WMR) is much less common, in part due to extra engineering required to handle its higher pressures. Furthermore, the .22 Magnum gives up much velocity in short barrels. Essentially, its ballistics will be like those of a fast .22 LR load from a rifle.

The .25 ACP is listed in deference to very small pistols like FN's appropriately named "Vest Pocket Pistol," which appeared around 1905. The "Baby Browning" is another example of tiny guns that fired this equally tiny, semi-rimmed centerfire cartridge (also known as the 6.5x16mm).

Another very old centerfire caliber associated with smaller concealment-type pistols is the .32 Automatic (.32 ACP). It has always been marginal for self-defense. This caliber is more widespread in Europe where it is known as the 7.65x17mm. Among the many pistols in circulation, one that stands out is the Walther PPK of James Bond fame.

The .380 ACP is around the same age. The .380 ACP is also known as the 9mm Kurz or 9x17mm (among others). It has long been considered the practical minimum for self-defense, which hasn't deterred sales. Part of the attraction relates to the abundance of very small pistols, but improved bullets help.

Popular small auto cartridges (L-R): .22 LR, .25 ACP, .32 ACP, and .380 ACP. Shorter lengths permit smaller pistols, but the little .25 Auto is in a league of its own.

The double-action Makarov shares features common to many .380 blow-back designs through the use of a similar cartridge. Note the heel-mounted magazine release.

The 9x18 Makarov was Russia's Cold War answer to the Walther PPK in .380 ACP. Enough Makarov pistols have shown up in the U.S. to justify putting this cartridge on the board. Bullet weights are similar, but velocities are a bit faster. Whereas the .380 uses a .355 bullet, the Makarov fires one measuring .365.

Pistols chambered for the above cartridges typically function as blow-back designs, meaning they don't require some sort of locked breech. Instead, slide mass and stiff springs can be used to temporarily delay opening until pressure subsides. An exception is the recent crop of micro .380 pistols with minimal slide-mass. They require the sort of locking delay seen with the next crop of cartridges.

Mid calibers. The 9mm Luger leads this pack. It will also be listed at times as 9mm Parabellum or 9x19mm NATO. Don't confuse it with the non-interchangeable 9mm Kurz (.380 ACP), which operates at much lower pressure. The ever popular 9mm Luger has been going strong since 1902, and though it may be old, it appears to have grown new legs! Thanks to improved bullets, the latest genre of plastic pistols combine adequate terminal performance with good ergonomics, light weight, and mild recoil.

A cartridge that causes some confusion is the semi-rimmed .38 Super Automatic, a more powerful evolution of the older .38 ACP (not a .380 ACP!). Because both cartridges share the same dimensions, the .38 Super could be viewed as a +P load. In fact, current brass is often stamped .38 Super +P to indicate the difference, and it should never be fired in a .38 ACP! When it appeared during the 1920s, the .38 Super offered near .357 Magnum power from a Colt 1911 Pistol. It might have caught on in a bigger way if not for the subsequent arrival of S&W's hot new magnum during a revolver era. Today, the .38 Super is primarily a match load, used by 1911 shooters to achieve IPSC power factor advantages. Its semi-rimmed design can cause fussiness with feeding, but competition shooters know how to make their Supers run.

The .40 S&W falls between the 9mm Luger and .45 ACP, but it will fit most 9mm pistol frames while offering a fair compromise of magazine capacity and power. Recoil from the .40 is stouter than a 9mm, but generally manageable in a standard-size pistol. The .40 S&W took off like a rocket from its 1990 launch, solving longstanding concerns about 9mm effectiveness. In fact, it looked like the .40 S&W would completely eclipse the ubiquitous 9mm Luger, at least in law enforcement circles. The new load was based on a shortened 10mm cartridge, itself adopted by the FBI to replace their 9mm pistols. Ironically, the same ballistic protocols that inspired the 10mm switch (and subsequent .40 S&W birth) sparked further research, resulting in better 9mm bullets. Today, the FBI is headed back to the 9mm and many other agencies are following suit. Nevertheless, the .40 S&W is a proven defensive round, nearly on par with the .357 Magnum and .45 ACP. As such, it's in no danger of disappearing overnight.

The .357 SIG is an offshoot of the .40 S&W and 10mm, created by necking down the latter's case. It was introduced in 1994 to offer true .357 Magnum ballistics from a semiauto pistol. A major agency in our state adopted it to replace their aging S&W M-65s and, supposedly, upper management bought in at least in part because of the familiar ".357" ring. This strange-looking bottleneck cartridge will feed very well from most .40 S&W magazines. A replacement barrel can thus provide a dual-caliber pistol, although zeros will probably be different. The .357 SIG is fairly hot, so a stiffer recoil spring could be necessary, along with more frequent replacements. SIG succeeded in achieving their .357 Magnum goal though, driving 125-grain .355 diameter JHPs to nearly 1400 fps!

Large calibers. Although the .40 S&W and 10mm share the same diameter bullet, the 10mm Automatic is a hotter pistol caliber, producing stiff recoil and muzzle blast. The .45 ACP is perhaps a bit more tolerable, but both are typically built on similar larger-frame platforms.

The original 10mm Bren Ten was a flop, but Colt followed with their Delta Elite after a few simple 1911 modifications. Since a 10mm cartridge was too long to fit in common 9mm-sized pistols, S&W retooled their bigger D/A .45 to accommodate this round. The increase in power over a 9mm was reassuring but came with a price.

The .380 (L) is shown beside popular mid-size cartridges, including 9mm Luger, .38 Super, and .357 Sig. All use .355 -.357-diameter bullets.

Shortly after the FBI adopted the 10mm version, qualification scores declined. A watered down 10mm load cut recoil to a more manageable level, which got other people thinking: how about a shortened case that would fit in a 9mm-sized platform? Soon after, the .40 S&W appeared. It looked like the 10mm would fade to niche status, but improved 9mm bullets caused the opposite effect. As the .40 declines, the 10mm is growing new legs in large pistols built for serious handgunners. Many will no doubt be used during close-range wild hog encounters.

The large-caliber pistol trio includes (L) the .40 S&W, 10mm Automatic, and .45 ACP.

Until the 1980s, the serious pistol calibers for defensive use were either the 9mm or the .45 ACP. The latter was the fight-stopping gold standard against which all other *pistol* calibers were measured. Since the .45 Automatic Colt Pistol appeared with the 1911 Government Model, this platform remains its most popular host, but there are also good double-action and striker-fired designs. The cartridges are fatter and longer than 9mm or .40 S&W rounds so a somewhat larger grip is necessary. Ammunition is generally available although cost is somewhat more. The .45 ACP spits out a large chunk of lead, resulting in a fair amount of recoil, but it still makes a great choice for experienced shooters of average build. Others would be better off with something lighter like a 9mm. In fact, the latest 1911 trend involves a proliferation of 9mm alternatives.

Oddities. There are other intriguing calibers like the huge .50 Action Express, but such ammo will be harder to locate and it's *always* expensive, even in the best of times. The FN 5.7x28mm and Armscor.22 TCM are in the same boat, albeit with much smaller cartridges. The latter can also be purchased as part of a 1911 kit, providing a switch-barrel 9mm option.

TOP PISTOL CARTRIDGE PICKS

The chart below lists approximate velocities with standard loads (except for .38 Super). Both 9mm and .45 ACP are also offered in +P velocities. Use them if you must, but you'll also pay a price. Beyond more recoil and muzzle-flash, the life of your pistol may be reduced without careful recoil spring monitoring. For what it's worth, "standard" is arbitrary. Again, using the 9mm and .45 ACP as examples, their listed 115 and 230-grain standard weights reflect their original loads. Nowadays, so many other options exist that the lines are greatly blurred. Regarding the 10mm, a 6" barrel is shown to reflect this increasingly popular, velocity-boosting length. But not shown is a 1030 fps Federal Hydra-Shok 180-grain "light load" designed to replicate 40 S&W velocity.

A representative sampling of pistol cartridges:

Caliber	Weights	Standard	Bbl	MV	Use
.22 LR	29-40 grains	40 grains	5"	1000 fps	Targets, plinking & small game
.380 ACP	90-100	90	2.75"	1000	Defense in smaller pistols

9mm Makarov	93-115	95	3.75"	1000	Defense in smaller pistols
9mm Luger	95-147	115	4"	1150	Defense; game up to coyote-size
.38 Super +P	115-147	130	5"	1200	Defense; game up to smaller deer within 50 yards
.357 SIG	125-147	125	4"	1300	Defense; game up to smaller deer within 50 yards
.40 S&W	135-180	180	4"	980	Defense; game up to smaller deer within 50 yards
10mm	155-200	180	6"	1300	Hogs, deer, black bear within 75 yards; defense
.45 ACP	185-230	230	5"	830	Defense; close-range hogs, deer, black bear

Note: more common loads are shown. Extreme variations are sometimes available.

Some people will recommend buying the largest manageable caliber, and while that's fair advice, for our purposes cost and availability also count. The 9mm holds an advantage here, although its versatility narrows. For revolver use, the .357 Magnum is just so versatile that it deserves a top revolver ranking, thanks in part to .38 special capabilities. Too bad that's not the case with the 10mm and .40 S&W, but alas, they headspace off their case mouths. Firing a .40 S&W in a 10mm is unsafe. I've seen it done but trouble is inevitable. The only way to use both calibers within one gun would be to find a 10mm moon clip revolver - or become a 1911 guru. You *could* buy one in 10mm and fit an extra .40 barrel, but you'd also want different recoil springs. You'd probably also need dedicated magazines, and your zeros would likely change. In the end, a separate upper assembly would make more sense.

Or better yet, just keep things simple and go with one of these mainstream calibers. The final choice may boil down to how much recoil you can tolerate; and the size of your hands:

9mm Luger: lowest recommended power threshold; mild recoil and highest capacity.

.40 S&W: strikes a good balance of gun-size, power, recoil, and capacity.

.45 ACP: the benchmark classic, but with more recoil and less capacity, usually in a larger pistol.

Of late, smaller single-stack pistols have become popular CCW picks, and many share the same 8 +1 capacity in either 9mm or .40. The .45 versions usually forfeit at least one round, which may be a fair trade for those able to handle its recoil. To help decide, let's take a closer look at "the big three" pistol choices…

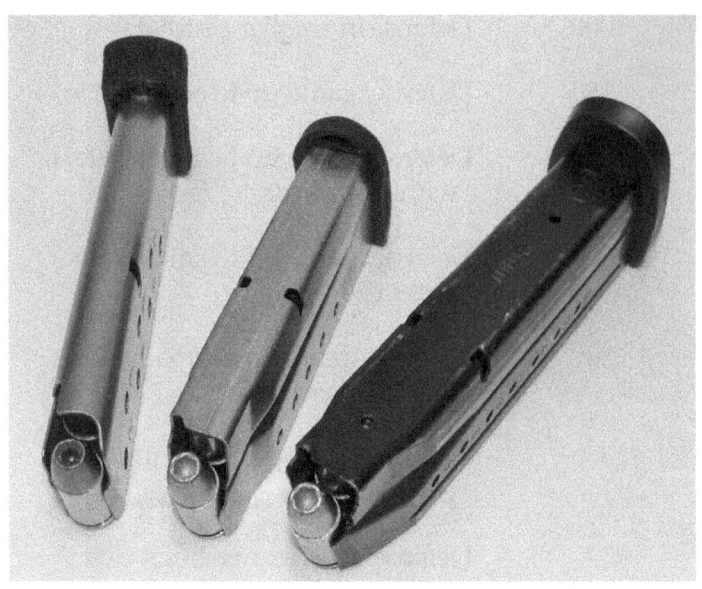

Three common magazine types: Single-stack (L), hi-capacity double-stack (R), and a hybrid-type seen in some compact pistols. Two have slots for reversible mag buttons.

9mm Luger. Originally developed by George Luger for his famous namesake pistol, the 9mm remains the most widely used pistol cartridge on the planet. Domestically, its popularity is attributable to increased capacity, moderate recoil, and lower cost.

Listing all of today's bullet choices would be a project, so I'll share a narrow sampling. We had a recent opportunity to run a few loads through the FBI test-protocols. As a recap, using ballistic gelatin, bullets are fired through several barriers including denim, drywall, and glass. Meaningful data about penetration, expansion, and weight-retention can be gathered for comparative study. If properly conducted, it's a fair test and one I trust. We were not disappointed by our present service load: CCI Speer 9mm 124-grain Gold Dot jacketed hollow-point. But honestly, just about all the mainstream U.S. ammunition manufacturers offer good, dependable loads. Many are built to the above criteria and listed accordingly with published performance data. However, because the 9mm is loaded globally, there is some variation in ammunition. NATO maximum average pressure (MAP) is higher than SAAMI limits. Some foreign variations are even hotter, so for extended pistol life (and safety), the better bet is to stick with established domestic brands.

I'd hunt deer with a good defensive JHP if a 9mm was all I had, but I'd shoot very carefully and try to stay within closer distances. This might also be an instance where I'd switch to a +P load (using a pistol so rated). Ideally, I'd look for a Barnes solid-copper VOR-TX hunting load, but it's only listed as a handgun offering in 10mm. This by itself is telling, but you can buy a Barnes TAC-XP 9mm +P, which fires an all-copper 115 grain HP at 1125 fps. Defensively, this load is no slouch with near .70 expansion and 13" FBI clothed penetration. A heavier version *might* be reassuring, but the good news is Barnes copper bullets are tough enough to act like heavier bullets. With no jacket to shed, weight retention

Today's better bullets explain recent 9mm confidence. Note the cavitation from high RPMs which also affect expansion.

222 | Handguns: A Buyer's And Shooter's Guide

is nearly 100%, meaning we could expect at least 124 grain JHP penetration – if not more. To promote expansion, consider a barrel with adequate length to generate good velocity. For optimum performance, a full-size gun would be the better bet, and adjustable sights would prove useful. Premium loads are expensive, but Q-load FMJs remain affordable, and practice makes perfect!

With less hunting in the mix, any number of good JHPs should do. As mentioned, we use Speer 124 Gold Dot JHPs. Our training or Q-load is most often Federal American Eagle124 grain FMJ. Both loads have similar POIs and recoil, and although AE is less expensive, its accuracy has been good-to-great from a large assortment of pistols, carbines, and SMGs.

The smallest 9mm pistols can generate enough recoil to cause issues for some shooters. To address this issue, Hornady now sells a 9mm Luger Critical Defense Lite, which develops an advertised MV of 1125 fps with a 100-grain FTX bullet. Based on FBI Protocol testing we witnessed with their similar .380 load, performance should be good, with recoil more in this range as well. Food for thought: suddenly, a 9mm pistol like S&W's smaller Shield could stand in for the lighter caliber. Because the 9mm Luger is a widely-distributed centerfire pistol caliber, high-volume production has kept a lid on its cost.

.40 S&W. This cartridge bridges the gap between the 9mm and .45 ACP. Based on a shortened 10mm case, it's one of those few compromises that works well. You get more magazine capacity than a .45 and more punch than a 9mm – but in the same sized gun as a nine. Recoil falls somewhere in between, permitting reasonable control for any follow-up shots. I happened to know one of S&W's M-4006 designers and his focus was on gun size more than anything. The team figured out how to stuff a carefully shortened 10mm cartridge into a 9mm Model 5906 frame and, viola, two birds were killed with one stone:

#1: Concerns about the 9mm's marginal "stopping power" were assuaged.

#2: Gun size remained manageable despite the caliber boost.

The latter was a big deal by 1990 due to an increasingly diverse LEO presence. At that time, there weren't nearly as many plastic pistols with interchangeable grip inserts to fit smaller hands. As for terminal performance, .40 S&W 165 JHPs soon established performance on par with 125-grain .357 loads (per Marshall & Sanow). Enough agencies embraced the idea to position the .40 S&W beyond the realm of tin-foil hat wearers, although early misinformation included accusations of mediocre accuracy. Our testing ran contrary, so I sat down at a bench with a match-grade S&W Performance Center Model 4006 and proceeded to shoot phenomenal 25-yard groups, later duplicated with higher-end 1911-type pistols. Conclusion: the .40 S&W will shoot just fine! Most of the .40 grumbling was early on (forty short & weak), followed by a longer period of fewer complaints. However, the .40 S&W runs warm enough to warrant a supported chamber.

Useful Pistol Cartridges

The modern-day .40 S&W (R) is dwarfed by the 19th century .38/40, but size can be deceiving. Although their exterior ballistics are similar, the .40 benefits from recent bullet research.

Ballistically, the .40 is darned close to the 19th century .38 WCF, right down to a true .40-caliber bullet. All sorts of critters were laid low by .38/40 Winchester rifles, backed up by Colt revolvers. We can achieve this power in a 9mm-sized pistol while taking advantage of much better .40-caliber bullets. Again, with JHPs weighing 155-165 grains, terminal performance is on par with the highly regarded .357 Magnum; with much greater capacity. Of course, there is no free lunch, so recoil will be greater than a 9mm. In a standard duty-sized pistol, the difference will be noticeable but not extreme, but in a smaller gun, the .40 can be snappy. To me at least, the same effect is even noted in a full-size 5" 1911, where recoil seems similar from a .45 ACP. By comparison, a 9mm 1911 seems closer to a .22 LR. Go figure.

Since the .40 S&W is hotter than a 9mm, stronger recoil springs will be needed, and replacement frequency may need to increase. Many .40 S&W pistols are really offshoots of 9mm designs, and although both types will handle a fair amount of shooting, the 9mms seem less subject to wear and tear - probably a non-issue for the majority of shooters.

No doubt about it - the .40 S&W was created strictly for defense. In that role, it has succeeded admirably, but unlike its warmer 10MM parent, it gets little hunting fanfare. I'd give it a go on deer with the right bullet and one that comes to mind is the .40 S&W Barnes 140 grain TAC-XP, listed with a MV of 1120 fps. Since we won't be chasing critters through the boonies with our agency .40s, we use Speer 165 God Dot JHPs, which perform very well in the FBI protocols, while producing only minimal muzzle flash. We support this load with Federal 165 AE FMJs, both of which share similar POIs. Like today's 9mm, there are plenty of other great bullet choices.

.45 ACP. Dissatisfied with existing handgun performance, the U.S. Army adopted a round with plenty of thump. Appearing in 1904, the .45 Automatic Colt Pistol cartridge fired a heavy 230-grain bullet at roughly 850 fps. Concurrent refinement of a promising new pistol resulted in the Model 1911 Government Model with a 7 +1 capacity, which soon proved itself in the trenches of World War I. Both the pistol and the cartridge have been going strong ever since. For those who can handle it, the .45 ACP still makes a great choice. Recoil is stiffer than the 9mm or .40, and, depending on the type of pistol, size can increase.

U.S. Military forces (as well as many others) are bound by the terms of the 1899 Hague Convention. Signatories are limited to non-expanding bullets, in which case bigger is usually better, given similar penetration. Battlefield results have validated this principle, but rumors to the contrary, a "forty-five" will not sweep an adversary off his feet, so a good, expanding bullet will be the better choice. In fact, data based on actual events shows smaller-caliber bullets so designed will be more effective than good, old-fashioned hard-ball, 230-grain FMJ .45 ACP.

In its seldom-used metric designation, the .45 Automatic Colt Pistol caliber is 11.43x23mm; obviously longer than a 9x19 Luger. A standard 1911's frame size will remain constant regardless of whether the pistol is chambered for this caliber or any smaller cartridges. On the other hand, most modern pistols are scaled to 9mm or .40 size rounds. A pistol like a .45 ACP Glock is thus chunkier- something to consider for those with smaller hands. When big fat cartridges are stuffed into double-column magazines, simple physics take over so the grip must be larger. This is less of a concern with

When limited to non-expanding bullets, the superiority of .45 ACP 230-grain hardball is well-established. But, contrary to urban legends, a good expanding 9mm bullet (L) can level the field.

some of the newer single-stack .45 ACP pistols, which maintain good ergonomics for a broad class of users. I recently wrapped my mitts around an S&W .45 ACP Shield which handled surprisingly well. For that matter, the standard 1911 really isn't bad. The weight disparity between an empty or loaded 8-shot Government Model is also less dramatic than some of the 12-15 round plastic pistols. In fact, extra ammo should also be factored in to all weight calculations; including a reserve beyond spare magazines.

The age-old bullet weight is 230 grains – double that of a standard 9mm. It remains a stalwart .45 ACP choice, made better by a good selection of expanding bullets. Common target loads employ 185-grain lead or jacketed SWC bullets designed for punching paper, and although they have little defensive value, several similar-weight, higher-velocity JHPs do. Hornady's 185 grain Flex-Tip incorporates a soft polymer nose-insert which not only initiates expansion, but also improves feeding. Speer sells a Gold Dot JHP of the same weight and Barnes catalogs a copper 185 TAC-XPD. These lighter bullets increase velocity somewhat while reducing recoil. You can even go lighter, but don't forget about an equivalent weight practice load. The 200 grain bullets are a great compromise and many people are happy with the standard 230 weight in a good expanding JHP, which all the manufacturers load. Such middle-of-the-road loads are more likely to function reliably while shooting closer to fixed sights.

The .45 ACP has also evolved to +P levels for modest velocity gains. These loads will be harder on a gun and not all are rated for such pressures. More frequent recoil spring changes would be a wise precaution, but those of heavier poundage could also be necessary. Reliability issues can also occur

The .45 ACP has aged well. Today, there's something for everyone (the 185-grain jacketed SWC (L) is a target load).

when .45 ACP +P loads are fired in shorter-barreled 1911 pistols. Increased slide velocity is an issue by itself, so the extra pressures further affect cycling dynamics, and the frame can incur more pounding. But even without +P loads, there are plenty of hard-hitting choices.

A FEW SECONDARY CHOICES

The above choices were based on their recognized ability to cover numerous bases using manageable and affordable platforms. These traits account for widespread availability of ammunition, which has an impact on cost. As an example of how the whole thing works, we'll soon examine the .380 ACP, which *should* be less expensive than 9mm Luger ammo since it shares the same bore diameter, while using less component materials. Although the .380 is a popular caliber, it has less punch, relegating it primarily to concealed-carry use in smaller pistols. By exiting the general-purpose handgun field, distribution decreases with an attendant spike in prices. For this reason, as useful as the .380 is, it makes the secondary list. Same story for the great 10mm. Power is certainly a non-issue, but recoil and cost are. The .22 Long Rifle is just too useful to ignore, offering a host of good qualities - except for power. Thus, it makes second-tier billing. Of these three good niche loads let's start with the relative newcomer.

10mm Automatic. I remember being at S&W when the .40 S&W was under development. The project was a big secret. I had an off-the-record conversation about it inside an elevator, where it was referred to as "the Centimeter" (described in whispers). Shortly thereafter, I had a .40 S&W Glock and 4006 T&E pistols to play with. I also had a custom 10mm Delta Elite for comparison. The 10mm seemed snappier (accounting for its heavier recoil spring), and as things played out, the 1911 did in fact suffer from increased punishment. A standard frame could easily handle the 20,000 PSI pressure of a .45 ACP cartridge, but the 35,000 PSI 10mm proved a bit much. Shorter gun-life and even cracked frames resulted, which didn't help 10mm sales. On top of that, the larger .45 ACP-sized guns were less manageable for smaller shooters. The FBI dropped their new S&W 10mm Model 1076s like hot potatoes once the .40 was established, and it looked like the 10mm would fade to semi-obscurity.

Surprise: it didn't. In fact, the 10mm is making a well-deserved comeback, quite often in long-slide form to exploit its full velocity potential. The latest crop of six-inch 1911s is most certainly geared toward hunting. The extra inch of barrel will boost velocity 50-70 fps and provide a longer sight-radius at the expense of a large pistol, but a five-inch 10mm is no bigger than any other 1911. Glock devotees can bump up to a 15 +1 capacity without any weight penalty. Its loaded weight of roughly 40 ounces is about the same as an empty 8 +1 steel-framed 1911.

Do enough research and you'll see a blur between some .40 and 10mm factory velocities. A recent example involved a 1911 long-slide 10mm test involving three 180-grain loads. A couple ran around 1,100 fps (not bad), but another clocked 1,000. A 175 did 1080, and a 155 averaged 1,000. Again, these are from a 10mm long-slide. By comparison, our 165 Speer Gold Dot .40 S&W duty load averages around 1,150 from a 4 ¼" barrel and the 180s run around 1,000 fps. The .40/10mm difference with heavier bullets is there, but you really have to shop 10mm performance. I'm guessing many folks won't.

Fortunately, things are changing for the better. Barnes lists one solid-copper 10mm load; their 155 grain TAC-XP, rated at 1,150 fps. Its solid-copper construction is tough enough to behave like a heavier conventional projectile. Power-wise, it approaches the well-respected .41 Magnum. Speer came out with a new 10mm Gold Dot JHP which drives a 200-grain bullet around 1,100 – 1,150 fps, depending on barrel length; not shabby by any stretch. Neither is Federal's new 180-grain Vital-Shok JSP which can supposedly clock 1,300 fps or more! The surprise comeback of the 10mm is clearly now beyond a fad, with earnest efforts by ammo builders to increase performance. If we want to believe the latest chronograph results, some 200-grain loads are hitting 1,500 fps, assisted by 6" barrels! Numbers like these really do put the 10mm into .41 Magnum territories, which means semiauto pistol devotees can finally have a serious hunting tool.

Today's 10mm 1911s are also built with better metallurgy, more able to resist the higher pressure of this cartridge. No doubt, manufacturers of other types have followed suit. Based on our experience with 9mm and .40 pistols, it seems logical to expect shorter gun-life in a 10mm pistol with less than anal maintenance. Ammo availability and cost could be further concerns. My old tricked-out Colt Delta Elite was a real sweetheart, regrettably traded off during the new .40 S&W boom; but all things considered, it may have been for the best since I can't say I miss chasing fired 10mm brass. Then again, the latest Ruger new moon clip Super Redhawk solves this problem quite nicely!

.380 ACP. Although some of the latest 9mm versions are coming close in size, the .380 still has a size edge. For many users, it will be an auxiliary purchase, intended for deep-cover carry when a larger pistol isn't practical. However, some will employ a .380 as their principle handgun to cut down on recoil, going a size larger than the micro-pistols which often have some snap. Browning recently came out with such a pistol in their scaled down 1911, which operates per its larger cousin's locked-breech design. It uses a lighter recoil spring than most blow-back .380s, resulting in easier slide manipulation. Same story for S&W's latest .380 EZ Shield, sized between their 9mm Shields and Compact M&Ps. Dropping down a full notch in size, Kimber, SIG, and Springfield Armory now sell .380 1911-type micro pistols with manageable slides; but the smaller we go, the more felt-recoil will increase due to simple physics.

Many small .380s employ 6-7 round magazines. JHPs offer some reassurance, but short barrels can hamstring expansion. Bullet placement still counts!

The .380 Automatic Colt Pistol cartridge uses the same diameter .355 bullets as a 9mm Luger, but their weight and velocity are less. The age-old .380 standard was a 95-grain FMJ loaded to around 950 fps, making it a marginal defensive choice. Fortunately, today's bullet improvements now extend to this caliber. I asked a trusted .380 LE user what his favorite load was and he said, "**I carry nothing but the Winchester PDX1 95 grain. It surpasses the FBI protocols as well as my own. It also passes my function/reliability testing with a 100% grade in both my Walther PP and Sig P232.**" Another load I'd add to the short-list is Hornady's 90-grain FTX Critical Defense (1,000 fps MV). We recently saw excellent results with this load during FBI-Protocol testing, and unlike many other .380 defensive loads, expansion was consistent during the clothed gel-block samples. Supposedly, the flexible plastic nose-insert will initiate reliable expansion without the possibility of becoming clogged by fabric - unlike conventional JHP bullets.

Extremely short barrels might benefit from lighter 85-90-grain bullets, which could give velocity a nudge to increase expansion, while marginally reducing recoil. Sometimes non-standard weights can affect POI, but for these close-range guns, reliability is the greater concern. Once a trusted load has been established, shop for an equivalent-weight FMJ practice load and work on shot placement.

.22 Long Rifle. This load got good billing as a revolver option, and it deserves a second look here. An understudy .22 LR pistol that shares similar (or better yet, identical) function can provide valuable practice for much less cost than any centerfire. A milder rimfire can also help work through less easily noticed bad habits like an all-too-common flinch. We maintain a couple .22 duty-pistol clones for exactly this reason - and they're fun to shoot!

Defensively, the .22 LR is too light. Not that a hit can't prove fatal; it most certainly can. Cattle are killed by .22 LR handguns from surgically-placed head shots, and cemeteries are full of hapless rimfire victims, so a .22 rimfire of any type is certainly no toy! However, reliable pistol function is dependent upon a balance of pressures and springs, so unlike a revolver, rimfire ammo options become more limited. A smattering of high-end .22 rimfire target pistols have been chambered specifically for low-recoil .22 Shorts, but they won't function in most .22 LR semiautos. That means lesser-powered .22 CB Caps are also out unless single-loaded (a nuisance). I have manually cycled .22 CB Longs through a pistol and CCI .22 "Quiets" to field a low-signature report. In rifle barrels, these loads are nearly silent, but in a revolver they have an identifiable signature. A pistol is perhaps a tad better, but the loading hassle kills the whole idea as far as I'm concerned.

Most listed velocities are based on rifle barrels. Plain and simple, any rimfire handgun of a practical length is going to forfeit speed, so most 40-grain high-speed loads will run around 1,000 fps. I ran some zippy CCI .22 LR 40-grain Velocitors through a 5-inch barrel and they clocked 1,176 fps; good for a pistol, but still way below the advertised rifle velocity of 1,435 fps. CCI .22 LR Stingers are notoriously fast and the box advertises their lighter 32-grain bullets at 1,640 fps, but from the same barrel I recorded 1,300 - quite respectable! CCI 36-grain Mini-Mags averaged an efficient 1,111 fps compared to their 1,235 fps rifle velocity. I wish I had a .22 WMR pistol on-hand with the same 5-inch barrel, but no such luck. However, if memory serves me right, an old .22 Magnum AMT I tested didn't do much better. But don't despair when it comes to small game hunting with a .22 pistol. The above .22 LR loads and many others are fully up to the task. Plenty of trappers and raccoon hunters use .22 LR handguns, placing their shots carefully; often in the head. Squirrels or cottontail rabbits can be laid low with chest shots, and milder HP loads will do a good job of stopping them in their tracks while minimizing meat damage.

As is the case with a .22 rifle, handgun accuracy can vary depending on the load, and reliability may as well. Many sporting-type rimfires do better with high-speeds, while some target pistols may prefer standard-velocity ammo. Do some testing before buying in bulk. Also, give your pistol some periodic maintenance since .22 LR ammo runs dirty. These guns are blow-back designs that deposit powder fouling and lead throughout their actions, so once again, ease of disassembly counts.

Mainstream calibers translate to lower costs, more choices, and completive designs. The .22 LR, .380, .9mm, .40, 10mm, and .45 ACP all qualify - with greater odds of finding them!

CLOSING COMMENTS

Note the absence of rifle cartridges like the 5.56mm NATO/.223 Remington loads common to AR-15s. The .300 Blackout is another up-and-coming cartridge specifically designed for this platform with sound-suppressors (silencers). As mentioned early on, AR-type "pistols" are just not practical for general holster-carry purposes; furthermore, they are *really* loud. The exception is special sub-sonic .300 Blackout variants when fired with a suppressor, but size will increase due to the "can," and the NFA hurdles must be negotiated. Nevertheless, due to their growing popularity, these AR-15 "pistols" (as well as those in 9mm) will receive attention later. Meanwhile, especially if funds or storage space are tight, consider a more immediately useful conventional centerfire pistol chambered for 9mm Luger, .40 S&W, or .45 ACP. Perhaps backed up by a .22 LR pistol sharing similar operation.

CHAPTER 19
SINGLE-ACTION PISTOLS

Chronologically, single-action pistols constitute an appropriate starting point regarding semiautomatic handgun design. Preceding the earlier part of the 20th century, all sorts of S/A types were produced including a number of smaller-caliber blow-back types. Many were fitted with small thumb-safeties and tiny sights, obviously intended for little more than close-quarter use. Other large designs broke new military ground, and although most have since faded away, one survives as the perennial forerunner.

The iconic single-action pistol is most certainly John Browning's brilliant .45-caliber Model 1911 Government Model. It has reigned supreme since 1911 and has yet to concede its well-worn, if somewhat faded, crown. A follow-up stroke of genius is the Browning P-35 Hi-power, although Browning himself never lived long enough to see its completion by FN in Belgium. The Hi-Power appeared during 1935 as a somewhat simplified, high-capacity 9mm version of the 1911, but steel construction, visible hammers, and frame-mounted safety levers are common to both. The term "cocked and locked" applies to both, although most of us will connect it with a 1911. Either is intended to be carried with its external hammer cocked. When a safety is swiped upward, the sear is blocked and the lever engages a corresponding slide cut. The slide will thus remain locked into battery during rough conditions, which in 1911, included horse-mounted carry. The 1911 also has a grip-safety which must be depressed before it can fire. The circa 1935 Browning 9mm Hi-power eliminated the grip-safety and some recent, smaller 1911-type pistols also dispense with this feature.

The single-action Soviet Torkarev is plow-share tough and simple, to the point where an external safety is absent!

Interestingly, Browning's original 1911 design had no external safety. The Army asked for one during pistol trials, establishing a longstanding and sensible trend. The rugged 7.62x25 Soviet Torkarev TT-33 Pistol functions similarly to a 1911, but has no external *or* grip safety - although commercial U.S. versions have one to meet import requirements (some are 9mm Luger). The Torkarev finally gave way to a safer double-action 9x18 Makarov in 1952. Among the many other single-action pistols fielded globally, our attention will focus on just a few, beginning with 'Ol Slabsides.

THE MODEL 1911 GOVERNMENT MODEL

After more than a century of continuous use, the 1911 remains a top choice for experienced shooters. The general design has been developed to meet every need from full-blown competition to CCW use. Ergonomics are excellent which, combined with a consistent but light trigger, results in a highly shootable handgun. Beyond standard parts, the huge assortment of aftermarket options form the basis of many highly-customized pistols and some of our best-known pistol-smiths owe their livelihood to this endeavor. As for factory-issue 1911s, an original GI-type pistol is harder to find than one loaded with extra features. Of every company manufacturing 1911s – of which there are a bunch – most sell base-line guns which would have been custom offerings during the 1980s. Accuracy has also greatly improved thanks to precision manufacturing.

You can buy everything from compact little three-inch fighting pistols to 6-inch, long-slide target models. The standard and most widespread variant is still a steel-frame .45 ACP Government Model with a five-inch barrel. The smaller 4 ¼" Commander is a popular concealed-carry choice that probably holds second-place, built with either a steel or aluminum frame; sometimes now with a 9mm choice. In fact, S&W recently jumped in with even lighter scandium-frame offerings. The fact that they produce 1911s at all is telling. One might think an established gun-maker would be getting out of a century-old design, but like Ruger, SIG, and others, this is not the case.

As for availability of parts, magazine options alone are daunting. By today's standards, the 1911 is a low-capacity pistol. As originally designed, its magazine held only seven .45-caliber rounds.

Nowadays, 8-shot mags are common, and other extended types could offer more (although reliability might be iffy). Having carried one in harm's way, I never felt compromised by the 7 +1 version. Those big, fat rounds are serious medicine and speedy reloads can be easily executed. But since hi-cap is in, newer wide-body types have evolved with staggered-column magazines capable of exceeding 20 rounds in 9mm. As originally conceived, John Browning's design was old-school construction relying on forged frames and tool-steel components.

A few of many 1911 configurations: 6" target-type long-slide, standard 5", and 4 ¼" Commander-size.

While most upper-receiver parts remain unchanged, one can purchase high-capacity 1911s as complete guns or lower receivers made from polymer materials. Bottom line: if you can't find what you're looking for with a Government Model platform, you probably don't need it.

The Model 1911's strong suits center on reliable function with plenty of power. As originally designed to battlefield tolerances, accuracy was so-so, but with careful fitting, match-grade accuracy is attainable. The trick is to achieve such accuracy without sacrificing reliability. Nevertheless, most garden-variety 1911s are capable of service-grade accuracy, averaging 5-shot groups of 3 inches or better at 25 yards from a machine rest. Carefully-built pistols may do this at 50 yards! This level of accuracy requires tight tolerances with less room for accumulation of fouling and dirt, so with price factored in, a true match-grade pistol is probably unnecessary.

1911 carry modes. Let's start with "cocked & locked." After inserting a loaded magazine, the slide can be manually racked to chamber a round. This action will also cock the external hammer, at which point the safety lever can be applied. The pistol can then be holstered (the separate grip safety provides additional security) in its intended carry condition. If desired, the magazine can be disengaged and topped off with an extra cartridge, affording full 7 +1 capacity (or greater depending on the magazine and caliber).

To clear a round from the chamber, the first step involves removing the magazine. Next, the safety must be disengaged from the corresponding slide notch that locks it into battery. Once "off safe," the slide can be manually retracted to extract a live round from the chamber. Obviously, caution is necessary, *so the pistol must be pointed in a safe direction with the trigger finger outside the trigger guard.*

You'll sometimes see a 1911 carried with the hammer down on a live round. Others will carry it on half-cock. The latter is a huge mistake and neither is recommended. The half-cock notch serves to intercept the hammer if it fails to remain at full-cock. The firing pin of a 1911 is shorter than its slide-tunnel, but a surrounding coil spring presents its tail for a blow from the hammer. In theory, even with the hammer fully lowered, the firing pin's tip will remain inside the tunnel, meaning a blow shouldn't fire the gun. BUT, there have been instances where a dropped 1911 fired strictly from firing pin inertia! If this can happen, what about a blow to a hammer on half-cock?

Don't carry a 1911 on half-cock. It's just there to intercept a hammer that fails to remain cocked during cycling. A hard blow could cause a discharge.

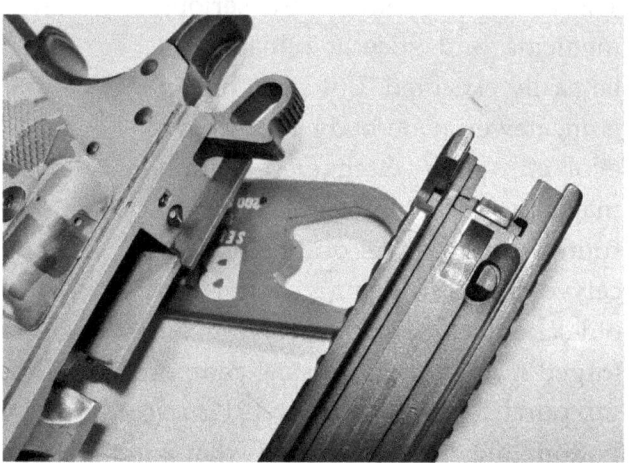

The "Series 80" describes several designs using a slide-mounted plunger to block firing pin movement. The plunger is depressed by a small linkage, visible on the frame.

A subsequent modification was Colt's so-called "Series 80" firing pin system, which introduced a slide-mounted plunger. The firing pin could only travel forward if the plunger was depressed through a connecting linkage activated by the shooter's grip. Some manufacturers also embraced this concept, harnessing leverage from trigger parts or the grip safety. (Pistols without this feature have since been generically referred to as "Series 70s".) Colt also changed the hammer's half-cock notch to a stronger shelf, with some other makers following suit. Eventually, "speed bumps" were added to grip safeties, providing more positive depression for reliable ignition. Lighter Titanium firing pins with stronger springs have also been used in lieu of linkage-type blocking systems to solve complaints about heavier trigger pulls. No system is totally foolproof, though. One of the darndest episodes I can recall involved an LEO armed with a series-80 1911 in close proximity to a hospital MRI. When the machine turned on, the magnetic force sucked the pistol from its holster, against the unit. Perhaps the strong field was enough to realign the pistols internals – because it fired upon impact! This just goes to show no mechanical device is foolproof. Good chance a holster with an improved retention feature has since been procured by this officer.

Onward to carry: three conditions are often used to define the acceptable methods:

<u>Condition One.</u> The previously described cocked and locked, with a round in the chamber, hammer

back, and the safety "on" (which also locks the slide forward).

Condition Two. Fully loaded (per Condition One), but with the hammer down. Owing to its design, the safety must remain off. So, to fire the pistol, the hammer must first be manually cocked. However, it will also need to be un-cocked before re-holstering or after chambering a round. Obviously, this process must proceed with caution.

Condition Three. Chamber empty and hammer down, with a loaded magazine inserted. This was often the standard military carry condition for situations short of imminent combat. It's the safest, but getting the pistol into action is a slower, two-handed affair since the slide must first be manually cycled.

Cocked & locked (top) is the preferred 1911 carry condition. Condition-two can be less safe with older variants that lack a drop-safe firing pin.

Cocked and locked remains the preferred defensive carry mode, making darned sure the safety is applied. If you're a bit confused, it makes a point: the 1911 is among the more complicated handguns. For dedicated shooters, it will work just fine. For occasional users, a simpler design may be better.

1911 evolutions. With its five-inch slide and all-steel construction, a standard-size government model is thin but by no means small. Over the years, several variations have appeared to address size and weight. Colt's original Commander used a shortened 3 ½-inch slide and full-size aluminum frame for significant weight savings. Recoil was snappy, so a steel-frame Combat Commander was developed, whereupon the aluminum version became Colt's Lightweight Commander. A subsequent Officers Model employed the same 3 ½" slide but used a shortened grip-frame, reducing capacity to 6 +1. Eventually, Colt unleashed their Defender with an Officer frame and even shorter 3-inch slide. The latter iteration pretty well killed the Officers Model, and somewhere along the way, Commander-type pistols stretched to 4 ¼" slides. Given the numerous makers and various configurations, the above is no more than a loose representation of the many possibilities.

Getting shorter 1911s to run reliably was a feat due to sharper barrel unlocking angles and increased slide velocities. We got there eventually, but the 4 ¼" offshoots remain forgiving choices. Long-slides seemed to come and go, but the 10mm seems to have brought them home to roost, simply because a six-inch barrel maximizes the velocity of this potent round.

I'll admit to having a very large soft spot for just about any 1911 pistol. I've owned dozens in various configurations; including high-cap models from Para Ordnance and STI. I still have a shorter 9mm Wilson KZ-9, which has a 4-inch slide and 14 +1 capacity. It shoots like a house afire and never fails to

Wilson Combat's double-stack 9mm KZ-9 is a 14 +1 steel/synthetic hybrid. Although no longer catalogued, an intriguing all-metal EDC version recently filled this void.

function. Other than this high-capacity spin-off, the others have departed in favor of the original, more ergonomic frame size. I now own several single-stacks in 9mm, .40 S&W, and .45 ACP; and through a decades-long process of natural selection, only the most accurate survive. My 6-inch STI 9mm Trojan kicks like a .22 and shoots sub-three inch groups at 50 yards with plain old 124-grain Federal FMJ. A second 5-inch .40 STI shoots nearly as well. I own it only because I can shoot it for free, but without this luxury I'd skip a .40. Good magazines are harder to find, and recoil is more on par with a .45, so I'd just go with this larger caliber and call it good.

The latest compact pistols often employ lightweight aluminum frames which can be feisty with full-house .45s. I know several knowledgeable gun people who have switched to 9mms for this reason. With more confidence in today's bullets, they're willing to trade any remaining ballistic gap for increased recoil control, while also boosting magazine capacity by an extra round or two.

Commander-size 9mms like Kimber's aluminum-frame Tactical Pro have gained ground thanks to recent bullet advances (this one has an adjustable MMC rear sight).

Under the hood. What follows is not a manual by any stretch. Instead, the goal is to provide more information pertaining to function. Although the foundation remains the same, all sorts of interesting 1911 variations have evolved, some being competition driven.

The original 1911 employs a separate, removable bushing to help align the barrel with the front end of the slide. During cycling, the slide-mounted bushing travels rearward around the barrel, providing just enough clearance for its rearward tilt and unlocking. The lower portion of the bushing also has ears, which capture a hollow steel plug that contains the recoil spring (located in a separate slide tunnel underneath the muzzle).

Standard disassembly begins by removing the magazine and clearing the pistol! Make any loaded ammo go away, including those in the magazine. Next, check the pistol one more time! You'll be working around its business-end so you can't be too careful.

In its standard G.I. form, SOP involves depression of the plug so the bushing can be rotated 90 degrees - *with the slide forward on a cleared gun!* At that point, the plug will want to launch, propelled by the recoil spring. But by exercising cautious control, the plug can be withdrawn through the front, relieving spring pressure for the next step: alignment of the frame-mounted slide-stop with a small disassembly notch in the slide. Plucking out the slide-stop will draw its axle through the pivoting barrel link. Once disconnected, the slide and barrel assembly can be pulled forward off the frame. The barrel can be separated from the slide after removing the bushing (which is captured by a lug). A reverse twist of the bushing will allow it and the barrel to be removed from the front of the slide. Other loose pieces will be the recoil-spring and short guide rod that butts against the frame. The parts on your bench should be a slide, bushing, barrel, recoil-spring, guide-rod, slide-stop, lower-receiver assembly (or frame), and empty magazine. At this point, consider the pistol field-stripped.

This field-stripped 1911 has a barrel-bushing. But, its solid recoil-spring plug has been replaced by a hollow collar to accommodate a full-length guide rod (reversed in the photo).

Nearly every 1911 owner will want a bushing wrench or two. A range bag is a good home for a spare.

As we can see, disassembly is a bit "fiddly;" at least, compared to more modern designs; so is reassembly without practice. A useful 1911 tool is a flat bushing wrench with an opening that surrounds the bushing. Many Government Models – particularly the most accurate ones – use snuggly fitted bushings to minimize muzzle slop. The wrench will provide extra leverage while also helping to restrain the spring-loaded plug. More than one plug is still in orbit, so don a set of safety glasses before performing any firearm maintenance, and do so in an area conducive to its recovery.

A field-striped 1911 provides a good opportunity to examine its main parts while gaining a better understanding of its general function. As far as BATF is concerned, the serial-numbered frame is the actual firearm, so we might as well begin here.

Frames. You could actually start from scratch with a stripped frame and assemble the various parts needed to create a personalized 1911. Unlike an AR-15, there is more going on than just bolting things together. Since careful fitting is required, most of us will be better with a good factory pistol, adding perhaps, a few extra niceties. But think about how far you want to go before committing to a purchase. For example, metal checkering is a custom touch appreciated by many Government Model aficionados. Unless offered as a factory feature, it'll require the services of a skilled gunsmith or a factory's custom shop. This treatment won't work though on a pistol with a serrated front-strap - something of lesser concern from a purely practical point of view.

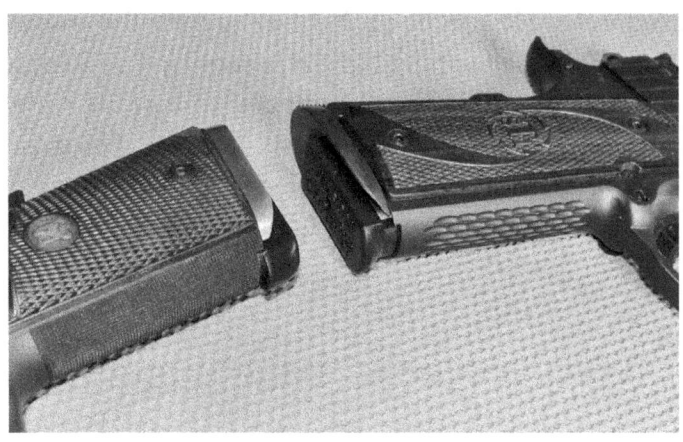

Two examples of factory metal checkering: The chain-link pattern is easier on clothing. Both frames are fitted with add-on magazine funnels.

The latest vogue is an integral accessory rail machined integral with the frame for the attachment of a light or laser. Holsters exist to accommodate this design, but the extra metal can boost a steel 1911's weight to over 40 ounces. Of course, aluminum-framed 1911s will shave weight, and scandium can lighten a gun significantly, but rails are much less common. So, the pistol's caliber and intended use will probably best determine its construction. I'd take lighter materials with a shorter Commander-sized pistol meant for EDC. On the other hand, a 10mm would benefit from steel to help resist the effects of its greater recoil. To that end, some frames are advertised as "high cut" types, designed to improve recoil control. If so, material is relieved below the trigger guard, permitting a grip closer to the bore axis. Some frames also include a "bevel-cut" to assist in the insertion of magazines. It's a worthwhile touch for a serious defensive pistol, and more streamlined than add-on mag funnels.

A standard 1911 frame can handle numerous calibers. The smaller 9mm functions via magazine spacers and modified feed lips.

Regardless of caliber, a 1911's frame will be sized for .45 ACP cartridges. Except for ejectors and slide-stops, adaptation to other calibers is accomplished through magazine spacers and tweaked feed-lips. An intriguing exception is Springfield Armory's Enhanced Micro Pistol. Chambered for 9mm and .40, the EMPs use shallower frames to match these shorter cartridges. The result is a unique and very comfortable-feeling smaller 1911, ideal for concealed-carry. A downside is less commonality of parts and the need for special magazines. Several high-cap variants are in the

238 | *Handguns: A Buyer's And Shooter's Guide*

same boat and some are noticeably larger in girth. Use of a supported chamber (ramped barrel) will require a corresponding frame cut; of which there are at least two versions. The upcoming barrel section will provide more info.

Slides. We have plenty of options here from sight cuts through breech-faces. The old G.I. design uses a staked front sight and a small fixed rear, mounted in a dovetail cut. But as pistol 'smiths wrung out better accuracy, refined sights were called for. So, Bo-Mar stepped up with "melted" adjustable target rear sights which required slide machining. Many of today's adjustable sights follow the low-profile Bo-Mar pattern, but subtle dimensional variations can exist. Another variation is a Novak Cut, machined for this popular fixed sight (and new adjustable versions). Up front, a dovetailed cut solves the problem of loose staked sights, while permitting various choices from F/O beads to night sights. The assortment of combat-type sights presents plenty of other options, but again, they must match their slide cuts.

The .45, .40/10mm, and 9mm each have unique breech-face recesses, although some people manage to run a 9mm off a .40 breech. Slide lengths usually correspond with barrels, and the materials will be carbon or stainless steel. One popular ejection enhancement is a scalloped port, which was formerly a custom touch. Same story for the slide serrations machined to assist manual cycling. Some shooters like an extra forward set while others prefer the original rear-only design. Some slides have upper flats instead of a radius, with longitudinal serrations to soften reflected light. A less common custom touch is a serrated rear slide-face for the same reason.

External dimensions remain constant regardless of caliber. The .45 ACP, .40 S&W, and 9mm Luger have forward slide serrations, full-length guide rods, and hollow plugs.

A firing pin stop can be seen within a slot at the rear of the slide, and it's retained by the tail of the firing pin. The stop is just a small sliding plate with a hole, and depressing the tail of the pin will allow it to slide downward for removal. The spring-loaded firing pin can then be withdrawn from the slide. The stop-plate is also the key to withdrawal of an internal extractor, which will be visible as a small circular seam to its left. Some newer 1911s have foregone this design in favor of an "external extractor," in which case it'll be a clearly visible separate arm, pinned to the right side of the slide.

A peek inside the roof of a field-stripped slide will reveal its locking-lug mortises, located ahead of the ejection port. The barrel lugs engage these cuts when the pistol is in battery. The muzzle-end will be machined to correspond with the small lug of the separate bushing that normally guides and supports the barrel. Sometimes in shorter pistols, a forward, coned barrel section serves the same

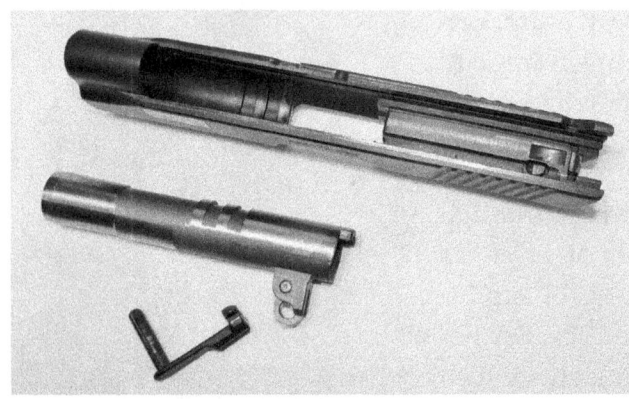

When locked, the two lugs on the barrel engage corresponding mortices in the slide. Camming action is provided by a link surrounding the slide-stop's axle, and the barrel's lower lug. Peak accuracy requires careful fitting.

purpose by centering it against the slide. Either way, you'll likely see a mortise corresponding to a bushing's lug.

Like the many other 1911 parts, you can purchase a separate slide, which is often used as the basis for a hand-built custom pistol. Many are machined to minimum tolerances, requiring hand-fitting to a frame, the goal being to achieve wiggle-free cycling. It's also worth noting that an extra slide could serve to create a complete switch-top upper.

Caliber conversions. A 9mm and .40 Government Model share the same frame-mounted ejector, making it possible to mount a properly-fitted slide assembly in either caliber to the same frame. Obviously, the barrels will be different, and each slide should have a caliber-specific breech-face for proper function. Caliber-specific magazines are needed, but with everything figured out you could even add a 10mm upper to the mix!

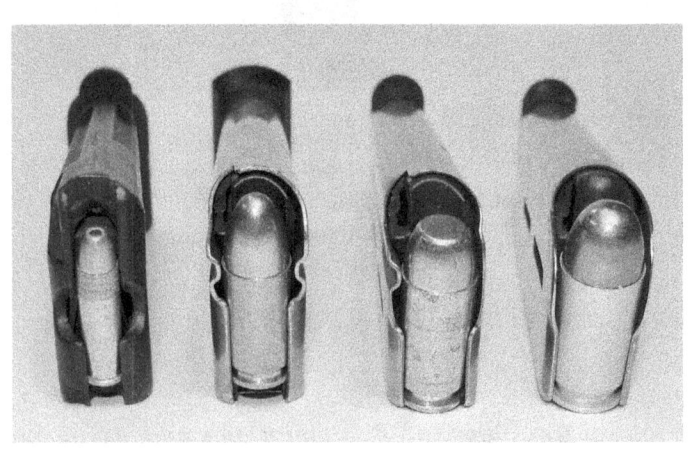

Caliber-specific 1911 magazines offer a range of cartridge possibilities from (L-R) .22 LR, through 9mm Luger, .40 S&W, and of course, the original .45 ACP.

The .45 has a different ejector, but a standard 1911 will work with many purpose-built .22 LR conversion units, permitting a useful switch-top .45/.22 LR. It's a great combination that will provide meaningful practice with the same trigger pull and feel. Installation of most will require a standard frame of the original design. A .45 ACP will probably be built this way anyway, whereas some 9mms and most .40s may have a ramped barrel frame cut (see below). If so, .22 conversion kit options could become more challenging. The ejector spacing can also be problematic with a 9mm or .40 1911s, and although this pinned part can be exchanged for a .45 ACP version, it's just enough of a hassle to discourage the process. The takeaway here is to research compatibility of a .22 unit before making a purchase. I've used Colt Ace and Kimber units on several .45 ACP frames without encountering any problems whatsoever. Rimfire conversions will receive more coverage in the rimfire pistol chapter.

Barrels. The original .45 ACP 1911 uses part of the frame to guide bullets toward the chamber. The lower rear edge of the barrel has a sloping radius ground to match the frame contour underneath. Both surfaces are often polished to provide smoother feeding, and if you ever see mention of a "polished throat," that's what it means. The trick is not to go overboard since even an unmodified the lower chamber edge does expose a small portion of cartridge brass. With a lower-pressure .45 ACP round, this is no big deal, but hotter calibers can stress the brass to the point of failure. When cartridge cases rupture they often do so at the juncture of the sidewall and base-web, so increased chamber support is good insurance.

The "ramped-barrel" design was a popular 1911 modification that grew legs during IPSC-type combat matches where a "power factor" helped determine scoring. The factor was based on bullet weight and velocity, which classified calibers as "major" or "minor." The .45 ACP was the major-power benchmark, providing extra scoring leeway with peripheral hits using standard ammunition. Then savvy handloaders realized they could boost .38 Super velocities (and sometimes 9mm) to major classification by increasing pressure. The lighter bullets cut down on recoil to help shorten time-based scores, but occasional case ruptures resulted in "Super Face;" an unsafe experience that could blow grips off frames while spewing magazine parts and live rounds in various directions. One fix was the extended feed-ramp which more fully enclosed the chamber. The extra material also reinforced the lower barrel-lug area, which helped prevent cracking. The integral extension required a corresponding cut in the frame, but this modification proved worthwhile. At least two designs have since evolved with minor dimensional differences, so a matching frame cut and barrel are necessary.

Beyond .38 Super, a "ramped barrel" can provide an extra safety margin for higher-pressure, .357 SIG, .40 S&W, and 10mm cartridges. I don't worry about a ramped barrel in a .45 ACP, but I prefer one with the others. Although not an essential 9mm feature, I'll still take a ramp and examination of the latest polymer wonders will reveal similar construction.

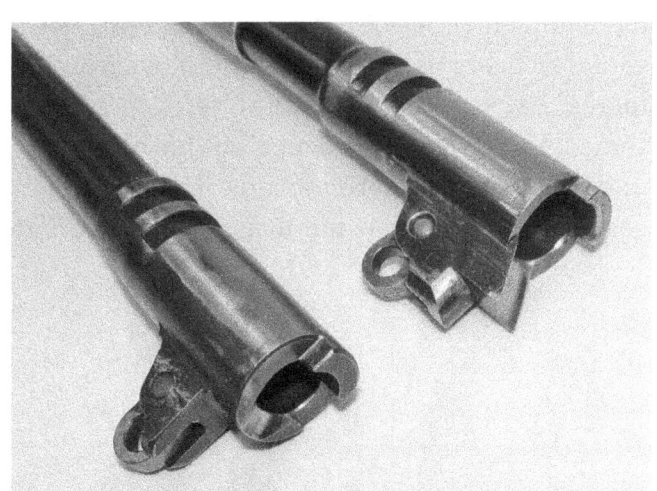

A "ramped barrel" (top) contains higher-pressure cartridges through increased chamber support, but a corresponding frame cut is required. This example also has a polished throat to improve feeding.

The age of the "silencer" has finally arrived in the United States despite additional ownership hurdles. For this reason, several new 1911s are hitting the market with threaded muzzle sections that protrude beyond their slides. A knurled sleeve is supplied to protect its threads if a suppressor (silencer) is not in use. Legalities and costs aside, function and practical carry methods must be considered. Taller sights will also be needed to clear a suppressor's larger diameter.

Fitting and accuracy. After-market "match barrels" are popular and some are sold as "drop-ins," while others need gunsmith fitting. The latter normally require careful removal of material in several key locations, plus a carefully matched barrel bushing. A drop-in type *might* help accuracy, but any dramatic improvement will probably result from luck-of-the draw tolerances. For maximum accuracy, when the gun is in battery, very little play should be evident. Beyond slide fit, both ends of the barrel play a role, plus its upper and lower lugs – not to mention the link. Fortunately, CNC machining now permits decent fitting from many factory-built pistols.

Supposedly, the fit of the barrel to the slide has a greater effect on accuracy than slide-to-frame fit, but both are related. It stands to reason that if everything falls back into consistent alignment, better accuracy should result. The trick is to maintain reliable function during less-than-ideal conditions, meaning dirt needs a place to go. My old captured WWII .45 rattled like grandpa's dentures on the north end of a jack-hammer, but it always ran. When shopping for a new 1911, I can stand a small amount of slide wobble but I'll check for snug barrel/slide fit. You can too: with the gun in battery, try pressing downward on the barrel through the ejection port. Absence of vertical play is a good omen. With the slide shoved forward, try wobbling the muzzle within the slide. Looseness could result from a poorly fitted bushing, barrel, or both. If things seem fairly solid at both ends, results on paper should be good – assuming the barrel itself is a quality product.

Barrel-bushings. A serious fighting pistol could need service on the fly, so tool-less removal of the bushing can help. Yes, accuracy will be degraded to some extent, but the trade-off is probably worthwhile. Colt once sold a collet-bushing with springy fingers, which seemed good in principle – until its metal fingers broke off. The later series-80s saw a return to the solid bushing. Briley has produced a spherical bushing design which employs a captured rotating ball, bored to the barrel's diameter. Like more conventional designs, it's offered in various dimensions to match different barrel ODs. I've shot some great groups with them, but for hard use, simple is better. A few bushings are also sold with integral "compensator" sections. The short-vented extensions will supposedly redirect propellant gasses to reduce recoil, but their primary attribute boils down to a questionable "looks cool" factor.

Colt's short-barrel collet bushing (L) allowed for increased barrel tilt, but its springy fingers sometimes broke. Bushing-less coned muzzles are a fail-safe solution.

Shorter 1911 barrels and slides increase the amount of barrel tilt during unlocking, so many dispense with a bushing altogether in favor of belled or coned muzzles. The tapered surfaces serve as bearings, while providing consistent barrel/slide alignment during closure. However, lacking a bushing to capture that energetic plug, an alternate system is necessary. The solution is a plug that slips inside the slide's spring tunnel from the rear. A shoulder on the plug prevents it from launching through the slide while providing a flush muzzle fit for its solid end.

A further variation is a bored-through collar-plug for use with a full-length guide rod. In theory, the rod's extra length provides better spring support. This supposed advantage is debatable and excludes use of a "press-check" technique to verify a chambered round. Why? Because, as the slide travels rearward, the stationary rod will extend through the collar-plug (like the barrel protruding through the slide). Since these plugs are essentially modified originals, they're often retained by the ears on a standard bushing. The rod will be just short enough to clear the bushing as it's compressed and rotated during disassembly. At that point, like the G.I. type, the plug will want to launch from the force of the recoil spring.

Guide rods. The full-length guide rod options are typically one or two-piece designs. The latter has a hollow tip machined to accept a hex-wrench, permitting removal of the front section from the threaded rear. Disassembly is no big deal, but aligning both sections during reassembly can be fiddly.

When possible, I prefer a one-piece guide rod with some type of pass-through collar bushing. After locking the slide open, the short leg of an L-shaped paperclip can be slipped through a strategically located small hole in the rod. If the slide is then permitted to travel forward a bit, it will capture the plug, spring, and rod, as one unit against the paperclip, relieving slide tension for easy dismounting.

A well-fitted bushing works well in most 1911s (note the plastic buffer). The compensated system (L) employs a self-centering cone, a hollow reversed plug, and two-piece guide rod. The bushing-less short-barrel system (R) employs a reversed pass-through plug to contain its one-piece guide rod and spring.

These captive parts can be plucked rearward from the slide after disassembly without flying parts. It works with either a barrel-bushing design or a coned barrel, but not with a 6" long-slide due its longer slide tunnel. Hence, the two-piece rod effectively shortens its rear section, allowing enough tilt for removal. With the one-piece rod/paperclip method, the only real hassle involves lining the barrel-link up with the frame-hole and slide-stop during reassembly.

Since there are several barrel and guide-rod options, the best way to gain understanding of the system is to do some research. Some people add a "shock buffer" to a rod, which is just a soft plastic spacer that abuts its flange. In theory, it'll ease slide/frame battering; however, the slide will then stop a bit short of its normal travel by the equivalent thickness of the buffer, which could cause insufficient travel for reliable last-shot lock-back. Furthermore, shock-buffers are sold in sets for a reason. Sooner or later they'll become chewed up, and loose plastic pieces in a defensive pistol are an obvious liability. The right poundage recoil spring is a better alternative, especially when a replacement schedule is maintained.

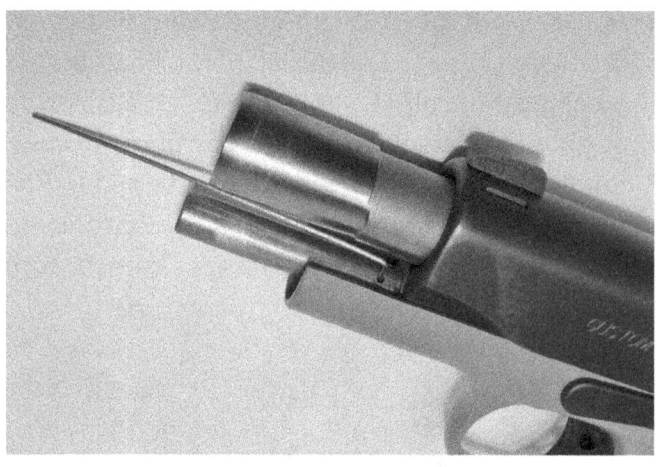

The standard solid plug has been replaced by a hollow collar to function with a full-length guide rod. The longer rod will protrude when the slide is rearward. Prior to disassembly, a bent paperclip can be inserted through a small hole in the rod.

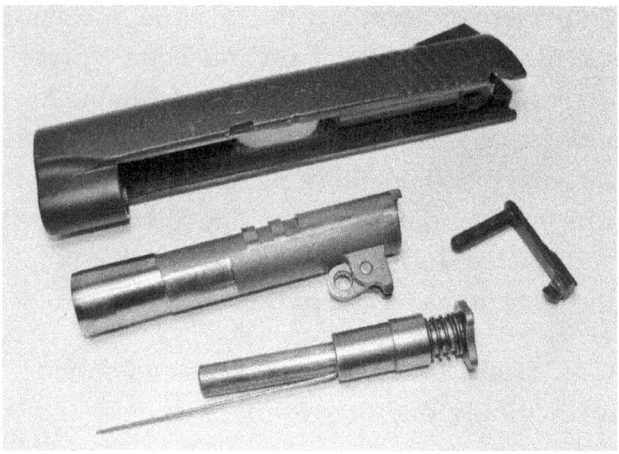

With spring tension relieved, the slide can be removed after pulling out the slide-stop. The captured collar and spring can then be plucked out as a unit. The coned barrel eliminates the need for a bushing, but still comes out through the front.

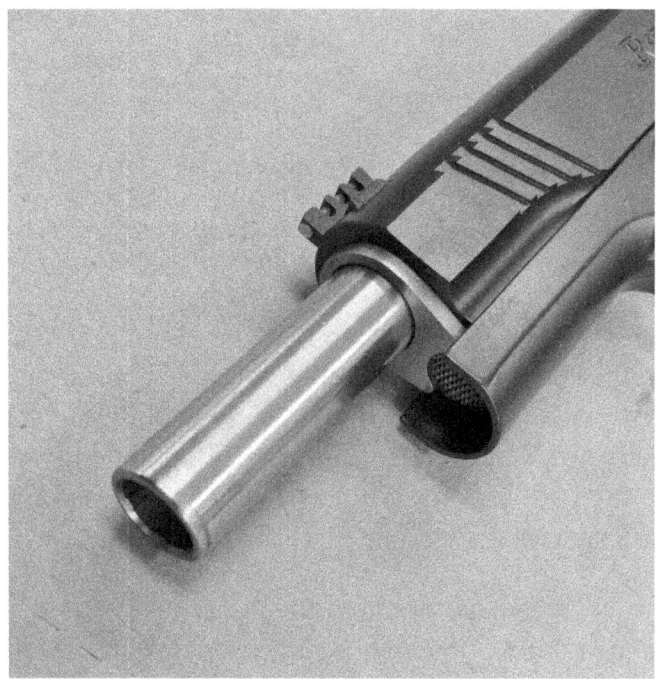

A standard 1911 permits a press-check. The solid plug captures the recoil spring and its short guide-rod won't protrude.

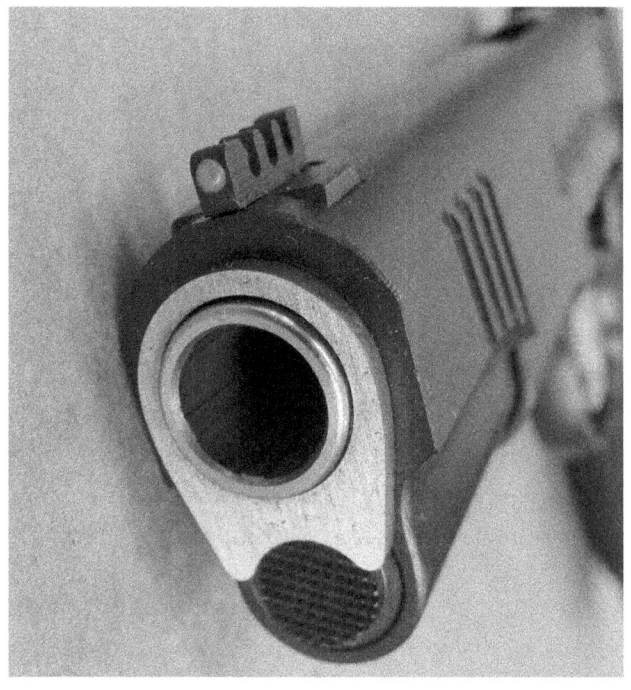

Disassembly begins with the slide forward. The bushing is rotated until its ears clear the plug. The recoil spring behind it is under tension so safety glasses are advised!

Springs. Of several 1911 springs, the one receiving the most attention is the recoil spring. As we know, it surrounds the guide-rod. It not only drives the slide forward after firing, but it also regulates the unlocking process. Recoil springs are rated by compression in pounds, with more being needed for hotter calibers; although slide mass also factors in. A standard five-inch .45 ACP pistol will typically run well with a 16-18-pound spring. A shorter four-inch Commander may need a 20 lb unit. A five-inch 10mm might use a stiffer 22-pound spring, while a 9mm may require a 10-12 lb. type.

The right weight is essential, not only for proper function, but also for gun longevity. Too much weight could impede cycling. Too little could cause premature unlocking, resulting in damage from excessive slide velocity. Even the right recoil spring has a finite life, which could be *approximately* 2,000 – 3,000 rounds, depending on the load, etc. Some shooters switch recoil springs to match specific loads, using reduced poundage with less energetic ones. One concern with a used gun is the condition of this spring, which could take a "set" over time, losing some of its tension. By starting with a standard load, you can observe ejected brass patterns. Ideally, fired cases will land around six feet to the right. More violent ejection (10-12') indicates the need for a stiffer spring, whereas those that dribble out could stand a lighter one. If the slide stops slightly out of battery during feeding, there's a good chance the recoil spring is weak. Among other vendors, Wolf sells a broad variety of springs which are rated by poundage. Some 1911 manufacturers also list their recommended recoil spring weights and replacement intervals.

The hammer spring and its plunger are located within the removeable mainspring housing, and captured by a small pin. The spring's force not only affects ignition but also, to some extent, unlocking. A pistol carried "cocked and locked" will benefit from occasional replacement of the mainspring every 3,000 – 5,000 rounds. The housing itself can be easily removed by driving out the thick pin at the bottom rear corner of the frame. From there it can be worked downward and off.

Magazine springs can also account for unexplained stoppages. I was having a heck of a time achieving reliable function with a .40 S&W 1911. The lower breech-face edge of the slide would occasionally fetch up on a nose-high cartridge, more often as the magazine became depleted. The fix was as simple as an "extra-power" magazine spring, which more quickly presented cartridges to the breech face of the fast-cycling slide.

The firing pin spring is also important. Cleaning and periodic replacement will keep it retracted for safe function, so it might as well be switched when the mainspring is changed. As noted, the small retaining plate on the rear of the slide captures the firing pin.

Extractors. The original 1911 uses an internal extractor, also captured by the firing pin stop. It should

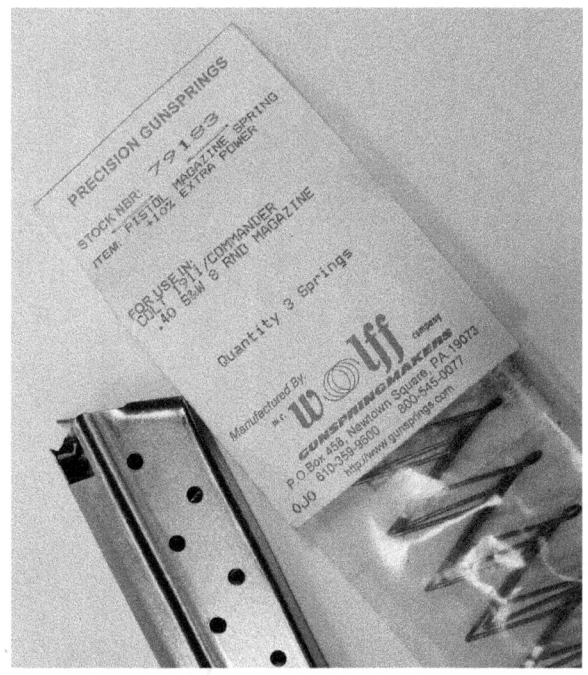

Many pistol malfunctions are magazine-related. Absent obvious damage, springs could solve feeding issues related to slide velocity.

be withdrawn through the rear of the slide for periodic cleaning. This part is caliber-specific, and the extractor on a properly tuned pistol will be set to a specific tension for proper rim engagement. Pre-chambering a cartridge can be hard on an extractor because the rim is normally fed through its claw from underneath (sometimes called controlled feeding). Lately, the external extractors common to many other pistols have appeared in 1911s. Either will work and the external spring-loaded claw does solve fussy tension issues.

Mainspring housings. The original design was a flat unit that followed the rear contour of the frame. A later "improvement" was an arched version, and the latest is a flat "bob-tail" with its lower corner removed for better concealment. The housings can be checkered, stippled, or grooved. Some look like steel but are actually plastic. In any case, the good news is that, like most other 1911 parts, the housing can easily be replaced with an after-market unit. Arched or flat, there really isn't one "best" type. Removal of the mainspring housing will relieve pressure on the hammer strut for subsequent disassembly, and besides containing the mainspring, it also captures the three-fingered spring that powers the sear, grip safety, and trigger bow.

Thumb safeties. Minimalist G.I. levers have given way to more generous pads and many are now two-sided designs that permit ambidextrous operation. Competition versions tend to be large but plenty of practical carry types exist. The bilateral versions often use the right-side grip panel to retain the extra lever – something to consider with after-market grips.

Today's popular features, rolled into this 1911, include the grip safety's extra speed-bump, and flat, checkered mainspring housing. The softened rear sight blade is another nice touch.

The left-side safety is the key to direct removal of the grip safety and other fire-control parts. With the mainspring housing removed, careful manipulation to an in-between setting will allow it to be drawn free when the hammer is back (attention should be paid to the detent plunger and spring). Other than the grip screws and mainspring housing, 1911 disassembly is pretty much tool-free.

A fitted arm on the safety extends within the frame to block the sear, so it should snap on and off in a positive manner. It needs to stay on "safe" in a holster, and it shouldn't bounce during recoil when "off safe." If the latter occurs, the slide's notch could eventually shear off the paddle from its axle. As for operation, the safety should remain engaged until the sights begin to index on a target!

Grip safeties. This second layer of safety *should* prevent a 1911 to fire unless it is fully depressed. However, the occasional pistol is out there with its grip safety pinned forward, serving as a ticking time-bomb. Be sure to check for proper function.

The old G.I. unit works, but some shooters can experience hammer bite related to its narrow profile. One hallmark of modern 1911 production is a beavertail version, which provides better looks and comfort with increased protection from the hammer. Refitting from the original Spartan design requires frame modification for most installations, so it's a gunsmith job. An extra speed-bump is a good idea; more so with a firing pin blocking design since the grip-safety needs full depression for reliable ignition. Fortunately, a beavertail grip safety is now a standard feature on many of today's 1911s.

Hammers. The original spur is largely passé in favor of "rowel" or "commander" hammers which typically sport a rounded thumb extension and milled-out center. Most are contoured for adequate beavertail grip safety clearance, with less chance of hammer-bite to boot. Occasionally, one could contact the bottom of an overhanging adjustable rear sight blade cranked down to its lowest setting; and again, note that although half-cock should be present, this setting is not a safe carry option!

Slide-stops. Some people add extended types, but a defensive pistol is better off without one. It could be accidentally bumped by a shooter's hand during recoil, locking the slide open prematurely. The extra mass could also cause the same problem through upward bounce.

Slide-stops are caliber-specific. To see how one works, insert the slide-stop into a field-stripped frame. Then *slowly* slide in an empty magazine while observing the activation of its arm upon contact of a small shelf on the follower. You can also try this with a loaded magazine to check for arm/bullet-nose clearance. The slide-stop's axle captures the barrel link after penetrating both sides of the frame. The forward spring-loaded detent in the plunger-tube housing helps hold it in place. Sometimes, the challenge is to avoid scratching the frame during reassembly.

Magazine releases. The standard low-profile button offers good protection from the inadvertent release of a magazine (caused by a holster or thumb during firing). Most right-handed shooters can reliably execute reloads through a simple flip of the pistol (lefties can use their trigger finger). I do own a few extended types with oversized buttons, but their use is confined to range work. Options include complete assembles or separate buttons and paddles. The latter types will require drilling and tapping of the standard release for mounting with a screw, while the complete after-market assemblies already have this work covered. In any case, a 1911's magazine release is removable. A small screw on its opposite side can be turned free from the frame as the button is partially depressed. Having gone the D&T route, I'd spring for a complete assembly.

Magazine wells (guides or chutes). A single-stack magazine can be more difficult to insert than a double-column type because of its un-tapered profile and a narrower frame opening. Some 1911s have beveled bottom edges, but competitors often upgrade to some sort of "speed-chute" guide. Some simple after-market magwells (Wilson) have thin ears that hook over the lower grip bushings between the grip panels and frame. Others are integral extensions of the mainspring housings, and

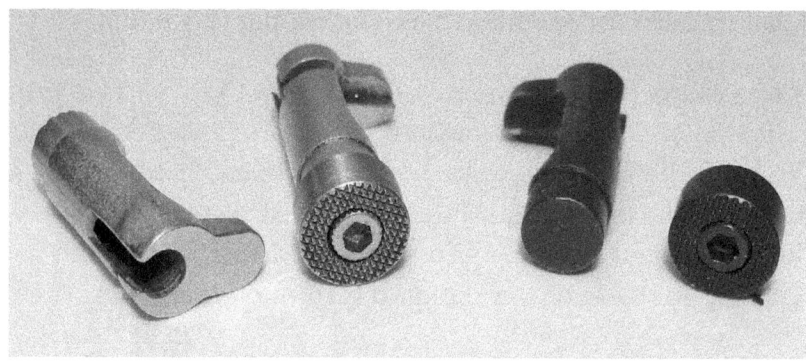

Aftermarket 1911 magazine release choices include add-on buttons or complete assemblies. The latter can be exchanged after rotating the small right-side screw 90 degrees. But for serious business, the standard design is more foolproof.

a few even offer detachable chutes. Some add bulk while other slim-line types are streamlined (when paired with thin grip panels). I've used all types with success, finding them useful in the dark. However, effective magazine insertion will usually require bumper-pad extensions. These rubber or plastic parts are often secured with two self-tapping screws – if corresponding magazine holes exist. So, think about compatible magazines before buying a mag-well - assuming you even need one.

I survived a war with the standard G.I frame and thanks to regular use, reloads became a subconscious act.

Mag-funnels can speed up reloads, but reliable seating will require bumper-pads. Actually, a factory-beveled frame will get you by and both pistols already have them.

Magazines. Seems like everyone and their uncle has built a 1911 magazine. The trick is to nail a good one because even the best pistol won't run reliably with so-so magazines. The original .45 type held seven rounds, with slightly tapered feed-lips that were narrower toward the rear for proper release of RN G.I. hardball rounds, but as other loads caught on including SWC types, lips were reconfigured to parallel and most of today's .45 ACP mags are built this way. Eventually, 8-round versions appeared. I have more confidence in 7-round types, but there are good brands of either capacity. Extended 10-rounders are also available, but they can exacerbate an uncommonly recognized problem.

The contents of a fully loaded .45 ACP magazine can develop plenty of inertia during seating, especially during lock-back reloads. During tactical reloads (round still in chamber) the underside of a forward slide will arrest the efforts of rounds to surge upward, whereas during lock-backs, brisk magazine seating can exert extra force on the lips. Eventually, they may spread, causing the top round to pop upward during chambering. The resulting ugly stoppage can't be cleared through normal "tap & rack" procedures since the rear part of the cartridge is typically wedged beneath the feed-lips, with its upper portion trapped between the barrel and slide face. At that point, the slide must be manually locked open so the magazine can be ripped free.

Shorter 9mm and .40 cartridges present less mass, but feeding is controlled by a spacer running inside the magazine's rear edge. Reliability may suffer simply because the 1911 was never designed to function this way. But Wilson Combat has saved the day more than once, and their 9mm type provides 10 +1 capacity with reliable feeding. But regardless of the caliber, occasional spring replacement won't hurt, especially with those seeing heavier use.

The Wilsons (and others) provide easier disassembly than the G.I. types, thanks to a bottom detent system (common to more modern pistols). Their removable base-pads are available in different thicknesses. I sometimes use bumper-pad types with or without a magwell, although the shallowest versions work fine with stock frames. Cushioned bottoms help prevent damage during speed-reloads (involving dropped mags), and provide extra purchase in the event of a stuck magazine. Regarding the 10-round .45 ACP issue, Chip Mc Cormick Corporation's (CMC) Railed Power Mags offer a great new solution through reinforced lips, formed by a dual-wall layer of stainless steel (also sold as 8 rd. types). Wilson Combat recently acquired CMC along with their well-known Shooting Star line that more closely follows the original 1911 pattern.

The original design with its welded bottom appears to have no ready means for disassembly. The trick is to load a few rounds and then insert something like a small screwdriver through a set of corresponding holes, which will trap a spring coil. Tension can be relieved as rounds are stripped out. Once emptied, the follower can be plucked out with the spring.

You might want to save one magazine as a reference guide for reassembly of the others. Numbering each tube can also help since, as often as not, stoppages can be traced to a faulty magazine.

Triggers. The original G.I. trigger was short but serviceable; however, since a Government Model can be disassembled by its user, aftermarket triggers soon appeared. Many are so-called "match triggers," sold with three-hole trigger bows that have set-screws in their faces. The initial idea behind the holes was to eliminate trigger mass for less chance bumping off a sear. These fancier triggers look cool, but the screw won't lighten your trigger pull; it's just there to limit excess travel during release. Ideally, a small amount should be present when the hammer drops; enough for proper sear clearance. At least an extra quarter turn is recommended, at which point the set-screw should be secured with a thread-locking compound. You can damage the sear/hammer engagement of a well-tuned 1911 by dropping its slide on an empty chamber. Without some cartridge resistance, the slide will slam home with extra force, causing hammer-bounce and burring of the sear. An improperly adjusted trigger screw or haphazard un-cocking technique can create the same effect as both parts rub together, so to drop the hammer on a match-grade trigger, either dry-fire the pistol or hold the hammer fully rearward while pulling the trigger until it can be eased down without sear contact.

Most commercial 1911s are sold with serviceable triggers, averaging somewhere around five pounds. Serious match shooters may run scary-light pulls below three pounds, but they're too light for defensive use. One attribute of all 1911 triggers is a distinct sear re-set point. With practice, it can be acquired for optimum trigger control and, at that point a 4 ½ - 5 lb trigger will serve admirably.

Plunger tubes. The Achilles Heel of the 1911 is the small horizontal housing above the left grip. It contains a tiny spring and two opposing detent-plungers which bear against the safety-lever and slide-stop. The "plunger tube" is secured to the frame by its two integral studs, staked from inside the magazine well. If the housing starts to separate, have it re-staked. (A few manufacturers, like Ruger, have machined plunger-tubers integral with the frame, effectively eliminating this problem.) The thumb-safety holds both plungers and their spring in place. The small spring will often have a small kink applied at its midpoint to prevent it from leaping out of the plunger-tube during disassembly, so if yours has a kink, that's a good thing.

The match-type 1911 trigger has an overtravel screw. Other features include an oversize mag button, checkered frame, magwell, and low-profile bumper pad. The Pachmayer grip panels are retained by hex-screws. The plunger tube is visible above it.

Most ambi safeties are retained by an arm extending beneath the right-side grip panel. Factor this in when shopping for replacements.

Grips. Plenty of great options exist here and adding a new set only requires a screwdriver. Each panel is secured by two screws which should be periodically checked for loosening. Each one threads into to a separate, shallow steel bushing, which is screwed to the frame by its slot in its face. Don't over-tighten your grip screws or they could drag out the bushings during removal. A bit of thread-sealer on the bushings is good extra insurance – but *not* on the screws. Thin panels are an option that can reduce grip size, but special shorter grip bushings will probably be required (otherwise, they'll protrude within the magwell). Some shooters may wind up with an ambidextrous safety, either as a factory feature or aftermarket addition. If so, there's a good chance the right paddle will be retained by a flat arm that extends beneath the grip panel. For this reason, a corresponding relief-cut is often machined into aftermarket grips; something to consider in advance.

Compensators and porting. A Google search of "race guns" will reveal all sorts of photos, showing modifications designed to reduce recoil. Muzzle-mounted "compensators" work by redirecting high-pressure gas through slots or ports. Most require special fitting to modified barrels and slides. They also work better with hotter calibers like .38 Super, simply because more high-pressure gas is available. That said, recoil was noticeably less in a compensated .45 ACP Clark-built pistol I owned. The compensator's chamber accumulated lots of hard-to-remove fouling, especially when lead bullets were fired.

Mag-na-port is a well-established firm that went another route, creating small ports in a barrel near its muzzle that vent pressure upwards. Their "Autoporting" design adds corresponding vents to semiauto slides. This $145 modification works, although recoil reduction is often less than a full-blown comp. Part of this is attributable to the extra mass of a compensator, which can change function dynamics (usually requiring a lighter recoil spring).

There are other issues to consider. Regarding compensators, holster fit may become a challenge. Although porting raises no such concerns, it can introduce hazards during some circumstances. Hip-shots are not recommended due to vented high-pressure gasses – no great loss as far as I'm concerned. Some projectile types can also raise havoc. S&W strongly advises against the use of lead bullets with a Performance Center compensator. Springfield Armory cautions against use of frangible loads with their ported Competition XD semiautos. It might be best to skip the whole idea on a carry gun due to increased size (compensators), increased muzzle-flash, and cost. Instead, invest the money in magazines, gear, and ammo.

Melted edges. Subtle rounding of corners or edges can improve ergonomics and carry comfort. This treatment is usually a custom upgrade, but you may also see it on some higher-end production guns. Compare a Kimber CDP (Custom Defensive Package) to their more pedestrian versions and you'll see the difference. Like metal-checkered frames, this "melt treatment" is sweet, but it jacks up the cost. The world won't end without it.

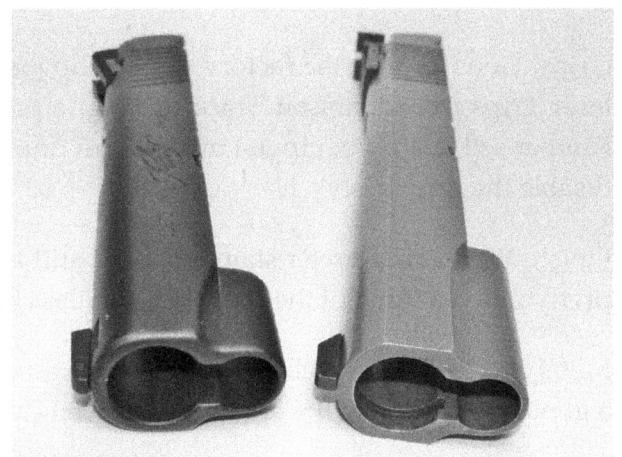

The softened corners of the Kimber slide are "melted". The dovetailed front sight is an improvement over the original staked design. The coned barrel accounts for the absence of an internal bushing slot.

Essential versus overboard. Many highly-customized Government Models are true eye candy, but the question is: how far do we really need to go? Money talks and many have a starting point of $3,000 or more. Don't despair. With a budget of under $1,000, somewhere between the original G.I. configuration and the higher-end pistols, a serviceable .45 ACP or 9mm 1911 can be found with a few useful enhancements:

Grip safety. A beavertail is worthwhile. Most of today's good 1911 candidates already have one. A speed-bump is good extra insurance for those who shoot with their support thumb under the dominant thumb.

Thumb safety. The G.I. type is skimpy and the race-gun types are often too large for practical use. I like ambidextrous types, but they add extra cost and complexity. A single-sided safety with a mid-size paddle will do and fortune smiles here, thanks to the competitive 1911 market.

Forward cocking serrations. They're nice but not essential, and they can be hard on holsters. They can also encourage careless placement of fingers near a muzzle.

Guide rod. Either type works, but a one piece full-length rod does permit easier disassembly with the paperclip trick. Don't let one affect your pistol choice, though. You can easily switch later for minimal cost.

Ramped barrel. If you skip a supported chamber in .45 ACP, .22 conversion unit options may increase, and that's how a .45 will probably come anyway. This feature is not essential with 9mm chamberings, but it is recommended for .38 Supers, .40s, or 10mms.

Magwell. The lowest-profile add-on chutes are nice, but a factory-applied beveled magwell will suffice. Beyond cost, an accessory well adds some bulk; although a slim-line version helps (better with matching thin grips). You can always upgrade later, and if going this route, a new mainspring housing is usually part of the well. Ed Brown, Smith & Alexander, Wilson, Dawson Precision, etc. are good sources.

Grips. Good chance the factory set will do just fine. If not, you can always change them later. The laser grips from Crimson Trace or Hogue present interesting possibilities, and some makers like Kimber sell factory-equipped models, but don't add a rubber slip-on grip-enhancing sleeve or you'll disable the grip safety!

Finish. Your call. I prefer stainless, but I still treat one as if it was blued steel. Nowadays, galling is pretty much a thing of the past with stainless frames and slides, but I also keep my slide-rails lubed.

Metal checkering. A well-checkered grip frame is a joy to behold, but it will increase cost. Truthfully, a good set of grips will work almost as well (while saving wear on clothing).

Sights. Again, your call, but think about any future upgrades and compatibility with your slide. I shop for rear sights with a forward-facing edge that can be driven against a belt for emergency single-hand slide racking. A fixed version is more durable, and can save some money, but it may not be spot-on. Adjustable sights will solve this problem while accommodating different loads. Some of the newest types are also quite compact and rugged. Either way, rounded blade corners can help avoid snagging. Consider Tritium night sights for 24/7 use.

Accessory rails. There's no disputing the value of a weapon-mounted light, but gun weight will increase and holster options may shrink. As for lasers, integral grip versions are practical alternatives for 1911s without rails.

Final contenders. Given the huge number of choices, an evaluation of every 1911 on the market just isn't feasible. Fortunately, there are a few solid choices from the middle of the pack. Cost will be greater than a basic run-of-the-mill Government Model, but the crowded market will guarantee features that were previously expensive extras. You'll find such pistols within the "production with enhancements" category below. Of course, everyone's situation is different, so some folks may choose to shop the higher tiers.

Custom 1911s. The pistols in this category come from highly-regarded pistol smiths. The gun itself could evolve from a customer-supplied 1911 or begin using in-house parts. Either way, rest assured the final product will be a precisely-fitted example of fine gunmaking with hand-checkered metal and other personalized details. The lead time could be long and the price *will* be steep, running into thousands of dollars. Among the prominent firms, you'll find Wilson Combat, Ed Brown, and Nighthawk Custom, etc. Many of these pistols start well above $3,500, although some also offer batch-built versions of semi-production status.

Semi-production. Here we'll find excellent limited-run pistols built with hand-fitted tool-steel parts, produced by Les Baer, Dan Wesson, STI, etc. Depending on final details, costs and waiting times could approach true custom builds, but most are sold with cataloged features for less. They'll often be found within the supply chain at either side of $2,000.

Production with enhancements. These off-the-shelf 1911s come from mainstream manufacturers and include the features listed above: beavertail grip safeties, extended safeties, etc. They make a great starting point, or for that matter, a completely serviceable pistol as is. Check out Colt, Kimber, Remington, Ruger, Springfield Armory, S&W, SIG, STI, and Taurus. Colt had some of its thunder stolen by the upstarts on the list, but they're back with a vengeance, the Competition Model being one good example. Springfield Armory's Range Officer line is laid out similarly, and with no disrespect to the others, Kimber alone can make your head spin. Ruger has also expanded its 1911 line. Like the rest, many of their well-appointed pistols retail at either side of $1,000. Street-pricing can be closer to $800, making the built-in extras more than worthwhile.

Basic. If you go this route, don't be surprised to find yourself shopping for extras that would've been included above – assuming they'll fit. A basic 1911 can be a good deal, coming in below $600, but some are built offshore with non mil-spec parts. Some custom 'smiths won't work on them for exactly this reason.

Whatever route you chose, spring for a few good magazines. Reliable function is impossible without them!

SEMI-GOVERNMENT MODEL CLONES

The explosion of concealed carry interest has resulted in many demure pistols chambered for .380 ACP and 9mm Luger cartridges. Their very small size precludes the use of a manageable blow-back design, and minimal space exists for a reliable striker-fired system, so back to the future we go with single-action designs that use a locked-breech system. Within the S/A category we'll find some interesting scaled down pistols that have much in common with a classic 1911.

Kimber's Micro-9s follow the general 1911 theme, but there are differences, one being the absence of a grip safety.

Browning. A close 1911 example is Browning's 1911 .380, which is 15% smaller than a standard .45 Government Model. That said, it isn't a true miniaturized copy; nor for that matter are most of the others. What sets the Browning apart is its in-between size, smaller than a true 1911, but large enough to remain shootable. It reminds me of my old Spanish-built .380 Llama. Browning also offers a neat .22 LR version.

Colt. The latest Mustang is an extension of their previous S/A .380s, which resembled 1911s on a much smaller scale. A grip safety is missing, but the Mustang Lite shares the polymer frame construction of the latest .380 Browning. An aluminum-frame Pocketlite is another option, and on both models, the Mustang's cocked & locked slide-notch is absent (common throughout many of these miniaturized clones).

Kimber. Known for an extensive line of 1911s, they have aggressively entered the miniature 1911 market with a series of Micro Pistols. The Micro 9 is indeed small, and the Micro .380 is even smaller. These aluminum-framed pistols lack a grip-safety, and the safety-locked slide feature is absent. However, at first glance, you can't help but feel you are looking at a 1911. The hardest part of buying a Micro would be sorting through the numerous options since everything is there, from melted surfaces to laser-grip options.

SIG. This well-respected pistol builder is another heavyweight miniature-1911 competitor. Their P-238 .380s follows the Kimber line with similar 1911-type controls. Like Kimber, they offer a small 9mm, in this case a "micro-compact," sold as the P-938 Equinox. Things get interesting due to a .22 LR version of the P-938, which can also accept 9mm conversion parts.

Springfield Armory. New for 2018 is another scaled-down 1911-type .380 like those sold by Sig and Kimber. This one is the Model 911, which also lacks a grip-safety or slide-locking safety. Being another locked-breech design, it's advertised as having an easy-to-cycle slide.

All the small 1911-type pistols are intriguing. The size difference between the .380 and 9mm Kimber or SIG pistols is minimal, so a final choice might be predicated more on recoil. These locked-breech pistols are, for the most part, easier to cycle than blow-back designs, but since they wind up in all sorts of unorthodox carry locations, their triggers trend heavier than standard 1911s. They can also be harder for some shooters to operate due to their smaller size, but practice should solve that issue. Of course, magazine capacity will be less, for the most part averaging around 6 rounds. Still, they make a sensible addition for 1911 owners seeking a backup-size pistol, thanks to a familiar manual-of-arms. Their drawback is use of proprietary parts, but that's less of a concern for a gun filling a secondary role.

THE P-35 BROWNING HI-POWER

Although this design pre-dates World War II, it's still one heck of a pistol. In fact, armed forces from both sides of the pond used P-35s as service arms. Although originally developed through the Belgian firm of Fabrique Nationale to meet new French service pistol specs, it was never adopted by France. Belgium, on the other hand, capitalized on a ready new source of innovative pistols. When the Germans captured FN's factory in 1940, they simply took over production of P-35s and applied Nazi markings. The Canadians among others were at the same time cranking out Inglis High-Powers, built from examples gathered through Britain. The result was an interesting collection of P-35s and globally-distributed spare parts. In all, Hi-Power pattern pistols have been used by 50 countries and more than a million have been built.

Current status. Until 2018, you could buy a Browning Hi-Power manufactured with Belgian parts and assembled in Portugal. Although Browning now lists it as "out of production," no doubt there are plenty new Hi-Powers still in circulation, along with lots of perfectly serviceable used versions. Seemingly out of the blue, to fill the recent void, LKCI began selling a Turkish-built P-35 as the Regent BR9, available in black Cerakote or stainless steel. Turkey now plays a significant role in the U.S. firearm industry thanks to modernized production technologies and less expensive labor costs. The success of this copy remains to be seen, but quality is supposedly quite good and cost is around $500 - $550, depending on the model. A remaining question based on mixed reports is the interchangeability of the Regent's parts.

Browning's 9mm Hi-Power was a high-capacity breakthrough offering excellent ergonomics. These features and its reputation for reliability still make the P-35 a good choice.

The platform. Count me as a fan of the BHP, which fits my hand better than just about anything else. Only the most recent spate of poly-

Single-Action Pistols | 255

mer pistols can give it a fair run in this regard. The Hi-Power is an old-school steel pistol, but -that's not necessarily a bad thing! It feels solid in the hand while maintaining liveliness, despite its generous capacity. Like the 1911, the P-35 is meant to be carried with its hammer cocked and on "safe," which means each trigger-pull is consistent, supporting a practical level of accuracy. The double-column 9mm magazine holds 13 rounds, plus one in the spout. It's great ergonomics and mild recoil make it a very shoot-able pistol.

Ammo and function. After the introduction of the .40 S&W, Browning adapted the High Power to this cartridge. The .40 required a slightly larger slide, resulting in a somewhat heavier gun. This caliber eventually disappeared, leaving just the 9mm Luger offering. Its 4 5/8-inch barrel and 32-ounce weight seem about perfect for all-around use. For most shooters, the grip angle makes it a natural pointer as well.

Reliability is excellent with modern Hi-Powers. Browning's imports were tuned to feed JHPs when expanding bullets became common, but hotter +P loads should be avoided. Some of the pistol's grace is attributable to less mass than other steel designs. The downside here is that, when factoring in the various licensed (or unlicensed) P-35 manufacturers, metallurgy can vary, so with hotter SMG-type loads thrown in the mix, cracked slides and frames can occur. On top of that, P-35 copies of questionable heritage have been built, so the safer bet is a commercial Browning or FN product. If buying a used Hi-Power, have a trusted gunsmith look it over. Assuming it passes muster, expect it to run a long time with good American-made FMJ practice loads in standard 115 or 124-grain weights. Run a couple boxes of defensive ammo through the gun to ensure reliability and note POI. Odds will be better of positive function if only 12 rounds are loaded into each magazine.

Again, spare magazines, parts, and grips are not a problem. Field-stripping is a cinch; much simpler than a 1911. Locking the safety into a disassembly notch will hold the slide rearward for easy removal of the slide-stop. At that point, the safety can be disengaged and the slide can move forward off the frame. Like many current pistol designs, the guide-rod/recoil spring and barrel can then be plucked out of the slide for easy cleaning.

Complaints. The Hi-Power has a magazine-disconnect feature, which prevents it from firing when removed. There are instances where I like this feature, but it can be a nuisance with the Browning. As designed, it impedes magazine removal. Instead of popping free, P-35 magazines need to be tugged out. More recent Browning magazines have a spring-loaded assist feature to overcome this hindrance, but any competent gunsmith can just remove the disconnect parts to solve the problem. Just remember: when done, the pistol WILL fire without a magazine (and any such modification could later be revisited during civil litigation). Another gripe with the P-35 involves its trigger. As issued it's okay, but far from match-grade. Due to its somewhat convoluted design, achieving a light pull is difficult and a distinct sear re-set point is absent, meaning you need to ride it all the way forward for subsequent shots; and the original safety was small and difficult to disengage. Browning's modern HPs solve this problem, and larger after-market levers can also be installed. Some people get pinched in the fleshy part of their hand by the hammer due in part to a short tang, but an average-size paw will be okay.

Upgrades. As an admitted High-Power junkie, I've rarely experienced hammer-bite. I wish it had a better trigger, but the pull can be improved to some degree by a competent gunsmith. The magazine issue is fixable. Accuracy can be tweaked from service-grade to slightly better with after-market barrels. Most of the commercial BHPs I've tested produced 5-shot groups averaging around 3-inches at 25 yards, although one did an honest 2 inches. Good sights help. Like most other pistols from this era, early P-35 sights were minimal. The recent commercial versions are better, but owing to the long-standing popularity of the Hi-Power, after-market sights are available.

There are several custom pistol smiths who specialize in Hi-Powers, as well as after-market parts. Nighthawk's gorgeous rendition is a recent example of the ultimate Hi-Power, replete with everything from fine finish to an extended beavertail tang. Cylinder & Slide Shop is another great BHP resource. BH Spring Solutions is also into Hi-Powers, including the new Turkish-built Regents.

A Browning I sorely miss was a hard-chrome version with adjustable sights and extended Cylinder & Slide Shop safety. A few odd-ball length Hi-Powers have been built, but unlike Government Model pistols, they're rare. Although the standard barrel length is around 4.7 inches, I have owned a couple of 6-inch GPs, imported by FN as competition pistols. They were interesting, but not nearly as practical in the long run.

Although imperfect, the H-Power is still a great pistol. I've owned somewhere around seven during the past thirty years. I was headed toward number eight – until another entirely new design appeared with equally great ergonomics. We'll give that one a look in the striker-fired section.

A VIABLE CHOICE?

A single-action pistol may or may not be the best option, depending upon personal factors. But if so, beyond the obligatory minimum of three magazines, plus a pouch and holster, a pistol-specific shop manual will also be worthwhile. If you buy a 1911 you may also want a bushing wrench. Even though a single-action pistol remains a great design, remember; the U.S. Military generally carried their 1911s in Condition Three. Internationally, so did most troops armed with P-35s. Another telling example is American law enforcement where, although a handful of agencies do carry Government Models, most do not. Most cops only shoot when you pay them to, but they still have an advantage over civilian users because of daily handling. Infrequent shooting *and* less handling make a case for a less complex system.

CHAPTER 20
DOUBLE-ACTION PISTOLS

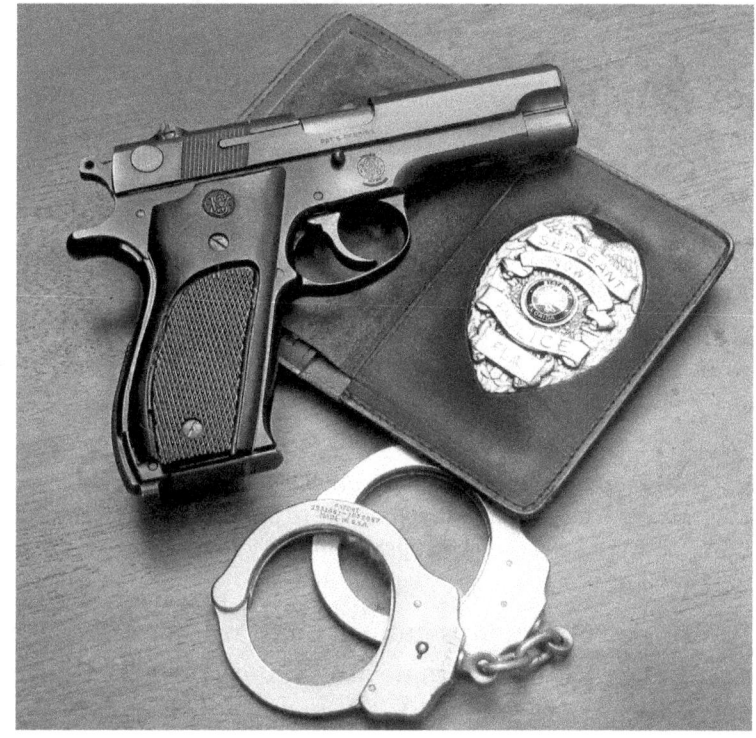

Let's clear the air. Some confusion surrounds "double-action" pistols, resulting from reference of semiauto designs that don't always fit this category. A garden-variety double-action revolver has a hammer which can either be trigger-actuated or manually cocked. In theory, a double-action pistol should function similarly, but "double-action" has been stretched to guns with heavier trigger-pulls - including striker-fired semiautos. For our purposes, a D/A pistol will be one with a trigger-actuated hammer. It may fire exclusively from this "double-action only" mode (DAO), or have true "double-action/single-action" capability (DA/SA).

Striker-fired pistols have made serious inroads into DA/SA sales, no doubt because of their relative simplicity, but a recent bobble in "the force" indicates renewed appreciation for semiautos that can be carried hammer-forward. Springfield Armory's new XD-E looks a lot like their striker-fired XD-series pistols. Look closer and you'll see an external hammer. On the other hand, the differences between Germany's pre-war hammerless Luger P-08 and its groundbreaking successor are much more obvious.

DOUBLE-ACTION/SINGLE-ACTION EVOLUTION

Walther really put the double-action pistol on the map with the battle-proven P-38, adopted by the German Army in 1938 as replacement for their aging P-08s. In fact, the 9mm Pistole 38 was a locked-breech adaptation of another immortal design: the blow-back circa-1930 Walther PPK. These DA/

Double-Action Pistols | 259

SA pistols are carried with their hammers un-cocked, like double-action revolvers. The difference is, after the initial long double-action trigger stroke, the pistol's reciprocating slide will automatically re-cock the hammer. The effort needed to deliver the first shot requires a very deliberate trigger stroke, whereas follow-ups can benefit from a shorter, lighter pull. However, the hammer will remain cocked when the shooting stops, requiring a conscious return to safer D/A trigger function. Manually controlling the trigger and hammer introduces the risk of accidental discharge during un-cocking, particularly during stress, so Walther came up with a mechanical alternative.

Walther's P-38 established the double-action pistol as a viable service design. More affordable to produce, it replaced the German Luger during WW II.

Traditional double-action. Walther's solution was a slide-mounted de-cocking/safety lever feature that's still in use today. Activation of the lever will safely drop the hammer, eliminating the need for trigger contact. The firing pin will be blocked while the trigger returns to its forward D/A position. Furthermore, if the lever is left in its downward de-cocking position, the pistol will be "on safe." The P-38's general features are recognizable in the U.S. M-9; itself a military version of the famous Beretta 92 FS. Pistols sharing similar function are sometimes called traditional double-actions (TDAs) - a fair description given their lineage.

As other manufacturers jumped on board, the DA/SA bandwagon, they preserved the basic function, but developed alternate de-cocking systems. These pistols are thus referred to as double-action/single-actions; "tradition" being omitted.

Double-action-only. Eventually, some pistols appeared with no single-action capability at all. Instead, each shot is initiated with the hammer at rest, through a long DAO trigger pull. This eliminates concerns over de-cocking as well as the related controls, resulting in an easy-to-operate design.

MORE ON DOUBLE-ACTION SYSTEMS

As it turns out, a hammer-fired pistol beyond the classic 1911 has appeal. In our experience, some shooters just want a visible hammer (like those common to SA/DA designs). It'll serve as an obvious cocking indicator, and the extra reassurance offered by hammer-down carry is the other attraction. The DA/SA negatives are extra complexity related to de-cocking, and disparate trigger pulls. Although both concerns disappear with DAO designs, the trade-off is a heavier trigger. Compounding this negative, DAO is more common in smaller guns, which can be inherently more difficult to shoot well regardless of their design. Fortunately, these supposed disadvantages can be overcome through structured practice.

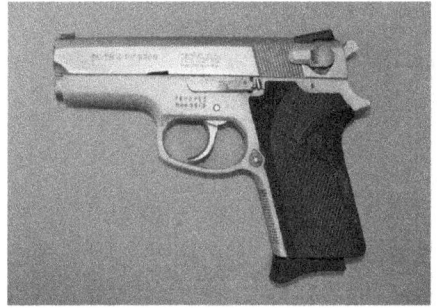  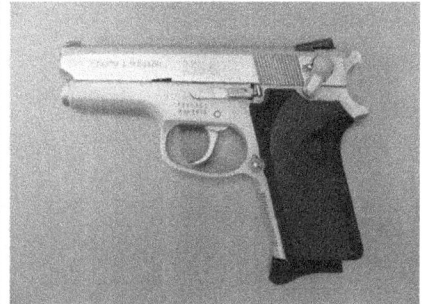

Traditional DA/SA modes (L-R): Double-action for carry, single-action, and de-cocked/on-safe. The lever also shields the firing pin from hammer contact (note its slightly rearward position).

DA/SA function. A TDA design like the P-38 won't discharge unless its slide-mounted de-cocking lever is returned to the fire position. For this reason, some DA/SA variants have been built with spring-loaded levers that *can't* be left on safe. S&W developed this option for their 3rd Gen pistols, and Beretta offers a de-cocking-only system for their M-92 platform, along with an aftermarket conversion kit. Sig went another route. Their practical frame-mounted de-cocking design employs a user-friendly spring-loaded lever that will safely drop the hammer through a swipe of the thumb. As soon as pressure is released, it'll pop back up to the fire-mode.

The Cold War era 9mm CZ-75 is a classic DA/SA design known for its good ergonomics and accuracy. It also uses a frame-mounted lever, but this one serves strictly as a safety. When applied, the pistol can be carried cocked like an S/A Browning Hi-Power or 1911. However, returning a CZ 75's function to first-shot D/A requires cautious manual un-cocking – after the safety is moved to its "fire" position.

A few other manufacturers including H&K have developed clever multi-purpose levers that can serve as both single-action safeties *and* de-cockers. If the hammer is cocked, the lever can be thumbed upward, placing the pistol "on safe," for S/A carry (like a 1911 or CZ-75). The normal downward swipe will return it to "fire" mode, BUT an extra deliberate pressure will safely de-cock the hammer. Of course, this active control must be properly positioned to the chosen mode of carry *before* the gun is returned to its holster!

FN pistols are held in high regard. Their DA/SA system incorporates a bilateral, multipurpose, de-cocker/safety.

Double-Action Pistols | 261

Note: one concern for DA/SA shoppers should be ambidextrous operation. Many are sold with bilateral de-cocking systems – something to consider for left-handed shooters.

De-cockers as safeties. During the time when SA/DA pistols reigned supreme, our agency went with manually operated de-cockers for an added disabling feature during some unique operational environments. Throughout the years, several LEO saves have been documented during struggles by quick-thinking application of a lever.

One might logically ask, "Why not just keep it on safe?" Well, over the course of one summer I tried to master the slide-mounted safety of a .45 ACP S&W Model 745 pistol, factory-equipped for competition. It functioned similarly, but wouldn't drop the hammer because this model was S/A-only. After weeks of enduring a beat-up thumb, I finally gave up. There were periods when I thought I had it nailed, but the inevitable fumble would follow. Finally, the light came on and I switched to a 1911, enjoying the positive ergonomics of a frame-mounted lever. We always gave our troops the option to carry their D/A 3rd-Gen S&Ws on "safe," but they had to demonstrate proficiency during live-fire. When the dust settled, nary an officer went this route, which is the unfortunate reality of a control so located.

Note: nationally, most folks just leave their slide-mounted levers in the fire mode, relying on the long first-shot trigger pull for safe carry. However, it is possible to inadvertently rotate the lever of a TDA design "on safe" during slide manipulations, and the often-taught "over-the-top" slide-grasp/release is one way to do this. We prefer the "sling-shot" technique with fingers intentionally indexed below the levers to keep them horizontal – or better yet, use the slide release during lock-back reloads.

S&W's Gen III Model 4006 embodied mid-1990 DA/SA design. Chambered for the upstart .40 S&W, it was built to last, and offered 12 +1 capacity.

DA/SA trigger skills. Effective use of a double-action pistol requires mastery of two different trigger pulls, but it's not an impossible task. The military has been using Berettas for over thirty years. The Illinois State Police adopted S&W 9mm Model 39s way back in the late 1950s. We used S&W Model 3913 and 4006, which were 3rd Generation types, for years with good results. It all boils down to proper training. In our experience, marginal shooters often cranked their first D/A shot, causing misses at further ranges. On the other hand, most of our seasoned revolver shooters made the transition without difficulty. A series of "controlled pair" drills with de-cocking in-between proved beneficial for everyone.

DAO trigger skills. Double-action revolver shooters will relate. Just think "revolver" with a long and heavy pull. On a positive note, each DAO pistol's pull will be consistent, if heavier than a striker-fired design. Yes, trigger-cocking a hammer requires extra effort, but in tight confines like pockets or purses, this isn't necessarily bad!

The double-action pistol today. Despite much stronger striker-fired sales, true DA/SA pistols are in no immediate danger of drying up. In fact, today's list is much longer than the few choices covered here. Hands-on experience drives our coverage. Let's start with a well-vetted U.S. Military pistol spanning three decades of steady use.

BERETTA PISTOLS

Just about all handgun-trained military personnel who served since 1985 will be familiar with Beretta's flagship TDA 9mm pistol. Same story for many law enforcement professionals whose agencies jumped on board the semiauto bandwagon shortly after the U.S. Military adopted the M-9. This era marked the start of wholesale transition from revolvers to semiautos, and since choices were more limited, the civilian M-92 FS version of the military M-9 was a logical pick. On the military side, plenty of grumbling ensued from old soldiers who reluctantly surrendered their proven 45-caliber 1911s. Some of it was no doubt justified given the status of mid-80s 9mm Luger projectiles, hampered more so by military FMJs. However, for better or worse, adoption did align US forces with other NATO elements, resulting in a handgun that could fire 9mm NATO cartridges.

Beretta 92 Series. The present 92 FS is an evolution of previous M-92 versions dating to 1975, and to some extent, it's fair to say this gun is still a work in progress. Beretta's basic TDA design has much in common with the German P-38, including an open-topped slide and locking-block system without a tilting barrel. The result is a reliable pistol with straight-line chambering from a double-column magazine (shades of a P-35), which eliminates the need for a feed-ramp. Since the upper surface of the slide is almost entirely absent, ejection is very positive with an added benefit of reduced mass. Disassembly is also simple. Furthermore, the 92 delivers good accuracy while offering a generous capacity of 15 +1 9mm rounds. It has decent ergonomics for most users - although it is a large pistol. Molded hi-cap polymer frames were still over the horizon during the birth of the 92, accounting for its larger dimensions, which were common to metal-frame guns. Weight was offset by a lighter aluminum frame, but no matter how we slice it, the Beretta's five-inch barrel translates to a "full size" pistol. Eventually, the 92 FS/M-9 led to all sorts of variants including shorter, "compact" models. The function of the Walther-type slide-mounted de-cocker/safety has been modified to meet various requests, and some guns have been built as DAO variants, with or without safeties. The increasing popularity of the .40 S&W resulted in a 96 FS, which was essentially the same pistol.

We have some experience with 9mm Beretta 92s, including joint military programs that were hosted on our range. As such, we'll defer to the T&E process that preceded M-9 selection, as well as its extensive use. Most of the malfunctions we noted were encountered by smaller shooters who had trou-

Adoption of Beretta's M-9 by U.S. Military forces during the 1980s ensured instant civilian success. Before long, equivalent 9mm Model 92s were everywhere.

ble establishing solid grips. We saw a few pistols choke during extremely cold weather, which we believe was attributable to lubricants. These stoppages were slightly out-of-battery slide returns, easily remedied by a bump from the shooter. I always enjoyed an opportunity to jump into a vacant slot with a borrowed M-9, finding each one eminently shootable thanks to its decent sights with longer radius. Recoil was extremely mild, permitting quick follow-up shots, and the generous 15-round magazines were handy during fast-paced combat course stages.

Meanwhile, one of our satellite state agencies procured a batch of .40 Beretta 96s. Compared to the 9mm 92/M-9 pistols, recoil was noticeably snappier. Gun life was shorter than expected, which may have been due to an improper maintenance regimen. As we understand it, Beretta has since made improvements to increase durability across the 92/96 series. A new .40 Brigadier also appeared with a beefed-up frame in the area surrounding the locking-block area. The larger .40 S&W rounds decrease capacity to 12 +1, still useful a useful compromise considering the same grip-frame size.

One often-cited Beretta liability involves the disassembly procedure, which some detractors claim is *too* easy. Some claim the slide can be ripped from its frame almost instantaneously through one fast grab that simultaneously activates the take-down lever. Having heard enough stories from reputable military witnesses, we believe it. No doubt, lots of practice is required to pull this off (literally), but the carry methods of most private citizens should minimize such risk. Ease of disassembly will then become a virtue, promoting regular maintenance. Another rumor involves catastrophic slide separations. Early on, some of these dangerous live-fire M-9 events were encountered, but a redesign ironed out this concern.

Recent improvements include a dovetail-cut slide permitting front sight replacement, and a stronger Picatinny-railed frame that can handle lights or lasers. For better or worse, a few polymer parts appeared to replace previous steel guide rods, trigger blades, de-cocking levers, and magazine releases. Beretta's metal-frame easily accommodates replacement grips including the excellent Crimson Trace laser types. The non-tilting barrel also works well when suppressed for those entertaining this option. Numerous other after-market parts are also sold for user customization. Since .22 LR conversion kits are available, a very useful pistol can evolve as resources permit. In fact, the ultimate Beretta has to be Wilson Combat's customized Brigadier Tactical, upgraded and tuned for total reliability.

The Beretta is well-made - and it runs. A 9mm 92FS may be an ideal choice from a prepping point of view, because of parts and G.I. magazines, the latter remaining abundant thanks to decades of military service. Somewhat ironically, although Beretta's M-92 series has achieved near-perfection resulting from 30+ years of improvements, the whole DA/SA concept is now overshadowed by a burgeoning line of striker-fired alternatives. One just appeared from Beretta, and another from Sig gave our M-9 the boot.

SIG SAUER PISTOLS

This company was founded as a joint Swiss and German venture, but has undergone some realignment since its 1976 inception. The present SIG Sauer, Inc. is based out of Newington, NH and has seen enormous recent growth. Having toured the plant, their manufacturing process appears state of the art; efficiently churning out a diverse line of U.S. built firearms.

P220 Series: This line began using welded-steel stampings, but a switch to CNC machined-steel parts appeared with U.S. manufacturing. No one doubts its solid construction, and Sig's hi-cap P226 has seen use around the globe as a military-issue evolution of their single-stack P220, both enjoying well-established records of reliability. The P226 is still sold in several configurations and calibers including 9mm, .40 S&W, and .357 SIG.

Here is my conundrum: Sig is an obvious frontrunner, by no one in our FTU circle has sufficient experience with these pistols from which to form evidence-based conclusions. The same can be said of several other great manufacturers, but in this case I have a trusted source. I'd bet my life on his opinions, because in this case he's done so, having carried Sigs on duty for most of a storied LEO career. But before drawing upon his experience, a quick overview of Sig's DA/SA pistols is in order.

Sig's P226 is a proven SA/DA design known for its great ergonomics. The frame-mounted de-cocking lever (above the mag button) moves vertically.

For starters, Sig opted for a strong alternative to the slide and barrel locking lugs common to previous 1911-based designs. Instead, an enlarged chamber portion of the barrel was redesigned to solidly mesh with a generous ejection port, providing an ultra-strong connection now in use by other manufacturers. Unlike many DA/SA pistols, the slide de-cocking system was eliminated in favor of the frame-mounted lever, located for easy single-handed operation. A downward swipe of the lever safely drops the cocked hammer, and upon release, its spring-loaded function immediately restores the gun to "fire" mode. No unwelcome surprises here; just remember to de-

Double-Action Pistols | 265

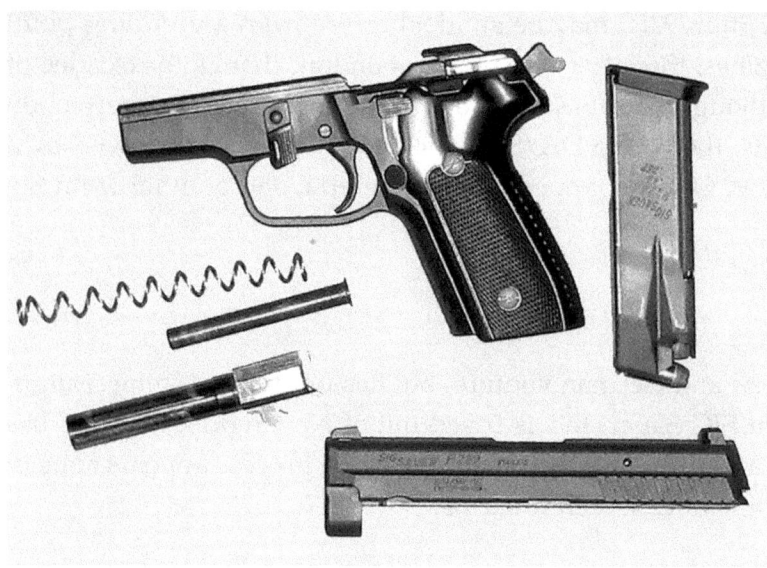

Like other Sigs, the P229 can be easily field-stripped after rotating a takedown lever above the trigger guard (photo by Domenic Leonard).

cock the pistol once any excitement ceases. There is no active safety, per se. Instead, inadvertent firing is avoided through use of a long, deliberate DA trigger stroke (Sig offers a few alternatives that shorten its length and reset). Of course, the hammer can also be manually cocked.

Beyond the spring-loaded de-cocking lever on the left side of the frame, a standard magazine release and slide release are the other active controls. Disassembly for field-stripping is easily accomplished via a rotating takedown lever ahead of the trigger guard. The frames are aluminum, and the slides can be carbon or stainless steel, with various finish options. The sights are dovetailed, and accessory-rail models are sold to accommodate lights or lasers. A useful bonus resulting from metal-frame construction is Crimson Trace's laser-grip panels, which work nicely with most existing holsters. Add a QD light to the rail and you can benefit from both as finances permit.

Perhaps the greatest attribute of all is a Sig's ergonomics. These pistols just seem to melt into the hands of most shooters, providing a natural target index. Of course, durability is a given, but accuracy is also renowned, often approaching match-grade levels without any compromise in reliability. Double-stack magazines offer plenty of capacity, and big-bore aficionados are in luck thanks to .45 ACP versions. Although metal-frame pistols tend to run heavier than most polymer types, a Sig's aluminum construction keeps a lid on overall weight, averaging around 34 ounces for a full-size 9mm P226. Recoil is surprisingly controllable thanks again to the ergonomics.

<u>Now, on to some first-hand experience from Sgt. Leonard, recently retired.</u> **Once upon a time, just after we started carrying the P-226 9mms, I was at the range with our traffic sergeant. I remarked that the Sig was probably the ugliest pistol I'd ever carried. He said something that is worth quoting: "The more you shoot it the prettier it gets."**

On ergonomics, Sigs had a revolution in grip design and they made a good grip a great grip. They offer Siglite night sights (Tritium), a shorter trigger for short fingers, and an, "Action Enhancement Package." Only some little old man locked in a vault under Mt. Washington knows what the hell they do, but they send your pistol back with pounds off the double action pull and ounces off the single action pull.

My first issued P-226 9 mm, came with shiny black plastic grips bearing cheap-looking molded checkering, but they fit the hand so well I never felt the need to mess with them. I don't remember the year but Sig "upgraded" their grips, but the new ones can be identified by the pebble grain finish on the panels. They look much nicer. Unfortunately, they make the grip too thick for my hands. I was surprised to find the thinnest grips were Pachmayrs. They usually make grips fatter, but not in this case. We switched to the P-226 in .40 S&W and I would have switched grips on my duty gun, but my time was running out so I didn't bother.

I was given a farewell gift of a new P-229 and I put the Pachmayrs on it. That's my current Sig. I then discovered Hogue had a new (at that time) line of aluminum grips that were very thin. I bought them and they're perfect. They look good, feel good, and are an excellent fit for my hands. I also had night sights and the enhancement package done to this P229.

As a Sig Armorer, I use to get lots of literature from Sig and one day I saw an update on 2,000 round servicing. There's a spring involved and it told the story of the real reason Sig went from the plain-but-comfortable grips to the nice-looking pebble-grain grips that turn the pistol into a club. Take off the right grip panel, and if it doesn't pop out and hit you in the eye, you'll see a spring; the trigger's action-bar return spring. This pushes a Sig trigger forward after firing. It hooks on at the front, and at the rear there is a nice little hole to hook it into. The problem is the hole is *not* where it goes. It goes on a rather crude notch cut into the plate that everything rides on. We are told repeatedly to instruct officers to NOT remove the right grip panel. It's considered part of the pistol's operating system and should be taken off only by a certified armorer. There is a groove cut into the inner face of the grip panel and the spring rides in this groove. If the spring comes off, or if you take it off, you'll invariably put the left end of the spring in that little hole and thus render the pistol unsafe. Do not take off the grips! There's nothing in there that needs cleaning or lube. The armorer will clean the two years of accumulated rubbish out and lube the pistol. The first time around I'd always catch one or two that took their grips off. Never after that, as they'd found out I knew they'd done it, and didn't know exactly *how* (Voodoo). We're getting to the point here.

Why did Sig go to these pretty but cumbersome grips? That spring had a service life of 10,000 actuations before breaking from fatigue. Sig instructs armorers to replace them every 5,000. They decided to fix the problem and came out with a new spring with a helix at the breaking point. The helix absorbed the fatigue and the springs never broke after that. But they introduced a problem of their own. Because of the coil, they were thicker than the old-style springs. Sig had to cut the channel in the grip panel deeper, but they just weren't thick enough to do that; the real reason Sig went with thicker grips.

For those with older Sigs who want to do the recommended service, you must know which spring you have. If you have the older spring, the grips won't go back on the gun when you put the new type in. Simple solution: just get the new Hogue aluminum grips and be better off all around. My advice? Send the gun to New Hampshire, have them do the Action Enhancement package, replacing an older spring with the new style. Send a pair of the new Hogues with the gun and request they put them on before they return it.

Sig's nearly indestructible P229 has been enhanced through aluminum Hogue grips (photo by Domenick Leonard).

I have been quoted as saying that Sig-Sauer makes the most durable, accurate, and reliable combat pistol in the world, bar none. Our original 9 mms? Twelve years without a single failure. Sigs don't break. Drop one in the dirt and when you fire it, it will clear itself. Over-lube it and when you fire it you'll see two streams of lube shooting out the front as it clears the rails.

Sgt. Leonard's final note: check out the Sig website for the new P-229 Legion Compact!

Sig's Legion. Nice! The Legion is a semi-custom Sig of sorts, with some useful Grayguns Inc. after-market features. In 9mm you get a 15+1 pistol with a 3.9" barrel that weighs 34.4 ounces – not a flyweight, but still manageable considering its integral accessory rail. A gray PVD finish graces the alloy receiver and stainless slide, which is fitted with tactically-designed, high-visibility "day/night sights." The frame is cut for a higher grip with nice metal-checkering and is graced with G-10 grips. The short reset trigger (SRT) reduces travel by a claimed 60%. Controls are slimmed for no-snag carry and front slide serrations are standard. The Legion is also available as a full-sized P226 in 9mm, .357 SIG, and .40 S&W (12+ 1); and all three calibers ship with three magazines. Looks like Sig has managed to build a nigh-perfect carry gun, complete with extra touches that many experienced shooters would add, but without going overboard. The sights and tuned trigger are the icing on the cake. The Legion was obviously designed with input from serious professionals.

Other Sigs. Another variant of note is Sig's all-stainless P226 Elite. Beyond a much heavier stainless steel frame with a beavertail extension, a checkered front-strap is included. An integral rail section permits use of lights or lasers, but night sights are provided as well. Sig's short reset trigger comes standard, forward cocking serrations adorn the slide, and the crowning touch is a pretty set of custom wooden grips. At a listed weight of over 42 ounces, this super-strong pistol may well be among the last surviving artifacts on Earth.

The $1,400 retail pricing of a Legion or Elite isn't cheap, but all things considered, these pistols are still a bargain since a standard P226 costs around $1,000. Of course, actual street prices are often considerably less. Those shopping for a smaller pistol may appreciate one of the P229 offerings. The

M11-A1 Compact comes to mind for a cost of around $1,100.

Speaking of costs, Sig also sells a less expensive .22 rimfire companion version of their P226, which is functionally identical. They have also gone after the competition market with a few single-action centerfire pistols, designed to compete with 1911s.

For down and dirty use though, the original DA/SA type is a practical choice, made even better when paired with a rimfire version. For that matter, Sig even sells centerfire conversion uppers for it, made possible by using one common frame!

CZ PISTOLS

While attending an out-of-state special-weapons program during the early 1980s, I noticed one federal participant with an interesting pistol that turned out to be an early CZ-75. When I asked him how he got it, the answer was "don't ask." At that time, Czechoslovakia was part of the Iron Curtain, so Czech-built arms were scarce. Still, word of an excellent double-action "Wondernine" had begun to seep out. Sure enough, this early specimen bore the reported painted finish instead of classic blued-steel. Fortunately, the curtain has since been cast aside, permitting CZ to prosper as a global player. The result is an ever-expanding line of CZ-75s - not to mention the establishment of CZ USA!

CZ 75 series. The all-steel CZ-75 is a classic example of old-school, solid steel machining. The pistol is an amalgamation of several good concepts including Browning's tilting barrel, a hi-cap magazine, true DA/SA capability, and a frame-mounted safety that provides a single-action carry option. The original CZ-75 version employs no de-cocking feature beyond the user's common sense. Ergonomics are outstanding, and accuracy is very good thanks in part to a reverse slide/frame interface with very little play. Whereas most slides surround their frame rails, a CZ-75's slide travels inside its frame, benefitting further from careful fitting. Disassembly is as simple as aligning both by two simple index marks, followed by removal of the slide-stop. From that point, field-stripping follows other common pistols for trouble-free maintenance. When it appeared, the dean of modern pistol craft, Col. Cooper, rated it as the best double-action; perhaps the most solid endorsement one could expect considering his strong preference for 1911s.

The 9mm CZ-75 earned early praise as a solid SA/DA design with a single-action option. Initially obscure in North America, the line has since expanded through CZ USA. Internationally, CZ pistols remain serious contenders.

A downside to the CZ-75 from the manufacturer's point of view was no patent, resulting in several close copies. The collapse of the Soviet Union resulted in expanded marketing opportunities, so an improved and patented CZ-85 appeared with a few new features including an ambidextrous slide-stop and safety. The further evolved CZ-85 B added a firing pin blocking mechanism and several cosmetic upgrades, and the excellent CZ-75 foundation remained intact. In fact, the pistol has come full circle thanks to the latest CZ-75 B designation, which incorporates numerous upgrades without compromising its nice lines. CZ advertises the 75-B as the most widely used military and LE pistol in the world, something which may come as a surprise to the tactical Tupperware crowd. The B-designation indicates continuation of the firing pin block, designed to prevent discharge if the pistol is ever dropped. Capacities are 16 +1 in 9mm and 10 +1 in .40 S&W. Being all-steel, it's no flyweight, but at 2.2 lbs (empty), neither is it a slug. Perhaps its strongest suit is a suggested retail price of around $600; quite a bargain for a well-machined steel handgun. Shooters looking for additional thump may consider the 97-B in .45 ACP. The CZ line has expanded to a large array of other variants, including some with polymer frames, de-cocking systems, and even dedicated competition models. One enduring attribute is reasonable cost of a CZ pistol despite solid and careful machining. A .22 rimfire conversion kit is another option for those seeking an affordable practice alternative.

MORE DA/SA PISTOLS

I still have my trusty S&W Model 3913. It's a compact 9mm with an aluminum frame and I've shot the hell out of it for more than two decades without so much as a single malfunction. I'm not positive of the exact year in which I bought it, but suspect it was during the late 1980s. Thanks to its 3 ½" barrel and single-stack frame, this lightweight 8 +1 pistol hides very well. Our Model 4006 .40 S&Ws were large, heavy, stainless steel pistols with a 12 +1 capacity, but they soaked up recoil and they worked. Of course, many such metal-frame D/A designs are now gone (including the above S&Ws), having given way to the latest bevy of polymer wonder-guns. Still, they can be found lurking in the nether regions of gun shop display cases. Comparing my M-3913 to S&W's latest 9mm Shield, capacity is identical and there's not a whole lot of difference in size.

S&W's Model 3913 9mm may be old-school by today's standards, but it works! One complaint involved slippery grips, remedied here with a soldering iron.

Most interestingly, Springfield Armory has unveiled a compact D/A polymer pistol which looks much like their striker-fired XDs. One obvious difference is the XDE's external hammer. Size-wise, it's similar to my trusty old M-3913, but its controls are more user-friendly and reminiscent of a 1911, meaning it can also be carried cocked and on-safe.

As for DA/SA pistols that offer an on-safe S/A carry alternative, I guess it can't hurt to have this feature. But for me at least, it defeats the pistol's main purpose; namely, the reassurance offered by hammer-down carry.

DOUBLE-ACTION-ONLY PISTOLS

The pistols dominating this field are mostly smaller-sized guns, the largest being more on the order of today's "compacts." Many others are pocket-sized types, chambered for .380 ACP or 9mm Luger. Their heavier DAO triggers can provide an extra measure of assurance during deep-cover carry, but capacity will be limited along with range and terminal effects. So, for the most part, a DAO pistol is a better second-gun choice when concealment becomes the priority.

As such, these semiautos fill niches formerly occupied by small D/A revolvers. Most have shorter track records, although some now qualify as "widely distributed." A few with which we have some experience are Kel-Tec's P-series, Ruger's LCP series, and S&W's Bodyguard. All three are locked-breech, polymer-frame DAOs that won't drain a savings account. Others mentioned for reference include the North American Arms Guardian, Remington RM380, SCCY CPX series, Taurus Curve, Beretta Pico, etc.

Kel-Tec. One of our instructors regularly carried a 6 +1, P-3AT .380, thanks in part to its feathery weight of around 8 ounces! One of his gripes was the lack of a last-shot lock-back feature, and the other was a slight predisposition to rust because of a carbon-steel slide. A somewhat larger 9mm PF-9 remains untried by us, but weighs less than 13 ounces – with an accessory rail to boot.

Ruger. Other cadre and trusted friends use .380 Ruger DAOs, which have morphed through several iterations. Ruger's 6 +1 LCP weighs a shade under 10 ounces. The LCP II adds a lock-back feature and a Glock-like trigger for a reason. It's a single-action version, reducing trigger-pull weight from over 10-pounds down to 6-ish. The LC380 jumps up a full notch dimensionally, offering a 17-ounce, compact size pistol with less recoil than a 9mm in an easy-to-operate 7 +1 package. The similarly-sized 9mm LC-9s are actually striker-fired guns.

S&W. I own a .380 Bodyguard for the reasons detailed. This DAO pistol met some personal requirements beyond small size, such as replaceable sights and a lock-back feature. It also possessed features common to the larger, striker-fired M&Ps in my possession. At around 12 ounces, the 6 +1 Bodyguard is still a small pistol. I chose an external-safety version sans the factory laser option, and just added high-visibility after-market sights. Since then, S&W has acquired Crimson Trace, bringing integral lasers home to roost with more affordable pricing.

DAO limitations. A size-driven challenge for most of these guns is establishment of an effective grip.

S&W .380 Bodyguards, shown with and without a laser. Not much difference size-wise, or in cost.

Usually, the pinky of the firing hand will be adrift if not its adjacent finger. While extended magazine floor-plates are sometimes an option, they can also be self-defeating given the primary mission of reduced gun size. Access to controls can also pose problems, especially for those of us schooled on more conventionally-sized pistols. It may also take some doing to develop an effective DAO shooting technique, but that's a valid reason for extra range time. A good starting point is 5-7 yards, but with practice you might see useful accuracy at double these distances. Of course, DAO pistols generally lack a hammer-spur since manual cocking isn't possible. Many such designs locate it deeper within the slide for increased protection from snagging.

Some other small pistols from Kahr and Ruger appear to be DAOs, but are actually striker designs. Regardless, most of these small pistols are carried a whole lot more than they are fired. For this reason, long-term durability is less of a concern.

D/A SUMMARY

For those already comfortable with a double-action trigger, a DA/SA pistol remains a viable choice. Military personnel trained on the Beretta M-9 come immediately to mind. For others, a look at the latest genre of striker-fired, polymer-framed pistols might be the better bet. In fact, the military is now making this move through a switch to their polymer SIG. Unlike many other simple striker-fired offerings, this one will have a frame-mounted safety lever. Shades of the 1911, perhaps?

CHAPTER 21
STRIKER-FIRED PISTOLS

A striker-fired pistol design is nothing new by itself. What is new is the incorporation of molded polymer frames and modular grip inserts that offer good ergonomics and a tailored fit without undue expense. The material seems to soak up some recoil, more so in conjunction with a closer grip-to-bore axis now seen with greater frequency. We can thank Glock for popularizing the general concept.

Inevitably, other makers followed suit with their own polymer-frame pistols, most of which employ steel inserts to gain a durable slide interface. The latest is a move from permanently molded-in rails to replaceable steel chassis, some complex enough to constitute a serial-numbered firearm; at least, as far as ATF is concerned. An advantage of such modularity is the possibility of different grip shells, sometimes offered with various length slides, that permit a multi-purpose handgun. Another evolution is polymer-pistol accuracy, which seems to have improved across the board, with 25-yard five-shot groups of two inches (or sometimes less) becoming common. As for weight, aluminum was the lighter option until polymer arrived. Manufacturing costs are also cheaper since frames can be molded instead of machined, so it's beginning to look like the days of steel-framed pistols may be numbered.

Striker function. A striker is a spring-loaded firing pin that does the job of a pivoting hammer. In most pistols, the striker is partially cocked during cycling, which shortens and lightens the trigger pull. A more complete description of striker function is forthcoming in the Glock section, a pistol which shares inherent disassembly concerns common to other striker-fired brands. Mainly, some means must exist for the striker to disengage from its sear during the disassembly process, explaining why a Glock must be dry-fired prior to field-stripping. A modicum of common sense would dictate unloading the pistol first. Nevertheless, some people continue to jeopardize the gene pool by surviving disassembly-related ADs. Recognizing this pitfall, other striker-fired manufacturers have come up with alternate disassembly systems. With an S&W M&P, a small sear-release can be tripped through the open slide - or you could just dry-fire the pistol, which S&W is not about to suggest.

A partially-cocked striker alleviates concerns (whether warranted or not) about a fully cocked hammer, and complete cocking requires less effort than most conventional DA systems. A manageable trigger can be produced with the added advantage of a consistent release. To prevent the striker from being inadvertently compressed to the point where ignition is possible, a trigger blocking system is commonly provided. Most often, it's a separate blade in the face of the trigger (Glock), which will disengage upon finger contact. Others (S&W) use a two-piece articulated trigger. The general idea is that the pistol can't fire unless trigger contact is established, so the primary safety is really between the shooter's ears.

Most striker-fired pistols employ a trigger-blocking system. S&W uses an articulated two-piece trigger with a small blocking tab, disengaged through pressure on its lower section.

THE GLOCK

When it appeared back in 1982, the Glock was an oddity. I remember looking at one and wondering who would ever buy one. Well, as it turned out, probably somewhere around half of the law enforcement community did, including me. The Glock's simple design, consistent trigger, and high capacity were the key selling points. A 9mm Glock 17 was a quantum leap above a 6-shot revolver, with three times the firepower, for no real increase in cost. The well-timed emergence of a hi-cap .40 S&W version didn't hurt Glock sales, either.

Any doubts about the durability of polymer pistols have long since been dispelled by numerous Glocks with ridiculously high round-counts. Within law enforcement circles, training was also simplified, compared to DA/SA pistols like Berettas, Sigs, or S&Ws. A Glock's active controls boiled down to a slide release and magazine release, with no need for de-cocking systems or cocked hammer concerns. Instead, Glock relies upon a "safe-action" trigger to block its partially-cocked striker. The striker is a heavy spring-loaded firing pin with a downward projecting lug, which becomes fully cocked by the trigger linkage as pressure is applied. When the striker is fully retracted, its lug disengages from the trigger linkage, permitting it to lunge forward as a firing pin. Upon discharge, the slide cycles, returning the striker to its partially-cocked, drop-safe condition. There is no second-strike capability, but simply racking the slide will restore the normal sequence.

As for the "safe-action" trigger, a narrow independent blade within its face must be simultaneously depressed for the trigger itself to articulate. In theory, if Rule #3 is observed (finger off trigger), the pistol shouldn't fire. Of course, during the 80s, semiauto pistols were relatively new to LE circles. Revolvers had ruled supreme, and their heavier D/A triggers apparently offset some sloppy trigger-finger discipline. A heavier

Similar function is good when multiple handguns are employed. Operation of this 9mm G-43 is identical to other Glocks, known for their simplicity.

"NY Trigger" was one early fix, but the real answer involved better training. Like other new technologies, a learning curve ensued which now extends to other striker-fired designs. Alternate carry methods and appropriate dress are recognized as essential concerns for protection from trigger interference. However, if nothing enters the trigger guard, you can drop a Glock off a tall building and it won't fire (good chance it won't break, either).

A web search of "accidental discharges" will reveal a number involving Glocks. Some will also relate to "kabooms," a reference to some sort of pressure excursion. As for ADs, Glock was really at the leading edge of many similar designs, primed to reveal obvious gun handling flaws and other less-appreciated hazards. The sheer volume of its distribution is no doubt another factor related to such web hits. As for kabooms, we suspect many could involve errant 9mm cartridges that become lodged in .40 bores during ammo mix-ups (something we go to great pains to avoid during range programs). Also, Glock chambers offer a bit less support than some other types, but the design is safe with quality ammo. However, plain lead bullets should be avoided, primarily because of Glock's rifling style which provides less bite, but also to preclude lead buildup in the forward chamber area that could prevent full cartridge seating. Disconnector timing is a bit more generous so the gun could *possibly* fire just a tad out of battery, resulting in case rupture - maybe.

Somewhere along the way in pistol training, use of slide-stops during lock-back reloads fell out of favor. Instead, an over-the-top slide grasp & release technique grew legs, justified by requiring less fine-motor-skill. We've always found this odd since nearby magazine release buttons seem to offer

With just two active controls excluding the trigger, Glocks are indeed simple. Disassembly requires a dry-fire, followed by depression of opposing metal tabs above the trigger.

Simplicity extends to reassembly. No fiddling with the tabs. Just slip the slide-assembly back on the frame and you're done.

Although known for polymer hi-cap pistols, Glock addressed CCW demand through a series of smaller versions. Shown top to bottom are a 9mm G-26 (Gen 4), a 9mm G-43, and a .380 G-42.

no such problems. However, a Glock slide release is a minimalist metal stamping which affords a bit less purchase than others. It may also be more susceptible to wear, possibly explaining a switch to the alternate release method. As for magazines, earlier polymer versions tended to bulge when loaded, making them more difficult to remove. We've also seen a few fly apart in the cold upon contact with hard ground (later types have a metal liner which seems to help). The sights are also plastic and more prone to damage, with the front sight sometimes becoming a casualty during single-handed tactical manipulations. For the most part though, this is all nitpicking. Bottom line: Glocks are good pistols.

With only 34 parts, it's a simple design, and unlike most all-steel pistols, no fitting is required. Disassembly is extremely simple, so maintenance is a breeze. However, the trigger must first be pulled, which can occasionally (and inexcusably) result in a very loud noise. Put your thinking cap on first, and ensure the gun is unloaded! Like most other pistols, this one will fire without a magazine, so find a home for it first, and then clear that chamber before pressing the trigger! Next comes the easy part: after pulling the slide rearward just a tad, retracting two small metal tabs will allow the slide-assembly to be drawn forward and clear of the frame. The recoil spring and guide-rod can then be plucked from the underside of the slide, along with the barrel. Reassembly is even easier since you don't have to mess with those tabs. Just slide the whole upper on to the frame!

A closer look at the G-42: Owners of full-size Glocks will be right at home with this scaled-down .380, or slightly larger 9mm.

This Gen 5, 9mm Glock 19, incorporates a Vortex Viper MRDS. BUT, a set of high backup iron sights are still there, just in case.

You can buy a Glock in several different calibers and configurations, from very small single-stacks, through full-size duty weapons, and longer competition models. One great selling point is that they all work pretty much the same, whether as a small .380 or a big 10mm. The larger M-21.45 ACP can be had as an SF version with reduced grip dimensions. The Gen 4 includes interchangeable back-strap sections, better grip texturing, reversible mag-releases, and captive dual recoil spring assemblies. The latest Gen 5 dispenses with molded in grip finger grooves and adds an ambidextrous slide-release along with a few other upgrades including a move to more conventional rifling.

GLOCK PISTOL SAMPLER

Model	Capacity	Caliber	Bbl	Wt. Empty	Wt. Loaded
42	6 +1	.380 ACP	3 ¼"	13. 76 oz	17.29 oz
26	10 +1	9mm	3 ½"	21.71 oz	26.12 oz
19	15 +1	9mm	4"	23.65 oz	30.18 oz
17	17 +1	9mm	4 ½"	25.06 oz	32.12 oz
27	9 +1	.40 S&W	3 ½'	21.89 oz	27 oz
22	15 +1	.40 S&W	4 ½"	25.59 oz	34.42 oz
30	10 +1	.45 ACP	3. ¾'	26.30 oz	33.71 oz
21	13 +1	.45 ACP	4.6"	29.84 oz	38.48 oz
20	15 +1	10mm	4.8"	30.89 oz	39.71 oz
40	15 +1	10mm	6"	28.15 oz	40.14 oz

Striker-Fired Pistols

The weight of a fully loaded 14-shot Glock Model 21 .45 ACP pistol is the equivalent of an empty 1911. Capacity was one advantage that put Glock on the map to begin with. Ironically, this truly innovative design has been eclipsed by several other feature-laden newcomers, so a few minimal concessions appeared like Gen 4 grips. Unlike some rivals (except for a military MHS submission), Glock has so far eschewed a manual safety lever, standing by their simplistic safe-action design. Nevertheless, Glock remains the undisputed polymer icon, even rivaling some steel-framed legends. A Government Model of some sort has always been THE American pistol, but Glock now appears to be standing head-to-head. A clear indicator is the emergence of custom after-market Glock parts, including match triggers, trick slides, threaded barrels, and even .22 LR conversion kits. Like the 1911, some gunsmiths also specialize in highly customized Glocks capable of generating polymer envy. No doubt about it; Glock is well-established.

Aftermarket parts and custom guns? Beyond its stippled frame, match barrel, and tuned trigger, this tricked-out Glock from ZEV sports a slide machined for optical and iron-sight inserts.

Some Glock owners may want a companion carbine, capable of sharing the same magazines. If so, several new 9mm AR-15s have appeared with dedicated Glock-magazine lower receivers. Unlike common gas-operated 5.56mm/.223 ARs, the pistol caliber versions run as blowback designs. They generate a bit more recoil, but are easy to disassemble and maintain. A shoulder-fired weapon that can run off pistol magazines has much appeal, but some Glock types lack a last-shot lock-back feature - something to consider before buying. A further concern for hunters will be 9mm carbine power, adequate for defense within reasonable ranges, but iffy on larger game like deer. Although velocity does improve somewhat in a 16-inch carbine barrel, the gain is much less than the several hundred feet-per-second we could expect from a .357 Magnum. With a 9mm, the increase may be more on the order of 100 fps or less. Still, the concept is a neat idea! Check out Ruger's latest PC-9 carbine with QD take-down capability.

One observation about Glock fans is their nearly religious devotion to this pistol. Any negative comments call for burning at the stake, preferably over a low flame. Regardless, many striker-fired alternatives have appeared, and some are darned good pistols. Imitation being the most-sincere form of flattery, most have a suspiciously similar trigger and an obligatory polymer hi-cap frame. Of course, each one is touted as the best, which can lead to some serious head-scratching by prospective buyers. I'm not even going to attempt to list all the polymer choices. Instead, I'll present a rival we've used extensively since 2008…

SMITH & WESSON'S MILITARY & POLICE PISTOL LINE

Don't confuse S&W's latest M&Ps with their older revolver line. We're talking about an entirely new semi-automatic pistol that bears strong resemblance to a Glock. Since its introduction in 2005, the M&P Pistol line has grown considerably to include a series of much smaller variants. But before getting into those, let's start with the standard-size pistols that form the backbone of this system.

The M&P Pistol. Our Firearms Training Unit tested various 9mm and .40 M&P versions during mid-2008. S&W sent us five models and we pretty much shot the hell out of them, cleaning only when our conscience got the better of us.

The first thing we liked was the ergonomics. These pistols felt great in our hands and were very shoot-able. As an old hand, I initially greeted the M&P with a loud yawn, but that opinion quickly changed after the first range session. Running a 4 ¼" 9mm against my custom 4" 9mm Wilson 1911, the S&W seemed simpler to use, and good hits were just as frequent. Say what? The M&P was death on falling plates and proved very effective during general combat-style speed shooting. The high grip, relative to its bore, really cut down on muzzle flip, permitting fast target transitions despite its 27-ounce weight (empty). Next, we broke out a 5" 9mm T&E Pro, which behaved more like a .22 rimfire. We switched out some 4 ¼" 9mm and .40 uppers because we could and the guns still ran fine. Their modular design also appeared armorer-friendly. Comparing it to other polymer wonder-guns, we really liked S&W's latest M&P.

S&W's Military & Police (M&P), shown here as a standard-size 4 ¼" model. The 9mm and .40 S&W are the same size.

Long story short, after adopting this system as a statewide replacement later in 2008, we ran our initial batch of 175 M&Ps hard. We've since added more, from which we feel qualified to draw a few conclusions. The comments that follow will mostly apply to 9mm and .40 S&W models with 4 ¼" barrels, minus any external safety levers. However, we've also played with compact and long-slide versions. I own a 5" 9mm Pro and have fired it extensively. S&W also sells other calibers including .357 Sig, .45 ACP (on a larger frame), a .22 LR version, and a new .380 ACP. The latest rimfire M&P is S&W's second variation, now built in-house, unlike their initial import. The .22s are externally similar, but internally they are totally different hammer-fired designs. The same is true of the latest .380, which is listed as a Shield, along with other small striker-fired pistols that evolved from M&Ps. In fact, S&W's entire M&P line is now a bit different because, after ten years of production, S&W used their experience to launch a second generation of M&Ps, known as 2.0s (the rimfire and Shield versions will be examined after a closer look at their progenitors).

As for our 1st Gen M&Ps, the feedback from several hundred agency users has been very positive. Each pistol came standard with three interchangeable grip inserts in small, medium, and large. The latest 2.0 includes a fourth medium-large for even better individualized fitting. They can all be switched out to provide a back-strap capable of accommodating just about any adult hand. The 18-degree grip angle was developed after much research and the gun seems to point naturally for a wide variety of shooters. The ability to personalize grip fit helps and the process is quite simple. A 90-degree twist of a bottom-mounted retaining pin will allow it be withdrawn, freeing up the insert. Each grip-insert is labeled on its underside to indicate the size. The inserts are flexible and the frame is textured, so overall grip purchase is positive. The 2.0's texturing is a bit more aggressive, which might raise complaints from *some* users. If so, S&W is still offering both generations.

A 3-slot rail section is molded into the dust-cover for attachment of lights or widgets. The sights are solidly mounted within dovetails, meaning they can be replaced, and they're steel, so durability is excellent. All our M&Ps have fixed night sights, which are properly regulated for our 124 gr. 9mm and 165 gr. .40 loads. The standard sights are three-dots, but other factory or after-market options are available. My Pro 9mm came with a fixed rear sight, and a fiber-optic front sight. It now sports a Dawson adjustable rear sight and correspondingly taller green F/O front.

More M&P models have surfaced, along with aftermarket parts. The Pro (top) has a custom barrel and sights, while S&W's V-Tac sports a racy FDE finish.

The M&P slides and barrel are stainless with an attractive, dark "Armornite" nitride finish (like Melonite) that has proven extremely durable. Besides good wear resistance, we've experienced no rust issues despite our coastal location. Some of 2.0s can be bought in a Cerecote FDE finish, which is applied on top of the standard corrosion-resistant nitride. A standard addition to all 2.0s is a smaller series of forward scallops for additional slide-grasping purposes. The barrel hoods have chamber-check ports and clear caliber markings (some 2.0 models also offer a new tactile loaded chamber indicator). The extractors are truly industrial strength, which is both reassuring and useful if a stuck cartridge ever needs to be cleared.

The metal magazines bear caliber markings and numbered round-count holes, with capacities of 17 & 15 rounds in 9mm and .40 (the .45s hold 10). The magazines drop free and quick reloads are a snap thanks to a generous well. The slide-stop is ambidextrous with a paddle on each side (although left-handed shooters may need extra effort to use it as a slide release). The magazine release can be switched to the opposite side without difficulty.

The trigger is an articulated two-piece design. Pressure on the tip cams a tab out of engagement with the frame so it can travel rearward. The pull of our service-grade models runs around 6 pounds and offers a tactile sear re-set point. The Pro-series trigger is lighter. Mine scales 4 ½ lbs and has a better re-set point. Meanwhile, the entire 2.0 line has since been upgraded to come closer to the Pro's trigger. The triggers all feel very good. I could've added an after-market trigger to my Pro, but it seemed fine as-is. A standard 2.0 trigger runs around 5 ½ pounds, but its reset is more in line with that of a Pro, so it should prove very shootable.

Our Gen 1 M&P accuracy is about on par with the other types of plastic pistols, running in the neighborhood of 3" at 25 yards. However, mechanical accuracy alone can be deceiving. Ergonomics play an important part in this equation. We watched shooting improve across the board after the switch from older 3rd-generation DA/SA S&Ws. Everyone fired 500+ rounds during the transition and they all left happy. It appears that the latest 2.0s might offer better accuracy, perhaps in part because of increased frame-rail engagement surfaces. Their new extended stainless chassis provides greater rigidity, and it also includes the pistol's serial number, which is visible through a port located in the polymer frame. Either gun is externally similar enough to fit existing M&P holsters.

Of course, just about any system has issues and the M&P is no exception. If you put a huge amount of ammo through an M&P fouling can accumulate in the striker (firing pin) channel. Cleaning the breech-face with it oriented up will allow solvent to seep into that area, and gunk will gradually build up until a light strike occurs. You won't get a second-strike until you rack the slide, which is basic remedial-action anyway. We've only seen this on one batch of range guns that saw daily use for several months. Another earlier issue supposedly involved "dead triggers," which occasionally failed to actuate the striker. Perhaps because we waited a while for the line to mature, despite a huge amount of use, we've never seen one.

S&W said we might notice a few right-hand slide-stop paddle breaks and we did see a handful, which were normally discovered by lefties. The pistol still runs fine since that control is ambidextrous, and this problem has since been fixed. We found a couple cracked forward chassis/rail sections, but these modular inserts were easily replaced. They occurred on a series of extremely high round-count .40s. Such an event with a steel-framed pistol would have wrecked the gun. In any event, the latest beefed up 2.0 chassis will probably solve this concern once and for all. We saw some chewed up plastic where the guide rod head contacts the frame. It doesn't affect function and the newest M&P frames have a reinforced steel contact surface.

Something we worry about with any striker-fired design is a discharge caused by a sweatshirt (or other foreign object) getting tangled up inside the trigger guard during re-holstering. Like any Glock owners, M&P users should dress with this in mind and select appropriate carry methods. External safety models are available along with key-lock variations. A lanyard-loop is another grip disassembly-pin option that can be quickly installed by the user. Some may disagree, but I think a manual thumb-safety on a striker-fired pistol is not a bad thing. The Model 1911 has been so-equipped for decades.

The longevity of a Glock is now legendary, but S&W's M&P may also be long-lived. Supposedly, there is a 9mm in Belgium with a documented round-count exceeding 200,000 rounds! Speaking from personal experience, our M&Ps have now seen nine years of steady use, and some have crossed the 25,000-round mark. Our multi-day basic pistol school continues to be a good test, during which each shooter fires 750+ rounds; often in miserable conditions. Snow and rain are common, so empty magazines take a beating as they lay in wet gravel and mud. We usually clean the pistols on the afternoon of day #2, saving the next session for last. We fire some frangible loads on reactive steel, and a huge amount of Federal American Eagle FMJ on cardboard targets. Older, recycled Speer Gold Dot JHP duty loads are reserved for night-fire stages. The M&Ps just eat them all up. One concession: we do maintain a collection of dedicated range magazines for the basic schools. They are possibly the most often-dropped objects in the state.

You can expect an M&P to run with only occasional cleaning, and it's so easy to disassemble that neglect is inexcusable. The grip retainer pin can also be used to flip the little sear-deactivation arm – a neat feature that circumvents the need for a trigger pull (I just use a pen). The takedown lever can then be rotated 90 degrees, permitting forward removal of the slide assembly. At that point, the captive recoil spring and barrel can be plucked out for cleaning. Reassembly is equally simple, and insertion of a magazine will restore sear function. I've grown to enjoy my M&P Pro, not only because it handles well, but also because it's so easy to clean. I often do that right on the range.

M&P disassembly doesn't require a trigger pull. Instead, just flip a small arm to disengage the sear from the striker. Then, rotate the takedown lever, and remove the slide assembly. Interchangeable grip inserts are retained by a pin, housed within the frame.

We also inventory a smattering of M&P 9Cs, which are chopped versions of the standard M&Ps. The Compacts have 3 ½' barrels and 12 +1 capacity (empty weight is similar but lighter when loaded because of 5 less rounds). The 9Cs run fine but we put the brakes on further procurement due to introduction of a new and even more compact S&W Shield.

I'm sure we'll hear some M&P horror stories – something that you'll run into with just about any system, but having run a good-sized batch of pistols for nearly a decade, we have confidence in our M&Ps. I still shoot custom 1911s, but I can grab an M&P off the rack and expect it to do nearly the same thing for around $600. Purchase the latest 2.0 version and you can take advantage of the various upgrades S&W has added. I'm battling a strong urge for the latest 4" compact 2.0, with its slightly shortened grip that still provides 15 +1 capacity in a 24-ounce 9mm. I'd go for the thumb-safety version, but you can have one either way.

These earlier M&Ps include a 5" Pro, standard 4 ¼", and 3 ½" Compact. The line has since expanded.

S&W's compact M&P Shield. This small pistol is for the most part a scaled-down M&P. However, the Shield is stoked by a quasi single-stack magazine. The result is a short, narrow grip, smaller than an M&P Compact model. The Shield is also bigger than a .380 Bodyguard, which places it within its own unique niche.

Upon its introduction, we procured two T&E Shields in 9mm and .40 S&W. Comparing them to my trusty old 9mm S&W M-3913, we found a Shield to be similar in size; maybe smaller by just a tad. Capacity of the 9mm Shield is the same 8 +1, so the latest S&W could possibly be viewed as a polymer alternative to older metal-frame D/A models. Regardless of the two calibers, the whole pistol is around 6" long and weighs 19 ounces. It's just less than 1" thick and certainly a whole lot flatter than a standard-size M&P. Funny thing; it still has a familiar feel. As such it would make a great companion piece, covering most bases with one standard manual-of-arms. Unlike some iterations of the full-size M&P line, the Shields will all fire with their magazines removed. Two are provided with each pistol. The 9mm had a flush-bottom 7-shot, and a longer 8-shot type with a grip extension.

A Shield feels good in the hand despite a lack of interchangeable grip inserts. I fired an 8-shot group on a miniature B-21 silhouette from offhand at 10 yards. Next, I backed up 22 paces to try my luck on a 10-inch steel disk. Firing two 5-round magazines as carefully as I could, all 10 rounds were well-centered, forming a 3-inch group. Of those, 8 measured 2-inches. These results were achieved without a rest, using Federal American Eagle 124-grain FMJ. Wow! Besides being well-regulated, the sights are easily visible, which no doubt helps. The trigger pull is decent as well. These factors, combined with a practical size, make the little S&W a very good, all-around carry-piece.

A Shield can be disassembled per its larger brethren, without dry-firing the pistol. The technique calls for deactivation of the sear after locking the slide to the rear. Visible beneath the breech-face is a small

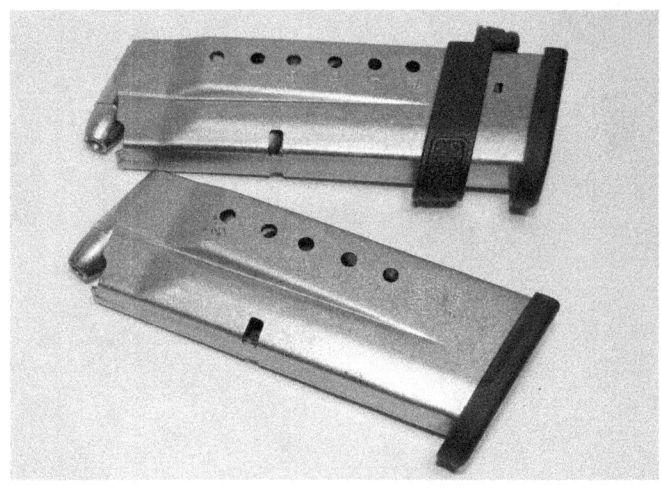
A 9mm Shield comes with two different magazines. The slightly longer 8-shot has a floating spacer to fill the gap when seated.

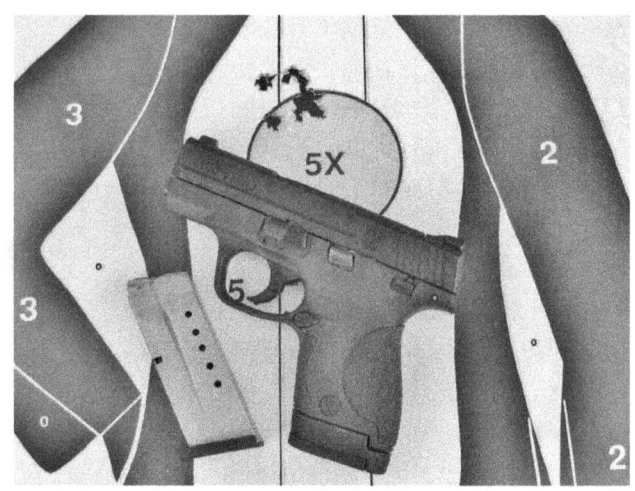
S&W's Shield impressed us right from the start. This version has an external safety. The 8-shot magazine is locked into the pistol.

dog-leg yellow wire, which can be folded forward and down. As this part protrudes within the mag-well, the sear will retract beneath the striker's tail, permitting forward removal of the slide assembly. It's an alternative to pulling the trigger and something we consider worthwhile. We recently saw a Glock AD during which its operator failed to clear the chamber. These things shouldn't happen - but they do. Rotating the take-down lever 90 degrees will allow the slide assembly to travel forward off the frame. Upon reassembly, insertion of a magazine will flip the little wire lever back to fire-mode. The procedure is very simple, and promotes regular maintenance. If it sounds familiar, that's because a full-size M&P uses the same process.

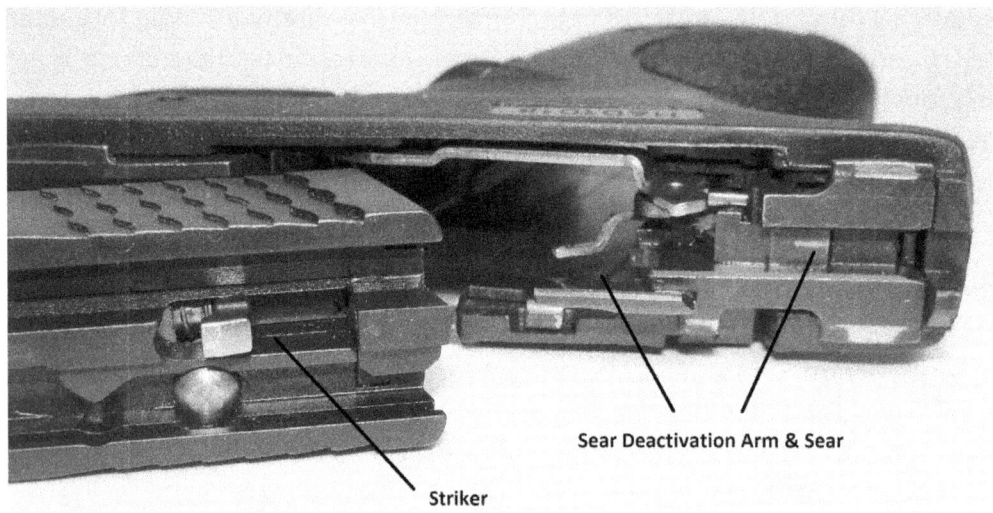
No need for a dry-fire with a Shield. Like an M&P, when folded forward, the small dogleg arm (visible in the mag-well) depresses the sear. The tail of the striker will then pass over it, permitting removal of the slide.

The recoil spring is actually two captive units that are fairly stout. You will probably first discover this upon retracting the slide. After reassembling the pistol, I had a heck of a time latching it open until realizing it wasn't fully rearward. Turns out the last bit of travel requires a bit of extra muscle, which should still be doable for most folks (for others, a remedy is the latest .380 EZ, specifically designed to rectify this complaint). Fully loading the magazines is a bit of a chore as well, especially when new.

The Shield has a gimpy little right-side safety reminiscent of some small-caliber pocket pistols. It shouldn't be too hard to master with a bit of practice, but after some initial struggling, we just skipped the safety entirely, relying instead on standard M&P function. Validating this practice, S&W has since come out with a "no safety" version. The slide release is manageable, but unlike a full-size M&P, it is not ambidextrous. The magazine release is in the same spot, but not reversible. Due to its short size, the Shield doesn't have a dust-cover Picatinny rail section.

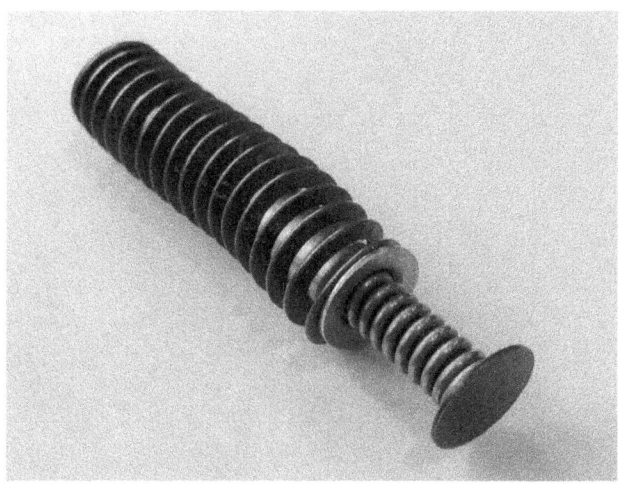

The Shield incorporates a secondary recoil spring, providing a compact system capable of handling recoil. The tradeoff: manual slide operation requires more effort.

S&W joined forces with several manufacturers to ensure accessories and holster options were available when the Shield was announced. This consumer-oriented step resulted in a street-ready carry package which has since expanded to numerous options, between Shield variants, after-market parts, and carry methods. A baseline Shield with 3-dot fixed sights still costs around $450. Night sight models and Performance Center Shields cost more, but they aren't exorbitantly priced despite extra goodies like ported slides and barrels.

We found .40 recoil to be stout, preferring the 9mm (which I subsequently purchased). A .45 ACP version has since been added, somehow with only a minor size increase. It feels surprisingly good in the hand and a couple cadre who sprung for .45s report manageable control. The 9mm version is no problem whatsoever, and carries perfectly in my small Desantis belt scabbard. Later, I added a set of "XS Sights Big Dot Tritium Express" night sights for rapid low-light use. The front is approximately the size of Jupiter and sits on a very shallow express-type "V" blade. It takes a bit of getting used to, but the sight picture is certainly a grabber. At 15 yards, bullets struck directly behind the bulbous bead, which at first seemed disconcerting. Then, thinking things through, it seemed simple enough to consider it a non-magnifying optical dot-sight. Suddenly everything clicked, and given the very coarse sight picture, groups were surprisingly good. Having hunted down extra magazines which are now readily available, I consider this 9mm Shield a real keeper!

Hot off the S&W line (October of 2017) is a Shield 2.0, with a better trigger and improved grip texturing. Models are available in 9mm and .40 S&W, with or without manual thumb safeties. Making matters better (or possibly worse given the extra temptation), Performance Center Shields can be purchased with ported barrels and better sights. The latest is a Shield with a built-in laser.

The Performance Center Shield comes with fiber-optic sights and porting. Per the warning on its slide, none of the Shields are fitted with a magazine disconnect.

M&P Shield .380 EZ. A bolt from the blue for 2018 was an unusual M&P variant geared perhaps for a growing segment of female shoppers seeking an easy-to-operate and soft-shooting pistol. The new EZ sorta looks like the aftermath of a Compact M&P and Shield that were tossed in a blender. It's bigger than a normal Shield, but not any heavier, with just enough extra length to include an accessory rail. One new feature across the EZ line is a grip-safety, with the further option of a frame-mounted thumb-safety, a combination that should provide a better mousetrap for unconventional carry methods. Function remains similar to the other locked-breech centerfire M&Ps, but the softer-shooting .380 allows use of a lighter recoil spring, eliminating complaints over manipulation of 9mm slides. The grip-safety imparts a somewhat odd look, but otherwise, the EZ is clearly a genesis of the M&P family. One difference not readily apparent is a switch to an internal hammer. As such, it really should be listed within other SA pistols, but the EZ more intuitively aligns with the rest of the M&P family. As it turns out, this M&P was not the first to use a hammer. In fact, its frame is a modified version of the next pistol on the list…

S&W's .380 Shield EZ has great potential for those with strength issues. It offers easy operation and low recoil, in a shootable pistol with reassuring safety features.

One departure from the M&P line is the EZ's internal hammer. Its grip safety is reminiscent of a 1911's, but pivots in reverse. An external safety lever is optional. Like other Shields, an EZ will fire with its magazine removed.

Model	Capacity	Caliber	Bbl	Wt. Empty	
M&P 22	10 +1	.22 LR	3 ½"	15.3 oz	Compact rimfire
Bodyguard	6 +1	.380 ACP	2 ¾"	12 oz	Ultra-compact DAO
Shield EZ	8 +1	.380 ACP	3.7"	18.5 oz	Semi-compact
Shield 2.0	8 +1	9mm	3.1"	18.3 oz	Compact
M&P 2.0	12 +1	9mm	3.6"	25.9 oz	Shortened M&P
M&P 2.0	15 +1	9mm	4"	27 oz	Compact M&P
M&P 2.0	17 +1	9mm	4 ¼"	25 oz	Standard-size M&P
M&P Pro	17 +1	9mm	5"	28.5 oz	Long-slide M&P
M&P 2.0	10 +1	.45 ACP	4.6"	30.1 oz	Standard-size M&P
Shield 2.0	7 +1	.45 ACP	3.3"	20.5 oz	Compact

Note: .40 S&W versions are dimensionally similar to the 9mms, with slightly less capacity.

M&P 22 Compact. I can envision a possible extra polymer S&W in my future. This one will be a rimfire M&P, chambered for .22 LR cartridges. Size-wise, the rimfire is a close cousin, running at about 90% scale. Internally, like the new .380 EZ, the .22 is a completely different single-action design that uses a concealed hammer instead of a striker. For this reason, a thumb-safety is provided. Its use is strongly advised since the hammer will be fully cocked whenever the slide cycles. By rights it should also be listed with single-actions, but even more so than the newer .380 EZ, this rimfire S&W just bears too much external resemblance for that. You'll find more about this pistol in the rimfire handguns chapter.

Matched M&Ps? Given the many choices within the whole M&P line, I'm feeling sorta like a one-eyed dog in a butcher shop. Putting an M&P collection together based on some restraint and logic, a full-sized pistol would be a good single-pistol choice. The addition of a smaller Shield could cover concealment needs, and a .22 would be an ideal plinker/practice piece. These three pistols would provide a versatile system capable of covering nearly any contingency.

For any other fanatics, a fourth 5-inch "Pro" would make a great range or combat-competition pistol. A possible alternative would be one of the new switch-top S&W Performance Center Slide Kits, permitting reconfiguration of an existing 1st Gen M&P.

Again, one thing worth considering in advance is external-safeties. Ideally, from a training point of view, function should be identical across the board – something worth considering regardless of the system. We scratched our heads on this after procuring a couple safety-equipped M&P-22s for remedial training purposes. Since our centerfires lacked this feature, our fix was to use them from an effective "ready," which also solved a safety-induced fit issue related to our duty holsters.

THE SPRINGFIELD ARMORY'S XD SERIES

Another heavy-hitter in the polymer pistol field is the Croatian-built XD. After examining a compact 9mm XD-M, I was immediately struck by its great handling qualities. Things improved from there when a beautiful little group formed at 15 paces, indicating near match-grade accuracy potential. Thinking it might be a fluke, a volley of 10 more shots clustered into nearly one ragged hole. In fact, there was little *not* to like about this pistol. It was well-designed, with interchangeable grip backstraps, positive slide-serrations and well laid-out controls. The relatively straight 13-degree grip angle put the pistol squarely in front of my face, presenting a useful and well-regulated set of sights. Considering the amount of ammunition an XD can accommodate, its ergonomics are also surprisingly good. In fact, the full-size 9mm has a stunning 19 +1 capacity!

Comparisons of Springfield Armory's XD to a Glock are inevitable. The triggers look familiar, but the XD incorporates several unique features. And, even this short version has a rail.

The polymer frame has imbedded steel rails and the trigger looks very much like a Glock's, with a central trigger-blocking tab. The reset is pronounced and pull-weight is about on par with the XD's stronger competitors. Tenifer Plus+ nitride steel is used on models other than those with bright stainless slides. A loaded-chamber indicator provides tactile reassurance during low-light, as does a cocking indicator.

Like a model 1911, the XD can't be fired until a grip-safety is disengaged by the web of the shooter's hand. This feature has merit on a striker-fired pistol. We continue to hear stories about those of various designs firing through trigger contact with some foreign object. For this reason, we prefer to recover a pistol with the thumb behind the slide. If it does begin to travel rearward, some holster-related interference may be the cause, whether it be a draw-string tab, sweatshirt, or pencil, etc. Using the thumb-behind-slide technique with an XD, the pistol shouldn't fire, thanks to loss of contact with the grip-safety. So, especially with an XD, this technique affords a bonus level of protection well worth having! We also appreciate the tactile assurance of the cocking-indicator stem that protrudes through the rear face of the slide. However, the grip-safety must be depressed before the slide can be cycled, and an XD will fire without a magazine (these, by the way, are metal).

Disassembly is relatively simple. A take-down lever on the left side of the frame can be rotated upward after the gun is cleared and its slide is locked open. The slide assembly will then travel forward for removal while the trigger is pulled, permitting the necessary striker/sear clearance. From there, recoil spring and barrel removal is standard. Recoil spring assemblies may or may not be captive, depending on the model. Reassembly is in reverse, sans any trigger manipulation, although the safety must remain off with any models so equipped. Springfield advises against excessive dry-firing of XDs, recommending use of snap-caps instead.

Although Springfield Armory, Inc. is a well-established firm, the company itself should not be confused with the original Springfield Armory in Massachusetts, established as a Federal Revolutionary War arsenal (now nothing more than a museum). Springfield Armory, Inc. was founded in 1974, and located in Geneseo, Illinois. Beyond XDs, they are known for a line of 1911 pistols, M-1A (M-14) rifles, and most recently, AR-15s. The X-treme Duty pistols are an evolution of a Croatian design, which appeared as the HS2000 back in 1999. It is still in use by Croatian military forces, and was briefly imported to the U.S., until Springfield picked up licensing rights in 2002. Since then, they have tweaked and greatly expanded the line of these imports.

Here's a look at the XD's cocking indicator and grip safety. Perhaps less obvious is the bilateral magazine release. Night-sights round out a list of very useful features.

Springfield Armory keeps adding new models from a 5.25" competition pistol to neat little XD-S single-stacks in 9mm and .45 ACP. The Mod.2 could well be an excellent choice thanks to refined ergonomics and reasonable size, with the 4" 9mm offering 16 +1 capacity, while coming in at 27 ½ ounces (empty). The entire lineup is somewhat mind-boggling with numerous choices falling into four XD categories (not counting their latest D/A variant). Some are even available with external thumb-safeties. I've seriously considered shooting a battery of XDs, but we can't own everything.

A less common XD variant is this .45 ACP, fitted with a thumb-safety. Sometimes what's old is new again.

Prior to adopting our agency S&Ws, we had a couple T&E XDs on the range with some M&Ps. Comments were favorable toward either. We wished we could have thrown 'em both in a blender, winding up with the best of both pistols. We went with S&Ws because of a long-standing relationship, the dreaded magazine-disconnect feature, and our proximity to the manufacturer. A local PD that uses our range adopted XDs as standard-issue, so we've had the chance to see them in action, gleaning favorable feedback from the force. My son's XD is still plugging along and works well enough that he added a second one.

SIG'S LATEST STRIKER-FIRED PISTOLS

A "well-established" firearm infers years of steady use - but there is another pathway to this end. If U. S. military forces adopt a firearm as a standard-issue weapon, it'll almost certainly become a mainstream commodity. Such should be the case with Sig Sauer's striker-fired P320, introduced in 2014, but already scheduled to replace the aging Beretta M-9. In fact, transition already began with the Army's 101st Airborne Division during late 2017. The new M-17 MHS is a product of *modular handgun system* trials, which gave the P320 a leg-up, right from the start. This pistol is a striker-fired polymer-frame evolution of the DAO P250, and its strong suit is modularity. The apparent loss of an appeal by Glock constitutes an ironic twist considering its dominant history, but innovation has triumphed and the Sig's selection now seems secure. Completion of initial M-17 orders should put a quarter-million new Sigs in circulation, not counting numerous LE and civilian orders that will follow. Of course, a compact spin-off was inevitable.

The P320. Here's a classic example of a design that uses a serial numbered chassis to house its fire-control parts. This feature allows users to purchase inexpensive polymer grip-frame shells, which can be swapped out to accommodate hands of different sizes. Complete slide assemblies can also be exchanged, permitting compact or full-size configurations, so much like an AR-15, this Sig is a true firearm transformer. The same grip frames will handle 9mm, .40 S&W, and .357 SIG options, while the .45 ACP requires some dedicated components. The various lower/upper possibilities provide full-size, compact, or sub-compact platforms (along with a few other options). Barrel lengths run from 4.7 inches down, and magazine capacity based on 9mm goes from 17 to 12 rounds, depending on the gun, with an even greater 21-round extended magazine version as an option. The weight of a 9mm varies from just under 30 to roughly 24 ounces. Use of stainless steel (nitride on the slides) provides a weather-resistant firearm that further benefits from easy disassembly for routine maintenance.

Polymer pistols can lack esthetics, but Sig's striker-fired P320 captures form and function through a brilliantly simple design. Note the location of its serial number.

Basic field-stripping also permits grip-frame exchanges. Like many other striker-fired pistols, the active controls are minimal, consisting of a slide-stop and magazine release. A simple disassembly lever is also present, but this one has an advantage in that no dry-firing or sear-deactivation system is required. After clearing the pistol, with its magazine removed, simply lock back the slide. At that point, a forward-mounted takedown lever can be rotated, permitting the upper receiver assembly to move forward off the frame (further stripping follows standard procedures). Extra wiggling of the takedown lever will allow it to be withdrawn from the left side of the frame so the fire-control chassis can be pulled out. The remaining grip frame then becomes nothing more than a light polymer shell with a magazine release. The first time I tried this I found the process a bit fiddly, but it was by no means difficult, and in any case, grip exchanges for most owners will probably be infrequent (one advantage is access of the self-contained fire-control module for periodic cleaning). The replaceable grip offers further possibilities like an integral laser version, but to keep a lid on initial cost, this tool-less upgrade can always occur later.

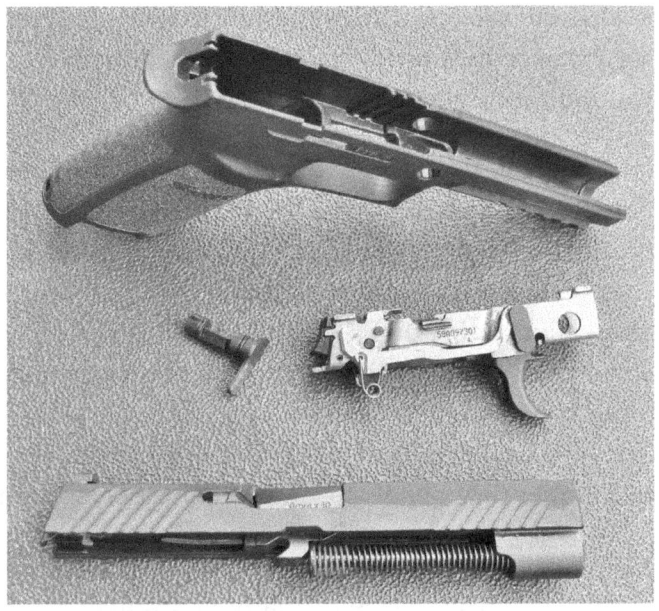

For legal purposes, the P320's removeable chassis constitutes the actual firearm. Modularity permits reconfiguration, and transformation is a snap. Long-term success is assured through adoption by the U.S. Military.

The grip-frame I tried was a "medium," which was clearly indicated on its forward right side. The rail section below was of ample length for any reasonable accessories, offering five slots. Although I'd probably opt for a "small" grip, this one felt darned good and pointed spot-on. Any ham-handed shooters would no doubt be happy with a "large." Recesses on the bottom edges of the generous magazine well provide extra purchase if a balky magazine needs a tug, and the pistol will fire with or without one in place. The magazine release can be reversed for use any south-paws, and the slide-stop/release is bilateral with unobtrusive but adequate pads. Combining these features with the various grips, a P-320 should accommodate just about anyone.

The full-size 9mm shown here is equipped with Tritium night sights, which are well-regulated for the 124-grain loads we tried. The front edge of the rear sight is cut for single-handed slide-racks and both sights are mounted in dovetails. Besides natural pointing, accuracy appeared to be surprisingly good; a product of quality construction, further enhanced by a generous sight radius. The trigger is also decent, running around 6 pounds with a distinct re-set point. No safety was offered with the standard civilian P320, but a striker block was incorporated to (in theory) prevent a discharge if the gun was dropped.

As it turned out, rare instances of firing were noted during accidental drops on hard surfaces from certain angles. Word spread like wildfire on the internet, including information that may or not have been accurate. The ultimate solution was a redesign and voluntary upgrade, requiring a return to Sig for the necessary modifications. Among them is a lighter trigger, and a striker with a new disconnector that requires machining of the slide.

As a testament to the already widespread distribution of the P320, aftermarket triggers are now available from outfits like Apex Tactical. Sig advertises the ability to "change caliber, size, and fit at will" within the 9mm, .40, and .357 SIG trio. Factory kits are available, along with various other goodies. Complete P-320s with threaded barrels and optics-ready slides further complement the line. It was almost inevitable that a civilian version of the Government's full-size M-17 and compact M-18 Sigs would appear, and that's exactly what happened in early 2018. The latest features include external ambidextrous safety levers and replaceable slide plates that can accommodate iron or optical sights. The best bet is to log into Sig's factory website for an in-depth visit. While you're there, note another newcomer destined to become a major player within the crowded CCW market.

SIG P365. This compact pistol launched in early 2018, so although an established track record is absent, its P320 lineage virtually guarantees success. The new CCW-oriented Sig P365 is similar in size to an S&W Shield, but offers greater capacity. The 9mm P-365 Micro-Compact is an honest 10 +1

Sig's smaller 9mm P365 would complement a P320. However, thanks to 12 +1 capacity, it could even stand on its own merit

pistol, achieving this feat through a cleverly engineered double-stack magazine, although its slim polymer grip belies this advantage. In fact, an extended magazine, designed to provide a bit of extra grip purchase, holds 12 rounds without ruining the P365's overall lines. Unlike some competing compact 9mms, it also has a built-in rail section. The catch is to make it fit, the rail is a proprietary design; however Sig is concurrently producing a new line of streamlined lights which lock on with only minimal bulk. Like the P-320, the actual "gun" is a separate chassis; explains why Sig lists the P-365 as a "steel-frame" pistol. Maintaining this design presents intrigue regarding future possibilities; meanwhile, looks like Sig has another winner that will nicely compliment their P320.

STRIKER-FIRED SUMMARY

The pistols covered here are good guns among *many* other choices. Glock devotees will settle for nothing less, with strong arguments to support their preference. Personal experience accounts for the increased focus on Smith & Wesson's M&P line; another good choice (in our case, manufactured within a five-hour's drive). However, starting from scratch, with perhaps with some allowance for extra teething, I'd give the P320 an extra-hard look. Although this pistol is a product of Sig Sauer, the gun itself is manufactured in New Hampshire. Location aside, the P320's military acceptance and useful features make it a serious contender.

Of course, we can't forget the other semiauto possibilities that further expand the list to good single-action or double-action choices. One thing they all have in common is the need for some accessories, so that's what we'll look at next, starting with an eye toward a few essentials that can control our "system cost."

CHAPTER 22
USEFUL PISTOL ACCESSORIES

Following our "system" approach, compared to a revolver, the list of pistol essentials will increase cost somewhat due to extra magazines and accessories that affect a true bottom line. I have a couple G.I. ammo cans full of pistol extras from recoil springs to slide-stops. By comparison, my revolver horde is pretty basic. Either way, costs are bearable with some common sense and restraint.

ESSENTIALS

No matter the handgun type, we're gonna need a holster. The costs for revolver speed-loader pouches aren't that different than mag types, but some magazines can be pricey, even without related extras like extended floor-plates or loading aids. So, here's a short list that shouldn't break the bank…

Holster. The holster, magazine pouch, and magazines really constitute the heart of a pistol system and although they all seem straight-forward, there's more going on with a holster than meets the eye. The cocked-and-locked aficionados and striker-fired crowd will need to pay more attention to details, but everyone will benefit from an educated approach to selection. Check out the holster chapters for more information.

Magazine pouch. I'll sometimes run an open-top, single magazine type with a QD belt mounting feature. Mostly, it's a range device, but if adequate tension can be applied, such a pouch can cover concealed carry. Trouble is, this use can differ from rough country demands where the safer bet is a pouch that offers secure closure. Snaps are quieter than Velcro and they last longer, but either will work. Pistol reloads normally involve the support hand; but that assumes both hands are working so it's worth considering access with either hand. Some combination OWB single mag-pouch/holsters are sold, and although they seem good in principle, normal support-hand access will be difficult from a 3:00 – 4:00 location. Still, plenty of single-magazine pouches are sold, mostly for CCW roles where concealment is a major concern. A double version offers greater challenges there, but will provide more firepower if ever needed while serving as a handy ammo organizer. Turns out, beyond preventing magazine loss, flaps can serve as useful indicators. As a right-handed shooter, the pistol remains in my right mitt during reloads while fresh magazines are fed with my left. I always start from the front, sweeping rearward for the next magazine. An empty pouch will remain unsnapped to indicate its status, prompting an instant shift to the next full magazine. Empty magazines *never* go back in a pouch. A partial might, *but only when no full magazines remain.*

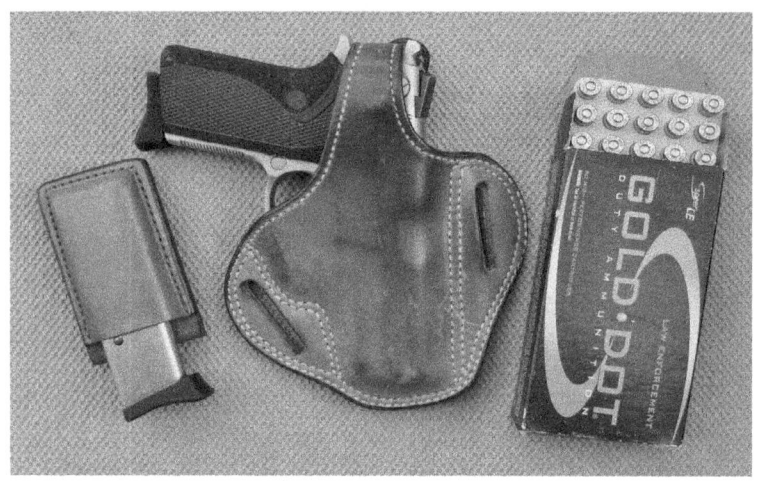

The pistol is just part of a larger system including, but not limited to, a holster, magazine pouch, spare mags, and ammo. CCW cost is sometimes less due to minimal equipment

Magazines. Three should be the minimum, but I like at least five for use with "working pistols" that see regular shooting. Magazines are often available as flush or extended floor-plate versions, and many CCW-type pistols ship with one of each. The flush-fits often trade one cartridge for more streamlined holster carry, while the extended ones tend to ride in pouches. This is a matter of preference, since the latter type can provide a better grip. Since oversize magwell funnels work poorly with standard floor-plates, shop for magazines with extended "bumper pads." They'll provide more reliable seating, and will also be appreciated on hard-surfaced ranges. In many cases, proprietary magazines will be required, but the more popular pistols like Glocks or 1911s offer additional aftermarket choices. In the latter case, given the numerous manufacturers spanning more than a century of production, quality varies. Don't skimp on quality.

Cleaning kit. A basic kit should cover most handgun needs. The actual cleaning rod is usually a sectioned type not ideal for match-grade rifle bores, but good enough to cover handguns on the fly. It'll probably include a few bore brushes, a slotted tip, some cleaning patches, solvent, and oil; all the basics necessary for routine handgun maintenance. A neat little kit designed for 1911s is sold by Real Avid. It includes a clever little "1911 Smart Wrench" for barrel-bushings; not needed for most other semiautos.

USEFUL EXTRAS

The following non-essential items could prove useful (although the first could rate as "essential" for folks with less hand strength).

Magazine loading tool. You may or may not need one, depending upon your fortitude. Some of the high-capacity magazines can be tough to load for nearly everyone during the last few rounds. There are some elaborate magazine loading devices on the market, good for high-volume refills, but simpler devices can provide enough of an assist to save a mangled thumb. You *may* appreciate a basic thumb-saver during high-volume shooting sessions. You'll probably *want* one during a multi-day training program.

Bushing wrench. This item is a specialty tool used to loosen snug-fitting 1911 barrel bushings. Most are just inexpensive flat steel or plastic plates with correspond bushing cutouts to help twist stubborn bushings until they'll disengage for removal.

Springs. You probably won't need any springs to start, but at some point, the recoil spring will need replacement. The interval can vary from 1,500 to 3,000 rounds. Others will need attention at some point, so more details will follow when maintenance is covered.

Dummy rounds. You might want to pick up a few A-Zoom aluminum packs. They're handy for malfunction-clearance exercises, as well as ball & dummy drills. Mix a few in with a magazine full of live ammo. Shoot with a friend and swap magazines, just to keep things honest. When the gun goes click it shouldn't move; affording great anti-flinching practice. You can even weave in immediate-action "tap & racks" to clear the duds. Dummy cartridges can also prove useful for development of initial loading and unloading techniques.

CUSTOM TOUCHES

In the revolver section, mention was made of not going overboard on customization due to increased liability concerns. Lately, legal use of deadly force can become clouded by the efforts of attorneys and so-called "expert witnesses" to portray a defendant as a "gun nut." This contention may be based upon the addition of extras that indicate a penchant for malevolent intent. Yeah, right.

Still, some features are just asking for trouble like logos or engravings with "threatening messages" (skull & crossbones, etc.). As an overstated example, good luck to any AR-15 owners who defend their premises with a bump-stock. So where do we draw the line? From a layman's point of view, a "hair trigger" might be troublesome, which could also implicate action jobs or aftermarket triggers. Odds would be better of justifying a more visible set of sights, better suited for old guys like me. A different set of grips (minus logos or language) might also be defensible as an improved control measure, intended to minimize risks for bystanders. Same story for a laser or light assuming their rationale was properly articulated.

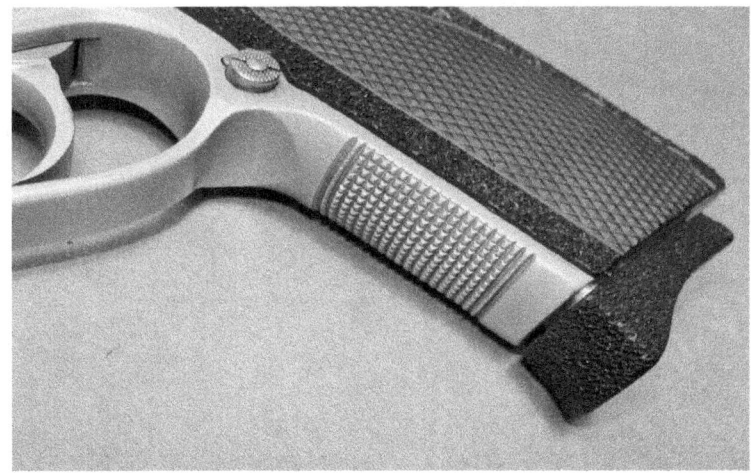

The fix for slippery plastic S&W M-3913 grips was patient stippling, applied by a soldering iron. But, a spare was in reserve – just in case things went badly.

Grips. Assuming your handgun can accommodate them, a replacement set of grips is an established method to improve fit or alter gun size. Polymer pistols often lack such capability, but those sold with factory inserts still provide a great way personalize fit. As for aftermarket grip panels, you can sometimes score a two-for-one with a Crimson Trace or Hogue laser set (such additions being legitimized thanks to integral rails). Rubber "hand-all" sleeves are another easy fix for those seeking greater girth, but don't use them with a grip-safety. Stair-tread or skate-board tape is often seen on competition pistols, but commercial die-cut adhesive grip-skins are a better way to increase traction.

Night sights: I don't have them on every pistol, but I like them on defensive handguns. Their small radioactive elements offer low-light capability, and work 24/7 with a useful life of 10 years or more. The best bet is to buy a pistol with factory-installed night sights. Cost is usually less in the long run, installation hassles are eliminated, and odds of proper regulation will be greater. That said, after-market night sights are sold to fit most of today's popular handguns, in some interesting new options such as dual fiber-optic/ Tritium designs. Before going this route, make sure a prospective handgun purchase will readily accept a sight change, and factor in any installation costs.

Trick triggers and controls. Owing to the popularity of striker-fired pistols, aftermarket kits have appeared. Some offer an improved reset, typically accompanied by a lighter pull; in some cases, *much* lighter. When we get down to a 3-4-pound trigger on a Glock or M&P, I have to ask if I'd be any worse off re-holstering a 1911 with its safety off. Heck, at least it has a grip safety! Some of these kits also include sexy looking anodized triggers with red or purple finishes, guaranteed to attract much attention whether desired or not. On a purely defensive pistol, the safest bet is stick with a factory-spec configuration, which tosses any related legal concerns back to the manufacturer.

RESTRAINT

The big takeaway here is, closer to stock form is better given the litigious state of our society. There's a big difference from a competition-type range pistol that drives much of the demand for neat extras and a working gun. Keep It Simple Stupid is also good since any spare funds can be prioritized toward training and practice! The main expense then will be ammunition, but such is the price for proficiency. A bonus in this regard will be familiarity with the field-stripping process necessary for proper cleaning, so that's where we're headed next.

CHAPTER 23
KEEP YOUR PISTOL RUNNING

Believe it or not, most semiauto pistol malfunctions are shooter-induced. Makes sense when we think about it. Given human nature, a likely cause involves maintenance, or lack thereof. Yes, basic field-stripping and cleaning is a necessity, but less obvious factors can include lubrication, springs, ammunition, and even a shooter's physique.

BASIC MAINTENANCE

First the obvious: you need to become comfortable with your pistol's disassembly process. We're only talking about basic field-stripping for proper cleaning. A surprising number of pistol owners remain uncertain of the exact procedures, resulting in either a haphazard approach or a lack of *any* attention. Given the many makes and models, a great reference is a manufacturer's manual, which will likely include step-by-step illustrations, along with lubrication points, and design-specific details. YouTube can be your friend as well. One thing they'll all have in common is a warning to make sure the gun is unloaded! Prior to getting started, check your pistol carefully and then check it again. This includes all magazines, too! Remove any live ammunition from the area and don a set of safety glasses. Besides energetic springs, solvents and bronze bristles are real threats to the eyes.

Most pistols field-strip to a frame, slide, barrel, and recoil-spring assembly. It's worth reiterating the above magazine cautions since, beyond live ammo worries, its removal will be necessary before proceeding. A less obvious concern is the recoil-spring assembly, which may or may not have a captive guide rod. If not, the rod can launch with authority. Same for magazine parts like springs and their retainers, so beyond the possibility of getting beaned, it's worth finding a spot where any airborne parts can be recovered. A magnetic parts tray is an inexpensive item that beats crawling under furniture.

Once the gun is disassembled, most of the carbon fouling and crud should be obvious; however, a few commonly missed spots include the slide's breech-face, the barrel's feed-ramp, and the frame's adjacent surfaces. The extractor also deserves periodic attention, and magazines shouldn't be ignored.

Brushes and solvents. The same general kit described for revolver maintenance will work with pistols. You can skip a stainless toothbrush in favor of a soft-bristled M-16 type (or even a regular toothbrush). Medical swabs or Q-tips are handy for frame and slide rail surfaces, and pipe cleaners may also prove useful.

Our general-purpose solvent is Shooter's Choice, which dissolves fouling and plastic shotgun wad residue. So far, we've never had a problem with polymer pistols, but it's probably best to try a small test spot first. The latest surface coatings are also worthy of caution. A small amount on the toothbrush will cut through fouling deposits, but avoid flooding the firing pin tunnel. This helps prevent an accumulation of glop that could eventually impede ignition.

During mass-cleaning sessions involving multiple pistols, we may also use an aerosol can of Gun Scrubber II to flush out crud from harder-to-reach areas, while exercising caution around night sights. They should be protected from aggressive solvents that could attack their seals. This makes it a good choice for cleaning magazines, unlike oil which attracts fouling and dirt.

A bronze bore-brush dipped in solvent should remove most fouling from a disassembled barrel, cleaning from the preferred breech-to-muzzle direction. The same .38/.357 brush used for a revolver will fit a .380, 9mm, or .357 Sig. Run it completely through before changing direction and let the rifling turn the brush. This process will occur more readily using a rod with a rotating handle. Several complete passes should get the job done when followed by a cleaning patch threaded into a slotted loop. Two or three patches are often sufficient and the last one works well for harder-to-reach locations like magazine wells and slide tunnels. Swabs or pipe cleaners can wipe fouling from areas like slide rails and most action recesses.

Lubrication. Since semiautomatic function involves at least some metal-on-metal contact, proper lubrication is the key to its longevity and reliability. Follow the manufacturer's recommendations.

Environmental factors can also raise concerns, especially in other than "normal" conditions. While total absence lubrication is almost universally bad, too much can raise havoc; especially in dusty or sandy theatres. The challenge can be to find a suitable balance. During my old military days, we operated in tropical climes involving monsoon rains and moisture. Rust-preventative lubricants were essential but additional problems arose from helicopter-driven flying debris. Conditions were so extreme that S&W Model 10 revolvers often became the handgun of choice for air crews. Desert operations are typically even more hostile, requiring sparing use of lubricants combined with non-stop firearm maintenance. Shooters who participate in combat-type matches like IDPA or IPSC can face similar problems during outdoor matches involving unforgiving terrain and weather, the latter involving extremes beyond heat. We've watched a few cold weather military sessions come to a screeching halt on our range due to improper lubrication protocols. Grease can really stiffen up in cold weather but so can some oils. Even if they don't, ice can immobilize an action (something a specialty holster like a UM-84 could help prevent).

We've had no such issues with military Break-Free CLP in all sorts of weather. CLP stands for "cleaner, lubricant, preservative." We buy it by the gallon, but a smaller 4-ounce plastic bottle is much more convenient for individual use. A gentle squeeze will dispense individual drops to prevent flooding of critical areas like fire-control parts.

If the manufacturer recommends one drop, then that's what should be applied (as opposed to flooding from stem to stern). Lacking a manual, I just go with a bit of common sense, applying lubricant sparingly to several common spots. These include one drop each to the corners of the frame rails, the barrel's muzzle, its slide-locking surfaces, and the guide rod. Depending on the pistol, the disconnector and hammer strut may also get a drop. Lubrication occurs after cleaning the field-stripped pistol, just prior to reassembly. Then the slide is run vigorously back and forth a few times, not only to detect any glitches, but also to distribute the lubricant. The final step is a wipe-down of all exposed metal surfaces with CLP, using a lightly moistened cleaning patch. Magazines remain clean but dry to prevent the attraction of grit. This process has served us well for decades in all sorts of weather and temperature extremes.

Although there are excellent task-specific solvents and lubes, Break-free covers lots of bases. For individual use, a smaller squeeze-bottle is the practical size.

Since technology moves quickly, I queried our current Chief Firearms Instructor. He's tried several newer alternatives. Here's his take: "I like M-Pro7 gun cleaner, M-Pro7 gun lube, and Qmaxx BLU premium gun and knife lube. I also use Qmaxx Black Diamond for pistol slides, AR-15 bolts and gas-operated shotguns because it works well. One other thing I use a lot is Frog Lube paste for slide rails (also AR-15 triggers) because it stays put, and works under heat. I know you were trying to keep this simple but is anything in Gun Land simple?"

Inspection. The normal field-stripping and cleaning process is a good time to check for problems. Besides anything obvious, you may discover sluggish slide cycling, a faulty slide-stop, or a sticking magazine. The latter two problems may be attributable to just one magazine. A cocked & locked design like a 1911 shouldn't fire when "on safe," nor should the hammer drop after the safety lever is moved to its fire position. The grip-safety should prevent firing until depressed. Most pistols also have a disconnector that prevents a discharge if the slide is out of battery. That function is easy to check (and understand) with an unloaded pistol.

It also won't hurt to inspect night sights in a dark location. Sometimes the cause of a dimming set (particularly the front sight) is nothing more than a gradual accumulation of carbon fouling that can be easily wiped off. Today's pistol sights are normally pressed into their dovetails with great force, but occasionally a loose one can be encountered. Aside from shifting POI, off-center installation is a good clue, typically involving the rear sight. Some pistols also rely on them to capture small spring-loaded firing pin interrupter parts, which means they need to stay put.

All steel-framed pistols should be periodically checked for corrosion, particularly under their grip panels. Loose screws can be another problem, and 1911s employ separate bushings which can loosen with the screws. Snug those up hard with blue thread sealant and then use less pressure on the grip screws. Make sure the plunger tube is staked to the frame, too. A firearm-type screwdriver kit with removable bits is a worthwhile addition that can cover lots of different guns.

FUNCTIONAL INSURANCE

Field-stripping is the practical limit of disassembly for most of us, but depending on the severity of use, more complex servicing will be necessary at some point. All our department-issued pistols receive (as a minimum) detailed annual armorer attention. Firing pins and extractors are removed, recoil springs are replaced, and the internals get a thorough cleaning. The same weapons also receive frequent inspections to nip potential problems in the bud. Inevitably, some will be found which illustrates the point: everyone should seek out a qualified gunsmith if for no other reason than peace of mind.

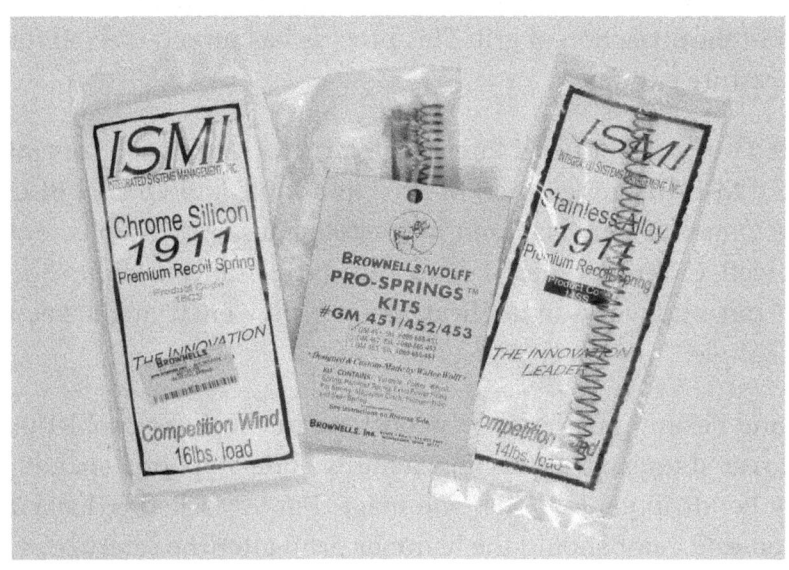

Semiautomatic function involves ongoing spring compressions. Sooner or later, most will need replacement. Popular pistols increase the odds of finding some.

Recoil-springs and others. Sooner or later, given enough shooting, a recoil spring will need replacement. The exact interval will depend on the pistol, and the types of rounds it fired. Using a 1911 as an example, you'll want springs suitable for given loads. A 16-pound recoil spring is often used for standard .45 ACP hard-ball cartridges. Lighter loads (or calibers) may need lighter springs. Firing hot ammo in low-poundage springs can really beat a pistol up (we gravitate toward non-+P for exactly this reason). With some stiff loads, recoil springs could stand replacement every 1,500 rounds. We generally change our M&P springs at 3,000 rounds, but intervals could be sooner due to extraneous effects like storing a pistol with its slide locked open, individual maintenance practices, cold weather use, etc. You can always tell a new spring from the old one; it'll be noticeably shorter. If your slide gets sluggish you may want to change the recoil spring. If it's on the edge, it may run okay while the pistol is clean, but get balky during the above conditions.

Magazine springs are another concern; in fact, some stoppages can be attributable to weak recoil *and* magazine springs. Tired magazine springs will also be shorter than new ones, and they may even develop unhealthy twists. Concerns about long-term storage of loaded magazines are somewhat overblown, but we've seen instances where replacement springs were called for. A series of unused fully-loaded 1911 magazines would probably feed after 25 years. On the other hand, an identical but well-used set could develop fatigue much sooner due to ongoing changes in spring tension.

A hammer-fired pistol (like a 1911) needs a stiff mainspring for dependable ignition, and to regulate the unlocking sequence. The latter is not a concern for a striker-fired pistol, but the ignition system is still spring-powered, and capable of accumulating fouling. In other words, regardless of the pistol type, periodic spring replacement and detailed gunsmith servicing is advised.

Beyond the manufacturers, after-market spring kits are sold for the more popular pistols like 1911s, Hi-Powers, Beretta 92s, etc. Wolf is but one of several vendors and Brownells has a good assortment to choose from.

Magazines. Using a vibratory engraver, Sharpie Pen, etc., you can number each one. Later, if you encounter malfunctions, this trick may help identify a suspect magazine. Run them dry and don't take them apart at the same time. That way, if you get confused during reassembly, another one can serve for reference.

Establishing reliability. Assuming you've already chosen a caliber, you'll want to think about a defensive load as well. You might want to stay within more common bullet-weights that correspond with practice loads. For example, we shoot literally tons of .40-caliber, 165-grain FMJ during training. It shoots to the same point-of-impact as our 165-grain JHP duty rounds. While getting comfortable with your pistol you can put lots of the cheaper FMJ through each magazine, while also monitoring feeding and ejection. Note where your empties

Numbered magazines can narrow down stoppage sources. Caliber markings can avoid further problems if similar pistols are involved. 1911 mags have only minor differences (the bumper-pads are add-ons).

are landing; if they're sailing half way across the range you probably need a heavier spring. If they barely dribble out, you'll want a lighter one. When all is well, a pile of empties should accumulate just a few feet to your right in one general area.

Whatever you choose for defensive use, shoot *at least one box*. For more assurance of positive function, shoot another half-a-box using your weak-hand only, through a somewhat dirty pistol. If it's on the ragged edge of reliability, this is where you'll likely see some stoppages. For a bit more confidence you can even cant the gun to 2:00 and 4:00 angles. Try some shots in low light, too. Most defensive loads are formulated for reduced flash signature, but you won't know until you shoot some. A brilliant flash will give you exactly one effective shot – which had better be a good one!

OTHER PISTOL-SPECIFIC CONCERNS

We always include pistol-specific cautions during pre-fire range safety briefings. These extras apply to semiauto shooters, although the first caution could easily include any revolver shooters on a crowded range.

Clothing. Dress to minimize the possibility of hot brass entering your clothing, and maintain muzzle control if it happens! Safety glasses are essential, but wear a hat with a visor to prevent a hot case from lodging between your glasses and eyes. Also, be aware of any loose garments or draw-string pulls that could wind up inside a trigger guard during re-holstering. *If resistance is felt, stop!*

Recovering pistol with thumb behind slide. A slide (or hammer) moving rearward as the pistol is re-holstered can indicate some type of obstruction, so position the strong thumb accordingly to detect potential disaster.

Thumb-over grip during firing. Position the support thumb to prevent contact with the reciprocating slide. Otherwise, you *might* dislocate the thumb. There is a better chance of drawing blood or uttering lots of naughty language - not to mention a stoppage.

Dropped magazines. Check any that contain ammo for proper cartridge orientation. Although unlikely, a tipped round could fire out of battery upon contact with a breech-face. There is a better chance of the magazine spitting out a round or picking up dirt, so give 'em a good looking over.

Malfunctions. Sooner or later you'll encounter one, and it's all too easy to be distracted by the problem. Control the muzzle during clearance attempts and be aware of your surroundings. Safety is the top priority!

Unloading. The big thing is always remove the ammunition supply (magazine) before clearing the chamber! Failure to do so will allow another round to feed when the slide is manually cycled. Sounds simple enough, but a huge amount of pistol ADs are attributable to this oversight. Don't try to catch an ejected live round, either. Let it go to the ground. Then, lock the slide rearward for a close inspection. Always double-check the chamber and magazine well before returning to standing.

Short or re-chambered cartridges. Some people store their handgun fully loaded (hopefully in a child-proof, secure container). Others will opt for an unloaded gun. Restoring a semiautomatic pistol to loaded status can be hard on ammo to the point where safety can be compromised. Repeat chamberings of the same cartridge can shorten its overall length through bullet impacts with the feed-ramp. The result will be decreased case volume that can elevate pressures to unsafe levels. Once in a blue moon we've even seen an opposite growing cartridge phenomenon. Of course, any changes to cartridge dimensions can negatively affect pistol function. You *could* drop a cartridge directly into the chamber and then let the slide slam home, but a pistol really isn't designed to work that way. Extractor damage may result. Even normal but repetitive unloading and loading subjects a cartridge to extractor bites that will eventually chew up its rim. A good rule of thumb is to NOT re-chamber the same pistol round more than three times. Rather than going for a fourth, strip the magazine, place this round in first, and then refill it. You can hit the used cartridge base with a black marking pen to indicate its position. When the other rounds have all had their turn in the barrel just head to the range and use them for practice. If you can fire them in low light, so much the better.

Chamber go/no-go gauge. A disassembled pistol barrel can serve as a handy ammo-checking gauge, especially on the fly. You'll see more on this shortly.

Segregation of ammo. Be sure to adopt some sort of segregation system when more than one caliber is in play. There's a good chance a 9mm round will lodge in a .40 barrel!

Press-checks. This seems to be the latest maneuver and it's even showing up in movies, probably because it looks cool. The idea is to draw the slide rearward just far enough to verify a loaded chamber. Granted, this step could offer extra reassurance before stepping into harm's way, but there is a downside: a properly designed pistol must be fully in-battery before it can fire. Otherwise, the unsupported case could rupture spewing out high-pressure gas and shrapnel, which accounts for inclusion of a disconnector. To ensure complete chambering, the slide should not be restrained during loading. Instead, it should be allowed to run home with full force, overcoming the disconnector. In other words, a press-check could be counter-productive.

Tactile loaded-chamber indicators solve this dilemma 24/7, but visual check-ports only work during adequate light. With a high-cap pistol, an alternative is to just rack the slide. There are other techniques as well, but I much prefer to spend a few extra moments for a tour of all potential problems during the initial loading process. It beats shooting off a finger-tip!

More on that disconnector. This feature is what interrupts the firing sequence during cycling. When working properly, it is carefully timed to prevent discharge until the pistol is fully back into battery. For the same reason, it can disable the gun if the slide is shoved just a small amount rearward. Beyond press-checks, a contact-distance struggle can shove a slide out of battery. A weak recoil spring can prevent its full return. The thumb-behind-slide re-holstering technique can identify another possible cause - a tight holster. FYI, old rumors to the contrary, the disconnector is NOT a safety! I was up to around a dozen stories of military 1911 instructors who shot themselves in a support-hand during demonstrations before I quit counting.

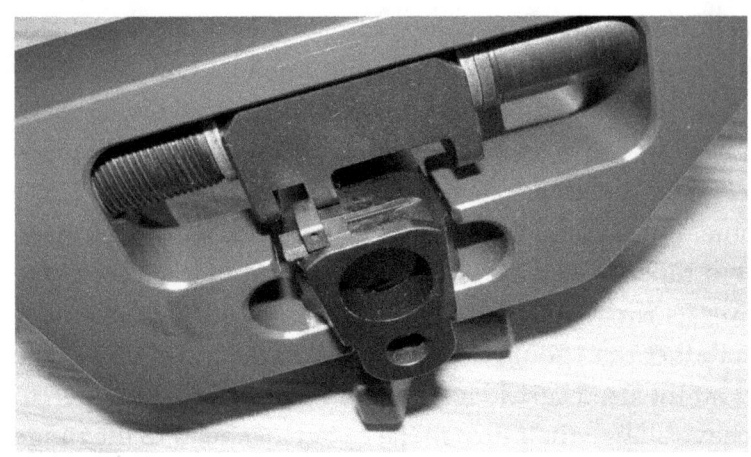

Sight replacement in progress after loss of a Tritium insert. The same effect can result from solvents that dissolve their seals. Don't pound on one, either!

Night sights ala carte. All our issued pistols are factory-equipped with these Tritium gas-powered sights. Durability has been excellent considering their hard use, but keep aggressive solvents away from the elements. You can't pound them in or out of their dovetails without risk of breaking a vial. The much safer bet is a proper sight-pushing fixture designed to exert gradual pressure (for that matter, many regular sights are installed with much force). Another seldom-mentioned issue is night sights can be surprisingly visible to others, even when the gun is holstered. We always point this out during night-fire ranges involving larger groups of shooters. The fix is a combination of awareness, appropriate clothing to cover the gun, and extra attention to your holster selection.

CLOSING THOUGHTS: SEMIAUTO PISTOL SECTION

Considering the extra worries over everything from magazines to springs, it appears a semiautomatic pistol would have to be less reliable than a revolver. In our experience, there's not a whole lot of difference between the two *so long as maintenance isn't ignored*.

If you go with a mainstream brand, feed it good ammo, and pay attention to the details, you can bet your life on one. John Browning figured that out before 1911 when his government trial submission digested 6,000 rounds! Since then, a century of refinement has extended such reliability to semiauto pistols as a whole.

SECTION IV
ALA CARTE HANDGUNS, CARRY SYSTEMS, GADGETS, AND OTHER CONCERNS

Chapter 24: CONVENTIONAL RIMFIRE HANDGUNS 309

Chapter 25: SINGLE-SHOT AND DERRINGER-TYPE HANDGUNS 323

Chapter 26: AN AR-15 PISTOL? 331

Chapter 27: INTO THE CARRY WEEDS; HOLSTERS, ETC. 345

Chapter 28: MORE ACCESSORIES: ESSENTIAL AND USEFUL ITEMS...... 361

Chapter 29: MORE ON AMMUNITION AND RELIABILITY 371

Chapter 30: DON'T FORGET TRANING! 381

CLOSING THOUGHTS 393

GLOSSARY... 395

CHAPTER 24
CONVENTIONAL RIMFIRE HANDGUNS

Although we've touched on rimfire handguns throughout this edition, they really deserve closer scrutiny. In this chapter, we'll address the more conventional types that share many features common to general-purpose centerfire revolvers and semiautos. The next chapter will cover a few less orthodox examples with, perhaps, some potential to fill a niche.

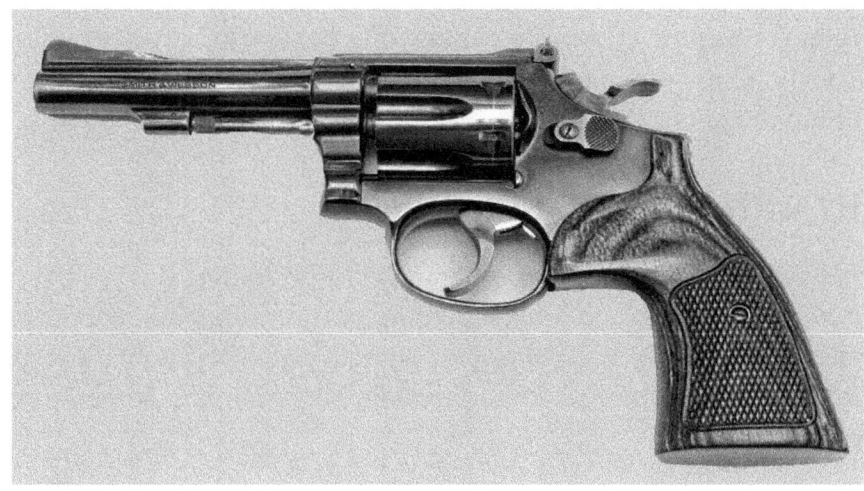

One thing they all offer is an affordable ammunition diet which can serve as a gateway to lots of extra shooting. As of early 2018, for the same cost, you could fire roughly five times as many rimfire rounds as centerfire cartridges. A 500-round brick of bulk-pack .22 LR shouldn't cost more than $25, roughly the same as two boxes of 9mm FMJ Q-loads. Good chance you'd leave the range without any of the latter remaining if meaningful practice was involved. On the other hand, 250 rounds is a fair amount of shooting; enough to leave half a brick of .22s for next time. If the rimfire works similarly to your centerfire handgun, then so much the better!

Options. For a .22 conversion unit, the cheapest route will be a conversion, assuming one is available. Centerfire revolver shooters will need a dedicated rimfire firearm (the only true "conversions" being a few dual-cylin-

How about five times the shooting for roughly the same cost? Skills are guaranteed to improve through a .22 LR handgun purchase.

Conventional Rimfire Handguns | 309

der .22 LR/.22 WMR types). Although many pistol shooters could be in the same boat, some guns like the 1911 offer switch-top uppers which may cost less than a complete rimfire. Most of 'em even work, although some trial and error could be necessary for satisfactory results. The revolver gang can recoup at least some of the expense thanks to self-contained firearms, which eliminate the need for costly spare magazines. In fact, everyone can keep a lid on associated expense through a bit of planning. Holsters and mag-pouches aren't cheap but careful pistol purchasing could eliminate the need for separate gear.

Sights. Many rimfire targets of opportunity run smaller, whether cans, metal spinners, or small game. A wrinkle is that .22 LR firearms can be fussy concerning ammo preferences, with no hard and fast rules concerning accurate combinations, so adjustable sights on rimfire handguns are worth having. They'll allow you to establish the precise zero needed to accommodate various loads, more reliably filling the pot.

RIMFIRE REVOLVERS

We touched upon a few companion rimfire options during the centerfire chapters. As it turns out, both single-action and double-action shoppers can reap benefits through a bit of planning. Commonality of function is all for the good, something most revolver manufacturers have already figured out. Rather than attempt to cover them all, let's maintain some relevancy with the previously covered centerfire players.

Ruger. The rimfire options are nicely covered with both SA and DA revolvers…

Single-action fanciers seeking a smaller revolver may like the kit-gun size .22 Bearcat, available with fixed or adjustable sights. The 4.2" barrel and 24-ounce weight provide a useful combination of carry-comfort and accuracy.

The larger Single-Six .22 is a better match for owners of larger centerfire SAs, and can be purchased as a dual-cylinder .22 LR/.22 WMR package. The smallest 4 5/8" version weighs 28 ounces. The original design has expanded to 10 or 9-shot Single Tens and Single Nines in .22 LR and .22 Magnum.

Ruger's Single-Six is available in several versions, and some even come with extra .22 Magnum cylinders.

Regarding double-actions, Ruger's centerfire LCRs, SP-101s and GP-100s are also sold as .22 LR versions. The small LCR-X or somewhat larger SP-101 would make a great DA kit-gun, while the full-size rimfire GP-100 would complement a general-purpose .357 Magnum. For that matter, either of the latter two rimfires would serve well with Ruger's larger Redhawk series.

Ruger's SAs vary in size commensurate with their chamberings, so you'll probably need a separate holster for a .22 Single-Six or Bearcat. On the other hand, the rimfire DA SP-101s and GP-100s are the same size as their centerfire counterparts.

S&W. A broad assortment of DA rimfire revolvers can be found in small or medium-frame choices that nicely match their centerfire counterparts. Essentially, you're buying the same gun so rimfire pricing is similar, BUT the actions feel the same, and the quality is there.

You can buy a .22 LR built on the same K-Frame as a .357 Model 66. Both 6 and 10-shot rimfire versions are offered and either is a first-rate choice. The stainless guns are 10-shot Model 617s, available with 4 or 6-inch, full-lug barrels. They look and handle more like larger L-Frames, and at nearly 39 ounces, even the shortest 4-inch version has plenty of heft. The blued-steel 6-shot Model 17 Masterpiece is aptly named, and has a 6-inch barrel. Weight is 40 ounces. All share the same lock-work as the center-fire models, meaning trigger pull will be familiar.

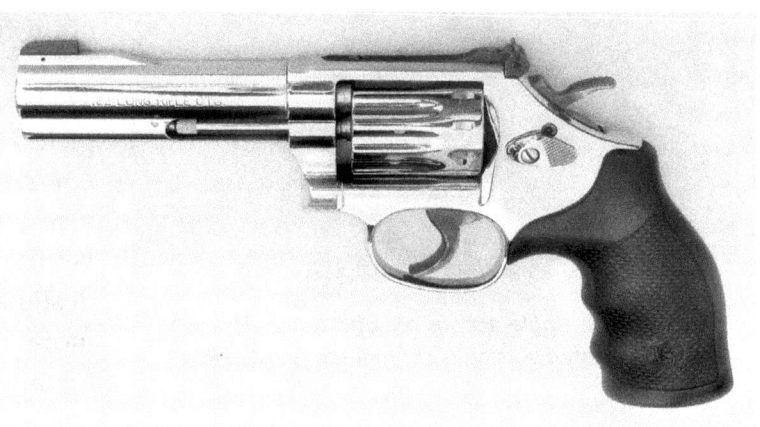

S&W's Model 617 is an elegant rimfire as is. This one received a custom factory polishing. Although stainless, its finish now looks like chrome (photo by Domenick Leonard).

If weight is a factor, don't forget S&W's neat little J-Frame "kit-guns." The feather-light 8-shot Model 317 has adjustable sights, a 3-inch barrel, and mostly-aluminum construction. The similar stainless steel Model 63 was my personal choice. It's still light at 26 ounces, but not *too* light. Featherweight guns are nice to carry, but less steady on target. The M-317 weighs less than half as much as the M-63; only 12.5 ounces! One thing to remember, a J-Frame in any caliber has a coil mainspring, which produces a different double-action trigger pull. It stacks a bit as the hammer sweeps rearward, unlike S&W's larger-framed guns. The J-Frames are still manageable in D/A mode, but they take some extra practice.

My M-63 choice was made easier since this J-frame fit a few holsters lurking in the attic, so further expense was limited to a couple small speed-strips. From a training point of view, a 6-shot .22 K-frame would've been the better match for my .357 Model 66. It would've also been easier to load, although the smaller "kit gun" rides well on my hip. By the way, despite extensive speed-loader experience, I skip them with .22 LR guns. Loading becomes difficult unless the chambers are squeaky-clean - which they won't be after a bit of shooting.

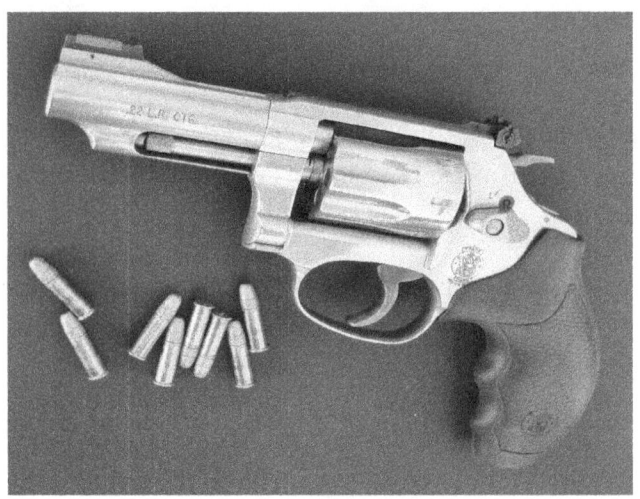

S&W's 8-shot stainless Model 63 could answer smaller .22 LR "kit gun" needs.

Other rimfire revolvers. Inexpensive Heritage .22s are available to plug a single-action rimfire gap. Among them is a 9-shot, dual-cylinder .22 LR/.22 WMR blued Combo with a 6 ½" barrel and adjustable sights

Charter Arms specializes in small double-actions revolvers. Their 4.2" .22 LR and .22 WMR Pathfinders are configured similarly to an S&W M-63 kit-gun, complete with adjustable sights. This .22 LR would be more useful than other Pathfinder versions sold as snubbies with fixed sights.

Taurus sells an interesting dual-cylinder .22LR/.22 WMR Tracker, which is closer to an S&W K-frame. It's available either as a 4-inch Ultralight, or a six-inch version. Both share a very clever QD cylinder exchange system, consisting of push-button that facilitates an easy exchange.

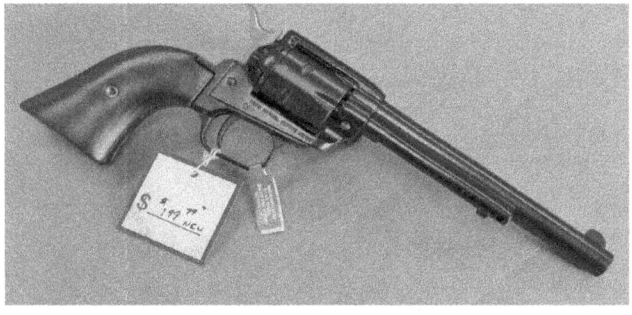

Heritage single-actions are affordable. This fixed-sighted version is chambered for .22 LR.

The above DA .22 LR revolvers would be logical picks for owners of equivalent centerfire models. An entirely different field is the series of miniature 5-shot S/A revolvers sold in .22LR and .22 WMR chamberings. Most are really niche items designed for deep concealment, so they'll receive more coverage with Derringers in Section IV. Meanwhile, on to semiautos…

RIMFIRE PISTOLS: CONVERSION OPTIONS

The idea of converting a centerfire pistol to accept rimfire .22 LR cartridges isn't new. The Colt Ace is one such design that first appeared as a complete rimfire pistol, back in the 1930s. Eventually, a 45-22 Conversion Kit appeared, which replaced the entire slide assembly of a 1911 .45 ACP Government Model. The external appearance and handling qualities of the centerfire were preserved, but internally the rimfire upper was quite different. Beyond creative ejector redesigning, a switch to a blow-back system was incorporated. The same idea has since been applied to several other centerfire pistol types popular enough to warrant the effort.

1911 Conversions. The Government Model is still the leader of the pack in rimfire conversion options. Owing to its long history, plenty of time has passed for refinement of several designs, beginning with the Ace.

Colt Ace Conversion Kit. The original locked-breech barrel and link arrangement was replaced by blow-back system incorporating a stationary barrel, secured to a standard frame by the slide-stop. Unlike most of today's versions, the Ace used a heavy steel slide that maintained .45 ACP handling qualities. To assist cycling with rimfire cartridges, extra impetus was imparted by a separate "floating chamber." Of course, a special .22 LR magazine was also necessary, but the last-shot lock-back feature was maintained. Since the conversion ran off the original frame, overall function remained identical right down to the same trigger-pull. The floating chamber, being designed to give the slide an extra boot, also increased recoil somewhat, providing more relevant practice. The boxed Colt 45-22 Conversion Kit I owned ran like a top on several frames

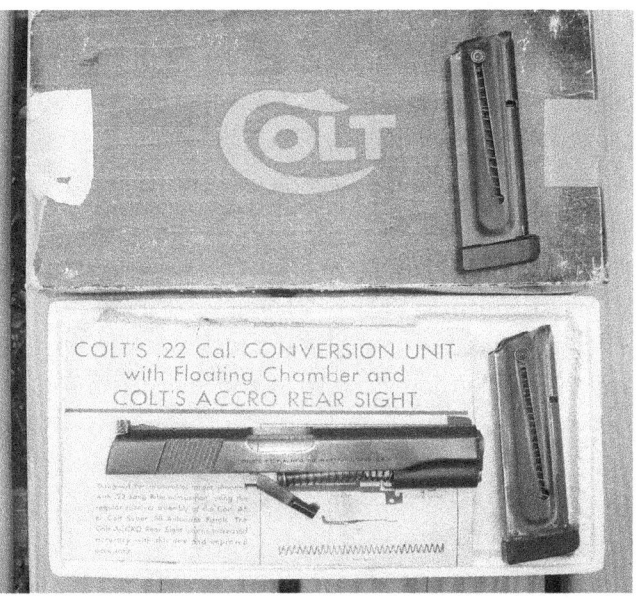

Colt's .22 LR Conversion Kit provided an earlier 1911 alternative to expensive centerfire practice.

1911 frames of different manufacture. The trick was to do some ammo testing and keep that floating chamber-insert clean. Although it was never a tack-driver, useful accuracy was attainable (around 1 ½" at 25 yards), and the identical function was appreciated. It was also a blast to shoot on smaller reactive targets geared for .22s. Today, a Colt unit is more of a collector's item. It's mentioned here because it set the stage for other designs, most of which are a whole lot simpler. One change commonly seen is use of lighter aluminum slides, which can "blow back" with lower-powered rimfire ammo.

Kimber. I stumbled upon a used, adjustable-sight unit, complete in its factory plastic box and one 10-round polymer magazine. I removed the slide assembly from my Kimber .45 Eclipse, lubed any parts that seemed worthy of oil, and slipped on the .22 upper assembly, capturing it with the original slide-stop. Presto, I had a sharp-looking .22 LR 1911! The matte aluminum slide cycled normally and made a nice match for the brushed-stainless frame. The rimfire magazine also locked in with enough protrusion for a bumper-pad effect, mating nicely with an after-market mag-funnel. Out to the range I went with an assortment of .22 LR brands, focusing on high-speeds with plated bullets,

Kimber's .22 LR Conversion easily exchanged with the original .45 ACP slide assembly of an Eclipse.

Conventional Rimfire Handguns

like the CCI Mini Mags recommended by Kimber. Accuracy was surprisingly good, thanks in part to good Bo-Mar type target sights and the familiar trigger of my frame. Turned out mine liked affordable Remington .22 LR Golden Bullets, which functioned reliably while forming tight clusters from 25 yards on a white-surfaced steel plate. Such was not the case with standard-velocity plain lead loads that produced occasional stoppages from sluggish slide cycling. Despite a lighter aluminum slide, the general handling qualities of the pistol were maintained, so my only complaint was the lack of a last-shot lock-back feature (although Kimber sanctions dry-firing). You can manually engage the slide-stop to clear and inspect the chamber, but the notch in the softer aluminum slide would eventually suffer peening if a lock-back feature was incorporated. I've since picked up a couple spare magazines which eject normally, permitting useful tactical-reloads. But one, being an off-brand, will engage the slide-stop, requiring more concentration for ammo management. Although they'll all hold ten .22 LR rounds, I usually load less for the sake of mental programing. Disassembly isn't much different from a normal 1911 and reassembly is a bit easier, promoting regular cleaning that ensures proper function. Overall, I'd rate this Kimber Rimfire Target Conversion kit as worthwhile investment. Suggested retail cost is around $340 for an adjustable-sight version finished either bright, or with dark anodizing.

Useful Kimber Conversion accuracy: This tight cluster of .22 Remington "Golden Bullets" was fired from an impromptu rest at 25 yards.

Short of buying a complete Kimber .22 pistol, their conversion unit is the simplest route, especially for owners of Kimber centerfire 1911s. Supposedly, it'll also fit shorter Commander-length pistols, and a new Compact Conversion has even appeared for shorter 1911s. But there are others…

<u>Jonathan Arthur Ciener (JAC).</u> This firm has been producing conversion units for years, for several firearms beyond Government Models. The Ciener 1911 conversion looks a lot like Kimber's unit. It's worth mentioning calibers and ejector spacing regarding these units, which are designed for .45 ACP 1911s. Cost for a JAC is around $250.

<u>Marvel.</u> I've come close to buying one of these on several occasions! These appropriately-named units are available in several configurations, including some designed for optical sights. They also have a reputation for stellar accuracy; good enough for use as true .22 bullseye pistols. Now sold with a lock-back capability, some will fit hi-cap STI and Para Ordnance frames. They appear to be well worth their $500 cost.

<u>Advantage Arms.</u> These units look like the Marvels, and are also advertised as being lock-back capable. AA says they won't fit Springfield Armory's "Range Officer" 1911s; indicative of possible fitting concerns among other combinations. Cost runs around $300.

Tactical Solutions. Well known for tricked-out Ruger .22 rifle and pistol goodies, TS also sells some sharp-looking 1911 conversion units geared toward rimfire action-shooting disciplines. Because their slides are steel, they permit incorporation of a lock-back feature. Besides providing relevant practice, these kits should be hell on metal spinners or cans! Pricing runs $410 - $480.

Further 1911 conversion-kit notes. Do your homework before committing to a purchase. Some units aren't compatible with Commander-length frames, or those cut for ramped barrels. A few will work with wide-body frames (Para Ordnance or STI) using wider proprietary magazines, but most are designed for singe-stack 1911s. Even at that, you might encounter fitting issues with certain frames. A mainspring (hammer spring) could also create possible hassles with some combinations, requiring less tension to achieve reliable function. And again, some units won't offer a last-shot hold-open feature due to use of aluminum slides. If so, try counting shots to minimize dry-fires, a beneficial practice by itself. Most have hardened breech-faces and firing pins spaced to minimize damage, but a peened chamber is at least worthy of concern.

Ejector spacing can cause further complications since it will vary among those calibers smaller than .45 ACP. Using a 9mm as an example, the ejector must be located closer to the center of the frame. This could prevent its engagement with the corresponding slot in a .22 conversion unit's slide. Some manufacturers will just exclude the use of their kits with smaller calibers like 9mm, .38 Super, .357 Sig, or .40 S&W, while others will advise replacement of such ejectors with a .45 version, done by drifting out the retaining pin. I'd much prefer to stick with a compatible combination for easy installation and removal.

Given all the variables, a check with the conversion manufacturer could save wasted cash and lots of aggravation.

Rimfire conversions for other pistols. One good test of "wide distribution" is availability of .22 conversion kits, but a pistol's cost can play a part. Take S&W's M&P pistol listings for example. So far, conversion kits are absent, which makes sense given the relatively low cost of a complete .22 LR M&P pistol; but two other hugely popular striker-fired pistol manufacturers, Glock and Springfield Armory (XDs), offer no equivalent rimfire models, presenting opportunities for entrepreneurs (no doubt, it's only a matter of time before some rimfire version of a Sig P320 appears). The single-action Browning Hi-Power and double-action Beretta 92/96 pistols are ripe conversion kit candidates, along with those from CZ. No doubt there are more, but lacking much experience with the units listed below, descriptions will remain brief.

Advantage Arms. They sell conversions for Glocks and XDs, but owing to the variations, consult their website to see what works. A last-shot hold-open feature is advertised for these units.

JAC (Ciener). They offer affordable, easy-to-switch kits for SA Browning Hi-Powers, DA Beretta 92/96 FS, and similar Taurus PT-92/99s. However, a de-cocking lever is omitted on the latter two, and none have a last-shot lock-back feature. JAC previously offered Glock units, but they're now listed as unavailable. (They still sell simple AR-15 .22 LR conversion kits that replace the bolt assemblies of 5.56 types.)

Tactical Solutions. TS lists kits for some Glock models which, unlike previous versions, now install per the extremely simple, standard field-stripping process. Although these kits are more expensive than some others, like their 1911 versions, slides are machined from steel permitting last-shot lockback.

Beretta. Recently, a Beretta-branded conversion kit appeared for Model 92/96 pistols, complete with a functional de-cocking system. A switch to the rimfire unit is a breeze thanks to an easy disassembly process, which also supports regular maintenance. The rimfire's slide is aluminum but will supposedly lock open on the last shot. Due to variations of Beretta's M-92 based pistols, check for compatibility before a purchase.

CZ: The Kadet Conversion Kit is advertised to work with the CZ-75/85 Pistol-Series. It gets good reviews for quality, and the rimfire slides are machined from steel, featuring adjustable sights. Two 10-shot magazines are included which offer last-shot hold-open with a CZ-75, but not the CZ-85. Since CZ made numerous versions of these pistols, check to see which ones will accept a .22 Kadet conversion – and which ones won't.

Conversion notes. Regardless of the unit, a break-in period may be needed to attain reliable function. You could also encounter fussiness regarding ammunition, with hi-speed plated bullet loads often being the better bet. Some fitting could be required due to dimensional variations among frames and slides, If in doubt, contact the conversion's manufacturer.

DEDICATED RIMFIRE HANDGUNS

Revolver shooters will need a separate gun since conversion kits are out, but those entertaining a .22 semiauto pistol might also opt for this approach. There are some darned good rimfire semiautos on the market that don't cost appreciably more than some conversion .22 LR kits, and a few could be less expensive. The only wrinkle is, if *identical* feel and function are top priorities, the choices become limited. It's better to view .22 LR pistols as representative facsimiles rather than true centerfire reproductions. Beyond the fact that most operate differently as straight blow-backs, some incorporate less expensive zinc alloys, and a few are produced by entirely different manufacturers.

The GSG double-action .22 LR facsimile bears a close resemblance to a centerfire Sig – but has an extra slide-mounted safety.

1911 rimfire copies. Some reasonably-priced, complete .22 LR Model 1911 clones have appeared which *might* be worth a look. Sig dropped theirs, but two other firms sell similar versions.

Tactical Imports/GSG. These blow-back 1911 copies shoot fairly well (thanks to stationary barrels), but costs are held down through the generous use of zinc alloys. Several versions are offered which imitate popular centerfire 1911s.

Chiappa Firearms. Same comments as above, priced similarly at around $300.

Kimber. The complete .22 LR pistols are classy, but here's the rub: looks like Kimber has suspended their production. Their 2018 listings show a few .45 ACP 1911s which include accessory .22 conversion kits, but no complete rimfire pistols, but since they were only recently dropped, plenty are still in the supply chain as both new or used guns.

Browning. These scaled down 1911-22s are another option. The original Black Label appeared during 2011 with a polymer frame, sized to 85% of a centerfire Government Model. Since then the line has expanded, and Browning now list aluminum-framed versions, all of which run off slides of the same alloy. Barrels are more Commander-size but the guns impart a classic appearance. Disassembly is like a centerfire 1911, and prices begin at around $500.

Sig. The P938-22 Target Micro- Compact should be a perfect .22 LR companion to Sig's smaller 1911-type centerfire single-actions. Controls are laid out the same way in classic 1911 fashion, and the locking system is preserved. The 10-shot rimfire is a tad larger than a P238 .380 because its built on the slightly larger frame of a P938 9mm. Thus, it can be converted to this caliber, resulting in a dual-use pistol. In rimfire form, a nice set of adjustable sights come standard with a longer 4-inch barrel, perfect for a day on the range.

Double-action copies. The two examples shown below actually match up closely with their DA centerfire counterparts.

Beretta. The latest M9A1-22 is a leader among rimfire pistols marketed to replicate centerfire form and function. Anyone conversant on 92 FS or M-9 operation will be right at home with Beretta's rimfire. The controls function identically and disassembly is the same. In fact, the .22 will even accept the same grip panels and fit in the same holsters. In addition to its useful lock-back feature, a great training bonus is the rimfire's 15-round capacity, which matches that of a 9mm. This model also features an accessory rail, so all things considered, its $400 price seems more than fair.

Sig. Another nearly identical centerfire champ is the P226-22 Nitron Full-size. How similar is it? Well, centerfire Caliber Exchange Kits are available in 9mm, .357 Sig, and .40 S&W! Yup, the rimfire uses the same frame. Capacity is a bit less due to a single-stack magazine that holds ten .22 LR rounds. Adjustable sights will accommodate various loads. Function and size are essentially the same, eliminating the need for extra holsters and gear. Cost for the .22 pistol is around $600; well worth it given its centerfire capability.

Striker-fired knock-offs. This field is a bit sparse. Part of the reason may be the extra engineering required to build a rimfire version. For example…

<u>S&W's .22 M&P Compact.</u> Here's a classic example of a striker-fired clone that isn't. This rimfire is a hammer-fired pistol, explaining the presence of an external safety system on each of the several .22 M&P variants. Another difference is lack of any interchangeable grip inserts, but from a practical sense, the rimfire M&P is pretty much the same pistol. We bought a few for agency use during remedial pistol programs. Our main goal was to instill greater confidence among a few serious trigger-jerking and flinching cases during structured low-recoil engagement of reactive targets. Even a couple reluctant participants wound up having a great time, and everyone agreed the positive results more than justified this effort. The switch between either pistol went smoothly thanks to the similarity of the rimfire M&Ps.

Unlike S&W's striker-fired centerfires, the M&P .22 LR Compact has an internal hammer (note the external safety). However, function and feel remain surprisingly similar.

The rimfire's sights are mostly plastic. The rear is protected by a steel housing and is adjustable. Per its centerfire cousins, the front sight is mounted in a dovetail, but being a blow-back design, the slide is aluminum to allow for rimfire momentum. This lighter alloy also translates to less overall weight, but the .22 is similar enough in other respects to provide relevant M&P practice. Some ranges restrict their hours due to noise, but a milder .22 could permit low-light work using a mounted light or laser, in this case possible because a rail section is present.

The .22 M&P has undergone a minor metamorphosis because the original version was produced by Walther. The current M&P-22 Compact is produced in-house by S&W, in several variations related to size, capacity, and finish. Many even have threaded muzzles to meet the latest suppressor craze. These pistols are a tad smaller than their centerfire counterparts (but still ship with two magazines). The rimfires also incorporate a magazine-disconnect safety and an internal locking system. A small loaded-chamber inspection port is provided, helpful in adequate light. An articulated trigger like the centerfire M&Ps is standard, although it's best viewed as an extra safety layer.

Disassembly is a bit different but by no means difficult. First, clear the pistol like any other with its magazine removed. Since the .22 isn't striker-fired, no sear disengagement tricks are needed. Instead, after locking the slide open, pivot the familiar take-down lever 90 degrees. At that point the slide must be drawn fully rearward. Lifting its rear will then allow the slide to move forward, off the frame. The captive recoil spring can then be removed, and since the barrel is pinned in place, that's the extent of the field-stripping process. Reassembly is no harder, and messing with the trigger isn't necessary.

The stationary barrel also has a positive effect on accuracy, which is useful if not match-grade. The garden-variety .22 LR loads we tried all worked, and reliability was quite good. We mostly shoot plated high-velocity .22 LR cartridges which are bought in bulk as CCIs or Federals, and shot-groups run a bit tighter than those from the centerfire M&Ps.

You *may* find the safety-lever interferes with some centerfire M&P holsters. After running into this issue with our Walther-built .22s, we just had everyone shoot from a "ready position;" not ideal but still preferable to bad habits resulting from a different holster. In fact, to maintain proper skills, we finish each range session with some centerfire holster drills (inert "blue-guns" will do the same thing). Once the trainees clear the range, an instructor plinking session is inevitable. It's just too much fun to resist!

OTHER GOOD .22 PISTOL PICKS

If identical function is foregone in favor of loosely similar features, the rimfire field expands for the better. There are many good pistols to choose from. The few that follow are based on hands-on experience. They're all single-action .22 LR blow-back semiautos with internal hammers, factory-tuned for decent trigger-pulls, and enhanced by excellent sights. Furthermore, they're designed so their rear sights remain stationary which, combined with a fixed barrel, results in excellent accuracy. Two use reciprocating breech-bolts which are housed in tubular receivers reflective of many .22 rifle designs. These pistols will all serve admirably as is, although numerous aftermarket upgrades can be installed by their owners. Beyond racy custom features like fiber-wrapped barrels, optical sight provisions are available, either from the factories or as accessories. Costs for factory-issue pistols start at around $400, although it's easy to run amuck given the plethora of higher-end models. Leave some wiggle-room for a proper holster, since each will be different enough to require a new one.

Browning. The .22 Buckmark has been in production for years. Several versions are now offered, but no matter which one you buy, it will be a sweet pistol. Its slide is a massive chunk of steel that travels below a stable top-rail designed to accommodate sighting systems. The controls make lots of sense, and should operate intuitively for Government Model shooters. For starters, the Buckmark's aluminum frame incorporates the same type of pushbutton magazine release common to most centerfire pistols. Its manual safety lever also functions similarly to 1911s, and the slide-stop will be familiar. A big departure (common to many .22 semiautos) is the Buckmark's internal hammer that provides a crisp SA trigger pull. Browning sells enough variations to satisfy nearly anyone, and they keep abreast of current trends by offering pistols with extended top-rails for optical sights, threaded muzzles for suppressors, and various finishes. The disassembly process is easy enough to encourage regular cleaning. Prices start at just above $400, creeping upward depending on the model. When money is less of a concern, the biggest challenge might involve settling on the finalist.

Browning's .22 LR Buckmark series is expansive. This one sports a Burris Fast-Fire, mounted on an accessory rail (photo by Domenick Leonard).

The Buckmark's rail has a built-in rear sight to address various aiming preferences (photo by Domenic Leonard)

Ruger. When it appeared in 1949, the Standard took off like a rocket. Since then it has morphed through several "Mark" iterations. The latest Mark IV series represents a real breakthrough by solving a complaint common to the others; namely, reassembly was a royal pain. Now it's crisis over, thanks to the Mark IV's new pushbutton release which allows the tubular upper receiver to pivot downward upon its front hinge. From there, the cylindrical reciprocating breech-bolt can be easily withdrawn in a manner reminiscent of an AR-15. There are lots of great used Rugers in circulation, but this improvement alone justifies the cost for a Mark IV. Around $400 (or less) will get you into a perfectly serviceable version, but there are higher-end models equipped to satisfy the latest trends like optics and suppressors. The 22/45 versions may interest 1911 owners. Some neat, tricked-out, polymer-frame Lite models are also sold, which could be useful where weight is a concern. The similar Tacticals use aluminum, and the Competitions are stainless, whereas traditionalists might be happy with a $450 Mark IV Standard that harkens back to 1949. The plain, steel-framed 22/45 is another basic-but-practical choice at around $410. The controls are all laid out similarly to a Buckmark's,. All Mark IVs include ambidextrous safety levers and magazine-disconnects. Meanwhile, owners of older Rugers can avoid some reassembly anguish through an aftermarket Majestic Arms Speed Strip Kit.

Ruger has been building great .22 pistols since 1949. Their 22/45 will serve well for owners of centerfire 1911 Government Models.

S&W. My trusty Model 41 dates to the 1950s, and the same pistol is still cataloged today after 50 years of production. The M-41 is a real Cadillac, but at around $1,500 it ain't exactly cheap. The good news though is we can come darned close to the performance of this target pistol for around one fourth the cost. S&WS's

Ruger's new MK IV "Lite" makes a handy trail companion as is, with the flexibility to add optics; or even a suppressor.

The MK IV also solves previous field-stripping headaches. Just depress the large button at the rear of the frame. The upper receiver will then swing open for easy servicing.

Victory is a relative youngster but has been selling like hotcakes from the get-go, pushing it into the realm of "well distributed" firearms. Controls are laid out similarly to the Buckmark's and Ruger's, and the Victory also uses an internal hammer. In a sense, it's a loose amalgamation of both with a Ruger-like bolt that travels within a tubular receiver, but a detachable barrel similar to a Buckmark.

This early S&W Model 41 .22 LR target pistol dates to the 1950s. Known for great accuracy, it's still in production - but cost reflects its quality.

An Allen wrench will permit easy field-stripping of a Victory, and equally easy barrel removal. Two standard stainless versions are sold with plain or threaded muzzles, and either will shoot to match-grade accuracy standards. Several Performance Center Victories also just appeared.

Aftermarket goodies. Any of the above .22 pistols should be perfectly serviceable as purchased. Some owners might opt for another set of easily replaceable grips while fanatics could wind up with completely different space-gun barrels sold by firms like Volquartsen or Tactical Solutions. The Buckmark and Victory barrels can be exchanged by their owners, whereas Ruger upgrades require a complete upper receiver unit (still replaceable on a kitchen table). Different sights, trick triggers, slide-rackers, and other widgets are also available. If the basic pistol doesn't have some sort of optical mounting system, there's a good chance one will be available from the above sources or B-Square. But the first thing I'd shop for beyond a good holster would be at least one spare magazine – even if my pistol shipped with two.

S&W's new "Victory" is the affordable alternative to a Model 41. It'll shoot extremely well right out of the box (photo by Domenick Leonard).

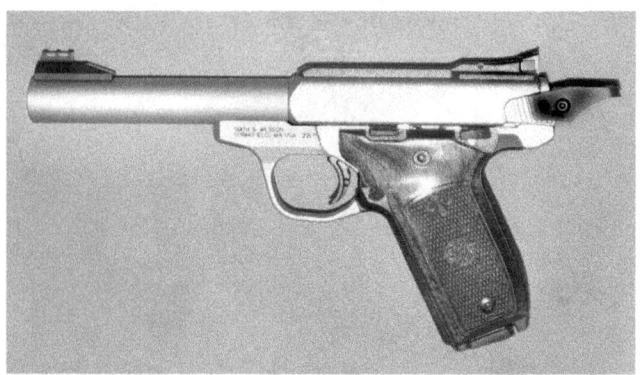

Aftermarket Victory parts soon followed. The custom touches are a Halo charging ring and set of Altamont grips (photo by Domenick Leonard).

What about a .22 Magnum? Choices are limited. Lacking any first-hand experience with Kel-Tec's PMR-30, I'll defer to others who claim this one works. Like other Kel-Tec firearms, the novel .22 WMR relies heavily on plastic, thus lightening this full-size pistol to only 14 ounces. The model number indicates its magazine capacity of an amazing 30 rounds, and it's held in place by a European-type heel release. The design is advertised as a hybrid blow-back, and though it looks a bit odd, it fires from an S/A trigger, incorporating an external thumb-safety (ambidextrous) similar to the above .22 LR types. Since the barrel is 4.3", this .22 WMR will give up much of its velocity potential, with an increase in muzzle-flash as well as ammo expense.

.22 Magnum pistol choices are relatively scarce. One unique example is the 30-shot Kel-Tec. It's fairly large, but surprisingly lightweight.

RIMFIRE SUMMARY

Centerfire handgun shoppers might consider availability of similar rimfires to avoid the further cost of separate holsters and gear. Go this route and the lower price of .22 ammo can result in even more savings related to practice. One possible downside is rimfire magazine capacity might differ affecting ammo management programming, but assuming the .22 holds more, the fix could be as simple as down-loading your magazines. Training concerns aside, and beyond its subsistence potential, a .22 rimfire handgun can offer lots of entertainment. Plinking session on cans, metal spinners, or other reactive targets won't trash the weekly grocery budget and marksmanship skills should noticeably improve.

CHAPTER 25
SINGLE-SHOT AND DERRINGER-TYPE HANDGUNS

Next come a series of rimfire and centerfire "niche guns," for lack of a better term. A single-shot handgun fits this category. Although it could address certain specialized needs, I'd scratch one off the list for use as a primary handgun since, defensively, one round just won't cut it. Today's versions run the full gamut from very small hide-out types to huge "hand-rifles" capable of firing high-powered rifle cartridges. The latter are dedicated hunting tools for use by serious sportsman, whereas the former constitute some means for a last-ditch response.

One 19th century "improvement" was a relatively small break-action, single-action Derringer with two barrels. This design still survives with modernized features such as interchangeable barrels that offer some pretty wild caliber options. The occasional four-barreled version also appears, most often in the smallest calibers to keep a lid on size. Given the abundance of small magazine-fed pistols, I'd lump them into niche or novelty status.

Although technically not a true Derringer (if there even is such a beast), a series of tiny 5-shot single-action revolvers seem most at home here. These well-made little guns will virtually disappear in a pocket or ride unnoticed in an ankle-holster. These "repeaters" should be viewed as secondary handgun choices. They're invariably chambered for .22 LR or .22 WMR, and either gives up much velocity in barrels as short as these.

Single-Shot And Derringer-Type Handguns | 323

SPECIALTY SINGLE-SHOT HANDGUNS

Large centerfire bolt-action handguns were popular for a while, driven to some extent by the sport of long-range Metallic Silhouette. Varmint hunters also enjoyed the extra challenge of engaging small prairie dogs at distances measured in football fields. Most are now gone, though Keystone Sporting Arms sells some neat rimfire bolt-actions.

Keystone's Crickett (and Chipmunk) rimfires. These petit bolt-action pistols evolved from Keystone's longstanding line of tiny .22 single-shot rifles scaled for children. The action is essentially the same and cocks from a separate knob behind the bolt. The one-piece stocks are racy designs offered in synthetic, walnut, or laminated wood. The 2 ½ pound single-shot pistol is far from compact but it'll fit in many packs with a few boxes of ammo. Both .22 LR and .22 WMR versions are offered. My experience involves a Chipmunk Hunter stamped .22 S. L. or LR. As such, its 10 ½-inch barrel can fire some intriguingly quiet rimfire alternatives including .22 CB Caps, Shorts, and Long Rifle CCI Quiets. These loads present clandestine subsistence-hunting possibilities for small game, and in my case, a way to wreak vengeance on highly annoying, chattering red squirrels that always seem to bust our bowhunting setups.

My laminated Chipmunk produced excellent accuracy during a series of 25-yard tests. I initially planned on adding a small dot-sight, but the Williams F/O green rifle-type open sights were both visible and precise. The forend also nested nicely in a sandbag rest, so despite a so-so trigger, the pistol almost shot itself as groups formed close to the sights using the factory setting.

Chipmunk 10 ½" Pistol	Grn	MV	Group	5 shots at 25 yards (temp 75 F)
Fed GMT .22 LR *	40	1085	1"	Typical .22 LR report. Great accuracy!
CCI "Quiet" .22 LR	40	685	1"	Louder than CBs, but quieter than Shorts. POI close to .22 LR
CCI CB Longs	29	630	2 ½"	Quietest load except for Colibri
CCI Target Shorts	29	930	2"	Louder than expected with an obvious report
Aguila Colibri	20	415	6+"	Almost silent, but accuracy was abysmal, with -5" POI

*Federal Gold Medal Target

Picking a quiet alternative to a .22 LR load was a bit challenging for me. Based on noise, CCI CB Longs were the clear winner. However, the most practical low-signature choice turned out to be CCI Quiets, simply because of their POI and accuracy. Results would be even better with an optical sight. A small scope-base was included with the gun for use with tip-off rings; the type that mount to grooved .22 receivers. The front receiver ring is drilled and tapped with two holes, but the base is designed to extend forward for anchoring with the rear sight's screw hole, meaning it must be removed during installation. The kicker is, most of the appropriately sized miniature dot-sights are designed to mount to Weaver or Picatinny-type bases. I had a couple adapters that would slide on the dovetailed rails, but the Chipmunk's sights work so well that I may leave things as they are. Being close to the bore-line, allowance for sight offset on small targets at close ranges will thus become unnecessary. However, one addition will be QD sling studs since a holster is impractical. During fall, this unorthodox handgun will reside in a small archery pack.

The inexpensive .22 LR Chipmunk Hunter shoots great and will handle lower-powered loads. The 10 ½" barrel boosts velocity while cutting noise, but it's no holster gun.

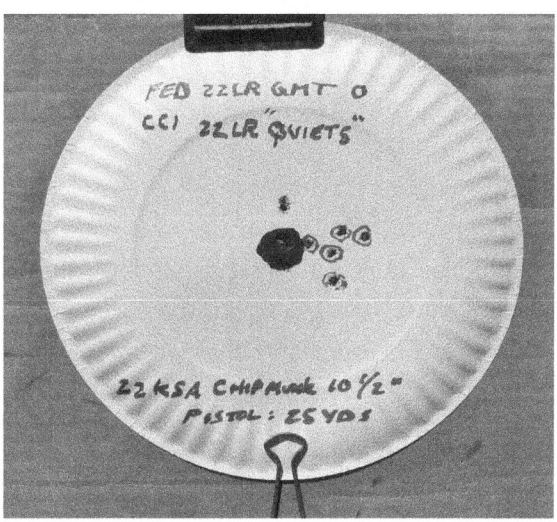

Two 5-shot groups fired off a sand-bag rest, with the Chipmunk's open sights. Those marked with circles are .22 LR Federal Gold Medal Targets. The unmarked holes were shot with .22 LR CCI Quiets. POI remained surprisingly close at 25 yards.

The Thompson/Center revolution. A few break-barrel single-shots endure but the most popular by far are built by Thompson/Center. They revolutionized the sporting handgun industry during the 1960s by offering a switch-barrel Contender pistol chambered for a growing list of popular calibers from .22 LR through .45/70. The rimfire option was possible thanks to a selectable dual-firing pin arrangement housed within its external hammer. Barrels came in various lengths (10-14") and most were designed to accept scopes. Before long, handgun devotees were roaming the woods with deer rifle calibers like .30/30 or .35 Remington. Off-season, a simple barrel change permitted use of cartridges like .22 Hornet or .223 Remington for leisurely varmint expeditions. I often cruised my area with such a 10-inch version that was stashed within the saddlebag of a motorcycle. These calibers (and others) shot as accurately as most rifles although velocity was compromised to some extent. Still, considering they were handguns, their maximum potential could be realized. At one point, I picked up a second frame and equipped it as a rifle thanks to T/C's extensive line of barrels, stocks, and accessories.

One supposed shortcoming of the Contender was its inability to handle popular full-power cartridges like the .308, .30/06, etc. T/C eventually rectified this by offering a beefed-up Encore which, like their Contender, could be configured as a pistol or shoulder-fired gun. The latter was not only sold in full-power chamberings, but also as a muzzle-loader. Barrel interchangeability remained although Contender and Encores are NOT compatible (no rimfires in the latter, either).

Since our focus on T/C's pistol offerings, here's a cautionary note: installing a pistol barrel (one shorter than 16") on a firearm sold as a rifle will violate the National Firearms Act by transforming it into a tightly regulated "short-barreled rifle." Like a suppressor, an SBR requires a $200 fee and NFA paperwork, issued through ATF (more to follow on this in the AR Pistol Chapter). It's easier and safer to avoid mixing the two T/C configurations!

The Encore is no doubt more popular due to its ability to handle hot calibers, but as a pistol, I'd still prefer the lighter Contender G-2. Not that it'll be small. My Contender (and Remington XP-100 .223 single-shot) had 14-inch barrels, but their reports were still concussive and their velocities suffered to some extent. Being scoped, they were also gargantuan. Forego the hotter calibers and things begin to improve. A lighter and shorter barrel helps and here's one that comes to mind…

HG-25 Pistol TC Contender: *The T/C Contender offers all sorts of possibilities – but only one shot.*

Thompson/Center's G-2 Contender. This can be purchased with 12 or 14-inch .45/.410 vent-rib barrels machined for special choke-tubes. The removable tube serves to constrict shot patterns just like any normal shotgun, but it also has deep parallel lugs to help arrest rifling-induced shot spin. These lugs provide engagement for a small included wrench, so the tube can be removed for use of conventional .45 Colt bullets. My 12-inch version worked better than expected with 2 ½" or 3" .410 shells, and shooting flying claybirds was doable with concentration - if I got on them fairly quickly. As a bow hunter from a state with a one-deer limit, I sometimes used this T/C from archery ground blinds after filling my tag. Some of the makeshift blinds were situated near wild apple trees that attracted ruffed grouse, so it was fun to sit in camo archery clothes with the Contender in hand. Any grouse that filtered in were shot from trees or the ground, harder than it seemed. A 3" dose of # 7 ½ shot did the trick with careful shooting inside 20 yards. Although the T/C barrel has a small folding rear sight, I never did try slugs or .45 bullets through it. Supposedly the latter shoot with decent accuracy. If bullets were called for I just switched to a different barrel, an option that is still available. The clever dual-firing pin design with a hammer-mounted selector will even permit installation of a .22 LR barrel. Of course, at around 3 ½ pounds, a Contender is no flyweight. This relegates it to sporting or survival use (accounting for its appearance here). I carried mine with a sling.

OTHER SINGLE-SHOTS

Continuing with the .45 Colt/.410 theme, a couple less well-known alternatives exist.

The Eagle Imports Comanche. Same idea as a T/C; without interchangeable barrels for much less cost. It is offered in several barrel lengths and finishes, with the 10-inch version more likely to produce optimum .410 patterns. For around $200, you could own a simple break-barrel gun that would fit in a backpack, bug-out bag, or other small space, providing a possible means of subsistence.

Heizer Defense. They sell the most unusual break-action .45/.410 gun of them all, mainly because of its size. Weighing only 21 ounces, the single-shot PS1 Pocket Shotgun is for all intents and purposes a hammerless derringer. This applies to not only its size, but also its range limitations. Although off-topic here, things get even more interesting with this pocket-blaster because of interchangeable rifle-caliber barrels, chambered in .223 and 7.62x39! Their muzzle-blasts are spectacular, although the concept does provide a last-ditch response for those toting carbines in these calibers.

TWO-BARRELED DERRINGERS

Several firms sell so-called "Derringers," a generic description perhaps analogous to Xerox, but in this case describing small hammer-fired break-action handguns. Since their inception, Derringers have been marketed as inexpensive concealment pieces, an idea that made more sense during the era of larger single-action peacemakers. Typically, they fire from a non-selective S/A hammer, but their over/under barrels are hinged at the top. The trigger is usually a low-profile "spur" type that lacks any sort of trigger guard. Barrels are short and chambered for less innocuous calibers like .38 Special. Another dazzling chambering is the .22 WMR, which puts out plenty of fire and noise while shedding most of its velocity. More recently, some other interesting calibers have appeared along with innovative upgrades that justify a greater cost. To that end, among today's manufacturers, a major player is Bond Arms.

Bond Arms. These guns are built in Texas by a well-established firm with a strong commitment to tank-grade durability. Choices are numerous with more than a dozen models in various calibers and barrel lengths. Judging by the features, it appears Bond went through the Derringer design with an eye toward improving any of its shortcomings. The result is a stainless steel gun with several safety improvements including a covered trigger guard. The most prominent feature is interchangeable barrels which can be ordered from the factory in most popular calibers including .45 Colt/.410 (or just buy one as a complete gun)! Barrel lengths run from 2 ½ - 6" and nearly all of the popular calibers are offered. As a primary sidearm, I'd want more capacity, but a Bond could have appeal as a

Two-shot derringers were an early pocket-pistol design. They still have a following and a few shoot big bullets. Competing semiautos offer more capacity, mostly in smaller calibers.

secondary gun sharing common ammunition. Of course, the .410 version is another intriguing option within a league of its own. Prices run from $400 - $500 reflecting Bond's excellent quality.

MINIATURE REVOLVERS

By the end of the 19th century, a number of small revolvers appeared and many were of questionable quality. They've since faded into obscurity, but the idea survived and one modern manufacturer has captured the market through a series of ultra-small rimfire single-actions.

North American Arms. Picture a tiny Derringer fitted with a 5-shot cylinder. How tiny? How about a .22 Short with a 1 1/8" barrel that weighs 4 ounces? Some others aren't much bigger since the equivalent .22 LR versions only adds 0.6 oz. The combination of polished stainless steel and pretty rosewood grips presents a distinctive aura, more on the order of jewelry. More utilitarian models are offered with synthetic grips, useful sights, and longer barrels. The .22 WMR chambering is there as well for those who appreciate fireworks. The most unusual Earl sports a 6" barrel to wring out the most velocity, and comes with a spare 5-shot .22 LR cylinder; but most NAA models fall in between, reflecting their intended use as last-ditch firearms that virtually disappear until needed. The initial design being minimalist, lacked an ejection system, instead requiring removal of the cylinder so it's axle can be used to punch out fired cases. More recently, a swing-out cylinder Sidewinder appeared, followed by a clever top-break model. The Ranger MC-BTII comes with a pair of 5-shot cylinders in .22 LR and .22 WMR. Switching them is a breeze since the gun breaks open on a lower hinge, presenting the cylinder for removal; or just reload the exposed rear face since opening the action activates an ejector-star (shades of the 19th century Schoefield). Despite these extra niceties, weight is only 6.9 ounces. The short 1.63" barrel maintains its small size, but velocity will suffer greatly – especially in .22 Magnum. Common to all models is a spur trigger and single-action hammer. All 5 chambers can be safely carried through use of special safety notches machined between each chamber. Lowering the hammer's firing pin into a notch will isolate it from a cartridge rim, but cocking will index the cylinder. NAA offers a few neat accessories designed for carry, as well as a LaserLyte grip option. The latter works similarly to Crimson Trace's laser-grips, and should greatly improve hit probability. Depending on what you lust after, prices will run from $230 - $575.

NICHE-GUN SUMMARY

These firearms are for the most part oddballs that could prove useful in more specialized circumstances. Except for smaller handguns (like Derringers), one challenge may involve a practical carry solution. Necessity being the mother of invention, unorthodox methods can evolve. One fix for the largest types like T/Cs could be a sling, but more will probably wind up cached, stashed in vehicles, or stowed in packs and bug-out kits - meaning they won't always offer an immediate response. For this reason, most of us would be better off starting with a general-purpose handgun. In fact, the next example goes beyond "niche," to specialized at best – or, possibly, even useless…

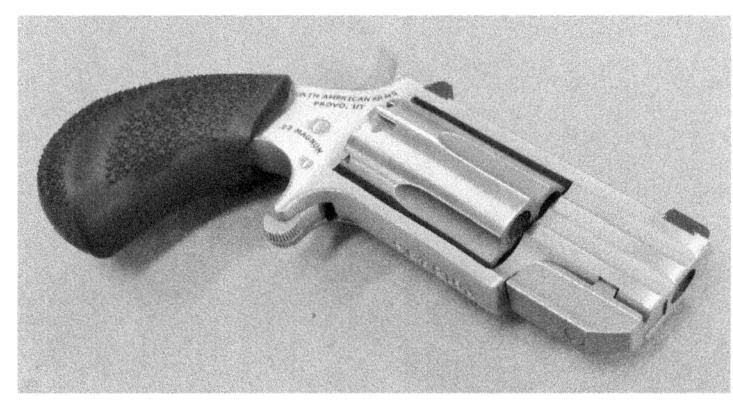

Jewelry that shoots through a tiny North American Arms revolver, chambered for .22 Magnum cartridges.

CHAPTER 26
AN AR-15 PISTOL?

My first encounter with an AR handgun involved a sawed-off M-16, recaptured during the Vietnam War. At some point, the other side may have attempted to revive a damaged battlefield pickup, but whatever the story, this ill-fated specimen made an interesting souvenir. The solid stock had been removed, along with the stock and forend. The barrel had been shortened to around ten inches, and feeding required manual operation with the charging handle. Of course, it just begged to fired, so we took it for a spin. Besides a dazzling muzzle flash, this thing was *loud!* It was still relatively large, too. The same issues were noted years later while playing with single-shot .223 pistols. An AR-15 is a bit worse regarding size, due to the need for a buffer-tube that extends rearward from the receiver. Bottom line, an AR pistol is both noisy and large; and lacking shoulder support (AKA stock), it'll also be hard to shoot well.

A good muzzle device can dramatically reduce muzzle flash, but it takes a suppressor to significantly reduce noise, and even with conventional 5.56 rounds, the report from a short-barreled AR-15 will be roughly equivalent to a .22 Magnum cartridge fired from a rifle. Also, both a "short-barreled rifle" (SBR) and suppressor are NFA items that must clear additional legal hurdles, with a $200 federal stamp-fee for each; so a suppressed SBR would cost $400, not to mention the price of the "can." Some AR manufacturers have begun permanently welding a suppressor's outer tube to the muzzle of an SBR, thereby extending barrel length to reach the non-NFA 16-inch minimum. Adding the internal

As configured with a sub-16" barrel, this AR constitutes an SBR, requiring extra NFA hurdles. Gotta speak the language...

suppressor parts still requires the stamp, but total cost falls to only $200..

An expedient fix is a short-barreled AR (less than 16") without a stock. The stubby bare buffer-tube extending from the rear of the receiver is just there to house necessary parts, and not "designed" for shoulder-fired use. As such, an AR so configured constitutes an ATF-sanctioned pistol, subject to no federal restrictions beyond those for an S&W revolver or a Glock. Yes, you could add a suppressor after jumping through the legal hoops, but your AR "pistol" will be plenty big without one!

The next items of concern are stocks and sights. As noted, the addition of a stock intended for shoulder use will automatically turn a pistol into an SBR. Adding a scope will only make things worse since ATF frowns upon either in conjunction with AR pistols, so the safer bet for legal purposes is to preserve the general pistol design. Interestingly, even ATF wrestled with this concept upon the appearance of "arm braces." These short plastic sleeves were advertised as stabilizers, designed to be

One expedient legal fix is an AR "pistol" with a stubby barrel and shortened buffer tube. Expect significant velocity loss and lots of noise in 5.56 NATO/.223 chamberings.

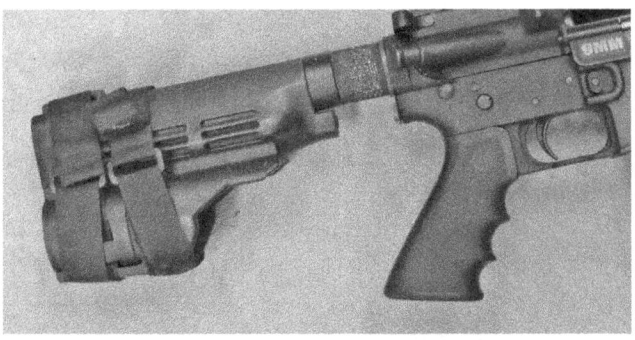

An SB Arm Brace came next. As designed, the idea was to strap it around your forearm and fire it one-handed. After a rocky start with ATF, looks like it's here to stay.

secured to a shooter's forearm by straps. The brace attached to the buffer tube in a manner similar to a telescoping carbine stock, and though not "designed" for shoulder use, a flat rear surface offered at least that temptation. ATF went back and forth over rulings, but finally sanctioned the concept. Dot-sights are increasingly popular with handguns across the board, but a scope on a brace-equipped AR pistol could tilt it towards the slippery slope of SBR territory.

The serial-numbered lower receiver, as originally configured, can also raise legal concerns. One virtue of the AR is its transformer-like design. One lower can accommodate a wide variety of upper-receiver assemblies in all sorts of barrel-lengths and calibers. A conversion is as simple as pulling two takedown pins, so total reconfiguration requires only several seconds; but according to The National Firearms Act of 1934, if your rifle starts out in that configuration, it must stay that way. Some enthusiasts like to assemble their own customized ARs, starting with a stripped lower receiver. This serial-numbered part constitutes the "firearm," so how it was listed on ATF Form 4473 will determine its legal status. Again, adding an upper with a barrel shorter than 16-inches to a rifle receiver makes it an SBR.

The spare 24" .223 will mount to the 16" .300 Blackout carbine in seconds. However, adding an upper with a barrel shorter than 16" requires special NFA registration!

Overall length also counts. Angled foregrips are okay, but forward pistol grips are out on AR pistols shorter than 26 inches. Measure from the actual muzzle.

There are a few other technicalities, so a safer bet is to buy an AR pistol and keep it that way. Or better yet, buy a 16" carbine with a telescoping stock and back it up with a conventional pistol!

POSSIBLE AR PISTOL ALTERNATIVES

Having trashed the AR pistol idea, I'll now admit to owning one. It's not a 5.56/.223 though…

We have experience with a couple other calibers more amenable to short-barreled AR platforms. Both burn less powder than a standard .223 Remington/5.56 NATO cartridge, resulting in more efficient combustion within so-called pistol-length barrels. The two immediate dividends are less noise and muzzle-flash. These factors are major concerns during tactical operations, which for us often involve confined spaces with steel or concrete surfaces. Beyond collateral damage, firing a full-strength major rifle cartridge from a short barrel in this type of environment will result in everyone being pretty much blind and deaf. For that matter, most private structures won't be a whole lot better. Yes, good muzzle devices and suppressors can help, but you are back at extra length and costs.

One interesting .223/5.56 AR pistol alternative is a less common but increasingly popular caliber that offers interesting capabilities for more technically-minded shooters. The second is a simpler blowback type that runs off a popular pistol cartridge. Both could be good AR pistol *or* carbine choices, but our focus is on the former.

Among many chamberings, three often used in AR pistols are (L-R): 5.56 NATO/.223, .300 Blackout (subsonic and supersonic), and 9mm Luger.

.300 Blackout. This interesting little cartridge was initially designed to fire subsonic loads through suppressed AR-15 carbines. Originally conceived as the .300 Whisper, AAC seized upon the idea to complement their line of suppressors, resulting in the present .300 Blackout iteration. The concept works very well, and with the right loads, it's almost mouse-fart silent. The key is elimination of a supersonic crack common to bullets exceeding the speed of sound. Normally, everyone is fixated on the highest velocities possible, but in this case, the objective is the opposite.

Instead, the idea is to launch an extremely heavy .30-caliber bullet at just above 1,000 fps. That way, with the right propellants, enough pressure can be generated to reliably cycle a gas-operated AR (not practical with a .223 because of insufficient bullet weight). I make my own .300 Blackout cases from shortened and reformed 5.56 NATO brass, but factory ammunition is now readily available. In either instance, the shortened cases loaded with longer ultra-heavy bullets permit an overall cartridge length that will still fit inside standard AR magazines. I often shoot 220-grain Hornady RN SPs, but some people use "lighter" 190-200 grain Spitzers. Of course, when the objective is to stay below the speed of sound, the price will be a loopy trajectory approaching that of a brick. As for terminal effects, expansion is unlikely with most projectiles, although some tumbling may result. Hornady just introduced a special Sub-X 190-grain semi-spitzer with a flat Flex-tip that they claim will expand down to 900 fps. I wouldn't doubt it after witnessing a recent FBI-protocol bare gel test that revealed excellent penetration *and* expansion.

A fast rate-of-twist is needed to stabilize such long-for-caliber projectiles. The four 16" .300 Blackout barrels I use are all 1x8 (one 360-degree twist within 8"). Five-shot groups at 100 yards run 2" or less (sometimes closer to an inch) with heavy 220-grain RN, but a slight amount of bullet yawing can be evident (barrels chambered for conventional cartridges like the .308 are often rifled 1x12). Yawing was more pronounced in a 10 ½" barrel and accuracy suffered, but a switch to 190-grain Hornady SUB-X provided the cure, placing 5 shots inside 1.75" at 100 yards.

Lighter-bullet supersonic loads can also be used, resulting in carbine-length ballistics similar to that of a Soviet 7.62x39 AK-47. Most of my .300 Blkt experience involves 110-grain spitzers that develop MVs of 2,350 – 2,400 fps from 16-inch barrels. Accuracy is useful but not stellar, averaging around 1.5 MOA, probably due to faster-twist rifling. When fired suppressed, their report still has a nasty supersonic crack; quieter, but still loud. However, trajectory is flat enough for use to 200 yards or thereabouts with 110 -120 grain bullets. So far, we've cleanly harvested two deer using 110 and 120-grain

Hornady's new 190-grain .300 Blackout "Sub-X" delivers subsonic accuracy and expansion – even from shorter barrels.

SUB-X trajectory: The yellow (unmarked) two-shot groups were fired at 50, 75, and 100 yards. The chart on the box shows a drop of 33" at 200 yards!

Barnes solid-copper TAC-TX loads. Neither bullet was recovered due to pass-through penetration, but based on previous Barnes experience, we'd bet on classic expansion with at least 95% weight retention. Although we haven't shot these Barnes loads in gel, we have witnessed results with factory-loaded 110 Hornady GMX solid-copper bullets from a carbine. Penetration was excellent and the expanded bullets appeared to be dead-ringers for other Barnes bullets we've recovered from game.

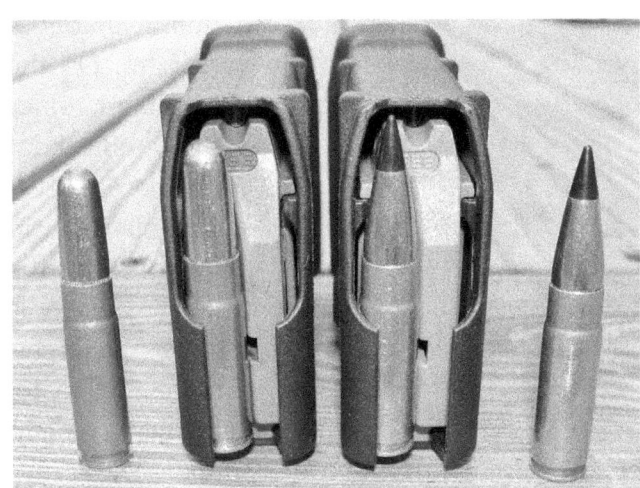

Two different .300 Blackout approaches: The heavy 220-grain RN (L) is for subsonic use. The 110-grain Barnes TAC-TX is a supersonic alternative. Its long plastic tip provides an overall length similar to 5.56mm cartridges for better feeding in AR magazines.

Hornady's .300 Blackout SUB-X (L) and monolithic GMX produced classic expansion with deep penetration during this bare-gel test.

The same properties that make such homogenous bullets great penetrators also raise concerns about indoor use. Heavier subsonic loads of any type are in the same boat since their bullets are really designed for .30-caliber high-power rifles like a .308, .30/06, or the .300 Magnums. Being tough, they won't expand at around 1,000 fps, instead just punching through barriers, driven onward by their increased mass.

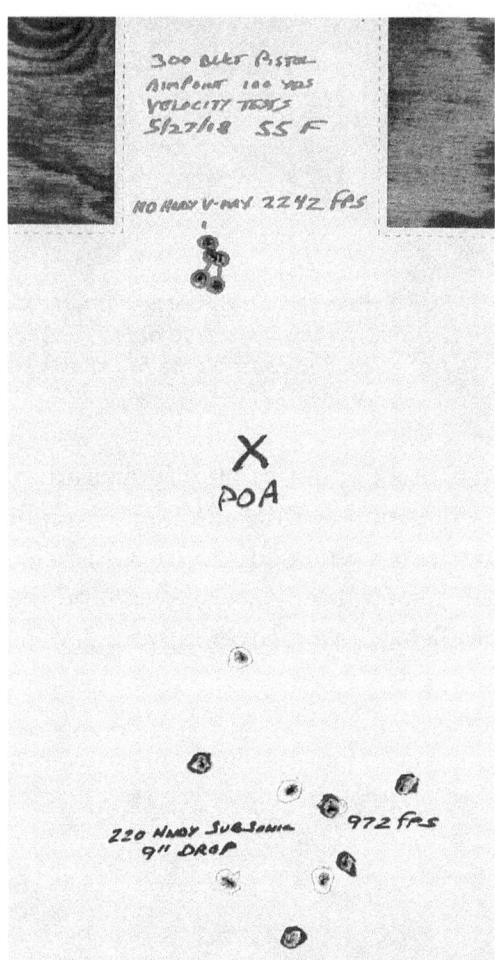

Another big issue is the great disparity in POI between supersonic and subsonic loads. With 16" carbine barrels, when using 110-grain supersonics zeroed for 100 yards, slow and heavy subsonics require around an extra foot of hold-over! Obviously, one common zero won't work.

Using the same loads, I see less drop in a 10 ½" pistol barrel; more on the order of eight inches. Seems weird at first, but the supersonics are slower due to incomplete powder combustion. As such, more elevation is necessary to maintain that 100-yard zero. On the other hand, since a .300 Blackout pistol bore of reasonable length can fully consume the smaller subsonic powder charges, carbine and pistol velocities remain similar. The result-

Beyond vastly different POIs, accuracy suffered with heavy 220-grain subsonics in a 10 ½" pistol barrel (rifled 1x8). Key-holing indicates poor stability – a contrast from 110 supersonics.

A switch to Hornady's lighter subsonic 190-grain Sub-X provided much better accuracy. It also eliminated concerns about suppressor baffle strikes.

ing disparity is evident downrange through less apparent drop when switching to subsonic loads.

BUT let's not forget the negative. Supersonic loads loose more velocity with each inch of barrel reduction while noise and flash increase. For this reason, I'm more interested in a longish pistol barrel of around 10 ½". Since gas-tube lengths and other dynamics must be balanced for reliable function (even more of a challenge once a suppressor is mounted), this length is also closest to the proven 16" carbine design. And for what it's worth, .300 Blackout velocity loss is much less than an equivalent .223. The combination of less propellant and greater bore volume contributes to more efficient combustion.

Comparative muzzle velocity loss	16" barrel	10½" barrel	Loss
.223 Rem 55-grain Federal AE FMJ	2840 fps *	2530 fps	310 fps
.300 Blackout 110-grain Hornady V-MAX	2350 fps *	2242 fps	108 fps
.300 Blackout 190-grain Hornady SUB-X	1050 fps	1025 fps	25 fps

Note: Common light-weight supersonics used to illustrate the full velocity potential of each caliber.

Although the .223's loss in a 10 ½" barrel is around 300 fps, its advantage over the .300 Blkt is still that amount greater. This could lend credence to the AR .233 pistol concept, but bullet weight is less; in a much smaller caliber initially designed for optimum performance from 20" rifle barrels (3100 fps +). Furthermore, these are muzzle velocities. The U.S. Military encountered stopping power issues in Afghanistan with 14" M-4s (shorter M-16s), as ranges approached 200 meters. Many .223 AR pistols employ even shorter barrels, meaning velocity will suffer more, while muzzle-blast will exponentially increase.

I'd be none-too-anxious to tackle deer or similar-sized animate targets with an SB .223 for these reasons. If not for the NFA requirements, the best of both worlds would be separate carbine and pistol-length uppers that could run off one AR lower.

Regarding the addition of a .300 Blackout, the only major AR-15 difference between a .223/5.56 NATO is the barrel. In fact, both calibers will even run off the same bolt assembles and magazines. A few years back, the .300 Blackout was an oddball load, but this situation has since changed. Still, if ammo availability does pose concerns, a separate pistol-length .223 upper could serve as a reassuring spare. Just pop two pins, pull off one complete upper receiver assembly, and switch it for the other within seconds. Viola, the ultimate transformer!

Exchanging an AR's upper-receiver is as easy as retracting the two captive pins in its lower half.

In my case, with a bunch of AR parts and .300 Blackout ammo on hand, a dedicated 10 ½" AR pistol seemed somewhat justifiable. It was procured as a niche item for use in tight spaces, which *could* include the home if fragile bullets are employed – like Hornady's 110-grain V-MAX offered through their Black ammo line. However, the main use for this AR pistol will be the confines of small winter coyote blinds, where maneuvering a suppressed carbine can present challenges. I hand-load 110 V-MAX bullets, achieving speeds similar to Hornady's posted MV of around 2350 fps from 16-inch carbine barrels. The 10 ½" pistol barrel only gives up 100 fps, making it plenty potent for use against our big northern hybrid wolf/coyotes. Any two-legged varmints would likely be in similar trouble. Recoil is minimal.

My AR pistol is a "build" that evolved using a bunch of parts on hand, but it runs surprisingly well, and shoots as accurately as its longer carbine cousins. Noise is somewhat worse with a bare muzzle, but I mostly shoot it suppressed. With the can attached (using a QD muzzle device), the subsonic report is similar to 16" carbines. Its overall length is also the same as a bare-muzzle 16" carbine, although the suppressor does add extra heft. The sight is an Aimpoint Comp-2, which has settings compatible with night vision devices. Muzzle-flash becomes a major concern in low light, more so with NVDs. A suppressor solves this issue. Lacking one, an effective muzzle device will be required. Those sold by Yankee Hill Machine, Sure-fire, Smith Enterprises (Vortex), and others will work amazingly well. As far as complete .300 Blackout AR pistol manufacturers, we have the most experience with Rock River and Windham Weaponry, but the list is growing, no doubt due to the popularity of this cartridge in carbines.

The shorter barrel of the 10 ½" AR pistol leaves room for a suppressor. Overall length remains close to a 16" carbine.

If the whole thing sounds like an especially convoluted AR pistol process, well, it is! Take hunting off the table though and things can get a whole lot simpler…

The 9mm option. We have lots of history with various 9mm ARs, including semiauto 16" carbines, and SBR-configured select-fire SMGs. Recoil, report, and flash from a 16" carbine is more like a .22 rimfire, but even the stumpy buzz-guns are compact and controllable. Unsuppressed, the report from their pistol-length barrels is mild, with minimal muzzle-flash in low light. The wide variety of 9mm loads includes everything from frangible to homogenous projectiles. Common 148-grain subsonic offerings function well and are extremely quiet when suppressed.

Generally speaking, the velocity from a carbine will be higher than from a pistol. However, the combination of small 9mm powder charges and ample bore volume translates to rapid combustion, offering little additional gain, even in a 16-inch barrel. Assuming the increased MV is only around

100 fps, 9mm SBR or AR pistol owners won't give up much in their shorter barrels. Even our 7-inch SMGs permit easy hits on combat silhouettes at 100 yards when fired in semiauto mode. Their M-4 shoulder stocks and Trijicon dot-sights are a big help, but the former is prohibited on a normal AR pistol. Perhaps one consolation is that longer-range terminal 9mm punch will decrease regardless of the platform. An offset is lots of extra AR shots will probably be available for those without magazine restrictions, and a hit by only one would ruin someone's day.

Our Agency SMGs have dedicated 9mm lowers, which run off common 32-round Sten Gun magazines. They feed reliably, although the last several rounds are a real bear to load. Actually, a generic AR-15 5.56 NATO lower receiver can be made to work with these magazines. A special 9mm adapter is simply inserted like a standard magazine, where it serves as a spacer of sorts. In theory, the addition of a 9mm upper receiver unit should then result in a functional AR-15 (a different hammer and buffer could be needed for proper function). Some manufacturers pin these adapters to 9mm designated receivers, creating permanent installations. It's a wonder they work as well as the do, given the large jump needed for a short 9mm to reach its chamber.

A 9mm SMG, shown with a Trijicon Reflex Sight and folding backup iron sights (BUIS). Accuracy is surprisingly good in semiauto mode. Note the pins in its mag-well, which capture an adapter block.

In fact, the internals are different from a standard 5.56 rifle, starting with the absence of a gas system. Instead, 9mm ARs run as blow-backs, using highly modified bolt-carriers. Unlocking is delayed through their mass, and timing is regulated by pinned-on weights. Things can get a bit touchy regarding feeding with some loads, more often when a suppressor is introduced. We were interested in shooting frangible 9mm loads for specialized confined-space ops, but experienced lots of stoppages until tinkering with different weights. Since everything is a balancing act, the trick is to establish function before laying in a large supply of ammo – preferably from the same lot number!

Once it gets moving, the heavy bolt travels with authority so, despite the small cartridge, recoil is more pronounced. The effects are less with a shoulder-stock, but expect some jump in an AR pistol. On a positive note, the simplified internals make cleaning easier. There's no separate bolt-head or cam-pin, and no gas-tube to maneuver around. The carrier is a giant one-piece bolt. In a pistol-size AR, it's easy to access the internals of both receiver halves after popping the two pins that hold them together. At that point both halves will also store in a very small space.

One promising concept is the appearance of AR lowers designed specifically for Glock magazines (including a few in .40 S&W or .45 ACP). One thing to keep in mind is that some lack a last shot lockback feature. It takes extra engineering to devise such a system with smaller pistol magazines, and that can drive up cost. Not having this capability would drive me nuts, but AKs don't lock open either and they're everywhere. Meanwhile, I've been holding out for a dedicated receiver capable of accepting S&W M&P magazines. Things are percolating and a few are now appearing, including some with modular magwells. Initial development seems to center on carbines, but much of the same technology extends to AR pistols.

The Shockwave Technologies KAK-type unit is a very basic AR pistol brace. Just forward of the Aimpoint sight is a QD Caldwell brass-catcher mount.

The AR 9mm pistol I envision would be nothing super-short. Instead, it would be sort of a quasi-pistol/carbine with a now-common flat-top upper receiver, a barrel running around 8 to 10 ½ inches, and a railed, free-floated forend. A smallish pistol brace (like a KAK unit) would be added to the stubby buffer-tube, and a dot-sight would be mounted for 24/7 aiming. The forend's Picatinny-rail surface would also accommodate back-up iron sights (BUIS), and other sections would allow easy attachment of a light, laser, or combination thereof. A threaded muzzle would accommodate various muzzle devices as well as any future suppressor. The result would be a good bump-in-the-night package; fairly maneuverable, and much less concussive than rifle-cartridge versions. In fact, other than the 9mm chambering and slight concession to barrel length, it would mirror my .300 Blackout pistol, but by comparison, a 9mm is much simpler. Buy a box of 9mm *something*, fill its magazine, and get to shooting. Yes, you'll want hearing protection, but you won't defoliate the surrounding area from muzzle blast or shake paint off adjacent surfaces.

In fact, Nordic Components already offers pretty much what I'm looking for. Their 8.5" AR 9mm pistol even has a modular magwell assembly, permitting configurations for use with Glock or M&P pistol

The A.R.M.S. 40-L folding rear sight backs up an Aimpoint Pro.

magazines. A last shot hold-open capability is listed for either, but the list price of $1,600 reflects the extra engineering necessary for such versatility. Wilson Combat offers another attractive candidate with their AR9, which comes as a carbine or SBR. Unfortunately, no pistol version is listed. Nevertheless, it's worthy of mention because of purpose-built lower receivers that accept Glock or Beretta magazines (also advertised was an M&P version). Anything built by Wilson is of excellent quality, accounting for the higher cost; in this case around $1,900, depending on final specs. Go with a more basic design though and prices fall in line with most other AR-15s. Rock River's LAR-9 can be configured lots of different ways, and other interesting 9mm options are appearing as shooters begin to appreciate the usefulness of this design.

.223/5.56mm option. Some AR-15 owners will no doubt consider a .223/5.56 pistol because of existing rifles and accumulated extras from magazines through spare parts and, of course, ammo. If so, many manufacturers now offer AR pistols, SBRs, and carbines. While I might go with a shorter barrel in some other AR pistol calibers, I'd prefer at least a 10 ½" barrel in this caliber (many SBRs are 11 ½" for this reason). Actually, we're talking about two different calibers, a topic which often cause some confusion. So, the 5.56 x45 mm NATO is hotter version of the civilian .223 Remington load, with a few minor dimensional chamber differences thrown in to accommodate the former's higher pressures.

You can safely fire .223 Remington ammo in a 5.56 chamber, but the reverse can be unsafe due to resulting high pressure. The "Wylde Chamber" is dimensioned to safely fire either, often with increased accuracy, the minor improvement being mostly moot for our purposes. Stick with a 5.56 NATO chamber and all bases will be covered. You may also see a barrel-stamping like 1x7 which indicates the rifling's rate of twist, this one being common among many 5.56 AR-15s, as well as U.S. Military versions. So designated, the bullet will spin one full turn (360 degrees) within 7-inches of bore travel. A 1x8 is increasingly popular, and a 1x9 is a decent choice for all but the heaviest bullets (as a rule of thumb, heavier or longer types require faster twists for stability). However, shorter barrels may benefit from faster twists, as we'll see in a moment.

An effective muzzle device is a must, given the much more noticeable flash of shorter 5.56 barrels. It's the product of unburned powder, accounting for velocity loss and concussive business-end effects. When configured as a pistol, the platform is not a long-range weapon anyway. Assuming the more exciting fireworks are tolerable, it'll be a more effective defensive alternative to a 9mm AR of any type, with an added boost in range. Put a good dot-sight on it and you should be good for 150 yards with a

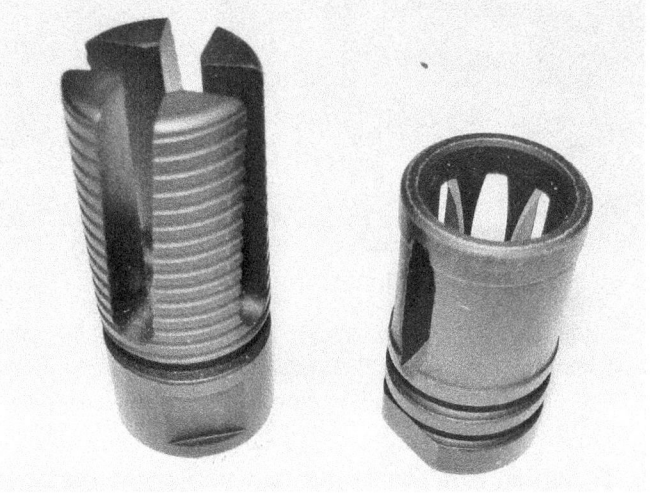

While a G.I. flash-hider (R) is better than nothing, the effectiveness of a good muzzle device is amazing. The Smith Enterprises rates highly.

Some devices provide QD suppressor attachment. The actual flash-hider section of this YHM is their effective "Phantom". Its concentric design prevents baffle-strikes.

100-yard zero. Since terminal effects should also be considered, this most likely a reasonable limit for a barrel under 12-inches. Hornady recently addressed this growing issue through a special SBR load that uses a 75-grain bullet, rated for 2,300 fps (MV) from a 10 ½" barrel. Thanks to much creative development, muzzle-flash is greatly reduced. A nicely expanded bullet we examined penetrated 17 inches during an FBI bare-gel test. A bullet of this weight will need a faster twist, even in a carbine barrel, so it's safe to assume you'll need a 1x7 in those of shorter length. Of further concern for those considering a suppressor, catastrophic damage could result from improperly stabilized bullets and baffle strikes.

MORE ON AR PISTOLS

If nothing else, the AR-15 is a versatile design. The transformer concept has gone beyond different upper receivers to modular magazine wells and rimfire conversion kits.

Windham Weaponry MCS Kit: This one covers 5.56 NATO/.223, .300 Blackout, and 7.62x39 Russian. Note the modular magazine-wells and different bolt assemblies (the Russian needs its own).

Further possibilities. Windham Weaponry is a firm we're very familiar with. WW doesn't list a 9mm pistol but they do catalog a sharp-looking carbine, as well as pistol versions chambered for some interesting calibers, including the globally available 7.62x39 AK-47 cartridge. Another unusual offering is their carbine-length Bug-out Bag System, which combines a modular lower-receiver assembly with two interchangeable uppers chambered for .223/5.56 NATO and 9mm. An extra .22 LR conversion kit is provided for the .223, which functions via easily replaceable magazine-well modules. A quick switch from one module to the next permits a wholesale conversion to 9mm. At around $2,500, this MCS backpack system isn't cheap, but it will cover just about everything.

You can also buy .22 LR AR-type pistols, including S&W's mostly polymer version. I own a 16" S&W carbine and it runs like a top, functioning identically to centerfire AR-15s. Other than for possible use as a trainer, I'm not sure what I'd do with a rimfire AR pistol. In fact, carrying one in a manner that free both hands could be a challenge…

.22 rimfire conversion kits are another possibility. Most, like this CMMG, install without tools. Simply swap one with a centerfire's bolt assembly.

Carry methods. Obviously, an AR pistol is not the ideal holster candidate. Good luck with any type of conventional concealed-carry, which doesn't rule out unconventional methods based on cases. Some are deliberately built to resemble sporting gear or musical instrument types, and won't attract much attention. I've even used a small hard-shell spotting-scope case after separating an upper from its lower. But mostly, I rely on a soft AR "assault case" with sewn on magazine pouches, an accessory pocket, and shoulder-strap. My 10 ½" AR will fit nicely in a shorter version even with a suppressor attached, and the whole package stows nicely in a vehicle. The other practical option is a sling, and there are a number of AR-specific mounting systems to accommodate one. The configuration of the AR will dictate the best choices. I often sandwich a thin steel sling-loop plate between a buffer-tube and the lower receiver. Even though I'm not a big fan of a single-point sling, a snap-ring QD type works well with an SBR or pistol-type AR if muzzle discipline is maintained. Of course, you can tuck a sling in a soft-case or just leave it on the gun.

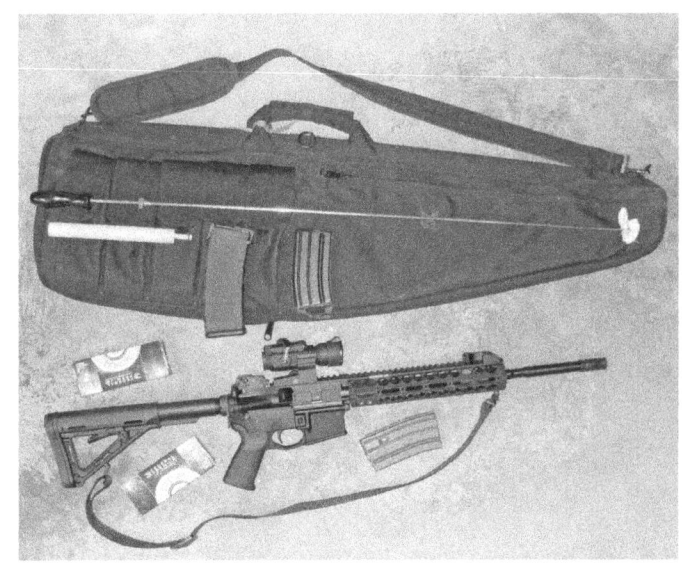

Purpose-built AR soft-cases are available in several lengths. They make nice self-contained organizers.

ALA CARTE HANDGUN WRAP-UP

By any stretch, an AR pistol is an odd duck. It's just too big to cover handgun needs, raising concerns about costs compared to practical benefits. Not that I wouldn't mind having one in a vehicle if things turned nasty, but for increased versatility, I prefer a 16-inch AR-15 carbine in 9mm (maybe .300 Blackout), or certainly .223/5.56 NATO. Its collapsible stock would still facilitate compact storage in a soft AR-type case with four or five spare magazines. The other niche-type handguns could address unique requirements – maybe, but a .22 rimfire handgun would make a great addition to a general-purpose centerfire. The others warrant third-tier status at best, and before even entertaining such an addition, the primary choices will still require essentials. So that's where we're headed next, starting with practical carry methods.

CHAPTER 27
INTO THE CARRY WEEDS: HOLSTERS, ETC.

Defensively, the number-one rule is to actually have a gun! Hopefully, at this point you'll have a better handle on what constitutes a practical choice so it doesn't stay behind. Compact pistols now satisfy the needs of many, although plenty of larger handguns ride comfortably in well-chosen holsters. Comfort, access, and retention are three big concerns and the odds for tracking down a workable solution increase with the more popular guns. The newest, or those with odd-ball barrel lengths, can cause headaches, not to mention lights and lasers, many of which mount underneath a gun. Grip-mounted lasers can solve holster issues, assuming they're available, but all these details are best considered *prior* to purchasing a firearm.

The good news is many manufacturers are now selling holsters cut for accessories. In fact, some new designs will accept various pistols, using just one holster. The makers are getting innovative on retention technologies and the rail-section common to many pistols can serve as a latching point. Retention, by the way, is a huge concern. We don't want to lose the gun or have anyone else take it from us! To that end, LEO holsters are rated by various levels of security, often commensurate with their operational complexity.

On top of that, besides OWB or IWB, there are alternate carry methods extending beyond shoulder or ankle rigs, etc. Comfort should always a big concern. For example, a system that seems tolerable in standing could become miserable while seated. Access is a further issue, especially when seat belts or chairs are introduced. Sometimes, efforts to ease discomfort can shift a holster to the point where the gun is inaccessible without major gyrations.

The bottom line is comfortable carry translates to regular carry, improving the odds of having a gun! Here's where gear and clothing comes into play.

BELTS AND CLOTHING

These two items are key components of a defensive handgun system. Let's start with the seemingly innocuous belt.

Belts. As it turns out, this seemingly minor item is actually a key piece. A good, rugged belt will secure the holster to its user while facilitating a positive draw-stroke. One that allows the holster to ride up with the gun will defeat the whole process, and on top of that, the most secure holster in the world will be rendered moot by a weak belt. It's worth spending a few extra bucks for a purpose-built model from a maker like Galco. Some even have a dress-belt appearance, which helps during concealment.

A full-blown duty/tactical belt will just attract attention while adding extra weight, although it's the better bet when lots of heavy extras are involved. Any such external belt should be worn with a set of "keepers," to prevent sagging or holster slippage. A set at least four simple snap-on keepers will lock the heavy outer belt to an inner trouser belt between its loops. We occasionally see uniformed personnel in BDU-type clothing with un-tucked shirts which present no ready keeper options. The downside here is that the entire belt can rotate far enough in a struggle to prevent retention efforts. We've even seen a few buckles that were inadvertently released, dumping an entire duty-belt on the ground. For this reason, we specify a buckle with a multi-step release system. One thing to remember is that some plastic parts may break after prolonged storage extreme cold.

Safariland's Level III holster is a large duty-type, properly secured here with keepers.

Life becomes simpler with a strong belt which threads through a rugged set of trouser loops to help nail everything down. You'll spend a bit more for a purpose-built gun belt but the extra security is well worth its cost, amortized through longer service. Just remember, holsters and spare ammo carriers should closely match belt width. Same story for trouser loops. My #1907 Gould & Goodrich double-stitched 1 ½" belt has seen daily use for several years and is still going strong.

Trousers. Watch the latest TV gun shows and you'll see plenty of episodes featuring shooters in tactical pants. We use 'em for range duties, but their downside is they scream "gun." The benefits include lots of strong pockets and sturdy belt loops. Truthfully, a set of rugged Carhartts will work nearly as well, and for that matter, jeans will get you by (most even have a small watch-pocket that will accept a speed-strip). Try not to skip belt-loops when wearing a holster, and cinch the belt to keep everything in place. A consistent location is essential to development of muscle-memory necessary for a fast draw, and an immobile holster will better support handgun retention. Some holsters have a belt-slide cut to straddle a loop, and it's worth the extra effort to thread everything together. An IWB holster may require going up one waist size for comfort. Some lady's clothing and holster combinations can locate a gun extremely close to the armpit, making any sort of rapid presentation difficult, so women can benefit from pants cut for men, style being offset by improved holster access. Of course, positioning of the handgun plays a further role. Going to extremes, I'm no fan of ankle-holsters, but many small back-up guns are carried this way by LEOs and others.

Shirts and jackets. I feel less vulnerable when the gun is out of sight. Even if someone does think I'm armed, they won't know what I'm carrying or how it's secured. In my case, the gun will be located on my right hip, covered by a garment - which won't be a cool-looking tactical vest. Defensively, whatever I'm wearing will also remain open in the front regardless of the weather for better access of the gun. Assuming it's a coat, a bit of weight will be added to a lower holster-side pocket, which will help flip it rearward. Generally, when concealment is less of an issue, an OWB holster will ride well on a belt at around 3:00. Warmer weather typically calls for an IWB system to maintain the lowest profile. An un-tucked shirt will work well with many smaller guns, and some of the latest IWB creations will work with a tucked-in shirt.

A sweatshirt seems like another easy alternative, although fast access can become problematic. Loose clothing can also pose hazards during re-holstering; especially with today's "safe-action" triggers. If any bunched-up clothing finds its way inside the trigger guard, an unpleasant outcome is possible. Because we run cold-weather outdoor range programs, dress is always considered. An easy fix is to tuck in any loose sweaters or windbreakers, which further eliminates a draw-cord concern: the plastic pull-ends can wind up inside holsters!

Lately, some interesting jackets have appeared with pockets for carry options. While they have merit, one concern involves responsible custody. If you use one, don't take it off! Lost & Found Departments are full of jackets and coats, but not too many belts.

HOLSTER GUIDELINES

Most experienced handgunners have established carry preferences. They also have the well-developed muscle memory necessary for instantaneous access of a gun. Safe bet everything is located to the point where it's a ritual. They know a random approach coupled with infrequent carry just won't cut it.

Default carry position. The establishment of a general-purpose carry location is a good first step.

When training uniformed staff, concealment is a non-issue. Also, lots of extras beyond hi-cap magazines are involved including handcuffs, lights, radios, etc. So, a duty-belt is the expedient solution with the holster firmly attached at around 3:00 (for a right-handed shooter). We consider this the general "default location" for a holster-carried handgun. Most LEOs use it but the same location works well for many civilian users, minus a separate belt or extraneous equipment. This simplifies the process, leaving a holster (still positioned at 3:00), and a magazine pouch at around 10:00, or speed-loaders at roughly 2:00; all attached to a sturdy belt.

To that end, our plain-clothes personnel are probably more in tune with CCW civilians. Carry latitude is granted since concealment is a major factor. The gun will typically be located higher to disappear under a jacket or blazer, and since bulk is an issue, a less obvious holster system helps. The fix is a stylish but purpose-built dress belt, combined with a lower-profile holster, positioned for access *and* concealment; sometimes a bit further rearward at 3:30 to 4:00.

Since either approach is fairly basic, they make good starting points for less experienced handgunners. Skip exotic carry options for the time being so basic holster skills can be *safely* developed. An OWB design is a good way to get comfortable with a handgun carried in a holster.

Basic features. Because a main emphasis here is on defense, two concerns are quick deployment *and* positive retention. Choices abound, with more appearing every day, some employing innovative release mechanisms for secure but rapid responses. Experienced handgunners probably won't need a lecture as to what they should choose, but others could benefit through a few guidelines intended to improve safety. We suggest a holster with the following key features:

Strong-side design, capable of being secured firmly to a belt. Shoulder-holsters look cool and do have their place. Under a heavy coat, access is much easier. However, we've seen some pretty scary gun-handling with such designs. Remember Rule #2: don't point your muzzle at something you don't want to shoot! This includes you as well as any bystanders. Watch where the muzzle points in a horizontal shoulder rig, and then think about Rule #2 again. Cross-draw rigs are fast and safer – but only if you're alone.

Snug fit via a weapon-specific design. Stick with reputable makers and you'll probably be on solid ground. Still, some gun and holster combinations can create surprises, which could be attributable to after-market parts including oversize controls. You don't want to wipe off a 1911 safety, pop your magazine or worse, discharge a round in the holster! Makeshift use of a holster on hand for different type of handgun could increase such hazards. That said, a few recent holster designs work well with various pistol makes and models. A list should accompany the product.

Covered trigger guard. This feature is safer overall and can prevent you from inserting your trigger finger during a draw (along with any loose clothing).

An active retention device, permitting release upon establishment of a proper grip. A separate motion is slow. Straps with snaps are often seen on sporting-type holsters, which require such a release. On the other hand, a thumb-break design will release with a grip that has been established in the holster (a swipe of the thumb will break the snap). This design has been around forever, and is more secure than an open-top holster. Granted, the level of retention is somewhat marginal, but it's still better than nothing. Some newer designs have hidden latches which can be accessed by the thumb while a shooting grip is established. We're not overly fond of releases activated by the trigger finger. It's too easy for that digit to wind up on the trigger as the gun clears its holster. Some CCW folks eschew any active retention device, relying instead on firm holster fit and concealment. Unlike LEOs, they probably won't be wrestling with drunks; but for more rigorous use including rough-country travel, additional security is worthwhile.

Non-collapsible construction, permitting single-hand recovery of the handgun. Anything requiring both hands for re-holstering is fundamentally unsafe. It'll only be a matter of time until the support hand winds up in front of the muzzle. From there, things can get ugly in a hurry. Soft nylon holsters usually collapse when empty, resulting in some fiddling with the support hand during recovery. Eventually, this turns into a habit. The latest spate of rigid IWB holsters are a marked improvement.

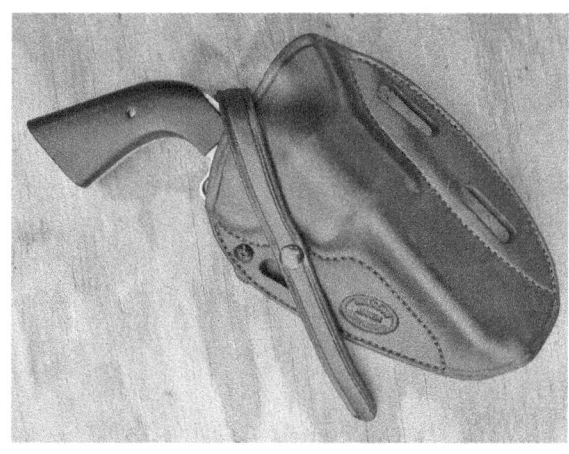

This sporting/CCW amalgamation by "Simply Rugged" incorporates a strap with a pancake design, sized large enough to handle serious single-actions.

Open bottom (for striker-fired pistols). Stuffing a "safe-action" pistol into a holster that contains a foreign object could cause an accidental discharge. The downside is a possible introduction of snow – assuming you're tough enough to sit in it (check if you fall on your keister).

Access to the magazine release while holstered (especially for mag-disconnect models). We train our troops to pop their magazines with their pistols still in their holsters. It's a safer first step during unloading, and it also disables any magazine-disconnect type pistols. If it takes some doing, we consider this a plus. Our holster procurement process factors this in.

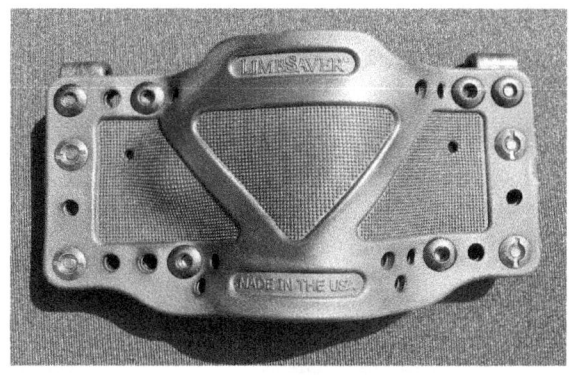

Limbsaver's versatile "Crosstech" covers IWB and OWB carry. Form it to your handgun with a hairdryer!

Adjustable drop & cant: This feature isn't necessary, but it's at least worth considering. Depending on physique and body location, a personalized holster angle can prove useful. Lately, thanks to synthetics and modular designs, such capabilities are more common.

Secure belt engagement: A durable belt is essential, but the holster needs to stay put! That means it should attach without undue play. Check belt and holster-slot dimensions before purchasing to ensure proper fit.

More on drop and cant. Drop is the vertical location of a holster relative to the belt, and cant is the angle of the gun. Concealed-carry holsters typically have minimal or even no drop, OWB general-purpose/duty holsters may have a bit, and tactical rigs sometimes have enough drop to wind up at thigh-level. The right amount is a personal choice governed by common sense and physique. Obviously, OWB concealed-carry is improved with a higher holster. When this is of less concern, minimal drop works

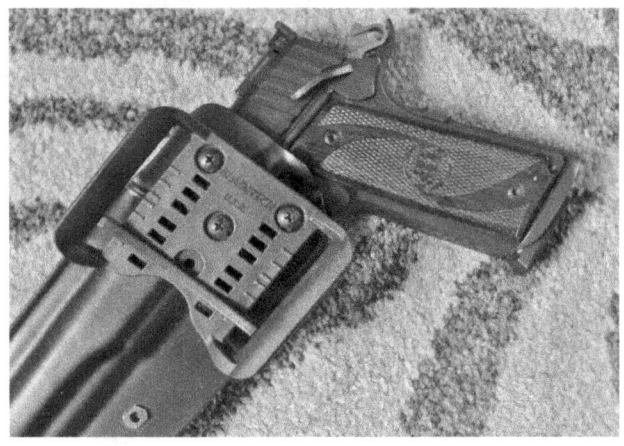

Blade-Tech covers different belt widths through an adjustable backer.

well, accounting for its common use by LEOs, who must also factor in body armor. Increased drop can degrade stability, and at some point, retention will become a concern. Thigh-rigs make the most sense for specialized tactical units equipped with ballistic body armor and shoulder-fired weapons. Our operators use them only because they need to, and their holsters are strapped securely to their thighs. Everyone else will be better-served by less extreme examples. However, shooters with higher waists may appreciate some extra drop. The modularity of some holster designs can permit personalized options for not only drop but cant.

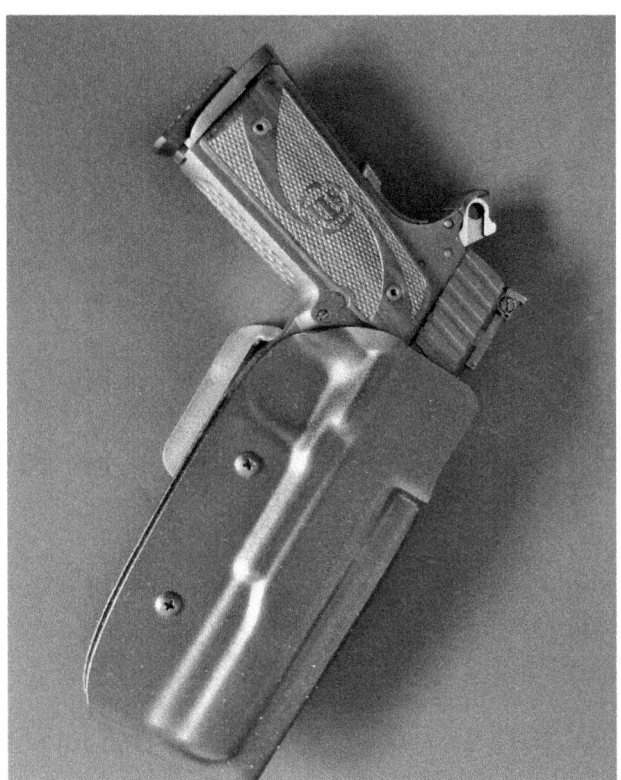

Same Blade-Tech viewed from the front. The synthetic holster is a molded shell. Tension can be varied by adjusting its screws.

A tactical-type thigh holster provides drop to the extreme. But, even when properly secured by belt-keepers and straps, exposure could raise concerns.

As for cant, conventional OWB holsters typically fall into three categories which determine the angle of a holstered gun, relative to the belt (assuming the gun will be carried on the shooter's dominant-hand side).

Negative cant. Positions the gun at a muzzle-forward angle. Holsters of this design are often seen during combat matches like IPSC, and may be worn at 2:00. Such an OWB arrangement may be uncomfortable when seated for any length of time; more so with a longer-barreled handgun. This rake works well for cross-draw carry by providing butt-forward access.

Neutral cant: Otherwise known as "straight-drop," there is no gun lean. This angle works well for OWB or IWB carry with most reasonably-sized handguns. Establishment of a firing grip often seems natural and a holstered gun can be shielded by the forearm. Recovery to the holster is also a fumble-free process so safety is improved.

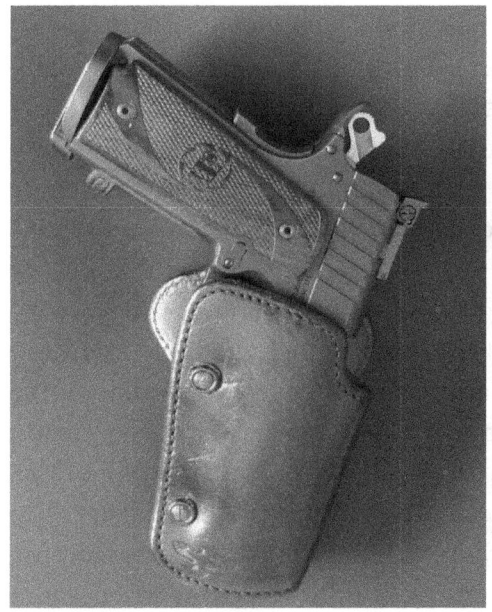

Galco's leather "Gunsite" sees lots of use, primarily on ranges, from instructors and competitors. It's a neutral design with two tension screws, designed for 1911s.

A rear view shows the Gunsite's straight-drop and belt-slot, configured for classic OWB carry.

Positive cant: Some shooters recognize this as "the FBI tilt," which angles the muzzle rearward for butt-forward access. This popular design is intended for concealed-carry when the gun is worn a bit rearward, at around 3:30 – 4:00. Pancake holsters are a classic example, often cut higher to help hide a gun inside a jacket. I use a few with compact handguns, enjoying great comfort (especially when seated), for a minor sacrifice in speed. The grip angle feels less natural, and re-holstering can be difficult without lots of extra practice. Use one regularly though, and it'll all come together.

IWBA (appendix) designs may have a negative cant, but they work since the guns are typically among the smallest types. IWB holsters are usually neutral, or close to it.

Materials. Leather was king for eons, and though it still makes a great choice, numerous synthetic alternatives now give it stiff competition. Slight play on words here since new leather can be stiff, requiring some break-in. One thing I like about a plain stainless steel firearm is that an unlined leather holster will work, whereas bluing will last much longer if the holster has a soft but more expensive lining. Some newer synthetic holsters also incorporate a lining, while other Kydex types are basic shells, often molded for improved fit. Soft nylon is another popular material, frequently built for generic fitting such as "4-inch large revolver," etc. Be wary of pancake types that collapse when the gun is withdrawn. They often require use of both hands during recovery, thereby promoting a tendency to sweep the support hand.

Retention. Most LE holsters are advertised with retention ratings; Level One through Level Three being common - although one can even find a Level Four or Five. There is no UL-type standard, and the whole classification process is poorly understood. A simplified explanation is the ratings reflect timed resistance to snatch attempts during deactivation of any retention controls. Rather than wade through the whole process, think of the higher levels providing enhanced security by additional layers of latches, hoods, or similar devices.

Fobus is known for Kydex holsters. The "memory" of the springy shell snaps around a handgun's contours. No collapse concerns during re-holstering.

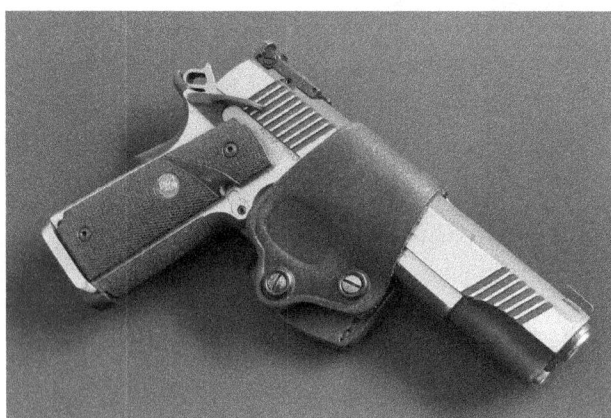

The Yaqui-slide is better than a pistol stuffed inside the waist but, with Level-Zero retention, scratch it off the list for open carry.

Many CCW holsters are open-top designs without a retention system other than friction-fit, enhanced perhaps, by concealment. They're really Level-Zero. I own several but often look for more security; especially during conditions analogous to survival. Loss of a weapon is possible on the move in rough country, explaining why numerous military-type holsters include flaps (that keep out weather and debris). A good example is the adaptable Bianchi UM84, which has seen steady U.S. military use in far-flung places. At one time, we issued these "Universal Military Holsters" to our K-9 handlers for strenuous back-country use (often at night). The handlers never worried about losing their handguns, Presentation was slower, but at least they had it! Eventually, we standardized on a Level IV Safariland holster. It not only offered excellent retention, but was also quick (in the hands of a trained user). Therein lays the rub. Our transition encompassed several days of holster work, perfected through a structured process. The shooters encountered challenges related to vehicles, oddball positions, and even support hand-only draws. Since a program like this could be a stretch for civilian shooters, a simpler system with at least *some* retention capability may be the better bet.

If I ever do a cartwheel, it will be entirely by accident. Nevertheless, this move does provide a non-hostile retention assessment as does an upside-down holster shake test, also with its retention device disabled for extra assurance (using an unloaded gun, of course). All our trainees perform this check upon initial holster issuance, and the tension screws are tweaked if necessary. Many of today's holsters incorporate *some* type of tension-adjustment to regulate fit – either as the sole retention feature or as part of an active-control design. For rough duty, I'll take both.

Although most civilians won't face these extremes, retention is worth considering, especially when tough conditions are possible. Horses, ATVs, and snowmobiles also count.

A pet holster is one we've used extensively with S&W M&P pistols for some plain-clothes roles. *Safariland's Model 6377 ALS* is a somewhat stripped-down but more compact version of a Level IV rig we issue to uniformed staff. The M-6377

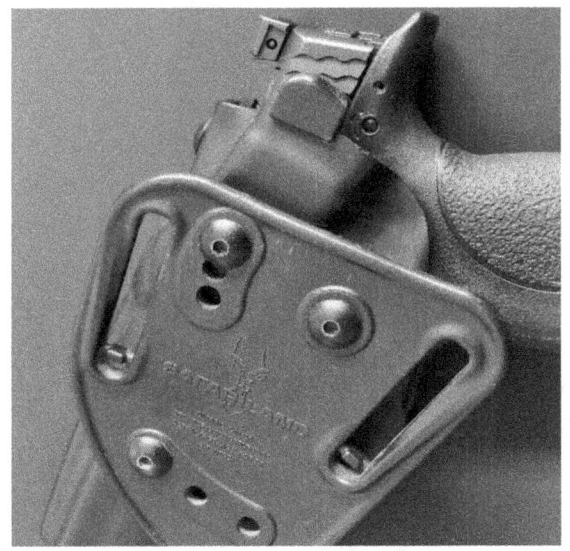

Safariland's ALS design is secure and fast, but unobtrusive. A rearward swipe of the tab frees the pistol. The latch will automatically reengage upon re-holstering. Separate plates accommodate drop preferences. Cant is easily adjusted. The latest 2019 version covers everything!

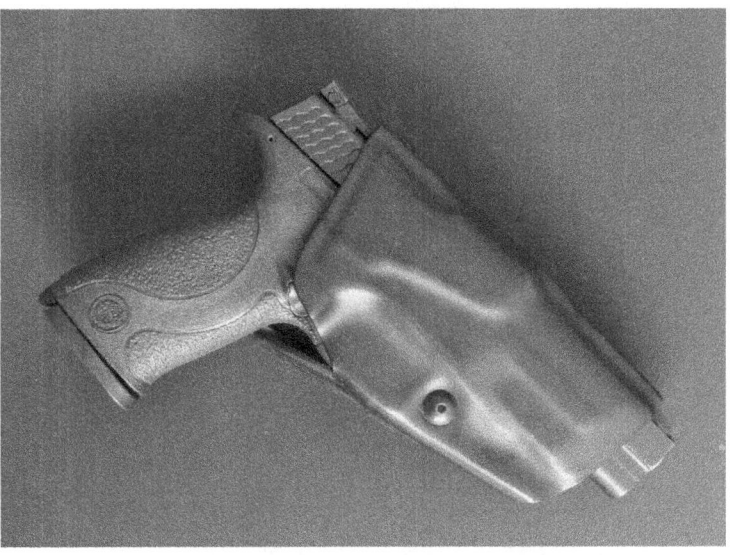

Safariland's M-6377 holster. The ALS release remains hidden during normal carry. An extra screw regulates tension.

looks like a basic open-top holster but its clever Automatic Locking System (ALS) provides Level II security. As soon as the pistol goes in the holster it's firmly locked back in, thanks to a hidden device located behind the grip. A release tab is perfectly indexed for disengagement by the thumb, and a tension-screw regulates resistance. The system is an easy one to master and draws seem as fast as any open-top rig, with the benefit of greatly increased security.

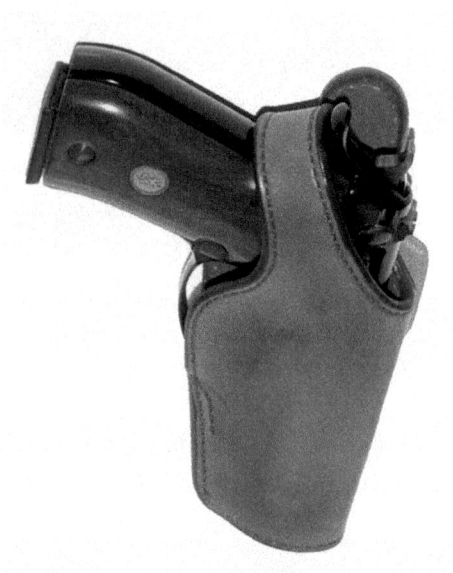

The thumb-break is a classic design. This well-crafted Bianchi contains a .380 Browning BDA (photo by Domenic Leonard).

Thumb-break holsters have been around for ages and are still good designs. With the shooter's grip established on the gun, the thumb will be well-positioned to swipe and unsnap a short retention strap. Material may be synthetic or leather, the latter often needing time to break in. A pancake type is wider to help wrap around the body for closer, form-fitting carry; beyond concealment, it also works in the bush. Comfort is such that it's easy to forget I'm armed. Many of the leather models are molded to fit specific guns, which further improves retention.

Some holsters like the DeSantis Speed and Mini-Scabbard dispense with a thumb-break feature, relying instead on a well-molded fit. My X-7 Mini-Scabbard also has a tension screw, permitting positive retention for an S&W 9mm Shield, carried OWB, underneath a jacket. Its belt slide is open at the center to straddle a belt loop, locking it solidly in place. My small Galco Hornet OWB holster is a more minimalist design with a one-piece belt slide, but its molded shape melds well around a small S&W J-frame .22 LR revolver. Less gun mass translates to less inertia when rigorous activity is encountered, which helps keep the gun where it belongs. Proper mindset is essential when it comes to maintaining custody of a handgun.

Modularity and programming. Some of the latest holster systems are truly ingenious, offering different carry possibilities thanks to their modular construction. Being big fans of Safariland, we have used their quick-disconnect holster and belt-mount systems with great success, while maintaining Level III retention. We may also switch out a standard belt-mounting plate for one with extra drop to accommodate high-waisted users or tactical operators. Thanks to total modularity the options are nearly endless! However, sometimes

Galco's OWB Hornet is cut for cross-draw, but also works for strong-side carry. Smaller guns are more likely to stay put in open-top holsters.

creativity can wreak havoc on tuned muscle-memory. I once added an extended drop plate to my duty holster for a range-test session. The difference seemed subtle, but actual use proved otherwise, as evidenced by numerous fumbled draws. I came close to having a stroke around twice per minute during subconscious weapon-custody checks. Having narrowly survived a gun-snatch, I'm now programmed to maintain gun contact using the inner part of my forearm. Trouble was, the increased drop was just enough to prevent this reassuring practice. After a couple hours, I'd had enough and went back to my established carry regimen.

Paddle-holsters. Threading a belt through holster slots can be inconvenient when frequent removal is necessary. A popular alternative is a paddle-holster, which dispenses with belt slots in favor of a large backer (the paddle) and hook arrangement. The flexible "paddle" slips inside the trousers (or under a belt), and the hook clips over the belt where it will *hopefully* restrain the holster during a draw. Some work better than others and, once again, the *correct* belt is an important component. Thanks to modularity, we sometimes configure holsters for our plainclothes staff with paddles - BUT, attachment or removal must never occur with a pistol in the holster!

<u>Handling holstered guns.</u> *We see this often, even with experienced handgunners. Paddles are prime but not exclusive offenders. Watch the act in progress and odds are, Rule #2 will be violated in short order as the gun sweeps its owner. Furthermore, a gun can fall out of its holster during this process. A safer SOP is to secure the handgun prior to donning or removal of a holster.*

Small-of-the back. A larger handgun can disappear in this location, but access will be more difficult, and prolonged seating will probably cause discomfort. Having wound up flat on my back a couple times, I'll pass. Icy pavement is unforgiving!

Appendix-carry (AIWB or IWBA). This IWB carry method is increasingly popular for several, but the big concern is Rule #2. For a right-handed shooter, the gun will position at around 2:00. The muzzle will thus be pointed toward anatomical items of deep concern. From a seated position its direction will probably shift, covering the upper thigh and its femoral artery. IWBA may cause some discomfort for those of us with a cherubic physique. On a positive note, access is usually both fast and ambidextrous. I'd feel more comfortable with a DAO handgun (like my small S&W .380 Bodyguard); with a safety "on" for added measure. But I'd feel much safer by not violating Rule #2, and some well-respected trainers won't sanction IWBA carry for exactly this reason.

Cross-draw. In this carry mode, a right-handed shooter will be wearing the holster somewhere around 10:00, with the gun's grip facing forward. People who spend most their time in vehicles are proponents of a cross-draw system, and some sportsmen also employ this method for use with heavy coats. The holster will typically position the butt-forward in what would normally constitute a negative cant design. My previously described Galco Hornet is engineered for these purposes but the J-frame/holster combination is small enough to work fine during 3:00 use. That's where it sits for me because that's where I'm programmed to go. Odds of sweeping others (or my support arm) are also reduced. These issues are real concerns on ranges with adjacent shooters!

Shoulder. One shoulder option is horizontal-carry, which is fast but not without issues including the need for a secure retention feature - and that pesky Rule #2. Even with a vertical-carry rig,1 it's darned easy to sweep parts of you, and most shoulder holsters also require two-handed recovery. However, a cross-chest rig is a valid system for rough-country use involving large handguns. Diamond D Leather is perfectly located as an Alaskan firm that specializes in such rigs for big guns. Most provide good support through use of harness systems, but they do take some doing to climb into - something to consider for those who address weather conditions through a layered clothing approach.

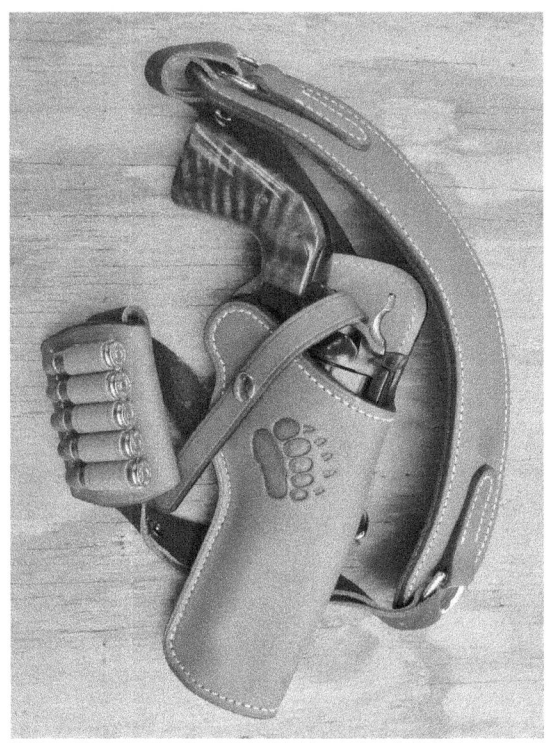

Large handguns call for specialized carry methods. A cross-chest system works, combing comfort with rapid access.

Ankle. This system requires lots of practice, good flexibility, and a very small gun. Right-handed users typically locate the holster inside the calf of the left leg, and access is accomplished with the right knee on the ground. We view as a last-ditch alternative reserved for a small secondary back-up gun. Good luck running with it, let alone anything bigger! However, depending on an individual's physique and vehicle layout, an ankle rig could make some sense for people who log lots of mileage.

Pocket. A few small holsters have recently appeared for pocket-carry, and most of the major manufacturers offer one. Some are just simple pouches with tacky exteriors while others are more like wallets. They are a much better idea than simply stuffing a handgun in a pocket. A loose gun is a real invitation to an AD, especially when other items lurk within. A carry system with a shielded trigger guard makes a lot more sense, but the pocket should still be reserved exclusively for the gun. A well-thought out design can also orient the handgun for establishment of a surreptitious grip when the hair on your neck begins to stand up.

Miscellaneous carries. I installed a Techna Clip on my S&W .380 Bodyguard. The Clipdraw is a similar product with a springy metal finger that mounts directly to the gun for holsterless IWB (or pocket) carry. This system is a concealed-carry option for use with smaller handguns. So is the DeSantis Clip-Grip, which can be used either with or without most holsters. Made for small S&W J-frame revolvers, the system uses a pair of replacement grips. The top edge of the right panel incorporates a small ledge designed to hook over a belt for unobtrusive IWB use - a big improvement over any "Mexican Carry" technique. Barami's Hip-Grip works the same way, using a more pronounced hook for positive belt engagement, and if memory serves me right, it was the original design. These variations beat holsterless Mexican Carry or a gun stuffed in a pocket, but none are as good as a proper holster.

You can find belt-mounted systems designed to replicate cell phone pouches. The Sneaky Pete version has bogus logos to support the illusion of electronic or medical devices, and the top-flap is secured by rare-earth magnets. EAA even has a product featuring coded access and an electronic locating feature. The sky is the limit now, with other clever designs from wrap-around belly bands to bra holsters, etc. These are at their best with small back-up handguns.

A fanny-pack can accommodate a larger gun, but it won't be as discreet. Muzzle orientation and rapid access are further concerns. I once encountered a surgeon with some handgun experience during a CCW course. He showed up with a very flat single-action Colt Model 1908 .380 carried cross-draw in a small fanny-pack. I was skeptical, but since no other shooters were involved and his confidence level seemed high, I decided to see what would happen. Turned out he was fast as greased lightning, unzipping the pack with his support hand while simultaneously executing a dominant-hand cross-draw. On the way to a two-handed position, he racked the slide to chamber a round, which alleviated concerns about an AD within his pack. Since the gun was carried with an empty chamber he chose to leave the safety off. There was no debating his speed OR accuracy, but this strategy was doomed without use of both hands; a risk he was prepared to accept.

Regarding slings, I first tried this years earlier as a practical way to carry a fairly large T/C single-shot Contender, installing QD studs in its forend and grip-bottom so a basic (but long) nylon sling could be attached. After tweaking its adjustment, I arrived at a length that would loop over my neck, allowing the gun to hang inverted and muzzle forward below my right shoulder. In a two-handed firing position the tensioned sling also became a shooting aid that greatly improved stability. I've since used this system with S&W .44 Magnums, substituting the bottom grip screw of a Hogue rubber grip for QD stud. A second stud was then installed in an 8 3/8" N-frame after drilling and tapping its full-lug barrel. A PC M-629 with a thin under-rib was simpler since it just needed a hole for the sling swivel. Overall, the concept has worked well with any type of clothing, but one huge caution remains. Since the gun hangs horizontally, its muzzle-forward position is bad news for others, limiting its use to solo outings.

Slings are another large-handgun possibility. They can also serve as braces. However, muzzle control must be closely managed during carry!

Spare ammo options. With respect to Murphy's Law, it's worth carrying at least one reload. When discretion is called for, a revolver speed-strip is not compact but better than loose rounds. As for pistols, ideally I'll situate magazines for access with either hand at around 10:00. However, this position is often a bit too far forward concealed carry clothing, meaning either a shift rearward may

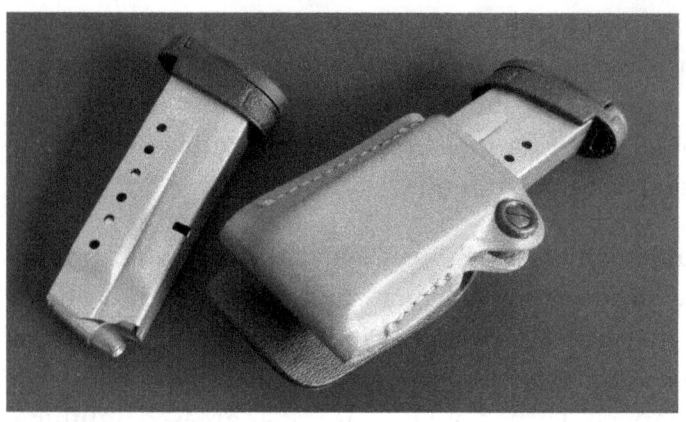
This CCW-type mag pouch has a screw to regulate tension. It also has a paddle with a hook to eliminate belt-threading.

be needed – or a less obvious system. As it turns out, the rectangular nylon pouch for my Buck #422 folding pocket knife fits some single-stack pistol magazines nicely; its Velcro closure is secure and the minimal profile is unobtrusive. Of course, there are plenty of good mag pouches in both closed and open-top form. For the latter, a tension-screw type can increase security while accommodating various magazines.

Holster and gear sources. With apologies to any omitted:

Aker Leather
Alessi Holsters
Alien Gear
Barranti Leather
Bear Armz Tactical
Bianchi
Black Dog
Blackhawk
Blade-tech
Bravo Concealment
Bulldog Custom Gun Leather
Cerisse
Clinger Holster
Cobra Tactical Products
Comp-Tac
Concealment Express
Cook
Crossbreed
CYA Supply Co.
Daltech Force
DeSantis
Diamond D Leather
Don Hume

Fobus
Galco
Gary Kramer
Gun Goddess
Gun Fighters Inc
High Noon Holsters
Hunter
International Handgun Leather
Kirkpatrick Leather
Limbsaver
Mernickle
Milt Sparks
Mitch Rosen
N82 Tactical
Outlaw Holsters
Raven Concealment Systems
Recluse
R&R Holsters
Safariland
Soteria Leather
Sneaky Pete
Sticky Holsters
Ted Blocker

Elite Survival Systems
El Paso Saddelry
Etsy Holsters
European Armory
Fancy Pants Holsters
Fierce Defender

Tulster
Uncle Mikes
Vedder
Versacarry
Wilson Combat
Wright Leather

CUSTODY CONCERNS

Whenever the gun leaves our immediate possession, concerns over custody increase. Take purses for example. Many can be seen in shopping carts or other detached locations, which increases their susceptibility to theft, pilfering, or loss. The same is true of gym bags, brief cases, or bug-out kits.

Vehicles. Beyond theft of the actual vehicle or its contents, we should consider liabilities incurred during servicing or any use by others. Some states have strict CCW laws restricting custody of firearms by non-credentialed persons, and more than one family member has wound up in legal trouble after a handgun was left in a vehicle. My state is much freer and our crime rate is relatively low, but since I still worry about any unattended weapons, an expedient fix is to simply wear the gun.

Bathroom breaks, travel, etc. Think loss of a handgun is unlikely? We encountered several cases where they were stolen from vehicles. An acquaintance left two handguns in out-of-state motel rooms on two different occasions, three decades apart. Despite training to the contrary, we also dealt with two lost handguns, one of which was temporarily misplaced at home, causing immediate concerns over its discovery by children. The other fiasco involved a pistol left on a toilet tank in a public bathroom. The latter makes a good case for a shoulder holster, but common sense works, too. We tell our magazine-disconnect pistol users to first pop the magazine and then place the gun in their underwear, thus increasing the odds of remembering its location. There is a loaded magazine lurking in our on-range outhouse; so far, no one has stepped forward to retrieve it as it slowly gets buried. In a restroom, plan on going fishing. A dedicated locking gun box will solve many home storage concerns. A gun underneath a pillow won't, accounting for the two motel stories. Our troops travel with lock-boxes, but a handgun stuffed in a boot overnight will work in a pinch. The safest bet is to either wear the gun or secure it!

CARRY WRAP-UP

Many casual shooters will view a holster as just an incidental purchase, which we now know is far from the case. Indeed, the handgun itself is just part of a larger system that requires well-chosen carry methods. Individual circumstances will dictate the details. To this end, don't forget to budget for any static defense and/or home storage measures. We're not done shopping…

CHAPTER 28

MORE ACCESSORIES: ESSENTIAL AND USEFUL ITEMS

In the interest of economy (and having run amuck with guns), it's time to consider some generic necessities. The costlier "lights or lasers" are nice, but shooting skills are paramount, so we might as well start with basic range gear. The following "essentials" and "useful items" should set you up for trigger time without need for a second mortgage.

ESSENTIALS

Although a range bag might seem more like a "useful extra," let's face it - practice IS essential. This means you'll need a practical way to lug your handgun, plus a holster, magazines or speed-loaders, and various other items on this list – beginning with ammo.

Ammunition. Okay, maybe ammo doesn't constitute an accessory in the truest sense of the word, but you'll still need some, and it won't grow on trees. Assuming you're serious about developing a reasonable degree of proficiency, the pathway to success will mirror the route to Carnegie Hall - practice! But before investing in large quantities, skip forward to the next chapter. The detour could save you some money needed for other items.

Holster and related gear. Some ranges are tightly controlled, with firing restricted to booths. If so, the rules may relegate all firearm handling to a bench-top, eliminating the immediate need for a holster, but sooner or later you'll want some sort of practical carry system. Those of us in less formal settings will reap the benefits of hands-free carry and custody. So, beyond factoring in the cost for a holster and ammo-pouch, don't forget a good belt.

Speed-loaders or magazines. Revolver shooters could live with two speed-loaders, although a speed-strip or two might be an acceptable alternative for small-frame types. Either way, they're simple and thus less prone to fussiness. Magazines can sometimes be more cantankerous so I feel better with at least three, counting the one that came with the pistol.

Hearing and eye protection. Don't participate in shooting activities unless properly equipped with both! Glasses should be shatter-resistant. We maintain a stash of Wiley X Saber Advanced Shooting Glasses in our range building, for daily issuance to our shooters. They hold up well, come in different tints, and are reasonably priced at around $35. We also require each participant to wear a hat with a visor, which helps prevent any ejected cases from becoming lodged between a lens and eyeball. As for hearing protection, electronic muffs permit normal conversations, but switch off from the concussion of a shot. So far, our inventory of affordable Brownell's Premiums ($40) have been working well. They're powered by two AAA batteries, and they fold for compact storage. Electronic types are nice (especially when range commands are involved), but a basic set of shooting muffs will do. Indoor ranges can be *really* loud, bad enough to justify the extra use of ear plugs. In fact, younger shooters and some ladies will benefit from this approach on any type of range. I always keep a set of disposable industrial foam plugs in a pocket, but something better is advised, accounting for my most frequent reply - "Huh?"

Safety glasses and hearing protection should be part of every range kit. Don't be afraid to double-up with muffs AND ear plugs, especially on indoor ranges!

HG-28 Safety Glasses: First-aid kit. Better to be safe than sorry. The occasional less dramatic boo-boo can occur, like a sliced finger. It might heal on its own, but blood will raise hell with steel surfaces, at which point you'll appreciate band-aids. But since we're dealing with bullets, shop for that type of kit which will also include compresses and a tourniquet.

Range bag. Life on the range is a lot simpler when all the necessary gear is in one grab n' go location. My range bag remains permanently set up with a stapler, hearing and eye protection, a small multi-tool, a condensed cleaning kit, targets, and various other items (including first-aid supplies). Beyond dividers to organize this stuff, padded compartments provide a ready means to pack handguns, holsters, ammo, spare magazines, etc. Having used a few rigid types, I much prefer a durable fabric version, in part because it will inflict less damage to walls and furniture, but also for easier stowage behind a truck seat. Fully loaded, you'll be dealing with some weight, so the shoulder strap common to most will be appreciated. Most of the well-known shooting emporiums sell good range bags in soft and hard-shell cases. The latter type may be a legal necessity during transportation. You can peruse Brownell's, Cabelas, Midway USA (and others) for examples that'll cover your needs. Prices start around $50, but even the more elaborate types can be had for less than $100.

Security measures. Here's another place-holder which was previously covered. Everyone's situation is different and a full-size gun safe won't be necessary for those with just a handgun. In that case, an affordable solution could be a handgun-size container built for security purposes (which might even double as a carry-case).

Cleaning kit and supplies. We covered these items in the respective revolver and pistol chapters, so their appearance here serves as a reminder – assuming you need one, which rifle-shooters may not. Anyhow, a basic kit should get you started. One do-all classic example is Hoppe's Deluxe Cleaning Kit, which sells for around $40. But there are basic versions for less, which can sometimes be more portable.

A range bag is more than just a carry device. It's also great organizer. Permanent contents should include your safety gear. Might as well spring for a dedicated staple-gun, too.

USEFUL EXTRAS

Here you'll see a few items useful as part of a range kit. They're all basic except for the shot-timer which, although extremely useful, could wait pending a piggy bank infusion. Steel reactive targets go together with timers like ice cream and apple pie, but they're heavy and expensive enough to warrant some creative alternatives.

Targets, with a couple handy extras. We do a lot of shooting on steel targets, but we don't need to lug them around. On the other hand, paper plates are cheap, portable, and easy to staple to backers. Attach six to a horizontal 2x4 and you'll gain a makeshift plate-rack (in this case, literally). Cardboard IPSC or IDPA silhouettes are a costlier, but they'll take a lot of hits while providing extra use as backers. You can stretch the life of either by circling hits with permanent markers, identifying various stages through different colors. Markers are fast, cheap, and easier than target pasties, too. In fact, you can use a coffee can lid as a template to draw a few circles on an IPSC Target (those sold with a white side work great). Next, a good stapler is almost worth its weight in gold, especially on a windy day. Mine is an Arrow Heavy-Duty Model T-50-P fed by ½" staples, which will anchor cardboard to wooden frames. Don't forget an extra box of staples, and stash this stuff in your range bag.

Shot-timer. Many combat-type matches rely on these devices, which capture the reports of individual shots to capture draw-times, shot intervals, and the total times of stages, all displayed to the nearest hundredth of a second. A shot-timer is also a useful practice tool which will also work when shooting solo thanks to programmable start tones with random delays and par times, etc. You can clip one on a belt or hand it to a buddy, switching off for some friendly rivalry while improving holster and reloading skills (those paper plates will work). There are several good choices, but most of our experience involves Competition Electronics, a similar current model being their Pro-Timer IV ($200). I always keep one in my range bag with a couple spare 9-volt batteries. PACT and a few others also sell good products, some of which are less expensive and more compact.

This timer displays a shot fired 2.14 seconds after its start-tone. Multiple shots will also be captured for review.

Loading aids. I don't use one very often but a simple plastic ADCO Super-Thumb has permanent residence in my range bag. Even tough old fingers can struggle to overcome some magazines; especially after sustaining the inevitable sliced thumb resulting from a sharp feed-lip. Extra shooting raises those odds, but there are some techy devices for higher-volume refills. Most revolver shooters will survive without speed-loader refill trays, but the moon clip crowd will want the tools.

Ammo cans. The metal OD-green G.I. types with handles are always useful for storage of ammo or parts, although they do have penchant for dinging everything in their path. Lately, useful molded-plastic alternatives have appeared in various sizes. In fact, MTM's 4-Can Ammo Crate system ($30) even includes a handy storage bin with handles. An advantage of either design is their airtight interiors, which permit dependable long-term ammunition storage. They also work for solvents and cleaning gear (but not when mixed with ammo).

LIGHTS AND LASERS

Do you really need these items? Both technologies have value, but for self-defense, a light is really an indispensable item since target ID is crucial. At this point, costs are adding up, so the challenge is locating products that can cover your needs without breaking the bank. While a dual-purpose light and laser device *could* kill two birds with one stone, it won't be cheap. It will also require a fixed attachment method to maintain consistent laser zero, which along with an attendant increase in size, will probably complicate holster-fit. However, there are simpler alternatives…

Lights. Products abound with some excellent choices. Some are purely hand-held, while others provide a weapon-mounted capability. A few address either use.

Safariland's Rapid Light System. As a budget-driven compromise, we've been using the RLS. The light resembles other tubular types, but unlike some, this one runs on three AAA batteries. A main difference with the RLS is a pivoting mount which can be slipped on to a pistol's accessory rail. At that point, the light can be swung to port or starboard until a small tab engages a rail slot, locking the light in place. When properly engaged, the light's tail-button can be positioned for activation with a thumb, either in a constant-on, or momentary mode. I slip mine on and pivot it left so my support-hand (left) thumb can activate the light. After a bit of practice, mounting is quick and positive. Don't judge its effectiveness without a gun, since rotating the mount when unattached is difficult. When we unwrapped our first T&E samples we almost gave up. Then we slipped one on an M&P and viola; piece of cake! At 190 lumens, the RLS won't rival some other dedicated weapon systems, but it's still plenty bright. Run time is more than adequate, and battery changes are easy. I have two, one of which stays on an AR-15. The second is often used in hand-held mode, but if I want it on a pistol, mounting is almost instantaneous. It won't fit in a holster, but dismounting is equally fast. A built-in clip will hook on a belt, or a furnished extra rail-type belt adapter piece can be used. Cost is under $100.

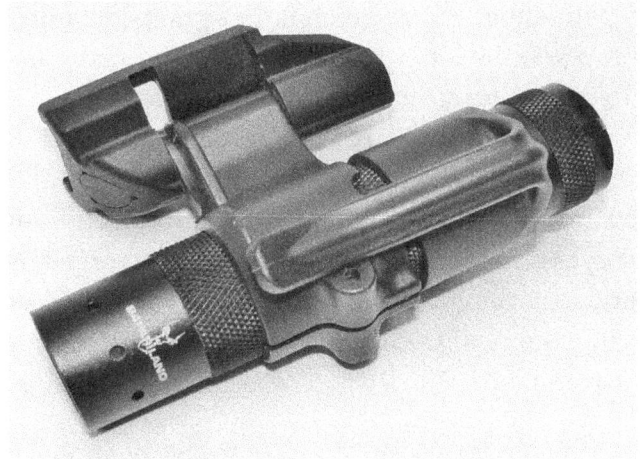

Safariland's RLS may not be the brightest, but it is affordable and versatile. It also runs on AAA batteries.

Streamlight is another well-respected manufacturer of tactical-type lights, including the small ProTac.

<u>Coast TX9R.</u> This light is a hand-held alternative which we've issued to several personnel with good results. It offers 300 Lumen high, 30 Lumen low, a strobe setting, and a beam-focusing feature – all in a compact unit with one other useful capability: you can run it on a lithium-ion rechargeable insert or four AA batteries. The rechargeable option will work in or outside the light using a micro-USB and the light has a lifetime warranty for around $100. Don't rule out the effectiveness of a hand-held light in conjunction with a handgun. There are several good techniques which, for safety's sake alone, are best developed through professional training.

Lasers. Since many unseemly things can happen after dark, lasers do have merit. Even when firing from contorted positions, if you can paste the beam on a target, you'll be able to make a hit. Most our experience involves Crimson Trace products (although Hogue now sells similar items). The replaceable-grip versions with built-in lasers won't interfere with holsters, so on a revolver or metal-frame pistol they make a lot of sense. Just switch out the standard panels for a CT unit, aim at target from 15 yards, and adjust the beam to coincide with your sights. Compressing an integral grip-pad activates the laser, and an on/off switch will shut it down. The beam is emitted from the upper right panel, high enough to clear the hand. On a small-frame revolver, it's a great addition; especially for those with older eyes. Run time in red is up to 4 hours, with a green version roughly half (off two #2032 batteries). The more affordable red-beam Lasergrip starts at around $229. The new genre of polymer pistols need a different mounting system since their grips are an integral portion of the frame. The wrap-around units generally work well, but some seem a tad ungainly. If a pistol has a rail section, it may be easier to mount a separate laser - although holstering could become problematic. The Crimson Trace Rail Master is but one example for around $160.

Streamlight's TLR-6 is a popular light & laser system - mounted to a Glock, of course.

Combination light & laser units. The Rail Master Pro Universal is another Crimson Trace product, which will mount to an accessory rail. Its tactical light is rated at 100 Lumens, with either red or green laser options, retailing for $289 to $379; the latter being preferred by many users due to its greater visibility. Run time can be up to a couple hours from one CR2 battery. Streamlight's TLR-6 is another popular option with similar light output and an integral red laser, powered by a CR-1/3-N Lithium battery. Beyond a rail mount, a trigger guard version is offered and cost for either type is affordable, starting at around $100. But really, we're just scratching the surface of what's available.

Sources. Crimson Trace is now part of the S&W family; a logical connection. There are many other manufacturers like Fenix, Streamlight, and Surefire, just to name a few.

Laser-training possibilities. LASERLYTE sells some interesting technologies that many of us could benefit from. Their products include a muzzle insert that "shoots" a small beam of light from your existing handgun to a target sensor, or a stand-alone firearm simulator package. The Quick Tyme Laser Trainer Kit provides an excellent means to safely develop holster skills from inside the home.

WHAT ABOUT A SILENCER?

First some concerns. For starters, these devices (otherwise known as suppressors) aren't truly silent. Furthermore, their full effect can't be realized with every type of handgun or load. On top of that, the requirements for ownership are more complex.

Legalities. One common misconception is that silencers are illegal. They're not, at least on a federal level, but being classified as National Firearms Act (NFA) items, a federal registration process is required, starting with submission of paperwork through ATF, including a $200 check to cover a special tax stamp. Since the federal permit will also list the suppressor's serial number, the "can" must be purchased up front so its number can be assigned. Meanwhile, it will languish on hold at the SOT (Special Occupational Tax) dealer - a classification beyond that of normal FFL holders. The initial expense will incur the cost of the device as well as federal fees, resulting in a substantial outlay. Finally, after a lengthy wait (months) for an FBI check and processing, unless background issues arise, the requisite paperwork will arrive along with an NFA tax stamp. At that point the device will be considered a firearm, requiring completion of a standard Form 4473 before its release to the owner. Note that this federal process doesn't account for state obligations or restrictions.

Physics. On a positive note, suppressors have recently caught on in a big way, so localized prohibitions are easing. Following this trend, handgun manufacturers now regularly offer threaded muzzles and taller sights. These efforts center on pistols since "silenced" revolvers will still be noisy due to their barrel/cylinder gaps. Pistols solve this problem, but will still emit a sharp supersonic crack unless subsonic loads are employed. Most .45 ACP loads fit this requirement, as do slower 147-grain 9mms, and some .40 S&W rounds. Although such combinations won't be truly silent (as in the movies), they can be safely fired without hearing protection. Some other calibers can be problematic due to velocity/pressure parameters affecting both noise and function. In fact, suppressors can have a generalized effect on function due to their increased mass and slide dynamics. For this reason, some combinations can require a nudge from a small spring-loaded booster, positioned between the can and slide, to improve function. Also, the diameter of many silencers can obstruct a pistol's sights, and size is a further issue regarding practical carry methods. Suppressors are typically built to their intended uses, with rifle-rated types being the strongest and heaviest to handle high pressures. Pistol versions can be smaller and lighter, with larger bores to accommodate 9mm or .45 ACP rounds. With any version, caliber compatibility and alignment are critical for safe bullet passage and prevention of internal baffle strikes.

Further details. Some units employ quick-disconnect mounting couplers, while others direct-thread to a barrel. Either way, the correct thread patterns are essential. Many .22 rimfires and 5.56/.223 barrels have 1/2x28 threads. A common .30-caliber pitch is 5/8x24, while larger calibers including most pistols require different patterns. I use a single Yankee Hill Machine .30-caliber suppressor on a few .223, .300 Blackout, and .308 firearms, all of which have threaded barrels fitted with QD devices. YHM makes this possible through use of thread-patterns compatible with the calibers of their couplers, thereby preventing a disastrous mix-up. An exchange is nearly instantaneous and sound suppression remains surprisingly effective throughout this caliber range. Although mine is rated through .300 Win. Mag., it seems right at home on a .300 Blackout AR pistol. Mine runs well with it attached, too. That's because it was built with a suppressor in mind, which can change pressure dynamics. Some gas-operated systems can become unreliable for this reason.

I'd be interested in a smaller 9mm unit, but not for use in a conventional sense. Instead, it would go on a 9mm AR pistol, affording very quiet shooting with readily available 147-grain subsonic loads and no concerns about gas-port pressures. Cost for such a device is generally less than rifle-rated types with many under $600. Trouble is, I'd need a different suppressor since its internals won't accommodate such larger-diameter projectiles, so the total cost would be closer to $800.

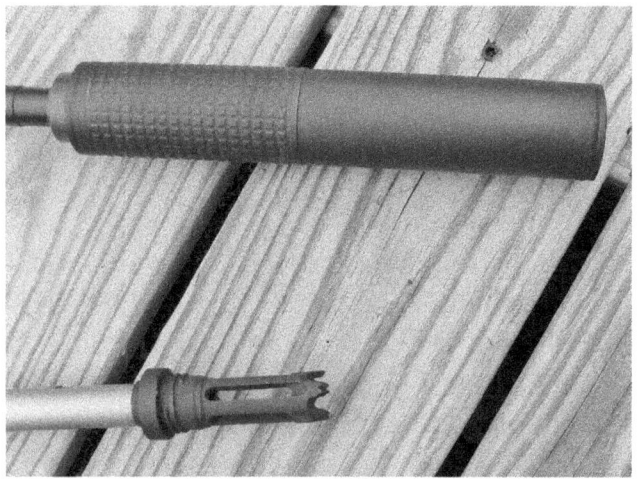

Given the costs associated with suppressor ownership, adaptibilty helps. This YHM system can mount to QD adapters, preinstalled on threaded barrels.

Direct-thread suppressors are popular for rimfires, and also for precision centerfire rifles. This semi-permanent Thunderbeast eliminates zero variations.

Of great interest for me is a .22 rimfire unit. Many .22 LR loads are subsonic in pistol-length barrels so ammo isn't as big a concern. Their barrels are generally fixed, so threaded versions permit easy attachment without concerns over function. The rimfire types are smaller and lighter because they can be. Instead of steel, titanium, or Inconel, the body can be aluminum with a provision for disassembly. Their internal series of baffles can thus be removed for periodic cleaning. The 1/2x28 muzzle of Ruger's short MK-IV Lite just begs for a slim unit, which would probably fit in many holsters. It would be really quiet! The only kicker with .22 units is the large amount of fouling they accumulate. Periodic disassembly is essential to prevent clogged (or seized) baffles. Although I *could* use my rifle-rated YHM can, I won't because of its welded and sealed construction (cleaned via occasional dips in an ultrasonic bath). A separate rimfire device is the better bet and some run below $400. So meanwhile, I'm shooting .22 CB Caps or Shorts through a 10 ½" single-shot Crickett pistol, a quiet and hassle-free alternative that won't break the bank.

The whole field is intriguing. Those interested in the finer points of suppressors will find much information online. In fact, The Silencer Shop specializes in this field, which is growing by leaps and bounds.

ALA CARTE AMMO OPTIONS

We've touched on some of these previously, but they're worth a closer look.

Quiet loads. Starting with .22 rimfire options, even the mildest .22 CB Caps, Shorts, and CCI Quiets will still have a noticeable report in most pistols. This is especially true in revolvers due to their necessary barrel/cylinder gaps. In fact, enough pressure can bleed off to raise concerns over stuck bullets in some combinations. Things improve in semiautos, more so with longer barrels, but function will likely be abysmal in all types. However, ".22 LR subsonics" will often work and are at least somewhat quieter in bare-muzzle pistols. For all intents and purposes, an unsuppressed 9mm pistol will be as loud with 147 subsonics as lighter, faster loads.

Shot loads on the side. How 'bout an instant shotgun? The .45 Colt/.410 shotshell concept was explored through specialized revolvers, but many conventional handguns can also be pressed into close-range shot-load service. You can buy conventional shot cartridges in rimfire or centerfire form for revolvers *or* pistols. The rimfire payloads are miniscule. The centerfire handgun loads are somewhat better but still well below a .410's ca-

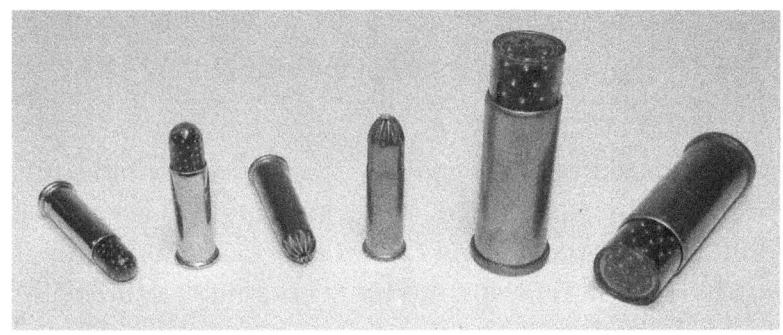

Metallic cartridge shot-loads are strictly close-range affairs. The .22 LRs are encapsulated CCIs, and simpler crimped Winchesters. The .44 Magnums employ Speer's disintegrating shot capsules.

pacity. The handgun-caliber loads often employ small charges of fine shot, contained within disintegrating, bullet-shaped plastic capsules. CCI offers a full line of these handgun loads for the popular calibers, and the largest payload is 150 grains (.45 Colt) while the others are under 100 grains (9mm). Shot size varies but #4 and #9 pellets are two common choices. The higher the shot number, the smaller the pellet, so in theory, smaller pellets should help improve pattern density. In a rifled bore, pellet deformation can result in wider patterns, increased even more from centrifugal forces. A good way to explore these effects would be to buy a sample of shot loads, staple up a large target, back up

around 5 paces, and let 'em fly. Don't expect miracles, though. As a frame of reference, a 2 ½" .410 shell holds ½ ounce of shot. Since there are 437 grains in an ounce, its 218-grain payload will seem like a magnum compared to a 100-grain .357 shot load.

In a dimly lit barn full of rats, conventional-caliber shot-loads can prove useful at close range. In very tight quarters such loads could *possibly* serve for defense, but a head-shot would be necessary, with hopes of some hits to the eyes. God only knows what might happen after that. A better target is a snake at a distance measured in steps.

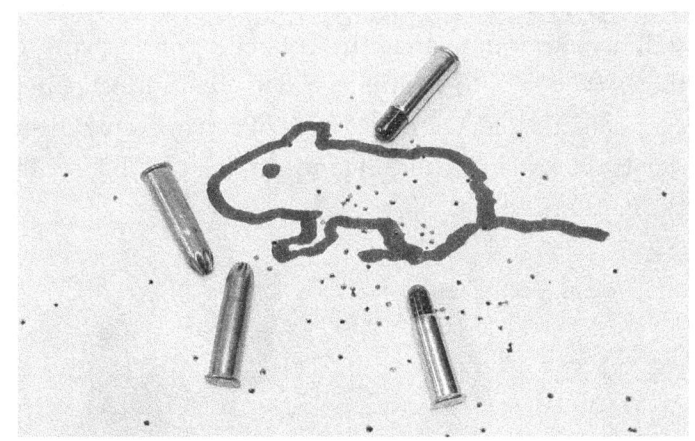

This 3-yard .22 LR pattern was produced by encapsulated CCIs, fired through a rifle barrel. Handgun results won't be any better.

Note: testing is essential. Semiautomatic pistols may not function reliably with shot-loads, due to their lighter payloads and bore-sealing characteristics.

Dummy cartridges to go. Gunsmiths often use inert "action proving" dummy cartridges to perform safe function checks within their shops. "Snap caps" serve a different purpose, providing a way to dry-fire guns that would be otherwise be damaged with empty chambers (double-barreled shotguns, lever-action rifles, and rimfires of all types are a few examples of guns that shouldn't be dry-fired). Action-proving dummies are designed to simulate the weight of loaded cartridges, whereas some snap-caps are lightweight plastic units with a shock-absorbing firing pin cushions. Fortunately, A-Zoom dummies fill both roles nicely.

Revolver shooters willing to invest in at least a cylinder full will have a safe means to practice reloads from speed-loader devices. Make sure the gun is empty first and secure live ammo elsewhere. As proficiency improves, you can turn off the lights. Standing over a bed (empty in the interest of domestic tranquility) will save chasing dummy cartridges. Newer pistol shooters can practice loading and unloading while developing an understanding of semiauto function.

All shooters can benefit further from "ball & dummy" live-fire drills, during which a few inert cartridges are mixed with live rounds. Any tendency to flinch will be painfully obvious upon a "click," presenting a great opportunity to note and correct this problem. Revolver shooters have it easy since a few random fired cases will work with the spin of a cylinder. Pistol shooters will need to mix a few dummies with a magazine of live rounds. The ensuing duds will also serve nicely for malfunction clearance practice, starting with the "tap-rack" technique.

FINAL ACCESORY THOUGHTS

The good news is you don't need to buy everything at once, but over time most gun people amass an impressive collection of trinkets, whether necessary or not. Perhaps the biggest expense is one that will accommodate an entire collection of firearms, namely a gun safe! Security matters and a safe is the best means to maintain it with the added benefit of some fire protection with better models. A gun safe also serves nicely as a handy organizer for magazines, lights, optics, and of course, shoulder-fired guns. If you buy one, go one size bigger than you hoped for, because sooner or later you'll probably fill it up.

CHAPTER 29
MORE ON AMMUNITION AND RELIABILITY

As noted, most malfunctions are shooter-induced, whether directly or indirectly. Ammunition may share part of the blame either way, so a reputable manufacturer is good insurance. Stick with a quality product and problems will be rare. On the flip side, anything goes with reloaded cartridges. I've been rolling my own for decades without any significant incidents, so at this point I have confidence in my reloads. That said, the process has been a learning curve which smoothed out over time. I tend to be anal about things that go bang. Others, sometimes not so much. Most established gun shops will have at least one interesting example of a handloading effort that ended badly. A common one is a revolver with part of its cylinder blown off, often accompanied by a severely bowed top-strap. For this reason, many firearms manufacturers refuse to warranty their guns if reloaded ammunition is used.

Of course, no man-made item is immune from failure. Overall, the ammo makers do one heck of a job producing safe and problem-free cartridges. Some shooters may never see a problem at all, but given the huge amount of ammunition produced annually in the USA alone, the odds guarantee at least a few misadventures. We're far from the biggest ammo consumer, but we have burned enough to see some weird stuff. In fact, within a one-week period, we saw two pistols blow up with factory ammo; all of which were from big-name manufacturers. Since we require shooting glasses, nobody was hurt. Others have been less lucky. Fortunately, many such incidents are less catastrophic.

Sticky extraction and/or split cases are sure signs of trouble. These commercially reloaded .44 Magnums were purchased from a major retailer. The first few rounds resulted in quarantine of the box.

AMMUNITION INSPECTION

It's easy to take quality control for granted, but knowing "stuff" happens, a good time to identify any practice-ammo defects is just prior to loading. There are handy volume loading devices, good for filling hi-cap magazines. You dump in slews of loose rounds and start cranking levers as they automatically feed into attached magazines. It's a testament to the quality of today's ammo that such systems normally produce reliable results; but we don't use them. Instead, we tell our troops to visually inspect each cartridge as it's loaded manually into a magazine. Occasionally, they find a defect. For example…

Primer anomalies. Backward-seated centerfire primers crop up now and then. They won't fire, but they're easy to spot in good lighting. A stranger version involved a few dud rounds that produced audible pops. Turned out several primers were seated sideways within a case of .40 S&W cartridges. They still fired but the powder charges never ignited. The factory shares the blame with the shooter who should've spotted them. Interestingly, he was just experienced enough to take QC for granted.

One of these is different than the others. Even major-brand ammunition isn't immune from the occasional defect – like a backward primer.

A "high primer" is one not fully seated. It often produces a failure to fire, due to the firing pin's blow being absorbed during impact. Afterward, the primer's depth may appear normal, although a light strike can be evident, presenting the false read of a light strike. It may or may not go off during a repeat attempt. High primers can be dangerous during semiauto feeding because they can be impacted by a fast-cycling slide (military primers are crimped in place, partly for this reason). High primers in revolvers won't face this problem, but they can impede or even halt cylinder rotation.

Missing primers are a less common occurrence, but easy to spot in decent light. In fact, the flash-hole will sometimes leak a bit of powder that winds up loose in the box. The darndest defect we saw was

Although relatively uncommon, each of these five cartridges displays a factory defect. Some are pretty weird!

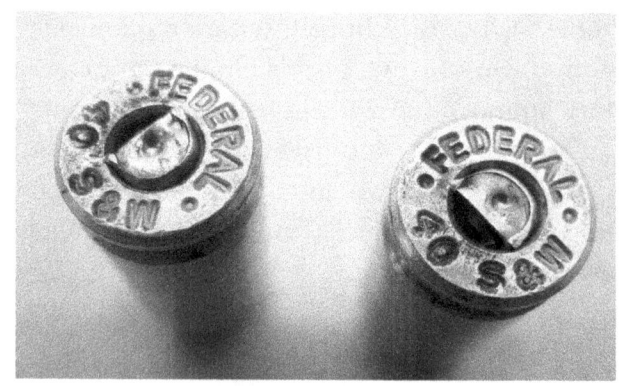

These sideways-seated primers actually detonated. Fortunately, their powder charges never ignited.

372 | Handguns: A Buyer's And Shooter's Guide

a major-brand 9mm round with no primer or primer pocket! It was essentially a dummy round containing a powder charge.

Cartridge cases and bullets. Dented or damaged cases are not uncommon and most occur during shipping. Occasionally, a bullet can be seated off-center, causing part of a case mouth to peel back. Odds are it won't chamber, but if it does, it may not fire; particularly if it's a rimless pistol cartridge that head-spaces off its mouth. Play it safe and don't shoot these rounds.

Once in a blue moon you might even encounter a bullet seated backward. It'll be pretty obvious, but if missed, I'm not sure a pistol would even feed one. I hope not because if it somehow chambered, the action might not go fully into battery. Theoretically, the disconnector would prevent the gun from firing but you never know…

Rarely, we've seen a wrong caliber cartridge in box of ammo. One I clearly remember was a lone .41 Magnum in a box of factory .44 Magnums. It just looked a bit different, sitting base-up within the full box. Another involved pistol ammo, the calibers since lost to time. The much more common screw-up involves a shooter grabbing the wrong box of ammo. Firing a box of 9mm Kurz (.380 ACP) in a 9mm Luger chamber would never be wise. We take pains to isolate any on-range 9mm Luger cartridges from the clutches of .40 shooters.

Dimensional checks. Defensive ammo *must* work, so beyond visual inspection, it's worth checking chamber fit. People who shoot multiple guns (and hand-loaders) will often invest in a chamber-checking gauge, a metal drum or block with a chamber cut to minimum SAAMI dimensions. Individual cartridges are inserted to ensure each will fully seat, via a simple go/no-go process. You can do the same thing with your pistol after removing its barrel. Carefully eyeball each round and then drop it in the chamber with the muzzle oriented downward. The cartridge should drop in, coming to an abrupt halt. Most pistols have a hooded barrel section which contacts the breech-face. The base of each round should stop somewhere adjacent to its terminus. If in doubt, try several to indicate the spot.

Rimmed revolver rounds are easy. They'll either drop in a cylinder or not, so range ammo gets checked when loading. Defensive cartridges are another matter. Close visual inspection *should* reveal high primers and thick rims, but the surest method is to load up the cylinder and manually rotate it while closed. This involves pulling the hammer part way back until hand and stop are retracted. The cylinder should then

A commercial chamber-checking gauge is good insurance, especially when several guns of the same caliber are involved. This .300 Blackout round is obviously out of spec.

spin free of any drag. Don't do this in your kitchen! It's a range thing. Also, don't forget any spare rounds in speed-loaders or moon clips, the latter of which can be easily bent.

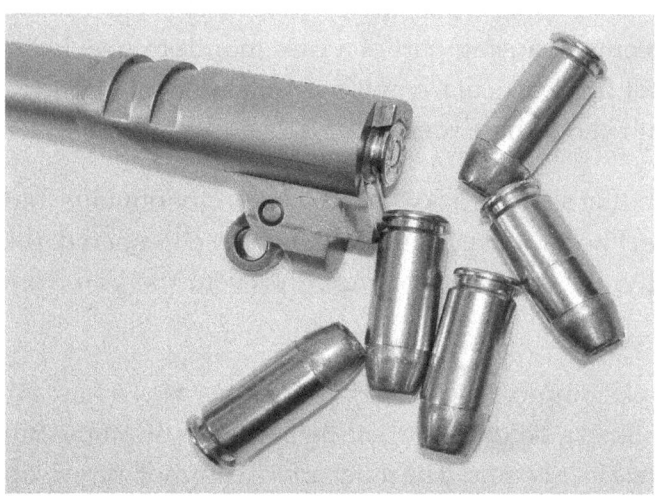

A disassembled barrel pistol can also serve as chamber-check gauge. Insert several cartridges to determine normal seating.

LIVE-FIRE TESTING

Assuming you have identified a good defensive load, avoid stocking up before firing *at least* 50 rounds. As noted in the pistol chapters, shoot a couple magazines using the support hand exclusively for a better indication of its function threshold. Preferably, wait until it's dirty for a clearer picture of load tolerance. Revolver shooters should check for any recoil-induced bullet creep, and regardless of the firearm, don't forget about low light muzzle-flash.

Compatibility. A load that functions well in your buddy's pistol could choke in yours. Using +P ammo as an example, increased slide velocity could cause it to overrun a magazine spring, creating unexplained stoppages. The not-too-obvious fix could be as simple as extra-power magazine springs, a heavier recoil spring, or both. Bullet profiles and feed-ramps are also part of the mix. Some older pistols (like the 1911 or BHP) were designed for FMJ RN, so larger-cavity JHPs won't always feed reliably. A switch to different magazines could also solve malfunctions, either alone, or as part of the larger picture. Sometimes you can solve a feeding mystery by locking a loaded magazine into a field-stripped frame. The location of the top bullet nose might not align well with the feed-ramp, or the slide-stop could throw you a curve. A malfunction that gave me fits was caused by a truncated-cone bullet with a shallower ogive that rubbed against the slide-stop arm. A simple ammo switch was all it took to fix this problem.

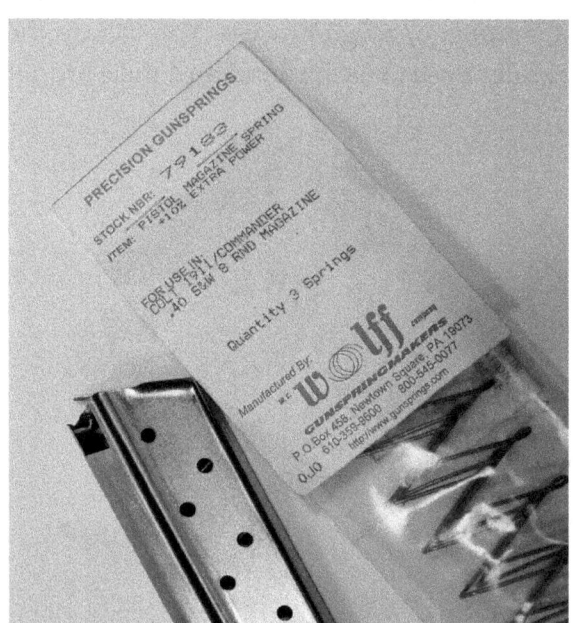

Snappy loads can increase slide velocity enough to override magazine feeding. Sometimes an extra-power spring is all it takes to fix this problem.

POI and function. Fixed-sighted handguns (most service-types) are designed for "average" loads, so a mid-weight bullet often makes a good initial choice. Using a 9mm as an example, the popular bullet-weights seem to be 115, 124, and 147 grains. A 124 could be a good choice when starting from a clean slate. Odds are the sights will be close to on the money, and function may also be a bit more positive. But, if a minor POI divergence is evident, it might be correctable through a load with a different velocity. Low hits could be raised a tad by switching to a heavier 147 which, due to its lower velocity, will spend extra time in the barrel as the gun recoils. Regardless of the caliber, we shoot tons of less expensive Q-load FMJs at paper, maintaining similar defensive-load POIs through identical velocities and weights. We also shoot some frangible bullets at reactive steel targets. They're lighter than their lead counterparts, so POI can be lower (higher velocity/less bore-time); which is more of a concern beyond 20 yards. Reliability can also suffer due to different cycling dynamics, but since it's just training ammo, troops get some stoppage-clearance practice. Still, you should shoot the first box of frangible ammo carefully to note any unlikely surprises. We've had a few rare instances where bullet noses snapped off upon contact with feed-ramps. A baffle-strike in a suppressor could be disastrous. Fortunately, the technology has improved, and most of these loads are now also "lead free," making them good indoor range choices. Cost is greater by around a third but lead toxicity is no joke (done that, been there).

DEFENSIVE AMMUNITION TIPS

The best defensive firearm in the world is only as good as its ammunition. The right type helps, but a few extra precautions could also save the day.

Nickel-plated defensive loads. Distinctive cartridge cases can help segregate non-expanding Q-loads from defensive ammunition. Shiny nickel-plated cases are also more visible in chamber-checking ports. Plus, their increased lubricity improves feeding, while offering better resistance to corrosion.

Ammo exchange. Our SOP includes annual replacement of all service ammo, regardless of its appearance. Replacement could happen sooner, depending on circumstances. If your defensive loads look grubby just swap them out. You can save the accumulation of recycled rounds for practice. We shoot ours during night-fire ranges, providing relevant muzzle-flash experience.

Solvents. Take care to avoid exposure of ammunition to lubri-

Note the low 25-yard POI caused by light frangible .38 Special bullets. However, at combat distances POI should be close enough, and safer for use on steel targets. No function issues with a revolver, either!

Color-coded insurance: The nickel-plated cartridge, visible in the chamber-port, indicates a defensive round.

cants or solvents since some can penetrate primers, causing duds. More than one handgun owner with a lazy streak has used a can of WD-40 in lieu of proper maintenance - and a few have paid for this mistake with their lives. Oiled cartridges and/or chambers can also increase breech thrust which is hard on a gun. Clean, dry ammo is also much less likely to attract dust or dirt.

Odd-length cartridges. Out-of-spec ammo is bad enough on a range, but defensively it could spell doom. The pistol chapter explained how repeat chambering of the same cartridge could drive a bullet deeper into its case through feed-ramp impacts. Besides unsafe pressure, function can be affected, so if a cartridge's overall length looks different, don't risk shooting it. We know that revolver rounds can sometimes grow because of inertial recoil effects. Forward bullet creep may not elevate pressure but it could tie up the gun.

Although more commonly encountered with revolver cartridges, even pistol bullets aren't immune from forward creep.

Storage. A cool, dry, and environmentally stable location is just the ticket. Heat and/or moisture are not. My personal defensive loads are stored in G.I. ammo cans for a bit of extra insurance. Since each is labeled, I can grab one on the fly if necessary.

LIVE-FIRE HAZARDS

Major-brand domestic ammunition is manufactured to SAAMI standards which specify velocity and pressure, but any sort of blockage within the barrel – even snow – could spike pressures high enough for a cartridge case, cylinder, or barrel to fail. This leads us to…

Squib-loads, hang-fires, and duds. Years ago, I was coaching a concealed-carry course for civilian shooters. Part of the curriculum involved misfire and squib-load/bore obstruction cautions. Long story short, one attendee with his head stuck in a foul place wound up with four commercially reloaded lead .38 bullets stuck halfway up a 6-inch D/A Colt revolver barrel. The initial alarm was raised only through an unexplained lack of holes on his target. The shooter was part of a group firing on a loud indoor range, and the combination of hearing protection and adjacent shots apparently resulted in a false assumption that he was experiencing misfires. These rounds were "squib loads," most likely resulting from low or missing powder charges. Externally, the old Colt showed no ill effects. At some later point the gun reappeared with a section of its barrel cut away for use as a training prop.

I previously mentioned a few of our M-65s having ringed barrels. This condition refers to a slightly enlarged bore section, usually caused by an obstruction. For a brief period, we were shooting a batch of "lead free" .38 rounds with a new priming mix. We soon discovered the compound was especially sensitive to any sort of moisture, resulting in wild velocity spreads and squibs (today, primer sealant is used). During the time it took to figure this out, we speculate that our fast-paced revolver sessions resulted in stuck bullets, which were blown free by subsequent rounds in the heat of the moment. This is by no means a recommended way to clear a bore, but luckily in our case the damage was minimal. Furthermore, no appreciable deterioration in accuracy was noted, and no exterior bulges could be seen in these heavy-barreled 4-inch guns. The average semiautomatic pistol barrel is thinner, so the outcome could be worse. Firing another round on top of an obstruction could bulge or even rupture the barrel, unleashing dangerous high pressure gas capable of destroying the gun and injuring the shooter. The same outcome is possible with revolvers, especially with hotter loads.

Any formal semiauto pistol training program will include malfunction clearance drills and the most common is an immediate-action "tap-rack-bang." The shooter smacks the magazine to ensure full seating, racks the slide to chamber a round, and immediately fires. Especially on a line full of shooters, a squib can be easy to mistake for a failure-to-feed or dud. A good autoloading squib indicator is a fired case that remains in the chamber, with a trace of smoke evident during its removal. There's also a good chance the under-powered cartridge will fail to fully cycle a slide, leaving a semiauto uncocked. Except for a shoot-out, this is *not* the best time to execute a fast clearance maneuver. Better to cease fire and unload for a close inspection. If a bore obstruction is discovered, often it'll be possible to disassemble a semi-auto pistol so the barrel can be removed for repairs.

Concerning the above Model 65s, some readers will now be howling over a failure on our part to provide misfire and squib-load cautions, including a cease-fire SOP. Well, it's part of every pre-fire safety briefing. When encountering an unusual report, you *should* cease fire immediately, but put a bunch of amped up people on high-speed stages and this may not happen. In fact, they may never know the difference.

Hang-fire caution. If a misfire or unusual report is encountered, cease fire, wait 30 seconds before opening the cylinder *and keep the gun pointed downrange*. Although rare, a hang-fire is a real phenomenon. The detonation of the primer is followed by a delay before the main powder charge ignites. We've seen a few involving rifles and handguns; hence the 30-second rule of thumb! Completely unload before conducting a thorough inspection.

Lodged bullets. We keep a range-rod handy to drive out stuck bullets. The occurrence is rare but it happens (even with good factory ammo). Often the bullet will be lodged near the chamber but we've seen some that protruded in a cartoonish manner, part way out of the muzzle. Application of a highly viscous lubricant is the first corrective step beyond initial safety precautions, followed by time for penetration. If things look grim, a dose of highly penetrating Dri-Slide can work its magic overnight. Then try an exploratory tap from the rod toward the direction of least bullet travel. Better yet, locate a gunsmith. There's a good chance the bullet will be deformed during attempts to hammer it out. If that happens, it may become hopelessly lodged within the bore. This is especially true with jacketed bullets which are the type most commonly fired, so better to be safe than sorry. If live ammo is involved, secure the gun before explaining the situation to the gunsmith!

Disconcerting as it may seem, the best way to survive a nasty encounter may be to aim at your assailant in hopes of shooting an obstruction out. Raising your non-gun hand while hollering "cease fire" in the middle of a gun fight is less effective.

Caliber mix-ups. We sometimes run multi-caliber pistol programs where ammo mix-ups are a huge concern. To illustrate the point, we'll randomly select a .40 S&W pistol, field-strip it, and drop a loaded 9mm cartridge into the chamber. Depending on tolerances, it may pass through, emerging from the muzzle - but there is also a good chance it won't. Big problems could occur if both calibers were loaded in a .40 S&W magazine. The 9mm *could* be held by the extractor, permitting it to fire. If so, the brass will emerge as an unusual curio, but it could just as easily split, venting dangerous pressure. Worse, the entire live round could wind up inside the barrel where, if mistaken for a failure to feed, a tap-rack-bang could quickly turn ugly. There are plenty of "kaboom" stories circulating through the Internet and we suspect at least some are based on such events.

One more example: an experienced shooter joined me for some fun on the range. He broke out an S&W .45 ACP Model 625 Revolver and the results of his first volley resembled a buckshot blast. Turned out he'd brought a bunch of moon clips intended for his nearly identical Model 610. Both guns are moon clip fed, but the M-610 is a 10mm - which will also fire .40s. Luckily, the fired cases swelled without splitting in the larger .45-caliber chambers. The undersized .40 bullets also rattled through the bore with no ill effect, although his dual-caliber belled brass cases certainly looked odd!

Be sure to segregate your ammunition!

Steel targets. Reactive steel targets are popular and can provide instant feedback, but bullet splatter can pose hazards, and ricochets are possible. A pockmark can turn a bullet 180 degrees, so undamaged surfaces are essential - along with properly hardened steel! Recommended minimum range for conventional projectiles can vary, but we go with 12 yards, using targets that are properly angled to defect fragments downward. In fact, we stick with frangible ammunition. The beauty of these bullets is their instant disintegration upon contact with *smooth* hard surfaces (not concrete). We've tried to make them ricochet through steeply angled shots on steel silhouettes, using adjacent cardboard targets to capture hits. Invariably, they just blow up which, for range purposes, is a good thing! As such, some users shorten the minimum distance to just a few steps. We don't because of Murphy's Law, which ensures an inevitable ammo mix-up.

This commercial steel IPSC target was wrecked by .223 impacts. It'll shoot back if another bullet enters the crater! Those dimples aren't safe, either.

LEAD TOXICITY

We all know lead paint is a concern, especially where children are present. Less appreciated is the shooting aspect. In fact, you can import hazards into family spaces from contaminated clothing, contact with furniture, or even through residual lead in vehicles. In other words, there are advantages to lead-free ammunition extending beyond the range!

Lead exposure for shooters. An exposed lead bullet is a major source, but all conventional loads will generate *some* lead. In fact, the mere act of handling cartridges can cause residual exposure. As for live-fire sources, standard, non-corrosive primers employ lead styphnate compositions that emit airborne lead during ignition. Additional lead can be generated during passage of a projectile through the gun, from both heat and friction. The bullet's impact can distribute more lead than the other sources combined, but the shooter is in closer proximity to the first sources. If we throw a poorly ventilated (or maintained) indoor range into the mix, some degree of unhealthy lead exposure is guaranteed. Back home, gun cleaning can make matters even worse. So, lead hygiene is as important as proper hearing and eye protection.

Casual shooters need not worry with a bit of common sense. Don't pick up fired brass with your hat and wash before smoking, eating, driving, etc. Jacketed bullets also help, although most have exposed bases that emit some ignition-generated lead. Plated bullets solve much of this problem by encapsulating the entire lead core. Products advertised as "lead-free" employ non-lead priming compounds, either in addition to the encapsulated lead projectile or, more commonly, with a frangible bullet using a plated, sintered-copper core. Besides less ricochet danger, they won't coat reactive steel targets and adjacent surfaces with lead – something to consider when resetting steel plates.

On the job, we don't shoot any plain-lead bullets. A substantial portion are FMJs - adequate for most outdoor range programs. We shoot lead-free frangible rounds during steel-plate stages. They cost more but they do allay concerns about exposure and ricochets. We're planning a new indoor range and, owing to our volume of shooting, lead-free rounds will be mandatory. It doesn't take long for lead residue to accumulate on every surface; something I found out the hard way years ago. On a more positive note, good old soap and water will solve most outdoor range concerns.

Reactive steel plates are lots of fun as long as the proper precautions are observed - including hygiene. They'll transfer lead residue during handling.

MANAGED PURCHASING

As ammunition stocks return to a previous state of normalcy, prices have become more competitive, with some attractive deals offered for bulk purchases. Still, the safer bet over the long run, defensively and monetarily, is to resist stocking up on specific ammo brands until a proven track-record has been established in *your* firearm. So, before springing for 1000 rounds or more, consider an incremental approach. Beyond the 3-4 boxes suggested to start, return for maybe another five boxes of practice rounds, plus a couple more boxes (of similar-weight) defensive loads. Then, assuming success continues, try scoring on a larger quantity of the same lot number, usually printed somewhere on a box flap. If two or more lots are procured, you can easily identify each series by marking the boxes with a simple code of your choosing. If nothing else, it'll help manage consumption of your inventory.

Of course, true reliability can only be established through lots of shooting - and that presents an excellent opportunity to weave in skill development.

CHAPTER 30
DON'T FORGET TRAINING!

Yes, the hardware is important, but so is proper training. A good, multi-day school is recommended for all handgunners, but those starting from a clean slate might want to begin with a basic course. The NRA offers solid basic handgun programs and many states require similar training for issuance of CCW credentials. Duration is often measured in hours instead of days, but the information can provide a good foundation for later in-depth training oriented toward defense. Fees will be involved, but most basic programs remain affordable with minimal gear requirements. An actual academy-type school will cost more and will probably specify requirements such as lights, magazines, and a substantial supply of ammunition. There's a good chance travel will be involved as well. It's money well spent but the party's not over.

Since marksmanship – particularly handgun shooting – is a perishable skill, ongoing practice will be necessary. A budget should allow for extra ammo. Don't forget about localized travel costs and range fees. Will everyone go this route? No, but they should.

Reality check. Note that a level of basic competency is different from true proficiency. To attain the latter, shooters should be able to run their weapons on demand, from any position, with either hand, in any light. On demand means "right now," without hesitation! Such advanced skills typically require more comprehensive training, maintained through ongoing, disciplined practice. The realities of everyday life will probably position even the more serious gun owners somewhere in the middle, beyond the basics of loading and unloading, but short of true Ninja status. That might be okay since, for safety's sake, it's best to not put the cart before the horse. Baseline competency should be developed before getting fancy.

For what it's worth, there is a direct relationship between all these factors and a practical handgun choice. If immediate danger calls for a gun, you'll need it like nothing else you've ever needed before. A survivable outcome will require full attention to all threats!

DEFENSIVE HANDGUN TRAINING: KEY COMPONENTS

First off, don't consider defensively-oriented shooting as a sport. Range work can be fun, but it ain't golf. it's closer to a martial art, meaning marksmanship is part of a much larger puzzle. When designing such a program, we view a few key pieces as building blocks. The first one is the cornerstone needed to support the rest.

Maturity/Judgment. Beyond common sense, moral and legal defensive tenets must be understood *and followed*. The same holds true for safety rules. There are people who shouldn't be around power tools or steering wheels. Firearms also apply (consider golf instead).

Safety. Here's the second key piece. Our observation is that even many self-proclaimed shooters are less than completely safe, so regardless of their background, all our trainees get a thorough safety class before touching a firearm. Novices don't know what they don't know, but on a positive note, they have no bad habits either. Often, they wind up the safest of the bunch, although everyone with judgment is trainable. Suffice to say that adherence to firearms safety rules is of paramount importance. Don't be afraid to be your worse critic, and carefully observe others in your proximity.

Operation. Now we're into the nuts and bolts. Proficiency includes the ability to perform basic operational tasks like loading, unloading, and clearance - *all without hesitation*. Operation also extends beyond these basic mechanics to clearing malfunctions, cleaning, etc. We've seen shooters who could post good target scores while never appearing completely comfortable with their weapons. Gun handling skills are perishable and can only be maintained through regular practice. Those remiss in this regard are painfully obvious from behind the firing line.

Marksmanship. Speed counts but accuracy is final. Hit probability from trained personnel like LEOs is now around 20%. How can this be? Well, things are different in the real deal! Unlike the movies, spray & pray doesn't work. The fundamentals governing marksmanship (stance, grip, breath-control, sight-picture, and trigger-control) must be mastered, so accuracy won't happen overnight. It also takes real discipline to employ these fundamentals under duress! The typical frame of reference involves stationary targets in bright light, engaged from static positions on level ground. But turn off the lights, get everything moving, and all bets are off – even if the scenario is just a range stage.

Holster skills. Since we don't walk around with a gun in hand, effective holster skills are essential. An efficient draw counts, but less often appreciated are proper ways to return a handgun to a holster *and* maintain its custody. A fast draw is just smooth compilation of scripted steps which become fluid through economy of motion. Watch footage of top-flight competitive shooters to understand the mechanics. Holster skills require the right techniques and plenty of practice – *initially with an empty handgun*. Same story for others like reloading…

Reloading skills. Since your handgun is not belt-fed, ammo and equipment management strategies should be refined. You'll want to account for rounds fired, and hopefully remaining. Since efficient reloads can minimize periods of vulnerability, any expended items (like fired brass, empty speed-loaders, or magazines) should become expendable. Proper training and techniques will increase speed while preventing harmful habits. Done right, these expendables should wind up on the ground. On the other hand, partially loaded magazines may not. Hence the need for effective "management strategies."

Tactics. A few other proven strategies can be incorporated to increase our longevity. Maximized readiness is the underlying theme, including not putting the gun away too soon. Identification and address of any threats must be balanced against handgun custody. Proper use of cover is also important since a great shot will die quicker in the open than a mediocre one who can exploit some sort of bullet-proof barrier. Murphy's Law dictates some single-hand shooting. Further realities mandate shooting on the move, engagement of moving targets, low-light techniques, and combinations thereof. Vehicular deployment may be relevant for some, and everyone will benefit from scenario-based exercises.

Legal obligations. Assuming we know how to shoot, we'll need to know when we legally can - or can't! Scenario-based "shoot/don't shoot" exercises are valuable learning experiences, but the inevitable litigious aftermath should also be fully understood.

Bottom line. Let's face it; most of us won't gain this information on our own. A good school is the better plan!

FIREARM SAFETY

Proper gun handling is imperative regardless of the situation. Think of the Universal Safety Rules as "the rules of the road." We know things will end badly if we disregard traffic lights, run stop signs, or drive on the opposite side of double yellow lines. Firearm safety rules carry just as much weight! Distracted handling is just as dangerous as distracted driving, and any muzzle-control issues will be exacerbated with a handgun, simply because the slightest move can steer it toward an unsafe direction. Picture the muzzle as a death ray capable of destroying whomever it sweeps. It doesn't matter if the safety is on; that's a lame excuse for bad gun handling! Besides, a safety is a mechanical device subject to failure, just like anything else. Like traffic rules, firearm safety rules can vary a bit from one good source to another, but most have enough in common to work in anywhere.

Universal Safety Rules. Most defensive handgun schools will present a strict list of The Four Basic Firearm Safety Rules (in bold print). The remaining six constitute our proprietary set of rules, which also reflect common practice:

1. **Treat all firearms as if they are loaded –** *always!*
2. *Never* **point a firearm at anyone or anything you do not intend to destroy.**
3. **Keep your finger <u>off</u> the trigger until weapon is on target.**
4. **Be sure of your target and backstop.**
5. Check it, <u>check it again</u>.
6. <u>Never</u> give a firearm to, or take a firearm from anyone, unless action is open and the firearm is unloaded.
7. If you don't know how a particular firearm operates, *leave it alone.*
8. <u>Never</u> leave a loaded firearm unattended.

Don't Forget Training!

9. Store firearms and ammunition separately, secure from unsupervised use.
10. Don't mix alcohol or drugs with firearms.

Back to Rule #2, beyond inattention, we sometimes see poor muzzle control resulting from the effects of excessive recoil – something to consider *before* buying a gun. Rule #2 often goes down the drain during re-holstering or malfunction-clearance attempts. The latter is a classic case of "distracted" handling! Gun cleaning has potential for similar sloppy handling. Furthermore, you don't have to see someone to violate the safety rules. Bullets will penetrate drywall with ease.

Accidental discharges (ADs). Set a fully loaded revolver on a bench with its hammer cocked, and then back up a couple steps. Now wait for it to "accidentally" fire. Think you might be waiting a while? Good chance it'll be a lifetime – as long as someone doesn't step forward to handle it. In that case, any ensuing "accidental" discharge will most likely relate to Rules #3 and #7 – among others.

Not that weird things can't happen; they can – like a case involving a fully loaded S/A .44 Magnum that was parked atop a few targets on a bench while its owner went downrange. The wind came up, the targets blew, and the old-style revolver landed on its uncocked hammer spur – at which point the gun discharged, striking its owner in the posterior. An accident? Maybe, but it really was shooter-induced negligence as nearly all ADs are. In fact, this explains why many critics refer to them as "negligent discharges." It's a fair point. Trouble is, just about every long-time shooter I know has experienced one, which was most certainly a watershed moment not likely to reoccur. What normally saved their day was the observance of Rule #2.

As for the guy with the .44 hole in his butt, he can start with Rule #8 and then consider Rules #1, #2, and #4 (since he survived, there's a good chance he will). If we follow all Universal Safety Rules religiously, safe gun handling should be assured. When in the proximity of those who don't, pack up and leave immediately.

A WORD ABOUT TACTICS

Defensive events often erupt with little warning. A purely reactive response will afford no time for any conscious planning, and adrenaline will kick in afterward. If the action continues, this natural reaction to stress will quickly manifest – especially if things begin to take unexpected twists. For example, picture trying to reload a backward magazine; bad enough in daylight, let alone in the dark! Not that it's as likely for civilians, but a running gun battle can introduce numerous unforeseen challenges. In that case, pure marksmanship can become just part of a larger picture involving movement, use of cover, ammo-management, etc. The key to survival will be proper use of tactics, reinforced by plenty of relevant training.

KISS approach. Simple is good. In our opinion, much of what appears in print or video is greatly overblown. For EDC purposes, do we seriously need to be wearing a spiffy tactical vest full of magazines, a 900 Lumen light, two tactical knives, maybe a fighting axe, multi-tool, para-cord bracelet, tourniquet-kit, etc.? Unless things go completely to hell, a bug-out kit or pack would be a better spot for this stuff. Meanwhile, how about a more simplistic approach involving consistent gear location? If something goes south in a hurry, two immediate concerns will be the gun and extra ammo. Sure, I have a folding knife, and I *might* even have a small light at times, but the blade is more often an everyday tool.

Readiness. Simple strategies are easier to follow but situational awareness should never be discounted. All sorts of firearms personalities appear on camera during fast-paced holster presentations. A fast draw is accompanied by 2-3 shots, followed by an immediate dismount to a tight chest-level "ready." In theory, this position will best permit scanning for additional threats. Trouble is, constant repetition often relegates the process to little more than a choreographed "looks cool" move. For starters, how 'bout ensuring the threat is actually neutralized before coming off target? Next, since there may be other threats to deal with, how about actually *looking around* once back in that "ready"? This and many other so-called "tactical" moves can devolve to nothing more than meaningless habits through unvarying repetitions. Better to expect the unexpected and train accordingly.

Mindset. As we can see, marksmanship by itself is not the final answer. It's important, but might account for less than half of a larger picture involving tactics and one other trait...

We like trainees who have a "coyote mindset." These are people who have strong survivor instincts. They can pull a rabbit out of a hat or turn things around by exploiting the smallest opportunity. Thinking back, the best soldiers, cops, or hunters I've known were probably coyotes in another life. They certainly weren't sheep! We often get an opportunity to observe those most wired to win during fast-paced combat course stages where, sooner or later, everyone will screw up *something*. Reloading fiascos or miscounted rounds are always educational to watch from behind a line of shooters. Sheeple may just melt down and forfeit needed rounds, but coyotes will figure out some way to bail themselves out. Good chance they'll even "cheat" to regain lost points. If a stage calls for say, three shots, but only two are fired, we might note four rounds going off next time. It'll often happen so fast that it becomes hard to detect, but firearms instructors get paid to watch the line. Yes, we could gig a shooter for this, but if the solution is safe, we'd rather see someone instantly dig their way out of a hole. All's fair in love or war and this type of stuff ain't romance. Innovative solutions sure beat a blank look with an empty weapon. Good chance some of the more resourceful types will show up later for advanced special operations training.

A TRAINING EXAMPLE

The outline shown below reflects our week-long basic handgun training program. It's presented to illustrate our take on the nuts and bolts of defensive handgun skills. We run it at a fast pace and each shooter will fire a minimum of 750 rounds, but being a "basic program," it's just a starting point. The general firearm safety class is backed up by on-range protocol and extra handgun-specific safety briefings. Live-fire is also preceded by a thorough marksmanship class, hands-on operation (manual-of-arms), and dry-fire exercises. Many of the live-fire drills are preceded by explanations, and some incorporate instructor demonstrations. Most drills also incorporate initial trainee dry-fire (empty gun) run-throughs. Better to start out slowly before learning to run!

- Legal issues/use-of-force (classroom).
- General firearm safety (classroom).
- On-range safety protocols & weapon-specific safety.
- System management and tactical strategies.
- Retention and disabling techniques.
- Basic holster skills: Draw & recovery.
- Basic loading skills: Loading, unloading, and clearance.
- Basic marksmanship drills.
- Malfunctions and clearance drills.
- Advanced accuracy drills.
- Advanced reloading drills.
- Use of cover: Strategies and drills.
- Engagement of multiple targets / ammo management drills.
- Single-hand operation and shooting drills.
- Advanced holster drills.
- Combat-sighting CQB drills.
- Pivots, turns, and shooting on the move.
- Moving targets.
- Integration of vehicles.
- Low-light/illuminated shooting.
- Use-of-force review.
- Shooting-decision/alternative-force scenarios.
- Cleaning & maintenance.
- Security & storage.

The point of this example is to illustrate there is more going on than just popping off a few rounds at a local range or sand-pit. Take "single-hand shooting and operation," for example. Think you could get in trouble trying to execute a support hand-only reload? Yep. Fast holster work can also get dicey, and there are several ways to shoot yourself while trying to hold a light. Better to seek a level of professional training appropriate for your experience.

TRAINING SOURCES

When it comes to firearms training, one size won't fit all. Personal experience should be a primary concern during course selection, but even those with substantial trigger time may wish to err toward basic programs – a safer bet than getting in over one's head. Reputable trainers know this and structure their curriculum accordingly. We gear our basic schools toward those with little-to-no firearms experience even though attendance is often a mixed-bag. Those with some credentials (military, LEO, serious sporting) have a leg up initially, but they don't always finish first. The trainees with zero experience have lots to digest but they're also blank slates without bad habits. As such, we find the outcome amusing, much to the chagrin of the more "experienced" shooters who still appreciate the broadening of their horizons.

Each firearms training source will have its own unique culture, including somewhat different approaches to the same objectives. Expect some variations as personal horizons expand through any subsequent programs, and sort out what works best for you. Hopefully, a program will be worth its costs, but even a few mediocre schools we've attended yielded useful informational nuggets, frequently from others in attendance!

For now, let's back up and start from the perspective of a new shooter. The playing field could level here since CCW applicants could be required to complete some type of basic course regardless of their experience, simply as a condition of issuance.

Basic courses. The NRA is a great starting point. Their online NRA Explore is a gateway to numerous resources including several handgun-oriented programs. You can even narrow down localized courses through a search engine permitting state or zip-code entries. The Basic Pistol Shooting Course is a one-day event that will cost around $125. The focus will be on firearms safety and basic marksmanship, although more advanced courses are also offered.

Local training sources can be explored. Those that incorporate defensive aspects may use temporary props; adequate so long as the doctrine is sound.

CCW requirements can vary from one locale to the next, but since many states specify training requirements, their issuing authorities are often a good source for local programs. In fact, there's a good chance the NRA will be involved either directly or indirectly through a gun club or commercial range. Content and duration can vary but many constitute one or two days between class room and live-fire (sometimes with a marksmanship standard).

Multi-day academies. The number of "shooting academies" has blossomed during recent years. Prior-military folks account for much of this growth, working off previous specialized training and combat experience gleaned through sandbox operations. As such, much of the content (often very good) will have strong tactical leanings.

Established academies often have the resources to cover necessary topics like moving targets. This system, with its two independent arrays, can incorporate overlapping shoot/no-shoot targets.

More resource benefits: The vertical panels are plug-in cover props (barricades). The tower is used during shoulder-fired moving target stages.

Some other schools like the well-established Gunsite Academy offer multifaceted training geared toward civilians as well as LE or military types. They pretty much wrote the book on the art of "modern pistol," based on the doctrine of their well-known founder, Col. Jeff Cooper. The Colonel is no longer with us but his legacy survives in the Prescott, Arizona region and the school still stands as an excellent example of a good training source. Several handgun programs are offered at Gunsite, starting with a very basic one-day CCW course. But the flagship five-day 250 Pistol Class is much the better bet. It's also a prerequisite for further intermediate and advanced courses. Tuition is around $1,700, which doesn't include 1000+ rounds and some necessary equipment. For most of us, travel-related expenses will also be involved (although courses are sometimes offered at regional U.S. locations).

Of course, there are other good schools that offer programs of varying durations, with many running 2-3 days. As touched upon previously, it's also worth noting that many list "pistol courses" which could be problematic for revolver shooters, particularly when younger military-type cadre are involved. At one recent civilian instructor certification program we attended, a participating high-speed attendee had no idea .38 Special loads could be fired through a .357 Magnum revolver. It pays to shop. Nowadays, it's easy enough to do some on-line searching not only for content, but geographic location.

Informal training? Some beginners may opt to latch on the coattails of acquaintances, either to prime the pump prior to formalized training, or in lieu of the latter. However, a little knowledge can be a dangerous thing. Proceed with caution concerning the former strategy, but assuming a good level of trust exists, the experience can provide some very basic familiarization. Still, treat it as that and nothing more, keeping an open mind later during formalized training. This rules out the latter strategy, which often involves colorful gun club members with questionable verbal resumes, equipped with much misinformation. Be especially wary of those festooned with patches or ornamentations and expect to get what you pay for. Those really in the know won't be publicly advertising their credentials or prowess.

Benefits of formal training. A reputable school will offer more than marksmanship development, beyond firearms safety and tactics. Most will issue a completion certificate which could come in handy later either as a testament of competency regarding issuance of permits, for use during litigation, or (better yet) avoidance of same. In fact, most include at least a class room segment dedicated to potential liabilities. If scenario-based drills involving shoot-houses or simulators are included, this experience alone will be well worth the price of admission!

SKILL DEVELOPMENT AND MAINTENANCE

Since marksmanship is a perishable skill, formal training needs follow-up commitment. Most schools have a defensive slant which, like other martial arts, requires discipline and structured practice. Balancing range time against work and other obligations can be tough, but a monthly range trip is well worth the effort. Go for quality instead of rounds indiscriminately blasted downrange. Better yet is a weekly regimen which could also develop a social aspect with, perhaps, unanticipated benefits…

Shoot with someone better than you. Those who befriend an above-average shooter (or two) can benefit greatly though some amicable rivalry, assuming safety remains the top priority. Your "rivals" don't need to be professional-class; just good enough to keep you on your toes. Since these folks will be regular shooters, they'll probably frequent local ranges, many of which will be maintained by fish & game clubs. They're often the perfect place to establish good connections, and most active shooters are also regular gun shop customers. Any shops in the area will be familiar with ranges and related activities, so they often make a good starting point. You'll be treated as a potential customer, with strong odds of receiving a friendly welcome during an exploratory club visit.

Join a club. Participants of NRA-sponsored handgun courses could already be familiar with local clubs by virtue of attendance. If not, many have a website listing available activities, hours, membership requirements, rules, and rates. As often as not, an initiation fee will be required, following by less expensive annual membership rates. Occasionally, work-party participation may also be part of the deal, but the payoff will likely be a good range facility. That's where you'll run into above-average shooters. Some may also indulge in some formalized competitive events, opening further opportunities.

Attend a competitive event. An ongoing debate is the relevancy of so-called combat competition courses to actual incidents. For starters, gamesmanship is a frequent byproduct of many competitive events, resulting in tricked-out guns and gear ill-suited for practical defense. Tactics can also suffer, and scenarios can become elaborate, resulting in high round-count matches that don't reflect reality. But one exception (for the most part) is the International Defensive Pistol Association (IDPA). Since IDPA was founded to recapture realism, basic guns are the norm, including many covered within this edition. Distances are usually shorter and concealed carry is woven in, along with some movement to cover, no-shoot targets, and (when possible) low-light stages. Scoring is based on both hits and times, with penalties assigned for improper use of tactics or failure to neutralize. To maintain fairness, magazine limits are imposed to support capacity-neutral stages. The guns are also broken into several classes from enhanced pistol to stock service revolver, and even smaller back-up guns. The result is an affordable proving ground requiring little more than basic range gear.

If nothing else, it's worth showing up as a spectator, just to gather information. You'll see handguns in use from the several classifications, as well as holsters and other gear. Regarding the latter, a fast-paced course is a great way to iron out any shortcomings, including ammo management failures. In fact, this aspect may be one of IDPA's most valuable aspects. Watch the competitors in action and you'll see they all have system, well-grounded in the KISS principle.

Most importantly, a formal competition course is guaranteed to generate stress. Virtually all the competitors will experience match nerves, but those posting higher scores prevail through experience and organization. The learning curve typically involves all sorts of mini-fiascos, but they'll serve well to reveal weaknesses that can be corrected over time. Don't despair and keep at it. Sooner or later, expect to enter a new level of subconscious performance that will cover any likely circumstance. Refining this process on a range beats the alternative, too!

On a lighter note, some clubs offer less formal events involving any number of targets from stationary clay pigeons to bowling pins. Some are even .22 rimfire shoots involving reactive targets like knock-down steel plates and spinners. The atmosphere is often more relaxed with some courses even designed for junior shooters. These venues present further opportunities to sharpen skills, with an added benefit of less ammo expense when rimfire shoots are offered. The fun factor can be hard to beat.

GOING IT ALONE

The big risks involve compromised safety and other bad habits. Strict adherence to the Universal Safety Rules will address most of those concerns, but there are other range-related protocols such as not handling firearms while others are downrange. In our experience, many experienced-but-untrained shooters will exhibit sloppy handgun control.

Other detrimental habits can become ingrained through lack of tactical education, resulting in compromised readiness, inefficient reloads, and other pitfalls made worse through improper system organization. Marksmanship can also suffer, from a general lack of basic tenets to specific maladies, a built-in flinch being one common but unrecognized fault. A flinch is tough to correct once established and the cure requires specialized techniques, thus illustrating the need for education.

CLOSING THOUGHTS

We carry a handgun because it's expedient to do so. Other than in very tight quarters, a shoulder-fired gun is by far a better defensive bet. Plus, it could feed you in a pinch. Trouble is, a trip to the local Ready Mart with a shotgun is guaranteed to generate too much excitement. Things probably won't calm down with a dreaded black rifle either, so mundane goings on call for more discretion. Hence the quest for a truly useful handgun with a practical means of carry, preferably for a reasonable cost.

The higher-end items are nice, but they won't guarantee success. A well-trained user of serviceable-but-basic equipment is much more likely to survive a nasty encounter than someone with so-so skills and the latest, greatest firearm. Add a jolt of adrenaline and Murphy's Law is guaranteed to take effect when given the slightest opportunity. The brutal truth is expect a major degradation in accuracy, perhaps on the order of 50%, even without complications. Throw in an empty chamber or stove-pipe stoppage, an inaccessible reload, or a backwards magazine, and the wheels will come completely off.

So, the KISS approach isn't a bad one, and it's also often cheaper to boot. Remember, we still need wiggle room for accessories and ammo. Some formal training would also be nice. Start light on hardware and you might recoup costs that would otherwise be blown on unnecessary items. A good school can provide guidance here – not to mention a life-altering experience more memorable than any vacation.

To that end, careful shopping can field a foundational centerfire handgun system with latitude for further growth. A similar .22 LR handgun offers a cost-efficient means to maintain, or even improve upon essential shooting skills. At some point, a backup gun could follow, although as we've seen, one well-chosen handgun can cover many bases.

Lastly, membership in The National Rifle Association is strongly recommended. Without this organization, safe to say the 2nd Amendment would be gutted, and many types of firearms would be banned. The "black rifle" would certainly make the list and handguns would likely follow. But beyond politics, the NRA is also a good informational source for training and local ranges, supported by regional coordinators. An annual membership is reasonable and includes extra benefits, including monthly magazine subscriptions.

GLOSSARY & QUICK REFERENCE GUIDE

The world of firearms certainly has its share of jargon. Most experienced shooters have learned the vernacular, but that's of little consolation for others. Making matters worse, even manufacturers resort to obscure terminologies and hard-to-decipher abbreviations. Since many appear within these pages, references are grouped by topics instead of alphabetical listings, loosely follow the chapter-based progression.

HANDGUN TYPES

Revolver. A handgun with a revolving cylinder that contains multiple chambers, each of which, when properly timed, will index with the barrel. The cylinders of many double-actions swings open for loading or unloading from the left side of the frame.

Semiautomatic. A self-loading pistol that harnesses recoil energy to eject fired cases and chamber fresh cartridges from a self-contained source; typically, a detachable magazine. A semiauto requires a separate trigger-pull for each shot.

Pistol (other). For purposes of this edition; a handgun other than a revolver or semiauto (like a single-shot or Derringer).

Locked-breech semiauto. A popular design that locks the barrel and breech-face (or slide) together, safely containing the higher pressures associated with hotter cartridges (like 9mm or .40 S&W). This connection is mechanically timed to unlock upon discharge, but only after the bullet leaves the barrel and pressure subsides.

Blow-back semiauto. A simpler non-locked design for milder cartridges like .22 LR, .32 ACP, etc., which employs the inertial resistance of a slide (or bolt) and recoil spring to delay cycling upon discharge, long enough for pressure to subside.

Striker-fired pistol. A heavy, spring-loaded firing pin, employed in lieu of a hammer. In most (but not all) designs, the striker becomes partially cocked during slide-cycling. Pulling the trigger completes cocking and then trips the striker. A classic example is the Glock, which offers a consistent trigger pull lighter than a most double-action pistols. Nevertheless, some striker-fired pistols are advertised as D/As due to their loosely similar trigger weights.

Hammer-fired. The traditional design, composed of several variations…

S/A revolvers and pistols. A single-action fires from a pre-cocked hammer. Cocking may be manual, or can be caused by the cycling of a slide, either resulting in a short and light trigger pull. A classic S/A revolver is Colt's Six-Shooter, which must be manually cocked. An S/A pistol like the 1911 .45 Pistol is normally cocked during slide-cycling, but has a manual option. A D/A revolver (below) typically offers S/A and D/A options.

D/A revolver. A double-action employs a trigger-cocking linkage to cycle and release the hammer through a longer, heavier trigger stroke. A classic example is S&W's Model 10 Revolver, designed to be safely carried with its hammer un-cocked. Although pre-cocking to S/A is possible, a quicker defensive response is available through the D/A mode.

DA/SA pistols. Double-action/single-action types fire either way (so, technically the S&W M-10 qualifies). Beretta's semiauto Model 92F/military M-9 is a classic example, designed to be carried un-cocked for a D/A first-shot response. Subsequent shots can be fired S/A since slide-cycling will automatically re-cock the hammer. A manual de-cocking system is incorporated so the pistol can be returned to D/A mode for safe carry.

DAO revolvers and pistols. These handguns fire from double-action only, so a S/A feature is absent. Although each shot requires a longer and heavier trigger stroke, the pull is consistent, and the hammer remains at rest when carried. In fact, many DAO handguns – both revolvers and pistols - have shrouded hammers for no-snag carry. A manual safety is sometimes incorporated with pistols, but DAOs of all types remain popular back-up guns.

AMMUNITION ABCs

Abbreviations are particularly common on the end-flap of cartridge boxes (9mm Luger-124 Gr. JHP). If in doubt, don't attempt to chamber or fire a cartridge. My *Survival Guns* book has more information on this subject.

Caliber (Cal). Technically $1/100^{th}$ of an inch, although reality often dictates otherwise. A .45 ACP is close, firing bullets that measure around 0.451" in diameter. But .44 Magnum bullets run around 0.429," and .38 Specials average 0.357" – the same as a .357 Magnum. Great license has been used throughout the years, resulting in justifiable confusion. In any case, the diameter (caliber) of bullet and bore should closely match, along with the forward sections (throats) of each revolver chamber.

Millimeter (mm). Metric cartridge designations are more definitive. A "millimeter" is roughly 0.04" (actually 0.3937"), so a 9mm Luger bullet is close to .36-caliber (actually 0.355). Globally, there are several other 9mm cartridges, so this one is known as the 9x19mm, the second number indicating the cartridge's case length; which differs from the 9x17 (.380 ACP), or 9x18 Makarov. Those 9x19mm case-heads stamped 9mm NATO indicate military ammunition.

Head Stamp. Most cartridges have identifying marks on their bases. U.S. civilian head stamps indicate the caliber and maker (WW 9mm Luger). Military cartridges (and some foreign types) are another matter. Instead, they may be stamped with arsenal abbreviations and the year of manufacture, such as LC 72 (Lake City 1972).

Primer. The small, separate, explosive mixture used to ignite the main propellant.

Propellant. The powder, unlike a primer, burns at a rapid rate, generating high-pressure gas to expel a projectile.

Grns. A unit of measure (not individual flakes), used to express the weight of a powder charge or bullet. There are 7000 grains per pound/437.5 per ounce. Most pistol charges are relatively small, running from 3-25 Grs (as opposed to 60 grs or more for some rifles). A typical 230 Gr. .45 ACP bullet is twice as heavy as 115 Gr 9mm, but it still only weighs a tad over ½ ounce.

Rimfire ammunition. The series of smaller rimmed cartridges including .22 Short, Long, Long Rifle (.22 LR), .22 Winchester Rimfire Magnum (.22 WRM), .17 Hornady Magnum Rimfire (.17 HMR) - and several others. The rim contains a small annular deposit of priming compound. A firing pin blow to the outer edge pinches it to cause ignition. As such, the case material must be thin, limiting rimfire use to lower-intensity ammunition. Rimfire cartridges are impractical to reload.

Centerfire ammunition. Includes nearly all other ammunition. A centerfire system can handle higher pressures since thicker cartridge heads can be used. Ignition occurs from a blow to a central primer, and two common systems are used…

Berdan-primed. A European design in which part of the ignition system is integral with the cartridge case. Manufacturers of steel or aluminum-cased cartridges employ Berdan priming to discourage reloading (possible only with special tooling), because these materials lack elasticity for safe resizing. Some surplus types may be corrosive, but the U.S. built loads from Hornady, CCI, or Winchester are non-corrosive.

Boxer-primed. Conventional U.S.-type reloadable priming design, with a cartridge-case pocket and central flash-hole. Primers are self-contained metallic cups. Fired primers can be "de-primed" and replaced with new ones. New U.S. ammo should be non-corrosive but old rounds (including some surplus imports) may contain mercuric priming which can quickly cause rust.

Non-corrosive priming. Nowadays, non-corrosive priming mixes are standard throughout the U.S., but that wasn't always true. The original mercuric compounds explain why many older barrels are pitted, due to lack of prompt attention after firing. There are still corrosive-primed surplus rounds in circulation, including some imported types. If in doubt, clean the barrel thoroughly after firing, or better yet, buy something else.

LF. Lead-free priming is an alternative to common lead-based compositions, and is often combined with non-lead or frangible bullets to eliminate lead hazards on indoor ranges.

Cannelure. A knurled band that encircles some bullets to accommodate cartridge-case crimps. Most revolver bullets have cannelures to prevent recoil-induced creep.

Crimp. The small rolled-in section of a cartridge case mouth that engages a bullet's cannelures. A roll-crimp is often employed with revolver ammunition to help hold a projectile in place. Pistol cartridges typically use a taper-crimp instead because they head-space off the edge of the case mouth.

RN (or RNL). A bullet of round nose design, either jacketed or lead (RNL). Either is a poor defensive load and lead is largely passé, but the pistol versions remain popular for practice and training. *Caution: a blunt tip is needed with the tubular magazines of lever-action rifles to prevent the detonation of adjacent primers during recoil.*

FMJ. A bullet design where the lead core is clad in a Full Metal Jacket, not designed to expand upon impact. Most military rifle bullets are so designed.

JHP (or HP). A jacketed hollow-point bullet design, with a nose-cavity for rapid expansion. Many are defensive loads. The solid-copper Barnes TSX is another type of HP, which lacks a jacket due to its homogenous composition.

JSP (or SP). A jacketed soft-point like a JHP design, but minus a cavity, with an exposed lead tip to initiate expansion.

TC. A truncated cone bullet is common to many .40 S&W loads. The conical nose has a flattened tip to fit within 9mm frames, but the taper is more gradual to provide the necessary increase in a .40's bullet weight.

WC. Cylindrical wad-cutter bullets employ a flat face, designed to punch clean holes in targets. Feeding is a challenge in semiautos so most appear as revolver loads, usually in .38 Special, with flush-seated lead bullets that are tough to chamber with speed-loaders.

SWC. The addition of a tapered and flat-tipped nose section to a WC, results in a semi-wadcutter bullet. Jacket types improve pistol feeding (.45 ACP target loads), and lead versions were common in LE revolvers. Some SWC-HPs incorporated a hollow-point, offering effective terminal performance.

Frangible. A specialty bullet, designed to disintegrate upon impact with hard surfaces, minimizing ricochet hazards. The core is often sintered-copper and polymer mix, clad with copper plating.

Chronograph. An instrument used to "see" bullets and record their velocities, displaying speeds in FPS.

FPS. A projectile's velocity when expressed as feet-per-second (1000 fps), common for the USA.

MV. Muzzle velocity is usually recorded 15 feet beyond a muzzle, to minimize the effects of blast on a chronograph. The bullet's speed is expressed in FPS.

ME/Ft lbs. Muzzle energy is expressed as foot-pounds, used to quantify projectile energy through mass (grains) and velocity (fps). What it won't factor in is the design of a bullet.

MAP. Maximum Average Pressure, established in the USA by SAAMI to govern ammunition production. For example, a 9mm and .40 S&W have a published MAP of 35,000 PSI.

+P. A cartridge loaded to higher pressure than the original load, normally by around 10%. The standard .38 Special's MAP is 17,000 PSI, whereas .38 +P is 18,500 PSI. The .357 Magnum MAP is 35,000 PSI.

SAAMI. The Sporting Arms and Manufacturing Institute is an industry body that provides consistent standards for the manufacturing of American sporting firearms and ammunition. Using domestic 9mm Luger as an example, upon its acceptance by SAAMI, a set of dimensional drawings was published to govern tolerances. The U.S.-built load is thus a safer bet than some obscure surplus imports. Further SAAMI standards specify pressure and velocity parameters.

CHAMBERS, BARRELS, AND ACTIONS

Breech. The rear end of a barrel. Also, an action's abutting surfaces (like the breech-face of a slide or recoil-plate of a revolver).

Chamber. The breech-end cavity of a barrel, precisely dimensioned to accept a cartridge. The "chambering" (or caliber) is typically stamped to the barrel's exterior.

Headspace. A carefully controlled chamber dimension that limits breech face clearance for safe containment of pressure. Many revolver cartridges, like the .357 Magnum, headspace on their rims. Rimless pistol cartridges (9mm, .45 ACP, etc.) develop headspace through abutment of their case mouths with a corresponding chamber ledge, and the breech face. In all cases, proper fit is critical for containment of pressure!

Bore. The center of a barrel through which a bullet passes. Its smoothness and dimensions can affect accuracy or fouling. The "bore" itself can also create some confusion. Turns out some other nations have used the smaller-diameter rifling surfaces (lands) to determine caliber. This makes sense since the bore is drilled to that dimension prior to cutting the grooves. But, see below…

Rifling. The spiral cuts machined into a barrel's bore, which engrave and stabilize a bullet. The "lands" are the high surfaces that separate "grooves," but the latter constitute the bore diameter or caliber (i.e. .357 Magnum) in the U.S. Some makers (among them Glock) have used polygonal or rounded lands, claiming improved gas sealing, with reduced friction and fouling. Some can provide less "bite" when used with softer bullets (plain lead) creating accuracy problems.

Rate-of-twist (ROT). Refers to a barrel's rifling twist-rate. A 1x10 twist will spin a bullet 360 degrees within 10-inches of passage through the rifling. Heavier or longer bullets generally require faster twists to develop adequate stability. A shorter or lighter bullet can tolerate a slower ROT. A 1x10 is a common 9mm twist, while 1x15-ish is a popular .45 ACP rate.

Crown. The muzzle surface that contacts the bore. It's often recessed, affording some protection from accuracy-robbing nicks or dings.

Compensator. A device attached to a muzzle, with ports to vent pressure upward, thereby reducing climb during recoil. Alternately, the porting could be cut directly into a barrel near the muzzle. Effectiveness is related to cartridge intensity but flash will typically increase.

Fouling (and leading). An accumulation of carbon or copper deposits which, in rifling, can cause deteriorating accuracy if not removed. Lead deposits are worse since they can eventually elevate pressures to unsafe levels. They're also a hassle to remove from a compensator!

Frame. The lower, action-section of a handgun. *A frame-assembly* contains the various fire-control parts like a hammer, trigger, etc., as well as a magazine or cylinder, and grips. In accordance with ATF statutes the frame constitutes a firearm and must therefore bear a serial number. Although some new modular designs (like the Sig P320) employ a removeable chassis assembly in lieu of a complete frame, they are still considered the actual pistol, subject to federal purchasing statutes.

Slide. The upper section of a semiautomatic pistol that reciprocates on its frame through discharge forces, causing extraction, ejection, and feeding of cartridges (from a magazine). *A slide-assembly* typically contains a firing pin or striker, an extractor, barrel, guide-rod, related springs, and the sights. The assembly cycles on corresponding frame rails, but is a non-regulated part.

Extractor. The spring-loaded claw that grasps the head of a cartridge to extract it from a chamber, usually mounted in the slide of semiauto pistols (see below for revolvers).

Ejector. The part that ejects a spent cartridge after extraction. A frame-mounted blade is common to many semiauto pistols. AR-15s (and some others) employ a spring-loaded plunger in the bolt-face. S/A revolvers rely on a long manually-operated retractable rod contained in separate barrel housing. A D/A *cylinder assembly* typically contains a spring-loaded dual-purpose extractor/ejector

Stoppage. A malfunction. The common types include a failure to feed, fire, extract, or eject.

TARGETS, ACCURACY, AND SIGHTS

Group. A cluster of shots, often measured to quantify accuracy. Five shot groups (often at 25 yards) are a common handgun standard. Measurements are taken from the centers of the furthest shots and expressed in inches (3" group).

Flier. An errant shot, often revealed as an aggravating deviation from a shot group.

Zero. The range at which our handgun is "sighted in" for a dead-on hold. At other ranges, an adjusted POA could be necessary.

POA. Point of aim describes the aiming point. It may be different from a target's center to allow for the effects of gravity and trajectory. With a 25-yard zero, using many handgun calibers, our POA might need to be several inches high at 50 yards. The higher POA should account for drop, hopefully producing a centered hit.

POI. Point of impact indicates the deviation of a shot-group from point of aim. In the above example, without that correction, our 50-yard POI would be several inches low.

Elevation. Refers to vertical sight corrections, usually through minor movements of an adjustable rear sight. Raising it will elevate POI for that 50-yard shot.

Windage. Applies to horizontal aiming corrections. "Kentucky Windage" refers to allowance for an incorrect zero in lieu of a sight adjustment. When possible, moving the rear sight will make life much more bearable.

Fixed Sights. Describes sights without the means to correct POI. Those built integral with a gun offer durability at the expense of adjustments. Others, installed as separate parts, may offer limited adjustments, most often for windage through horizontal "drifting" of the rear sight. However, most are tightly fitted, and some contain other parts, so a sight-pushing fixture is recommended.

Adjustable sights. These permit POI corrections through small screws, which can change the relationship of the sighting plane to the bore. Typically, one screw adjusts elevation (U or D), while a second applies windage (L or R). The small moving parts increase fragility to some extent, but can compensate for various loads. Fixed or adjustable, here's the rule to remember: Always move the rear sight in the same direction you want the bullet to go.

Dot sight/MRDS. Not to be confused with a laser (which projects a beam), these sights work like a scope but contain a small aiming dot instead of crosshairs. Most are battery-powered and the smallest versions are known as miniaturized, red-dot sights.

Reticle. Refers to the crosshairs or dot within an optical sight used for aiming. Scope reticles are normally mounted within a separate interior housing, to permit adjustments. Dot-sights employ a reflected dot which is typically illuminated by an electronic diode.

MOA. The size of a dot-sights reticle (the dot) is commonly expressed as <u>minute-of-angle</u>, approximating one inch at 100 yards (actually 1.047"). So, a 2 MOA dot would cover (or subtend) two inches at that range.

Eye relief/EER. The distance from the rear (ocular) lens of an optical device to a user's eye, where a full image is visible. This will occur with many rifle scopes at around 3-4 inches, allowing for recoil protection. Pistol and scout scopes are often advertised as EER models with <u>extended eye relief</u> for use at arm's length.

Picatinny Rail. The military mounting system, <u>like an accessory rail</u>, which uses precisely specified dimensions that accommodate scope rings, lights, lasers, and other accessories.

QD System. A <u>quick disconnect</u> design for easy dismounting of scope rings, sling swivels, etc.

CARRY JARGON

OC. <u>Open carry</u> refers to a firearm carried in plain sight. Although lawful in some states, OC is not necessarily advised for other than outdoor or sporting purposes.

CCW. <u>Concealed-carry weapon</u>, often used to reference concealed-carry or CCW permit holders.

EDC. <u>Every day carry</u>, the current term in vogue to describe a handgun, usually of smaller size, amenable to regular carry without inconvenience.

OWB. An <u>outside-the-waistband</u> holster or carry method.

IWB. An <u>inside-the-waistband holster</u> or carry method, intended to improve concealment.

IWB-A. An IWB system designed to be located more forward, in the <u>appendix</u> region.

LEGAL CONCERNS

BATF (ATF). The <u>Bureau of Alcohol, Tobacco, Firearms, and Explosives</u> which regulates FFLs, SOT holders, NFA items, and other firearms. Airguns and muzzleloaders including percussion revolvers are exempt and can be ordered by mail - if no local restrictions exist.

FFL. <u>Federal Firearms License</u>, held by firearms dealers (non-NFA). A gun shop is a typical FFL example. We can also buy a firearm through the Internet, but it will need to be shipped to an FFL holder in the purchaser's state of residence. From there a Form 4473 must be completed. The dealer will next contact ATF for a NICS check (National Instant Check System). Upon clearance of the NICS process, the buyer (transferee) can assume ownership of the firearm. A transfer fee ($25-$50) is commonly part of the deal, and covers an FFL holder's efforts. Check your local laws before proceeding.

Firearm. A "firearm" must have serial-numbered part; normally its receiver. Purchase of a serial-numbered AR lower will require the Form 4473 and NICs process. Upper AR-15 receivers aren't numbered and can be purchased like scopes or boots. The same applies for extra upper pistol assemblies, or the accessory barrels used on T/C or CVA single-shots.

NFA. National Firearms Act, which regulates the sale and transfer of silencers, SBRs, etc.

Carbine. A generic, shorter-barreled rifle of compact size. For our purposes, it will also have a finished barrel at least 16-inches long to avoid additional NFA restrictions (see SBR).

SBR. A "Short-Barreled Rifle" has a shoulder-stock and barrel less than 16-inches in length. As such, it requires a special $200 federal stamp and permitting process through ATF.

Suppressor. Another word for a silencer. Like an SBR, ownership is legal through the federal permit process. The actual device is serial-numbered in the same way as a firearm, and must be registered to its legal owner upon issuance of the $200 federal stamp. Some state or local jurisdictions impose further limits.

Full-Auto. Another NFA firearm, like a machinegun, which can fire multiple rounds through one trigger pull. Submachineguns (SMGs) fire smaller pistol-type cartridges. Either may also offer a select-fire option.

Select-fire. This term describes firearms which can be fired in semi-automatic or full-auto modes. The latter is tightly regulated as an NFA firearm which, like SBRs and silencers, is subject to special permits and fees. Some firearms are strictly full-auto, but either constitutes a machinegun.

SOT. Special Occupational Tax status for dealers and manufacturers of NFA items. Purchasers of SBRs and suppressors will need to use an SOT Dealer.

www.ingramcontent.com/pod-product-compliance
Lightning Source LLC
Chambersburg PA
CBHW081202170426
43197CB00018B/2893